CLYMER®

POLARIS

ATVs • 1985-1995

The world's finest publisher of mechanical how-to manuals

PRIMEDIA
Information Data Products

P.O. Box 12901, Overland Park, Kansas 66282-2901

Copyright ©1996 PRIMEDIA Business Magazines & Media Inc.

FIRST EDITION
First Printing June, 1996
Second Printing October, 1997
Third Printing June, 1998
Fourth Printing July, 1999
Fifth Printing November, 2000
Sixth Printing July, 2002
Seventh Printing December, 2003
Eighth Printing September, 2005

Printed in U.S.A.

CLYMER and colophon are registered trademarks of PRIMEDIA Business Magazines & Media Inc.

ISBN: 0-89287-668-9

Library of Congress: 96-75544

TECHNICAL PHOTOGRAPHY: Mark Jacobs.

TECHNICAL ILLUSTRATIONS: Michael St. Clair.

WIRING DIAGRAMS: Robert Caldwell.

TECHNICAL ASSISTANCE:
  Don Anderson, Instructor/Technical Supervisor
  Northwest Technical College
  Outdoor Power Equipment & Snowmobile Technology Department
  Detroit Lakes, Minnesota 56501

  Dale Fett, Technical Advisor
  Fett Brothers Performance, Inc.
  Route 4, Box 383C
  Frazee, Minnesota 56544

  Charlie Okeson
  Okeson Offtrail Sales
  Route 2, Box 130
  Detroit Lakes, Minnesota 56501

TOOLS AND EQUIPMENT: K&L Supply Co. at www.klsupply.com

COVER: Photographed by Mark Clifford, Mark Clifford Photography, Los Angeles, California.

PRODUCTION: Veronica Bollin.

CLYMER®

Publisher Shawn Etheridge

EDITORIAL

Managing Editor
James Grooms

Associate Editors
Lee Buell

Technical Writers
Jay Bogart
Jon Engleman
Michael Morlan
George Parise
Mark Rolling
Ed Scott
Ron Wright

Editorial Production Manager
Dylan Goodwin

Senior Production Editor
Greg Araujo

Production Editors
Holly Messinger
Darin Watson

Associate Production Editors
Susan Hartington
Julie Jantzer-Ward
Justin Marciniak

Technical Illustrators
Steve Amos
Errol McCarthy
Mitzi McCarthy
Bob Meyer

MARKETING/SALES AND ADMINISTRATION

Marketing Director
Rod Cain

Trade Show & Retention Marketing Manager
Elda Starke

Sales Channel & Brand Marketing Coordinator
Melissa Abbott Mudd

New Business Marketing Manager
Gabriele Udell

Art Director
Jennifer Knight
Chris Paxton

Sales Managers
Justin Henton
Dutch Sadler
Matt Tusken

Business Manager
Ron Rogers

Customer Service Manager
Terri Cannon

Customer Service Representatives
Shawna Davis
Courtney Hollars
Susan Kohlmeyer
Jennifer Lassiter
April LeBlond

Warehouse & Inventory Manager
Leah Hicks

PRIMEDIA
Business Magazines & Media

P.O. Box 12901, Overland Park, KS 66282-2901 • 800-262-1954 • 913-967-1719

The following books and guides are published by PRIMEDIA Information Data Products.

More information available at *primediabooks.com*

CONTENTS

QUICK REFERENCE DATA

POLARIS MODEL NUMBERS

Year/Model	Model number
1985	
Scrambler	W857027
Trail Boss	W857527
1986	
Scrambler	W867027
Trail Boss	W867527
Trail Boss	W867627
1987	
Trail Boss	W877527
Cyclone	W877828
Trail Boss 4 × 4	W878027
Trail Boss 4 × 4	W878127
Trail Boss 4 × 4	W878327
1988	
Trail Boss 2 × 4	W887527
Trail Boss 4 × 4	W888127
Trail Boss 250 R/ES	X888528
Trail Boss 250 R/ES	W888528
1989	
Trail Boss	W898527
Trail Boss 2 × 4	W897527
Trail Boss 4 × 4	W898127
Big Boss 4 × 6	X898627
Big Boss 4 × 6	W898627
1990	
Trail Blazer	W907221
Trail Boss 250	W908527
Trail Boss 2 × 4	W907527
Trail Boss 2 × 4 - 350L	W907539
Trail Boss 4 × 4	W908127
Trail Boss 4 × 4 - 350L	W908139
Big Boss 4 × 6	W908627
1991	
Trail Blazer	W917221
Trail Boss 250	W918527
Trail Boss 2 × 4	W917527
Trail Boss 2 × 4 - 350L	W917539
Trail Boss 4 × 4	W918127
Trail Boss 4 × 4 - 350L	W918139
Big Boss 4 × 6	W918627
Big Boss 6 × 6	W918727
1992	
Trail Blazer	W927221
Trail Boss 250	W928527
Trail Boss 2 × 4	W927527
Trail Boss 2 × 4 - 350L	W927539
Trail Boss 4 × 4	W928127
Trail Boss 4 × 4 - 350L	W928139
Big Boss 4 × 6	W928627
Big Boss 6 × 6	W928727

(continued)

POLARIS MODEL NUMBERS (continued)

Year/Model	Model number
1993	
Trail Blazer	W937221
Trail Boss	W938527
Sportsman	W938039
250 2 × 4	W937527
350 2 × 4	W937539
250 4 × 4	W938127
350 4 × 4	W938139
250 6 × 6	W938727
350 6 × 6	W938739
1994	
Trail Blazer 2W	W947221
Trail Boss 2W	W948527
Sport	W948540
Sportsman	W948040
300 2 × 4	W947530
400 2 × 4	W947540
300 4 × 4	W948130
400 4 × 4	W948140
300 6 × 6	W948730
400 6 × 6	W948740
1995	
Trail Blazer	W957221
Trail Boss	W958527
300 2 × 4	W957530
400 2 × 4	W957540
300 4 × 4	W958130
Scrambler	W957840
Sport	W958540
Sportsman 4 × 4	W958040
Xplorer 4 × 4	W959140
Magnum 2 × 4	W957444
Magnum 4 × 4	W958144
400 6 × 6	W958740

W is the first letter of the Vehicle Identification Number for Standard production models.
X is the first letter of the Vehicle Identification Number for limited production pilot build models.
The first two numeric digits indicate the model year designation.
The third and fourth numeric digits indicate the chassis designation.
The fifth and sixth numeric digits indicate the engine used.

GENERAL DIMENSIONS

Model	Length cm (in.)	Width cm (in.)	Wheel base cm (in.)
1985			
Scrambler W857027	188.0 (74.00)	109.2 (43.00)	121.9 (48.00)
Trail Boss W857527	188.0 (74.00)	109.2 (43.00)	121.9 (48.00)
1986			
Scrambler W867027	188.0 (74.00)	109.2 (43.00)	116.8 (46.0C)
Trail Boss W867527	188.0 (74.00)	109.2 (43.00)	116.8 (46.00)
Trail Boss W867627	188.0 (74.00)	109.2 (43.00)	116.8 (46.00)

(continued)

GENERAL DIMENSIONS (continued)

Model	Length cm (in.)	Width cm (in.)	Wheel base cm (in.)
1987			
Trail Boss W877527	177.8 (70.00)	110.5 (43.50)	115.6 (45.50)
Cyclone W877828	198.1 (78.00)	110.5 (43.50)	127.0 (50.00)
Trail Boss 4 × 4 W878027	177.8 (70.00)	113.0 (44.50)	120.7 (47.50)
Trail Boss 4 × 4 W878127	177.8 (70.00)	113.0 (44.50)	120.7 (47.50)
Trail Boss 4 × 4 W878327	177.8 (70.00)	113.0 (44.50)	120.7 (47.50)
1988			
Trail Boss 2 × 4 W887527	177.8 (70.00)	110.5 (43.50)	115.6 (45.50)
Trail Boss 4 × 4 W888127	117.8 (70.00)	113.0 (44.50)	120.7 (47.50)
Trail Boss 250 R/ES X888528	185.9 (73.20)	111.0 (43.70)	125.7 (49.50)
Trail Boss 250 R/ES W888528	185.9 (73.20)	111.0 (43.70)	125.7 (49.50)
1989			
Trail Boss W898527	185.9 (73.20)	111.8 (44.00)	125.7 (49.50)
Trail Boss 2 × 4 W897527	185.9 (73.20)	111.8 (44.00)	125.7 (49.50)
Trail Boss 4 × 4 W898127	185.9 (73.20)	113.0 (44.50)	125.7 (49.50)
Big Boss 4 × 6 X898627	247.7 (97.50)	113.0 (44.50)	190.5 (75.00)
Big Boss 4 × 6 W898627	247.7 (97.50)	113.0 (44.50)	190.5 (75.00)
1990			
Trail Blazer W907221	185.9 (73.20)	111.8 (44.00)	125.7 (49.50)
Trail Boss 250 W908527	185.9 (73.20)	111.8 (44.00)	125.7 (49.50)
Trail Boss 2 × 4			
250 Air cooled W907527	185.9 (73.20)	111.8 (44.00)	125.7 (49.50)
350 Liquid cooled W907539	195.6 (77.00)	111.8 (44.00)	126.4 (49.75)
Trail Boss 4 × 4			
250 Air cooled W908127	185.9 (73.20)	113.0 (44.50)	126.4 (49.75)
350 Liquid cooled W908139	195.6 (77.00)	113.0 (44.50)	126.4 (49.75)
Big Boss 4 × 6 W908627	247.7 (97.50)	112.8 (44.40)	190.5 (75.00)
1991			
Trail Blazer W917221	185.9 (73.20)	111.8 (44.00)	125.7 (49.50)
Trail Boss 250 W918527	185.9 (73.20)	111.8 (44.00)	125.7 (49.50)
Trail Boss 2 × 4			
250 Air cooled W917527	185.9 (73.20)	111.8 (44.00)	125.7 (49.50)

(continued)

GENERAL DIMENSIONS (continued)

Model	Length cm (in.)	Width cm (in.)	Wheel base cm (in.)
1991 (continued)			
Trail Boss 2 × 4 (continued)			
350 Liquid cooled W917539	195.6 (77.00)	111.8 (44.00)	125.7 (49.75)
Trail Boss 4 × 4			
250 Air cooled W918127	185.9 (73.20)	113.0 (44.50)	126.4 (49.75)
Trail Boss 4 × 4			
350 Liquid cooled W918139	195.6 (77.00)	113.0 (44.50)	126.4 (49.75)
Big Boss 4 × 6 W918627	247.7 (97.50)	112.8 (44.40)	190.5 (75.00)
Big Boss 6 × 6 W918727	247.7 (97.50)	116.1 (45.70)	190.5 (75.00)
1992			
Trail Blazer W927221	185.9 (73.20)	111.8 (44.00)	125.7 (49.50)
Trail Boss 250 W928527	185.9 (73.20)	111.8 (44.00)	125.7 (49.50)
Trail Boss 2 × 4			
250 Air cooled W927527	185.9 (73.20)	111.8 (44.00)	125.7 (49.50)
350 Liquid cooled W927539	195.6 (77.00)	111.8 (44.00)	126.4 (49.75)
Trail Boss 4 × 4			
250 Air cooled W928127	185.9 (73.20)	113.0 (44.50)	126.4 (49.75)
350 Liquid cooled W928139	195.6 (77.00)	113.0 (44.50)	126.4 (49.75)
Big Boss 4 × 6 W928627	247.7 (97.50)	112.8 (44.40)	190.5 (75.00)
Big Boss 6 × 6 W928727	247.7 (97.50)	116.1 (45.70)	190.5 (75.00)
1993			
Trail Blazer W937221	185.9 (73.20)	111.8 (44.00)	125.7 (49.50)
Trail Boss W938527	185.9 (73.20)	111.8 (44.00)	125.7 (49.50)
Sportsman W938039	195.6 (77.00)	113.0 (44.50)	126.4 (49.75)
250 2 × 4 W937527	185.9 (73.20)	111.8 (44.00)	125.7 (49.50)
350 2 × 4 W937539	195.6 (77.00)	111.8 (44.00)	126.4 (49.75)
250 4 × 4 W938127	185.9 (73.20)	113.0 (44.50)	126.4 (49.75)
350 4 × 4 W938139	195.6 (77.00)	113.0 (44.50)	126.4 (49.75)
250 6 × 6 W938727	247.7 (97.50)	112.8 (44.40)	190.5 (75.00)
350 6 × 6 W938739	261.6 (103)	116.1 (45.70)	190.5 (75.00)
1994			
Trail Blazer 2W W947221	185.9 (73.2)	111.2 (44)	125.7 (49.5)

(continued)

GENERAL DIMENSIONS (continued)

Model	Length cm (in.)	Width cm (in.)	Wheel base cm (in.)
1994 (continued)			
Trail Boss 2W W948527	185.9 (73.2)	111.2 (44)	125.7 (49.5)
Sport W948540	182.9 (72)	111.2 (44)	126.4 (49.75)
Sportsman 4 × 4 W948040	195.6 (77)	116.8 (46)	126.4 (49.75)
Sportsman 4 × 4 W948040			
300 2 × 4 W947530	185.9 (73.2)	111.2 (44)	125.7 (49.5)
400 2 × 4 W947540	195.6 (77)	111.2 (44)	126.4 (49.75)
300 4 × 4 W948130	185.9 (73.2)	113 (44.5)	126.4 (49.75)
400 4 × 4 W948140	195.6 (77)	116.8 (46)	126.4 (49.75)
300 6 × 6 W948730	247.6 (97.5)	116.1 (45.7)	190.5 (75)
400 6 × 6 W948740	261.6 (103)	116.1 (45.7)	190.5 (75)
1995			
Trail Blazer W957221	185.9 (73.2)	111.8 (44)	125.7 (49.5)
Trail Boss W958527	185.9 (73.2	111.8 (44)	125.7 (49.5)
300 2 × 4 W957530	185.9 (73.2)	111.8 (44)	126.4 (49.75)
400 2 × 4 W957540	195.6 (77)	111.8 (44)	126.4 (49.75)
300 4 × 4 W958130	185.9 (73.2)	113 (44.5)	126.4 (49.75)
Scrambler W957840	189.2 (74.5)	115.6 (45.5)	123.2 (48.5)
Sport W958540	182.9 (72)	111.8 (44)	126.4 (49.75)
Sportsman 4 × 4 W958040	195.6 (77)	116.8 (46)	126.4 (49.75)
Xplorer 4 × 4 W959140	195.6 (77)	116.8 (46)	126.4 (49.75)
Magnum 2 × 4 W957444	195.6 (77)	118.1 (46.5)	126.4 (49.75)
Magnum 4 × 4 W958144	195.6 (77)	116.8 (46)	126.4 (49.75)
400 6 × 6 W958740	261.5 (103)	116.8 (46)	190.5 (75)

TECHNICAL ABBREVIATIONS

ABDC	After bottom dead center
ATDC	After top dead center
BBDC	Before bottom dead center
BDC	Bottom dead center
BTDC	Before top dead center
C	Celsius (Centigrade)
cc	Cubic centimeters

(continued)

CDI	Capacitor discharge ignition
cu. in.	Cubic inches
F	Fahrenheit
ft.-lb.	Foot-pounds
gal.	Gallons
H/A	High altitude
hp	Horsepower
in.	Inches
kg	Kilogram
kg/cm^2	Kilograms per square centimeter
kgm	Kilogram meters
km	Kilometer
l	Liter
m	Meter
MAG	Magneto
ml	Milliliter
mm	Millimeter
N•m	Newton-meters
oz.	Ounce
psi	Pounds per square inch
PTO	Power take off
pt.	Pints
qt.	Quarts
rpm	Revolutions per minute

RECOMMENDED LUBRICANTS

Item	Lubricant type
Ball-joints	A
Brake fluid	B
Control cables (throttle, choke, etc.)	D
Engine counterbalancer (models so equipped)	E
Engine injection oil (2-stroke models)	F
Engine oil (4-stroke models)	G
Front A arm pivot shafts	A
Front axle bearings (without front wheel drive)	A
Rear axle bearings	A
Steering post bushings	A
Swing arm bushings	A
Tie rod ends	A
Transmission	
Chain type (Type I, Table 6)	D
Gear type (Type II, Table 6)	H
Chain and gear type (Type III, Table 6)	D
Output shaft (with front wheel drive only)	A
EZ Shift selector (Type III, Table 6)	G

A. Grease that conforms to NLG1 No. 2, such as "Conoco Superlube M" or "Mobilgrease Special."
B. Brake fluid, DOT 3 only.
C. Polaris Cable Lube (number 2870510).
D. Polaris Chain Lube (number 2870464).
E. SAE 10W/30 engine oil.
F. Polaris Injection Oil.
G. Polaris SAE 40 (part No. 2871271) is recommended. API type SE or SF with SAE 10W/40 viscosity may be used.
H. SAE 30W engine oil.

APPROXIMATE REFILL CAPACITY

Oil injection reservoir		
2-stroke engines	1.89 L	2 qt.
Dry sump reservoir		
4-stroke engines	1.89 L	2 qt.
Liquid cooling system		
2-stroke engines (so equipped)	1.89 L	2 qt.
4-stroke engines	2.4 L	2.25 qt.
Fuel tank		
All 2-stroke models	15.12 L	4 gal.
4-stroke models	13.25 L	3.5 gal.
Transmission		
1985-1986 chain type	0.47 L	0.5 qt.
1987-1993 gear type	0.47 L	0.5 qt.
1993-1995 gear & chain EZ shift		
High-reverse shift	0.47 L	0.5 qt.
High/low/reverse shift	0.59 L	0.6 qt.

SPARK PLUGS

Model	NGK type	Champion type	Gap mm (in.)
1985-1987	BR8ES	RN4YC	0.51 (0.020)
1988	–	RN4YC	0.64 (0.025)
1989	BR8ES	RN4YC	0.70 (0.028)
1990-1995			
2-stroke models	BR8ES	–	0.70 (0.028)
4-stroke magnum	BKR6ES	–	0.64 (0.025)

IGNITION TIMING (WITH DIAL INDICATOR)*

	Figure 73	Degrees	mm	in.
1985-1987				
All models except Cyclone				
At 3,000 rpm	"A"	23-27	3.482	0.137
At 6,000 rpm	"A"	17.5-21.5	2.145	0.084
Cyclone				
At 3,000 rpm	"A"	21-25	2.959	0.117
At 6,000 rpm	"A"	15.5-19.5	1.729	0.068
1988				
EC25PF-03 engine				
At 3,000 rpm	"A" or "B"	23-27	3.482	0.137
At 6,000 rpm	"A" or "B"	19.5	2.145	0.084
EC25PF-04 engine				
At 3,000 rpm	"C"	27-31	4.646	0.183
At 6,000 rpm	"C"	19.5	2.145	0.084
1989				
All models				
At 3,000 rpm	"B"	25	3.482	0.137
At 6,000 rpm	"B"	20	2.249	0.089
1990-1995				
250 models				
At 3,000 rpm	"B"	25	3.482	0.137
At 6,000 rpm	"B"	20	2.249	0.089
300 models				
At 3,000 rpm	"B"	25	3.482	0.137
At 6,000 rpm	"B"	17	1.632	0.064

(continued)

IGNITION TIMING (WITH DIAL INDICATOR)* (continued)

	Figure 73	Degrees	mm	in.
1990-1995 (continued)				
350 & 400 models				
At 3,000 rpm	"D"	23.5	−3.504	−0.140
At 6,000 rpm	"D"	18	2.164	0.085
425 Magnum models				
At 3,000 rpm	"E"	30	–	–
* All specifications are before top dead center (BTDC).				

VALVE CLEARANCE

	mm	in.
4-stroke engines		
Exhaust valves	0.15	0.006
Inlet valves	0.15	0.006

CHAPTER ONE

GENERAL INFORMATION

This Clymer shop manual covers the 1985-1995 Polaris Scrambler, Trail Blazer, Trail Boss, Cyclone, Big Boss, Xplorer, Sport, Sportsman, and Magnum models. The text gives complete information on maintenance, tune-up, repair and overhaul. Hundreds of photos and drawings guide you through every step. This book includes all of the information you need to know to keep your Polaris running right.

A shop manual is a reference. You want to be able to find information fast. As in all Clymer books, this one is designed with you in mind. All chapters are thumb tabbed. Important items are extensively indexed at the rear of the book. All procedures, tables, photos and illustrations in this manual are for the reader who may be working on the ATV or using this manual for the first time. All the most frequently used specifications and capacities are summarized in the *Quick Reference Data* pages at the front of the book.

Keep the book handy in your tool box. It will help you to better understand how the ATV runs, lower repair and maintenance costs and generally improve your satisfaction with your Polaris ATV.

MANUAL ORGANIZATION

All dimensions and capacities are expressed in English units familiar to U.S. mechanics as well as in metric units. This chapter discusses equipment and tools useful both for preventative maintenance and troubleshooting. Refer to *Basic Hand Tools* in this chapter for the recommended tools that should be on hand for simple home repair and/or major overhaul.

Chapter Two provides methods and suggestions for quick and accurate diagnosis and repair of problems. Troubleshooting procedures discuss typical symptoms and logical methods to pinpoint the trouble.

Chapter Three explains all periodic lubrication and routine maintenance necessary to keep the ATV running well. Chapter Three also includes recommended tune-up procedures, eliminating the need to consult chapters constantly on the various assemblies.

Subsequent chapters describe specific systems such as the engine, clutch/belt drive, transmission, fuel, exhaust, electrical, suspension and brakes.

Each chapter provides disassembly, repair, and assembly procedures in simple step-by-step form. If a repair is impractical for a home mechanic, it is so indicated. It is usually faster and less expensive to take such repairs to a dealer or competent repair shop. Specifications concerning a particular system are included at the end of the appropriate chapter.

Some of the procedures in this manual specify special tools. In most cases, the tool is illustrated either in actual use or alone. Well equipped mechanics may find they can substitute similar tools already on hand or can fabricate their own.

Table 1 lists model number coverage.

General dimensions are listed in **Table 2**.

Table 3 lists vehicle weight.

Metric and U.S. standards are used throughout this manual. U.S. to metric conversion is given in **Table 4**.

Critical torque specifications are found in table form at the end of each chapter (as required). The general torque specifications listed in **Table 5** can be used when a torque specification is not listed for a specific component or assembly.

A list of general technical abbreviations is given in **Table 6**.

Metric tap drill sizes can be found in **Table 7**.

Table 8 lists windchill factors.

Tables 1-8 are found at the end of this chapter.

NOTES, CAUTIONS AND WARNINGS

The terms NOTE, CAUTION and WARNING have specific meanings in this manual. A NOTE provides additional information to make a step or procedure easier or clearer. Disregarding a NOTE could cause inconvenience, but would not cause damage or personal injury.

A CAUTION emphasizes an area where equipment damage could occur. Disregarding a CAUTION could cause permanent mechanical damage; however, personal injury is unlikely.

A WARNING emphasizes an area where personal injury or even death could result from negligence. Mechanical damage may also occur. WARNINGS *are to be taken seriously*. In some cases, serious injury and death have resulted from disregarding similar warnings.

SERVICE HINTS

Most of the service procedures covered are straightforward and can be performed by anyone reasonably handy with tools. It is suggested, however, that you consider your own capabilities carefully before attempting any operation involving major disassembly.

1. "Front," as used in this manual, refers to the front of the ATV; the front of any component is the end closest to the front of the vehicle. The "left" and "right" sides refer to the position of the parts as viewed by a rider sitting and facing forward. For example, the throttle control is on the right-hand side. These rules are simple, but confusion can cause a major inconvenience during service. See **Figure 1**.

2. When disassembling any engine or drive component, mark the parts for location. Also mark all parts which mate together. Small parts, such as bolts, can

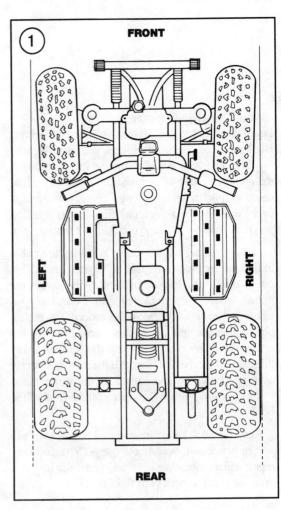

be identified by placing them in plastic sandwich bags (**Figure 2**). Seal the bags and label them with masking tape and a marking pen. When reassembly will take place immediately, an accepted practice is to place nuts and bolts in a cupcake tin or egg carton in the order of disassembly.

3. Finished surfaces should be protected from physical damage or corrosion. Keep gasoline and hydraulic brake fluid off painted surfaces.

4. Use penetrating oil on frozen or tight bolts, then strike the bolt head a few times with a hammer and punch (use a screwdriver on screws). Avoid the use of heat where possible, as it can warp, melt or affect the temper of parts. Heat also ruins finishes, especially paint and plastics.

5. No parts (other than bushings and bearings) in the procedures given in this manual should require unusual force during disassembly or assembly. If a part is difficult to remove or install, find out why before proceeding.

6. Cover all openings after removing parts or components to prevent dirt, small tools or other contamination from falling in.

7. Read each procedure *completely* while looking at the actual parts before starting a job. Make sure you *thoroughly* understand what is to be done and then carefully follow the procedure, step-by-step.

8. Recommendations are occasionally made to refer service or maintenance to a Polaris dealer or a specialist in a particular field. In these cases, the work will be done more quickly and economically than if you performed the job yourself.

9. In procedural steps, the term "replace" means to discard a defective part and replace it with a new or exchange unit. "Overhaul" means to remove, disas-semble, inspect, measure, repair or replace defective parts, reassemble and install major systems or parts.

10. Some operations require the use of a hydraulic press. It is wiser to have these operations performed by a shop equipped for such work, rather than to try to do the job yourself with makeshift equipment that may damage your machine.

11. Repairs go much faster and easier if your machine is clean before you begin work. There are many special cleaners on the market, like Bel-Ray Degreaser, for washing the engine and related parts. Follow the manufacturer's directions on the container for the best results. Clean all oily or greasy parts with cleaning solvent as you remove them.

> *WARNING*
> *Never use gasoline as a cleaning agent. It presents an extreme fire hazard. Be sure to work in a well-ventilated area when using cleaning solvent. Keep a fire extinguisher, rated for gasoline fires, handy in any case.*

12. Much of the labor charge for repairs made by a dealer are for the time involved during the removal, disassembly, assembly, and reinstallation of other parts in order to reach the defective part. It is frequently possible to perform the preliminary operations yourself and then take the defective unit to the dealer for repair at considerable savings.

13. If special tools are required, make arrangements to get them before you start. It is frustrating and time consuming to get partly into a job and then be unable to complete it.

14. Make diagrams (take a video or Polaroid picture) wherever similar-appearing parts are found. For instance, crankcase bolts are often not the same length. You may think you can remember where everything came from—but mistakes are costly. There is also the possibility that you may be sidetracked and not return to work for days or even weeks—in which the time carefully laid out parts may have become disturbed.

15. When assembling parts, be sure all shims and washers are replaced exactly as they came out.

16. Whenever a rotating part butts against a stationary part, look for a shim or washer.

17. Use new gaskets if there is any doubt about the condition of the old ones. A thin coat of silicone sealant on non-pressure type gaskets may help them seal more effectively. If it is necessary to make a

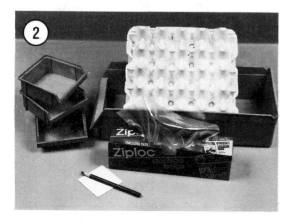

cover gasket and you do not have a suitable old gasket to use as a guide, you can use the outline of the cover and gasket material to make a new gasket. Apply engine oil to the cover gasket surface. Then place the cover on the new gasket material and apply pressure with your hands. The oil will leave a very accurate outline on the gasket material that can be cut around.

> *CAUTION*
> *When purchasing gasket material to make a gasket, measure the thickness of the old gasket (at an uncompressed point) and purchase gasket material with the same approximate thickness.*

18. Heavy grease can be used to hold small parts in place if they tend to fall out during assembly. Be sure to keep grease and oil away from electrical components.

19. A carburetor is best cleaned by disassembling it and cleaning the parts in hot soap and water. Never soak gaskets and rubber parts in commercial carburetor cleaner. Never use wire to clean out jets and air passages, because they are easily damaged. Use compressed air to blow out the carburetor only if the float has been removed first.

20. Take your time and do the job right. Do not forget that a newly rebuilt engine must be broken in just like a new one.

TORQUE SPECIFICATIONS

Torque specifications throughout this manual are given in Newton meters (N•m) and foot pounds (ft.-lb.). Newton meters have been adopted in place of kilogram meters (mkg) in accordance with the International Modernized Metric System. Many tool manufacturers offer torque wrenches calibrated in both Newton meters and foot pounds.

Early torque wrenches calibrated in kilogram meters can be used by performing a simple conversion. All you have to do is move the decimal point one place to the right. For example: 4.7 mkg = 47 N•m. This conversion is accurate enough for mechanical work even though the exact mathematical conversion is 46.09 N•m.

SAFETY FIRST

Professional mechanics can work for years and never sustain a serious injury. If you observe a few rules of common sense and safety, you can enjoy many safe hours servicing your own machine. If you ignore these rules you can hurt yourself or damage the equipment.

1. Never use gasoline as a cleaning solvent.

2. Never smoke or use a torch in the vicinity of flammable liquids, such as cleaning solvent in an open container.

3. If welding or brazing is required on the machine, remove the fuel tank to a safe distance, at least 50 feet away.

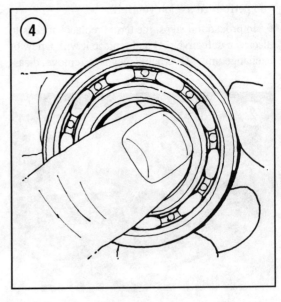

1

4. Use the proper sized wrenches to avoid damage to fasteners and injury to yourself.

5. When loosening a tight or stuck nut, be guided by what would happen if the wrench slips. Be careful; protect yourself accordingly.

6. When replacing a fastener, always use one with the same measurements and strength as the old one. Incorrect or mismatched fasteners can result in damage to the vehicle and possible personal injury. Beware of fastener kits that are filled with cheap and poorly made nuts, bolts, washers and cotter pins. Refer to *Fasteners* in this chapter for additional information.

7. Keep all hand and power tools in good condition. Wipe greasy and oily tools after using them. They are difficult to hold and can cause injury. Replace or repair worn or damaged tools.

8. Keep your work area clean and uncluttered.

9. Wear safety goggles during all operations involving drilling, grinding, the use of a cold chisel or *anytime* you feel unsure about the safety of your eyes. Safety goggles should also be worn anytime solvent and compressed air is used to clean parts.

10. Keep an approved fire extinguisher (**Figure 3**) nearby. Be sure it is rated for gasoline (Class B) and electrical (Class C) fires.

11. When drying bearings or other rotating parts with compressed air, never allow the air jet to rotate the bearing or part. The air jet is capable of rotating them at speeds far in excess of those for which they were designed. The bearing or rotating part is very likely to disintegrate and cause serious injury and damage. To prevent injury and bearing damage when

using compressed air, hold the inner bearing race (**Figure 4**) by hand.

EXPENDABLE SUPPLIES

Certain expendable supplies (**Figure 5**) are required during maintenance and repair work. These include grease, oil, gasket cement, wiping cloths and cleaning solvent. Ask your dealer for the special locking compounds, special lubricants or other products which may be suggested by the manufacturer for maintenance or repair. Cleaning solvents may be available from servicing dealers or some hardware stores.

> *WARNING*
> *Having a stack of clean shop cloths on hand is important when performing engine and suspension service work. Clean shop cloths should be stored safely, but present less danger than solvent and lubricant soaked cloths. Most local fire codes require that used shop cloths be stored in a sealed, metal container with a self-closing lid until they can be washed or discarded.*

> *WARNING*
> *Even mild solvents and other chemicals can be absorbed into your skin while cleaning parts. Health hazards ranging from mild discomfort to major infections can often be avoided by using a pair of petroleum-resistant gloves. These can be purchased from industrial supply houses or many hardware stores.*

ENGINE AND CHASSIS SERIAL NUMBERS

Polaris all-terrain vehicles are identified by frame and engine identification numbers. The frame or Vehicle Identification Number (VIN) is stamped on the frame tube at one of the locations shown in **Figure 6**.

On 1985 and 1986 models, the vehicle's model number is located at A, **Figure 6** and the serial number is located at B, **Figure 6**.

On 1987 and 1988 models except 1988 R/ES model, the vehicle's model number is located at C, **Figure 6** and the serial number is located at D,

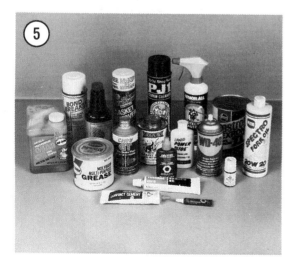
5

Figure 6. On 1988 R/ES model, the model and serial numbers are located at location D, **Figure 6**.

On 1989 and newer models, the vehicle's serial number is located at E, **Figure 6**.

The engine number of all models is stamped on the right-hand side of the crankcase as shown in **Figure 7**.

Figure 8 shows the breakdown of the model number found on Polaris vehicles covered in this manual. The first letter will be either a "W" or "X" and indicates if the model is a limited production (pilot) machine designated by "X" or a regular production machine designated by "W." The next two digits represent the year that the vehicle was manufactured. The last two digits in the vehicle's model number indicate the engine model. The model numbers are listed in **Table 1**.

Write down all serial and model numbers applicable to your machine and carry the numbers with you when you order parts from a dealer. Always order by year and engine and machine numbers. If possible, compare the old parts with the new ones before purchasing them. If the parts are not alike, have the parts manager explain the reason for the difference

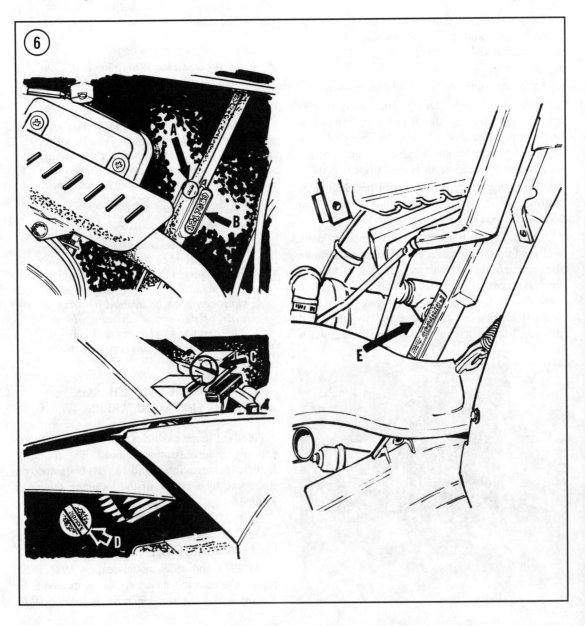

and insist on assurance that the new parts will fit and are correct.

BASIC HAND TOOLS

Many of the procedures in this manual can be carried out with simple hand tools and test equipment familiar to the mechanic. Keep your tools clean and in a tool box. Keep them organized with home related tools stored together. After using a tool, wipe

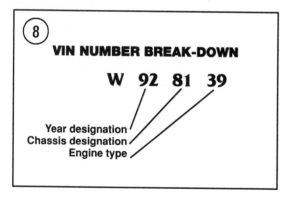

VIN NUMBER BREAK-DOWN

W 92 81 39

Year designation
Chassis designation
Engine type

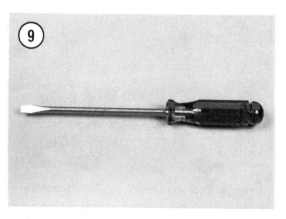

off dirt and grease with a clean cloth and return the tool to its correct place.

Top quality tools are essential; they are also more economical in the long run. If you are now starting to build your tool collection, avoid the "advertised specials" featured at some parts houses, discount stores and chain drug stores. These are usually a poor grade tool that can be sold cheaply and that is exactly what they are—*cheap*. They are usually made of inferior material and are thick, heavy and clumsy. Their rough finish makes them difficult to clean and they usually don't last very long. If it is ever your misfortune to use such tools you will probably find out that the wrenches do not fit the heads of fasteners correctly and will often damage the fastener.

Quality tools are made of alloy steel and are heat treated for greater strength. They are lighter and better balanced than cheap ones. Their surface is smooth, making them a pleasure to work with and easy to clean. The initial cost of good quality tools may be more but they are cheaper in the long run. Don't try to buy everything in all sizes in the beginning; do it a little at a time until you have the necessary tools.

The following tools are required to perform virtually any repair job. Each tool is described and the recommended sizes given for starting a tool collection. Additional tools and some duplicates may be added as you become familiar with the vehicle. Polaris all-terrain vehicles are built with metric and U.S. standard fasteners—so if you are starting your collection now, buy both sizes.

Screwdrivers

The screwdriver is a very basic tool, but if used improperly it will do more damage than good. The slot on a screw has a definite dimension and shape. A screwdriver must be selected to conform with that shape. Use a small screwdriver for small screws and a large one for large screws or the screw head will be damaged.

Two basic types of screwdrivers are required: common (flat-blade) screwdrivers (**Figure 9**) and Phillips screwdrivers (**Figure 10**).

Screwdrivers are available in sets which often include an assortment of common and Phillips blades. If you buy them individually, buy at least the following:

    a. Common screwdriver—5/16 × 6 in. blade.

b. Common screwdriver—3/8 × 12 in. blade.

c. Phillips screwdriver—size 2 tip, 6 in. blade.

Use screwdrivers only for driving screws. Never use a screwdriver for prying or chiseling metal. Do not try to remove a Phillips or Allen head screw with a common screwdriver (unless the screw has a combination head that will accept either type); you can damage the head so that even the proper tool will be unable to remove it.

Keep screwdrivers in the proper condition and they will last longer and perform better. Always keep the tip of a common screwdriver in good condition. **Figure 11** shows how to grind the tip to the proper shape if it becomes damaged. Note the symmetrical sides of the tip.

Pliers

Pliers come in a wide range of types and sizes. Pliers are useful for holding, cutting, bending and crimping. They should never be used to cut hardened objects or to turn bolts or nuts. **Figure 12** shows several pliers useful in ATV repair.

Each type of pliers has a specialized function. Slip-joint pliers and are used mainly for holding things and for bending. Needlenose pliers are used to hold or bend small objects. Groove-joint pliers (commonly referred to as channel locks) can be adjusted to hold various sizes of objects such as pipe or tubing. There are many more types of pliers, but the ones described are the most suitable for ATV repair.

> *CAUTION*
> *Pliers should not be used for loosening or tightening nuts or bolts. The pliers' sharp teeth will cut into the corners of the nut or bolt and damage the fastener.*

> *CAUTION*
> *If it is necessary to use slip-joint pliers to hold an object with a finished surface that can be easily damaged, wrap the object with tape or cardboard for protection.*

Locking (Vise-grip) Pliers

Locking pliers (**Figure 13**) hold objects very tightly like a vise. Because locking pliers exert more force than regular pliers, their sharp jaws can perma-

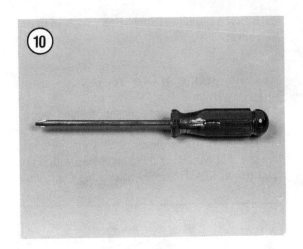

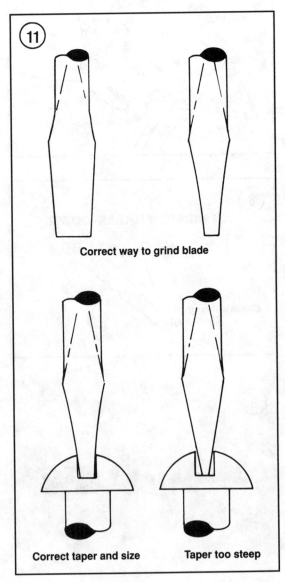

Correct way to grind blade

Correct taper and size Taper too steep

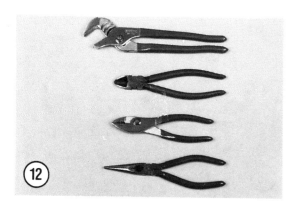

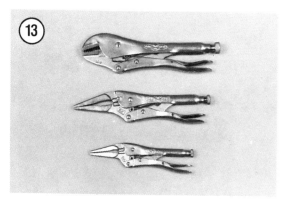

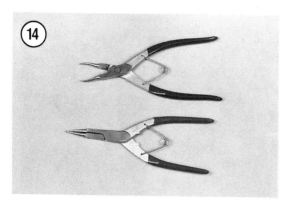

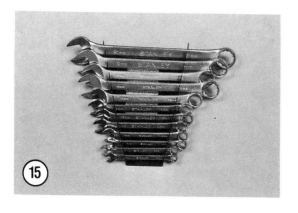

nently scar any object that is held. In addition, when locking pliers are locked in position, they can crush or deform thin wall material. Locking pliers are available in many types for specific tasks.

Snap Ring (Circlip) Pliers

Snap ring pliers (**Figure 14**) are made for removing and installing snap rings and should not be used for any other purpose. External pliers (spreading or expanding) are used to remove snap rings from the outside of a shaft or other similar part. Internal snap rings are located inside a tube, gear or housing and require pliers that squeeze the ends of the snap ring together so that the snap ring can be removed.

Box-end, Open-end and Combination Wrenches

Box-end and open-end wrenches (**Figure 15**) are available in sets or separately in a variety of sizes. The number stamped on open and box-end wrenches refers to the distance between 2 parallel flats of a nut or bolt head. Combination wrenches have a box-end wrench on one end and an open-end wrench of the same size on the other end. The wrench size is stamped near the center of combination wrenches.

Open-end wrenches are speedy and work best in areas with limited overhead access. Their wide jaws make them unsuitable for situations where the bolt or nut is sunken in a well or close to the edge of a casting. These wrenches only grip on two flats of a fastener so if either the fastener head or wrench jaws are worn, the wrench may slip off.

The fastener must have overhead access to use box-end wrenches, but they grip all six corners of a fastener for a very secure grip. Box-end wrenches may be either 6-point or 12-point. The 12-point box-end wrench permits operation in situations where there is only a small amount of room to turn the wrench. The 6-point gives superior holding power and durability but requires a greater swinging radius.

No matter what style of wrench you choose, proper use is important to prevent personal injury. When using any wrench, get in the habit of pulling the wrench toward you. This reduces the risk of injuring your hand if the wrench should slip. If you have to push the wrench away from you to loosen or tighten a fastener, open and push with the palm of your hand. This technique gets your fingers and knuckles out of the way should the wrench slip. Before using a wrench, always consider what could happen if the wrench slips or if the fastener breaks.

Adjustable Wrenches

An adjustable wrench (sometimes called a Crescent wrench) can be adjusted to fit nearly any nut or bolt head which has clear access around its entire perimeter. Adjustable wrenches **Figure 16** are best used as a backup wrench to keep a large nut or bolt from turning while the other end is being loosened or tightened with a proper wrench.

Adjustable wrenches have only two gripping surfaces and one is designed to move. The usually large physical size and the adjustable feature make this type of wrench more apt to slip off the fastener, damaging the part and possibly injuring your hand.

These wrenches are directional; the solid jaw must be the one transmitting the force. Apply force in the direction indicated by the arrow in **Figure 16**. If you use the adjustable jaw to transmit the force, it may loosen, allowing the wrench to slip off.

Adjustable wrenches come in several sizes but a 6 or 8 in. size is recommended as an all-purpose wrench.

Socket Wrenches

This type is undoubtedly the fastest, safest and most convenient to use. Sockets which attach to a ratchet handle are available with 6-point or 12-point openings and 1/4, 3/8 and 1/2 in. drives (**Figure 17**). The drive size indicates the size of the square hole which mates with the ratchet handle.

Torque Wrench

A torque wrench (**Figure 18**) is used with a socket to measure how tightly a nut or bolt is installed. They come in a wide price range and with 1/4, 3/8, or 1/2 in. square drive. The drive size indicates the size of the square drive which mates with the socket.

Impact Driver

This tool makes removal of tight fasteners easy and reduces the chance for damage to bolts and screw slots. Impact drivers and interchangeable bits

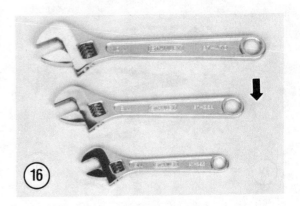

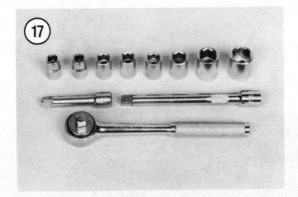

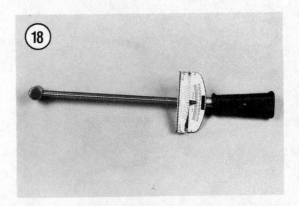

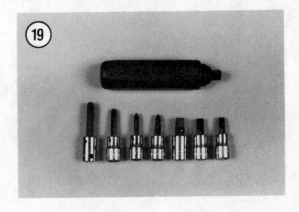

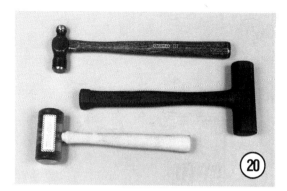

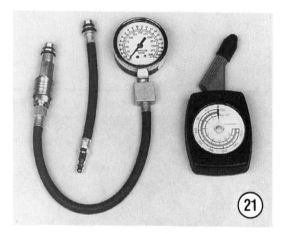

(**Figure 19**) are available at most large hardware, ATV and motorcycle dealers. Sockets can also be used with some hand impact drivers; however, make sure the socket is designed for impact use. Regular hand type sockets may shatter if used on an impact driver.

Hammers

The correct hammer (**Figure 20**) is necessary for certain repairs. A hammer with a face (or head) of rubber or plastic or the soft-faced hammer that is filled with lead shot is sometimes necessary during engine teardowns. *Never* use a metal-faced hammer on engine or suspension parts, as severe damage will result in most cases. You can usually produce the same amount of force with a soft-faced hammer. A metal-faced hammer, however, is required when using a hand impact driver or cold chisel.

PRECISION MEASURING TOOLS

Measurement is an important part of vehicle and engine service. When performing many of the service procedures in this manual, you will be required to make a number of measurements. These include basic checks such as engine compression (**Figure 21**) and spark plug gap (**Figure 22**). As you get deeper into engine disassembly and service, measurements will be required to determine the condition of the piston and cylinder bore, crankshaft runout and so on. When making these measurements, the degree of accuracy dictates which tool is required. Precision measuring tools are expensive. If this is your first experience at engine service, it may be more worthwhile to have the checks made at a dealer. However, as your skills and enthusiasm increase for doing your own service work, you may want to purchase some of these specialized tools. The following is a description of the measuring tools required to perform the service procedures described in this manual.

Feeler Gauge

Feeler gauges are available in sets of various sizes (**Figure 23**). The gauge is made of either a piece of a flat or round hardened steel of a specified thickness. Wire gauges are used to measure spark plug

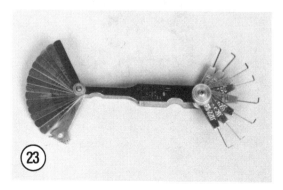

gap. Flat gauges are used for most other measurements.

Vernier Caliper

This tool (**Figure 24**) is invaluable for reading inside, outside and depth measurements to close precision. Common uses of a vernier caliper are measuring the length of springs, the thickness of shims or the depth of a bearing bore. Although a vernier caliper is not as precise as a micrometer, it allows reasonably accurate measurements, typically to within 0.001 in. (0.025 mm).

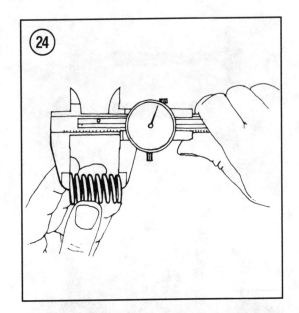

Outside Micrometers

An outside micrometer (**Figure 25**) is one of the most reliable instuments for precision measurement. Outside micrometers are required to precisely measure piston diameter, piston pin diameter, crankshft journal and crankpin diameter. Used with a telescopic gauge, an outside micrometer can be used to measure cylinder bore size and to determine cylinder taper and out-of-round. Outside micrometers are delicate instruments; if dropped on the floor, they most certainly will be knocked out of calibration. Always handle and use micrometers carefully to ensure accuracy. Store micrometers in their padded case when not in use to prevent damage.

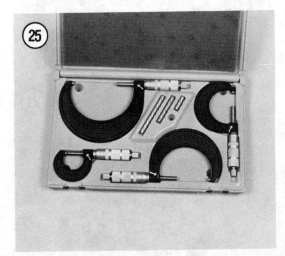

Dial Indicator

Dial indicators (**Figure 26**) are precision tools used to check differences in machined surfaces, such as the runout of a crankshaft or brake disc. A dial indicator may also be used to locate the piston at a specific position when checking ignition timing. For ATV repair, select a dial indicator with a continuous dial (**Figure 27**). Several different mounting types are available, including a magnetic stand that attaches to iron surfaces, a clamp that can be attached to various components and a spark plug adapter that locates the probe of the dial indicator through the spark plug hole. See *Magnetic Stand* in this chapter. The various mounts are required for specific measuring requirements. The text will indicate the type of mounting necessary.

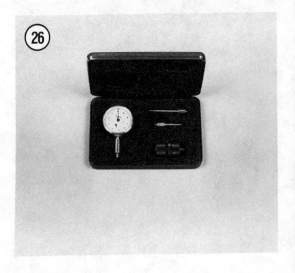

Degree Wheel

A degree wheel (**Figure 28**) is a specific tool used to measure parts of a circle or angle. A degree wheel can be a valuable aid in positioning the engine crankshaft to determine the exact timing of the ignition or port opening. A degree wheel can be ordered through most parts suppliers.

Compression Gauge

An engine with low compression cannot be properly tuned and will not develop full power. A compression gauge (**Figure 29**) measures engine compression. The one shown on the left has a flexible stem with an extension that allows you to hold it while operating the starter. Open the throttle all the way when checking engine compression. See Chapter Three.

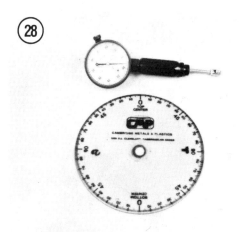

Strobe Timing Light

This instrument is used to check ignition timing accurately. By flashing a light at the precise instant the spark plug fires, the position of the timing mark can be seen. The flashing light makes the moving mark appear to stand still so that it can be viewed in relation to the stationary mark.

Suitable lights range from inexpensive neon bulb types to powerful xenon strobe lights. See **Figure 30** for a typical timing light. A light with an inductive pickup is recommended to eliminate any possible damage to ignition wiring. The timing light should be attached and used according to the instructions provided by its manufacturer.

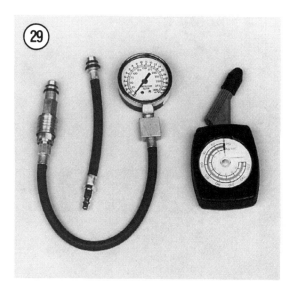

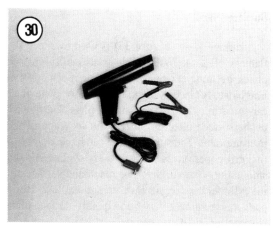

Multimeter or VOM

A VOM (Volt and Ohm Meter) is a valuable tool for all electrical system troubleshooting (**Figure 31**). The voltmeter application is used to indicate the voltage applied or available to various components. The ohmmeter can be used to check for continuity and to measure resistance. Some tests are easily accomplished using a meter with sweeping needle, but other components should be checked with a digital VOM.

Screw Pitch Gauge

A screw pitch gauge (**Figure 32**) determines the thread pitch of bolts, screws or studs. The gauge is made up of a number of thin plates. Each plate has a thread shape cut on one edge to match one thread pitch. When using a screw pitch gauge to determine a thread pitch size, try to fit different blade sizes onto the bolt thread until both threads match exactly.

Magnetic Stand

A magnetic stand (**Figure 33**) often used to securely hold a dial indicator when checking the runout of a round object or when checking the end play of a shaft.

V-Blocks

V-blocks (**Figure 34**) are precision ground blocks that are used to hold a round object when checking its runout or condition.

Surface Plate

A surface plate (**Figure 35**) is used to check the flatness of parts. While industrial quality surface plates are quite expensive, the home mechanic can improvise. A piece of thick, flat metal or plate glass can sometimes be used as a surface plate. The quality of the surface plate will affect the accuracy of the measurement. The surface plate can have a piece of fine grit paper on its surface to assist cleaning and smoothing a flat surface. The machined surfaces of the cylinder head, crankcase, and other close fitting parts may require a very good quality surface plate to smooth nicked or damaged surfaces.

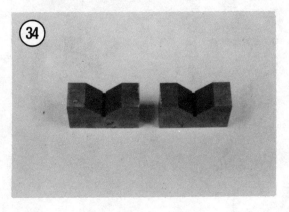

NOTE
Check with a local machine shop, fabricating shop or school offering a machine shop course for the availability of a metal plate that can be resurfaced and used as a surface plate.

SPECIAL TOOLS

This section describes special tools that may be unique to Polaris all-terrain vehicles and engine service and repair. These tools are often a valuable asset even if used infrequently and most can be ordered through your Polaris dealer. It is often necessary to know the specific vehicle or engine model for selecting the correct special tools.

Flywheel Puller

A flywheel puller (**Figure 36**) is required whenever it is necessary to remove the flywheel and service the stator plate assembly or when adjusting the ignition timing. In addition, when disassembling the engine, the flywheel must be removed before the crankcase can be split. There is no satisfactory substitute for this tool. Because the flywheel is a taper fit on the crankshaft, makeshift removal often results in crankshaft and flywheel damage. Don't think about removing the flywheel without this tool. A puller can be ordered through Polaris dealers.

Clutch Tools

A number of special tools are required for clutch service. These are described in Chapter Eight.

MECHANIC'S TIPS

Removing Frozen Nuts and Screws

When a fastener rusts and cannot be removed, several methods may be used to loosen it. First, apply penetrating oil such as Liquid Wrench or WD-40 (available at hardware or auto supply stores). Apply it liberally and let it penetrate for 10-15 minutes, then tap the fastener several times with a small hammer. Do not hit it hard enough to cause damage. Reapply the penetrating oil if necessary. Using an impact driver as described in this chapter will often loosen a stuck bolt or screw.

CAUTION
Do not pound on screwdrivers unless the steel shank of the tool extends all the way through the handle. Pounding on a plastic–handled screwdriver is a sure way to destroy the tool.

For frozen screws, apply additional penetrating oil as described, insert a screwdriver in the slot and tap the top of the screwdriver with a hammer. This loosens the rust so the screw can be removed in the normal way. If the screw head is too chewed up to use this method, grip the head with vise-grip pliers and twist the screw out.

Avoid applying heat unless specifically instructed, as it may melt, warp or remove the temper from parts.

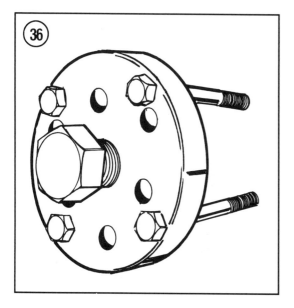

Removing Broken Screws or Bolts

When the head breaks off a screw or bolt, several methods are available to remove the remaining portion.

If a large portion of the remainder projects out, try gripping it with vise-grips. If the projecting portion is too small, file it to fit a wrench or cut a slot in it to fit a screwdriver. See **Figure 37**.

If the head breaks off flush, use a screw extractor. To do this, centerpunch as close as possible to the exact center of the remaining part of the screw or bolt. Drill a small hole in the screw and tap the extractor into the hole. Back the screw out with a wrench on the extractor. See **Figure 38**.

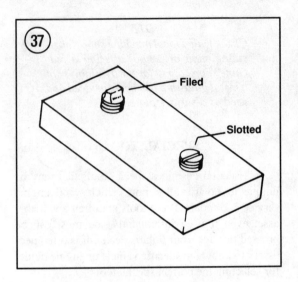

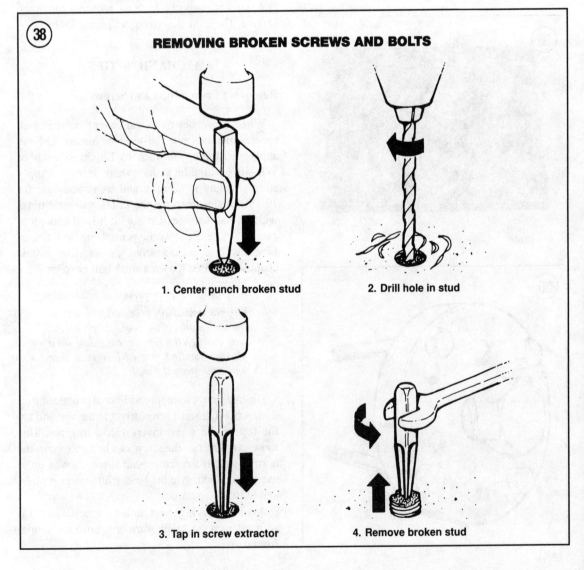

REMOVING BROKEN SCREWS AND BOLTS

1. Center punch broken stud

2. Drill hole in stud

3. Tap in screw extractor

4. Remove broken stud

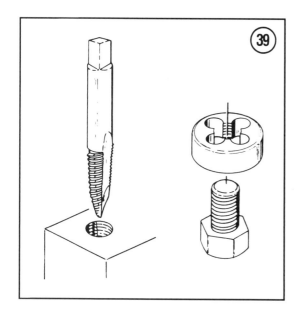

Remedying Stripped Threads

Occasionally, fastner threads are damaged during service or repair. Sometimes the threads can be cleaned up by running a tap (for internal threads on nuts) or die (for external threads on bolts) through the threads. See **Figure 39**. To clean or repair spark plug threads, a spark plug tap can be used.

NOTE
Tap and dies can be purchased individually or in a set as shown in **Figure 40**.

If an internal thread is damaged, it may be necessary to install a Helicoil (**Figure 41**) or some other type of thread insert. Follow the manufacturer's instructions when installing their insert.

If it is necessary to drill and tap a hole, refer to **Table 7** for metric tap drill sizes.

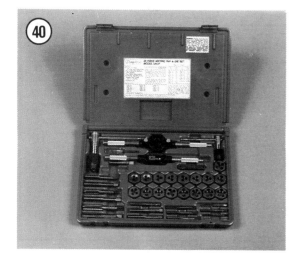

Removing Broken or Damaged Studs

If some threads of a stud are damaged, but some threads remain (**Figure 42**), the old stud can be removed as follows. A tube of Loctite 271 (red), 2 nuts, 2 wrenches and a new stud are required during this procedure.

1. Thread two nuts onto the damaged stud (**Figure 43**), then tighten the 2 nuts against each other so that they are locked.

NOTE
If the threads on the damaged stud do not allow installation of the 2 nuts, you may be able to remove the stud with locking (vise-grip) pliers.

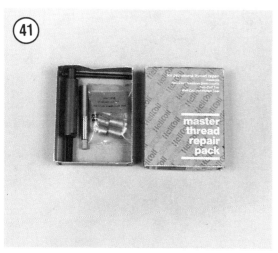

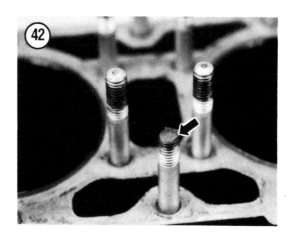

2. Turn the bottom nut counterclockwise (**Figure 44**) and unscrew the stud.

3. Clean the threads with solvent or electrical contact cleaner and allow to dry thoroughly.

4. Install 2 nuts on the top half of the new stud as in Step 1. Make sure they are locked securely.

5. Coat the bottom half of a new stud with Loctite 271 (red).

6. Turn the top nut clockwise and thread the new stud in completely.

7. Remove the nuts and repeat for each stud as required.

8. Follow Loctite's directions on cure time before assembling the component.

Ball Bearing Replacement

Ball bearings (**Figure 45**) are used throughout the engine and chassis to reduce power loss, heat and noise resulting from friction. Because ball bearings are precision made parts, they must be maintained by proper lubrication and maintenance. If a bearing is found to be damaged, it should be replaced immediately. However, when installing a new bearing, care should be taken to prevent damage to the new bearing. While bearing replacement is described in the individual chapters where applicable, the following should be used as a guideline.

NOTE
Unless otherwise specified, install bearings with the manufacturer's mark or number facing outward.

Removal

While bearings are normally removed only if damaged, there may be times when it is necessary to remove a bearing that is in good condition. However, improper bearing removal will damage the bearing and maybe the shaft or case half. Observe the following when removing bearings.

1. When using a puller to remove a bearing from a shaft, care must be taken so shaft is not damaged. Always place a spacer (**Figure 46**) between the end of the shaft and the puller screw. In addition, place the puller arms next to the inner bearing race.

2. When using a hammer to remove a bearing from a shaft, do not strike the hammer directly against the shaft. Instead, support the bearing races with

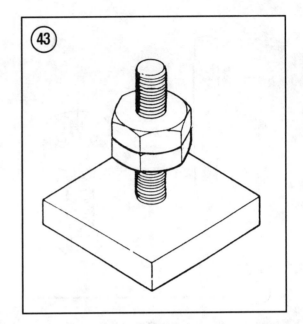

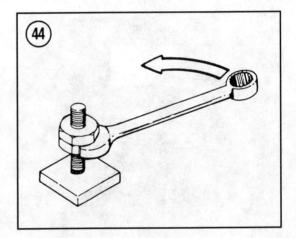

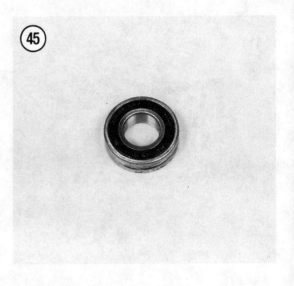

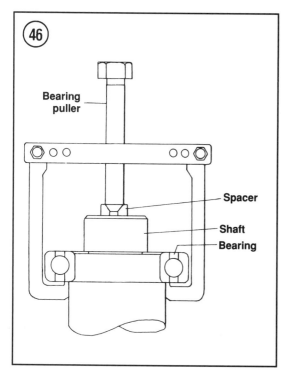

46

Bearing puller

Spacer

Shaft

Bearing

wooden blocks (**Figure 47**) and use a brass or aluminum rod between the hammer and shaft.

WARNING
Failure to use proper precautions will probably result in damaged parts and may cause personal injury.

3. The ideal method of bearing removal is with a hydraulic press. However, certain procedures must be followed or damage may occur to the bearing, shaft or case half. Observe the following when using a press:

   a. Always support the inner and outer bearing races with the proper size wooden or aluminum spacer (**Figure 48**). If only the outer race is supported, the balls and/or the inner race will be damaged.

   b. Always make sure the press ram aligns with the center of the shaft. If the ram is not centered, it may damage the bearing and/or shaft.

   c. The moment the shaft is free of the bearing, it will drop to the floor. Secure or hold the shaft to prevent it from falling.

Installation

Refer to the following when installing bearings.

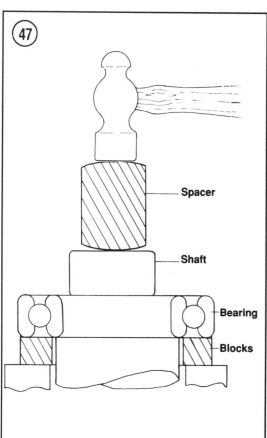

47

Spacer

Shaft

Bearing

Blocks

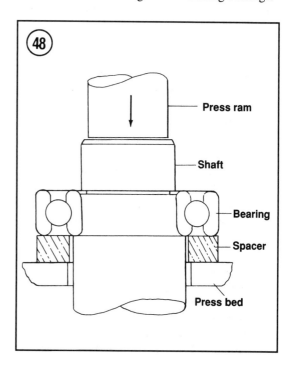

48

Press ram

Shaft

Bearing

Spacer

Press bed

1. When installing a bearing in a housing, pressure must be applied to the *outer* bearing race (**Figure 49**). When installing a bearing on a shaft, pressure must be applied to the *inner* bearing race.

2. When installing a bearing as described in Step 1, some type of driver is required. Never strike the bearing directly with a hammer or the bearing will be damaged. When installing a bearing, a piece of pipe or a socket with an outer diameter that matches the bearing race is required. **Figure 50** shows the correct way to use a socket and hammer when installing a bearing.

3. Step 1 describes how to install a bearing in a case half and over a shaft. However, when installing over a shaft and into a housing at the same time, a snug fit is required for both outer and inner bearing races. In this situation, a spacer must be installed underneath the driver tool so that pressure is applied evenly across *both* races. If the outer race is not supported as shown in **Figure 51**, the balls will push against the outer bearing race and damage it.

Shrink Fit

1. *Installing a bearing over a shaft*—If a tight fit is required, the bearing inside diameter will be smaller than the shaft. In this case, driving the bearing on the shaft using normal methods may cause bearing damage. Instead, the bearing should be heated before installation. Note the following:

   a. Secure the shaft so that it can be ready for bearing installation.

   b. Clean the bearing surface on the shaft of all residue. Remove burrs with a file or sandpaper.

   c. Fill a suitable pot or beaker with clean mineral oil. Place a thermometer (rated higher than 120° C [248° F]) in the oil. Support the thermometer so it does not rest on the bottom or side of the pot.

   d. Secure the bearing with a piece of heavy wire bent to hold it in the pot. Hang the bearing in the pot so it does not touch the bottom or sides of the pot.

   e. Turn the heat on and monitor the thermometer. When the oil temperature rises to approximately 120° C (248° F), remove the bearing from the pot and quickly install it. If necessary, place a socket against the inner bearing race (**Figure 52**) and tap the bearing into place. As

the bearing chills, it will tighten on the shaft so you must work quickly when installing it. Make sure the bearing is installed all the way.

2. *Installing a bearing in a housing*—Bearings are generally installed in a housing with a slight interference fit. Driving the bearing into the housing using normal methods may damage the housing or cause bearing damage. Instead, the housing should be heated before the bearing is installed. Note the following:

CAUTION
Before heating the housing in this procedure to remove the bearings, wash the

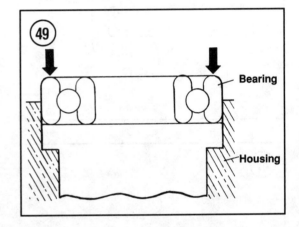

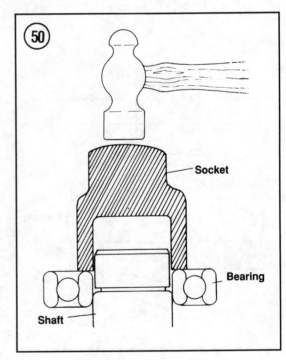

housing thoroughly with detergent and water. Rinse and rewash the housing as required to remove all traces of oil and other chemical deposits.

a. Heat the housing to about 100° C (212° F) in an oven or on a hot plate. An easy way to see if it is at the proper temperature is to drop tiny drops of water on the housing; if they sizzle and evaporate immediately, the temperature is correct. Heat only one housing at a time.

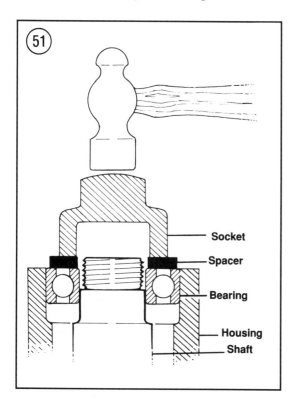

51

Socket
Spacer
Bearing
Housing
Shaft

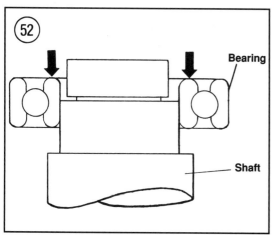

52

Bearing

Shaft

CAUTION
Do not heat the housing with a torch (propane or acetylene)—never bring open flames into contact with the bearing or housing. The direct heat will destroy the case hardening of the bearing and will likely warp the housing.

b. Remove the housing from the oven or hot plate. Hold onto the housing with a kitchen pot holder, heavy gloves or heavy shop cloths—*it is hot.*

NOTE
A suitable size socket and extension works well for removing and installing bearings.

c. Hold the housing with the bearing side down and tap the bearing out. Repeat for all bearings in the housing.
d. While heating the housing, place the new bearings in a freezer if possible. Chilling them will slightly reduce their overall diameter while the hot housing assembly is slightly larger due to heat expansion. This will make installation much easier.

NOTE
Always install bearings with their manufacturer's mark or number facing outward unless the text directs otherwise.

e. While the housing is still hot, install the new bearing(s) into the housing. Install the bearings by hand, if possible. If necessary, lightly tap the bearing(s) into the housing with a socket placed on the outer bearing race. *Do not install new bearings by driving on the inner bearing race.* Install the bearing(s) until it seats completely.

Oil Seals

Oil seals (**Figure 53**) are used to prevent leakage of oil, grease or combustion gasses from between a housing and a shaft. Improper procedures to remove a seal can damage the housing or the shaft. Improper installation can damage the seal. Note the following:

a. Prying is generally the easiest and most effective method of removing a seal from a housing. However, always place a rag underneath the pry tool to prevent damage to the housing.

b. A low–temperature grease should be packed in the seal lips before the seal is installed.

c. Oil seals should always be installed so their manufacturer's numbers or marks face out.

NOTE
A socket of the correct size can often be used as a seal driver. Select a socket that fits the seal's outer diameter properly and clears any protruding shafts.

d. Oil seals should be installed with a seal driver placed against the outside of the seal. Make sure the seal is driven squarely into the housing. Never install a seal by hitting directly against the top of the seal with a hammer.

OPERATING TIPS

Areas set aside by the federal government, state or local agencies for off-road riding are continuing to disappear. The loss of these areas is usually due to the inappropriate actions of a few who really don't care if they ruin the sport for other more responsible riders. Areas may be closed to protect wildlife habitat, historical sites, vegetation, geological formations or to set aside the area for use by those who do not favor powered equipment. Whatever the reason, *DO NOT* enter areas that prohibit ATV's (or all powered vehicles) because doing so can result in an expensive citation and may result in closures of more land. By following basic rules, you and others will have areas open for enjoying ATV's.

1. Never operate the vehicle in congested areas or steer toward people.

2. Always be aware of the terrain and avoid operating the ATV at excessive speed. Unfamiliar terrain may contain hidden obstructions, low hanging tree limbs, unseen ditches, hikers or even animals. Avoid operation near dangerous terrain.

3. Cross highways (where permitted) at a 90° angle after looking both directions and determining that it is safe to cross. If a group is crossing, post traffic crossing guards.

4. Do not ride on or near railroad tracks. The engine and exhaust noise can drown out the sound of an oncoming train.

5. Keep the headlight and taillight clean. When riding at night, always have the headlight and taillight ON.

6. Do not tailgate. Rear end collisions can cause injury and damage.

7. Keep both feet on the foot pegs. Don't let your feet hang out in an attempt to stabilize the vehicle in turns or in near-spill situations. Broken limbs may result. Slow down and avoid dangerous maneuvers.

WARNING
To provide protection against head injury, always wear an approved helmet when riding.

Rules For Operating Off the Road

When riding, always observe the practice of good sportsmanship and recognize that other people will judge all off-road vehicle riders by your actions.

1. NEVER mix alcohol or drugs with riding.

2. Don't litter the trails and camping areas. If possible, pick up any trash left by other people and leave the area cleaner than it was before you came.

3. Don't pollute lakes, streams or the oceans. Many streams are already in danger and "just kicking up a few rocks" may muddy the water enough to kill stream life.

4. Be careful not to damage living trees, shrubs or other natural terrain. The beauty of a field of wild flowers is not improved by the addition of ATV tracks.

5. Respect the rights of other people and their property.

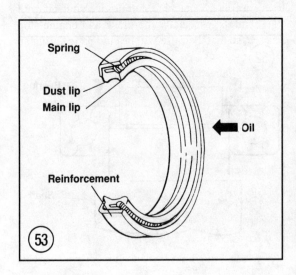

Spring
Dust lip
Main lip
Oil
Reinforcement
(53)

6. Help anyone found in distress.

7. Make yourself and your vehicle available for assistance in any search and rescue parties.

8. Don't harass other people using the same area as you. Never operate a machine in congested areas or steer toward people. Respect the rights of others enjoying the recreation area.

9. Be sure to obey all federal, state, provincial and other local rules regulating the operation of your ATV.

10. Inform public officials when using public land.

11. Don't harass wildlife and stay out of areas posted for the protection and feeding of wildlife.

12. Keep your exhaust noise to a minimum.

13. When riding in the snow, stay away from carefully groomed snowmobile trails. Snowmobilers get pretty upset when ATV's spoil the trails they have worked hard to make for their sport.

Pre-start Inspection

ATV's are ideal machines for getting around otherwise inaccessible areas; however, they should be checked before each ride and properly maintained to prevent break-downs in a remote location. A pre-start inspection should always be performed before heading out. While the following list may look exhaustive, it can be performed rather quickly after a few times.

1. Familiarize yourself with your vehicle. If the throttle sticks, don't panic. Stop the engine with the emergency stop switch, stop the vehicle and correct the problem. If your machine is new or if you are using a friend's machine, familiarize yourself with the controls, especially the brake and engine stop switch, so that their use will be automatic during an emergency.

2. Make sure the vehicle is clean before starting. The vehicle should be cleaned after riding and it should only need to be wiped off with a clean damp cloth. Do not use gasoline, solvents or abrasive cleaners.

3. Check chain tension (Chapter Three) and adjust if necessary.

4. Check the emergency stop switch for proper operation.

5. Check the brake operation. Be sure the brake system is correctly adjusted and operates properly. Be sure to release the parking brake before riding. If the parking brake is left ON, the rear brake may not operate properly and will be damaged.

6. Check the fuel level and top it up if necessary. Also, check your fuel supply regularly while riding.

7. Check the oil injection tank. Use only approved oil and make sure the tank is full before starting.

8. On liquid cooled models, check the coolant level. On air cooled models, make sure that the cooling fins are clean and air flow is not obstructed.

9. Operate the throttle lever. It should open and close smoothly.

10. Remove the belt guard and visually inspect the drive belt. If the belt seems worn or damaged, replace it. Chapter Eight lists drive belt wear limit specifications. Install the belt guard after inspecting the belt. Make sure the belt guard mounts are not loose or damaged.

11. Visually inspect all hoses, fittings and parts for looseness or damage. Check the tightness of all bolts and nuts. Tighten as required.

12. Check the handlebar and steering components for looseness or damage. Do not ride the vehicle if any steering component is damaged. Tighten loose fasteners as required.

13. Check the tires for wear or damage and the wheels for proper alignment (Chapter Three).

14. Check the front and rear suspension for proper movement. Repair any worn or damaged components as necessary.

> *WARNING*
> *When starting the engine, be sure that no bystanders are in front or behind the vehicle. A sudden lurch of the machine could cause serious injury.*

15. Start the engine and make sure that all lights are working.

> *NOTE*
> *If an abnormal noise is noticed after starting the engine, locate and repair the problem before operating the vehicle.*

> *NOTE*
> *Refer to the appropriate chapter for tightening torques and service procedures.*

Tools and Spare Parts

Before leaving on a trip, make sure that you carry tools and spare parts in case of emergency. A tool kit should include the following:

a. Flashlight.
b. Rope.
c. Tools.
d. Tape.
e. Tire patch kit.
f. Tire inflator pump.

Some suggested contents of a spare parts kit are:

a. Spark plug.
b. Light bulbs.
c. Drive belt.
d. Throttle cable.
e. Brake cable.
f. This book...just in case.

If you are planning a long trip, extra oil and fuel should also be carried. If the ATV is being operated at different altitudes, it may be necessary to install a different size carburetor main jet.

2-Stroke Engine Oil

CAUTION
Oil designed for use in a 4-stroke engine is different from oil designed for a 2-stroke engine. The engines used in all Polaris ATV models, except Magnum, are 2-stroke engines and only 2-stroke oil should be used.

Lubrication for a 2-stroke engine is provided either by oil mixed with the incoming fuel/air mixture or by oil injected into the fuel/air mixture. The 2-stroke engines included in this manual are equipped with an oil injection system. Some of the oil settles out in the crankcase, lubricating the crankshaft and lower end of the connecting rods. The rest of the oil enters the combustion chamber to lubricate the piston rings and cylinder walls. This oil is burned during the combustion process, then expelled with the engine's exhaust.

Engine oil must have several special qualities to work well in the Polaris 2-stroke engine. The oil must flow freely in cold temperatures, lubricate the engine sufficiently and burn easily during combustion. It can't leave behind excessive deposits and it must be appropriate for the high operating tempera-

tures associated with 2-stroke engines. Refer to *Engine Lubrication* in Chapter Three.

4-Stroke Engine Oil

CAUTION
Oil designed for use in a 4-stroke engine is different from oil designed for use in a 2-stroke engine. Polaris Magnum models are equipped with 4-stroke engines. All other models are equipped with 2-stroke engines. Be certain the correct oil is used.

Oil for use in the 4-stroke engines is graded by the American Petroleum Institute (API) and the Society of Automotive Engineers (SAE) in several categories. Oil containers display these ratings on the top or label.

API oil grade is indicated by letters; oil for gasoline engines is identified by an "S," such as "SE, SF, SG" or "SH."

Viscosity is an indication of the oil's thickness or ability to flow at a specific temperature. The SAE uses numbers to indicate viscosity; thin oils have low numbers while thick oils have high numbers. A "W" after the number indicates that the viscosity testing was done at low temperature to simulate cold-weather operation. Engine oils fall into the 5 to 50 range.

Multigrade oils (for example 5W-20) have been changed by additives that modify the oil to be less viscous (thinner) at low temperatures and more viscous (thicker) at high temperatures. This allows the oil to perform efficiently across a wide range of engine operating conditions. The lower the number, the easier the engine will start in cold climates. Higher numbers are usually recommended during hot weather operation.

Grease

Greases are graded by the National Lubricating Grease Institute (NLGI). Greases are graded by number according to the consistency of the grease; these range from No. 000 to No. 6, with No. 6 being the most solid. A typical multipurpose grease is NLGI No. 2. For specific applications, equipment manufacturers may require grease with an additive such as molybdenum disulfide (MOS2).

NOTE
A low–temperature grease should be used wherever grease is required as a lubricant. Chapter Three lists low temperature grease recommended by Polaris.

RTV GASKET SEALANT

Room temperature vulcanizing (RTV) sealant is used on some preformed gaskets and to seal some components. RTV is a silicone gel supplied in tubes and can be purchased in a number of different colors.

Moisture in the air causes RTV to cure. Always place the cap on the tube as soon as possible when using RTV. RTV has a shelf life of one year and will not cure properly when the shelf life has expired. Check the expiration date on RTV tubes before using and keep partially used tubes tightly sealed.

Applying RTV Sealant

Clean all gasket residue from mating surfaces. Surfaces must be clean and free of oil and dirt. Remove all RTV gasket material from blind attaching holes, as it can cause a "hydraulic" lock and affect bolt torque.

Apply RTV sealant in a continuous bead 2-3 mm (0.08-0.12 in.) thick. Circle all mounting holes unless otherwise specified. Torque mating parts within 10 minutes after application.

THREADLOCK

Because of the vehicle's operating conditions, a threadlock (**Figure 54**) is required to help secure many of the fasteners. A threadlock will lock fasteners against vibration loosening and seal against

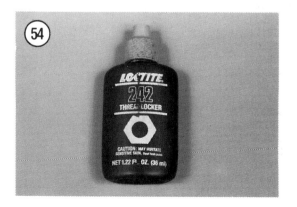

leaks. Loctite 242 (blue) and 271 (red) are recommended for many threadlock requirements described in this manual.

Loctite 242 (blue) is a medium strength threadlock for general purpose use. Component disassembly can be performed with normal hand tools. Loctite 271 (red) is a high strength threadlock that is normally used on studs or critical fasteners. Heat or special tools, such as a press or puller, may be required for component disassembly.

Applying Threadlock

Surfaces must be clean and free of oil and dirt. If a threadlock was previously applied to the component, this residue should also be removed.

Shake the Loctite container thoroughly and apply to both parts. Assemble parts and/or tighten fasteners.

GASKET REMOVER

Stubborn gaskets can present a problem during engine service as they can take a long time to remove. Consequently, there is the added problem of secondary damage occurring to the gasket mating surfaces from the incorrect or accidental use of a gasket scraping tool. To quickly and safely remove stubborn gaskets, use a spray gasket remover. Spray gasket remover can be purchased from automotive parts houses. Following the manufacturer's directions for use.

PARTS REPLACEMENT

Always be ready to provide the frame and engine numbers when purchasing or ordering replacement parts. Frequently design changes are made during manufacture and some are relatively major. The vehicle serial number is located on the plate (**Figure 6**) attached to the frame. The engine serial number (**Figure 7**) is located on the plate attached to the left-hand side of the engine crankcase.

WARNING
Use caution when servicing an engine or vehicle if either serial number plate is missing, because it will be much more difficult to identify the specific parts to install. It may also indicate that the vehicle or engine has been stolen.

Table 1 POLARIS MODEL NUMBERS

Year/Model	Model number
1985	
Scrambler	W857027
Trail Boss	W857527
1986	
Scrambler	W867027
Trail Boss	W867527
Trail Boss	W867627
1987	
Trail Boss	W877527
Cyclone	W877828
Trail Boss 4 × 4	W878027
Trail Boss 4 × 4	W878127
Trail Boss 4 × 4	W878327
1988	
Trail Boss 2 × 4	W887527
Trail Boss 4 × 4	W888127
Trail Boss 250 R/ES	X888528
Trail Boss 250 R/ES	W888528
1989	
Trail Boss	W898527
Trail Boss 2 × 4	W897527
Trail Boss 4 × 4	W898127
Big Boss 4 × 6	X898627
Big Boss 4 × 6	W898627
1990	
Trail Blazer	W907221
Trail Boss 250	W908527
Trail Boss 2 × 4	W907527
Trail Boss 2 × 4 - 350L	W907539
Trail Boss 4 × 4	W908127
Trail Boss 4 × 4 - 350L	W908139
Big Boss 4 × 6	W908627
1991	
Trail Blazer	W917221
Trail Boss 250	W918527
Trail Boss 2 × 4	W917527
Trail Boss 2 × 4 - 350L	W917539
Trail Boss 4 × 4	W918127
Trail Boss 4 × 4 - 350L	W918139
Big Boss 4 × 6	W918627
Big Boss 6 × 6	W918727
1992	
Trail Blazer	W927221
Trail Boss 250	W928527
Trail Boss 2 × 4	W927527
Trail Boss 2 × 4 - 350L	W927539
Trail Boss 4 × 4	W928127
Trail Boss 4 × 4 - 350L	W928139
Big Boss 4 × 6	W928627
Big Boss 6 × 6	W928727
1993	
Trail Blazer	W937221
Trail Boss	W938527
Sportsman	W938039
250 2 × 4	W937527
350 2 × 4	W937539
250 4 × 4	W938127
(continued)	

Table 1 POLARIS MODEL NUMBERS (continued)

Year/Model	Model number
Sportsman (continued)	
350 4 × 4	W938139
250 6 × 6	W938727
350 6 × 6	W938739
1994	
Trail Blazer 2W	W947221
Trail Boss 2W	W948527
Sport	W948540
Sportsman	W948040
300 2 × 4	W947530
400 2 × 4	W947540
300 4 × 4	W948130
400 4 × 4	W948140
300 6 × 6	W948730
400 6 × 6	W948740
1995	
Trail Blazer	W957221
Trail Boss	W958527
300 2 × 4	W957530
400 2 × 4	W957540
300 4 × 4	W958130
Scrambler	W957840
Sport	W958540
Sportsman 4 × 4	W958040
Xplorer 4 × 4	W959140
Magnum 2 × 4	W957444
Magnum 4 × 4	W958144
400 6 × 6	W958740

W is the first letter of the Vehicle Identification Number for standard production models.
X is the first letter of the Vehicle Identification Number for limited production pilot build models.
The first two numeric digits indicate the model year designation.
The third and fourth numeric digits indicate the chassis designation.
The fifth and sixth numeric digits indicate the engine used.

Table 2 GENERAL DIMENSIONS

Model	Length cm (in.)	Width cm (in.)	Wheel base cm (in.)
1985			
Scrambler W857027	188.0 (74.00)	109.2 (43.00)	121.9 (48.00)
Trail Boss W857527	188.0 (74.00)	109.2 (43.00)	121.9 (48.00)
1986			
Scrambler W867027	188.0 (74.00)	109.2 (43.00)	116.8 (46.00)
Trail Boss W867527	188.0 (74.00)	109.2 (43.00)	116.8 (46.00)
Trail Boss W867627	188.0 (74.00)	109.2 (43.00)	116.8 (46.00)
1987			
Trail Boss W877527	177.8 (70.00)	110.5 (43.50)	115.6 (45.50)
Cyclone W877828	198.1 (78.00)	110.5 (43.50)	127.0 (50.00)

(continued)

Table 2 GENERAL DIMENSIONS (continued)

Model	Length cm (in.)	Width cm (in.)	Wheel base cm (in.)
1987 (continued)			
Trail Boss 4 × 4 W878027	177.8 (70.00)	113.0 (44.50)	120.7 (47.50)
Trail Boss 4 × 4 W878127	177.8 (70.00)	113.0 (44.50)	120.7 (47.50)
Trail Boss 4 × 4 W878327	177.8 (70.00)	113.0 (44.50)	120.7 (47.50)
1988			
Trail Boss 2 × 4 W887527	177.8 (70.00)	110.5 (43.50)	115.6 (45.50)
Trail Boss 4 × 4 W888127	117.8 (70.00)	113.0 (44.50)	120.7 (47.50)
Trail Boss 250 R/ES X888528	185.9 (73.20)	111.0 (43.70)	125.7 (49.50)
Trail Boss 250 R/ES W888528	185.9 (73.20)	111.0 (43.70)	125.7 (49.50)
1989			
Trail Boss W898527	185.9 (73.20)	111.8 (44.00)	125.7 (49.50)
Trail Boss 2 × 4 W897527	185.9 (73.20)	111.8 (44.00)	125.7 (49.50)
Trail Boss 4 × 4 W898127	185.9 (73.20)	113.0 (44.50)	125.7 (49.50)
Big Boss 4 × 6 X898627	247.7 (97.50)	113.0 (44.50)	190.5 (75.00)
Big Boss 4 × 6 W898627	247.7 (97.50)	113.0 (44.50)	190.5 (75.00)
1990			
Trail Blazer W907221	185.9 (73.20)	111.8 (44.00)	125.7 (49.50)
Trail Boss 250 W908527	185.9 (73.20)	111.8 (44.00)	125.7 (49.50)
Trail Boss 2 × 4			
250 Air cooled W907527	185.9 (73.20)	111.8 (44.00)	125.7 (49.50)
350 Liquid cooled W907539	195.6 (77.00)	111.8 (44.00)	126.4 (49.75)
Trail Boss 4 × 4			
250 Air cooled W908127	185.9 (73.20)	113.0 (44.50)	126.4 (49.75)
350 Liquid cooled W908139	195.6 (77.00)	113.0 (44.50)	126.4 (49.75)
Big Boss 4 × 6 W908627	247.7 (97.50)	112.8 (44.40)	190.5 (75.00)
1991			
Trail Blazer W917221	185.9 (73.20)	111.8 (44.00)	125.7 (49.50)
Trail Boss 250 W918527	185.9 (73.20)	111.8 (44.00)	125.7 (49.50)
Trail Boss 2 × 4			
250 Air cooled W917527	185.9 (73.20)	111.8 (44.00)	125.7 (49.50)
350 Liquid cooled W917539	195.6 (77.00)	111.8 (44.00)	125.7 (49.75)
Trail Boss 4 × 4			
250 Air cooled W918127	185.9 (73.20)	113.0 (44.50)	126.4 (49.75)

(continued)

Table 2 GENERAL DIMENSIONS (continued)

Model	Length cm (in.)	Width cm (in.)	Wheel base cm (in.)
1991 (continued)			
Trail Boss 4 × 4 (continued)			
350 Liquid cooled W918139	195.6 (77.00)	113.0 (44.50)	126.4 (49.75)
Big Boss 4 × 6 W918627	247.7 (97.50)	112.8 (44.40)	190.5 (75.00)
Big Boss 6 × 6 W918727	247.7 (97.50)	116.1 (45.70)	190.5 (75.00)
1992			
Trail Blazer W927221	185.9 (73.20)	111.8 (44.00)	125.7 (49.50)
Trail Boss 250 W928527	185.9 (73.20)	111.8 (44.00)	125.7 (49.50)
Trail Boss 2 × 4			
250 Air cooled W927527	185.9 (73.20)	111.8 (44.00)	125.7 (49.50)
350 Liquid cooled W927539	195.6 (77.00)	111.8 (44.00)	126.4 (49.75)
Trail Boss 4 × 4			
250 Air cooled W928127	185.9 (73.20)	113.0 (44.50)	126.4 (49.75)
350 Liquid cooled W928139	195.6 (77.00)	113.0 (44.50)	126.4 (49.75)
Big Boss 4 × 6 W928627	247.7 (97.50)	112.8 (44.40)	190.5 (75.00)
Big Boss 6 × 6 W928727	247.7 (97.50)	116.1 (45.70)	190.5 (75.00)
1993			
Trail Blazer W937221	185.9 (73.20)	111.8 (44.00)	125.7 (49.50)
Trail Boss W938527	185.9 (73.20)	111.8 (44.00)	125.7 (49.50)
Sportsman W938039	195.6 (77.00)	113.0 (44.50)	126.4 (49.75)
250 2 × 4 W937527	185.9 (73.20)	111.8 (44.00)	125.7 (49.50)
350 2 × 4 W937539	195.6 (77.00)	111.8 (44.00)	126.4 (49.75)
250 4 × 4 W938127	185.9 (73.20)	113.0 (44.50)	126.4 (49.75)
350 4 × 4 W938139	195.6 (77.00)	113.0 (44.50)	126.4 (49.75)
250 6 × 6 W938727	247.7 (97.50)	112.8 (44.40)	190.5 (75.00)
350 6 × 6 W938739	261.6 (103)	116.1 (45.70)	190.5 (75.00)
1994			
Trail Blazer 2W W947221	185.9 (73.2)	111.2 (44)	125.7 (49.5)
Trail Boss 2W W948527	185.9 (73.2)	111.2 (44)	125.7 (49.5)
Sport W948540	182.9 (72)	111.2 (44)	126.4 (49.75)
Sportsman 4 × 4 W948040	195.6 (77)	116.8 (46)	126.4 (49.75)

(continued)

Table 2 GENERAL DIMENSIONS (continued)

Model	Length cm (in.)	Width cm (in.)	Wheel base cm (in.)
1994 (continued)			
Sportsman 4 × 4 W948040			
300 2 × 4 W947530	185.9 (73.2)	111.2 (44)	125.7 (49.5)
400 2 × 4 W947540	195.6 (77)	111.2 (44)	126.4 (49.75)
300 4 × 4 W948130	185.9 (73.2)	113 (44.5)	126.4 (49.75)
400 4 × 4 W948140	195.6 (77)	116.8 (46)	126.4 (49.75)
300 6 × 6 W948730	247.6 (97.5)	116.1 (45.7)	190.5 (75)
400 6 × 6 W948740	261.6 (103)	116.1 (45.7)	190.5 (75)
1995			
Trail Blazer W957221	185.9 (73.2)	111.8 (44)	125.7 (49.5)
Trail Boss W958527	185.9 (73.2	111.8 (44)	125.7 (49.5)
300 2 × 4 W957530	185.9 (73.2)	111.8 (44)	126.4 (49.75)
400 2 × 4 W957540	195.6 (77)	111.8 (44)	126.4 (49.75)
300 4 × 4 W958130	185.9 (73.2)	113 (44.5)	126.4 (49.75)
Scrambler W957840	189.2 (74.5)	115.6 (45.5)	123.2 (48.5)
Sport W958540	182.9 (72)	111.8 (44)	126.4 (49.75)
Sportsman 4 × 4 W958040	195.6 (77)	116.8 (46)	126.4 (49.75)
Xplorer 4 × 4 W959140	195.6 (77)	116.8 (46)	126.4 (49.75)
Magnum 2 × 4 W957444	195.6 (77)	118.1 (46.5)	126.4 (49.75)
Magnum 4 × 4 W958144	195.6 (77)	116.8 (46)	126.4 (49.75)
400 6 × 6 W958740	261.5 (103)	116.8 (46)	190.5 (75)

Table 3 VEHICLE WEIGHT

Model	kg	lb.
1985		
Scrambler W857027	172.4	380.0
Trail Boss W857527	199.6	440.0
1986		
Scrambler W867027	172.4	380.0
Trail Boss W867527	199.6	440.0
Trail Boss W867627	199.6	440.0
1987		
Trail Boss W877527	199.6	440.0
Cyclone W877828	181.4	400.0
Trail Boss 4 × 4 W878027	222.3	490.0
Trail Boss 4 × 4 W878127	222.3	490.0
Trail Boss 4 × 4 W878327	222.3	490.0

(continued)

Table 3 VEHICLE WEIGHT (continued)

Model	kg	lb.
1988		
Trail Boss 2 × 4 W887527	199.6	440.0
Trail Boss 4 × 4 W888127	222.3	490.0
Trail Boss 250 R/ES X888528	181.4	400.0
Trail Boss 250 R/ES W888528	181.4	400.0
1989		
Trail Boss W898527	181.4	400.0
Trail Boss 2 × 4 W897527	199.6	440.0
Trail Boss 4 × 4 W898127	222.3	490.0
Big Boss 4 × 6 X898627	294.8	650.0
Big Boss 4 × 6 W898627	294.8	650.0
1990		
Trail Blazer W907221	176.9	390.0
Trail Boss 250 W908527	192.8	425.0
Trail Boss 2 × 4		
250 Air cooled W907527	199.6	440.0
350 Liquid cooled W907539	222.3	490.0
Trail Boss 4 × 4		
250 Air cooled W908127	222.3	490.0
350 Liquid cooled W908139	254.0	560.0
Big Boss 4 × 6 W908627	294.8	650.0
1991		
Trail Blazer W917221	176.9	390.0
Trail Boss 250 W918527	192.8	425.0
Trail Boss 2 × 4		
250 Air cooled W917527	199.6	440.0
350 Liquid cooled W917539	222.3	490.0
Trail Boss 4 × 4		
250 Air cooled W918127	222.3	490.0
350 Liquid cooled W918139	254.0	560.0
Big Boss 4 × 6 W918627	294.8	650.0
Big Boss 6 × 6 W918727	340.2	750.0
1992		
Trail Blazer W927221	176.9	390.0
Trail Boss 250 W928527	192.8	425.0
Trail Boss 2 × 4		
250 Air cooled W927527	199.6	440.0
350 Liquid cooled W927539	222.3	490.0
Trail Boss 4 × 4		
250 Air cooled W928127	222.3	490.0
350 Liquid cooled W928139	254.0	560.0
Big Boss 4 × 6 W928627	294.8	650.0
Big Boss 6 × 6 W928727	340.2	750.0
1993		
Trail Blazer W937221	177	390.0
Trail Boss 250 W938527	192.8	425.0
Sportsman W938039	254.0	560.0
250 2 × 4 W937527	199.6	440.0
350 2 × 4 W937539	222.3	490.0
250 4 × 4 W938127	222.3	490.0
350 4 × 4 W938139	254.0	560.0
250 6 × 6 W938727	294.8	650.0
350 6 × 6 W938739	340.2	750.0
1994		
Trail Blazer 2W W947221	177.0	390.0
Trail Boss 2W W948527	192.8	425.0
Sport W948540	217.3	479.0

(continued)

Table 3 VEHICLE WEIGHT (continued)

Model	kg	lb.
1994 (continued)		
Sportsman 4 × 4 W948040	265.4	585.0
300 2 × 4 W947530	219.0	483.0
400 2 × 4 W947540	232.2	512.0
300 4 × 4 W948130	244.0	538.0
400 4 × 4 W948140	259.4	572.0
300 6 × 6 W948730	373.3	823.0
400 6 × 6 W948740	388.7	857.0
1995		
Trail Blazer W957221	177.0	390.0
Trail Boss W958527	193.0	425.0
300 2 × 4 W957530	219.0	483.0
400 2 × 4 W957540	232.0	512.0
300 4 × 4 W958130	244.0	538.0
Scrambler W957840	222.0	490.0
Sport W958540	217.0	479.0
Sportsman 4 × 4 W958040	265.4	585.0
Xplorer 4 × 4 W959140	258.6	570.0
Magnum 2 × 4 W957444	242.0	534.0
Magnum 4 × 4 W958144	270.0	595.0
400 6 × 6 W958740	389.0	857.0

Table 4 DECIMAL AND METRIC EQUIVALENTS

Fractions	Decimal in.	Metric mm	Fractions	Decimal in.	Metric mm
1/64	0.015625	0.39688	33/64	0.515625	13.09687
1/32	0.03125	0.79375	17/32	0.53125	13.49375
3/64	0.046875	1.19062	35/64	0.546875	13.89062
1/16	0.0625	1.58750	9/16	0.5625	14.28750
5/64	0.078125	1.98437	37/64	0.578125	14.68437
3/32	0.09375	2.38125	19/32	0.59375	15.08125
7/64	0.109375	2.77812	39/64	0.609375	15.47812
1/8	0.125	3.1750	5/8	0.625	15.87500
9/64	0.140625	3.57187	41/64	0.640625	16.27187
5/32	0.15625	3.96875	21/32	0.65625	16.66875
11/64	0.171875	4.36562	43/64	0.671875	17.06562
3/16	0.1875	4.76250	11/16	0.6875	17.46250
13/64	0.203125	5.15937	45/64	0.703125	17.85937
7/32	0.21875	5.55625	23/32	0.71875	18.25625
15/64	0.234375	5.95312	47/64	0.734375	18.65312
1/4	0.250	6.35000	3/4	0.750	19.05000
17/64	0.265625	6.74687	49/64	0.765625	19.44687
9/32	0.28125	7.14375	25/32	0.78125	19.84375
19/64	0.296875	7.54062	51/64	0.796875	20.24062
5/16	0.3125	7.93750	13/16	0.8125	20.63750
21/64	0.328125	8.33437	53/64	0.828125	21.03437
11/32	0.34375	8.73125	27/32	0.84375	21.43125
23/64	0.359375	9.12812	55/64	0.859375	22.82812
3/8	0.375	9.52500	7/8	0.875	22.22500
25/64	0.390625	9.92187	57/64	0.890625	22.62187
13/32	0.40625	10.31875	29/32	0.90625	23.01875
27/64	0.421875	10.71562	59/64	0.921875	23.41562
7/16	0.4375	11.11250	15/16	0.9375	23.81250
29/64	0.453125	11.50937	61/64	0.953125	24.20937
15/32	0.46875	11.90625	31/32	0.96875	24.60625
31/64	0.484375	12.30312	63/64	0.984375	25.00312
1/2	0.500	12.70000	1	1.00	25.40000

Table 5 GENERAL TORQUE SPECIFICATIONS

Item	N·m	ft.-lb.
Bolt		
6 mm	6	4.3
8 mm	15	11
10 mm	30	22
12 mm	55	40
14 mm	85	61
16 mm	130	94
Nut		
6 mm	6	4.3
8 mm	15	11
10 mm	30	22
12 mm	55	40
14 mm	85	61
16 mm	130	94

Table 6 TECHNICAL ABBREVIATIONS

ABDC	After bottom dead center
ATDC	After top dead center
BBDC	Before bottom dead center
BDC	Bottom dead center
BTDC	Before top dead center
C	Celsius (Centigrade)
cc	Cubic centimeters
CDI	Capacitor discharge ignition
cu. in.	Cubic inches
F	Fahrenheit
ft.-lb.	Foot-pound
gal.	Gallons
H/A	High altitude
hp	Horsepower
in.	Inches
kg	Kilogram
kg/cm^2	Kilograms per square centimeter
kgm	Kilogram meters
km	Kilometer
l	Liter
m	Meter
MAG	Magneto
ml	Milliliter
mm	Millimeter
N·m	Newton-meters
oz.	Ounce
psi	Pounds per square inch
PTO	Power take off
PVT	Polaris Variable Transmission
pt.	Pints
qt.	Quarts
rpm	Revolutions per minute

Table 7 METRIC TAP DRILL SIZES

Metric (mm)	Drill size	Decimal equivalent	Nearest fraction
3 × 0.50	No. 39	0.0995	3/32
3 × 0.60	3.32	0.0937	3/32
4 × 0.70	No. 30	0.1285	1/8
4 × 0.75	1/8	0.125	1/8
5 × 0.80	No. 19	0.166	11/64
5 × 0.90	No. 20	0.161	5/32
6 × 1.00	No. 9	0.196	13/64
7 × 1.00	16/64	0.234	15/64
8 × 1.00	J	0.277	9/32
8 × 1.25	17/64	0.265	17/64
9 × 1.00	5/16	0.3125	5/16
9 × 1.25	5/16	0.3125	5/16
10 × 1.25	11/32	0.3437	11/32
10 × 1.50	R	0.339	11/32
11 × 1.50	3/8	0.375	3/8
12 × 1.50	13/32	0.406	13/32
12 × 1.75	13/32	0.406	13/32

Table 8 WINDCHILL FACTORS

Estimated wind speed in mph	Actual thermometer reading (°F)											
	50	40	30	20	10	0	−10	−20	−30	−40	−50	−60
	Equivalent temperature (°F)											
Calm	50	40	30	20	10	0	−10	−20	−30	−40	−50	−60
5	48	37	27	16	6	−5	−15	−26	−36	−47	−57	−68
10	40	28	16	4	−9	−21	−33	−46	−58	−70	−83	−95
15	36	22	9	−5	−18	−36	−45	−58	−72	−85	−99	−112
20	32	18	4	−10	−25	−39	−53	−67	−82	−96	−110	−124
25	30	16	0	−15	−29	−44	−59	−74	−88	−104	−118	−133
30	28	13	−2	−18	−33	−48	−63	−79	−94	−109	−125	−140
35	27	11	−4	−20	−35	−49	−67	−82	−98	−113	−129	−145
40	26	10	−6	−21	−37	−53	−69	−85	−100	−116	−132	−148
*												
	Little danger (for properly clothed person)			Increasing danger				Great danger				
				• Danger from freezing of exposed flesh •								

*Wind speeds greater than 40 mph have little additional effect.

CHAPTER TWO

TROUBLESHOOTING

Diagnosing mechanical or electrical problems is relatively simple if you use orderly procedures and keep a few basic principles in mind. The first step in any troubleshooting procedure is to define the symptoms as closely as possible and then localize the problem. Subsequent steps involve testing and analyzing those areas which could cause the symptoms. A haphazard approach may eventually solve the problem, but it can be very costly in terms of wasted time and unnecessary parts replacement.

Proper lubrication, maintenance and periodic tune-ups as described in Chapter Three will reduce the necessity for troubleshooting. Even with the best of care, however, all vehicles are prone to problems which will require troubleshooting.

Never assume anything and do not overlook the obvious. If you are riding along and the engine suddenly quits, check the easiest, most accessible areas first. Has the spark plug wire fallen off? Is there fuel in the tank? Is the fuel shut-off valve turned ON?

If nothing obvious turns up in a quick check, look a little further. Learning to recognize and describe symptoms will make repairs easier for you or a mechanic at the shop. Describe problems accurately and fully. Did the engine lose power gradually and miss before stopping or did it stop suddenly with a bang? What color smoke (if any) came from the exhaust and so on.

After the symptoms are defined, areas which could cause problems can be tested and analyzed. Guessing at the cause of a problem may provide the solution, but it usually leads to frustration, wasted time and a series of expensive, unnecessary parts replacements.

You do not need expensive equipment or complicated test gear to determine whether you should attempt repairs at home. A few simple checks could save a large repair bill and lost time while your ATV sits in a dealer's service department. On the other hand, be realistic and *do not attempt repairs that are beyond your abilities*. Service departments tend to charge heavily for putting together an engine that someone else has disassembled. Some shops won't even take such a job, so use common sense and don't get in over your head.

OPERATING REQUIREMENTS

An engine needs 3 basics to run properly: correct fuel/air mixture, sufficient compression and a spark at the right time (**Figure 1**). If one basic requirement is missing, the engine will not run. Ignition problems are a frequent cause of breakdowns and the ignition system can be quickly and easily checked. Keep that in mind before you begin tampering with carburetor adjustments.

If the ATV has been sitting for any length of time and refuses to start, check and clean the spark plug. Then check the condition of the battery (if so equipped) to make sure it is fully charged. If these are okay, then inspect to the gasoline delivery system. This includes the tank, fuel shutoff valve, fuel pump and fuel line to the carburetor. Gasoline deposits may have gummed up the carburetor's fuel inlet needle, jets and small air passages. Gasoline tends to lose its potency after standing for long periods and condensation may contaminate it with water. Drain the old gas and try starting with a fresh tankful.

EMERGENCY TROUBLESHOOTING

If the ATV is difficult to start or won't start, it does not help to tear up the rewind starter or drain the battery using the electric starter (on models so equipped). Check for obvious problems even before getting out your tools. Go down the following list step by step. Do each one; you may be embarrassed to find that the emergency stop switch is in the OFF position, but it is better than draining the battery. If the engine still will not start, refer to the appropriate troubleshooting procedure which follows in this chapter.

1. Is there fuel in the tank? Open the filler cap and rock the vehicle. Listen for fuel sloshing around.

> *WARNING*
> *Do not use an open flame to check in the tank. A serious explosion and fire will probably result.*

2. Is the fuel shut-off in the ON position?
3. Make sure the emergency stop switch is not stuck in the OFF position.
4. Is the spark plug wire on tight? Push it on and rotate it slightly to clean the electrical connection between the spark plug and connector.

5. Is the starting enrichment (choke) knob in the correct position? A warm engine may be easily flooded by choking, but some engines may not start unless the mixture is enrichened. It helps to know the starting characteristics of the specific engine.

ENGINE STARTING

An engine that refuses to start or is difficult to start is very frustrating. More often than not, the problem

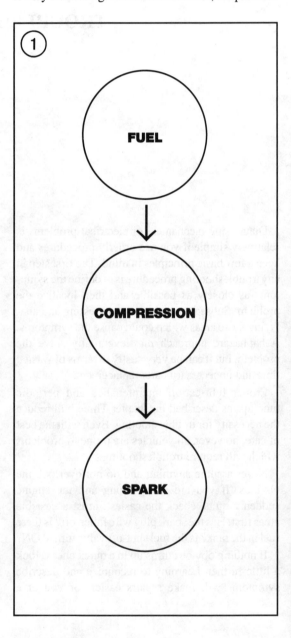

is very minor and can be found with a simple and logical troubleshooting procedure.

The following items show a beginning point from which to isolate engine starting problems.

Engine Fails to Start

Perform the following spark test to determine if the ignition system is operating properly.

1. Remove the spark plug.

NOTE
*A test plug (**Figure 2**) is a useful tool to check the ignition system. The clip makes attachment to a ground easier than a standard plug and the gap can be clearly viewed. Test plugs like the one shown are available from tool and parts suppliers that have ignition test equipment and service parts.*

2. Connect the spark plug wire and connector to the removed spark plug and touch the spark plug's base to a good ground like the bare aluminum of the engine cylinder head. Position the plug so that you can see the electrodes.

WARNING
If it is necessary to hold the high voltage lead, do so with an insulated pair of pliers. The high voltage generated by the ignition system could produce serious shocks that could be fatal.

3. Crank the engine with the electric or recoil starter and observe the spark plug electrodes exposed in Step 2. A fat blue spark should be evident across the electrodes.

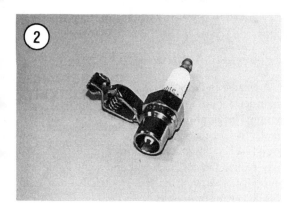

4. If the spark is good, the problem is probably a lack of fuel, but check the condition of the installed spark plug. If the plug's condition is questioned, install a new spark plug of the correct type and heat range. Check to make sure the starting enrichment (choke) is in the correct position. Fuel must enter the cylinder, but the cylinder must not be flooded with fuel.

5. If the spark is not good or does not occur regularly, check the following possible causes.
    a. Loose electrical connections.
    b. Broken or shorted spark plug high tension lead.
    c. Shorted engine stop switch or connecting wires.
    d. Damaged ignition high tension coil.
    e. Damaged CDI unit.

Engine is Difficult to Start

Check for one or more of the following possible malfunctions:
    a. Fouled spark plug.
    b. Starting enrichment (choke) is incorrectly set.
    c. Fuel system is contaminated.
    d. Carburetor incorrectly adjusted.
    e. Poor compression.
    f. Incorrect type or damaged ignition high tension coil.
    g. CDI unit faulty or improperly grounded.

Engine will not Crank

Check for one or more of the following possible malfunctions:
    a. Recoil starter mechanism broken.
    b. Discharged battery (models with electric starting).
    c. Damaged electric starter, solenoid etc. (models with electric starting).
    d. Internal engine damage, such as seized piston or crankshaft bearings.

ENGINE PERFORMANCE

In the following checklist, it is assumed that the engine runs, but is not operating at peak performance. This will serve as a starting point from which to isolate a performance problem.

The possible causes for each malfunction are listed in a logical sequence and in order of probability.

Engine is Hard to Start or Starts and Dies

a. Fuel tank empty or fuel tank vent is closed.
b. Obstructed fuel line, fuel shut-off valve or fuel filter.
c. Sticking carburetor float valve.
d. Carburetor incorrectly adjusted.
e. Improper operation of the starting enrichment (choke) valve.
f. Operator not allowing the engine to warm up before opening the throttle.
g. Fouled or improperly gapped spark plug.
h. Ignition timing incorrect.
i. Broken or damaged ignition coil.
j. Improper valve timing or improper valve clearance (4-stroke models).
k. Damaged reed valve (2-stroke models so equipped).
l. Clogged air filter element.
m. Contaminated fuel.
n. Engine flooded with fuel.
o. Damaged CDI unit.

Engine Will Not Idle or Irregular Idle

a. Carburetor incorrectly adjusted (either too lean or too rich).
b. Starting enrichment (choke) stuck or used improperly.
c. Fouled or improperly gapped spark plug.
d. Obstructed fuel line or fuel shut-off valve.
e. Vacuum leak between carburetor and cylinder.
f. Leaking compression (blown head gasket).
g. Incorrect ignition timing.
h. Improper valve timing or valve clearance (4-stroke models).
i. Low engine compression.

Engine Misses at High Speed

a. Fouled or improperly gapped spark plug.
b. Improper ignition timing.
c. Incorrect main jet installed.
d. Clogged carburetor jets.
e. Obstructed fuel line or fuel shut-off valve.

f. Incorrect valve timing (4-stroke models).
g. Damaged ignition coil or CDI unit.

Engine Overheating

a. Obstructed or broken cooling fins (air cooled models).
b. Obstructed radiator (liquid cooled models).
c. Low coolant level.
d. Improper ignition timing.
e. Improper spark plug heat range.
f. Vehicle overloaded.
g. Cooling fan not operating.
h. Fuel mixture too lean.

Engine Loses Power at Normal Riding Speed

a. Carburetor incorrectly adjusted.
b. Engine overheating.
c. Incorrect ignition timing.
d. Brake dragging (not releasing properly).

Engine Lacks Acceleration

a. Improperly adjusted carburetor (too lean).
b. Incorrect ignition timing.
c. Brake dragging.
d. Incorrect valve timing or valve clearance (4-stroke models).

Engine Backfires —Explosions in Muffler

a. Fouled or improperly gapped spark plug.
b. Incorrect ignition timing.
c. Contaminated fuel.
d. Lean fuel mixture.

ENGINE NOISES

A change in the sound is often the first clue that the rider notices indicating that something may be wrong. Noises are difficult to differentiate and even harder to describe. Experience is needed to diagnose sounds accurately, but identifying a problem quickly may reduce the cost of repair and some inconvenience. The following are some noises that may help locate sources of trouble.

Knocking or Pinging During Acceleration

a. Poor quality or contaminated fuel.
b. Spark plugs of the wrong heat range.

Slapping or Rattling Noise at Low Speed or During acceleration

a. May be piston slap caused by excessive piston-to-cylinder clearance.
b. May be caused by broken piston skirt.

Knocking or Rapping While Decelerating

May be caused by excessive (damaged) connecting rod bearing clearance.

Persistent Knocking and Vibration

May be caused by excessive (damaged) main bearing clearance.

Rapid On-Off Squeal

a. Compression leak around the head gasket.
b. Loose spark plug and compression leak around plug.

EXCESSIVE VIBRATION

Most reports of excessive vibration result from the engine not attached securely to the vehicle frame. Also liquid cooled 350, 400 and 425 models are equipped with an internal engine balancer that may be assembled incorrectly.

TESTING ELECTRICAL COMPONENTS

Most dealers and parts houses will not accept returns of any electrical parts. When testing electrical components, make sure that you perform the test procedures as described in this chapter and that your test equipment is working properly. If a test result shows that the component is defective it is still a good idea to have the component retested by a Polaris dealer to verify the test result before purchasing a new component. Refer to **Figure 3**.

POWER TRAIN

The following items provide a starting point from which to troubleshoot power train malfunctions. The possible causes for each malfunction are listed in a logical sequence.

Low Engine Operating Speed (Engine Running Properly, but Lugs)

a. Drive pulley spring broken or wrong spring.
b. Drive pulley weight too heavy.
c. Belt slipping.

Engine Operating Speed Too High

a. Incorrect drive pulley spring.
b. Drive pulley weights too light.
c. Drive pulley binding.
d. Driven pulley binding.

Engine Speed Erratic During Speed or Load Changes

a. Drive pulley binding.
b. Driven pulley binding.
c. Pulley grooves worn.

Harsh Engagement

a. Drive belt worn (too narrow).
b. Incorrect pulley-to-pulley clearance adjustment.

Drive Belt Not Operating Smoothly in Primary Sheave

a. Drive pulley face is rough, grooved, pitted or scored.
b. Defective drive belt.

Uneven Drive Belt Wear

a. Misaligned drive and driven pulleys.
b. Loose engine mounts.

Glazed Drive Belt

a. Excessive slippage. May be caused by stuck brakes.
b. Engine idle speed too high.

Drive Belt Too Tight at Idle

a. Engine idle speed too high.
b. Incorrect distance between pulleys.
c. Incorrect belt length.

Drive Belt Edge Cord Failure

a. Misaligned drive and driven pulleys.
b. Loose engine mounts.

Drive Belt Turns Over

a. Incorrect belt.
b. Incorrect belt alignment.
c. Engine mount broken or loose.

Brake Not Holding Properly

a. Incorrect brake adjustment.
b. Worn brake pads.
c. Worn brake disc.
d. Oil saturated brake pads.
e. Sheared key on brake disc.
f. Air in hydraulic lines on models with hydraulic brakes.

Brake Not Releasing Properly

a. Weak or broken return spring.
b. Bent or damaged brake lever.

c. Incorrect brake adjustment.

Excessive Chain Noise

a. Incorrect chain tension.
b. Excessive chain stretch.
c. Worn sprocket teeth.
d. Damaged chain and/or sprockets.

Chain Slippage

a. Incorrect chain tension.
b. Excessive chain stretch.
c. Worn sprocket teeth.

Leaking Transmission

a. Loose bolts.
b. Damaged gasket.
c. Damaged oil seal(s).
d. Cracked or broken case.

Rapid Chain and Sprocket Wear

a. Misaligned sprockets.
b. Incorrect chain tension.

Drive Clutch Engages Before Specified Engagement RPM

a. Worn spring.
b. Incorrect weight.

Drive Clutch Engages After Engagement RPM

a. Incorrect spring.
b. Worn or damaged secondary sheave buttons.

Erratic Shifting

a. Worn rollers and bushings.
b. Scuffed or damaged weights.
c. Dirty drive pulley assembly.
d. Worn or damaged driven pulley ramp buttons.

Engine Bogs During Engagement

a. Incorrect driven pulley width adjustment.

b. Drive belt worn too thin.

c. Incorrect distance between drive and driven pulleys.

Drive or Driven Pulley Sticks

a. Damaged pulley assembly.

b. Moveable pulley damaged.

c. Dirty pulley assembly.

STEERING

Descriptions of handling problems are subjective, but the following items will provide a starting point from which to troubleshoot handling and steering problems. Some possible causes for each malfunction are listed in a logical sequence.

Generally Poor or Unpredictable Handling

a. Improper tire inflation pressure.

b. Improperly adjusted wheel alignment.

c. Worn or damaged steering components.

d. Worn or damaged suspension components.

e. Bent or broken frame.

Loose Steering

a. Loose steering post, bushings or steering column fasteners.

b. Loose tie rod ends.

c. Worn spindle bushings.

Unequal Steering

a. Improperly adjusted tie rods.

b. Improperly adjusted steering stops.

c. Damaged steering components.

Steering Wanders

a. Loose or worn steering components.

b. Improperly adjusted toe-out.

c. Worn or damaged tires.

d. Damaged shock absorber.

e. Bent or broken frame.

ENGINE ELECTRICAL SYSTEM TROUBLESHOOTING

All models are equipped with a capacitor discharge ignition system. This section describes complete ignition and charging system troubleshooting.

This solid state system uses no contact breaker points or other moving parts. Because of the solid state design, problems with the capacitor discharge system are relatively few. Problems are usually limited to no spark, but that lack of spark might only occur when the engine is subjected to certain temperatures, loads or vibrations. It is often easier to find the cause of no spark than those with intermittent problems. If the ignition has no spark, first check for broken or damaged wires. Also make sure that the engine stop switch wires are not shorted to ground.

Test Equipment

Basic testing of the ignition and electrical system can be performed with an accurate ohmmeter. A visual inspection and tests with an ohmmeter will usually pinpoint electrical problems caused by dirty or damaged connectors, faulty or damaged wiring or electrical components that may have cracked or broken. If basic checks fail to locate the problem, take your ATV to a Polaris dealer and have them troubleshoot the electrical system.

Precautions

Certain measures must be taken to protect the capacitor discharge system while testing. Instantaneous damage to semiconductors in the system will occur if the following is not observed.

1. Do not crank the engine if the CDI unit is not grounded to the engine.

2. Do not touch or disconnect any ignition components if the engine is running or while the battery cables are connected.

3. Keep all connections between the various units clean and tight. Be sure that the wiring connectors are pushed together firmly.

Troubleshooting Preparation

Refer to the wiring diagram for your model at the end of this book when performing the following.

NOTE
To test the wiring harness for poor connections in Step 1, bend the molded rubber connector while checking each wire for resistance.

1. Check the wiring harness for visible signs of damage.

2. Make sure all of the connectors (**Figure 4**) are properly attached as follows:

NOTE
Never pull on the wires when separating an electrical connector. Pull only on the housing of the connector. See **Figure 5**.

a. Disconnect each electrical connector in the ignition circuit. Check for bent or damaged male connector pins (**Figure 6**). A bent pin will not connect properly and will cause an open circuit.

b. Check each female connector end. Make sure the metal connector at the end of each wire (**Figure 7**) is pushed all the way into the plastic connector. If not, use a small, narrow blade screwdriver to carefully push them in. Make sure you do not pinch or cut the wire. Also, make sure that you do not spread the connector.

c. Check the wires to make sure that each is properly attached to a metal connector inside the plastic connector.

d. Make sure all electrical connectors are clean and free of corrosion. If necessary, clean the connectors with an electrical contact cleaner.

e. After making sure that all of the individual connectors are alright, push the connectors together until they "click." Make sure they are fully engaged and locked together (**Figure 8**).

3. Check all electrical components for a good ground to the engine.

4. Check all wiring for short circuits or open circuits.

5. Make sure the fuel tank has an adequate supply of fresh fuel and that the oil tank is properly filled.

6. Check spark plug cable routing (**Figure 9**) and be sure the cable is properly connected to spark plug.

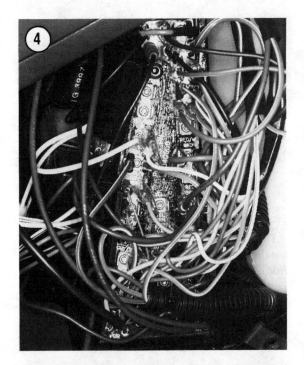

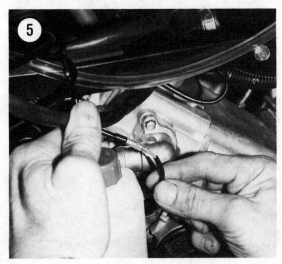

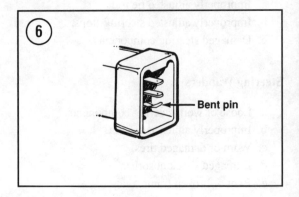
Bent pin

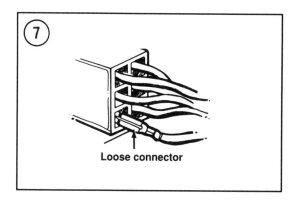

Loose connector

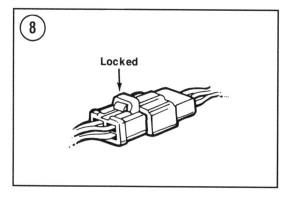

Locked

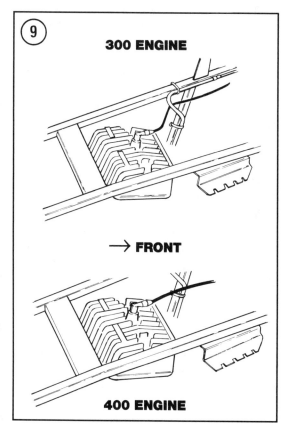

300 ENGINE

→ **FRONT**

400 ENGINE

CAUTION
To prevent expensive engine damage, refer to CAUTION under Spark Plug Removal in Chapter Three.

7. Remove the spark plug and check its condition. See Chapter Three.

8. Make the following spark test:

WARNING
During this test do not hold the spark plug, wire or connector with fingers or a serious electrical shock may result. If necessary, use a pair of insulated pliers to hold the spark plug wire.

a. Remove the spark plug.

NOTE
A special test plug such as the one shown in Figure 10 is available from many parts suppliers. The clip can be attached to a good engine ground.

b. Connect the spark plug cable connector to a spark plug that is known to be good (or the test plug) and touch the base of the spark plug base to a good ground like the engine cylinder head. Position the spark plug so you can see the electrode.

c. Turn the ignition switch ON and set the cut-out switches to the ON position.

d. Crank the engine with the starter. A fat blue spark should be evident across the spark plug electrode.

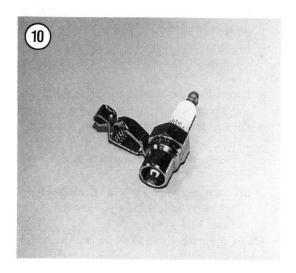

e. If there is no spark or only a weak one, check for loose connections at the coil. If all external wiring connections are good, check the remaining components of the ignition system.

f. Turn the ignition switch OFF.

Switch Tests

Test the ignition switch and the emergency cut-out switch as described in Chapter Eleven.

Ignition Component Resistance Test

An accurate ohmmeter is required to perform the following tests. Refer to **Figure 11** for 1985-1988 models with 250, 300 and 350L engines, **Figure 12** for models with 400L engine or **Figure 13** for Magnum models with 4-stroke engine.

Ignition high tension coil

Refer to **Figure 14**.

1. Locate the ignition high tension coil. It is attached to the frame above the engine. The coil is located under the headlight cover on late models.

2. Disconnect the black/yellow or black/white primary connector (A, **Figure 14**) from the high tension coil.

3. Check ignition coil primary resistance as follows:

a. If necessary, switch ohmmeter to the R × 1 scale.

b. Measure resistance between the small primary terminal and the coil ground. Refer to **Table 1** for specifications.

c. Disconnect the meter leads.

4. Check ignition coil secondary resistance as follows:

a. Disconnect the spark plug cable from the spark plug. Remove the spark plug cap from the end of the high-tension cable (B, **Figure 14**).

b. If necessary, switch ohmmeter to the R × 1000 scale.

c. Measure resistance between the high-tension (spark plug) cable and the coil ground. Refer to **Table 1** for specifications.

5. Check ignition coil insulation for cracks or other defects that would permit moisture to enter the coil.

Internal damage can be checked using additional test equipment. If condition is questioned, take the coil to a Polaris dealer for additional tests.

6. If resistance test results are not as specified in Steps 3-5, the coil is probably faulty. Have the dealer recheck the coil to verify that the unit is faulty before buying a replacement.

NOTE
Normal resistance in both the primary and secondary (high-tension) coil winding is not a guarantee that the unit is working properly; only an operational spark test can tell if a coil is producing an adequate spark from the input voltage. A Polaris dealer may have the equipment to test the coil's output. If not, substitute a known good coil to see if the problem is fixed.

Ignition system exciter and pulser coils (1885-1987 models)

The ignition system is equipped with an exciter coil and a pulser coil attached to the stator plate located behind the engine flywheel.

1. Locate the three wires and connector leading from under the engine flywheel to the ignition CDI ignition module.

2. Separate the 3-prong connector located between the engine and the CDI unit. This connector has 3 wires: white, black/red and brown/white.

3. Switch the ohmmeter to the R × 1 scale.

4. Attach the ohmmeter between the connectors for the brown/white and the white wires from the engine to check the exciter coil.

5. Compare the reading to the specification in **Table 2**. If the reading is not within specifications, replace the exciter coil assembly as described in Chapter Eleven.

6. Attach the ohmmeter between the connectors for the brown/white and the black/red wires from the engine to check the pulser coil.

7. Compare the reading to the specification in **Table 2**. If the reading is not within specifications, replace the Pulser and Exciter coil assembly as described in Chapter Eleven.

8. Reconnect the 3-prong connector.

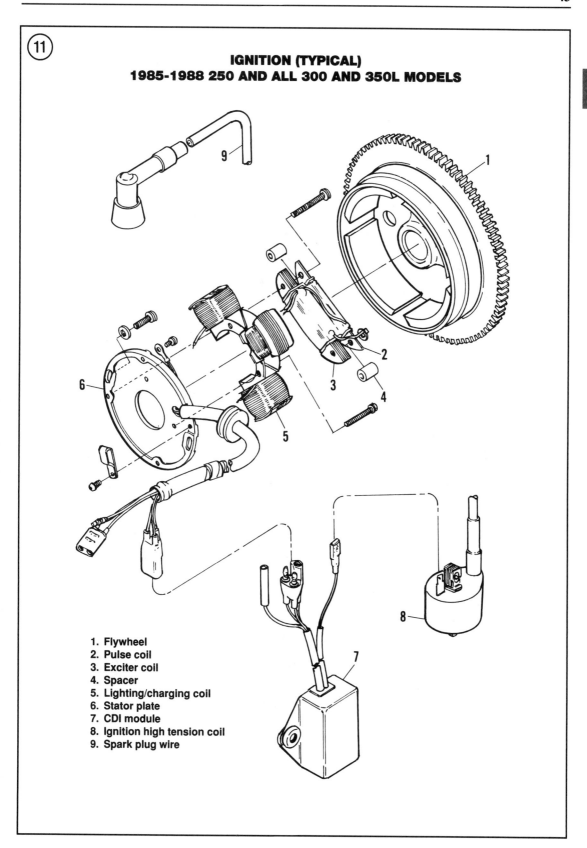

⑪

**IGNITION (TYPICAL)
1985-1988 250 AND ALL 300 AND 350L MODELS**

2

1. Flywheel
2. Pulse coil
3. Exciter coil
4. Spacer
5. Lighting/charging coil
6. Stator plate
7. CDI module
8. Ignition high tension coil
9. Spark plug wire

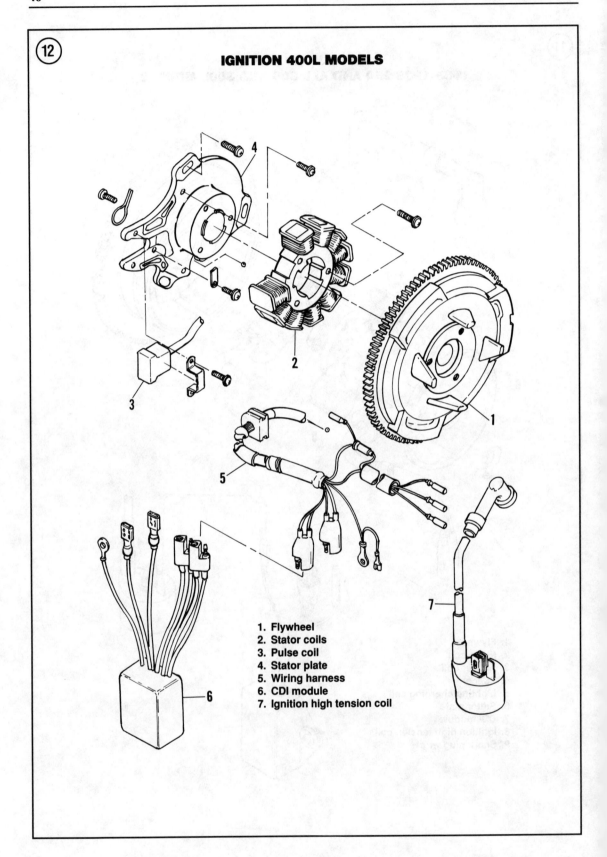

⑫

IGNITION 400L MODELS

1. Flywheel
2. Stator coils
3. Pulse coil
4. Stator plate
5. Wiring harness
6. CDI module
7. Ignition high tension coil

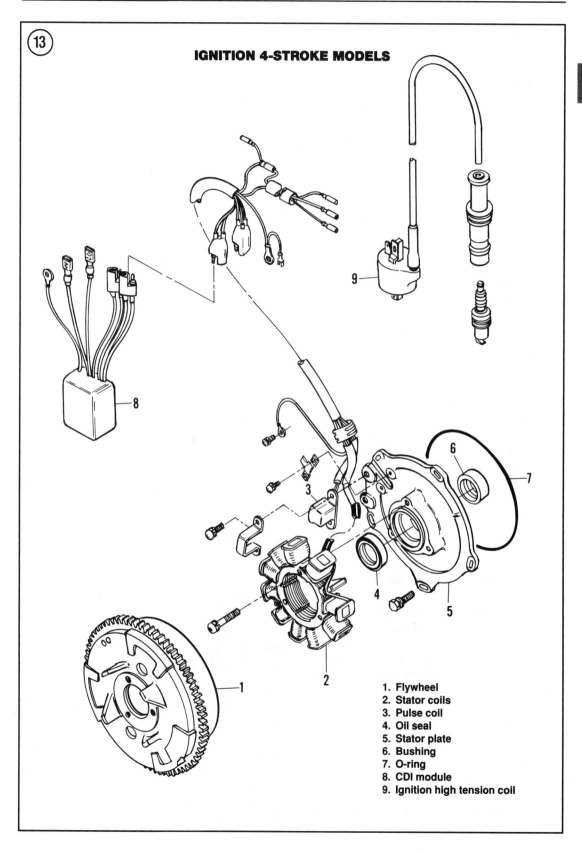

IGNITION 4-STROKE MODELS

1. Flywheel
2. Stator coils
3. Pulse coil
4. Oil seal
5. Stator plate
6. Bushing
7. O-ring
8. CDI module
9. Ignition high tension coil

Ignition system exciter coil (all 1988-on models with 150 watt alternator)

The ignition system is equipped with a single coil assembly that includes both the exciter coil (3, **Figure 11**) and the pulse coil (2, **Figure 11**). This coil assembly is attached to the stator plate located behind the engine flywheel.

1. Locate the three wires and connector leading from under the engine flywheel to the ignition CDI module.

2. Separate the connector located between the engine and the CDI unit. This connector contains the black/red and brown/white wires.

3. Switch the ohmmeter to the R × 1 scale.

4. Attach the ohmmeter between the brown/white and the black/red wires(end) from the engine to check the exciter coil.

5. Compare the reading to the specification in **Table 2**. If the measured resistance is not within specifications, replace the exciter/pulse coil assembly as described in Chapter Eleven.

6. Attach the ohmmeter between the connector for the black/red wire from the magneto and a good engine ground to test for a short circuit.

7. The test in Step 6 should indicate an open circuit (infinite resistance). If not, check the connecting wires for damage or replace the coil assembly as required.

8. Reattach the connectors.

Ignition system exciter and pulser coils (all models with 200 watt alternator)

The 400 and Magnum models equipped with 200 watt alternators are equipped with ignition system exciter and pulser coils attached to the stator plate. Magnum models are equipped with 2 exciter coils which must be tested separately. Refer to **Figures 12** and **13**.

1. Locate the wires leading from under the engine flywheel to the ignition CDI modlule. Locate the wire connectors.

2. Separate the wiring connectors located between the engine and CDI unit.

3. Switch the ohmmeter to the R × 1 scale.

4. Attach the ohmmeter between the connectors for the red and the black/red exciter coil wires.

5. Compare the reading of the specification in **Table 2**. If the resistance is not within specification, replace the exciter coil as described in Chapter Eleven.

6. On Magnum models, move the ohmmeter leads to the red and green exciter coil wires. Compare the reading to the specification in **Table 2**. Replace the exciter coil (Chapter Eleven) if resistance is not as specified.

7. To test the pulser coil, attach the ohmmeter between the connectors for the white/red and white wires leading from the engine.

8. Compare the resistance to the specification in **Table 2**. If the resistance is not within specification, inspect the pulser coil wires for damage and repair as necessary. If the wires are good, replace the pulser coil as described in Chapter Eleven.

9. Reattach all connectors.

Lighting coil (1985-1992 models)

> *NOTE*
> *Refer to Chapter Eleven **Electrical Systems** for battery charging system testing and service procedures.*

The lighting coil on these models is mounted on the stator plate behind the flywheel.

1. Locate the 2 wires (yellow/red and yellow) and connector leading from under the engine flywheel connected to a two wire connector.

2. Disconnect the two wire connector. One wire is yellow and the other is yellow/red.

3. Switch the ohmmeter to the R × 1 scale.

4. Attach the ohmmeter between the yellow/red and yellow wires leading from the engine.

5. Compare the reading to the specification in **Table 3**. If the reading is not within 10% of the listed specification, replace the lighting coil assembly as described in Chapter Eleven.

6. Reattach the wire connectors.

VOLTAGE REGULATOR

NOTE
Be sure the lighting coil is operating properly before testing the voltage regulator.

If you are experiencing blown bulbs or if all of the lights are dim (filaments barely light), test the voltage regulator as follows. In addition, check the bulb filament; an overcharged condition will usually melt the filament rather then break it.

1. Lift the front and rear of the vehicle, so that all wheels are off the ground. Block the position of the vehicle so that it is not able to move.

2. Locate the voltage regulator and remove the covers necessary to attach voltmeter leads to the wires attached to the voltage regulator.

3. Set the voltmeter to the 25 volt DC scale, then connect the black (negative) voltmeter lead to a good ground on the vehicle frame.

NOTE
Do not disconnect leads from the voltage regulator when testing voltage output.

4. Connect the other (positive/red) voltmeter lead to the voltage regulator red wire.

WARNING
When performing the following steps, be sure that the area is clear and that no

one walks behind the vehicle or serious injuries may result.

5. Have an assistant start the engine. When starting the engine, do not use the throttle to increase the engine speed more than necessary.

6. Slowly increase the engine rpm and observe the voltmeter reading. If the voltmeter indicates less than 13 volts or more than 14.6 volts, replace the voltage regulator.

7. Turn the engine off and disconnect the voltmeter.

8. Lower the ATV to the ground.

SPEED LIMITER

The reverse speed limiter is installed to prevent engine (and vehicle) speeds that are too fast for safe operation in reverse. The *OVERRIDE* switch (**Figure 15**) located on the left side of the handlebar permits the rider to manually override the safety speed limiting feature. In addition, some 1989 and later ATV's incorporate a safety feature called ETC (Electronic Throttle Control). If the throttle should stick at any position other than idle, the operator can return the throttle lever to idle. A switch incorporated into the throttle lever will energize the white wire to the speed limiter and prevent engine speeds above that of clutch engagement; thus preventing the vehicle from moving. Several different units have been used, so it is important to install the correct unit when replacing an old unit.

Many problems that cause a spark related miss are incorrectly blamed on the speed limiter. A quick check of the speed limiter can be accomplished by temporarily detaching the black wire from the speed limiter unit. If the engine operates satisfactorily with the black wire disconnected, first check the associated switches and wiring. Refer to the appropriate wiring diagrams. Repair or replace wiring, switches, or speed limiter as required. The speed limiter is a valuable safety device and the ATV should not be operated with the speed limiter disconnected or removed.

Throttle Lever Switch

To test the throttle lever switch (**Figure 16**) used on 1989 and later models, proceed as follows:

1. Disconnect the wires from the throttle lever switch.

2A. If the switch has two wires, proceed as follows.

a. Attach an ohmmeter to the white and red/white wires attached to the switch.

b. Move the throttle lever and check continuity between the white and red/white wires. Switch should be open (no continuity) when the throttle is open and closed (continuity) when the throttle is closed.

2B. If the switch has three wires, proceed as follows.

a. Attach an ohmmeter to the gray/white wire and to the red/white wire.

b. Move the throttle lever and check continuity between the gray/white wire and to the red/white wire. Switch should be open (no continuity) when the throttle is closed and closed (continuity) when the throttle is open.

3. If the throttle lever switch fails any of these tests, install a new switch.

Table 1 IGNITION HIGH TENSION COIL

	Primary resistance	Secondary resistance *
1985-1995	0.3 ohms	6.3 K ohms

* With the spark plug cap removed. Coil secondary resistance should not be tested with the spark plug cap installed. The resistance of the cap used on late models is 3.7-6.3 K ohms.

Table 2 IGNITION GENERATING COIL

	Resistance
1985-1987	
Pulser (black/red to brown/white)	23 ohms
Exciter (brown white to white)	120 ohms
1988-1995 (except 400 and 425 engines with 200 Watt)	
Stator coil (black/red to brown/white)	120 ohms
1994-1995 (400 engines with 200 Watt)	
Pulser (white/red to white)	97 ohms
Exciter (black/red to brown/white)	226 ohms
1995 (425 engines)	
Pulser (white/red to white)	97 ohms
Exciter (red to green)	3.2 ohms
Exciter (black/red to brown/white)	450 ohms

Table 3 LIGHTING COIL

	Resistance
1985-1988 with 100 watt alternator	
Models without battery	
(yellow to yellow/red or brown)	0.45-0.60 ohms
Models with battery	
(yellow/red to yellow)	0.45-0.60 ohms
1989-on with 150 watt alternator	
250, 300, 350 & 400 engines	
(yellow/red to yellow)	0.25-0.35 ohms
400 & 425 engines with 200 watt alternator	
(yellow/red to yellow)	0.34 ohms
(yellow/brown to yellow)	0.17 ohms

Table 4 REVERSE SPEED LIMITER

	Low limit	High limit	ETC* limit
1987			
Trail Boss**			
Type LR40 (4060079)	3,200 rpm	4,800 rpm	–
Cyclone			
Type LR41 (4060081)	4,650 rpm	–	–
1988			
All models except R/ES			
Type LR42 (4060082)	3,400 rpm	–	–
Trail Boss R/ES			
Type LR43 (4060084)	3,900 rpm	–	–
1989-1993			
All models except Trail Blazer			
Type LR44 (4060085)	3,400 rpm	–	1,800 rpm
1990-early 1991 Trail Blazer			
Type LR-41-1 (4060089)	–	–	1,900 rpm
Late 1991-1993 Trail Blazer			
(with F/N/R transmission)			
Type LR47 (4060093)	3,500	–	1,900
1994-1995			
Trail Blazer (1994)			
Type LR47 (4060093)	3,500	–	1,900
Sport models			
Type LR49 (4060114)	2,800	–	1,200
All 400 models except Sport,			
Scrambler and 425			
Type LR44-2 (4060112)	3,400	–	1,200

* Electronic Throttle Control.
** The LR40 unit can be retrofitted to earlier models.

CHAPTER THREE

LUBRICATION, MAINTENANCE, AND TUNE-UP

Your Polaris ATV requires periodic maintenance to operate efficiently without breaking down. This chapter covers the regular maintenance required to keep your ATV in top shape. Regular, careful maintenance is the best guarantee for a trouble-free, long lasting vehicle. All-terrain vehicles are high-performance vehicles that demand proper lubrication, maintenance and tune-ups to maintain a high level of performance, extend engine life and extract the maximum economy of operation.

You can do your own lubrication, maintenance and tune-ups if you follow the correct procedures and use common sense. Always remember that damage can result from improper tuning and adjustment. In addition, where special tools or testers are called for during a particular maintenance or adjustment procedure, the tool should be used or you should refer service to a qualified Polaris dealer or repair shop.

The following information is based on recommendations from Polaris that will help you keep your ATV operating at its peak level.

Tables 1-11 are at the end of this chapter.

PRE-RIDE CHECKS

The following checks should be performed before the first ride of the day. Refer also to **Table 1**.

1. Inspect all fuel lines and fittings for leakage. Repair any leaks and clean up any spilled fuel.
2. Make sure the fuel tank is full of fresh gasoline.
3. Make sure the engine oil levels are correct. Add the correct type of oil if necessary.

    a. Engine oil injection reservoir (2-stroke models).

    b. Engine counterbalancer compartment (350L and 400L liquid cooled 2-stroke models).

c. Engine oil reservoir (4-stroke models).

4. Make sure the transmission oil level is correct. Add the correct type of oil if necessary. Refer to **Table 4**.

5. Inspect cooling system before starting the engine.

  a. On liquid cooled models, check coolant level. If level is low, determine the cause of fluid loss. Also, make sure the outside of the radiator is clean.

  b. On air cooled models, make sure the cooling fins are clean.

6. Make sure the air filter is clean.

7. Check the throttle lever, brake lever and brake pedal for proper operation.

8. Check the brake fluid level (models with hydraulic brakes) of each master cylinder reservoir.

9. Check the front and rear suspension for proper operation and freedom of movement.

10. Check the drive chain(s) for excessive wear and correct tension. Adjust tension if necessary.

11. Check inflation of all tires. Refer to **Table 2**.

12. Check exhaust system for looseness or damage.

13. Check front wheel drive oil (models with front wheel drive).

14. Check wheels for tightness.

15. Check all lights, switches and other electrical systems for proper operation.

16. Make sure all fasteners are tight.

SERVICE INTERVALS

The service intervals shown in **Table 3** will help ensure long service under normal operating condition. However, if the vehicle is run in extremely

dusty or wet conditions, service should be more frequent.

For convenience when maintaining your vehicle, most of the services listed in **Table 3** are described in this chapter; however, the text may refer you to another chapter for more complex service.

TIRES AND WHEELS

Tire Pressure

Tire pressure should be checked and adjusted to maintain the smoothness of the tire, good traction and handling and to get the maximum life from the tire. The recommended tire pressure of 20.7-34.5 kPa (3-5 psi) is too low to be measured with a standard tire pressure gauge. Inexpensive, accurate, low pressure gauges (**Figure 1**) can be purchased from your Polaris dealer that can be carried in your tool box or on the ATV.

The tire pressures recommended in **Table 2** are for the type and size of tires originally installed on your Polaris. If you have installed different tires, follow the tire pressure recommendation specified by the tire manufacturer.

WARNING
Always inflate both tires on the same axle to the same pressure. If the ATV is operated with unequal air pressures on opposite sides of the same axle, the vehicle will pull to one side and will handle poorly.

CAUTION
*Do not overinflate the tires because they will be permanently distorted and damaged. If overinflated, they may bulge out similar to inflating an inner tube that is not within the constraints of a tire. If this happens the tire will **not** return to its original contour.*

Tire Inspection

The tires take a lot of punishment. Inspect them frequently for wear, cuts, abrasions or other damage. If you find a nail or other object in the tire, mark its location with a light colored crayon before removing it. This will help you locate the hole for repair. Refer to Chapter Twelve for tire changing and repair information.

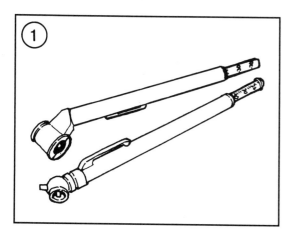

Measure the height of the tire tread (**Figure 2**) with a ruler. To obtain an accurate measurement of tire wear, measure a number of different knobs around the tire. If your inspection and measurements indicate that the tire is worn out, replace it as described in Chapter Twelve.

WARNING
Do not ride your vehicle with worn out or damaged tires. Flat, worn out or damaged tires can cause you to lose control of the ATV. Replace excessively worn or damaged tires immediately.

Rim Inspection

Inspect the condition of the wheel rims frequently, especially on the outer side. If the wheel has hit a tree or large rock, rim damage may be sufficient to cause an air leak. A bent wheel may also cause severe misalignment and vibration, resulting in an unsafe riding condition.

Make sure wheel mounting nuts are all in place and tight. Do not operate the vehicle if any of the wheel mounting studs are broken or missing or if any of the wheel mounting nuts are missing or loose.

BATTERY

All electric start models are equipped with a battery. In addition to checking and correcting the electrolyte level, the exterior of the battery, should be cleaned on a regular basis.

NOTE
Recycle your old battery. When you replace the old battery, be sure to turn in the old battery at that time. The lead plates and the plastic case can be recycled. Most ATV dealers will accept your old battery in trade when you purchase a new one. Never place an old battery in your household trash. It is illegal, in most states, to place any acid or lead (heavy metal) in landfills. There is also the danger of the battery being crushed in the trash truck and spraying acid on the truck or landfill operator.

Safety Precautions

When working with batteries, use extreme care to avoid spilling or splashing the electrolyte. This solution contains sulfuric acid, which can ruin clothing and cause serious chemical burns. If any electrolyte is spilled or splashed on clothing or skin, immediately neutralize it with a solution of baking soda and water, then flush with an abundance of clean water.

WARNING
Electrolyte splashed into the eyes is extremely harmful. Safety glasses should always be worn while working with batteries. If electrolyte enters eyes, call a physician immediately, then force your eyes open and flood them with cool clean water for approximately 15 minutes.

If electrolyte is spilled or splashed onto any surface, it should be neutralized immediately with a baking soda and water solution, then rinsed with clean water.

While batteries are being charged, highly explosive hydrogen gas forms in each cell. Some of this gas escapes through the filler cap openings and may form an explosive atmosphere in and around the battery. This condition can persist for several hours. Sparks, an open flame or a lighted cigarette can ignite the gas, causing an explosion and possible personal injury.

Take the following precautions to prevent an explosion:

1. Do not smoke or permit any open flame near any battery being charged or which has been recently charged.

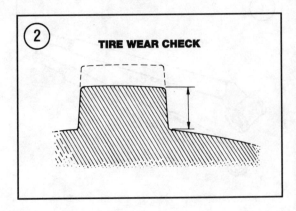
TIRE WEAR CHECK

2. Do not disconnect live circuits at the battery terminals since a spark usually occurs when a live circuit is broken.

3. Take care when connecting or disconnecting any battery charger. Be sure its power switch is OFF before making or breaking any connections. Poor connections are a common cause of electrical arcs which cause explosions.

4. Keep children and pets away from charging equipment and batteries.

For maximum battery life, check the electrolyte level and state of charge periodically. Also, check the battery and connections for corrosion. In hot, dry climates check the battery more frequently. The electrolyte level should always be between the 2 marks (A and B, **Figure 3**). The electrolyte level for each cell can be seen through the battery case. If the electrolyte is below the level of the lower mark in one or more cells, add distilled water as required. To ensure proper mixing of the water and acid, operate the engine or charge the battery immediately after adding water. *Never* add battery acid instead of water—this will shorten the battery's life.

On all models covered in this manual, the negative (–) terminal of the battery is grounded. When removing the battery, disconnect the grounded negative (–) cable before detaching the positive (+) cable. This will minimize the chances of a tool shorting to ground when disconnecting the "hot" positive cable.

WARNING
When performing the following procedure, protect your eyes, skin and clothing. If electrolyte gets in your eyes, flush

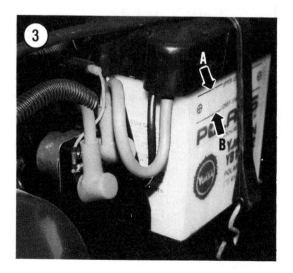

your eyes thoroughly with clean water and get prompt medical attention.

Battery Removal

The battery (**Figure 3**) is located under the left rear fender of models so equipped and provides power for electric starting. Observe the following when removing the battery:

1. Clean the battery case.

2. Disconnect the negative (–) battery lead from the battery before disconnecting the positive (+) lead.

3. Remove the battery hold down strap.

4. Detach the positive (+) lead from the battery terminal.

5. Disconnect the vent hose.

6. Lift the battery from the battery box (carrier).

7. Clean all dirt and corrosion from the outside of the battery case and from the battery box.

Battery Inspection and Servicing

The electrolyte level can be checked without removing the battery, but it should be removed and cleaned if electrolyte is added or if specific gravity is checked. The electrolyte level is visible through the battery case. Clean the battery case and observe the height of the fluid level in each cell. Maintain the electrolyte level between the 2 marks on the case (A and B, **Figure 3**). If the electrolyte level is low, remove and clean the battery thoroughly before servicing it.

1. Inspect the pad at the bottom of the battery box (carrier) for contamination or damage. Clean the battery box and pad with a solution of baking soda and water. Dry any bare metal, then repaint to protect surfaces from additional damage.

2. Check the entire battery case for cracks or other damage. If the battery case is warped, discolored or has a raised top, the battery has been overcharged or overheated.

3. Check the battery hold-down strap for acid damage, cracks or other damage. Replace the hold-down strap if required.

4. Check the battery terminal bolts, spacers and nuts for corrosion or other damage. Clean the parts in a solution of baking soda and water. Replace damaged parts.

NOTE
Keep cleaning solution out of the battery cells or the electrolyte will be seriously weakened.

5. Clean the top of the battery with a stiff bristle brush and water. If necessary, a solution of baking soda and water can be used to help clean, but be careful not to contaminate the electrolyte in the battery's cells with either soap or the baking soda solution.

6. Check the battery cable terminal ends for corrosion or other damage. If corrosion is minor, clean the battery cable clamps with a stiff wire brush. Install new cables if terminal ends or cables are severely damaged.

NOTE
Do not overfill the battery cells in Step 7. The electrolyte expands due to the heat of charging and will overflow if the level is above the upper level line.

7. Remove the caps from the battery cells and add distilled water, if necessary, to raise the level between the upper and lower level lines on the battery case.

Battery Testing

The best way to check the condition of a battery is to test the specific gravity of the electrolyte in each of the battery's cells using a hydrometer. Use a hydrometer that is marked with numbered graduations from 1.100 to 1.300 rather than one with color-coded bands. To use the hydrometer, proceed as follows:

1. Remove the battery.

NOTE
Keep cleaning solution out of the battery cells or the electrolyte will be seriously weakened.

2. Clean the top of the battery with a stiff bristle brush and water. If necessary, a solution of baking soda and water can be used to help clean, but be careful not to contaminate the electrolyte in the battery's cells.

NOTE
Do not attempt to test a battery with a hydrometer immediately after adding

water to the cells. If possible, wait until after testing the specific gravity to add distilled water. If necessary to add water, charge the battery for 15-20 minutes at a rate high enough to cause vigorous gassing before checking the specific gravity.

3. Remove the caps from the battery's cells and check the level of the electrolyte.

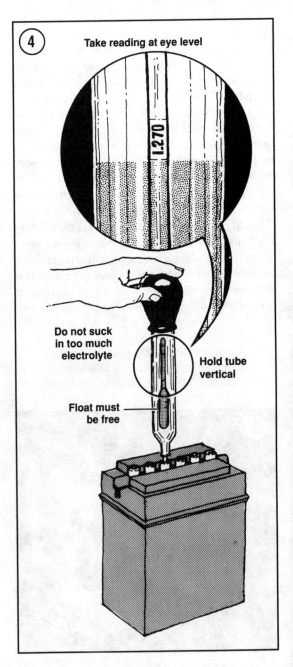

NOTE
Draw enough electrolyte into the hydrometer to allow the weighted float inside the hydrometer to be suspended in the fluid.

4. Squeeze the rubber ball of the hydrometer, insert the tip into one cell and release the ball to draw electrolyte up into the hydrometer. When using a temperature compensating hydrometer, release the electrolyte and repeat the process several times until the tester has adjusted to the temperature of the electrolyte.

5. Hold the hydrometer vertically and observe the numbered line aligned with the surface of the electrolyte (**Figure 4**). This is the specific gravity of this cell.

6. Return the electrolyte to the cell from which it came.

7. Repeat the test described in Steps 4-6 for the remaining cells.

NOTE
Specific gravity is a measurement of the density or weight of the electrolyte as compared to plain water. As the battery is charged, the electrolyte becomes more dense. Therefore, specific gravity indicates the battery's state of charge.

8. The specific gravity of the electrolyte in each cell is an excellent indication of that cell's condition. Refer to **Figure 5**. The electrolyte in a fully charged cell will have specific gravity of 1.260-1.280, a cell in good condition will have specific gravity of

1.230-1.250. Any cell reading 1.120 or less is weak and should be charged.

NOTE
If a temperature compensated hydrometer is not used, add 0.004 to the specific gravity for every 10° above 80° F (25° C). Subtract 0.004 to the specific gravity for every 10° below 80° F (25° C).

Battery Charging

While charging, the battery cells will bubble. If one cell does not have gas bubbles or if that cell's specific gravity is very low, the cell is probably defective.

If a battery loses its charge (when not in use) within a week or if the specific gravity drops quickly, the battery is defective. A good battery should only discharge approximately 1% each day.

CAUTION
Always remove the battery from the vehicle before connecting charging equipment.

WARNING
During charging, highly explosive hydrogen gas is released from the battery. The battery should be charged only in a well-ventilated area away from any open flames, cigarettes or other ignition sources. Never check the charge of a battery by arcing across the terminals. The resulting spark can ignite the hydrogen gas, causing an explosion.

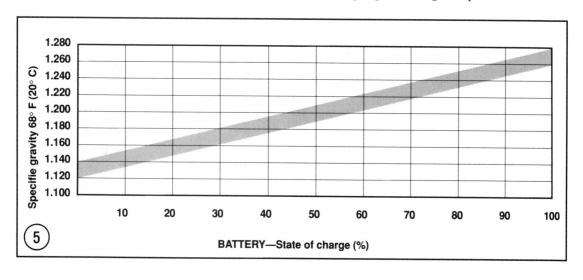

1. Remove the battery from the vehicle as described in this chapter.
2. Connect the positive (+) lead from the charger to the battery's positive terminal.
3. Connect the negative (–) lead from the charger to the battery's negative terminal.

> *CAUTION*
> *Maintain electrolyte at the upper level while charging. Refill with distilled water as necessary.*

4. Remove all of the vent caps from the battery and check electrolyte level. Leave caps off while charging.
5. Set the charger to 12 volts and turn the charger ON.

> *NOTE*
> *Charge the battery at a slow charge rate of 1/10 of its given capacity. The standard charging rate is approximately 1.2 amps.*

6. The charging time depends upon the discharged condition of the battery. Use the chart in **Figure 5** to determine the approximate charge times at different specific gravity readings. For example, if the specific gravity of your battery is 1.180, the approximate charging time would be 6 hours.
7. After the battery has been charged for the predetermined time, turn the charger OFF, disconnect the leads and check the specific gravity of each cell as described in this chapter.

Battery Installation

1. Make sure the rubber pad is in good condition, clean and correctly positioned in the bottom of the battery box before installing the battery.
2. Install the battery in the battery box (carrier) with the terminals facing as shown in **Figure 3**.
3. Connect and route the battery vent tube so that it is not kinked, pinched or plugged. Position the tube so that the hose outlet is located away from all metal components. Install a new vent tube if necessary.
4. Install the battery hold-down strap as shown in **Figure 3**.

> *CAUTION*
> *Be sure the cables are attached to the proper terminals on the battery. Con-*

> *necting the battery backwards will reverse the polarity and damage the rectifier and ignition system.*

5. Attach the positive (+) battery cable to the positive battery terminal.
6. Attach the negative (–) ground cable to the negative battery terminal.
7. Coat the battery terminals and cable ends with dielectric grease or petroleum jelly.

New Battery Installation

Before installing a new battery, check its electrolyte level and state of charge. Charge the battery as required before installing it, then check the specific gravity of the electrolyte. A hydrometer check should indicate the specific gravity of the electrolyte in each cell is 1.260-1.280. A new battery may be permanently damaged if the electrolyte level is too low when it is installed.

FLUID CHECKS

Vital fluids should be checked daily or before each ride to assure proper operation and prevent severe component damage. Refer to **Table 1**. Checking the fluids frequently will help the operator gauge their normal use and prevent damage from operation with insufficient lubrication.

BREAK-IN PROCEDURE

After extensive top end repair, such as boring, honing or new rings and major lower end work, the engine should be broken-in just as if it were new.

Refer to the *Break-In Procedure* described in Chapter Four or Chapter Five.

PERIODIC LUBRICATION

WARNING
Serious fire hazards always exist around gasoline and other petroleum products. Do not allow any smoking in areas where fuel is stored or while refueling your ATV. Always have a fire extinguisher, rated for gasoline and electrical fires, within reach just to play it safe.

Lubricating 2-Stroke Engines

Polaris 2-stroke engines are lubricated by oil injected into the intake manifold. This oil mixes with the incoming fuel charge and circulates through the crankcase and enters the combustion chamber where it is burned with the fuel. The internal engine components are lubricated by the oil as it passes through the crankcase and cylinder.

All Polaris 2-stroke engines are equipped with a variable-ratio oil injection system. The injection system automatically maintains the optimum fuel/oil ratio according to engine speed and load.

Checking Oil Level
(Models With 2-Stroke Engines)

The oil reservoir that supplies oil for the oil injection system is located at the front of the vehicle. Check the oil level in the reservoir (**Figure 6**) daily or each time the vehicle is refueled.

CAUTION
*Serious engine damage will occur if the oil system is allowed to run dry. If the oil lines are disconnected or if air has entered the oil line between the reservoir and the injection pump, refer to the **Oil Injection Pump Bleeding** procedure in this chapter.*

Use regular unleaded gasoline with a minimum octane rating of 87. Refer to **Table 4** for the recommended oil for use in the oil injection system on 2-stroke models.

Lubricating 4-Stroke Engines

Polaris 4-stroke engines are equipped with a dry sump type lubrication system that contains 1.89 L (2 qts.) of oil. The oil reservoir (tank) located on the left side (**Figure 7**) must always be filled with the type (**Table 4**) and quantity of oil recommended by the manufacturer. The various components of the engine are lubricated by the oil as it circulates within the engine. The oil then returns to the reservoir. The oil is used over and over as the 4-stroke engine operates. Engine heat is transferred to the oil, then the oil is allowed to cool while it is in the reservoir. The oil also becomes contaminated as it circulates within the engine and a filter is used to trap some of the particles.

Regular oil and filter changes will contribute to the longevity of the engine. The recommended engine oil and filter change intervals are specified in **Table 3**. These change intervals assume the vehicle is operated in moderate climates, under moderate loads and at moderate speeds. The oil should be changed more frequently if the vehicle is operated in dusty, wet, hot or cold conditions with heavy loads or at high speeds. Use only a high-quality oil of the type as listed in **Table 4**.

Check the oil level in the reservoir (**Figure 7**) daily or each time the vehicle is refueled. Use regular unleaded gasoline with a minimum pump octane rating of 87 to prevent detonation and excessive combustion chamber deposits.

Checking Oil Level
(Models With 4-Stroke Engines)

A dipstick is attached to the oil fill cap (**Figure 7**). The oil level should be maintained between the marks on the dipstick (**Figure 8**).

If the oil level is low, pour in the required amount and type of oil specified in **Table 4** and **Table 5**. Fill the tank until the oil level is at the top (full) mark.

Changing Engine Oil and Filter
(Models With 4-Stroke Engines)

Regular oil and filter changes will contribute to engine longevity. The recommended engine oil and filter change intervals are specified in **Table 3**. These change intervals assume the vehicle is operated in moderate climates, under moderate loads and at moderate speeds. If the vehicle is operated in dusty or wet conditions, under heavy loads or at high speed, change the oil and filter more frequently. Refer to **Table 4** for the recommended type of lubricant.

To change the engine oil and filter you need the following:

a. Drain pan.
b. Funnel.
c. Opener or pour spout.
d. Wrench and sockets.
e. 2 qts. of oil.
f. New oil filter.

There are a number of ways to discard the old oil safely and legally. Some service stations and oil retailers will accept your used engine oil for recycling.

> *NOTE*
> *Never dispose of motor oil in the trash, on the ground, or down a storm drain. Many service stations accept used motor oil and waste haulers provide curbside used motor oil collection. Do not combine other fluids with motor oil to be recycled. To locate a recycler, contact the American Petroleum Institute (API) at www.recycleoil.org.*

> *NOTE*
> *Running the engine before draining the oil allows the oil to heat up so that it will flow more freely. The warm, circulated oil will more easily carry contaminants and sludge buildup out when it is drained.*

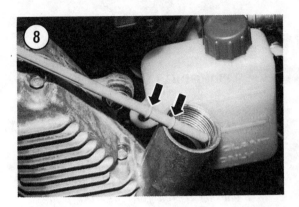

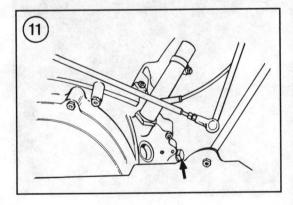

1. Start the engine and let it warm up approximately 2-3 minutes.

2. Place the vehicle on level ground and apply the parking brake.

3. Stop the engine and place a drain pan under the drain plug.

4. Remove the drain plug (**Figure 9**) and allow the engine oil to drain from the reservoir.

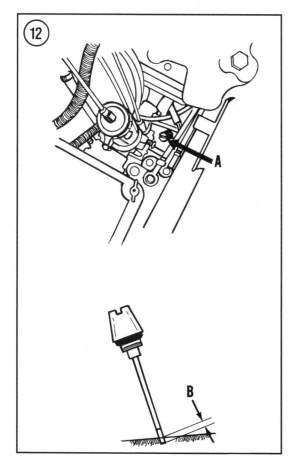

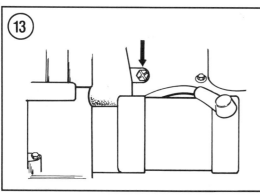

5. Remove the fill cap (**Figure 7**) to allow the oil to drain faster.

6. Allow the oil to drain for at least 15-20 minutes.

7. Reinstall the drain plug after all oil has drained.

8. Relocate the drain pan under the oil filter, then remove the filter (**Figure 10**).

9. Thoroughly clean the oil filter receptacle in the left crankcase. If necessary, clean any remaining oil sludge.

10. Install the new oil filter (**Figure 10**).

11. Make sure the drain plug is tight, then fill reservoir with 2 qts. of engine oil.

12. Start the engine, allow it to idle and check for oil leaks. If leakage is noted, stop the engine immediately and correct the leak.

WARNING
Avoid prolonged contact with used oil. It is advisable to wash your hands thoroughly with soap and water as soon as possible after handling or coming in contact with engine oil.

Engine Counterbalancer
(2-Stroke Engines So Equipped)

The 350L and 400L liquid cooled engines used by some models are equipped with a counterbalancer that is gear-driven by the crankshaft. The gears and shaft are lubricated by an oil bath. The oil should be changed every 100 hours of operation or once each year. Refer to **Table 4** for the correct type of oil.

1. Remove the bottom chain guard.

2A. Remove the fill plug (**Figure 11**) on 350L models.

2B. Remove the fill plug and dipstick (A, **Figure 12**) on 400L models.

3. Remove the drain plug (**Figure 13**) and allow the oil to drain.

4. Reinstall the drain plug.

5. Make sure vehicle is level, then fill the compartment with the correct type of oil.

6A. On 350L models, oil should be at the level of fill plug (**Figure 11**).

6B. On 400L models, oil level should be within the knurled area of the dipstick (B, **Figure 12**).

7. Install and tighten the fill plug.

Control Cables and Levers

All of the cables and levers should be inspected for freedom of movement and lubricated twice each year or at least every 50 hours of operation. Refer to **Table 4** for the recommended lubricant.

The throttle and mechanical brake cables (of models so equipped) should be cleaned and lubricated at intervals indicated in **Table 3**. The cables should also be checked for kinks and signs of wear, fraying or any damage that cause cables to fail or stick. Cables will not last forever even under the best conditions and the need to replace cables should expected.

The most positive method of control cable lubrication involves the use of a cable lubricator like the one shown in **Figure 14**. A can of cable lube is also required. Use only the cable lubricant listed in **Table 4**. *Do not* use chain lube as a cable lubricant.

1. Loosen the cable adjuster at the handlebar and disconnect the cable from the lever.
2. Attach the cable lubricator to the end of the cable housing following its manufacturer's instructions (**Figure 14**).
3. Insert the lubricant can nozzle into the lubricator, press the button on the cap and hold it down until the lubricant begins to flow from the other end of the cable housing.

NOTE
Place a shop cloth at the end of the cable to catch the excess oil as it drains out.

4. Detach the lubricant can from the lubricator, then remove the lubricator from the cable housing.
5. Apply a light coat of grease to the cable ends before reattaching them.
6. Reattach the cables. Adjust the cables as described in this chapter.
7. Operate the controls (throttle and brake) and check for smooth operation. If the controls do not operate smoothly, correct the cause or install a new cable and housing. Controls must not bind.

Transmission Oil

Oil contained in the transmission housing lubricates the chain and sprockets or gears. Different oil is recommended for models with a chain transmission (Type I, **Table 6**) than for models with a gear transmission (Type II, **Table 6**) or gear/chain transmission (Type III, **Table 6**). Refer to **Table 4** for the recommended lubricant type. If possible, always use one type and brand of oil. Different types or brands may vary slightly in their composition and a mixture of the two may not lubricate as well as either alone.

Oil Level Check

The oil level on models with a chain type (Forward-Reverse) transmission is checked by removing the level plug (A, **Figure 15**). The oil level on later models with a gear type or gear and chain type transmission is checked with the dipstick attached to the fill plug (A, **Figure 16** or A, **Figure 17**).

1. Park the vehicle on a level surface.

2A. On models with a chain transmission (Type I, **Table 6**), unscrew and remove the level plug (A, **Figure 15**) from the transmission housing.

2B. On models with a gear transmission (Type II, **Table 6**), the fill plug (A, **Figure 16**) has a dipstick attached. To check the oil level, unscrew and remove

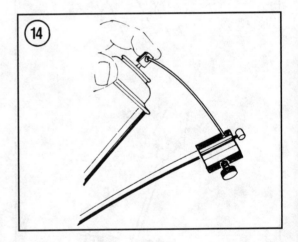

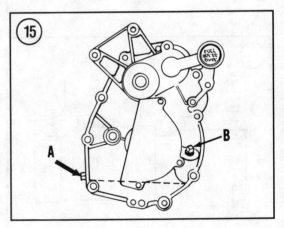

the fill plug (A, **Figure 16**) from the transmission housing. Wipe the dipstick off and insert it back into the housing. Do not screw the fill plug back into the cover.

2C. On models with a gear and chain transmission (Type III, **Table 6**), the fill plug (A, **Figure 17**) has a dipstick attached. To check oil level, pull the fill plug (A, **Figure 17**) from the transmission housing. Wipe the dipstick off and insert it back into the housing.

3A. On Type I models with the level plug (A, **Figure 15**), the oil level should be at the level of the removed plug.

3B. On models with a dipstick attached to the filler plug (A, **Figure 16** or A, **Figure 17**), the oil level should be within the knurled section of the dipstick.

4. If the oil level is low, top off with an oil recommended in **Table 4**. Do not overfill. Recheck the oil level.

5. Reinstall and tighten the removed plugs securely.

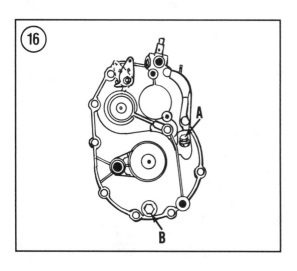

Changing transmission oil

Refer to **Table 3** for recommended oil change intervals and to **Table 4** for recommended type of oil.

1. Park the vehicle on a level surface.

2A. On models with a chain transmission (Type I, **Table 6**), unscrew and remove the level plug (A, **Figure 15**) and fill plug (B) from the transmission housing.

2B. On models with a gear transmission (Type II, **Table 6**), remove the fill plug (A, **Figure 16**) and drain plug (B) from the transmission housing.

2C. On models with a gear and chain transmission (Type III, **Table 6**), remove the fill plug (A, **Figure 17**) and drain plug (B, **Figure 17**) from the transmission housing.

3. Models with chain transmission (Type I, **Table 6**) are not equipped with a drain plug. Oil can be drained from these models by raising the front of the vehicle to allow most of the oil to drain from the level hole (A, **Figure 15**).

NOTE
Oil is easily spilled when draining and refilling the transmission. Try to prevent as much spillage as possible, then clean as much of the spilled oil in the shop cloths as possible.

NOTE
Store the oil soaked shop cloths in a suitable container until they can be cleaned.

4. If the drain plug was removed, proceed as follows:
   a. Inspect the magnet in the drain plug.
   b. Clean and reinstall plug.

5. Insert a funnel into the hole for the filler plug and fill the transmission housing with the correct type (**Table 4**) and quantity (**Table 5**) of oil.

6. Check the oil level as described in the previous procedure and reinstall the plugs.

Rear Axle Housing

The bearings for the rear axle are lubricated by grease that can be injected through the fitting (A, **Figure 18**). Refer to **Table 4** for recommended type of lubricant. The bearing should be greased at least every 50 hours or twice each year. If the vehicle is operated under severe service conditions or with heavy loads, perform this service more frequently.

Suspension

Grease fittings are provided on some suspension components. Refer to **Table 4** for the recommended lubricant. Inject grease into the fittings every 50 hours of operation or at least twice each year. If the vehicle is operated under severe service conditions or with heavy loads, perform this service more frequently.

Steering

Bushings for the steering shaft and tie rod ends should be greased every 50 hours of operation or at least twice each year. If the vehicle is operated under severe service conditions, perform this service more frequently. Refer to **Table 4** for the recommended lubricant.

Front Hub Wheel Bearings (Not Driven)

The front wheel bearings on models without front wheel drive should be removed, cleaned and repacked every 50 hours of operation or at least twice each year. Refer to **Table 4** for the recommended lubricant. The wheels should be removed and bearings cleaned, then repacked with grease as soon as possible if water has entered the bearings. New seals should be installed when assembling. Refer to Chapter Twelve for service.

Front Wheels (Driven)

Refer to **Table 4** for the recommended lubricant for use in the driven front wheel hubs. The oil should be changed twice each year or at least every 50 hours of operation. If vehicle is operated in wet conditions, check frequently for signs of water contamination. Drain the oil, flush the hub and fill with new oil as soon as possible if contamination is noticed.

1. Remove the plug (**Figure 19**) and rotate it to bottom, then allow the oil to drain.

2. Turn the hub until the hole for the plug is at about the 4 o'clock position, then fill the hub with oil. Hub should be just over half full of oil.

3. Allow the oil to settle and recheck to be sure oil is at the 4 o'clock position, then reinstall plug.

PERIODIC MAINTENANCE

Periodic maintenance intervals for specific items are listed in **Table 3**.

Drive Belt Check

Check the drive belt (**Figure 20**) for cracks, fraying or unusual wear as described in Chapter Eight. Replace the drive belt if any damage is noted or if it is worn as noted in Chapter Eight.

Rear Drive Chain Adjustment
(All Models Except Big Boss)

The rear drive chain should be inspected and adjusted periodically depending upon vehicle usage. Improper maintenance and neglect can cause premature failure of the chain and the sprockets.

To check the rear drive chain free play, the *suspension must be loaded* so the chain is at its tightest point in suspension travel. Measure chain free play midway between the sprockets, as shown in **Figure 21**. The rear drive chain should have 6.35 mm (1/4 in.) free play.

To adjust the rear drive chain free play, proceed as follows:

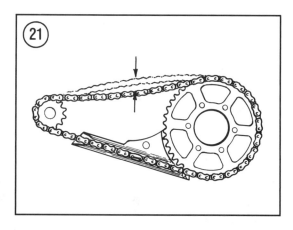

1. Loosen the rear axle clamp bolts (B, **Figure 18**).
2. Insert a pin (approximately 5/16 in. diameter) through the hole (**Figure 22**) in the rear sprocket hub and into the rear axle housing.
3. Move (rock) the vehicle so the pin forces the rear axle housing to rotate in its retaining clamps. The proper direction of rotation depends upon whether loosening or tightening is required.
4. Measure chain free play and adjust play as necessary.
5. When the chain free travel is correct, tighten the axle housing clamp bolts to the torque specified in **Table 7**.
6. Remove the pin and recheck chain free play.

Rear Drive Chain and Axle-to-Axle
Chain Adjustment
(Models With 6 Wheels)

The rear drive chain connects the output sprocket of the transmission with the first of the 2 rear drive axles. An axle-to-axle drive chain connects the 2 rear axles, providing drive to the rearmost axle. Adjustment of the rear drive chain affects the tension of the axle-to-axle chain, so the rear drive chain should be adjusted first.

The rear drive chain should be inspected and adjusted periodically depending upon vehicle usage. Improper maintenance and neglect can cause premature failure of the chain and the sprockets.

Rear drive chain

To *check* the rear drive chain free play on models with 6 wheels, the *suspension must be unloaded*. Chain free play when measured midway between the sprockets should be 38 mm (1.5 in.) as shown in **Figure 21**.

To *adjust* the rear drive chain free play, proceed as follows:
1. Loosen the rear axle housing clamp bolts (B, **Figure 18**).
2. Insert a pin (approximately 5/16 in. diameter) through the hole (**Figure 23**) in the top of the rear axle housing.
3. Move the vehicle so the pin engages a hole in the sprocket hub (**Figure 22**, typical).
4. Move (rock) the vehicle so the pin forces the rear axle housing to rotate in its retaining clamps. The

proper direction of rotation depends upon whether loosening or tightening is required.

5. Measure the chain free play and adjust play as necessary.

6. When the chain free travel is correct, tighten the axle housing clamp bolts to the torque specified in **Table 7**.

7. Remove the pin and recheck chain free play.

> *NOTE*
> *Changing the adjustment of the rear drive chain will affect the adjustment of the rear axle drive chain.*

8. Check and adjust the free play of the axle-to-axle drive chain that connects the drive axle with the rearmost axle as described in the following steps.

Axle-to-axle chain

The rear axle of all models with six wheels is driven by a chain connecting the rearmost (third) axle with the center (drive) axle. The axle-to-axle drive chain should be inspected and adjusted periodically depending upon vehicle usage. Improper maintenance and neglect can cause premature failure of the chain and sprockets. Refer to *Lubrication* section in this chapter.

Free play of the rear (axle-to-axle) drive chain should be 6.35 mm (1/4 in.) when measured midway between the sprockets.

To *adjust* the rear (axle-to-axle) drive chain, proceed as follows:

1. Loosen the rear axle clamp bolts (B, **Figure 18**).

2. Insert a pin through the rear sprocket (**Figure 22**) and into the axle center housing.

> *NOTE*
> *The proper direction of rotation depends upon whether loosening or tightening is required. Move the vehicle to the rear to tighten the chain.*

3. Move (rock) the vehicle so the axle center housing is forced to rotate as necessary to adjust the chain free play.

4. Install and tighten the clamp bolts (B, **Figure 18**).

5. Remove the pin, then recheck free play of the center drive chain.

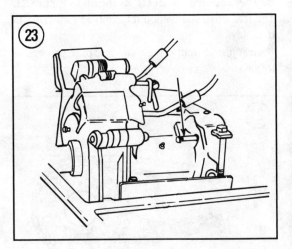

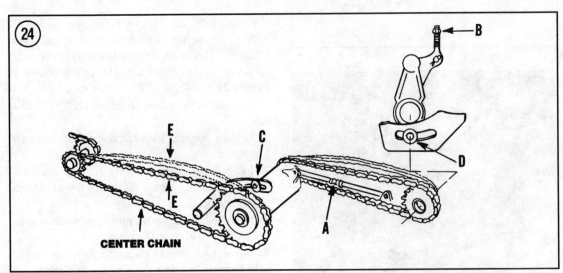

6. When chain free play is correct, tighten the clamp bolts to the torque specified in **Table 7**.

Center and Front Drive Chain Adjustment (1985-1987 Models With Front Wheel Drive)

The center and front drive chains should be inspected and adjusted periodically depending upon vehicle usage. Improper maintenance and neglect can cause premature failure of the chain and sprockets.

Free play of both the front and center drive chains should be 6.35 mm (1/4 in.) when measured midway between the sprockets E, **Figure 24**. The center drive chain must be adjusted first, because any changes to it will affect the free play of the front drive chain.

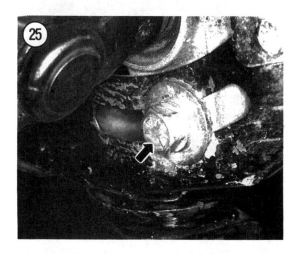

Center drive chain adjustment

1. Loosen the cap screw (C, **Figure 24**).
2. Change the length of the adjuster (A, **Figure 24**) as necessary to adjust the chain free play.
3. Tighten the cap screw (C, **Figure 24**).
4. Recheck free play after tightening the screw. After correctly adjusting the free play of the center drive chain, check and adjust the free play of the front drive chain.

Front drive chain adjustment

1. Loosen the cap screw (D, **Figure 24** or **Figure 25**).
2. Turn the adjuster nut (B, **Figure 24**) as necessary to adjust the chain free play.
3. Tighten the cap screw (D, **Figure 24** or **Figure 25**).
4. Recheck free play after tightening the screw.

Center and Front Drive Chain Adjustment (1988-on Models With Front Wheel Drive)

The center and front drive chains should be inspected and adjusted periodically depending upon vehicle usage. Improper maintenance and neglect can cause premature failure of the chain and sprockets. Refer to *Lubrication* section in this chapter.

Free play of both the front and center drive chains should be 6.35 mm (1/4 in.) when measured midway between the sprockets (Refer to **Figure 26**). The

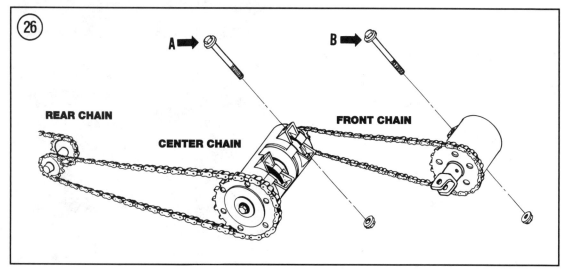

REAR CHAIN   FRONT CHAIN   CENTER CHAIN

center drive chain must be adjusted first, because any changes to it will affect the free play of the front drive chain.

Center drive chain adjustment

1. Disconnect, then remove the brake pedal linkage.
2. Detach the front fender mud flap from the foot board.
3. Remove the center chain guard.
4. Remove the front chain guard.
5. Loosen the clamp bolts (A, **Figure 27**) that secure the chain drive eccentric housing.
6. Rock the vehicle until the hole (B, **Figure 27**) in the housing aligns with the hole in the sprocket (sprocket is removed in **Figure 27**), then insert a pin through the holes.

> *NOTE*
> *The proper direction of rotation depends upon whether loosening or tightening is required. Move the vehicle to the rear to tighten the center chain.*

7. Move (rock) the vehicle so the center drive eccentric housing is forced to rotate as necessary to adjust the chain free play.
8. Install and tighten the clamp bolts (A, **Figure 27**).
9. Remove the pin, then recheck free play of the center drive chain. When free play of the center drive chain is correct, check and adjust the free play of the front drive chain.

Front drive chain adjustment

1. Loosen the clamp bolt (B, **Figure 26**) that clamps the front drive chain housing. Refer also to **Figure 28**.
2A. If spanner shown in **Figure 29** is available, insert the pins of the spanner wrench in the holes and rotate the eccentric front chain housing.
2B. If spanner is not available, align one of the holes in the front drive chain housing with a hole in the sprocket, then insert a pin through the holes. Rock the vehicle to turn the eccentric chain housing.

> *NOTE*
> *The proper direction of rotation depends upon whether loosening or tight-*

ening is required. Move the vehicle to the rear to tighten the chain.

3. Turn the front drive chain housing as necessary to adjust the chain free play.
4. Install and tighten the clamp bolt (**Figure 28**).
5. Remove the pin, if used, then recheck free play of the front drive chain.

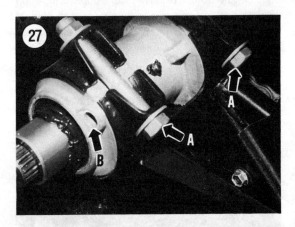

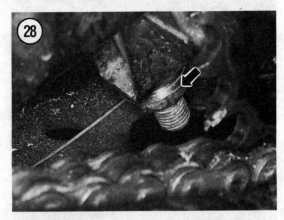

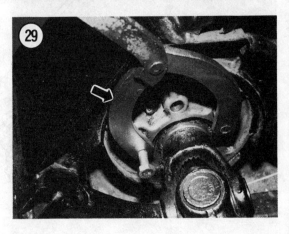

Brake Inspection and Adjustment (Models With Mechanical Type)

WARNING
The brake system is an important part of vehicle safety. If you are unsure about the condition of any brake component or assembly, have it checked by a Polaris dealer.

Mechanical drum type brakes are used on the front wheels and a mechanical disc type brake is used on the rear wheels of 1985-1987 Trail Boss models without front wheel drive. Periodic inspection, service and adjustment will help ensure proper operation of the brakes.

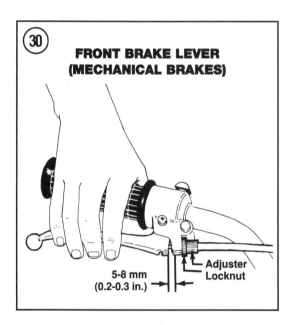

30
FRONT BRAKE LEVER (MECHANICAL BRAKES)

5-8 mm (0.2-0.3 in.)
Adjuster
Locknut

31

Front brakes

Both front brakes must operate evenly and stop the vehicle without pulling to either side when operating the front brake lever mounted on the right side of the handlebar. The front brake lever should have 5-8 mm (0.2-0.3 in.) free play (**Figure 30**). Brake lever free play is adjusted by turning the cable adjuster after loosening the locknut.

Adjust the front brake cables at the wheel ends of the cable (**Figure 31**) as follows:

1. Raise and support the front of the vehicle so the front wheels are off the ground and can be rotated.

2. Loosen the lock nut and turn the cable adjuster (**Figure 30**) into the housing. At this point, the handlebar lever should have too much free play.

3. Tighten the adjusting nuts (**Figure 31**) located at the wheel ends of the cables until the brake just starts to drag, then back the adjuster nut off slightly.

4. Turn the cable adjuster out of the housing until handlebar lever free play (**Figure 30**) is 5-8 mm (0.2-0.3 in.).

5. Check the cable joint (A, **Figure 32**) to be sure the joint block is level when the brake is applied. If the block is on an angle when the brake is applied, turn the adjusters (**Figure 31**) as required to equalize brake pressure.

Rear brake

The rear wheels are actuated by the rear brake lever mounted on the left side of the handlebar. Operating the handlebar lever should stop the vehicle without excessive pressure. The rear brake lever must have 6.0-6.5 mm (0.24-0.26 in.) free travel (**Figure 33**). Brake lever free play is adjusted by turning the cable adjuster (**Figure 33**) after loosening the locknut.

The rear brake caliper and disc are located on the right side of the transmission. Check the brake disc visually for cracks, deep scoring, heat discoloration, checking or excessive wear. Refer to Chapter Fourteen for brake service. Rear brakes are equipped with a self-adjusting brake mechanism. To adjust the rear brake caliper, squeeze the brake lever strongly several times to actuate the self-adjusting mechanism. If adjustment cannot be corrected by squeezing the brake lever, check the brake assembly as described in Chapter Fourteen.

NOTE
If brake adjustment is difficult or if you are unsure about its operation, refer adjustment to a Polaris dealer. Do not operate the vehicle without properly functioning brakes.

Brake System Inspection
(Models With Hydraulic Caliper)

WARNING
The brake system is an important part of machine safety. If you are unsure about the condition of any brake component or assembly, have it checked by a Polaris dealer.

The brake system should be inspected periodically. The front and rear brake systems are operated by the same brake lever. The front brake discs and calipers are located at each of the front wheels. The rear wheel brake caliper and disc is attached to the transmission and stops rotation of the transmission output shaft. The handlebar mounted master cylinder incorporates an integral reservoir.

Check the brake disc visually for cracks, deep scoring, heat discoloration, checking or excessive wear. Inspect the brake pads for cracks, chips, evidence of overheating or excessive wear. Install new pads if worn past the service limit groove or if the

remaining lining is less than 1.9 mm (0.075 in.) thick. Refer to Chapter Fourteen for brake service.

Servicing Brake Fluid
(Models With Hydraulic Caliper)

All models after 1987, and 1987 Trail Boss models with 4-wheel drive are equipped with hydraulically actuated front and rear brake systems. The condition and level of the hydraulic brake fluid is important to the operation of the brakes.

Proceed as follows to check the level and fill the reservoir with brake fluid:

1. Clean any dirt from the master cylinder reservoir cover.
2. Make sure the reservoir is level to prevent spilling brake fluid as the cover is removed. Remove the screws attaching the reservoir cover, then remove the cover and seal.
3. Check the level of the fluid. Brake fluid should be 3.2 mm (1/8 in.) below the top of the reservoir on 1987 and 1988 models or 6.35 mm (1/4 in.) below the top of the reservoir of 1989 and later models.

WARNING
Use only brake fluid marked DOT 3 (specified for disc brakes). Other brake fluids may vaporize and cause brake failure. Do not mix different brands or types of brake fluid, because they may

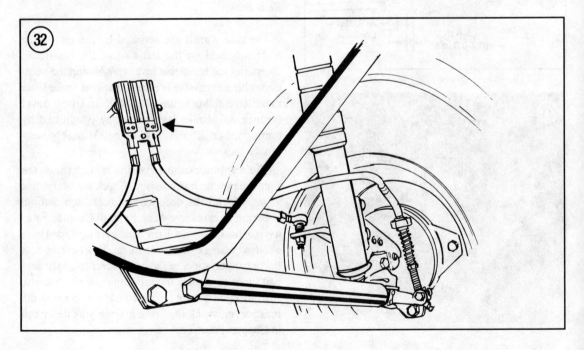

not be compatible. Mixing silicone based (DOT 5) brake fluid with DOT 3 fluid may cause brake system failure.

CAUTION
Be careful when adding brake fluid. Spilled brake fluid on painted or plated surfaces may damage the finish. If brake fluid is spilled on a painted surface, wash the area immediately with soapy water and rinse thoroughly with clean water.

4. Fill reservoir to the correct level, then install the cover.

Each time the reservoir cover is removed, a small amount of moisture and dirt can enter the brake system and be mixed with the brake fluid. The same thing can happen if a leak occurs or any part of the hydraulic brake system is loosened or disconnected. Dirt can cause unnecessary wear or clog the system.

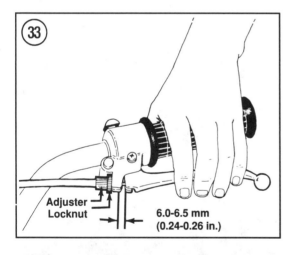

Adjuster
Locknut
6.0-6.5 mm
(0.24-0.26 in.)

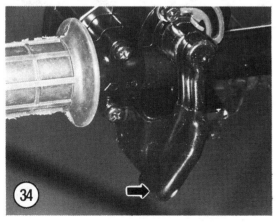

Water in the fluid can vaporize at high temperature and impair the brake's ability to stop. It is recommended that the brake fluid be drained and the system refilled with new fluid each year. To change the brake fluid, refer to *Bleeding the System* in Chapter Fourteen. Continue adding new fluid to the master cylinder until the brake fluid leaving the calipers is clean and free of contaminants.

Throttle Cable Free Play Adjustment

On models with 2-stroke engines, the carburetor (throttle) cable and the oil pump control cable are both attached to and controlled by the handlebar mounted throttle lever. Adjustment of one cable affects the adjustment of the other cable. It is important to check and adjust the carburetor idle speed, adjust the throttle lever free play and synchronize the movement of the oil injection pump to be sure the carburetor throttle and the oil injection are both properly controlled.

All models require some throttle cable play to prevent changes in the idle speed when you turn the handlebars. The recommended amount of cable free play is 1.6 mm (1/16 in.) when measured at the end of the throttle lever. Refer to **Figure 34**, typical. In time the cable(s) will stretch and the free play will become excessive.

NOTE
Check throttle cable free play at the handlebar lever. It is important that the throttle cable has the correct amount of play as described.

1. Set the engine idle speed as described under *Idle Speed Adjustment* in this chapter.
2. Start the engine and allow it to idle in NEUTRAL. Make sure the handlebar mounted speed control lever is at its slowest speed position.
3. With the engine running at idle speed, push the throttle lever to increase engine speed and observe the amount of movement (free play) required to increase the engine speed.
4. If the free play is more than 1.6 mm (1/16 in.), adjust as follows.

NOTE
Be careful not to remove all end play. The engine idle speed may be increased if no end play is present.

a. Loosen the lock nut on the cable adjuster (**Figure 35**, typical) near the handlebar mounted throttle lever and turn the adjuster OUT to reduce the amount of free play. If additional adjustment is required, a similar adjuster is located at the carburetor. Be sure the cable is not damaged.

b. When free play is correct, tighten the adjuster locknut to maintain the correct setting. Recheck free play after tightening the locknut.

5. If the throttle cable has no free play, perform the following:

a. Loosen the lock nut on the cable adjuster (**Figure 35**, typical) near the handlebar mounted throttle lever and turn the adjuster IN to increase the amount of free play.

b. When free play is correct, tighten the adjuster locknut to maintain the correct setting. Recheck free play after tightening the locknut.

6. Check throttle operation after adjusting. The idle speed must quickly return to idle speed when the throttle lever is released. If the idle speed changes when the handlebar is turned, check to be sure the cable is routed properly.

7. On models with 2-stroke engines, check the *Oil Injection Pump Adjustment* as described in the following procedure.

Oil Injection Pump Adjustment (Models With 2-Stroke Engines)

The oil pump injects lubricating oil into the engine. The amount of oil is determined by throttle position. Control cable adjustment is necessary because the cables will wear and stretch during normal use. Incorrect cable adjustment can cause too little or too much oil and may result in engine seizure and poor performance.

The oil pump cable adjustment should be checked once a year or whenever the throttle cable is adjusted, disconnected or replaced.

1. Adjust the carburetor as described under *Tune-Up* in this chapter.

> *CAUTION*
> *If the carburetor is not adjusted before adjusting the oil pump, engine damage may occur. The oil injection pump operation must be synchronized with the carburetor opening.*

2. Adjust the *Throttle Cable Free Play* as described in the previous procedure.

> *NOTE*
> *The oil injection pump (**Figure 36**, typical) on 250 and 400 air-cooled models is located on the rear of the engine crankcase. The pump (**Figure 37**, typical) on 350L and 400L liquid-cooled models is located on the front of the engine crankcase.*

3. Move the throttle lever until free play is just removed from the cables and the carburetor throttle just begins to move. The cable to the oil injection pump should also just begin to move the pump lever (A, **Figure 36** or A, **Figure 37**) and the mark (B, **Figure 36** or B, **Figure 37**) on the lever must be aligned with the mark on the pump housing.

CAUTION
It is important that all free play is re-moved from the cables, but the throttle should not move. If it is necessary to move the throttle to align the marks on pump, the oil injection control cable must be adjusted.

4. If the adjustment marks do not align:
   a. Loosen the locknut on the cable adjuster located near the pump.
   b. Turn the cable adjuster until the 2 marks (B, **Figure 36** or B, **Figure 37**) align.
   c. Tighten the cable adjuster locknut and recheck the adjustment.

Oil Filter Inspection/Replacement
(Models With 2-Stroke Engines)

On models with 2-stroke engines, an inline oil filter is installed between the injection oil tank and the oil pump. A clamp is used on each end of the filter. The oil filter is installed to prevent contaminants from entering the pump and obstructing oil passages or causing the pump to stick.

CAUTION
An oil filter that is contaminated and clogged will prevent oil from reaching the engine. Change the filter if contamination can be seen or is suspected. Engine seizure from lack of oil is more difficult to repair than installing a new filter.

Inspect the oil filter frequently for contamination or other obstruction. If the oil filter is contaminated, replace it and check the reservoir for additional contaminants. The connecting lines and the oil system reservoir should be removed, cleaned, then checked for contamination or damage. After the system has been cleaned, install a new oil filter, fill the reservoir with new approved oil, and bleed the oil pump as described in this chapter to make sure oil is being delivered to the engine.

When replacing the oil filter, note the following:
   a. Place a cloth underneath the oil filter to absorb oil spilled when the filter is removed.
   b. Loosen or remove the hose clamps from the filter nipples.
   c. Detach both hoses from the filter.
   d. Check the hose clamps for fatigue or damage. Install new clamps if required.
   e. Attach the hoses to the new filter.
   f. Install the clamps over each hose and filter nipple. Tighten the clamps securely.
   g. Fill the reservoir with new approved oil.
   h. Bleed the oil injection pump as described in this chapter.
   i. Remove and safely discard the cloth used to catch spilled oil.

Oil Filter Replacement
(Models With 4-Stroke Engines)

On models with 4-stroke engines, a cartridge type oil filter is attached to the left side of the engine, below the oil reservoir. Replace the filter cartridge each time the engine oil is changed.

To change the oil filter, refer to *Changing Engine Oil and Filter* in this chapter.

Air Filter Servicing

Remove and clean the air filter element (**Figure 38**, typical) every 25 hours of operation. Install a new filter after every 50 hours of operation, under normal operating conditions, or if the filter is damaged.

CAUTION
Operating the engine without the air filter or modifying the air intake system may result in engine damage. Any changes in the air intake system will also alter the fuel mixture adjustment.

To remove the filter element, remove the seat and support bracket, if needed. Remove the wing nuts attaching the cover (A, **Figure 39** or 1, **Figure 40**), then remove the cover and element.

CAUTION
Wear proper eye protection when cleaning the air filter using compressed air.

Tap the element lightly on a solid surface to dislodge debris. Direct low-pressure (approximately 5.8 kPa [40 psi]) compressed air at the outside of the filter element toward the inside to blow dirt away. Grease the top and bottom surfaces of the element (**Figure 38**) and reinstall by reversing the removal procedure.

Some models have a foam pre-filter (B, **Figure 39** or 2, **Figure 40**) covering the inlet to the filter. If this pre-filter requires service, remove the fuel tank cover. Clean the pre-filter with solvent followed by hot soapy water. Then rinse the pre-filter with clean water and dry thoroughly. Apply foam filter oil to the pre-filter and squeeze out all excess. The wire support located under the foam pre-filter must be correctly positioned so the foam will not restrict the air flow. The darker foam is used as a splash guard and noise suppression. Do not allow the darker foam to restrict the air flow.

Coolant Inspection and Change (Liquid Cooled Models)

The engine of some models is cooled using a small amount of coolant, circulating pump and a radiator. The system components should be inspected frequently for fluid level, evidence of leaks, and condition of the hoses. Since the system contains so little fluid, it is important to identify and repair even small leaks quickly. Refer to **Table 5** for the fluid capacity of the cooling system.

WARNING
Do not check, drain or otherwise service the liquid cooling system when the coolant is hot. The system is under pressure and serious burns can result from

the hot liquid or steam contacting your body. Allow the engine to cool before removing the radiator cap, opening the drain or disconnecting any of the hoses.

1. To drain coolant from the radiator, open the drain cock (**Figure 41**) and loosen the radiator cap (**Figure 42**). Some coolant will be trapped in the system and

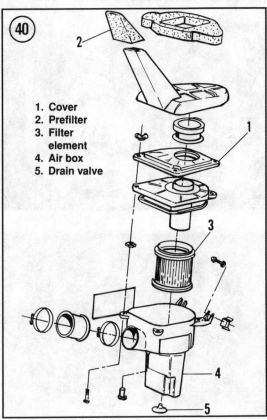

1. Cover
2. Prefilter
3. Filter element
4. Air box
5. Drain valve

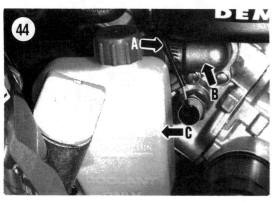

will be removed when the hoses or components are removed.

> *WARNING*
> *The EPA has classified ethylene glycol as an environmental toxic waste, which cannot be legally flushed down a drain or poured on the ground. Treat antifreeze that is to be discarded as you treat motor oil. Put it in suitable containers and dispose of it according to local regulations.*

> *WARNING*
> *Spilled antifreeze is very slippery on cement floors. Wipe up spilled antifreeze as soon as possible.*

2. The manufacturer recommends that only a mixture of 50 percent distilled water and 50 percent antifreeze be used in the cooling system. Use only antifreeze designated for use with aluminum engines and radiators.

3A. When filling the cooling system on 350L and 400L engines, it is necessary to remove the bleed screw (**Figure 43**) to allow air to escape from the cylinder head. Install the bleed screw when fluid without air is coming from the bleed screw hole.

3B. When filling the cooling system on 4-stroke Magnum models, be careful to fill the system completely. If the system is completely drained, loosen the clamp (A, **Figure 44**) on the hose to the thermostat housing (B, **Figure 44**). Pull the hose loose and fill the system with coolant at the radiator, while allowing air to escape from the loosened hose. When coolant begins to flow from the thermostat and hose connection, reattach the hose and tighten the clamp. Continue adding coolant to the radiator (**Figure 42**) and fill the reservoir (C, **Figure 44**).

4. Purge air from the cooling system on all models by squeezing the coolant hoses while filling with coolant.

5. Install the radiator cap (**Figure 42**) and fill the reservoir (C, **Figure 44**) before starting the engine.

> *NOTE*
> *After flushing the cooling system, the coolant level may drop when pockets of trapped air fill with coolant. To avoid operating the engine with a low coolant level, check the level at least once again before starting the engine. It may be necessary to allow the system to cool*

and bleed the system once again as outlined in Step 3A or 3B.

6. Operate the engine until it reaches normal temperature, then stop the engine. Allow the engine to cool then remove the cap from the reservoir and check the coolant level. Check the coolant level frequently.

Oil Injection Pump Bleeding (Models With 2-Stroke Engines)

The engine is lubricated by oil injected into the engine. Serious engine damage will occur if the oil system is allowed to run dry. If the oil lines are disconnected or if air has entered the oil line between the reservoir and the injection pump, refer to the following procedure to bleed air from the oil pump and lines.

CAUTION
*Some other causes of improper lubrication are incorrect engine idle speed, maladjusted throttle cable free play or incorrect synchronization of the oil injection pump. Insufficient lubrication regardless of the cause can result in severe engine damage. The carburetor (throttle) cable and the oil pump control cable are both attached to and controlled by the handlebar mounted throttle lever and adjustment of one cable affects the other cable. Refer to **Tune-Up** procedure in this chapter for adjusting the idle speed. Refer to **Throttle Cable Free Play Adjustment** in this chapter to adjust the throttle cable. Refer to **Oil Injection Pump Adjustment** in this chapter to adjust the oil injection pump control cable.*

1. Fill the oil reservoir before starting the engine.
2. Loosen the bleed screw (C, **Figure 36** or C, **Figure 37**) one full turn and allow oil to flow from the loosened screw for about 10 seconds to bleed air from the delivery line to pump.

CAUTION
Never allow the engine to run with the bleed screw loose.

3. Tighten the bleed screw when oil is flowing steadily.

4. Start the engine and allow it to run at slow idle speed.

NOTE
All air should be removed from the pressure line within about 10-20 seconds. If air is not bled from the system quickly, stop the engine and determine the cause.

5. With the engine at idle speed, turn the injection pump control lever (A, **Figure 36** or A, **Figure 37**) to deliver the maximum amount of oil for a short time.
6. Release the pump control lever and make sure the pump control cable is properly aligned.

Steering System and Front Suspension Inspection

Check the steering system and front suspension at the intervals listed in **Table 3**, following any hard spill or collision or if proper operation is questioned.
1. Park the vehicle on level ground and set the parking brake.
2. Visually inspect all components of the steering and front suspension for obvious problems. Pay

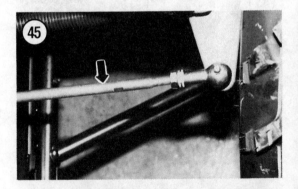

close attention to the tie rods (**Figure 45**), steering shaft and front struts (shock absorbers). Some suggested indicators of damage are:

    a. Bent or broken components. Especially check areas where paint is flaking or missing.

    b. Loose fasteners or locknuts.

    c. Excessively loose components that are normally tight fitting.

    d. Unable to move components that are normally free to move.

3. Check the handlebar holder bolts (**Figure 46**) for tightness. These screws are located under the cover (**Figure 47**).

4. Make sure the front wheel bolts (**Figure 48**) are tight.

5. Make sure all covers (caps) are in place on the front axle.

6. Make sure the front axle nut (models without front wheel drive) is tight and that the cotter pin is in place.

7. Check steering play as follows:

    a. To check the steering shaft for radial play, move the handlebar from side to side (without attempting to turn the wheels). If play is excessive, the upper bearings are probably worn and should be replaced.

    b. To check the steering shaft for axial (vertical) play, lift up and push down on the handlebar. If excessive play is noticed, check the cotter pin (**Figure 49**) located at the bottom of the steering shaft. If the cotter pin is in place and in good condition, check the thrust bearings located at the lower end of the steering shaft.

8. Turn the handlebar quickly from side to side and notice the following:

    a. If there is appreciable looseness at the tie rod ends, the ends may be worn.

    b. Observe the joint between the lower end of the strut and the A-arm. Noticeable looseness may indicate a worn ball-joint.

    c. Observe the joints at the inner ends of the A-arms. Noticeable looseness may indicate worn bushings.

    d. Check for missing cotter pins loose or missing fasteners.

Front Wheel Toe-out

Toe-out is a condition where the front of the tires is further apart than the back. Toe adjustment is accomplished by changing the length of the tie rods. Check and adjust the toe-out periodically or when the steering is imprecise or unpredictable. Inspect the steering assembly for damage and wear before adjusting the toe-out. Inflate the tires to the pressure listed in **Table 2**, then check the tires and wheels for damage. If a wheel might be bent, raise that wheel and rotate it to check more carefully.

To check the toe adjustment, proceed as follows:

1. Position the vehicle on a flat, smooth surface and set the handlebar straight ahead.

2. Raise one front wheel, rotate the tire and use chalk to mark the centerline all around the tire. Lift the other front wheel and mark the centerline of that tire in the same way.

3. Use a tape measure to measure the distance between the centerline at the front, then at the rear of the tires. The distance between the centerlines of the tires should be 3.18-6.35 mm (1/8-1/4 in.) more at the front than at the rear. The tires should toe-out slightly and should not toe-in.

4. If the measured distance is incorrect, change adjustment as follows:

   a. Loosen the inner and outer tie rod end lock nuts (A, **Figure 50**) on both tie rods. Both tie rods must be adjusted.

   b. Rotate the tie rods (B, **Figure 50**) the same amount on both sides to establish the recommended toe-out. The distance between the ball ends of the two tie rods should be the same to center the steering.

   c. Tighten the lock nuts (A, **Figure 50**) securely when adjustment is correct. Recheck to make sure toe-out is correct after tightening the lock nuts. Make sure the tie rod has full movement after tightening the lock nuts. The tie rod end should be square with each other (not cocked) after the lock nuts are tightened.

> *CAUTION*
> *The fasteners that attach the tie rod ends must be installed in a certain direction to prevent steering system interference and binding. In addition, the tie rod ends must be correctly positioned or interference can occur. If the inner tie rod end is attached with a through-bolt, the head of the through-bolt must face down and the nut must be on top. Furthermore, the threaded stud on the outer tie rod end must face up (nut on top). However, if both the inner and outer tie rod ends are attached with threaded studs, position the tie rod assembly so the threaded stud on the inner end is facing down (nut on the bottom) and the stud on the outer end is facing up (nut on top).*

Front Hub Wheel Bearings
(Models Without Front Wheel Drive)

Inspect the front hub bearings for excessive wear or damage at the intervals specified in **Table 3**. Refer to *Front Hub Wheel Bearings* in the *Periodic Lubrication* section of this chapter for lubrication requirements. Refer to Chapter Twelve for removing and installing the bearings and seals.

1. Support the vehicle with both front wheels off the ground.

2. Turn both wheels by hand. The wheels should rotate smoothly with no roughness, excessive noise, excessive play or other abnormal conditions.

3. If necessary, service the front hub bearings as described in Chapter Twelve.

Rear Axle Housing Bearings

The rear axle is supported by bearings contained in the rear axle center housing (**Figure 51**). Refer to *Rear Axle Bearings* in the *Periodic Lubrication* section of this chapter for lubrication requirements. Refer to Chapter Thirteen to remove and install the bearings and seals.

1. Support the vehicle with both rear wheels off the ground.

2. Turn the wheels by hand. The wheels should rotate smoothly with no roughness, excessive noise, excessive play or other abnormal conditions.

3. If necessary, service the bearings as described in Chapter Thirteen.

Nuts, Bolts, and Other Fasteners

Check the tightness of fasteners, as listed in **Table 3**. Constant vibration can loosen many of the fasteners and all should be checked for tightness, especially:

a. Engine mounting hardware.
b. Engine covers.
c. Handlebar mounting.
d. Exhaust system.

Spark Plugs

Periodically check the spark plugs for firing tip condition and the correct electrode gap. Refer to spark plug service under *Engine Tune-Up* in this chapter.

Exhaust System

The exhaust system is a vital link to the performance and operation of the Polaris engine. Check the

exhaust system from the exhaust port to the muffler for:

a. Damaged or leaking gaskets.
b. Loose or missing fasteners or retaining springs.
c. Cracked, dented or otherwise damaged components.

Refer to Chapter Six for cleaning, repair and other service to the exhaust system.

Fuel Shut-Off Valve and Filter

An inline fuel filter (**Figure 52**) is located between the fuel tank and the carburetor. The fuel filter traps particles which might otherwise enter the carburetor. Minute particles can cause the float valve (fuel inlet needle) to stick or clog one of the jets.

Valve attached to fuel tank

The fuel shut-off valve is attached to the bottom of the fuel tank (3, **Figure 53**) or in the fuel line below the bottom of the tank (3, **Figure 54**). To remove the valve from the bottom of the tank, proceed as follows:

1. Remove the seat.

2. Disconnect the ground cable from the battery on models so equipped.

3. Make sure the fuel valve is OFF or prepare to plug the fitting from the fuel tank, then loosen the hose clamp and disconnect the fuel line.

4. Open the shut-off valve and carefully drain all remaining fuel from the tank. If fuel can not be drained, siphon the fuel from the tank. The tank should be as empty as possible. Turn the shut-off valve to the OFF position when finished.

5. Unbolt and remove the fuel tank cover.

6. Remove the screw from the center of the shut-off handle (**Figure 55**), then remove the handle (4, **Figure 53**).

7. Unbolt and remove the fuel tank (2, **Figure 53**).

8. Remove the two screws attaching the shut-off valve (3, **Figure 53**) to the tank, then pull the shut-off valve assembly from the tank.

9. Install by reversing the removal procedure. Check for leaks after installing and filling with fuel.

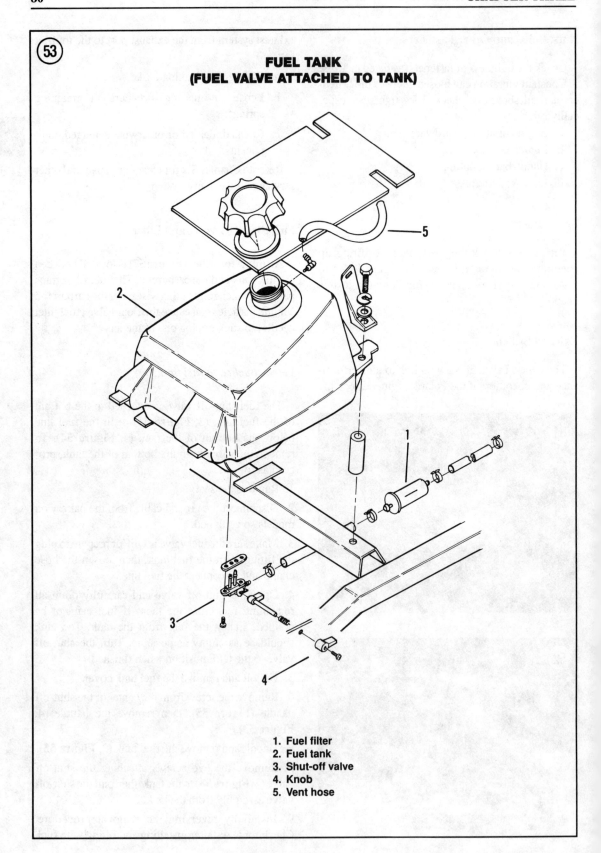

**FUEL TANK
(FUEL VALVE ATTACHED TO TANK)**

1. Fuel filter
2. Fuel tank
3. Shut-off valve
4. Knob
5. Vent hose

Valve connected inline with fuel hose

To remove the valve from Xplorer and other models with the shut-off valve located in the fuel line below the tank, proceed as follows:
1. Remove side cover.
2. Loosen the clamps on the fuel supply lines (4, **Figure 54**) to the shut-off valve.
3. Pinch one of the two fuel supply lines to stop the fuel, detach the line from the shut-off valve, then plug the line to keep it from leaking.
4. Detach the second fuel supply line from the shut-off valve as described in Step 3.
5. Loosen the hose clamp, then detach the fuel outlet line from the fuel shut-off valve.
6. Remove screw from the center of the fuel shut-off knob (5, **Figure 54**), then pull the knob from the shaft.
7. Remove the attaching nut (6, **Figure 54**) to remove the valve assembly.

Wire Harness, Control Cables and Hose Lines

Inspect all wiring, cables and hoses for proper routing. The spark plug wire for models with 300 cc engines should be held in place by routing the wire between the left frame and the brake line. The spark plug wire for 400L models should be routed directly to the front.

Secure loose components with cable ties. Secure hoses, cables and wires to the frame with cable ties. Tighten cable ties only enough to hold the components, but not tight enough to collapse the hoses.

Replace damaged wires, hoses and cables as required following the original routing. The original routing can sometimes be more easily followed by attaching a string to the old wire, cable or hose before withdrawing it. If carefully removed, the string can then be used to pull the new component through the same path as the old one.

Drive Pulley Adjustment

Refer to Chapter Eight.

Steering and Front Suspension Inspection

Check the steering assembly monthly. Wheel alignment cannot be maintained with bent or otherwise damaged steering components or with loose or missing fasteners.
1. Visually inspect all components of the steering. Pay close attention to the tie-rods (B, **Figure 50**) and steering shaft, especially after a hard spill or collision. If there is steering system damage, the steering components must be repaired as described in Chapter Twelve.
2. Check the handlebars for looseness. Tighten the clamp screws (**Figure 46**) or install new parts as required.
3. Check all bolts attaching steering and suspension parts for the correct tightness.
4. Refer to Chapter Twelve for additional checks.

General Inspection

Refer to *General Inspection and Maintenance* in this chapter.

Engine Mounts and Fasteners

Loose engine mounts will cause incorrect clutch alignment. Check the engine mounts and mounting screws to make sure they are tight. Check and tighten if necessary all accessible engine assembly fasteners.

NOTE
If the engine mount screws are loose, check clutch alignment as described in Chapter Eight after retightening the fasteners.

Cylinder Head Torque

If the engine is a 2-stroke model, refer to Chapter Four. If the engine is a 4-stroke model, refer to Chapter Five.

Ignition Timing

Refer to *Tune-Up* in this chapter.

Carburetor Adjustment

Refer to *Tune-Up* in this chapter.

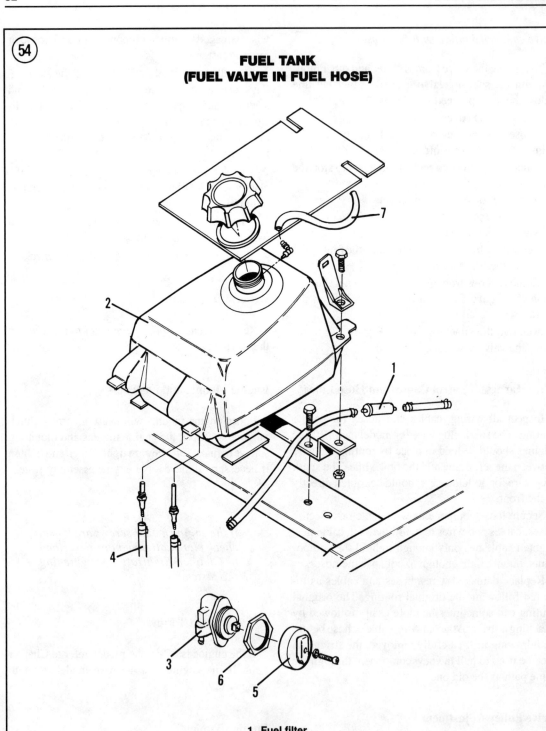

(54)

FUEL TANK
(FUEL VALVE IN FUEL HOSE)

1. Fuel filter
2. Fuel tank
3. Shut-off valve
4. Hoses from tank to valve
5. Knob
6. Nut
7. Vent hose

Throttle Cable Routing
(Models With 2-Stroke Engines)

The single throttle cable that begins at the thumb control is attached to two cables by a junction block. The two branched cables are connected to the carburetor and the oil injection pump. Check the throttle cable from the thumb throttle to the carburetor and

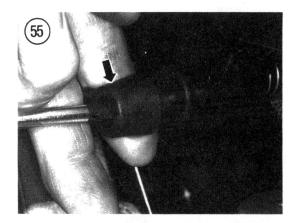

oil pump for proper routing. Check the cable ends for fraying or splitting that could cause the cable to stick in the housing or break.

Headlight

Refer to Chapter Eleven.

Cooling System Inspection
(Liquid Cooled Models)

> *WARNING*
> *When performing any service work to the engine or cooling system, never remove the radiator cap (**Figure 56**), open the coolant drain (**Figure 57**) or disconnect any hose while the engine is hot. Scalding fluid and steam may be blown out under pressure and cause serious injury.*

Check the following items once a year, or whenever troubleshooting the cooling system. If you do not have the test equipment, the tests can be done by a Polaris dealer, radiator shop or service station.

1. Loosen the radiator cap to its first detent and release the system pressure, then turn the cap to its second detent and remove it from the radiator. See **Figure 56**.

2. Check the rubber washers on the radiator cap for tears or cracks. Check for a bent or distorted cap. Raise the vacuum valve and rubber seal and rinse the cap under warm tap water to flush away any loose rust or dirt particles.

3. Inspect the radiator cap neck seat on the coolant tank for dents, distortion or contamination. Wipe the sealing surface with a clean cloth to remove any rust or dirt.

> *CAUTION*
> *Do not exceed 89.6 kPa (13 psi) when performing Steps 4 and 5 or damage to the cooling system will occur.*

4. Have the radiator cap pressure tested. The specified radiator cap relief pressure is 69 kPa (10 psi). The cap must be able to sustain this pressure. Replace the radiator cap if it does not hold pressure.

5. Leave the radiator cap off and have the entire cooling system pressure tested. The entire cooling system should be pressurized to 69 kPa (10 psi). The

system must be able to hold this pressure. Replace or repair any components that fail this test.

6. Check all cooling system hoses for damage or deterioration. Replace any hose that is in questionable condition. Make sure all hose clamps are tight.

7. Check the radiator for leaks or other damage. Repair or replace the radiator as necessary.

Coolant Check
(Liquid Cooled Models)

Most models have a coolant recovery system that includes the coolant recovery reservoir (**Figure 58**). Normal service includes making certain that coolant in the recovery tank remains between the minimum and maximum marks (**Figure 58**). The cap of the recovery tank is vented and can be removed to add coolant while hot. When heated, the liquid coolant will normally expand and raise the level of fluid in the recovery tank. Then as the engine cools (after stopping the engine) the coolant from the recovery tank will be drawn back into the engine.

> *WARNING*
> *Do not remove the radiator cap (**Figure** 56) when the engine is hot. Scalding hot coolant may be expelled onto your skin.*

To check and service coolant in the engine as well as in the recovery tank, proceed as follows.

1. Park the vehicle on level ground.

2. Remove the cover.

3. Loosen the radiator cap (**Figure 56**) to its first detent and release the system pressure, then turn the cap to its second detent and remove it from the radiator.

4. Check the level in the radiator. If the radiator is not completely filled, add a sufficient amount of antifreeze and water (in a 50:50 ratio) through the radiator cap opening as described under *Coolant Inspection and Change* in this chapter.

5. Reinstall the radiator cap (**Figure 56**).

6. Remove the cap from the coolant recovery tank (**Figure 58**) and add an antifreeze and water mixture (in a 50:50 ratio) until the coolant is between the minimum and maximum marks on the recovery tank. The cap of the recovery tank is vented and can be removed to add coolant while the engine is hot.

Coolant
(Liquid Cooled Models)

Use only a high-quality ethylene glycol based coolant compounded for aluminum engines. Mix the coolant with water at a 50:50 ratio. Coolant capacity is listed in **Table 5**. When mixing antifreeze with water, make sure to use only soft or distilled water. Distilled water can be purchased at supermarkets in gallon containers. Do not use tap or saltwater because it will damage engine parts.

> *CAUTION*
> *Always mix coolant in the proper ratio for the coldest temperature in your area. Pure antifreeze is more likely to freeze at a higher temperature than a 50/50 mixture of antifreeze and water.*

Coolant Change
(Liquid Cooled Models)

The cooling system should be completely drained and refilled once a year (preferably before off-season storage).

> *CAUTION*
> *Use only a high-quality ethylene glycol antifreeze specifically labeled for use with aluminum engines. Do not use an alcohol-based antifreeze.*

Follow the procedure described under *Coolant Inspection and Change* in this chapter while the engine is *cold*.

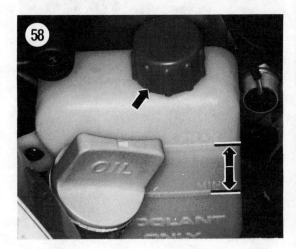

GENERAL INSPECTION
AND MAINTENANCE

Recoil Starter

Pull out the starter rope and inspect it for fraying. If its condition is questionable, replace the rope as described in Chapter Four or Chapter Five.

Check the action of the starter. It should be smooth, and when the rope is released, it should return all the way. If the starter action is rough or if the rope does not return, service the starter as described in Chapter Four or Chapter Five.

Body Inspection

Repair or replace damaged body panels.

Body Fasteners

Tighten any loose body fasteners. Replace loose rivets by first drilling out the old rivet and then installing a new one with a pop-riveter. This tool,

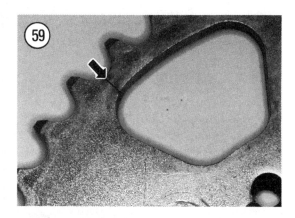

along with an assortment of rivets, is available through many hardware and auto parts stores. Follow the manufacturer's instructions for installing rivets.

Welded joints should be checked for cracks and damage. Damaged welded joints should be repaired by a competent welding shop.

Drive Axle Sprockets

Inspect the teeth on the drive axle sprockets for wear, cracks (**Figure 59**) and other damage. If the sprockets are damaged, replace them as described in the service section for the specific unit or system.

Fuel Tank and Lines

Inspect the fuel tank for cracks and abrasions. If the tank is damaged and leaking, replace it. See Chapter Six.

Oil Tank

Inspect the oil tank for cracks, abrasions or leaks. Replace the tank if its condition is in doubt.

Electrical System

Check all of the switches for proper operation. Refer to Chapter Eleven.

Electrical Connectors

Inspect the high-tension lead to the spark plug (**Figure 60**) for cracks and breaks in the insulation and replace the lead if it is not perfect. Breaks in the insulation allow the spark to arc to ground and will impair engine performance.

Check primary ignition wiring and lighting wiring for damaged insulation. Usually minor damage can be repaired by wrapping the damaged area with electrical insulating tape. If insulation damage is extensive, replace the damaged wires.

Abnormal Engine Noise

Start the engine and listen for abnormal noises. Often the first indication of developing trouble is a change in sound. An unusual rattle might indicate a loose fastener that can be easily repaired, or it could be the first indication of severe engine damage. After becoming familiar with the vehicle and with practice, you will be able to identify most new sounds. Periodic inspections and quick identification of abnormal engine noises can prevent a complete engine failure.

Oil and Fuel Lines

Inspect the oil and fuel lines for loose connections and damage. Tighten all connections and replace any lines that are cracked or damaged.

ENGINE TUNE-UP

The number of definitions of the term "tune-up" is probably equal to the number of people defining it. For the purposes of this book, a tune-up is general adjustment and maintenance to insure peak engine performance.

The following paragraphs discuss the different parts of a tune-up which should be performed in the order given. Have the new parts on hand before you begin.

To perform a tune-up on your vehicle, you need the following tools and equipment:
    a. A spark plug wrench.
    b. Socket wrench and assorted sockets.
    c. Phillips head screwdriver.
    d. Spark plug feeler gauge and gap adjusting tool.
    e. Dial indicator.
    f. Flywheel puller.
    g. Compression gauge.

Cylinder and Cylinder Head Nuts

The screws and nuts retaining the cylinder or cylinder head must be tight. If any are loose, the gasket may be damaged and leakage will continue even after tightening the fasteners. The engine must be at room temperature when tightening the retaining fasteners.

1. Remove any cowling necessary to access the cylinder and head fasteners.

2A. For models with 2-stroke engines, tighten each screw or nut retaining the cylinder and cylinder head in a crossing pattern to the torque listed in **Table 7**.

Additional cylinder head service is described in Chapter Four.

2B. For Magnum models (4-stroke engine), tighten the screws and nuts retaining the cylinder head as described in Chapter Five. The cylinder head must be removed to tighten the cylinder retaining fasteners.

Cylinder Compression

A compression check is one of the quickest ways to check the condition of the piston rings, valves, cylinder and head gasket. It's a good idea to check compression at each tune-up, record the compression of each cylinder, then compare the current compression with test results from earlier tune-ups. The first step is to write the measured compression of the cylinder and the date, so that it can be compared with tests recorded at the later tune-ups. A gradual change may indicate normal wear or may help you spot a developing problem.

1. Start and run the engine until it warms to normal operating temperature, then turn the engine off.

> *CAUTION*
> *To prevent expensive engine damage, use compressed air to blow dirt away from around the base of the spark plug. Dirt that accumulates around the plug may fall into the cylinder when the plug is removed and cause serious engine damage when the engine is restarted.*

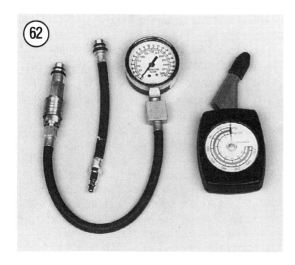

2. Remove the spark plug. Insert the plug in the cap, then ground the plug to the cylinder head or exhaust pipe. Refer to **Figure 61**.

> *CAUTION*
> *If the plug is not grounded during the compression test, the ignition could be damaged.*

3. Screw a compression gauge (**Figure 62**) into the spark plug hole or, if you have a press-in type gauge, hold it firmly in position.

4. Make sure the emergency cutout switch is in the OFF position.

5. Hold the throttle wide open and crank the engine several revolutions until the gauge gives its highest reading. Record the reading. Remove the compression gauge and release the pressure valve.

6. If the compression is very low, a ring could be broken or there may be a hole in the piston. On models with a 4-stroke engine, a valve may be stuck open or damaged.

Correct Spark Plug Heat Range

The proper spark plug is very important in obtaining maximum performance and reliability. The condition of a used spark plug can tell a trained mechanic a lot about engine condition and carburetion.

Select a plug of the heat range designed for the loads and conditions under which the vehicle will be run. Use of a spark plug with the incorrect heat range can result in a seized piston, scored cylinder wall or damaged piston crown.

> *CAUTION*
> *Do not install a plug that is much different from that specified by the manufacturer. The terms "Hot" and "Cold" are relative and should not be considered literal, except as they relate to the specific engine and the type of service. Refer to* ***Figure 63***.

In general, use a hot plug for low speeds and low temperatures. Use a cold plug for high speeds, high engine loads and high temperatures. The plug should operate hot enough to burn off unwanted deposits, but not so hot that it burns itself or causes preignition. The insulator of a spark plug that is the correct

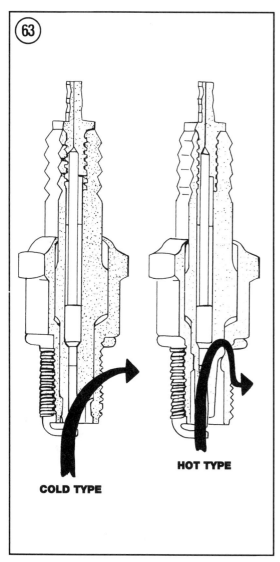

HOT TYPE

COLD TYPE

heat range will be a light tan color after the engine has operated for awhile. See **Figure 64**.

The reach (length) of a plug is also important. A shorter than normal plug will cause hard starting, reduced engine performance and carbon buildup on the exposed cylinder head threads. A spark plug that is longer than normal might interfere with the piston or may cause overheating. Physical damage to the piston or overheating often results in severe engine damage. Refer to **Figure 65**. If a spark plug extends into the combustion chamber too far (**Figure 65**), carbon buildup on the exposed threads may prevent the spark plug from being removed. Forcing the spark plug out will probably damage the threads in the cylinder head.

The standard heat range spark plug for the various models is listed in **Table 8**. It may be desirable to install a spark plug of a slightly different heat range than listed to match specific operating conditions.

Spark Plug Removal/Cleaning

1. Grasp the spark plug lead as near the plug as possible and pull it from the plug. If the spark plug cap (**Figure 66**) is stuck to the plug, twist the cap slightly to break it loose.

CAUTION
Dirt could fall into the cylinder when the plug is removed, causing serious engine damage when the engine is started.

2. Use compressed air to blow away any dirt that has accumulated next to the spark plug base.

NOTE
If the plug is difficult to remove, apply penetrating oil, like WD-40 or Liquid Wrench, around the base of the plug and let it soak. If the plug is still difficult to remove, apply additional penetrating oil and let it soak into threads again.

3. Remove the spark plug with a spark plug wrench.
4. Inspect the plug carefully. Look for a broken center porcelain, excessively eroded electrodes, and excessive carbon buildup or oil fouling. See **Figure 64**.

Gapping and Installing the Plug

The gap between electrodes of new spark plug should be carefully set before installation. A specific gap is necessary to ensure a reliable, consistent spark. Use a special spark plug gapping tool to bend the ground electrode and a wire feeler gauge to measure gap between electrodes.

NOTE
Never try to close the spark plug gap by tapping the spark plug on a solid surface. This can damage the plug internally. Always use the special tool to open or close the gap. Be careful not to bend the electrode enough to break to weaken it.

1. Insert a wire feeler gauge between the center and side electrode (**Figure 67**). The correct gap is listed in **Table 8**. If the gap is correct, you will feel a slight drag as you pull the wire through. If there is no drag, or the gauge won't pass through, bend the side (ground) electrode with a gapping tool (**Figure 68**) to set the proper gap.
2. Apply an anti-seize compound to the plug threads before installing the spark plug.

NOTE
Anti-seize compound can be purchased at most automotive parts stores.

3. Screw the spark plug in by hand until it seats. Very little effort should be required. If force is necessary, the plug is cross-threaded, the threads are dirty or the threads in the cylinder head are damaged. Unscrew the plug, clean the threads and try again.
4. Use a spark plug wrench and tighten the plug an additional 1/4 to 1/2 turn after the gasket has made contact with the head. If you are installing an old, regapped plug and reusing the old gasket, only tighten an additional 1/4 turn.

CAUTION
Do not overtighten the spark plug. This will only squash the gasket and destroy its sealing ability, causing compression leakage around the base of the plug. It is also important to tighten the spark plug sufficiently to provide a good seal. If the plug is too loose, hot exhaust gasses will pass around the threads and eventually make the plug difficult to re-

(64)

SPARK PLUG CONDITION

3

Normal

Gap bridged

Carbon fouled

Overheated

Oil fouled

Sustained preignition

move without damaging the threads in the cylinder head.

5. Install the spark plug wire. Make sure it snaps onto the top of the plug tightly.

> *CAUTION*
> *Make sure the spark plug wire is located away from the exhaust pipe. The spark plug wire on models with 300 cc engines should be held in place by routing the wire between the left frame and the brake line. The spark plug wire on 400L models should be routed directly to the front.*

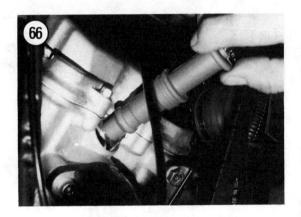

Reading Spark Plugs

Much information about engine and spark plug performance can be determined by careful examination of the spark plug. Refer to **Figure 64**.

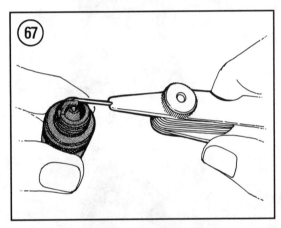

Ignition Timing

All models are equipped with a capacitor discharge ignition (CDI) and no breaker points are used. This ignition system is much less susceptible to failures caused by dirt, moisture and wear than conventional breaker-point ignition.

Check the dynamic ignition timing with the engine running at the rpm indicated in **Table 9**. The procedure for setting the *Dynamic Timing* is described in this chapter. When assembling the ignition system, refer to the *Initial Timing* procedure described in this chapter.

First check the static timing, then check the timing with the engine running (dynamic timing).

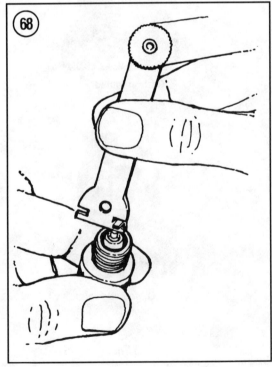

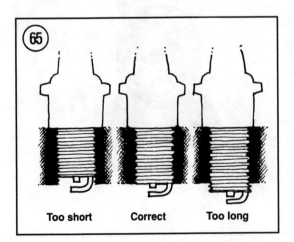

Too short   Correct   Too long

Static timing can be used to verify the flywheel timing marks before using a timing light to check the ignition timing with the engine running. The static timing procedure is used to:

a. Find the correct flywheel timing mark to use.

b. Detect a broken or missing flywheel Woodruff key.

c. Detect a twisted crankshaft.

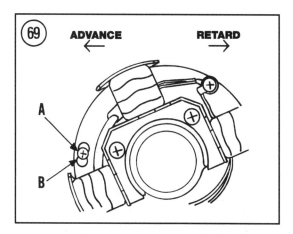

d. Scribe timing marks on a new flywheel.

Static timing requires the use of an accurate dial indicator to determine the piston position in relation to top dead center (TDC). Before making any timing adjustment, find exact TDC as described in the *Static Timing* paragraphs which follow in this chapter.

Dynamic engine timing uses a timing light connected to the spark plug lead. As the engine is cranked or run, the light flashes each time the spark plug fires. When the light is pointed at the moving flywheel, the mark on the flywheel appears to stand still. The correct mark on the flywheel should align with the stationary timing pointer on the engine.

The static timing and dynamic timing both depend upon operating parts and correct assembly. The initial timing procedure is used to assemble the parts close to the correct timing position.

Initial timing

Ignition timing is changed by relocating the stator plate that is located under the engine flywheel. When disassembling, note that the holes for the stator plate attaching screws are elongated.

On 2-stroke engines, refer to **Figure 69**. When assembling, align the mark on the stator plate with the center of the mounting screw as shown (A, **Figure 69**) for all models except Cyclone. On Cyclone models, mark (B, **Figure 69**) should be centered on the screw.

On 4-stroke engines, refer to **Figure 70**. When assembling, align the mark on the stator plate with the mark on the crankcase as shown in **Figure 70**.

It may be necessary to move the stator plate slightly when timing dynamically as described in this chapter.

Static timing

1. Remove any interfering cowling.

2. Remove the plug from the timing hole in the recoil starter (**Figure 71**, typical).

3. Remove the spark plug as described in this chapter.

4. Install a dial indicator and locate top dead center (TDC) as follows:

a. Screw the extension onto a dial indicator and insert the dial indicator into the adapter.

b. Screw the dial indicator adaptor into the cylinder head (**Figure 72**). Do not lock the dial indicator in the adapter at this time.

c. Rotate the flywheel (by turning the drive pulley) until the dial indicator rises all the way up in its holder (piston is approaching top dead center). Then slide the indicator far enough into the holder to obtain a reading.

d. Tighten the set screw holding the dial indicator adaptor to the dial gauge lightly.

e. Rotate the flywheel until the dial on the gauge stops and reverses direction. This is top dead center. Zero the dial gauge by aligning the zero with the dial.

5. Look at the flywheel, through the timing plug hole. Some, (not all) models are equipped with a "T" mark indicating top dead center (A, **Figure 73**). Note the timing advance marks at B, **Figure 73**.

6. Rotate the crankshaft counterclockwise (viewed from the right-hand side) until the gauge needle has made approximately 3 revolutions. This will back the engine up sufficiently to remove all play.

7. Carefully turn the crankshaft clockwise until the gauge indicates that the piston is the correct distance before top dead center as indicated in **Table 9**.

8. View the timing marks through the hole in the crankcase (**Figure 74**). The correct mark on the flywheel should align with the pointer or boss on the magneto housing as shown. If they do not, perform the following:

a. Make a new temporary mark on the flywheel that aligns with the crankcase mark similar to the correct marks shown in **Figure 74**. This temporary mark can be used as the reference when using the timing light.

NOTE
If the wrong flywheel is installed or if the flywheel is not correctly installed on the crankshaft, you will probably not be able to make the engine run until the correct flywheel is installed and correctly timed to the crankshaft.

b. Repeat the timing procedure to check the accuracy of the new mark. It is also a good idea to remove the recoil starter and check the flywheel for other marks. If the engine does not run and the factory marks are far off, the flywheel key may be sheared or missing.

9. Remove the dial gauge and adapter. Install the spark plug and connect the spark plug high-tension lead.

10. Check the ignition *Dynamic Timing* as described in this chapter.

Dynamic timing

Check ignition timing while the engine is cold, before warming to normal temperature. Timing may change as much as 2° when the engine warms.

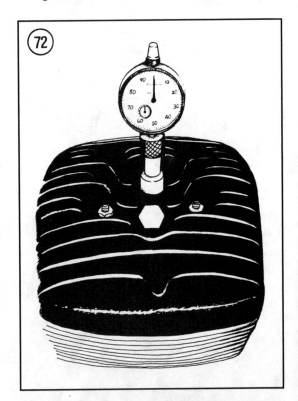

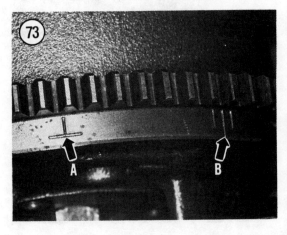

1. Perform the *Static Timing Check* in this chapter to make sure flywheel is correctly installed and the timing mark is correctly positioned. It will also allow you to identify correctly the proper mark and to color it with white paint or chalk so that it will be easier to see.

3. Attach a stroboscopic timing light to the spark plug lead. Follow the instructions provided by the manufacturer of the timing light.

4. Attach a tachometer according to its manufacturer's instructions.

5. Block the position of the vehicle's wheels, so the ATV can not move, and shift the transmission to neutral.

WARNING
Don't allow anyone to stand behind or in front of the vehicle when the engine is running, and take care to keep hands, feet and clothing away from the engine, belt and drive chains.

NOTE
Because ignition components are temperature sensitive, ignition timing should be checked, when the engine is cold.

6. Start the engine, allow it to idle for approximately 10-15 seconds, then increase the engine speed to the correct test rpm listed in **Table 9**.

7. Point the timing light at the crankcase timing inspection hole (**Figure 71**) and observe the flywheel timing mark that appears to be stopped in line with the timing pointer or boss on the magneto housing.

NOTE
The timing light will flash, appearing to stop the timing marks at the instant of ignition.

8. Increase the engine speed briefly and observe the timing mark that is aligned with the timing pointer or boss.

9. Refer to **Table 9** for the correct timing specifications. Compare the observed timing to the correct timing.

10. If timing is not correct, the ignition timing should be adjusted. Refer to *Setting Ignition Timing* in this chapter.

11. When timing is correct, turn the engine off, remove the timing light and tachometer. Install all of the covers that were removed.

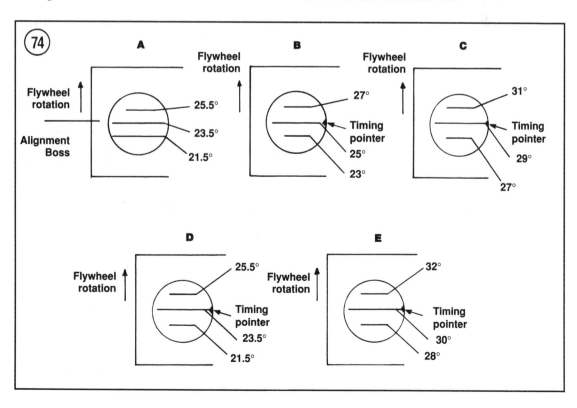

Setting ignition timing

The ignition must occur at a specific time for the engine to perform at its optimum. Refer to **Table 9** for the recommended timing for your specific model, then refer to the following procedure.

1. Before changing the ignition timing, refer to *Static Timing Check* in this chapter to make sure the timing marks are correctly located on the flywheel and the flywheel is correctly installed. After making sure the marks are correct, perform the *Dynamic Timing Check* as outlined in this chapter. Leave the timing light attached.

2. Remove the recoil starter assembly as described in Chapter Four (2-stroke engines) or Chapter Five (4-stroke engines).

3. Remove the flywheel as described in Chapter Four or Chapter Five. Refer to **Figure 75** for a typical flywheel puller attachment.

4. Ignition timing is changed by moving the stator plate (**Figure 76** or **Figure 77**). Observe the following:

   a. If the correct flywheel mark did not yet reach the timing pointer or boss, the ignition timing is advanced. To correct the timing, loosen the screws attaching the stator, then move the stator clockwise slightly.

   b. If the correct flywheel mark had passed the timing pointer or boss, the ignition timing is retarded. To correct the timing, loosen the screws attaching the stator, then move the stator counterclockwise slightly.

   c. Tighten the stator plate retaining screws.

   d. Reinstall the flywheel, starter pulley and recoil starter assembly.

5. Recheck the dynamic ignition timing. If timing is still not correct, repeat steps 3 and 4 until ignition timing is correct.

6. Install the timing hole plug and any removed covers.

Cam Chain Adjustment
(4-Stroke Engines)

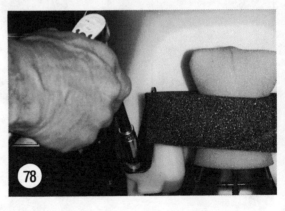

An automatic cam chain tensioner assembly is used and no manual adjustment is required.

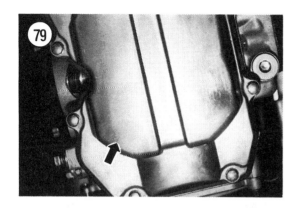

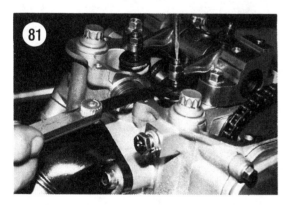

Valve Clearance
(4-Stroke Engine)

Check and adjust valve clearance with the engine cold. The exhaust valves are located at the front of the engine and the inlet valves are located the rear of the engine.

1. Place the ATV on a level surface and block the wheels to keep it from rolling.

2. Refer to Chapter Fifteen to remove the seat, side covers and fuel tank cover.

3. Shut the fuel off, disconnect the fuel lines, then unbolt and remove the fuel tank (**Figure 78**). Refer to Chapter Six.

4. Disconnect the spark plug high tension lead and remove the spark plug. Removing the spark plug will make it easier to rotate the engine.

5. Remove the screws attaching the cylinder head cover (**Figure 79**), then remove the cover.

6. Turn the engine until the two marked teeth (**Figure 80**) on the side of the cam sprocket are at the top. This will set the piston at (or near) Top Dead Center on the compression stroke and all of the valves will be closed. Check by moving each rocker arm by hand. There should be some side movement.

7. Check the clearance of both the intake valve and exhaust valves by inserting a flat feeler gauge between the rocker arm pad and the valve stem as shown in **Figure 81**. The correct valve clearances for the intake and exhaust valves are listed in **Table 10**. If the clearance is correct, there will be a slight resistance on the feeler gauge when it is inserted and withdrawn.

8. To correct the clearance, perform the following:

   a. Loosen the valve adjuster locknut.

   b. Use a screwdriver to turn the adjuster in or out so there is a slight resistance felt on the feeler gauge (**Figure 81**).

   c. Hold the adjuster to prevent it from turning and tighten the locknut to the torque specification listed in **Table 7**. An offset adapter must be used on the torque wrench as shown in **Figure 82**.

   d. Recheck the clearance to make sure the adjuster did not move when the locknut was tightened. Readjust the valve clearance if necessary.

9. Clean the gasket surfaces of the cylinder head and cover, then install a new gasket to the cylinder head cover.

10. Install the cylinder head cover and tighten the retaining screws to the torque listed in **Table 7**.

11. Complete assembly by reversing the disassembly procedure.

Carburetor Adjustment

Idle mixture

Adjustment of the pilot air screw controls the fuel and air mixture at idle speed. Turning the pilot air screw clockwise reduces the amount of air and richens the mixture.

1. Locate the pilot air screw.

　a. On 2-stroke engines, the pilot air screw (A, **Figure 83**) is on the right side of the carburetor.

　b. On 4-stroke (Magnum) engines, the pilot air screw is located on the bottom of the carburetor, nearest the engine (A, **Figure 84**).

2. Turn the pilot air screw in (clockwise) until it seats lightly.

> *NOTE*
> *Do not damage the seat or the tip of the pilot air screw by forcing it into its seat.*

3. Back the pilot air screw out the number of turns specified in **Table 11**. The standard setting should be nearly optimum for operation at air temperature of 15.6° C (60° F). The screw should be turned IN approximately 1/4 turn for each 30° below 60° F (or 1/4 turn for each 16° below 15.6° C). The pilot air screw should be turned OUT (counter-clockwise) about 1/4 turn for each 30° above 60° F (or 16° above 15.6° C).

> *CAUTION*
> *Do not use the pilot air screw to change engine idle speed. The pilot air screw must be set as specified or a "too lean" mixture and subsequent engine damage may result.*

Throttle cable adjustment

The throttle cable is attached to the handle bar mounted speed control (throttle) lever to change the engine speed by opening the carburetor's throttle valve. On models with a 2-stroke engine, the throttle also controls the amount of lubricating oil that the oil pump injects into the engine.

Maintaining correct cable free play is critical to proper speed control and to prevent cable damage. On models with a 2-stroke engine, it is also important to ensure correct engine lubrication.

1. Remove the cover from the handlebar housing (**Figure 85** or **Figure 86**).

2. Slide the rubber boot (A, **Figure 85** or A, **Figure 86**) away from the cable adjuster at the handlebar housing.

3. Lubricate the cable with Polaris Cable Lube.

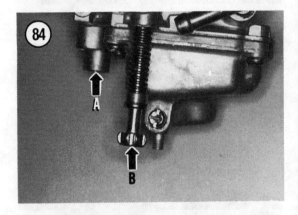

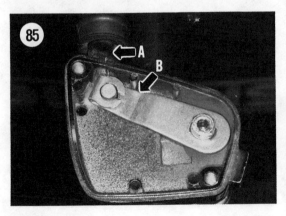

4. Start the engine and set the engine idle speed as described in this chapter.

5. Check the clearance between the internal lever and the boss (B, **Figure 85** or B, **Figure 86**) when the idle is set at the speed listed in **Table 11**.

6. If clearance is not 1.6 mm (1/16 in.), loosen the locknut, turn the adjuster into the handlebar housing, then tighten the locknut. If gap is incorrect, it may not be possible to set the engine idle speed or to maintain accurate control of the engine speed.

7. Another cable adjuster is located at the carburetor end of the cable, if additional adjustment is needed. On models with 2-stroke engines, it is necessary to adjust the oil pump if the position of the cable adjuster at the carburetor is changed. Refer to *Oil Injection Pump Adjustment* in this chapter.

Idle speed

The idle speed stop screw is shown at B, **Figure 83** for models with 2-stroke engines. The idle speed stop screw on Magnum models (4-stroke engine) is located as shown in **Figure 87**.

CAUTION
*Do not use the pilot air screw (A, **Figure 83** or A, **Figure 84**) to change the engine idle speed. The pilot air screw must be set as described in this chapter or the engine may be damaged by excessively lean air/fuel mixture.*

1. Locate the throttle stop screw (B, **Figure 83** or B, **Figure 84**).

2. Connect a tachometer according to its manufacturer's instructions.

3. Set the idle speed by turning the throttle stop screw in to increase or out to decrease idle speed. Refer to **Table 11** for the correct idle speed for your model.

STORAGE

Several months of inactivity can cause serious problems and a general deterioration of the ATV's condition. This is especially true in areas of weather extremes. During long period so of inactivity, it is advisable to prepare the vehicle for lay-up.

Selecting a Storage Area

Most owners store ATV's in their home garages; however facilities for long term ATV storage are readily available for rent or lease. Consider the following points when selecting a building for storage.

1. The storage area must be dry. Heating is not necessary (even in cold temperatures) but the building should be well insulated to minimize extreme variations in temperature.

2. Buildings with large windows should be avoided, or the windows should be covered to prevent direct sunlight from falling upon the ATv. Covering windows is also a good security measure.

Preparing Vehicle for Storage

Careful storage preparation will minimize deterioration and make it easier to restore the ATV to service later. Repair any known problems before storing the vehicle. The following is a satisfactory storage procedure.

1. Wash the vehicle completely. Make certain to remove all dirt from all of the hard-to-clean parts like

the cooling fins (on air cooled models) and the radiator (of liquid cooled models).

2. Operate the vehicle for about 20-30 minutes to warm the oil in the engine on 4-stroke models, balancer on 2-stroke models so equipped and the transmission on all models.

NOTE
Oil should be changed immediately before storage, regardless of time since a scheduled oil change.

3. While still warm, drain the oil from:

a. The engine reservoir on 4-stroke models.

b. The balancer on liquid cooled 2-stroke models.

c. The transmission on all models.

4. Refill with the quantity and type of oil listed in **Table 4** and **Table 5**.

5. Drain all gasoline from the fuel tank, connecting hoses and the carburetor. It is especially important to make sure all fuel is removed since the blends of gasolines have changed in recent years.

6. Clean and lubricate all drive chains and control cables. Refer to the procedures in this chapter.

7. Remove the spark plug and pour about one teaspoon of engine oil into the cylinder. Reinstall the spark plug and crank the engine by hand slowly to distribute the oil in the cylinder.

8. Tape or tie a plastic bag over the end of the silencer to prevent the entry of moisture.

9. Check the tire pressure and inflate to the correct pressure if necessary. Refer to **Table 2**.

10. Raise the ATV and place it securely on a stand with all the wheels suspended off the ground.

11. Cover the ATV with a tarp or heavy drop cloth. This cover serves mainly as a dust cover and must not hold moisture inside. Do not wrap this cover tightly, because it may trap condensed moisture. Leave room for air to circulate around the ATV.

Inspection During Storage

Try to inspect the vehicle at weekly intervals while in storage. Any deterioration should be corrected as soon as possible. For example, if corrosion is observed, coat it lightly with grease or silicone spray.

CAUTION
Do not start the engine while it is in storage.

If stored for an extremely long period, the engine should be cranked a couple of times to recoat the cylinder walls with oil.

Restoring Vehicle to Service

A vehicle that has been properly prepared and stored in a suitable building should require only light maintenance before returning it to service. It is advisable, however, to perform a spring tune-up.

1. Remove the cover from the ATV and check for visible signs of damage. Mice and other animals sometimes select an ATV as a homesite.

CAUTION
Tire pressure should be checked before lowering the ATV to the ground. Air loss during storage may have nearly flattened the tires.

2. Check tire pressure and inflate to the proper pressure. Refer to **Table 2** for recommended pressure for standard tires.

3. Fill the fuel tank with fresh gasoline.

4. Remove the spark plug and install a fresh one of the correct type and heat range.

5. Perform the standard tune-up as described earlier in this chapter.

6. Check the operation of the engine stop switch. Oxidation of the switch during storage may make it inoperative.

7. Clean and test ride the vehicle.

Table 1 DAILY INSPECTION

Check fuel lines for leaks
Make sure that enough gasoline is in fuel tank
Check engine oil levels
  Injection system oil level (2-stroke models)
  Engine counterbalancer oil level (350 and 400 liquid cooled 2-stroke models)
  Engine oil reservoir (4-stroke models)
Check transmission oil level
Inspect cooling system
  Check coolant level (liquid cooled models)
  Make sure that outside of radiator is clean and not obstructed
  Make sure cooling fins are clean (air cooled models)
Check condition of air filter
Check brake fluid level (models with hydraulic brakes)
Check operation of front and rear suspension
Check drive chain(s)
Check tires for correct inflation
Check exhaust system for looseness or damage
Check front wheel drive oil (models with front wheel drive)
Check wheels for tightness
Check operation of lights and other electrical components
Check that all fasteners are tight

Table 2 TIRE SIZE AND PRESSURE

	Front tires kPa (psi)	Rear tires kPa (psi)
1985		
Scrambler W857027		
Size	$22 \times 11.00 \times 8$	$22 \times 11.00 \times 10$
Pressure	20.7 (3)	20.7 (3)
Trail Boss W857527		
Size	$22 \times 8.00 \times 10$	$22 \times 11.00 \times 10$
Pressure	27.6 (4)	20.7 (3)
1986		
Scrambler W867027		
Size	$22 \times 11.00 \times 8$	$22 \times 11.00 \times 10$
Pressure	20.7 (3)	20.7 (3)
Trail Boss W867527		
Size	$22 \times 8.00 \times 10$	$22 \times 11.00 \times 10$
Pressure	27.6 (4)	20.7 (3)
Trail Boss W867627		
Size	$22 \times 8.00 \times 10$	$22 \times 11.00 \times 10$
Pressure	27.6 (4)	20.7 (3)
1987		
Trail Boss W877527		
Size	$22 \times 8.00 \times 8$	$22 \times 11.00 \times 10$
Pressure	27.6 (4)	20.7 (3)
Cyclone W877828		
Size	$22 \times 8.00 \times 10$	$22 \times 11.00 \times 10$
Pressure	27.6 (4)	20.7 (3)
Trail Boss 4 × 4 W878027		
Size	$22 \times 8.00 \times 10$	$22 \times 11.00 \times 10$
Pressure	27.6 (4)	20.7 (3)
Trail Boss 4 × 4 W878127		
Size	$22 \times 8.00 \times 10$	$22 \times 11.00 \times 10$
Pressure	27.6 (4)	20.7 (3)
	(continued)	

Table 2 TIRE SIZE AND PRESSURE (continued)

	Front tires kPa (psi)	Rear tires kPa (psi)
1987 (continued)		
Trail Boss 4 × 4 W878327		
Size	22 × 8.00 × 10	22 × 11.00 × 10
Pressure	27.6 (4)	20.7 (3)
1988		
Trail Boss 2 × 4 W887527		
Size	22 × 8.00 × 10	22 × 11.00 × 10
Pressure	27.6 (4)	20.7 (3)
Trail Boss 4 × 4 W888127		
Size	22 × 8.00 × 10	22 × 11.00 × 10
Pressure	27.6 (4)	20.7 (3)
Trail Boss 250 R/ES X888528		
Size	22 × 8.00 × 10	22 × 11.00 × 10
Pressure	27.6 (4)	20.7 (3)
Trail Boss 250 R/ES W888528		
Size	22 × 8.00 × 10	22 × 11.00 × 10
Pressure	27.6 (4)	20.7 (3)
1989		
Trail Boss W898527		
Size	22 × 8.00 × 10	22 × 11.00 × 10
Pressure	20.7 (3)	20.7 (3)
Trail Boss 2 × 4 W897527		
Size	22 × 8.00 × 10	22 × 11.00 × 10
Pressure	20.7 (3)	20.7 (3)
Trail Boss 4 × 4 W898127		
Size	22 × 8.00 × 10	22 × 11.00 × 10
Pressure	27.6 (4)	20.7 (3)
Big Boss 4 × 6 X898627		
Size	22 × 8.00 × 10	22 × 11.00 × 10
Pressure	27.6 (4)	34.5 (5)
Big Boss 4 × 6 W898627		
Size	22 × 8.00 × 10	22 × 11.00 × 10
Pressure	27.6 (4)	34.5 (5)
1990		
Trail Blazer W907221		
Size	22 × 8.00 × 10	22 × 11.00 × 10
Pressure	20.7 (3)	20.7 (3)
Trail Boss 250 W908527		
Size	22 × 8.00 × 10	22 × 11.00 × 10
Pressure	20.7 (3)	20.7 (3)
Trail Boss 2 × 4 W907527		
Size	22 × 8.00 × 10	24 × 11.00 × 10
Pressure	20.7 (3)	20.7 (3)
Trail Boss 2 × 4 - 350L W907539		
Size	22 × 8.00 × 10	24 × 11.00 × 10
Pressure	27.6 (4)	20.7 (3)
Trail Boss 4 × 4 W908127		
Size	22 × 8.00 × 10	24 × 11.00 × 10
Pressure	27.6 (4)	20.7 (3)
Trail Boss 4 × 4 - 350L W908139		
Size	25 × 8.00 × 12	25 × 12.00 × 10
Pressure	27.6 (4)	20.7 (3)
Big Boss 4 × 6 W908627		
Size	22 × 8.00 × 10	22 × 11.00 × 10
Pressure	34.5 (5)	34.5 (5)

(continued)

Table 2 TIRE SIZE AND PRESSURE (continued)

	Front tires kPa (psi)	Rear tires kPa (psi)
1991		
Trail Blazer W917221		
Size	22 × 8.00 × 10	22 × 11.00 × 10
Pressure	20.7 (3)	20.7 (3)
Trail Boss 250 W918527		
Size	22 × 8.00 × 10	22 × 11.00 × 10
Pressure	20.7 (3)	20.7 (3)
Trail Boss 2 × 4 W917527		
Size	22 × 8.00 × 10	24 × 11.00 × 10
Pressure	20.7 (3)	20.7 (3)
Trail Boss 2 × 4 350L W917539		
Size	22 × 8.00 × 10	24 × 11.00 × 10
Pressure	27.6 (4)	20.7 (3)
Trail Boss 4 × 4 W918127		
Size	22 × 8.00 × 10	24 × 11.00 × 10
Pressure	27.6 (4)	20.7 (3)
Trail Boss 4 × 4 - 350L W918139		
Size	25 × 8.00 × 12	25 × 12.00 × 10
Pressure	27.6 (4)	20.7 (3)
Big Boss 4 × 6 W918627		
Size	22 × 8.00 × 10	22 × 11.00 × 10
Pressure	34.5 (5)	34.5 (5)
Big Boss 6 × 6 W918727		
Size	22 × 8.00 × 10	22 × 11.00 × 10
Pressure	34.5 (5)	34.5 (5)
1992		
Trail Blazer W927221		
Size	22 × 8.00 × 10	22 × 11.00 × 10
Pressure	20.7 (3)	20.7 (3)
Trail Boss 250 W928527		
Size	22 × 8.00 × 10	22 × 11.00 × 10
Pressure	20.7 (3)	20.7 (3)
Trail Boss 2 × 4 W927527		
Size	22 × 8.00 × 10	24 × 11.00 × 10
Pressure	20.7 (3)	20.7 (3)
Trail Boss 2 × 4 350L W927539		
Size	22 × 8.00 × 10	24 × 11.00 × 10
Pressure	27.6 (4)	20.7 (3)
Trail Boss 4 × 4 W928127		
Size	22 × 8.00 × 10	24 × 11.00 × 25 × 10
Pressure	27.6 (4)	20.7 (3)
Trail Boss 4 × 4 350L W928139		
Size	25 × 8.00×12	25 × 12.00 × 10
Pressure	27.6 (4)	20.7 (3)
Big Boss 4 × 6 W928627		
Size	22 × 8.00 × 10	22 × 11.00 × 10
Pressure	34.5 (5)	34.5 (5)
Big Boss 6 × 6 W928727		
Size	22 × 8.00 × 10	22 × 11.00 × 10
Pressure	34.5 (5)	34.5 (5)
1993		
Trail Blazer W937221		
Size	22 × 8.00 × 10	22 × 11.00 × 10
Pressure	20.7 (3)	20.7 (3)
Trail Boss W938527		
Size	22 × 8.00 × 10	22 × 11.00 × 10
	(continued)	

3

Table 2 TIRE SIZE AND PRESSURE (continued)

	Front tires kPa (psi)	Rear tires kPa (psi)
1993 (continued)		
Trail Boss W938527 (continued)		
Pressure	20.7 (3)	20.7 (3)
Sportsman W938039		
Size	25 × 8.00× 12	25 × 12.00 × 10
Pressure	27.6 (4)	20.7 (3)
250 2 × 4 W937527		
Size	22 × 8.00 × 10	24 × 11.00 × 10
Pressure	20.7 (3)	20.7 (3)
350 2 × 4 W937539		
Size	22 × 8.00 × 10	24 × 11.00 × 10
Pressure	27.6 (4)	20.7 (3)
250 4 × 4 W938127		
Size	22 × 8.00 × 10	24 × 11.00 × 10
Pressure	27.6 (4)	20.7 (3)
350 4 × 4 W938139		
Size	25 × 8.00× 12	25 × 12.00 × 10
Pressure	27.6 (4)	20.7 (3)
250 6 × 6 W938727		
Size	22 × 8.00 × 10	22 × 11.00 × 10
Pressure	34.5 (5)	34.5 (5)
350 6 × 6 W938739		
Size	25 × 8.00 × 10	25 × 12.00 × 10
Pressure	34.5 (5)	34.5 (5)
1994		
Trail Blazer 2W W947221		
Size	22 × 8.00 × 10	22 × 11.00 × 10
Pressure	20.7 (3)	20.7 (3)
Trail Boss 2W W948527		
Size	22 × 8.00 × 10	22 × 11.00 × 10
Pressure	20.7 (3)	20.7 (3)
Sport W948540		
Size	22 × 8.00 × 10	22 × 11.00 × 10
Pressure	27.6 (4)	20.7 (3)
Sportsman 4 × 4 W948040		
Size	25 × 8.00× 12	25 × 12.00 × 10
Pressure	27.6 (4)	20.7 (3)
300 2 × 4 W947530		
Size	22 × 8.00 × 10	24 × 11.00 × 10
Pressure	20.7 (3)	20.7 (3)
400 2 × 4 W947540		
Size	22 × 8.00 × 10	24 × 11.00 × 10
Pressure	20.7 (3)	20.7 (3)
300 4 × 4 W948130		
Size	22 × 8.00 × 10	24 × 11.00 × 10
Pressure	20.7 (3)	20.7 (3)
400 4 × 4 W948140		
Size	25 × 8.00× 12	25 × 12.00 × 10
Pressure	27.6 (4)	20.7 (3)
300 6 × 6 W948730		
Size	22 × 8.00 × 10	22 × 11.00 × 10
Pressure	34.5 (5)	34.5 (5)
400 6 × 6 W948740		
Size	25 × 8.00× 12	25 × 12.00 × 10
Pressure	34.5 (5)	34.5 (5)

(continued)

Table 2 TIRE SIZE AND PRESSURE (continued)

	Front tires kPa (psi)	Rear tires kPa (psi)
1995		
Trail Blazer W957221		
Size	$22 \times 8.00 \times 10$	$22 \times 11.00 \times 10$
Pressure	20.7 (3)	20.7 (3)
Trail Boss W958527		
Size	$22 \times 8.00 \times 10$	$22 \times 11.00 \times 10$
Pressure	20.7 (3)	20.7 (3)
300 2 × 4 W957530		
Size	$22 \times 8.00 \times 10$	$24 \times 11.00 \times 10$
Pressure	20.7 (3)	20.7 (3)
400 2 × 4 W95754		
Size	$22 \times 8.00 \times 10$	$24 \times 11.00 \times 10$
Pressure	27.6 (4)	20.7 (3)
300 4 × 4 W958130		
Size	$22 \times 8.00 \times 10$	$24 \times 11.00 \times 10$
Pressure	27.6 (4)	20.7 (3)
Scrambler W957840		
Size	$23 \times 7.00 \times 10$	$22 \times 11.00 \times 10$
Pressure	27.6 (4)	20.7 (3)
Sport W958540		
Size	$23 \times 7.00 \times 10$	$22 \times 11.00 \times 10$
Pressure	27.6 (4)	20.7 (3)
Sportsman 4 × 4 W958040		
Size	$25 \times 8.00 \times 12$	$25 \times 12.00 \times 10$
Pressure	27.6 (4)	20.7 (3)
Xplorer 4 × 4 W959140		
Size	$25 \times 8.00 \times 12$	$25 \times 12.00 \times 10$
Pressure	27.6 (4)	20.7 (3)
Magnum 2 × 4 W957444		
Size	$23 \times 7.00 \times 10$	$24 \times 11.00 \times 10$
Pressure	27.6 (4)	20.7 (3)
Magnum 4 × 4 W958144		
Size	$25 \times 8.00 \times 12$	$25 \times 12.00 \times 10$
Pressure	27.6 (4)	20.7 (3)
400 6 × 6 W958740		
Size	$25 \times 8.00 \times 12$	$25 \times 12.00 \times 10$
Pressure	34.5 (5)	34.5 (5)

Table 3 PERIODIC MAINTENANCE

Every 6 months or after 50 hours of operation	Grease the front wheel bearings (without front wheel drive) Change front wheel drive oil (models with front wheel drive) Change engine oil and filter (models with 4-stroke engines) Grease the rear axle bearing Grease swing arm bushings Grease front ball-joints Grease front A-arm shafts Grease tie rod ends Grease steering post bushings Lubricate and check all control cables Grease transmission output shaft Check brake adjustment
	(continued)

Table 3 PERIODIC MAINTENANCE (continued)

Every 6 months or after 50 hours of operation (continued)	Check spark plug condition and gap
	Check and adjust tension of all drive chains
	Install new air filter element
	Visually inspect all wiring harness, control cable and hose assemblies for incorrect routing and missing fasteners
	Check the drive pulley for correct adjustment
	Visually check condition of tires
	Check all suspension components for missing fasteners and excessive play
	Check all steering components for missing fasteners and excessive play
	Check steering adjustments and adjust if necessary
	Check exhaust system for missing or damaged components and fasteners
	Check all fasteners for tightness
	Check all wiring for chafing or other damage
	Check all electrical connectors for looseness or damage
	Perform general inspection
Once a year or every 100 hours of operation	Change transmission oil (Chain and gear type transmissions)
	Change counterbalancer oil (350 and 400 liquid cooled engines)
	Change engine oil and filter (models with 4-stroke engines)
	Check torque of engine mount bolts
	Retorque cylinder head
	Check all control cables for routing and damage
	Check ignition timing
	Adjust carburetor
	Adjust oil injection pump (the carburetor must be adjusted before adjusting the oil injection pump)
	Check headlight and aim beam
	Check cooling system hoses for looseness or damage
	Replace coolant (liquid cooled models)
Once every 2 years	Drain all brake fluid from the system, refill with new DOT 3* fluid and bleed system

* Do not substitute any other type.

Table 4 RECOMMENDED LUBRICANTS

Item	Lubricant type
Ball-joints	A
Brake fluid	B
Control cables (throttle, choke, etc.)	D
Engine counterbalancer (models so equipped)	E
Engine injection oil (2-stroke models)	F
Engine oil (4-stroke models)	G
Front A arm pivot shafts	A
Front axle bearings (without front wheel drive)	A
Front hubs (with front wheel drive)	I
Rear axle bearings	A
Steering post bushings	A
Swing arm bushings	A
Tie rod ends	A
Transmission	
Chain type (Type I, Table 6)	D
	(continued)

Table 4 RECOMMENDED LUBRICANTS (continued)

Item	Lubricant type
Transmission (continued)	
Gear type (Type II, Table 6)	H
Chain and gear type (Type III, Table 6)	D
Output shaft (with front wheel drive only)	A
EZ Shift selector (Type III, Table 6)	G

A. Grease that conforms to NLG1NO.2, such as Conoco Superlube M or Mobilgrease Special.
B. Brake fluid, Dot 3 Only.
C. Polaris Cable Lube (part No. 2870510).
D. Polaris Chain Lube (part No. 2870464).
E. SAE 10W-30 engine oil.
F. Polaris Injection Oil.
G. Polaris SAE 40 engine oil (part No. 2871271) is recommended. API type SE or SF with SAE 10W/40 viscosity may be used.
H. SAE 30 engine oil.
I. Polaris Demand Drive Hub Fluid (part. No. 2871654) or type F automatic transmission fluid.

Table 5 APPROXIMATE REFILL CAPACITY

Oil injection reservoir		
2-stroke engines	1.89 L	2 qt.
Dry sump reservoir		
4-stroke engines	1.89 L	2 qt.
Liquid cooling system		
2-stroke engines (so equipped)	1.89 L	2 qt.
4-stroke engines	2.4 L	2.25 qt.
Fuel tank		
All 2-stroke models	15.12 L	4 gal.
4-stroke models	13.25 L	3.5 gal.
Transmission		
1985-1986 chain type	0.47 L	0.5 qt.
1987-1993 gear type	0.47 L	0.5 qt.
1993-1995 gear & chain EZ shift		
High-reverse shift	0.47 L	0.5 qt.
High/low/reverse shift	0.59 L	0.6 qt.

Table 6 TRANSMISSION APPLICATION

	Model No.	Transmission
1985 and 1986	Type I	Chain (15 links wide)
1987		
Trail Boss W877527	Type I	Chain (11 links wide)
Cyclone W877828	Type I	Chain (11 links wide)
Trail Boss 4 × 4 W878027	Type II	Gear (ME25P)
Trail Boss 4 × 4 W878127	Type II	Gear (ME25P)
Trail Boss 4 × 4 W878327	Type II	Gear (ME25P)
1988		
Trail Boss 2 × 4 W887527	Type II	Gear (ME25PR)
Trail Boss 4 × 4 W888127	Type II	Gear (ME25P3)
T. B. 250 R/ES × 888528	Type I	Chain (11 links wide)
T. B. 250 R/ES W888528	Type I	Chain (11 links wide)
1989		
Trail Boss W898527	Type I	Chain (11 links wide)
Trail Boss 2 × 4 W897527	Type II	Gear (ME25P6)
Trail Boss 4 × 4 W898127	Type II	Gear (ME25P3A or ME25P5)
Big Boss 4 × 6 X898627	Type II	Gear (ME25P6)
Big Boss 4 × 6 W898627	Type II	Gear (ME25P6)

(continued)

Table 6 TRANSMISSION APPLICATION (contnued)

	Model No.	Transmission
1990		
Trail Blazer W907221	Type I	Chain (11 links wide)
Trail Boss 250 W908527	Type II	Gear (ME25P10)
Trail Boss 2 × 4 W907527	Type II	Gear (ME25P8)
T.B. 2 × 4 350L W907539	Type II	Gear (ME25P10)
Trail Boss 4 × 4 W908127	Type II	Gear (ME25P7)
T.B. 4 × 4 350L W908139	Type II	Gear (ME35P1)
Big Boss 4 × 6 W908627	Type II	Gear (ME25P8)
1991		
Trail Blazer W917221	Type II	Gear (ME25P10)
Trail Boss 250 W918527	Type II	Gear (ME25P10)
Trail Boss 2 × 4 W917527	Type II	Gear (ME25P8)
T.B. 2 × 4 350L W917539	Type II	Gear (ME25P2)
Trail Boss 4 × 4 W918127	Type II	Gear (ME25P7)
T.B. 4 × 4 350L W918139	Type II	Gear (ME35P1)
Big Boss 4 × 6 W918627	Type II	Gear (ME25P8)
Big Boss 6 × 6 W918727	Type II	Gear (ME35P1)
1992		
Trail Blazer W927221	Type II	Gear (ME25P10)
Trail Boss 250 W928527	Type II	Gear (ME25P10)
Trail Boss 2 × 4 W927527	Type II	Gear (ME25P8)
T.B. 2 × 4 350L W927539	Type II	Gear (ME25P2)
Trail Boss 4 × 4 W928127	Type II	Gear (ME25P7)
T.B. 4 × 4 350L W928139	Type II	Gear (ME35P1)
Big Boss 4 × 6 W928627	Type II	Gear (ME25P8)
Big Boss 6 × 6 W928727	Type II	Gear (ME35P1)
1993		
Trail Blazer W937221	Type II	Gear (ME25P10)
Trail Boss W938527	Type II	Gear (ME25P10)
Sportsman W938039	Type III	Gear/chain (1341136)
250 2 × 4 W937527	Type II	Gear (ME25P8)
350 2 × 4 W937539	Type II	Gear (ME25P2)
250 4 × 4 W938127	Type II	Gear (ME25P7)
350 4 × 4 W938139	Type II	Gear (ME35P1)
250 6 × 6 W938727	Type II	Gear (ME35P1)
350 6 × 6 W938739 (w/o EZ Shift)	Type II	Gear (ME25P2)
Late 350 6 × 6 (with EZ Shift)	Type III	Gear/chain
1994		
Trail Blazer 2W W947221	Type III	Gear/chain (1341124)
Trail Boss 2W W948527	Type III	Gear/chain (1341124)
Sport W948540	Type III	Gear/chain (1341124)
Sportsman 4 × 4 W948040	Type III	Gear/chain (1341136)
300 2 × 4 W947530	Type III	Gear/chain (1341125)
400 2 × 4 W947540	Type III	Gear/chain (1341123)
300 4 × 4 W948130	Type III	Gear/chain (1341136)
400 4 × 4 W948140	Type III	Gear/chain (1341146)
300 6 × 6 W948730	Type III	Gear/chain (1341136)
400 6 × 6 W948740	Type III	Gear/chain (1341146)
1995		
Trail Blazer W957221	Type III	Gear/chain (1341124)
Trail Boss W958527	Type III	Gear/chain (1341124)
300 2 × 4 W957530	Type III	Gear/chain (1341125)
400 2 × 4 W957540	Type III	Gear/chain (1341123)
300 4 × 4 W958130	Type III	Gear/chain (1341136)
Scrambler W957840	Type III	Gear/chain (1341140)
Sport W958540	Type III	Gear/chain (1341124)

(continued)

Table 6 TRANSMISSION APPLICATION (continued)

	Model No.	Transmission
1995 (continued)		
Sportsman 4 × 4 W958040	Type III	Gear/chain (1341146)
Xplorer 4 × 4 W959140	Type III	Gear/chain (1341146)
Magnum 2 × 4 W957444	Type III	Gear/chain (1341139)
Magnum 4 × 4 W958144	Type III	Gear/chain (1341132)
400 6 × 6 W958740	Type III	Gear/chain (1341146)

Table 7 MAINTENANCE TIGHTENING TORQUES

	N·m	ft.-lb.
2-stroke engines		
Cylinder head	23-25	17-18
Cylinder base	34-39	25-29
Crankcase		
6mm	8-10	6-8
8mm	22-23	17-18
Crankshaft		
Right side slotted nut	39-60	29-44
Left side pulley screw	54	40
Engine mounts		
Exhaust screws or nuts		
Flywheel nut		
Air cooled	60-84	44-62
Liquid cooled	39-60	29-44
Other 6mm bolts	8-10	6-8
Magnum 4-stroke engines		
Breather union	8.97-15.2	6.5-11
Cam drive sprocket nut	48.3-70.4	35-51
Cam driven sprocket screws	6.9-8.28	5-6
Cam chain tensioner slider	6.9-8.28	5-6
Cam chain tensioner plug	19.3-26.2	14-19
Carburetor flange	16.6-19.3	12-14
Coolant pump cover	6.9-8.97	5-6.5
Coolant pump impeller	6.9-8.97	5-6.5
Crankcase		
8mm	19.3-20.7	14-15
Crankcase drain bolt	19.3-23.5	14-17
Cylinder head bolts		
6mm	8.29	6
11mm	See text for procedure	
Cylinder head cover	8.28	6
Cylinder base bolts		
6mm	6.9-8.28	5-6
10mm	62.1-67.6	45-49
Flywheel	80.0-99.4	59-73
Oil delivery pipe bolts	24.8-34.5	18-25
Oil filter union	49.7-59.3	36-43
Oil hose union	8.97-15.2	6.5-11
Oil pressure blind plug	8.97-15.2	6.5-11
Oil pump mount bolts	6.9-8.97	5-6.5
One way valve plug	19.26.2	14-19
Recoil starter	6.9-8.97	5-6.5
Rocker arm support brackets	11.0-12.4	8-9
Rocker arm adjuster locknut	8.28-9.66	6-7
Rocker shaft locating screw	8.28	6

(continued)

3

Table 7 MAINTENANCE TIGHTENING TORQUES (continued)

	N·m	ft.-lb.
Magnum 4-stroke engines (continued)		
Spark plug		
New	12.0-15.2	8.7-11
Old	23.5-27.6	17-20
Starter motor	6.9-8.97	5-6.5
Stator plate	6.9-8.97	5-6.5
Oil pump case screws	2.76	2 (24 in.-lbs.)
Vehicle		
Clutch screw	54	40
Rear axle housing clamp bolts	65	48

Table 8 SPARK PLUGS

Model	NGK type	Champion type	Gap mm (in.)
1985-1987	BR8ES	RN4YC	0.51 (0.020)
1988	–	RN4YC	0.64 (0.025)
1989	BR8ES	RN4YC	0.70 (0.028)
1990-1995			
2-stroke models	BR8ES	–	0.70 (0.028)
4-stroke magnum	BKR6ES	–	0.64 (0.025)

Table 9 IGNITION TIMING (WITH DIAL INDICATOR)*

	Figure 74	Degrees	mm	in.
1985-1987				
All models except Cyclone				
At 3,000 rpm	"A"	23-27	3.482	0.137
At 6,000 rpm	"A"	17.5-21.5	2.145	0.084
Cyclone				
At 3,000 rpm	"A"	21-25	2.959	0.117
At 6,000 rpm	"A"	15.5-19.5	1.729	0.068
1988				
EC25PF-03 engine				
At 3,000 rpm	"A" or "B"	23-27	3.482	0.137
At 6,000 rpm	"A" or "B"	19.5	2.145	0.084
EC25PF-04 engine				
At 3,000 rpm	"C"	27-31	4.646	0.183
At 6,000 rpm	"C"	19.5	2.145	0.084
1989				
All models				
At 3,000 rpm	"B"	25	3.482	0.137
At 6,000 rpm	"B"	20	2.249	0.089
1990-1995				
250 models				
At 3,000 rpm	"B"	25	3.482	0.137
At 6,000 rpm	"B"	20	2.249	0.089
300 models				
At 3,000 rpm	"B"	25	3.482	0.137
At 6,000 rpm	"B"	17	1.632	0.064
350 & 400 models				
At 3,000 rpm	"D"	23.5	−3.504	−0.140
At 6,000 rpm	"D"	18	2.164	0.085
425 Magnum models				
At 3,000 rpm	"E"	30	–	–

* All specifications are before top dead center (BTDC).

Table 10 VALVE CLEARANCE

	mm	in.
4-stroke engines		
Exhaust valves	0.15	0.006
Inlet valves	0.15	0.006

Table 11 CARBURETOR TUNE-UP SPECIFICATIONS

	Carb. model	Pilot jet	Pilot air screw turns out	Idle rpm
1985				
Scrambler & Trail Boss	VM30SS	30	1 1/2	800
1986				
Scrambler & Trail Boss	VM30SS	50	1	800
1987				
Trail Boss	VM30SS	50	1	800
Cyclone	VM34SS	40	1	800
Trail Boss 4 × 4	VM30SS	50	1	800
1988				
Trail Boss 2 × 4 & 4 × 4	VM30SS	35	1	800
Trail Boss 250 R/ES	VM38SS	45	1 1/2	800
1989				
All models	VM30SS	40	1	800
1990				
Trail Blazer, Trail Boss 250, 2 × 4, 4 × 4 and Big Boss 4 × 6	VM30SS	40	1	700
Trail Boss 2 × 4-350L and 4 × 4-350L	VM34SS	30	1 1/2	700
1991				
Trail Blazer, Trail Boss 250, 2 × 4, 4 × 4, Big Boss 4 × 6 and 6 × 6	VM30SS	40	1	700
Trail Boss 2 × 4-350L and 4 × 4-350L	VM34SS	30	3/4	700
1992				
Trail Blazer, Trail Boss 250, 2 × 4, 4 × 4, Big Boss 4 × 6 and 6 × 6	VM30SS	40	1	700
Trail Boss 2 × 4-350L and 4 × 4-350L	VM34SS	30	3/4	700
1993				
Trail Blazer, Trail Boss, 250 2 × 4, 250 4 × 4 and 250 6 × 6	VM30SS	40	1	700
Sportsman, 350 2 × 4, 4 × 4 and 6 × 6	VM34SS	30	3/4	700
1994				
Trail Blazer and Trail Boss	VM30SS	40	1	700
Sport, Sportsman 4 × 4, 400 2 × 4, 4 × 4 and 6 × 6	VM34SS	30	1 1/2	700
300 2 × 4, 4 × 4 and 6 × 6	VM30SS	40	1 1/2	700
1995				
Trail Blazer and Trail Boss	VM30SS	40	1	700
300 2 × 4, 4 × 4	VM30SS	40	1 1/2	700
Scrambler	VM34SS	30	1 1/2	700
400 2 × 4, 6 × 6, Sport, Sportsman 4 × 4 and Xplorer	VM34SS	30	1 1/2	700
Magnum 2 × 4 and 4 × 4	CVBST34	42.5	1 3/8	1,200

3

CHAPTER FOUR

ENGINE
(2-STROKE MODELS)

This chapter provides complete service and overhaul procedures, including disassembly, removal, inspection, service and reassembly for the 2-stroke engines used in all models except Magnum.

Refer to Chapter Five for service to the 4-stroke engine used in Magnum models.

Engines with 244 cc and 283 cc displacements are air cooled. The 244 cc engine is referred to as a "250" model and the 283 cc engine is referred to as a "300" model.

Engines with displacements of 352 cc and 378 cc are liquid cooled. The 352 cc engine is referred to as a "350L" model and the 378 cc engine is referred to as a "400L" model.

Before beginning any work, read the service hints in Chapter One. You will do a better job with this information fresh in your mind.

The text often refers to left and right sides of the engine as it sits in the ATV's frame, not as it happens to be sitting on your workbench. "Left" and "right" refers to the rider sitting on the seat of the ATV facing in the normal direction (forward).

Refer to **Table 1** for 2-stroke engine applications. **Tables 1-3** are at the end of this chapter.

ENGINE PRINCIPLES

Figure 1 explains how a 2-stroke engine operates. Understanding the principles and knowing what must happen for the engine to run will help you troubleshoot problems when it doesn't start or run properly.

ENGINE LUBRICATION

Polaris 2-stroke engines are lubricated by the oil injection system. Oil is injected into the engine, circulates through the crankcase, and eventually enters the combustion chamber with the fuel. The oil is burned with the fuel and expelled through the exhaust. The various components of the engine are lubricated by oil, which clings to the various parts as it passes through the crankcase and cylinders. The

①

2-STROKE OPERATING PRINCIPLES

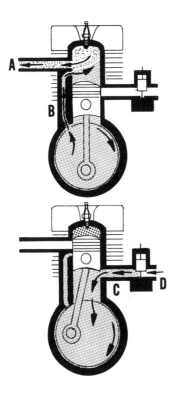

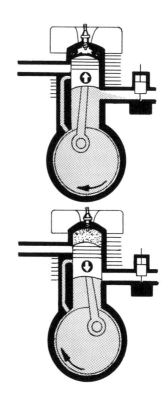

The crankshaft in this discussion is rotating in a clockwise direction.

As the piston travels downward, it uncovers the exhaust port (A) allowing the exhaust gases, which are under pressure, to leave the cylinder. A fresh fuel/air charge, which has been compressed slightly, travels from the crankcase into the cylinder through the transfer port (B). Since this charge enters under pressure, it also helps to push out the exhaust gases.

While the crankshaft continues to rotate, the piston moves upward, covering the transfer port (B) and exhaust port (A). The piston is now compressing the new fuel/air mixture and creating a low pressure area in the crankcase at the same time. As the piston continues to travel, it uncovers the intake port (C). A fresh fuel/air charge, from the carburetor (D), is drawn into the crankcase through the intake port, because of the low pressure within it.

Now, as the piston almost reaches the top of its travel, the spark plug fires, thus igniting the compressed fuel/air mixture. The piston continues to top dead center (TDC) and is pushed downward by the expanding gases.

As the piston travels down, the exhaust gases leave the cylinder and the complete cycle starts all over again.

oil is not reused and the amount of oil in the reservoir will diminish as the oil is being used.

The oil injection system automatically injects oil into the engine during operation at a variable ratio depending on engine rpm. Check the oil level in the reservoir (**Figure 2**) daily and each time the vehicle is being filled with fuel. Refer to Chapter Three for *Oil Injection Pump Bleeding* and for *Oil Injection Pump Adjustment*.

SERVICE PRECAUTIONS

Whenever you work on your Polaris ATV, there are several precautions that should be followed to help with disassembly, inspection, and reassembly.

1. In the text there is frequent mention of the left and right side of the engine. This refers to the engine as it is mounted in the frame, not as it sits on your workbench.

2. Always replace a worn or damaged fastener with one of the same size, type and torque requirements. Make sure to identify each screw before replacing it with another. Screw threads should be lubricated with engine oil, unless otherwise specified, before torque is applied. If a tightening torque is not listed in **Table 2** at the end of this chapter, refer to the torque and fastener information in Chapter One.

3. Use special tools where noted. In some cases, it may be possible to perform the procedure with makeshift tools, but this procedure is not recommended. The use of makeshift tools can damage the components and may cause serious personal injury. Where special snowmobile tools are required, these may be purchased through any Polaris dealer. Other tools can be purchased through your dealer, or from a motorcycle or automotive accessory store. When purchasing tools from automotive accessory dealer or store, remember that all threaded parts that screw into the engine must have metric threads.

4. Before removing the first screw or nut and to prevent frustration during assembly, get a number of boxes, plastic bags and containers. Use these containers to separate and organize the parts as they are removed. Also have a roll of masking tape and a permanent, waterproof marking pen to label each part or assembly. If your ATV was purchased second hand and it appears that some of the wiring may have been changed or replaced, label each electrical connection before separating it.

5. Use a vise with protective jaws to hold parts. If protective jaws are not available, insert wooden blocks on each side of the part(s) before clamping it in the vise.

6. Remove and install pressed-on parts with an appropriate mandrel, support and press. *Do not* try to pry, hammer or otherwise force them on or off.

7. Refer to **Table 2** at the end of the chapter for torque specifications. Proper torque is essential to assure long life and satisfactory service from your engine's components.

8. Discard all O-rings and seals during disassembly. Apply a small amount of grease to the inner lips of new seals to prevent damage when the engine is first started.

9. Keep a record of all shims as they are removed. As soon as the shims are removed, inspect them for damage and write down their thickness and location.

10. Work in an area where there is sufficient lighting and room for component storage.

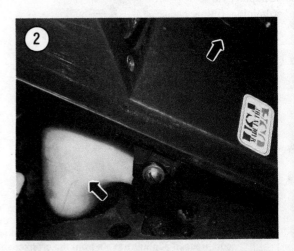

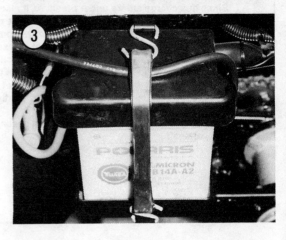

SERVICING THE ENGINE IN THE FRAME

The ATV's frame is a great holding fixture, especially when breaking loose stubborn bolts and nuts. The following components can be serviced while the engine is mounted in the frame.

a. Alternator and stator.
b. Cylinder.
c. Cylinder head.
d. Flywheel.
e. Piston and rings.
f. Starter motor and drive.

LIQUID COOLING

Some engines (350L and 400L models) are cooled by a mixture of antifreeze and water that is circulated by a pump through passages inside the engine and to a radiator located in front of the engine. Refer to Chapter Three for cooling system maintenance (draining, filling, bleeding and checking the coolant level). Refer to Chapter Seven for service to other components of the engine cooling system.

ENGINE REMOVAL AND INSTALLATION

Before removing the engine, clean the engine, frame and work area thoroughly. If water is used, be sure blow or wipe the engine dry before beginning removal.

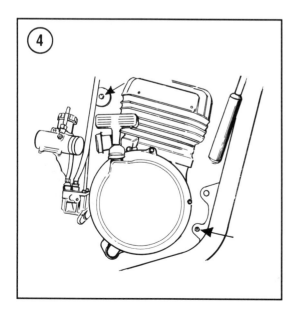

1. Place the ATV on a level surface and block the wheels to keep it from rolling.
2. Refer to Chapter Fifteen to remove the seat, side covers, fuel tank cover, rear rack and rear cab.
3. Disconnect the ground wire from the negative terminal of the battery (**Figure 3**).
4. On liquid cooled models, refer to Chapter Three and drain the coolant.
5. Remove the exhaust system as described in Chapter Six.
6. Remove the air filter and air box.
7. On models with all wheel drive, refer to Chapter Ten and remove the center drive and driven sprockets, and chain.
8. Refer to Chapter Eight and remove the PVT (Polaris variable transmission) outer cover, drive belt, drive pulley, driven pulley and inner cover from the left side.
9. Unbolt the carburetor from the engine and move it out of the way. It is not necessary to detach the throttle control and the carburetor can remain attached to the control cable.
10. Detach the oil lines from the oil injection pump and immediately plug the oil lines.
11. Unbolt the oil injection pump from the engine and relocate it out of the way. It is not necessary to disconnect the control cable, if the pump can be moved out of the way.
12. Detach the spark plug wire from the spark plug. Relocate the high tension lead (wire) out of the way.
13. On liquid cooled models, proceed as follows:
    a. Detach the cooling hoses from the engine.
    b. Disconnect the wire from the temperature sending unit.
14. Detach the battery ground from the engine on models equipped with an electric starter.
15. Detach the battery positive lead from the starter solenoid on models so equipped.
16. Remove the nuts from the bolts attaching the engine to the frame. See **Figure 4**. Withdraw the bolts so the engine can be removed. It may be necessary to loosen the mount bolts so that the bracket can swing out of the way.
17. Carefully lift the engine from the ATV frame.
18. Reinstall the engine by reversing the removal procedure, and observe the following:
    a. Refer to Chapter Three for *Oil Injection Pump Bleeding*.
    b. Make sure that the overflow tube from the carburetor is routed over the frame as shown

in **Figure 5**. Be sure that the vent tube is not bent, kinked or clogged.

> *CAUTION*
> *The engine and drive system can be damaged severely if any covers, cooling ducts, boots or cowling are left off. Cooling for many models includes a cooling fan (**Figure 6**) and ducts for the variable drive belt and clutch pulleys. It is important that all of the cooling system components are in good condition, installed and properly sealed.*

c. Refer to Chapter Eight for installing and sealing the clutch inner cover.
d. Refer to Chapter Eight for installation and adjustment of the clutch pulleys and drive belt.
e. On models with liquid cooled engines, refer to Chapter Three for filling and bleeding the cooling system.
f. Refer to Chapter Fifteen for installing the side covers, fuel tank cover, rear rack and rear cab.

CYLINDER HEAD

Removal of only the cylinder head and the exhaust pipe will permit inspection of the cylinder and piston. The cylinder head, cylinder and piston may be removed with the engine mounted in the frame; however, depending upon the expected extent of service, mechanics sometimes prefer to first remove the engine.

Removal/Installation

Allow the engine to cool to ambient temperature before removing the cylinder head.
1. Place the ATV on a suitable level surface and block the wheels to hold the vehicle in place.
2. Disconnect the battery ground on models so equipped.
3. Remove the seat, the rear rack and rear fender as described in Chapter Fifteen.

> *NOTE*
> *Removal of the front fender may not always be a required step, but it will often provide additional working room. It may also prevent components from getting dirty or being damaged.*

4. Remove the exhaust system as described in Chapter Six.

5. Remove air filter and air box.

6. On liquid cooled models, disconnect the wire from the cooling temperature sending unit, drain the cooling system and detach the coolant hose from the cylinder head.

7. Disconnect the high tension lead from the spark plug. Move the wire out of the way.

8. Loosen all of the fasteners attaching the cylinder head to the cylinder in the reverse of the order shown in **Figure 7**. The cylinder head on models with the 250 engine is attached with five retaining nuts. The cylinder head on models with other air cooled engines is attached with six retaining nuts. The cylinder head on liquid cooled models is attached with six retaining screws. Remove the fasteners after all are loose.

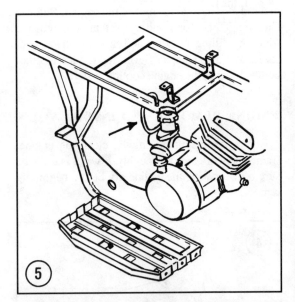

CAUTION
Use caution not to damage the cylinder, cylinder head or other parts by carelessly pounding on the cylinder head.

9. Loosen the cylinder head by bumping the perimeter of the head with a soft-faced mallet, then lift the cylinder head from the cylinder.

10. Remove and discard the cylinder head gasket.

11. Clean and inspect the gasket surfaces of the cylinder (**Figure 8**) and cylinder head before assembling. The seal between these two parts is important. The surfaces must not be nicked or gouged and all of the gasket must be removed before assembling.

12. Install the cylinder head gasket, observing the following.

    a. On liquid cooled models, the single round hole in the gasket (A, **Figure 9**) must be located directly below the coolant elbow cavity.

    b. If there is a difference, the wide side of the fire ring (B, **Figure 9**) should be down, against the cylinder.

    c. The gasket used on 400L models has a small hole above the exhaust port. This small hole is for the decompression aid for easier starting. Make sure that the correct gasket is installed.

13. Install the cylinder head and tighten retaining fasteners to the torque specified in **Table 2** in the order shown in **Figure 7**.

14. On liquid cooled models, refer to Chapter Three when filling and bleeding the cooling system.

Inspection

1. Inspect the cylinder head for warpage with a straightedge and flat feeler gauge. Replace the cylinder head if warped. If extent of warpage is slight, consult with a Polaris dealer about possible repair.

2. Check for cracks around the holes in the cylinder head. Also check for damaged threads in the spark plug hole. Cracked cylinder heads must be replaced, but usually threads for the spark plug can be repaired by a Polaris dealer or competent machine shop.

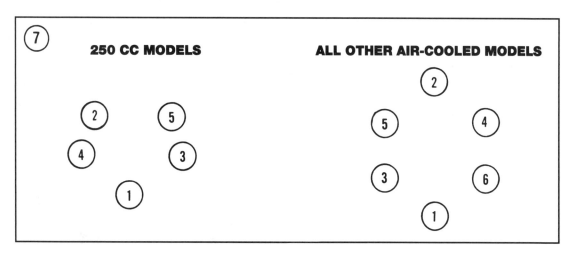

⑦ **250 CC MODELS**   **ALL OTHER AIR-COOLED MODELS**

3A. On air cooled engines, check for broken or cracked cooling fins (**Figure 10**). Missing cooling fins can result in localized hot spots that affect engine operation. If any fins are cracked, have the cylinder head inspected by a Polaris dealer.

3B. On liquid cooled models, check the water passages for corrosion or other blockage. If cylinder head passages are corroded, those in the cylinder (**Figure 11**) should also be carefully checked.

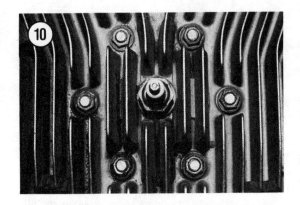

> *CAUTION*
> *Do not damage the cylinder head by cleaning with caustic solvents or hard scrapers. The soft material of the cylinder head is easily damaged by carelessness or harsh handling.*

4. Clean all carbon deposits from the combustion chamber. Use a soft scraper that will not damage the cylinder head. To finish cleaning, wipe the cylinder head with a shop cloth and cleaning solvent.

CYLINDER

Removal

1. Remove the cylinder head as described in this chapter.
2. Remove air filter and air box.
3. On models with all wheel drive, refer to Chapter Ten and remove the center drive and driven sprockets, and chain.
4. Refer to Chapter Eight and remove the PVT (Polaris variable transmission) outer cover, drive belt, drive pulley, driven pulley and inner cover from the left side.
5. Unbolt the carburetor from the engine and move it out of the way. It is not necessary to detach the throttle control and the carburetor can remain attached to the control cable.
6. Disconnect the oil injection line (A, **Figure 12** or A, **Figure 13**) from the cylinder near the inlet port or from the carburetor adapter.
7. On 350L and 400L models remove the reed valve assembly (and carburetor adapter) as described in this chapter.
8. On liquid cooled models, loosen the clamps, then detach the coolant transfer hose (**Figure 14**) from the cylinder.
9. Loosen the four nuts that attach the cylinder base to the crankcase. Refer to **Figure 15**. A 14 mm

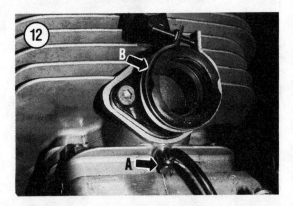

universal socket can be used on the two nuts at the front (exhaust) of engine, but an end wrench is required to loosen the nuts on the rear (inlet).

NOTE
The piston should slide smoothly from the cylinder bore and only light taps should be required to release the cylinder.

10. Tap the cylinder lightly with a soft hammer to separate the cylinder from the cylinder base gasket

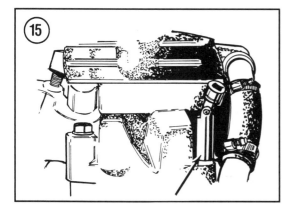

and the studs in the crankcase. Lift the cylinder from the piston and crankcase.

CAUTION
Stuff a shop towel around the connecting rod under the cylinder before the cylinder is completely removed to prevent dirt or any loose parts from falling into the crankcase. The shop towel will also keep the connecting rod and piston from falling when the cylinder is removed.

11A. On 250 and 300 engines, remove the carburetor adapter (B, **Figure 12**) from the cylinder to prevent it from becoming damaged while cleaning the cylinder.

11B. On 350L and 400L engines, unbolt and remove the carburetor adapter (B, **Figure 13**) and reed valve assembly from the rear of the cylinder. Be careful not to damage the reed valves. Inspect the reed valves as described in this chapter.

12. Remove the exhaust port spigot (**Figure 16**) to facilitate cleaning and to prevent it from being damaged while cleaning the port.

13. Remove the cylinder base gasket and discard it.

14. Soak any remaining gasket material with solvent, then scrape it from the cylinder base and crankcase. Be careful not to gouge the sealing surfaces.

Inspection

The following procedure requires the use of highly specialized and expensive measuring instruments. If such equipment is not readily available, have the measurements performed by a dealer or qualified machine shop.

1. Measure the cylinder bore with a cylinder bore gauge (**Figure 17**) or inside micrometer at the points shown in **Figure 18**. Measure both in line with the piston pin and at 90° to the pin. Measure the cylinder approximately 13 mm (1/2 in.) from the top of the cylinder, in the middle and approximately 13 mm (1/2 in.) from the bottom. If the taper or out-of-round exceeds the limits in **Table 3**, the cylinder must be rebored to the next oversize and fitted with a new piston, or a new standard size cylinder should be installed.

NOTE
Purchase the new piston before the cylinder is rebored so the piston can be measured by the machinist. Slight

manufacturing tolerances must be taken into account to determine the actual cylinder bore diameter and piston-to-cylinder clearance.

2. Check the cylinder bore for scratches or other obvious damage. Carefully inspect the cylinder around the exhaust and transfer ports.

> *NOTE*
> *It may be possible to repair a damaged cylinder by reboring, but if you have any question, have the part inspected by your Polaris dealer or machine shop specializing in this type of repair.*

3. Clean the cylinder and ports carefully. A broad-tipped, dull screwdriver or the end of a hacksaw blade can be used to scrape carbon from the ports, but be careful not to damage the cylinder.

4. Inspect the threaded holes and studs for damage and replace or repair as necessary.

5. Test the injection pump check valve located in the inlet passage as described in this chapter.

Installation

1. Check to be sure that all of the old gasket has been removed from the top surface of the crankcase and the bottom surface of the cylinder.

2. Make sure that the cylinder, piston, crankcase and work area are clean and undamaged.

3. Coat both sides of the cylinder base gasket with Loctite 515 Gasket Eliminator, be sure that all of the studs are in place in crankcase, then install a new cylinder base gasket over the studs.

4. Lubricate the cylinder bore, piston and rings with 2-stroke engine oil.

> *CAUTION*
> *Be careful not to break the ends of the piston rings when installing the cylinder. The ends are small so they surround the alignment pins in the ring grooves and therefore, can be easily broken.*

5. Make sure the piston ring gaps align with the pin in the piston grooves. Refer to **Figure 19**.

6. Compress the top ring and start the chamfered edge of the cylinder over the ring.

7. Compress the second ring and slide the cylinder down over the ring.

8. Continue to slide the cylinder down until it completely covers the rings. Slide the cylinder all the way down over the mounting studs, against the crankcase and base gasket.

9. Install the base nuts and tighten in a crossing pattern. Tighten the nuts to the torque listed in **Table 2**.

> *NOTE*
> *The two nuts on the front (exhaust side) of the engine can be tightened with a 14 mm universal socket as shown in **Figure 15**. A 14 mm crow's foot wrench must be used to torque the cylinder base nuts on the rear (inlet side) of the engine.*

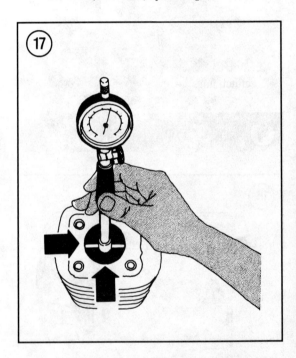

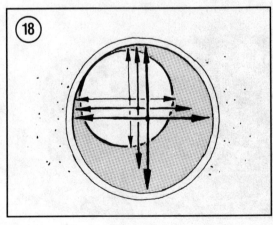

10. Complete reassembly of the engine by reversing the disassembly procedure and observe the following:

    a. Make sure that overflow tube from the carburetor is routed over the frame as shown in **Figure 5**. Be sure that vent tube is not bent, kinked or clogged.

> *CAUTION*
> *The engine and drive system can be damaged severely if any covers, cooling ducts, boots or cowling are left off. Cooling for many models includes a cooling fan (**Figure 6**) and ducts for the variable drive belt and clutch pulleys. It is important that all of the cooling system components are in good condition, installed and properly sealed.*

    b. Refer to Chapter Eight to install and seal the clutch inner cover.

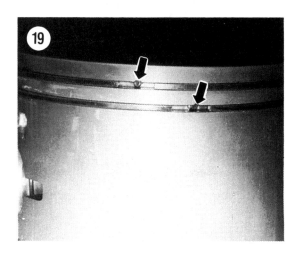

    c. Refer to Chapter Eight to install and adjust the clutch pulleys and drive belt.

    d. On models with liquid cooled engines, refer to Chapter Three to fill and bleed the cooling system.

    e. Refer to Chapter Fifteen to install the side covers, fuel tank cover, rear rack and rear cab.

REED VALVE ASSEMBLY

Engines with liquid cooling (350L and 400L) are equipped with a reed valve assembly installed in the intake port of the cylinder.

Special care must be taken when handling the reed valve assembly. The reeds are fragile and can be easily broken or bent by improper handling. A reed valve that doesn't open or close properly will cause severe performance loss and will lead to early engine failure.

Removal/Inspection/Installation

1. Place the ATV on a suitable level surface and block the wheels to hold the vehicle in place.
2. Disconnect the battery ground on models so equipped.
3. Remove the seat, the rear rack and rear fender as described in Chapter Fifteen.
4. Remove air filter and air box.
5. Unbolt the carburetor from the engine and move it out of the way. It is not necessary to detach the throttle control and the carburetor can remain attached to the control cable.
6. Disconnect the oil injection line (A, **Figure 12** or A, **Figure 13**) from the cylinder fitting or the carburetor adapter.

> *NOTE*
> *The fitting on the oil injection line at the cylinder or carburetor adapter is also the check valve for the oil injection system. The check valve should allow oil to pass into the inlet passage, but should prevent crankcase pressure from entering the oil line.*

7. Remove the 6 screws attaching the carburetor adapter (B, **Figure 13**) to the cylinder.
8. Carefully remove the carburetor adapter and check the adapter for cracks or other damage. Refer to **Figure 20**.

9. Remove the reed assembly (**Figure 21**). The reed housing on 400L models is equipped with a removable stuffer block, which is located nearest the carburetor. This reed stuffer block may also be installed in 350L models.

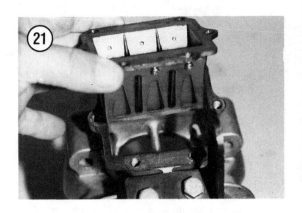

> *NOTE*
> *One early sign of reed failure is hard starting. Check the condition of the reeds whenever the reed assembly is removed. Be especially careful not to damage the reed petals when removing, checking, assembling or installing. The reed assembly (**Figure 22**) can be inspected without disassembly.*

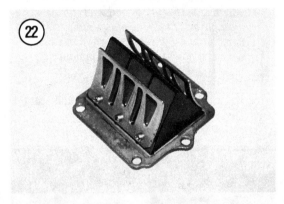

10. Measure the reed stop height. This is the distance between the reed valve stop and the reed housing. Refer to **Figure 23**. The recommended stop height is listed in **Table 3**. This height should not change during normal operation, but it may have been bumped. Make sure that the reed stop is smooth and straight so that it does not damage the reed petals.

11. Measure the reed air gap. Refer to **Figure 24**. This is the distance the reed stands away from the reed housing when the reed is at rest. Install new reed petals if the gap exceeds the maximum limit listed in **Table 3**.

12. Inspect the reed petals for white stress marks, which are indications that the reed petal is about to fail. Install new reed petals if any stress marks are noticed.

13. If the reed assembly (**Figure 22**) is disassembled, make sure that the petals are centered over the ports in the reed housing.

14. Reinstall the reed assembly by reversing the removal procedure.

PISTON, PISTON PIN AND RINGS

The piston is made of aluminum alloy and is fitted with Keystone type rings. The Keystone cross section is easily seen by positioning a straightedge across the ring as shown in **Figure 25**. The Keystone cross section is designed to move in and out in the groove to prevent carbon buildup. When installing the ring, make sure that the identification mark is toward the top of the piston.

The piston pin is made of steel and is a precision fit in the piston. The piston pin is held in place by a clip at each end of the bore in the piston.

Piston Removal

1. Remove the cylinder head and the cylinder as outlined in this chapter.

2. Before removing the piston, hold the rod tightly and rock the piston to detect excessive clearance

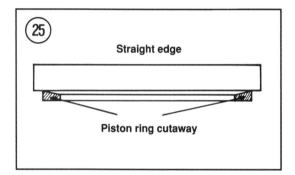

Straight edge

Piston ring cutaway

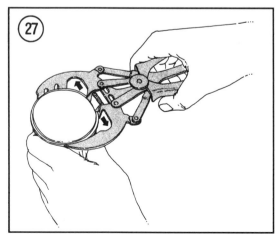

between the piston, piston pin and connecting rod. Refer to **Figure 26**. Do not confuse the normal sliding motion of the piston on the pin with rocking motion. Any perceptible rocking motion indicates wear on the piston pin, piston, connecting rod small end bearing or the connecting rod small end. Any excessive wear is probably a combination of the wear of all of these parts.

NOTE
Do not reuse the piston pin retaining clips. The clips are damaged during removal. Severe engine damage will result if a clip becomes loose while the engine is running.

3. Remove the clips from each side of the piston pin bore. The slot in the pin bore permits a small screwdriver to be used to remove the spring clip. Be careful to prevent the clips from springing out.

4. Use a suitable tool (part No. 2870386) to pull the piston pin from the bore in the piston.

CAUTION
Be careful when removing the piston pin to avoid damaging the connecting rod. The piston should be supported to either push or pull the pin from the pin bore. Be sure that lateral loads are not transmitted to the lower connecting rod bearing.

5. Lift the piston from the connecting rod.

NOTE
If the piston is to be left off for some time, protect the connecting rod by placing a piece of foam insulation tube over its end to protect it. Stuff a clean, lint free shop towel around the connecting rod to keep dirt from entering the crankcase.

WARNING
The edges of all piston rings are very sharp. Be very careful when handling them to avoid cutting your fingers.

6. Remove the top ring with a ring expander tool (**Figure 27**) or by spreading the ends with your thumbs (**Figure 28**) just enough to slide the ring up over the top of the piston. Repeat the procedure for the second ring.

Inspection

1. Carefully clean the carbon from the piston crown with a scraper. Do not damage the piston. Also notice the "F" mark or arrow cast into the piston crown. Refer to **Figure 29**.

> *CAUTION*
> *Do not use a wire brush to clean the piston skirt and do not gouge the piston while attempting to clean it. The soft aluminum of the piston is easily damaged by improper cleaning techniques. Notice that the ring grooves are Keystone shaped (**Figure 30**) and should not be cleaned with a tool that has straight sides.*

2. Examine each ring groove in the piston for carbon deposits or other conditions that reduce the width of the groove.

3. Examine each ring groove for gouges, bent lands or other conditions that increase the width of the groove.

4. Measure the *Piston Clearance* as described in this chapter.

5. Measure the diameter of the pin bore in the piston (**Figure 31**), then measure the piston pin diameter (**Figure 32**).

6. Subtract the diameter of the piston pin from the diameter of the pin hole in the piston to determine the pin-to-pin bore clearance.

7. Refer to the specifications listed in **Table 3** and replace parts as required.

8. If damage or wear indicates that the piston should be replaced, select a new piston as described in *Piston Clearance* in this chapter.

9. Inspect and install new piston rings as described in *Piston Ring Removal/Inspection/Installation* in this chapter.

Piston Clearance

1. Measure the piston diameter at a point 10 mm (0.40 in.) from the bottom of the piston skirt.

2. Measure the cylinder bore diameter with a cylinder bore gauge (**Figure 33**) or inside micrometer at the points shown in **Figure 34**. Measure in line with the piston pin and at 90° to the pin. If the taper or out-of-round exceeds the limits in **Table 3**, the cylinder must be rebored to the next oversize and fitted

with a new piston, or a new standard size cylinder should be installed.

3. Subtract the diameter of the piston skirt from the maximum diameter of the cylinder bore to determine the piston skirt-to-cylinder clearance.

4. The piston skirt-to-cylinder clearance should not exceed the limit listed in **Table 3**. It may be possible

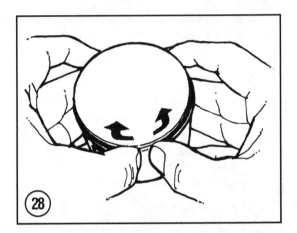

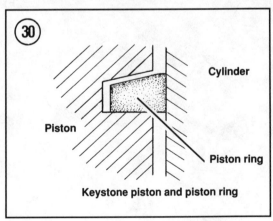

Keystone piston and piston ring

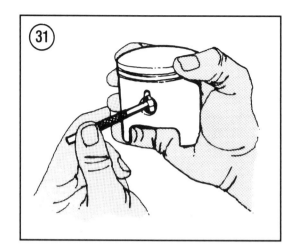

to repair a damaged cylinder by reboring, but if you have any question, have the parts inspected by your Polaris dealer or machine shop specializing in this type of repair.

NOTE
Purchase the new piston before the cylinder is rebored so that the piston can be measured by the machinist before any changes are made. Slight manufacturing tolerances must be taken into account to determine the bore diameter and piston-to-bore clearance.

Piston Installation

1. Coat the piston pin, pin bore, needle bearing and connecting rod small end bore in with clean engine oil.

CAUTION
Do not reuse old clips to retain the piston pin in the piston. The clips are deformed during removal and severe engine damage can result if the clips become loose while the engine is running. Always install new clips if the piston is removed. Use a special piston pin clip installer tool part No. 2870773 (or equivalent) to prevent damage to the pin retaining clips while installing. Be certain the clip properly engages the groove in the piston.

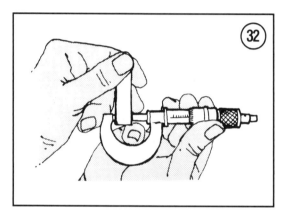

2. Install a new retaining clip in one end of the piston pin bore. The opening of the retaining ring should face down, toward the crankshaft (bottom of the piston).

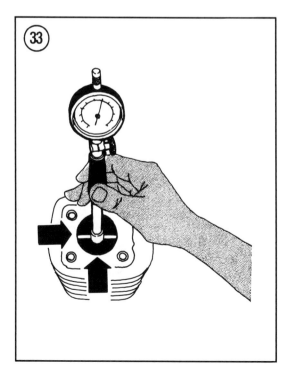

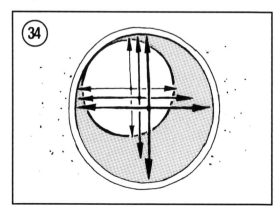

3. Insert the piston pin through the bore in the piston, until it extends slightly beyond the inside of the pin boss. Refer to **Figure 35**.

4. Place the piston over the connecting rod with the "F" mark or arrow (**Figure 29**) on the piston crown pointing toward the magneto (right) side of the engine.

5. Align the piston pin with the hole in the connecting rod and needle bearing, then push the pin through the connecting rod. Continue pushing the pin until it just contacts the previously installed retaining clip.

NOTE
The pin should be a smooth fit in the bore when the pin and the bores are lubricated. If the piston pin is tight, cool the pin and warm the piston slightly. Be careful not to transmit lateral shock to the connecting rod or otherwise damage parts by carelessly pounding on the side of the piston.

6. Install a new retaining clip in the piston pin bore, with the opening facing down, toward the bottom of the piston. Use a special piston pin clip installer tool part No. 2870773 (or equivalent) to prevent damage to the clips. Be sure that the clip properly engages the groove in the piston.

7. Check installation by rocking the piston back and forth around the pin axis, then sliding the piston from side to side. It should rotate freely without perceptible play.

8. Install the piston rings as described in this chapter.

9. Install the cylinder and cylinder head as described in this chapter.

Piston Ring Removal/Inspection/Installation

WARNING
The edges of all piston rings are very sharp. Be very careful when handling them to avoid cutting your fingers.

1. Remove the top ring with a ring expander or spread the ring with your thumbs just enough to slide the ring up over the top of the piston. Repeat the procedure for the remaining ring.

2. Clean the carbon from the ring grooves with a section of a broken ring as shown in **Figure 36**. Be careful not to cut your hand on the ring used as a

cleaning tool, or damage the piston. Do not gouge the aluminum piston; remove only the carbon.

CAUTION
Do not use a wire brush to clean the piston skirt. Do not gouge the piston while attempting to clean it. The soft aluminum of the piston is easily damaged by improper cleaning techniques.

3. Examine each ring groove in the piston for carbon deposits or other conditions that reduce the width of the groove.

NOTE
The groove for the top compression ring usually wears more than the other groove, but both should be carefully inspected.

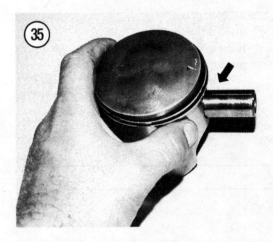

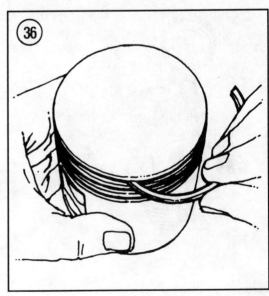

4. Examine each ring groove for gouges, bent lands or other conditions that increase the width of the groove.

5. Check each ring for binding in its groove. Clean or replace the piston as necessary.

6. Measure the end gap of each ring in the cylinder bore, before installing the ring on the piston as follows.

    a. Insert one ring into the cylinder. Make sure the ring is square in the cylinder by using the top of the piston to slide the ring up or down in the cylinder.

    b. Use a feeler gauge to measure the gap between the ends of the ring as shown in **Figure 37**.

    c. Check the end gap at several locations in the cylinder and always make sure that the ring is positioned squarely in the cylinder. Compare the measured end gap with the specifications listed in **Table 3**.

    d. If the gap is too wide, the rings will not seal properly. Some causes for the gap to be too wide are: the cylinder bore may be worn, the rings may be worn or the ring is not correct for the application.

    e. If the gap is less than the minimum specified in **Table 3**, make sure that the correct ring is being used. The rings may bind and break if the gap is not wide enough. Do not attempt to file the ends of the ring to enlarge the gap, because the ends of the rings must fit around the pins located in the grooves.

7. Make sure the piston ring grooves are absolutely clean. Identify the top of the piston ring. The top has the manufacturer's mark and is angled. The angle can be checked with a straight edge as shown in **Figure 25**.

CAUTION
If the ends of the ring are spread too far, the ring will probably break. Use care when installing the rings and spread the ends of the rings only enough to install without scratching the sides of the piston.

8. Install the bottom ring in the piston's lower groove, then install the top ring. Refer to **Figure 27** or **Figure 28** for the correct method of spreading the rings.

CAUTION
Be extremely careful not to damage the assembled piston or rings. It is suggested that the cylinder be installed as soon as possible after installing the rings in the piston grooves. Also, be careful not to break the ends of the piston rings when installing the cylinder. The ends of the rings are small so they surround the alignment pins in the ring grooves and therefore, can be easily broken by improper handling.

9. Follow the *Break-in Procedure* in this chapter if the cylinder was rebored, a new piston was installed or if new piston rings were fitted.

RECOIL STARTER (EARLY 250 MODELS)

Refer to the following for service to the recoil starter used on early 250 models. Refer to **Figure 38**.

Removal/Installation

1. Place the ATV on a level surface and block the wheels to keep it from rolling.

2. Remove the screws attaching the recoil starter, then remove the starter and gasket.

3. Install the recoil starter assembly and tighten the retaining screws.

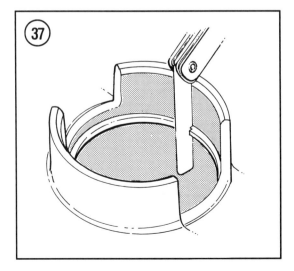

Disassembly and Starter Rope Removal

1. Pull the starter rope from the housing and tie a loose knot to keep the rope from recoiling, if the rope is not broken.

2. Remove the anchor from the starter handle and remove the handle from the end of the rope.

3. Hold the rope, untie the previously tied knot, then allow the rope to unwind slowly into the housing.

4. Remove the nut from the center post.

5. Remove the friction plate, ratchet pawl (**Figure 39**) and spring (A, **Figure 40**).

> *CAUTION*
> *The recoil spring is under pressure and may jump from the housing during disassembly. Its edges are sharp and may cut or cause eye injury. Wear safety glasses or a face shield and gloves when disassembling and assembling.*

6. Carefully lift the starter pulley and rope from the housing. Make sure that the recoil spring (**Figure 41**) remains in the starter housing.

7. Unwind and remove the rope from the starter pulley if replacement is required.

Inspection and Assembly

1. Clean all parts and dry thoroughly.

2. Inspect the friction plate, friction spring, ratchet pawl and pawl spring (**Figure 42**) for damage. Friction spring should grip the friction plate securely.

3. Check the rope for fraying or other damage. It is usually a good practice to replace a rope that has even slight damage, before it breaks.

4. Inspect the tabs at the ends of the recoil spring. To remove the spring, invert the starter housing and tap it on a solid surface. Allow the recoil spring to unwind inside the starter housing.

5A. If removed, reinstall the old recoil spring as follows:

   a. Hook the outer end of the recoil spring in the housing.

   b. Wind the spring into the housing in a counterclockwise direction until the spring is completely in the housing. Hold the coils in place while winding the spring in place.

   c. The installed spring should be positioned as shown in **Figure 41**.

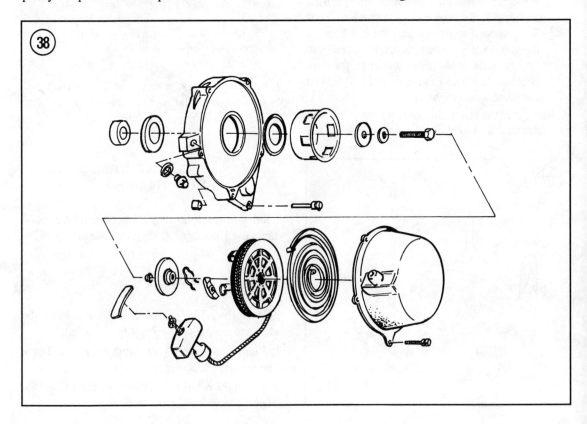

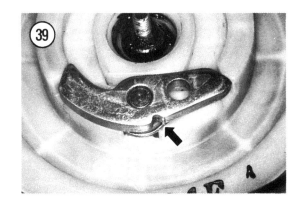

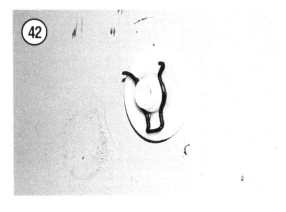

5B. New recoil springs are held compressed by a wire. Use the following instructions to install the new spring.

    a. Position the new spring in the housing so that it spirals inward in a counterclockwise direction and attach the outer end of the spring to the housing.

    b. Hold the spring in place and cut the retaining wire. The installed spring should be positioned as shown in **Figure 41**.

6. Lubricate the spring with a light, low temperature lubricant.

7. If the rope is detached from the pulley, attach the rope as follows:

    a. Tie a secure knot at one end of the rope and insert the other end through the hole in the pulley.

    b. Pull the rope through the pulley until the knot is firmly seated in the pocket of the pulley.

    c. Wind the rope into the pulley groove counterclockwise (as viewed from the side shown in **Figure 40**). The rope should be wound fairly tightly into the groove.

    d. When the rope is almost completely wound into the pulley, pull the end up through the notch (B, **Figure 40**). The end of the rope should lock into the notch.

8. Apply a small amount of low temperature grease to the center post in the starter housing and to the bushing in the center of the starter pulley.

9. Install the starter pulley over the center post making sure the inner end of the recoil spring engages the tab at the center of the pulley. Refer to **Figure 41**. Make sure that the pulley is fully seated (down) in the housing.

10. Preload the recoil spring as follows:

    a. Hold the pulley down in the housing.

    b. Grasp the end of the rope that extends from the notch in the pulley and wind the pulley counterclockwise four (4) turns.

    c. Hold the pulley to prevent the spring from pulling the rope back into the housing.

    d. Route the end of the rope out through the housing, while continuing to hold the pulley.

    e. When the rope exits the housing, pull enough rope out to tie a large knot in the rope to keep it from winding into the housing.

11. Install the pawl spring (A, **Figure 40**).

12. Install the pawl as shown in **Figure 39**. The pawl spring is located at the arrow.

13. Install the friction plate and spring (**Figure 42**) with each end of the spring located on the drive side of the ratchet.

14. Install the spring washer and nut on the center post. Tighten the nut securely.

15. Attach the handle to the starter rope and check operation of the recoil starter. If the rope is the correct length, but does not hold the handle against the housing, refer to Step 10 and preload the spring another turn. If the rope is too long, the coils of the rope may extend outside the pulley groove and bind against the housing.

RECOIL STARTER (ALL 300, 350L AND 400L MODELS AND LATE 250 MODELS)

Refer to the following for service to the recoil starter used on late 250 models and all 300, 350L and 400L models. Refer to **Figure 43**.

Removal/Installation

1. Place the ATV on a level surface and block the wheels to keep it from rolling.

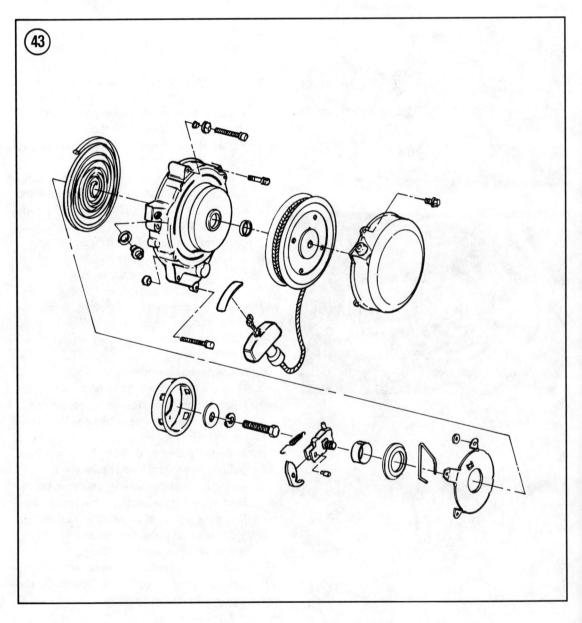

(43)

2. Remove the screws attaching the recoil starter, then remove the starter and gasket.

NOTE
The electric starter reduction drive assembly should remain with the engine. One end of the reduction drive assembly pilots in the rewind starter housing.

3. Install the recoil starter assembly and tighten the retaining screws.

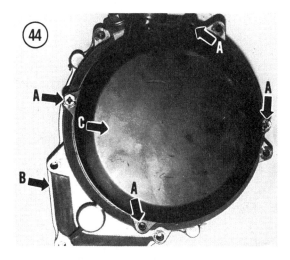

Rope Removal and Installation

The starter rope can be removed and a new rope installed as follows, without removing the starter assembly from the engine.

1. Remove the 4 screws (A, **Figure 44**) which attach the rope housing to the flywheel housing (B, **Figure 44**). If the rope is not broken, allow the rope housing to unwind slowly.

2. Lift the rope housing (C, **Figure 44**) from the starter and unwind the rope from the pulley.

3. Remove the starter handle from the rope and detach the rope from the pulley.

4. Attach a new rope to the pulley, thread the end of the rope through the rope housing (C, **Figure 44**), then attach the handle.

5. Pull the rope out of the rope housing as far as possible, then position the rope housing over the pulley.

NOTE
If the flywheel housing (B, Figure 44) is removed from the engine, hold the housing to keep it from turning while winding the rope onto the pulley in Step 6.

6. Turn the rope housing (C, **Figure 44**) clockwise until the handle is against the housing.

7. Turn the rope housing approximately three additional turns to preload the recoil spring and to point the handle in the correct direction. Align the holes in the rope housing with the threaded holes in the flywheel housing, then install the four screws (A, **Figure 44**).

Disassembly, Inspection and Assembly

1. Unbolt the flywheel housing (B, **Figure 44**) from the engine, then remove the complete flywheel housing and starter assembly.

2. Remove the starter rope as described in this chapter.

3. Clamp the ratchet pawl bracket (**Figure 45**) in a vise. Be careful not to damage the spring.

4. Hold the rope pulley with a cloth belt type strap wrench and remove the pulley by turning it counterclockwise.

5. Lift the ratchet pawl bracket, spring hook, ratchet friction ring and friction spring from the housing as an assembly. Refer to **Figure 46**.

6. Remove the 4 retaining screws (**Figure 47**) and lift the spring retainer plate from the housing.

> *CAUTION*
> *The recoil spring (**Figure 48**) is under pressure and may jump from the housing during disassembly. Its edges are sharp and may cut or cause eye injury. Wear safety glasses or a face shield and gloves when disassembling and assembling.*

7. Carefully lift the starter spring from the starter housing.

8. Clean all parts and dry thoroughly.

9. Inspect the friction plate, friction spring, ratchet pawl and pawl spring (**Figure 45** and **Figure 46**) for damage. The friction spring should grip the friction plate securely.

10. Check the rope for fraying or other damage. It is usually a good practice to replace a rope with even slight damage before it breaks.

11. Inspect the tabs at the ends of the recoil spring.

12A. Reinstall the old recoil spring as follows:

   a. Hook the outer end of the recoil spring in the housing as shown in **Figure 48**.

   b. Wind the spring into the housing in a counterclockwise direction until the spring is completely in the housing. Hold the coils in place while winding the spring in place.

   c. The installed spring should be as shown in **Figure 48**.

12B. New recoil springs are held compressed by a wire. Use the following instructions to install the new spring.

   a. Position the new spring in the housing so that it spirals inward in a counterclockwise direction and attach the outer end of the spring to the housing as shown in **Figure 48**.

   b. Hold the spring in place and cut the retaining wire. The installed spring should be as shown in **Figure 48**.

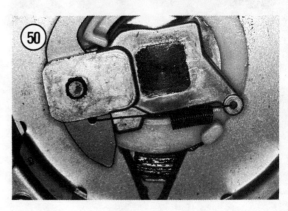

13. Lubricate the spring with a light, low-temperature lubricant.

14. Install the spring retainer plate (**Figure 49**).

15. Assemble the ratchet pawl bracket, spring hook, ratchet friction ring and friction spring as shown in **Figure 46**.

16. Apply a small amount of low-temperature grease to the center post, then insert the ratchet pawl

and friction assembly into the housing (**Figure 50**). Engage the spring hook with the end of the spring.

17. Hold the ratchet pawl tight against the housing and install the starter pulley on the threaded outer end.

18. Refer to *Rope Removal and Installation* to install the rope and preload the recoil spring.

19. The starter pulley cup on some models is attached to the flywheel as shown in **Figure 51**. On other models, the starter engagement dogs are cast into the flywheel as shown in **Figure 52**.

20. Apply Loctite 515 Gasket Eliminator to the mating surfaces and attach the starter assembly to the engine.

FLYWHEEL AND STATOR PLATE

Removal/Installation

Before removing the flywheel and stator plate, clean the engine, frame and work area thoroughly. If water is used, be sure blow or wipe the engine dry before beginning removal.

1. Place the ATV on a level surface and block the wheels to keep it from rolling.

2. Disconnect the ground wire from the negative terminal of the battery.

3. Refer to Chapter Three to drain oil from the engine and the reservoir.

4. Detach the spark plug high tension lead from the spark plug.

5. Remove the recoil starter as described in this chapter.

6. Remove the flywheel nut and washer. Then use a suitable puller (**Figure 53**) to remove the engine flywheel.

7. The mark on the stator plate should be aligned with the pointer on the engine crankcase. Refer to **Figure 54** and **Figure 55** for typical marks. If the stator plate is not already marked, mark the position of the stator plate in a similar way so the stator can be reinstalled at the same ignition timing position.

> *CAUTION*
> *Use care to prevent damage to seals, crankshaft, stator plate, armature wires or other parts when removing the stator plate and stator assembly.*

8. Remove the stator retaining screws and the screws (**Figure 56**) attaching the clamp for the sealing ring around the wires.

9. Carefully guide the stator wires out through the opening as shown in **Figure 57**.

10. Install the stator plate, making sure that the previously affixed timing marks (**Figure 54** or **Figure 55**) are aligned. Be sure that the stator is fully seated and tighten the retaining screws.

11. Seal the stator wire grommet (**Figure 56**) with an appropriate sealer.

12. Make sure that the Woodruff key is in place, then install the flywheel. Tighten the flywheel retaining nut to the torque recommended in **Table 2**.

13. Install the recoil starter and tighten the retaining screws.

COOLANT PUMP

The liquid coolant of 350L and 400L models is circulated by a pump located in the lower right side of the engine crankcase. The engine must be removed from the frame before the coolant pump shaft, seals and impeller can be serviced.

Remove the balance shaft as described in this chapter to service the coolant pump drive shaft. The coolant pump shaft is an extension on the right end of the balance shaft.

Removal/Installation

1. Remove the engine as described in this chapter.

2. Remove the rewind starter as described in this chapter.

3. Remove the flywheel and stator plate as described in this chapter.

4. Remove the electric starter as described in Chapter Eleven.

5. Loosen the clamps on the coolant transfer hose (**Figure 58**), then remove the hose.

> *NOTE*
> *The slotted nut (**Figure 59**) has left hand threads and is removed by turning the nut clockwise. A special tool, part No. 2870967, for removing this nut is available from Polaris dealers.*

6. Remove the slotted nut (**Figure 59**) from the right end of the crankshaft.

7. Remove the four nuts (8-11, **Figure 60**) with a 10 mm socket wrench.

8. Remove the two screws (6 and 7, **Figure 60**) with a 10 mm socket wrench.

9. Remove the five screws from position (1-5, **Figure 60**) with a 12 mm socket wrench.

10. Remove the cover from the right side of the engine. It will probably be necessary to use a soft-faced hammer to separate this cover from the crankcase.

NOTE
Shims may be located behind the impeller to adjust the clearance between the impeller blades and the cover. Do not lose these shims when removing the impeller.

11. Remove the retaining nut (A, **Figure 61**), then slide the impeller (B, **Figure 61**) and pump housing from the shaft.

12. Remove the seal collar (A, **Figure 62**), O-ring (B) and guide washer (C) from the engine crankshaft (D).

13. If additional disassembly is necessary, refer to the procedure described in this chapter for removing the balance shaft.

14. Inspect seals (**Figure 63**) for leakage. Install new seals and inspect the shaft for damage. Refer to the procedure described in this chapter for removing the balance shaft if the shaft is damaged.

15. Clean all old gasket material and sealer from the coolant pump housing, the mating surface of the crankcase and from the engine cover.

16. The impeller can be installed using the original shims if only new seals were installed. If other parts were installed or if clearance between the impeller

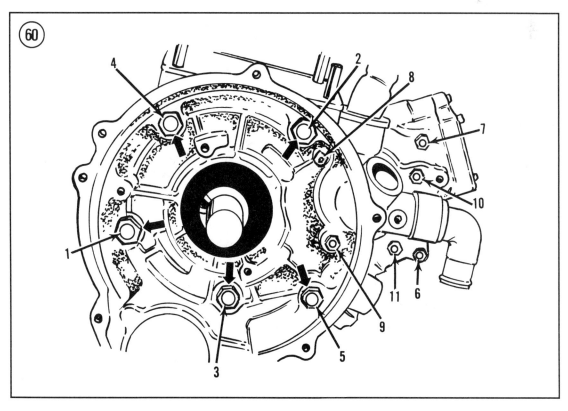

blades and the housing may have been wrong, measure the clearance as follows.

    a. Install the impeller using the shims that were originally installed between the shaft and the back of the impeller. Tighten the retaining nut securely.

    b. Stick a small amount of soft modeling clay on one impeller blade.

    c. Temporarily install the engine right side cover and tighten screws (1, 4, 5 and 6, **Figure 60**).

    d. Remove the four retaining screws and the engine right cover, then measure the thickness of the clay located on the impeller blade.

    e. Compare the measured clearance with the limit specified in **Table 3**. If the clearance is too small, the blades may grind against the cover. If the clearance is too great, the pump will cavitate.

    f. If the measured clearance is outside the limit, remove the impeller and change the thickness of the shims located between the shaft and the impeller. Recheck clearance by repeating sub-steps 16a through 16e.

    g. After the correct thickness of shims has been determined, remove the engine cover, impeller retaining nut, impeller and shims, then proceed to Step 17.

17. Lubricate the coolant pump shaft and install the pump housing and seals (**Figure 63**).

18. Install the selected shims and the pump impeller (B, **Figure 61**).

19. Apply Loctite 242 to the threads of the impeller retaining nut, then install and tighten the nut (A, **Figure 61**).

20. Coat the engine crankshaft with engine oil and install the collar, O-ring and guide washer (**Figure 62**).

21. Install a new gasket (A, **Figure 64**) and coat the mating surface of the pump housing (B, **Figure 64**) with Loctite Gasket Eliminator.

22. Coat the seal collar (**Figure 62**) and the seal in the engine right side cover with engine oil, then install the cover. Tighten the retaining screws and nuts in the order shown in **Figure 60**.

23. Install the slotted nut (**Figure 59**) and tighten the nut to the torque specified in **Table 2**.

24. The remainder of assembly is the reverse of the disassembly procedure. Fill the cooling system with a mixture of antifreeze and water as described in Chapter Three.

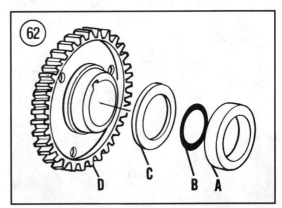

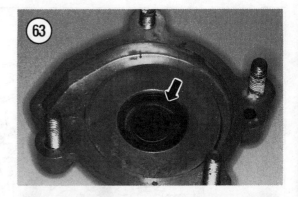

ENGINE BALANCER

Engine models 350L and 400L are equipped with a balance shaft that rotates at the same speed as the engine crankshaft. The engine must be removed and the coolant pump must be removed, as described in

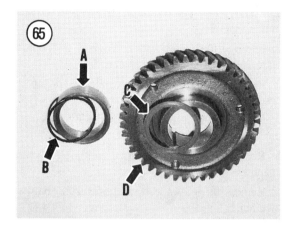

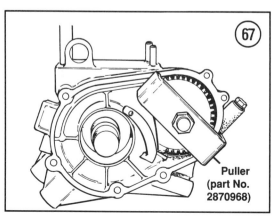

Puller
(part No.
2870968)

this chapter, before removing the balance shaft. The coolant pump shaft is an extension on the right end of the balance shaft.

Removal/Installation

1. Remove the engine from the frame as described in this chapter

2. Remove the engine right side cover and coolant pump as described in this chapter. Be careful not to damage the impeller (B, **Figure 61**) or the pump housing (B, **Figure 64**). Do not lose the shims located behind the pump impeller.

3. Remove the seal collar (A, **Figure 65**), O-ring (B, **Figure 65**), guide washer (C, **Figure 65**) and gear (D, **Figure 65**) from the engine crankshaft.

4. Remove the oil injection pump as described in this chapter.

> *CAUTION*
> *Damage will result if attempts are made to remove the balance shaft before removing the oil pump or the counterbalance bracket.*

5. Remove the two screws (**Figure 66**) attaching the counterbalance bracket.

> *CAUTION*
> *The balance shaft can be damaged severely by improper handling. Failure to heat the crankcase sufficiently or not using the correct puller may result in damage.*

6. Attach a puller (part No. 2870968) to the balance shaft as shown in **Figure 67**. Tighten the puller to apply tension, but do not attempt to pull the balance shaft without heating the crankcase as described in Step 7.

> *WARNING*
> *If the crankcase is heated with an open flame, be extremely careful to prevent damage or injury. Gasoline, oil and some other materials located in or around the engine are extremely flammable. The amount of heat suggested by the manufacturer is 1-2 minutes with a small propane torch no closer than 2.5 cm (1 in.) from the crankcase.*

7. Heat the crankcase at the locations indicated in **Figure 68**, while keeping tension on the attached puller.

8. Continue heating the crankcase, while tightening the puller until the balance shaft and bearings slide from the crankcase. Refer to **Figure 69**. If the inner (left) bearing remains in the crankcase, the crankcase should be separated to remove the bearing.

NOTE
The counterbalance retainer bracket must be in position when installing the balancer shaft assembly.

9. Position the counterbalance bracket (**Figure 66**) and guide the balancer and bearings assembly into the crankcase. When installing the balance shaft, it is necessary to heat the crankcase near the bearings as described in Step 7.

10. Install the crankshaft gear over the Woodruff key, aligning the marked tooth with the marked tooth of the balancer shaft gear as shown in **Figure 70**.

NOTE
After servicing the balance shaft, it is important to measure the clearance between the impeller blades and the cover. Refer to installing the coolant pump in this chapter.

11. Select the correct thickness of shims to install behind the coolant pump impeller as described in this chapter.

12. Install the coolant pump as described in this chapter.

13. Install the oil injection pump as described in this chapter.

14. The remainder of assembly is the reverse of the disassembly procedure. Fill the cooling system with a mixture of antifreeze and water as described in Chapter Three.

CRANKCASE

Disassembly

The crankcase contains the crankshaft and connecting rod assembly. The crankcase must be separated to remove the crankshaft. Service to the crankcase, crankshaft and connecting rod is often better performed by properly trained technicians. Use caution whenever you separate and rejoin the crankcase halves. The importance of absolute cleanliness cannot be over-emphasized when servicing internal parts of the engine.

Separation

1. Remove the engine from the frame as described in this chapter.

2. Remove the recoil starter, flywheel and stator plate as described in this chapter.

3. Remove the cylinder head, cylinder and piston as described in this chapter.

4. Remove the oil injection pump as described in this chapter.

5. Remove the balance shaft as outlined in this chapter.

6. Remove the screws securing the crankcase halves together.

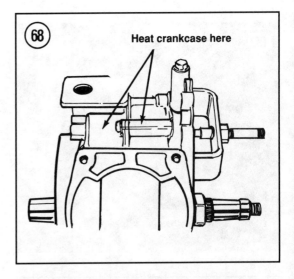

Heat crankcase here

CAUTION
The crankshaft can be easily damaged by pounding on its end while attempting to force the crankshaft and main bearing from the case. Using a puller as shown in **Figure 71** *reduces the risk of damage.*

7. Attach a suitable puller as shown in **Figure 71** to push the crankshaft out of the crankcase.

CAUTION
Shims washers may be located between the crankshaft and main bearings. Be careful not to lose or damage these washers.

8. Heat the crankcase around the main bearing area and tighten the puller (**Figure 71**) to pull the crankcase from the crankshaft.
9. After removing one crankcase half, attach a puller to the opposite side and push the crankshaft from that side in a similar way.

Assembly

Crankshaft end play is adjusted by changing the thickness of shims located between the inner races of the main bearings and the crankshaft. Refer to **Table 3** for recommended crankshaft end play. Refer to *Crankshaft* section in this chapter to determine the correct thickness of shims to install.

1. Make sure that all the oil seals are removed from the crankcase and that the crankcase is clean.
2. Heat one half of the crankcase around the main bearing bore and insert the crankshaft and main bearing assembly. Make sure that the bearing is fully seated.
3. Apply Loctite Gasket Eliminator 515 Sealant to the crankcase mating surface.

NOTE
If the crankcase has been heated sufficiently, it will not require excessive force to install it over the bearings.

4. Heat the uninstalled crankcase half around the main bearing bore and position it over the end of the crankshaft. Align the case halves and push the two halves together.
5. Apply a light coat of oil to the crankcase screw threads before installing them.
6. Install the crankcase screws and tighten by hand.
7. Tighten the screws attaching the halves together to the torque listed in **Table 2**. Make sure that the screws are tightened evenly.
8. Fill the lip cavities of the crankshaft seals with a low-temperature lithium base grease, then install the seals in the crankcase bores.
9. The remainder of the assembly is the reverse of the separation procedure.

CRANKSHAFT, BEARINGS AND SHIMS

Inspection/Adjustment

CAUTION
The crankshaft bearings are damaged during removal. Carefully inspect the bearings while still installed on the crankshaft. Do not remove the bearings unless replacement is necessary.

1. Use a suitable puller to remove the bearings and seals from the crankcase or crankshaft. Note the original direction of the shaft seals.

2. Clean the crankcase halves, both inside and out with a suitable solvent and dry thoroughly. Be sure to remove all traces of old gasket material and sealer from the mating surfaces.

3. Inspect the crankcase halves carefully for cracks, fractures or other damage. Inspect the bearing bores for damage.

4A. If new bearings are being installed, determine the correct thickness of the shims necessary to limit the end play of the crankshaft as follows.

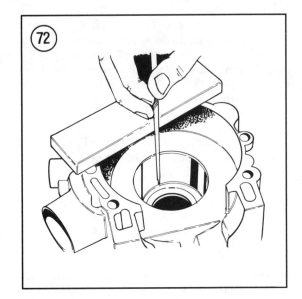

   a. Position a straightedge across the crankcase as shown in **Figure 72** and use a dial caliper to measure the distance from the top of the straightedge to the bottom of the bearing bore.

   b. Measure the thickness of the straightedge.

   c. Subtract the thickness of the straightedge (measured in sub-step b) from the distance measured in sub-step a to determine the actual depth of the main bearing bore from the crankcase parting surface. *Record this distance*.

   d. Measure the depth of the similar main bearing bore in the other crankcase half following sub-steps a through c. *Record the calculated depth of this bearing bore*.

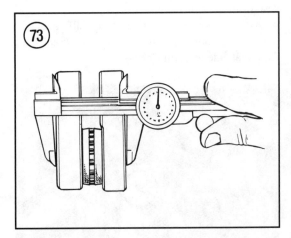

   e. Add the depth recorded in sub-step c and the depth recorded in sub-step d. This is the distance between the bearing bores of the assemble crankcase.

   f. Measure the distance between the shoulders at the ends of the crankshaft (**Figure 73**). *Record the measured length*.

   g. Measure the thickness of all of the main bearing outer races (**Figure 74**). Add all of the measured thicknesses to obtain the total main bearing thickness. *Record this total thickness*.

   h. Add the length of the crankshaft determined in sub-step f to the thickness of the main bearings calculated in sub-step g. This total is the total length of the crankcase and main bearings.

   i. Subtract the length of the crankshaft and main bearings (sub-step h) from the distance between the main bearing bores (sub-step e). This is the measured end play without shims.

   j. Select shims that will not cause the shaft to bind but will reduce the amount of end play to within the limit recommended in **Table 3**.

   k. Position the shims on the crankshaft, then use a suitable press to install the main bearings on the crankshaft.

4B. To check if the crankshaft end play is correct, proceed as follows.

a. Position a straightedge across the crankcase as shown in **Figure 72** and use a dial caliper to measure the distance from the top of the straightedge to the bottom of the bearing bore.

b. Measure the thickness of the straightedge.

c. Subtract the thickness of the straightedge (measured in sub-step b) from the distance measured in sub-step a to determine the actual depth of the main bearing bore from the crankcase parting surface. *Record this distance.*

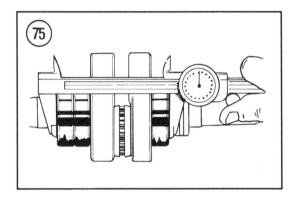

d. Measure the depth of the similar main bearing bore in the other crankcase half following sub-steps a through c. *Record the calculated depth of this bearing bore.*

e. Add the depth recorded in sub-step c and the depth recorded in sub-step d. This is the distance between the bearing bores of the assembled crankcase.

f. Make sure that the main bearings are fully seated on the crankshaft. Then measure the distance between the outer races of the main bearings (**Figure 75**). *Record the measured length.*

g. Subtract the length of the crankshaft and main bearings (sub-step f) from the distance between the main bearing bores (sub-step e). Compare the measured end play with the recommended limit listed in **Table 2**.

h. If the end play is not correct, the main bearings must be removed from the crankshaft to change the thickness of the shims. Add or remove shims equal to the amount necessary to correct the end play.

OIL INJECTION SYSTEM

The oil injection pump typical of air cooled 250 and 300 models is located on the rear of the crankcase as shown in **Figure 76**. The oil injection pump typical of liquid cooled 350L and 400L models is located at the front of the engine crankcase as shown in **Figure 77**.

It is important that the correct amount of oil is delivered to the engine. Refer to Chapter Three for adjusting the control cable and bleeding air from the system. Engine performance is adversely affected by improper oil delivery.

Pump
Removal/Installation

1. Detach the control cable from the control lever (A, **Figure 76** or A, **Figure 77**).

2. Disconnect the oil lines from the pump fittings and plug the lines.

3. Remove the two mounting screws (B, **Figure 76** or B, **Figure 77**).

4. Withdraw the pump from the bore in the crankcase.

CAUTION
Do not lose shims which may be located between the spigot at the bottom of the pump drive and the pump driven gear. These shims are used to set pump end play. Excessive end play may cause a noticeable noise when the engine is running at slow speed.

5. Withdraw the pump driven gear from the bore in the crankcase.

6. Using a vernier caliper, measure the distance from the pump mounting surface to the drive gear as shown in **Figure 78**.

7. Measure the depth of the pump mounting flange as shown in **Figure 79**.

8. Subtract the depth measured in Step 7 from the distance measured in Step 6. The result is the end play of the oil pump drive gear.

9. Compare the end play with the recommended end play listed in **Table 3**.

10. Add shims (**Figure 80**) between the pump drive gear and the pump mounting flange if clearance is excessive.

Oil Injection Check Valve

The oil injection check valve is located in the output line from the oil injection pump. The valve permits oil to be injected into the engine intake, but should stop crankcase pressure from entering the oil line. The check valve is located in the banjo fitting (C, **Figure 76**) on 250 models and in the injector

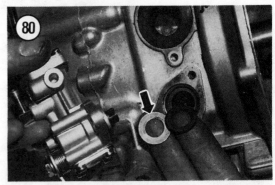

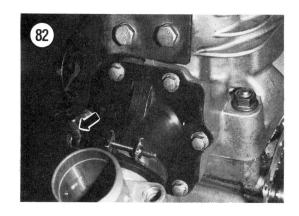

fitting (**Figure 81**), or in the banjo fitting (**Figure 82**) on all other models.

Test the check valve using a pressure tester (**Figure 83**). The valve should open when pressure exceeds 13.8-34.5 kPa (2-5 psi) in the direction of oil flow, but should close when a vacuum is applied. Install a new check valve if the old valve is faulty.

BREAK-IN PROCEDURE

If the rings are replaced, a new piston installed, the cylinder rebored or honed or major lower end work performed, the engine should be broken-in just as though it were new. The performance and service life of the engine depends greatly on a careful and sensible break-in.

For the first 5-10 hours of operation, use no more than one-third throttle and vary the speed as much as possible within the one-third throttle limit. Avoid prolonged steady running at one speed, no matter how moderate, as well as hard acceleration.

Following the first 5-10 hours use more throttle until the ATV has run for 100 hours. Then limit the throttle to short bursts of speed until 150 hours have been logged.

Table 1 2-STROKE ENGINE SPECIFICATIONS

Engine model	Bore mm (in.)	Stroke mm (in.)	Disp. cc (cid.)	Hp @ rpm
1985				
Scrambler				
EC25PF 01	72 (2.835)	60 (2.362)	244 (14.9)	22 @ 6,000
Trail Boss				
EC25PF 01	72 (2.835)	60 (2.362)	244 (14.9)	22 @ 6,000
1986				
Scrambler				
EC25PF 01	72 (2.835)	60 (2.362)	244 (14.9)	22 @ 6,000
Trail Boss				
EC25PF 01	72 (2.835)	60 (2.362)	244 (14.9)	22 @ 6,000
Trail Boss				
EC25PF 01	72 (2.835)	60 (2.362)	244 (14.9)	22 @ 6,000
		(continued)		

Table 1 2-STROKE ENGINE SPECIFICATIONS (continued)

Engine model	Bore mm (in.)	Stroke mm (in.)	Disp. cc (cid.)	Hp @ rpm
1987				
Trail Boss				
EC25PF 01, 03	72 (2.835)	60 (2.362)	244 (14.9)	22 @ 6,000
Cyclone				
EC25PF 02	72 (2.835)	60 (2.362)	244 (14.9)	30 @ 7,000
Trail Boss 4 × 4				
EC25PF 01, 03	72 (2.835)	60 (2.362)	244 (14.9)	22 @ 6,000
Trail Boss 4 × 4				
EC25PF 01, 03	72 (2.835)	60 (2.362)	244 (14.9)	22 @ 6,000
Trail Boss 4 × 4				
EC25PF 01, 03	72 (2.835)	60 (2.362)	244 (14.9)	22 @ 6,000
1988				
Trail Boss 2 × 4				
EC25PF 03	72 (2.835)	60 (2.362)	244 (14.9)	22 @ 6,000
Trail Boss 4 × 4				
EC25PF 03	72 (2.835)	60 (2.362)	244 (14.9)	22 @ 6,000
Trail Boss 250 R/ES				
EC25PF 04	72 (2.835)	60 (2.362)	244 (14.9)	27@ 6,600
Trail Boss 250 R/ES				
EC25PF 04	72 (2.835)	60 (2.362)	244 (14.9)	27 @ 6,600
1989				
Trail Boss				
EC25PF 05	72 (2.835)	60 (2.362)	244 (14.9)	22 @ 6,000
Trail Boss 2 × 4				
EC25PF 05	72 (2.835)	60 (2.362)	244 (14.9)	22 @ 6,000
Trail Boss 4 × 4				
EC25PF 05	72 (2.835)	60 (2.362)	244 (14.9)	22 @ 6,000
Big Boss 4 × 6				
EC25PF 05	72 (2.835)	60 (2.362)	244 (14.9)	22 @ 6,000
Big Boss 4 × 6				
EC25PF 05	72 (2.835)	60 (2.362)	244 (14.9)	22 @ 6,000
1990				
Trail Blazer				
EC25PF 07	72 (2.835)	60 (2.362)	244 (14.9)	22 @ 6,000
Trail Boss 250				
EC25PF 05	72 (2.835)	60 (2.362)	244 (14.9)	22 @ 6,000
Trail Boss 2 × 4				
EC25PF 05	72 (2.835)	60 (2.362)	244 (14.9)	22 @ 6,000

(continued)

Table 1 2-STROKE ENGINE SPECIFICATIONS (continued)

Engine model	Bore mm (in.)	Stroke mm (in.)	Disp. cc (cid.)	Hp @ rpm
1990 (continued)				
Trail Boss 4 × 4				
EC25PF 05	72 (2.835)	60 (2.362)	244 (14.9)	22 @ 6,000
Big Boss 4 × 6				
EC25PF 05	72 (2.835)	60 (2.362)	244 (14.9)	22 @ 6,000
Trail Boss 2 × 4-350L				
EC35PL 02	80 (3.152)	70 (2.758)	352 (21.5)	32 @ 5,800
Trail Boss 4 × 4-350L				
EC35PL 02	80 (3.152)	70 (2.758)	352 (21.5)	32 @ 5,800
1991				
Trail Blazer				
EC25PF 07	72 (2.835)	60 (2.362)	244 (14.9)	22 @ 6,000
Trail Boss 250				
EC25PF 05	72 (2.835)	60 (2.362)	244 (14.9)	22 @ 6,000
Trail Boss 2 × 4				
EC25PF 05	72 (2.835)	60 (2.362)	244 (14.9)	22 @ 6,000
Trail Boss 4 × 4				
EC25PF 05	72 (2.835)	60 (2.362)	244 (14.9)	22 @ 6,000
Big Boss 4 × 6				
EC25PF 05	72 (2.835)	60 (2.362)	244 (14.9)	22 @ 6,000
Big Boss 6 × 6				
EC25PF 05	72 (2.835)	60 (2.362)	244 (14.9)	22 @ 6,000
Trail Boss 2 × 4-350L				
EC35PL 02	80 (3.152)	70 (2.758)	352 (21.5)	32 @ 5,800
Trail Boss 4 × 4-350L				
EC35PL 02	80 (3.152)	70 (2.758)	352 (21.5)	32 @ 5,800
1992				
Trail Blazer				
EC25PF 07	72 (2.835)	60 (2.362)	244 (14.9)	22 @ 6,000
Trail Boss 250				
EC25PF 05	72 (2.835)	60 (2.362)	244 (14.9)	22 @ 6,000
Trail Boss 2 × 4				
EC25PF 05	72 (2.835)	60 (2.362)	244 (14.9)	22 @ 6,000
Trail Boss 4 × 4				
EC25PF 05	72 (2.835)	60 (2.362)	244 (14.9)	22 @ 6,000
Big Boss 4 × 6				
EC25PF 05	72 (2.835)	60 (2.362)	244 (14.9)	22 @ 6,000

4

(continued)

Table 1 2-STROKE ENGINE SPECIFICATIONS (continued)

Engine model	Bore mm (in.)	Stroke mm (in.)	Disp. cc (cid.)	Hp @ rpm
1992 (continued)				
Big Boss 6 × 6				
EC25PF 05	72 (2.835)	60 (2.362)	244 (14.9)	22 @ 6,000
Trail Boss 2 × 4-350L				
EC35PL 02	80 (3.152)	70 (2.758)	352 (21.5)	32 @ 5,800
Trail Boss 4 × 4-350L				
EC35PL 02	80 (3.152)	70 (2.758)	352 (21.5)	32 @ 5,800
1993				
Trail Blazer				
EC25PF 07, 09	72 (2.835)	60 (2.362)	244 (14.9)	22 @ 6,000
Trail Boss 250				
EC25PF 07, 09	72 (2.835)	60 (2.362)	244 (14.9)	22 @ 6,000
2 × 4 250				
EC25PF 05, 08	72 (2.835)	60 (2.362)	244 (14.9)	22 @ 6,000
2 × 4 350L				
EC35PL 02	80 (3.152)	70 (2.758)	352 (21.5)	32 @5 ,800
4 × 4 250				
EC25PF 05, 08	72 (2.835)	60 (2.362)	244 (14.9)	22 @ 6,000
4 × 4 350L				
EC35PL 02	80 (3.152)	70 (2.758)	352 (21.5)	32 @ 5,800
Big Boss 6 × 6 250				
EC25PF 05, 08	72 (2.835)	60 (2.362)	244 (14.9)	22 @ 6,000
Big Boss 6 × 6 350L				
EC35PL 02	80 (3.152)	70 (2.758)	352 (21.5)	32 @ 5,800
1994				
Trail Blazer				
EC25PF 09	72 (2.835)	60 (2.362)	244 (14.9)	22 @ 6,000
Trail Boss 250				
EC25PF 08	72 (2.835)	60 (2.362)	244 (14.9)	22 @ 6,000
2 × 4 300				
EC28PF 01	74.5 (2.935)	65 (2.561)	283 (17.3)	22 @ 6,000
4 × 4 300				
EC28PF 01	74.5 (2.935)	65 (2.561)	283 (17.3)	22 @ 6,000
2 × 4 400L				
EC38PL 01	83 (3.270)	70 (2.758)	378 (23.1)	35 @ 5,700
4 × 4 400L				
EC38PL 01	83 (3.270)	70 (2.758)	378 (23.1)	35 @ 5,700

(continued)

Table 1 2-STROKE ENGINE SPECIFICATIONS (continued)

Engine model	Bore mm (in.)	Stroke mm (in.)	Disp. cc (cid.)	Hp @ rpm
1994 (continued)				
Sport 400L				
EC38PL 01	83 (3.270)	70 (2.758)	378 (23.1)	35 @ 5,700
Sportsman 4 × 4				
EC38PL 01	83 (3.270)	70 (2.758)	378 (23.1)	35 @ 5,700
Big Boss 6 × 6 300				
EC28PF 01	74.5 (2.935)	65 (2.561)	283 (17.3)	22 @ 6,000
Big Boss 6 × 6 400L				
EC38PL 01	83 (3.270)	70 (2.758)	378 (23.1)	35 @ 5,700
1995				
Trail Blazer				
EC25PF 09	72 (2.835)	60 (2.362)	244 (14.9)	22 @ 6,000
Trail Boss				
EC25PF 08	72 (2.835)	60 (2.362)	244 (14.9)	22 @ 6,000
2 × 4 300				
EC28PFE 01	74.5 (2.935)	65 (2.561)	283 (17.3)	22 @ 6,000
4 × 4 300				
EC28PFE 01	74.5 (2.935)	65 (2.561)	283 (17.3)	22 @ 6,000
2 × 4 400L				
EC38PLE 01	83 (3.270)	70 (2.758)	378 (23.1)	35 @ 5,700
Scrambler				
EC38PLE 03	83 (3.270)	70 (2.758)	378 (23.1)	
Sport 400L				
EC38PLE 02	83 (3.270)	70 (2.758)	378 (23.1)	
Sportsman 4 × 4				
EC38PLE 01	83 (3.270)	70 (2.758)	378 (23.1)	35 @ 5,700
Xplorer 4 × 4				
EC38PLE 01	83 (3.270)	70 (2.758)	378 (23.1)	35 @ 5,700
6 × 6 300				
EC28PFE 01	74.5 (2.935)	65 (2.561)	283 (17.3)	22 @ 6,000
6 × 6 400L				
EC38PLE 01	83 (3.270)	70 (2.758)	378 (23.1)	35 @ 5,700

Table 2 TIGHTENING TORQUES

	N·m	ft.-lb.
2-stroke engines		
Cylinder head	23-25	17-18
Cylinder base	34-39	25-29

(continued)

Table 2 TIGHTENING TORQUES (continued)

	N·m	ft.-lb.
Crankcase		
6mm	8-10	6-8
8mm	22-23	16-17
Crankshaft		
Right side slotted nut	39-60	29-44
Left side pulley screw	54	40
Flywheel nut		
Air cooled	60-84	44-62
Liquid cooled	39-60	29-44
Other 6mm bolts	8-10	6-8

Table 3 SERVICE SPECIFICATIONS

	mm	in.
Coolant impeller blade clearance		
Minimum limit	0.05	0.020
Maximum limit	0.1	0.040
Crankshaft		
End play	0.20-0.40	0.008-0.016
Alignment		
Preferred	0.05	0.002
Limit	0.15	0.005
Oil injection pump		
End play	0.20-0.40	0.008-0.016
Piston ring end gap		
1985-1990 models	0.20-0.41	0.008-0.016
1991-1993 models		
250 (air cooled)	0.23-0.46	0.009-0.018
350L (liquid cooled)	0.26-0.53	0.010-0.021
1994 models		
250 (air cooled)	0.23-0.46	0.009-0.018
300 (air cooled)	0.30-0.56	0.012-0.022
400L (liquid cooled)	0.18-0.38	0.007-0.015
1995 models		
250 (air cooled)	0.23-0.46	0.009-0.018
300 (air cooled)	0.30-0.56	0.012-0.022
400L (liquid cooled)	0.18-0.38	0.007-0.015
Piston skirt clearance		
1985-1989 models	0.036-0.071	0.0014-0.0028
1990 models		
250 (air cooled)	0.036-0.071	0.0014-0.0028
350L (liquid cooled)	0.061-0.094	0.0024-0.0037
1991-1993 models		
250 (air cooled)	0.028-0.053	0.0011-0.0021
350L (liquid cooled)	0.061-0.095	0.0024-0.0037
1994 models		
250 (air cooled)	0.028-0.053	0.0011-0.0021
300 (air cooled)	0.030-0.066	0.0012-0.0026
400L (liquid cooled)	0.058-0.094	0.0023-0.0037
1995		
250 (air cooled)	0.028-0.053	0.0011-0.0021
300 (air cooled)	0.030-0.066	0.0012-0.0026
400L (liquid cooled)	0.058-0.094	0.0023-0.0037
Reed stop height		
350L and 400L models	9.0	0.350
Maximum reed petal air gap		
350L and 400L models	0.4	0.015

CHAPTER FIVE

ENGINE
(4-STROKE MODELS)

This chapter provides complete service and overhaul procedures, including removal, disassembly, inspection and reassembly on the 4-stroke engine used in Magnum models. Refer to Chapter Four for service on the 2-stroke engine used in other models.

Refer to **Table 1** for 4-stroke engine application. The one cylinder engine has a displacement of 425 cc and is liquid cooled. The single overhead camshaft is driven by a chain from the engine crankshaft. The two inlet and two exhaust valves are opened by rocker arms that are individually adjustable.

Before beginning any work, read the service hints in Chapter One. You will do a better job with this information fresh in your mind.

The text often refers to left and right sides of the engine as it sits in the ATV's frame, not as it happens to be sitting on your workbench. "Left" and "Right" refers to a rider sitting on the seat of the ATV facing in the normal direction (forward).

Tables 1-4 are at the end of this chapter.

ENGINE PRINCIPLES

Figure 1 explains how a 4-stroke engine operates. Understanding the principles and knowing what must happen for the engine to run will help you troubleshoot problems when it doesn't.

ENGINE COOLING

The engine is cooled by a mixture of antifreeze and water that is circulated by a pump through passages inside the engine and to a radiator located at the front of the engine. Refer to Chapter Three for cooling system maintenance and to Chapter Seven for service to the engine cooling system.

Carburetor

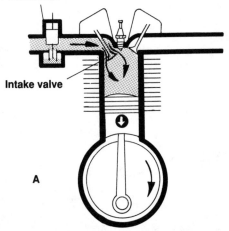

Intake valve

A

As the piston travels downward, the exhaust valve is closed and the intake valve opens, allowing the new air-fuel mixture from the carburetor to be drawn into the cylinder. When the piston reaches the bottom of its travel (BDC) the intake valve closes and remains closed for the next 1 1/2 revolutions of the crankshaft.

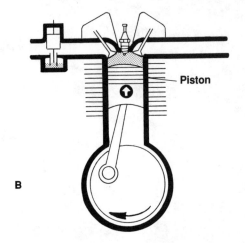

Piston

B

While the crankshaft continues to rotate, the piston moves upward, compressing the air-fuel mixture.

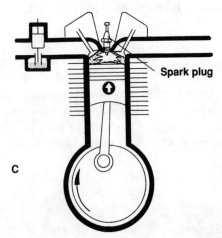

Spark plug

C

As the piston almost reaches the top of its travel, the spark plug fires, igniting the compressed air-fuel mixture. The piston continues to top dead center (TDC) and is pushed downward by the expanding gases.

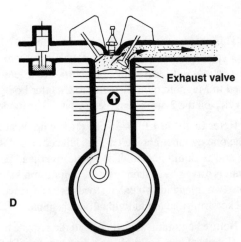

Exhaust valve

D

When the piston almost reaches BDC, the exhaust valve opens and remains open until the piston is near TDC. The upward travel of the piston forces the exhaust gases out of the cylinder. After the piston has reached TDC, the exhaust valve closes and the cycle starts all over again.

NOTE
Cooling is also assisted by the fins (A, Figure 2) on the oil reservoir located on the left side. Some heat from the engine is transferred to the oil, then radiated to the air flowing past the cooling fins in the reservoir. Service to the lubrication system is included in this chapter.

ENGINE LUBRICATION

Polaris 4-stroke engines are equipped with a dry sump type lubrication system that contains only a small (**Table 2**) amount of oil. The various components of the engine are lubricated by the oil as it is circulated within the engine, then back to the reservoir (tank). The oil is used over and over as the

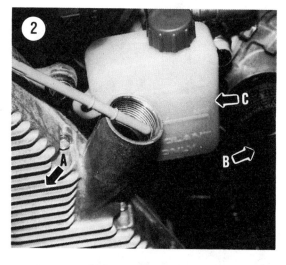

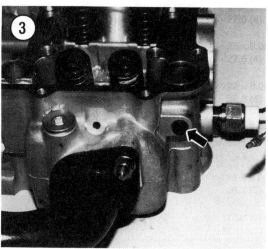

4-stroke engine operates. Engine heat is transferred to the oil, then the oil is allowed to cool while it is in the reservoir (A, **Figure 2**). The oil also becomes contaminated as it circulates within the engine and a filter is used to trap some of the particles.

The oil flows through a screen in the bottom of the oil reservoir, then through the supply hose to the oil pump. The oil pump forces oil through a one-way (check) valve that stops oil from draining into the engine when it is not running. After passing the check valve, oil flows to the oil filter. If the oil filter (B, **Figure 2**) is obstructed, a bypass valve in the filter allows the oil to pass without being filtered. After flowing through (or around) the oil filter, the oil is divided into 2 separate paths.

Part of the pressurized oil flows through the stud at the left front of the cylinder head to lubricate the camshaft and valve operating mechanism.

Some of the lubricating oil is directed to the crankcase main oil gallery. Oil from the main oil gallery is used to lubricate the crankshaft, connecting rod and engine balancer assembly. Oil thrown off lubricates the cylinder, rings, piston, connecting rod, piston pin bearing, oil/coolant pump drive gears, cam chain and drive sprockets.

Refer to Chapter Three for servicing the lubricating oil and the oil filter.

Oil Pressure Test

Pressurized oil is directed up through the stud at the left front of the cylinder head to lubricate the camshaft and valve operating mechanism. To check the engine oil pressure, proceed as follows:

1. Stop the engine and make sure that the reservoir is full of oil. If the condition of the oil filter is questionable, refer to Chapter Three and install a new oil filter.

2. Remove the blind plug (**Figure 3**), located at the lower front part of the cylinder head.

3. Connect a suitable oil pressure gauge with a 1/8 in. NPT (National Pipe Thread) pipe fitting, to the oil port.

4. Start and run the engine until it reaches operating temperature.

5. Run the engine at 5,500 rpm and observe the pressure indicated by the installed gauge.

CAUTION
Low oil pressure will quickly damage engine parts. Low oil pressure should be corrected as soon as possible.

6. After checking the pressure, remove the oil pressure gauge.

7. Coat the threads of the blind plug (**Figure 3**) with sealer before installing. Refer to **Table 3** for recommended tightening torque for the oil pressure blind plug.

SERVICING THE ENGINE IN THE FRAME

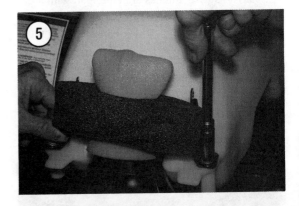

The ATV's frame is a great holding fixture, especially when breaking loose stubborn bolts and nuts. The following components can be serviced while the engine is mounted in the frame.

    a. Alternator and stator.
    b. Cam chain and sprockets.
    c. Cam chain tensioner and guides.
    d. Cylinder.
    e. Cylinder head.
    f. Flywheel.
    g. Rocker arms.
    h. Piston and rings.
    i. Starter motor and drive.

ENGINE REMOVAL AND INSTALLATION

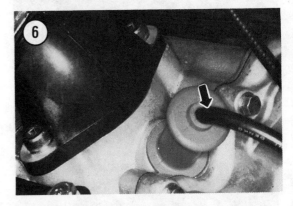

Depending upon the extent of the engine service, some mechanics prefer to remove the engine before servicing some internal components that do not require engine removal. Also, some disassembly of the engine before removal may make removal and installation easier. The engine must be removed from the frame to service the following components.

    a. Connecting rod.
    b. Coolant pump and mechanical seal.
    c. Counterbalancer.
    d. Crankcase.
    e. Crankshaft.
    f. Main bearings.
    g. Oil pump.

Before removing the engine, clean the engine, frame and work area thoroughly. If water is used, be sure blow or wipe the engine dry before beginning removal.

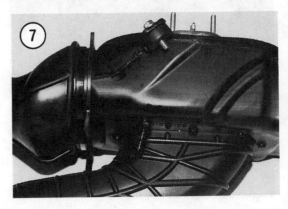

1. Place the ATV on a level surface and block the wheels to keep it from rolling.

2. Refer to Chapter Fifteen to remove the seat, side covers, fuel tank cover, rear rack and rear cab.

3. Disconnect the ground wire from the negative terminal of the battery (**Figure 4**).

4. Refer to Chapter Three and drain coolant.

5. Refer to Chapter Three to drain oil from the engine and the reservoir.

6. Shut the fuel off, disconnect the fuel lines, then unbolt and remove the fuel tank (**Figure 5**). Refer to Chapter Six.

7. Disconnect the spark plug high tension lead (**Figure 6**).

8. Detach the engine breather hose from the engine.

9. Remove the air filter and air box (**Figure 7**).

10. Detach the fuel lines and controls from the carburetor, then unbolt and remove the carburetor. Refer to Chapter Six. Insert a clean, lint free shop towel in the exposed port to prevent dirt from entering.

11. Detach the springs from the exhaust pipe, then remove the exhaust pipe.

12. On models with all wheel drive, refer to Chapter Ten and remove the center drive and driven sprockets, and chain.

CAUTION
Do not lose the spacers or the spacer retaining O-rings from the threaded ends of the screws that attach the PVT inner cover.

13. Refer to Chapter Eight and remove the PVT (Polaris variable transmission), drive belt, drive pulley, driven pulley and inner cover.

14. Unbolt and remove the recoil starter from the right side of the engine as described in this chapter.

CAUTION
Do not thread the puller attaching bolts into the flywheel more than 6 mm (1/4 in.), or the stator coils may be damaged.

15. Remove the flywheel nut and washer then use a suitable puller (**Figure 8**) to remove the engine flywheel.

NOTE
Do not lose the thrust washer located between the starter drive and the crankcase.

16. Remove the electric starter drive (**Figure 9**).

17. Mark the position of the stator plate on the crankcase (A, **Figure 10**), so the stator can be reinstalled in the same timing position.

CAUTION
Use care to prevent damage to seals, crankshaft, stator plate, armature wires or other parts when removing the stator plate and stator assembly.

18. Remove the stator retaining screws (B, **Figure 10**), then remove the stator plate and stator assembly.
19. Remove the sealing ring (**Figure 11**), then cover the end of the crankshaft with a clean, lint free shop towel to prevent damage or the entrance of dirt.
20. Detach the transmission shift linkage from the shift selector, then secure the linkage out of the way.
21. Detach the wire from the coolant temperature sender.

NOTE
Observe the position of the starter cable before detaching it from the starter. It is important to reconnect the cable without causing it to bind and short out.

22. Unbolt and remove the electric starter motor.
23. Loosen the hose clamps, then detach the oil delivery hose (A, **Figure 12**) and the return hose (B, **Figure 12**). Cover fittings and plug the lines to prevent the entrance of dirt.
24. Unbolt and remove the oil reservoir (A, **Figure 2**) and the coolant tank (C, **Figure 2**). The coolant tank can be secured out of the way.
25. Loosen the hose clamp, then detach the cooling hose from the thermostat housing located on the left side of the cylinder head.
26. Remove the engine oil filter (B, **Figure 2**).

NOTE
Mark the location of the engine mount bolts and studs before removing, to help with alignment when reinstalling the engine.

27. Remove the nut and disconnect the ground cable (**Figure 13**) from the upper right side engine mount.
28. Remove the two screws (**Figure 14**), then remove the engine mount and ground cable.
29. Remove the nut (**Figure 15**) and washer from the lower left engine mount bolt. Mark the location of the stud to help with alignment when installing.
30. Remove the nut from the rear engine mount (**Figure 16**).
31. Move the top of the engine to the left until the coolant supply hose clears the frame (on the right side), at the water pump.

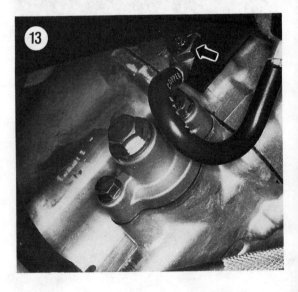

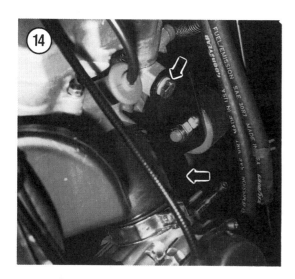

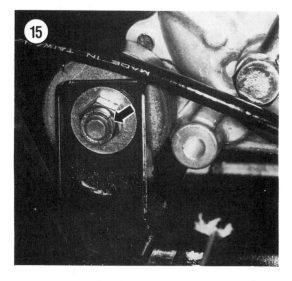

32. Lift and twist the engine clockwise until the engine mount stud at the left front is withdrawn from the frame mount and the coolant hoses (on the lower right side), are clear of the frame.

33. Support the engine with a board across the frame, under the engine.

WARNING
Coolant is slippery and can cause you to fall. Catch as much coolant as possible, then clean the work area after draining coolant.

34. Loosen the clamp on the upper coolant hose, detach the hose from the pump outlet and allow remaining coolant to drain. The hose can be reattached after draining.

35. Loosen both clamps and remove coolant pump lower (inlet) hose.

36. Lift the back of the engine while rotating the front clockwise, then remove the engine from the left side.

37. Install the engine from the left side. Install the rear engine mount washer and nut loosely before inserting into the slotted plate.

38. Attach the coolant hoses to the pump inlet and outlet, before final positioning of the engine.

NOTE
Make sure that coolant hoses and clamps are clear of the frame when engine is in position.

39. Locate the rear mount stud in the slotted plate, then roll the engine into position in the reverse of the removal procedure.

40. Install and tighten the engine mounts, aligning the previously installed marks.

NOTE
The drive pulleys should be temporarily installed to check the alignment of the engine in it mounts. If not aligned, it may be necessary to relocate the engine mounts.

41. Refer to Chapter Eight and temporarily install *and align* the drive pulleys.

42. Tighten the engine mount bolts and nuts, then remove the drive pulleys.

43. Complete assembly by reversing the removal procedure and observing the following.

a. Refer to this chapter to install the flywheel and stator plate.

b. Refer to Chapter Three to fill and bleed the cooling system.

c. Be sure that the oil feed hose from the oil tank is attached to the upper fitting (A, **Figure 12**) and the return hose to the oil tank is attached to the lower fitting (B, **Figure 12**).

d. Refer to Chapter Nine to adjust transmission shift linkage.

e. Coat all exhaust connections with high-temperature silicone sealer and make sure all retaining springs are in good condition.

f. Check and adjust engine controls if necessary.

CYLINDER HEAD COVER AND ROCKER ARM ASSEMBLY

Removal/Installation

1. Place the ATV on a level surface and block the wheels to keep it from rolling.

2. Refer to Chapter Fifteen to remove the seat, side covers and fuel tank cover.

3. Shut the fuel off, disconnect the fuel lines, then unbolt and remove the fuel tank (**Figure 5**). Refer to Chapter Six.

4. Disconnect the spark plug high tension lead (**Figure 6**) and remove the spark plug. Removing the spark plug will make it easier to rotate the engine.

5. Remove the screws attaching the cylinder head cover (**Figure 17**), then remove the cover.

6. Turn the engine until the cam sprocket pin (A, **Figure 18**) is straight up as shown. This will set the piston at (or near) top dead center on the compression stroke and all of the valves will be closed.

7. Loosen the rocker shaft retaining screw (B, **Figure 18**).

> *CAUTION*
> *Do not lose the dowel pins when removing the rocker arm assembly.*

8. Remove the 4 screws attaching the rocker arm shaft brackets, then lift the rocker arms and shaft assembly from the engine.

9. Inspect the wear surfaces (**Figure 19**) on the rocker arms and mating surfaces on valves and camshaft.

> *NOTE*
> *The ends of the adjusting screws are hardened and should not be resurfaced.*

10. Separate the brackets, rocker arms and shaft. Inspect the shaft surface and the rocker arm bores for wear or scoring. Recommended shaft diameter

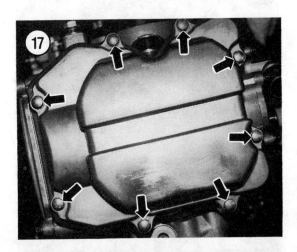

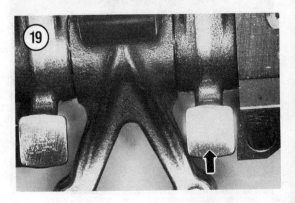

and bore clearance is listed in **Table 4**. Install new shaft and rocker arms if clearance exceeds the wear limit.

11. Coat the cam lobes and cam follower surfaces with molybdenum disulfide grease before installing the rocker arm assembly. Coat the threads of screws with a light film of engine oil.

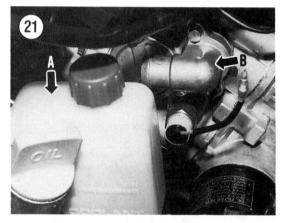

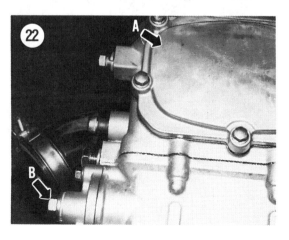

NOTE
If the camshaft has turned from top dead center on the compression stroke, turn the engine until the camshaft sprocket pin (A, Figure 18) is in the position shown.

12. Install the rocker arm assembly, tightening the screws to the torque values listed in **Table 3**.
13. Adjust valve clearance as described in Chapter Three.
14. Clean the gasket surfaces of the cylinder head and cover, then install a new gasket (**Figure 20**) on the cylinder head cover.
15. Install the cylinder head cover and tighten the retaining screws to the torque listed in **Table 3**.
16. Complete assembly by reversing the disassembly procedure.

CAMSHAFT

Removal

1. Place the ATV on a level surface and block the wheels to keep it from rolling.
2. Refer to Chapter Fifteen to remove the seat, side covers and fuel tank cover.
3. Shut the fuel off, disconnect the fuel lines, then unbolt and remove the fuel tank (**Figure 5**). Refer to Chapter Six.
4. Clean the engine and frame thoroughly.
5. Remove the cylinder head cover and rocker arms as outlined in this chapter.
6. Drain the cooling system.
7. Remove the coolant reservoir (A, **Figure 21**).
8. Loosen the hose clamp, then detach the hose from the thermostat housing (B, **Figure 21**).
9. Unbolt and remove the thermostat housing (B, **Figure 21**) and thermostat. Observe the location of the bleed holes in the thermostat and housing. When assembling, bleed holes should be together.
10. Unbolt and remove the camshaft end cap from the left side of the cylinder head.
11. Unbolt and remove the sprocket cover (A, **Figure 22**) from the right side of the cylinder head.

CAUTION
Plug (B, Figure 22) is under spring pressure. Push against the plug while removing to keep it from flying off. In Step 12, the plug only needs to be loos-

*ened, but it must be removed later to set
the tensioner.*

12. Loosen the plug (B, **Figure 22**), then remove the
two screws attaching the tensioner assembly to the
cylinder. Remove the tensioner assembly.

13. Turn the engine until the sprocket drive pin
(**Figure 23**) is at the top. The engine will be at (or
near) top dead center on the compression stroke.

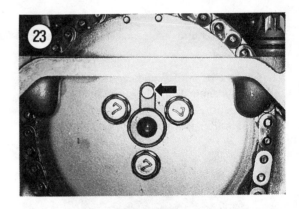

> *NOTE*
> *The flywheel TDC mark will be in the
> center of the timing port of the recoil
> starter housing when the crankshaft is
> at exactly top dead center.*

14. Stuff a clean shop cloth in the cavity below the
cam sprocket, then remove the 3 sprocket retaining
screws. Refer to **Figure 23**.

15. Slide the camshaft in (toward the left), then
remove the sprocket from the dowel pin and camshaft. Hold the chain up and remove the sprocket
from the chain and cylinder head.

16. Secure the cam chain with a wire to keep it from
falling.

17. Remove the camshaft from the left (PTO) side
of engine (**Figure 24**).

Inspection

1. The automatic compression release mechanism,
located in the camshaft, can be inspected as follows,
without removing the camshaft from the engine.

   a. Twist the release mechanism (**Figure 24**) in-
      side the camshaft and observe the smoothness
      of operation. There should be no roughness
      and the spring should return the weight against
      the stop pin.

   b. The actuator ball (**Figure 25**) should be held
      outward when the release mechanism is in the
      compression release position.

   c. Withdraw the release mechanism (**Figure 26**)
      from the camshaft. Inspect the shaft and spring
      for wear or damage.

   d. Inspect the lobe at the end of the release lever
      shaft (**Figure 26**) and the actuator ball for wear
      or damage. The actuator ball is not available
      separately from the camshaft.

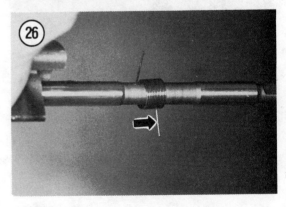

2. Thoroughly clean the camshaft and visually inspect all surfaces of the camshaft for wear or dam-

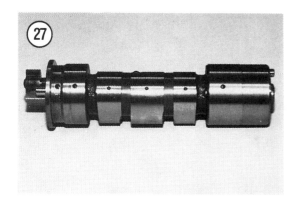

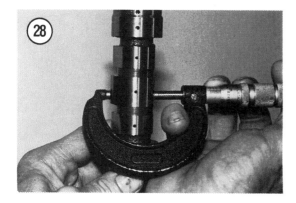

age. Be sure the oil feed holes (**Figure 27**) in the camshaft are open and clean.

3. Measure the height of each cam lobe (**Figure 28**) and compare with the specifications listed in **Table 4**.

4. Measure the diameter of the camshaft journals (**Figure 29**) and compare with the specifications listed in **Table 4**.

5. Calculate the bearing clearance by measuring the inside diameter of the bores in the cylinder head, then subtracting the journal diameters measured in Step 4.

6. Inspect the thrust face of the end cap (**Figure 30**) for wear. If the end cap is damaged, install new cap and carefully inspect the end of the camshaft.

Installation

> *CAUTION*
> *The camshaft must be correctly synchronized to open and close the valves at exactly the right time in relation to the position of the crankshaft. This exact timing is accomplished by installing the chain on the crankshaft and camshaft sprockets with the shafts in specific positions. Very expensive damage could result from improper installation.*

> *NOTE*
> *To install the automatic compression release mechanism (**Figure 26**), the actuator ball (**Figure 25**) must be held out. It may be necessary to use a small magnet to hold the actuator ball out while installing the compression release in the camshaft.*

1. Lubricate the automatic compression release with clean engine oil and install the mechanism with the ends of the spring positioned as shown in **Figure 31**. Check for correct operation before continuing assembly.

2. Coat the camshaft lobes and journals with molybdenum disulfide (or Polaris low temp grease part No. 2870577), then install the camshaft. Rotate the camshaft until the lobes are facing down, toward the cylinder head. The sprocket drive pin (**Figure 23**) will be straight up.

3A. If the alternator stator is not removed, time the camshaft as follows.

a. Check to be sure the flywheel TDC timing mark is aligned with the center of the timing port (**Figure 32**). If necessary, turn the engine crankshaft while guiding the timing chain as required.

b. Carefully remove the wire that was temporarily attached to keep the cam chain from falling and position the sprocket in the chain.

CAUTION
The camshaft must be correctly synchronized to open and close the valves at exactly the right time in relation to the position of the crankshaft. This exact timing is accomplished by installing the chain on the crankshaft and camshaft sprockets with the shafts in specific positions. Very expensive damage could result from improper installation.

c. Attempt to attach the sprocket to the camshaft, without moving the crankshaft or the camshaft. If the cam sprocket cannot be attached to the cam without moving either the camshaft or crankshaft, relocate the sprocket inside the chain.

d. When the cam chain is correctly installed, the flywheel TDC mark will be centered in the timing port hole (**Figure 32**) and the camshaft sprocket drive pin (**Figure 23**) will be straight up as shown. Camshaft sprocket marks (**Figure 33**) will be up as shown.

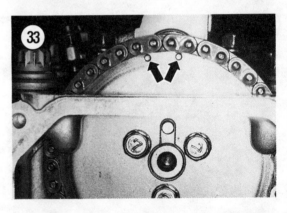

e. When the camshaft timing is correct, remove each of the screws attaching the cam sprocket, one at a time, coat the threads with Loctite 242 (or equivalent) and tighten to the torque listed in **Table 3**. Remove the shop cloth from the cavity below the cam sprocket when installation is complete.

3B. If the alternator stator plate is removed, time the camshaft to the crankshaft as follows.

a. Turn the engine crankshaft until the mark (**Figure 34**) on the crankshaft sprocket is facing down.

b. Use a wire to pull the chain up through the cylinder head.

c. Mesh the timing chain with the crankshaft sprocket so that the single plated link is aligned with the marked tooth as shown in **Figure 34**.

NOTE
Make sure the camshaft drive pin (A, Figure 35) is still facing straight up.

d. Carefully remove the wire that was temporarily attached to the cam chain and position the sprocket in the chain with the 2 marks aligned, with the two plated links (B, **Figure 35**), of the chain.

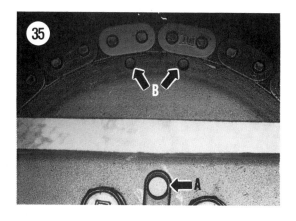

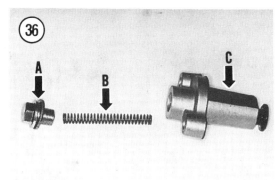

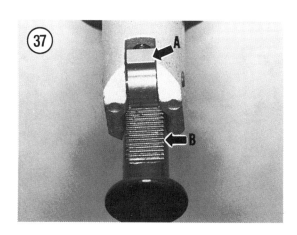

e. Attach the sprocket to the camshaft, without moving the crankshaft or the camshaft. It may be necessary to pry carefully on the bottom of the sprocket to attach the sprocket to the camshaft.

f. When correctly assembled, the crankshaft TDC marks (**Figure 34**) will be aligned and the camshaft sprocket drive pin (A, **Figure 35**) will be facing straight up as shown.

NOTE
Because of the number of links in the cam chain, the plated links will not align with the marked sprocket teeth every revolution. The plated links are only useful when assembling.

g. After the chain and sprockets are correctly installed, remove each of the screws attaching the cam sprocket, one at a time and coat the threads with Loctite 242 (or equivalent) and tighten to the torque listed in **Table 3**.

4. Apply Loctite 525, Loctite 518 Gasket Eliminator or equivalent to the camshaft end cap (**Figure 30**) and install a new O-ring, then install the end cap.

5. Set and install the cam chain tensioner body as follows.

NOTE
Plug (A, Figure 36) is under spring pressure. Push against the plug while removing to keep it from flying off. The plug must be removed to set the tensioner.

a. Remove the plug (A, **Figure 36**) and spring (B, **Figure 36**) from the tensioner body.

b. Lift the ratchet (A, **Figure 37**), then push the plunger (B, **Figure 37**) into the body.

NOTE
Do not install the plug (A, Figure 36) or spring (B, Figure 36) until after the tensioner body is installed.

c. Use a new gasket and install the tensioner body, plunger and ratchet in the cavity of the cylinder. Tighten the two retaining screws to the torque listed in **Table 3**.

d. Install tensioner spring (B, **Figure 36**) and plug (A, **Figure 36**). Tighten the plug to the torque specified in **Table 3**.

NOTE
Timing marks on the crankshaft and camshaft sprockets will align every other revolution of the crankshaft. Also, because of the number of chain links, the plated links sometimes used for timing will probably not be aligned after turning the crankshaft.

6. Rotate the engine crankshaft 2 or more revolutions and recheck alignment of the timing marks (**Figure 33** and **Figure 34**). If installing the chain tensioner changed the timing, remove the tensioner and repeat Steps 3-5.

7. Complete assembly by reversing the removal procedure. Refer to **Table 3** for recommended torque values.

CYLINDER HEAD

Removal

1. Remove the cylinder head cover, rocker arms and the camshaft as described in this chapter.
2. Detach the carburetor and exhaust pipe from the cylinder head. Refer to Chapter Six.
3. Remove the 2 flange head screws (**Figure 38**).
4. Loosen the 4 retaining screws (**Figure 39**) evenly in a crossing pattern, then remove the screws.

NOTE
The cylinder head may stick to the gasket and to the dowel pins in cylinder.

5. Separate the cylinder head from the cylinder and move the cylinder head to a suitable work area.

Disassembly/Inspection/Assembly

1. Remove all traces of gasket material from the cylinder and head mating surfaces.
2. Before removing the valves, remove all carbon deposits from the combustion chamber (**Figure 40**) and valve ports with a wire brush. A blunt screwdriver or similar scraper can be used, but care must be taken not to damage the cylinder head, valves or spark plug threads.
3. After the carbon is removed from the combustion chamber and ports, clean the entire cylinder head with solvent. Blow dry with compressed air.
4. Clean all carbon from the piston crown (**Figure 41**).

5. Check the cylinder head for cracks, erosion, stripped threads or other damage.

6. Place a straightedge across the cylinder head gasket surface and compare with the warpage limit listed in **Table 4**.

7. Inspect the camshaft bearing surfaces in the cylinder head for wear or scoring. Also check the oil delivery port (**Figure 42**) for blockage. Remove the blind plug in front of the oil delivery port to assist in

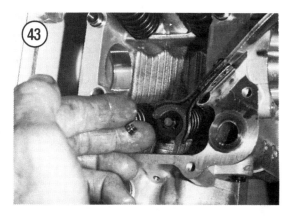

cleaning. Coat the threads of the blind plug (**Figure 3**) with sealer before installing. Refer to **Table 3** for recommended tightening torque for the oil pressure blind plug.

> *CAUTION*
> *The general practice is to take the cylinder head to a machine shop or dealer for inspection and valve service. The following procedure should be done only by properly trained and equipped technicians. Lost or damaged parts may be difficult or impossible to obtain and precision machining may be necessary.*

8. If the cylinder head is to be disassembled, use the following procedure.

> *NOTE*
> *Do not compress the valve spring more than necessary to remove the keepers.*

a. Use a suitable tool to compress the spring on one valve, remove the keepers (**Figure 43**), then release the compressor tool slowly. Repeat the procedure for the other valves.

> *NOTE*
> *Separate and mark the location of each valve and its related components. The front valve and components nearest the chain cavity can be identified as "X-R" (exhaust-right) and the similar components on the left side marked "X-L." The rear valves are inlet valves and can be similarly marked "I-R" for inlet-right and "I-L" for the inlet valves on the left side. Be sure to keep the parts separated and clearly identified, because components for all four valves are similar, but should not be interchanged.*

b. Remove the springs and keep the valve, springs, spring retainer and keepers together. Mark the components so they can be reinstalled in their original location.

> *NOTE*
> *Install new valve stem seals (**Figure 44**) whenever the cylinder head is disassembled. Hard, cracked or worn seals will result in excessive oil consumption, poor performance and carbon buildup.*

c. Measure the free length of the valve springs (**Figure 45**) and compare with the specifications in **Table 4**. The springs should also be square with the ends as shown in **Figure 46**.

> *NOTE*
> *The valves cannot be refaced and the ends of the stems should not be ground. Install a new valve if it is defective in any way.*

d. Inspect the seating surface of the valve for evidence of leakage.

e. Measure the diameter of the valve stem (**Figure 47**) and compare with the specification in **Table 4**.

f. Measure the inside diameter of the valve guide using the proper size hole gauge as shown in **Figure 48**. Use a micrometer to measure the hole gauge as shown in **Figure 49**.

g. Guides should only be removed and replaced by your Polaris dealer or competent machine shop specializing in this type of work. The cylinder head must be heated to 100° C (212° F) before pressing the old guides out. Heat the cylinder head and freeze the new guides before pressing new guides into place. Refer to **Table 4** for correct protrusion. The valve seat must be machined after installing a new guide.

h. Subtract the stem outside diameter (sub-step 8e) from the inside diameter of the guide (sub-step 8f) to determine the stem to guide clearance. Refer to **Table 4** for recommended limits.

i. Inspect the valve seat in the cylinder head for pitting, roughness, uneven surface, or evidence of burning. If the need for machining is questioned, have the head and valves inspected by your Polaris dealer or competent machine shop specializing in this type of work. Machining the valve seat in the cylinder head requires special equipment and training. Do not remove any more material than is necessary and check seating carefully.

j. Assemble new valve stem seals (**Figure 44**) onto the valve guides. The correct seal (part No. 3084857) for the inlet valves is black. The seal (part No. 3084859) for the exhaust valves is *brown*.

k. Lubricate the valve guide and seal with clean engine oil. Coat the valve stem with molybde-

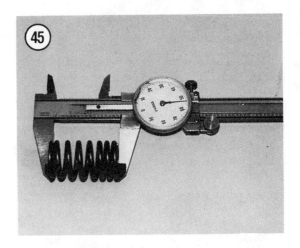

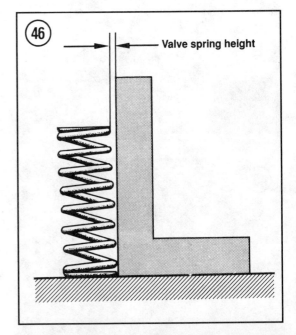

Valve spring height

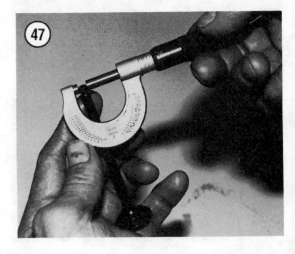

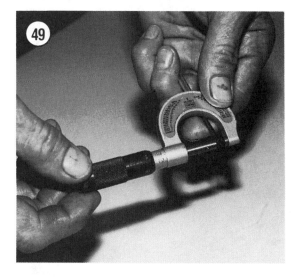

num disulfide grease and insert the valve into the guide and seal using a twisting motion.

l. Dip the valve spring in engine oil and position on the correct valve with the tightly wound coils toward the cylinder head.

m. Place a retainer on the spring and compress the spring just enough to install the split keepers (**Figure 43**). After the keepers are installed, tap the end of the valve stem with a soft faced hammer to seat the keepers.

Installation

1. Position the gasket on the cylinder dowels. The O-ring (**Figure 50**) seals the oil passage leading to the camshaft and valves. The O-ring should be part of the gasket.

2. Position the cylinder head over the dowels in the cylinder and install the six retaining screws finger tight.

> *CAUTION*
> *It is important to tighten the cylinder head*
> *retaining screws as described to provide*
> *a good seal and to prevent damage.*

3. Tighten the 4 larger bolts (**Figure 39**) in a crossing pattern evenly in the following steps:

   a. Tighten to 30 N•m (22 ft.-lb.).

   b. Tighten to 69 N•m (51 ft.-lb.).

   c. Loosen each of the 4 screws exactly 180° (1/2 turn).

   d. Loosen each of the four screws again exactly 180° (1/2 turn).

   e. Tighten to 15 N•m (11 ft.-lb.).

   f. Tighten each of the 4 screws exactly 90° (1/4 turn).

   g. Tighten each of the 4 screws exactly 90° (1/4 turn) more.

4. Tighten the 2 screws (**Figure 38**) to the torque listed in **Table 3**.

5. Install the cylinder head cover and the camshaft as described in this chapter.

6. Install the carburetor and attach the exhaust pipe to the cylinder head. Refer to Chapter Six.

CYLINDER

Removal

1. Remove the cylinder head cover, rocker arms and cylinder head as described in this chapter.

2. Lift the front cam chain guide strip (**Figure 51**) from the chain gallery.

3. Loosen the banjo bolts at the ends of both oil pipes (**Figure 52**). Remove the four banjo bolts, eight sealing washers and two oil pipes.

4. Loosen the clamp, then detach the coolant hose from the cylinder inlet fitting at the front of the cylinder.

5. Remove the 2 screws (**Figure 53**) from the right (cam chain) side of the cylinder.

NOTE
Remove the cylinder head gasket from the cylinder to locate the four cylinder base screws. The screws are located in the cooling passage surrounding the cylinder.

6. Loosen each of the four cylinder base screws 1/4 turn at a time in a crossing pattern. Remove the screws after all four are loose.

NOTE
The piston should slide smoothly in the cylinder bore and only light taps should be required to release the cylinder.

7. Tap the cylinder lightly with a soft hammer to separate the cylinder from the cylinder base gasket and the dowels in the crankcase.

CAUTION
Stuff a shop towel around the connecting rod under the cylinder before the cylinder is completely removed to prevent any loose parts from falling into the crankcase. The shop towel will also keep the connecting rod and piston from falling when the cylinder is removed.

8. Lift the cylinder from the piston and crankcase as shown in **Figure 54**. Notice that dowel pins are loose and may fall free when removing the cylinder.

9. Remove the cylinder base gasket and discard it.

10. Soak any remaining gasket material with solvent, then scrape it from the cylinder base and crankcase. Be careful not to gouge the sealing surfaces.

11. Install a piston holding fixture under the piston to protect the piston skirt from damage. This fixture may be purchased or fabricated from wood. See **Figure 55** for dimensions.

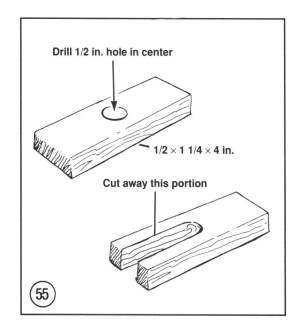

Drill 1/2 in. hole in center

1/2 × 1 1/4 × 4 in.

Cut away this portion

(55)

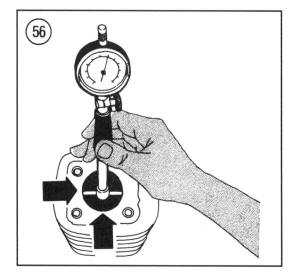

(56)

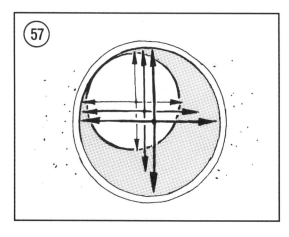

(57)

Inspection

The following procedure requires the use of highly specialized and expensive measuring instruments. If such equipment is not available, have the measurements performed by a dealer or qualified machine shop.

1. Measure the cylinder bore with a cylinder bore gauge (**Figure 56**), or inside micrometer at the points shown in **Figure 57**. Measure in line with the piston pin and at 90° to the pin. If the taper or out-of-round exceeds the limits in **Table 4**, the cylinder must be rebored to the next oversize and fitted with a new piston, or a new standard size cylinder should be installed.

NOTE
Purchase the new piston before the cylinder is rebored so the piston can be measured by the machinist before any changes are made. Slight manufacturing tolerances must be taken into account to determine the actual cylinder bore diameter and the final piston-to-bore clearance.

2. Check the cylinder bore for scratches or other obvious damage. It may be possible to repair a damaged cylinder by reboring, but if you have any question, have the part inspected by your Polaris dealer or machine shop specializing in this type of repair.

Installation

1. Check to be sure that all of the old gasket has been removed from the top surface of the crankcase and the bottom surface of the cylinder.
2. Make sure the cylinder, piston, crankcase and work area are clean and undamaged.
3. Be sure that all of the dowel pins are in place in the crankcase, then install a new cylinder base gasket over the dowel pins.
4. Lubricate the cylinder bore, piston and rings with engine oil.
5. Make sure the top rail of the oil ring is correctly positioned in the notch as shown in **Figure 58**. The gaps in the remaining rings should be spaced around the piston.

NOTE
The ring compressor must be the correct size and must be a type that is removable

from the bottom of the piston around the connecting rod.

6. Compress the rings into the grooves of the piston using a suitable ring compressing tool. Refer to **Figure 59**.

> *NOTE*
> *If the cam chain is still installed, carefully pull it up through the cylinder as the cylinder is lowered into position.*

7. Slide the cylinder over the piston and compressed rings, then remove the ring compressor and lower support tools. Then lower the cylinder against the gasket on the crankcase and over the dowel pins. Refer to **Figure 59**.

8. Install the cylinder retaining screws and tighten to the torque specified in **Table 3**. Tighten the 4 larger screws, located in the coolant passage, in a crossing pattern, before tightening the 2 smaller screws (**Figure 53**).

9. Install the front cam chain slipper (**Figure 60**). Make sure the lower end engages the notch (**Figure 61**) at the lower end correctly.

10. Install the cylinder head, camshaft, rocker arms and cylinder cover as outlined in this chapter.

11. Adjust the valve clearance as described in Chapter Three.

PISTON, PISTON PIN AND PISTON RINGS

The piston is made of an aluminum alloy. The piston pin is made of steel and is a precision fit in the piston. The piston pin is held in place by a clip at each end of the bore in the piston.

Piston Removal

1. Remove the cylinder head cover, cylinder head and cylinder as described in this chapter.

2. Before removing the piston, hold the rod tightly and rock the piston to detect excessive clearance between the piston, piston pin and connecting rod. Do not confuse the normal sliding motion of the piston on the pin with rocking motion. Any perceptible rocking motion indicates wear on the piston pin, piston, connecting rod small end bearing or the connecting rod small end. Any excessive wear is

probably a combination of the wear of all of these parts.

> *NOTE*
> *Do not reuse the piston pin retaining clips. The clips are damaged during removal and severe engine damage will result if a clip becomes loose while the engine is running.*

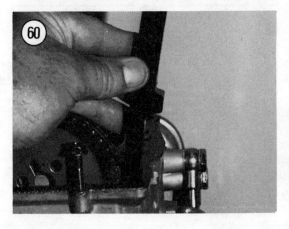

3. Remove the clips from each side of the piston pin bore (**Figure 62**). Be careful to prevent the clip from springing out.

4. Use a proper size wooden dowel or suitable tool (**Figure 63**) to push the piston pin from the bore in the piston.

CAUTION
Be careful when removing the piston pin to avoid damaging the connecting rod. The piston should be supported to

either push or pull the pin from the pin bore. Be sure that lateral loads are not transmitted to the lower connecting rod bearing.

5. Lift the piston from the connecting rod.

NOTE
If the piston is to be left off for some time, protect the connecting rod by placing a piece of foam insulation tube over its end. Stuff a clean, lint free shop towel around the connecting rod to keep dirt from entering the crankcase.

WARNING
The edges of all piston rings are very sharp. Be very careful when handling them to avoid cutting your fingers.

6. Remove the top ring with a ring expander tool or by spreading the ends with your thumbs just enough to slide the ring up over the top of the piston. Repeat the procedure for the remaining rings.

Inspection

1. Carefully clean the carbon from piston crown with a scraper. Do not damage the piston. Notice the arrow cast into the piston crown.

CAUTION
Do not use a wire brush to clean the piston skirt. Also, do not gouge the piston while attempting to clean it. The soft aluminum of the piston is easily damaged by improper cleaning techniques.

2. Examine each ring groove in the piston for burrs, dented edges, carbon deposits or other conditions that reduce the width of the groove.

NOTE
The groove for the top compression ring usually wears more than the other grooves, but all should be carefully inspected.

3. Examine each ring groove for gouges, bent lands or other conditions that increase the width of the groove.

4. Measure the *Piston Clearance* as described in this chapter.

5. Measure the diameter of the pin bore in the piston (**Figure 64**) and the piston pin diameter (**Figure 65**).

6. Subtract the diameter of the piston pin from the diameter of the pin bore in the piston to find the pin-to-pin bore clearance.

7. Refer to the specifications listed in **Table 4** and replace parts as required.

8. If damage or wear indicates that the piston should be replaced, select a new piston as described in *Piston Clearance* in this chapter.

9. Inspect and install new piston rings as described in *Piston Ring Removal/Inspection/Installation* in this chapter.

Piston Clearance

1. Measure the piston outside diameter at a point 5 mm (0.20 in.) from the bottom of the piston skirt. Refer to **Figure 66**.

2. Measure the diameter of the cylinder bore with a cylinder bore gauge (**Figure 56**) or inside micrometer at the points shown in **Figure 57**. Measure in line with the piston pin and at 90° to the pin. If the taper or out-of-round exceeds the limits in **Table 4**, the cylinder must be rebored to the next oversize and fitted with a new piston, or a new standard size cylinder installed.

3. Subtract the diameter of the piston skirt from the maximum diameter of the cylinder bore to determine the piston skirt-to-cylinder clearance.

4. The piston skirt-to-cylinder clearance should not exceed the limits listed in **Table 4**. It may be possible to repair a damaged cylinder by reboring, but if you have any question, have the parts inspected by your Polaris dealer or machine shop specializing in this type of repair.

NOTE
Purchase the new piston before the cylinder is rebored so the piston can be measured, by the machinist, before any changes are made. Slight manufacturing tolerances must be taken into account to determine the actual cylinder bore diameter and piston-to-bore clearance.

Piston Installation

1. Coat the piston pin, pin bore and connecting rod small end bore in with clean engine oil.

CAUTION
Do not reuse old clips to retain the piston pin in the piston. The clips are deformed during removal and severe engine damage can result if the clips become loose while the engine is running. Always install new clips if the piston is removed.

2. Install a new retaining clip in one end of the piston pin bore. Position the tang on the retaining

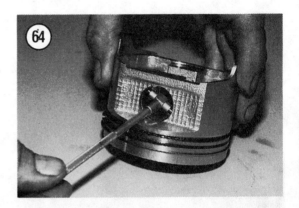

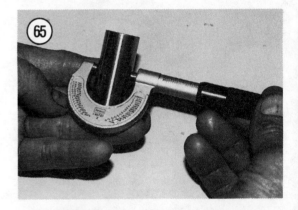

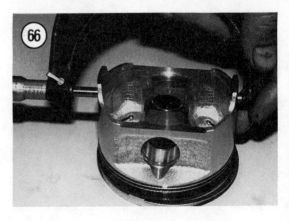

ring outward as shown in **Figure 67**, either toward the top or bottom of the piston.

3. Press the piston pin through the bore in the piston, which does not have the retaining clip, until it extends slightly beyond the inside of the pin boss.

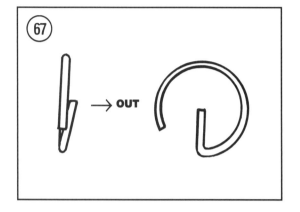

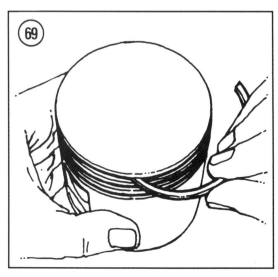

4. Place the piston over the connecting rod with the arrow (**Figure 68**) on the piston crown pointing toward the magneto (right) side of the engine.

5. Align the piston pin with the hole in the connecting rod, then push the pin through the connecting rod. Continue pushing the pin until it just contacts the previously installed retaining clip.

NOTE
The pin should be a smooth fit in the bore when the pin and the bores are lubricated and at 20° C (68° F). However, if the pin is too tight, cool the pin and warm the piston slightly. Be careful not to transmit lateral shock to the connecting rod or otherwise damage parts by carelessly pounding on the side of the piston.

6. Install a new retaining clip in the piston pin bore, with the tang projecting outward as shown in **Figure 67**. Position the tang either toward the top or bottom of the piston.

7. Check installation by rocking the piston back and forth around the pin axis, then sliding the piston from side to side. It should rotate freely without perceptible play.

8. Install the piston rings as described in this chapter.

9. Install the cylinder, cylinder head, camshaft, rocker arms and cylinder head cover as outlined in this chapter.

Piston Ring Removal/Inspection/Installation

WARNING
The edges of all piston rings are very sharp. Be very careful when handling them to avoid cutting your fingers.

1. Remove the top ring with a ring expander tool or by spreading the ends with your thumbs just enough to slide the ring up over the top of the piston. Repeat the procedure for the remaining rings.

2. Clean the carbon from the ring grooves in the piston with a broken ring or suitable tool. Refer to **Figure 69**. Be careful not to cut your hand on the ring used as a cleaning tool or damage the piston.

CAUTION
Do not use a wire brush to clean the piston skirt. Also, do not gouge the pis-

ton while attempting to clean it. The soft aluminum of the piston is easily damaged by improper cleaning techniques.

3. Examine each ring groove in the piston for burrs, dented edges, carbon deposits or other conditions that reduce the width of the groove.

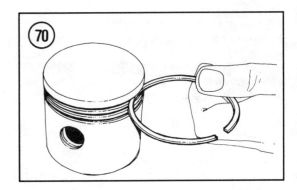

NOTE
The groove for the top compression ring usually wears more than the other grooves, but all should be carefully inspected.

4. Examine each ring groove for gouges, bent groove lands or other conditions that increase the width of the groove.

5. Roll each ring around its groove as shown in **Figure 70** to check for binding. Clean or replace the piston as necessary.

6. Measure the end gap of each ring in the cylinder bore, before installing the ring on the piston as follows.

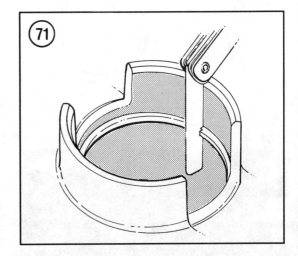

   a. Insert one ring into the cylinder. Make sure the ring is square in the cylinder by using the top of the piston to slide the ring up or down in the cylinder.

   b. Use a feeler gauge to measure the gap between the ends of the ring as shown in **Figure 71**.

   c. Check the end gap at several locations in the cylinder and always make sure the ring is positioned squarely in the cylinder. If the gap is too wide, the rings will not seal properly. If the gap is too small, the rings may bind and break when the engine is run.

   d. If the gap is too wide, the cylinder bore is worn, the rings are worn or the ring is not correct for the application.

   e. If the gap is less than the minimum specified, first make sure the correct ring is being used. The end gap can be enlarged by carefully filing the ends of the ring as shown in **Figure 72**. Use a fine cut file and be extremely careful when filing the ends of a ring.

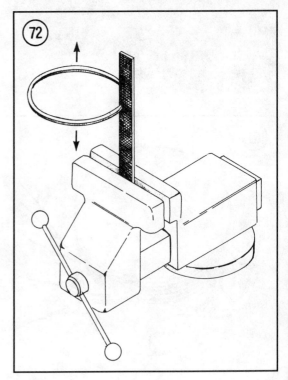

7. Measure the side clearance of the top and second piston rings in their grooves as shown in **Figure 73**. Always make sure the grooves are clean before measuring. Compare the measured side clearance with the specifications listed in **Table 4**. If the clearance of new rings in the piston grooves is greater than the wear limit, a new piston should be installed.

8. Make sure the piston is absolutely clean, then coat the rings and ring grooves with engine oil before installing the rings.

NOTE
The arrow on the piston faces toward the right (magneto) side of the engine.

9. Install the oil ring expander in the bottom groove with its ends toward the front of the piston. Make sure the ends do not overlap.

10. Install the top rail of the oil control ring over the expander installed in step 8. The tab of the top rail must engage the notch shown in **Figure 74**.

11. Install the bottom rail of the oil control ring over the expander with the gap at least 30° from the previously installed top rail.

12. Install the second ring with the "R" mark on its side toward the top (crown) of the piston. The second ring has a groove cut into the bottom outside diameter of the ring.

13. Install the top ring with the "R" mark on its side toward the top (crown) of the piston. The top ring is chrome plated and the inside diameter is chamfered at the top.

14. Position the second compression ring end gap toward the rear (inlet side) of the cylinder. Position the top ring with its end gap toward the front (exhaust) side of the engine.

CAUTION
Be extremely careful not to damage the assembled piston or rings. It is suggested that the piston and cylinder be installed as soon as possible after installing the rings in the piston grooves.

15. Follow the *Break-in Procedure* in this chapter if the cylinder was rebored, a new piston was installed or if new piston rings were fitted.

CAM CHAIN, SPROCKETS AND TENSIONER

The camshaft is driven by a chain located in a cavity in the right side of the engine. The chain is one piece, does not have a master link and should not be split. Removal of the cam chain and sprockets is usually part of a more complete disassembly and overhaul.

1. Refer to instructions in this chapter to remove the *Cylinder Head Cover and Rocker Arm Assembly*.

2. Clean the engine and frame thoroughly.

3. Unbolt and remove the sprocket cover (A, **Figure 75**) from the right side of the cylinder head.

CAUTION
*Plug (B, **Figure 75**) is under spring pressure. Push against the plug while removing to keep it from flying off. In Step 5, the plug only needs to be loosened, but it must be removed later to set the tensioner.*

4. Loosen the plug (B, **Figure 75**), then remove the two screws attaching the tensioner assembly to the cylinder. Remove the tensioner assembly.

5. Refer to this chapter and remove the recoil starter assembly.

6. Refer to this chapter and remove the flywheel and the alternator stator plate.

7. Turn the engine until the sprocket drive pin (**Figure 76**) is at the top. The engine will be at (or near) top dead center on the compression stroke.

8. Remove the three screws attaching the camshaft sprocket to the camshaft. Refer to **Figure 76**.

9. Slide the camshaft in (toward the left), then remove the sprocket from the dowel pin and camshaft. Hold the chain up and remove the sprocket from the chain and cylinder head.

10. Attach a wire to the cam chain, then lower the chain (A, **Figure 77**) while removing it from around the crankshaft.

11. If still in place, remove the nut and washer (B, **Figure 77**) from the end of the crankshaft.

12. Slide the cam drive sprocket from the crankshaft after removing the slotted nut (B, **Figure 77**). The nut has left-hand threads and is loosened by turning clockwise.

13. Inspect the chain and sprockets as follows:
   a. Stretch the chain on a flat surface (like a table), exerting approximately 4.53 kg (10 lb) force.
   b. Measure the length of a 20 pitch section of the chain.
   c. If the length of 20 rollers is more than 13.7 cm (5.394 in.), install a new chain.
   d. Check the sprocket teeth for wear or other damage. A damaged sprocket can quickly damage a new chain.
   e. Check the Woodruff key and slot in the lower (drive) sprocket for wear or damage.

14. Remove the screw (**Figure 78**) and lift out the rear tensioner slider. Inspect the tensioner slider for wear or damage. If the condition of the front slider is questioned, remove the cylinder head and remove the rear slider.

15. Install the tensioner slider and tighten the lower retaining screw to the torque listed in **Table 3**.

16. Install the Woodruff key for the lower sprocket, then install the lower sprocket with the marked tooth towards the outside.

17. Install the slotted nut (B, **Figure 77**) that retains the cam drive sprocket and tighten it to the torque listed in **Table 3**.

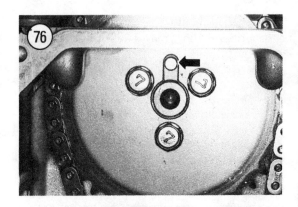

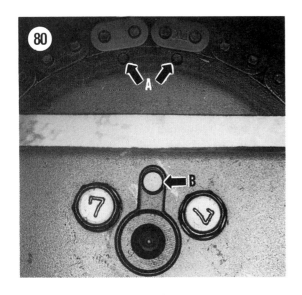

18. Make sure the marked tooth of the drive sprocket is facing the bottom after the nut is tightened.

19. Install the camshaft drive chain around the lower sprocket and use a wire to pull the chain up inside the chain cavity. The plated links of the chain should be toward the outside and the longer chain section between the plated links should be toward the rear of the engine.

20. Align the single plated link with the marked tooth of the lower (drive) sprocket and align the marked tooth with the crankcase mark as shown in **Figure 79**.

21. Locate the camshaft (driven) sprocket inside the chain near the camshaft. Align the two marked teeth on the sprocket with the two plated links as shown at A, **Figure 80**.

NOTE
If the plated links are not at the top of the chain, make sure the chain is straight and that the longer section of chain (between the plated links) is toward the rear of the engine.

22. Align the pin (B, **Figure 80**) in the camshaft with the hole in the sprocket and install the 3 screws attaching the sprocket. Tighten the screws to the torque listed in **Table 3**.

23. Set and install the cam chain tensioner body as follows.

NOTE
Plug (A, Figure 81) is under spring pressure. Push against the plug while removing to keep it from flying off. The plug must be removed to set the tensioner.

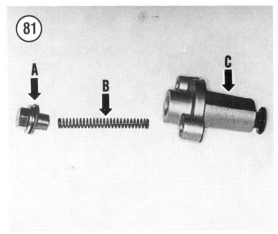

a. Remove the plug (A, **Figure 81**) and spring (B) from the tensioner body (C).

b. Lift the ratchet (A, **Figure 82**), then push the plunger (B, **Figure 82**) into the body.

NOTE
Do not reinstall the plug (A, Figure 81) or spring (B, Figure 81) until after the tensioner body is installed.

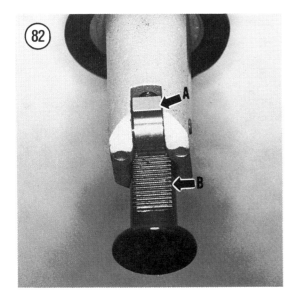

c. Install the tensioner body using a new gasket. Tighten the two retaining screws to the torque listed in **Table 3**.

d. Install tensioner spring (B, **Figure 81**) and plug (A, **Figure 81**). Tighten the plug to the torque specified in **Table 3**.

NOTE
Timing marks on the crankshaft and camshaft sprockets will align every other revolution of the crankshaft, but because of the number of chain links, the plated links previously used for timing will probably not be aligned after turning the crankshaft.

24. Rotate the engine crankshaft 2 or more revolutions and recheck alignment of the timing marks. The marked tooth on the lower drive sprocket should be aligned with the mark on the crankcase as shown in **Figure 79**. In addition, the two marked teeth and the alignment dowel on the cam (driven) sprocket should be at the top as shown in **Figure 80**. If installing the chain tensioner changed the timing, remove the tensioner, then repeat Steps 20-23.

25. Complete assembly by reversing the disassembly procedure. Refer to **Table 3** for recommended torque values.

RECOIL STARTER

Removal/Installation

1. Place the ATV on a level surface and block the wheels to keep it from rolling.
2. Remove the screws attaching the recoil starter, then remove the starter and gasket.

NOTE
The electric starter reduction drive assembly should remain with the engine. One end of the reduction drive assembly pilots in the rewind starter housing.

3. Install the recoil starter assembly and tighten the retaining screws to the torque listed in **Table 3**.

Disassembly and Starter Rope Removal

1. If the rope is not broken, pull it from the housing and tie a loose knot to keep the rope from rewinding.
2. Remove the anchor from the starter handle and remove the handle from the end of the rope.
3. Hold the rope, untie the previously tied knot, then allow the rope to wind slowly into the housing.

4. Remove the center screw (**Figure 83**).
5. Remove the friction plate (A, **Figure 84**), ratchet pawl (B) and spring (C).

CAUTION
The recoil spring is under pressure and may jump from the housing during disassembly. Its edges are sharp and may cut or cause eye injury. Wear safety glasses or a face shield and gloves when disassembling and assembling.

6. Carefully lift the starter pulley and rope from the housing. Make sure the recoil spring remains in the starter housing.
7. Unwind and remove the rope from the starter pulley if replacement is required.
8. To remove the recoil spring, invert the starter housing and tap it on a solid surface. The spring will fall free and unwind inside the starter housing.

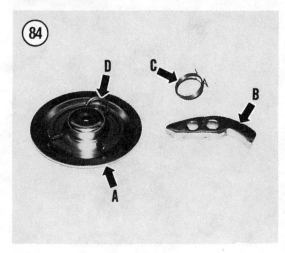

Inspection and Assembly

1. Clean all parts and dry thoroughly.

2. Inspect the friction plate (A, **Figure 84**), friction spring (D), ratchet pawl (B) and pawl spring (C) for damage. Friction spring should grip the friction plate securely.

3. Check the rope for fraying or other damage. It is usually a good practice to replace a rope with even slight damage, before it breaks.

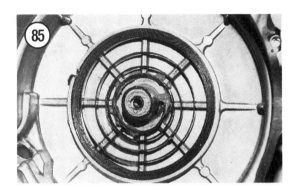

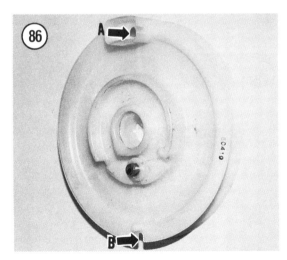

4. Inspect the tabs at the ends of the recoil spring.

5A. Reinstall the old recoil spring as follows:

   a. Hook the outer end of the recoil spring in the housing.

   b. Wind the spring into the housing in a counterclockwise direction until the spring is completely in the housing. Hold the coils in place while winding the spring into the hosing.

   c. The installed spring should be positioned as shown in **Figure 85**.

5B. New recoil springs are held compressed by a wire. Use the following instructions to install the new spring.

   a. Position the new spring in the housing so that it spirals inward in a counterclockwise direction and attach the outer end of the spring to the housing.

   b. Hold the spring in place and cut the retaining wire. The installed spring should be positioned as shown in **Figure 85**.

6. Lubricate the spring with a light, low-temperature lubricant such as Polaris Cable Lube (part No. 2870510).

7. If the rope is detached from the pulley, attach the rope as follows:

   a. Tie a secure knot at one end of the rope and insert the other end through the hole (A, **Figure 86**).

   b. Pull the rope through the pulley until the knot is firmly seated in the pocket of the pulley.

   c. Wind the rope into the pulley groove counterclockwise (as viewed from the side shown in **Figure 86**). The rope should be wound fairly tightly into the groove.

   d. When the rope is almost completely wound into the pulley, pull the end up through the notch (B, **Figure 86**). The end of the rope should lock into the notch.

8. Apply a small amount of Polaris low-temperature grease (or equivalent) to the center post in the starter housing and to the bushing in the center of the starter pulley.

9. Install the starter pulley over the center post making sure the inner end of the recoil spring engages the tab at the center of the pulley. Refer to **Figure 87**. Make sure the pulley is fully seated (down) in the housing.

10. Preload the recoil spring as follows:

   a. Hold the pulley down in the housing.

b. Grasp the end of the rope that extends from the notch (B, **Figure 86**) in the pulley and wind the pulley counterclockwise 4 turns.

c. Hold the pulley to prevent the spring from pulling the rope back into the housing.

d. Route the end of the rope out through the housing, while continuing to hold the pulley.

e. When the rope exits the housing, pull enough rope out to tie a large knot in the rope to keep it from winding into the housing.

11. Install the pawl spring (**Figure 88**).

12. Install the pawl as shown in **Figure 89**. The pawl spring is located at arrow.

13. Install the friction plate and spring (**Figure 90**) with each end of the spring located on the drive side of the ratchet.

14. Install the spring washer and center screw (**Figure 83**). Tighten the screw to the torque listed in **Table 3**.

15. Attach the handle to the starter rope and check operation of the recoil starter. If the rope is the correct length, but the recoil spring does not hold the handle against the housing, refer to Step 10 and preload the spring an additional turn. If the rope is too long, the coils of the rope may extend outside the pulley groove and bind against the housing.

FLYWHEEL AND STATOR PLATE

Removal/Installation

Before removing the flywheel and stator plate, clean the engine, frame and work area thoroughly. If water is used, be sure blow or wipe the engine dry before beginning removal.

1. Place the ATV on a level surface and block the wheels to keep it from rolling.

2. Disconnect the ground wire from the negative terminal of the battery.

3. Refer to Chapter Three to drain oil from the engine and the reservoir.

4. Detach the spark plug high tension lead from the spark plug.

5. Remove the recoil starter as described in this chapter.

> *CAUTION*
> *Do not thread puller attaching bolts into the flywheel more than 6 mm (1/4 in.), or the stator coils may be damaged.*

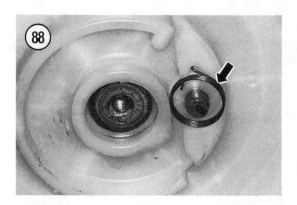

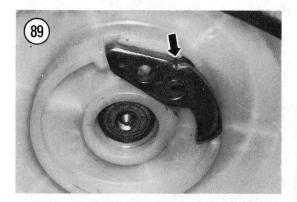

6. Remove the flywheel nut and washer then use a suitable puller (**Figure 91**) to remove the engine flywheel.

NOTE
Do not lose the thrust washer located between the starter drive and the crankcase.

7. Remove the electric starter drive (**Figure 92**).
8. Mark the position of the stator plate on the crankcase (A, **Figure 93**), so the stator can be reinstalled at the same ignition timing position.

CAUTION
Use care to prevent damage to seals, crankshaft, stator plate, armature wires or other parts when removing the stator plate and stator assembly.

9. Remove the stator retaining screws (B, **Figure 93**), then remove the stator plate and stator assembly.
10. Remove the sealing ring (**Figure 94**).
11. Check the bearing and seal surfaces for scratches or burrs.
12. Apply a light coating of grease to the crankshaft and the seal (A, **Figure 95**) located in the stator plate.
13. Coat the bushing (B, **Figure 95**) in the stator plate with molybdenum disulfide grease or assembly lube.
14. Install a new O-ring (**Figure 94**) in the recess of the engine crankcase.
15. Apply Loctite 515, Loctite 518 or equivalent sealer to the outer diameter of the stator and position a new O-ring on the stator plate. Refer to **Figure 96**.
16. Install the stator plate, making sure the previously affixed timing marks are aligned. Be sure the

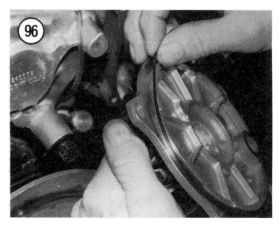

stator is fully seated and tighten the retaining screws to the torque listed in **Table 3**.

17. Seal the stator wire grommet (A, **Figure 97**) with an appropriate sealer.

18. Be sure the thrust washer is located on the back of the starter reduction gear (B, **Figure 97**). Apply a coating of grease to the bushing, then install the gear.

19. Make sure the Woodruff key is in place, then install the flywheel. Tighten the flywheel retaining nut to the torque recommended in **Table 3**.

20. Install the recoil starter and tighten the retaining screws.

COOLANT PUMP

The engine must be removed from the frame and the crankcase must be separated before the coolant pump shaft and seals can be serviced. However, the outer cover and impeller can be removed for inspection without removing the engine.

Remove the oil pump as described in this chapter to service the shaft oil seal and the coolant pump mechanical seal. The coolant pump shaft is an extension of the oil pump drive shaft.

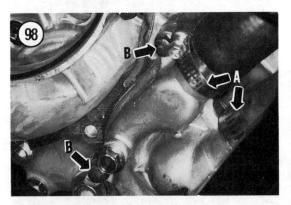

Removal/Installation

1. Drain the cooling system as described in Chapter Three.

2. Loosen the clamps (A, **Figure 98**) attaching the coolant hoses, then detach the hoses from the cover.

3. Remove the 4 screws (B, **Figure 98**) attaching the coolant pump cover.

4. Bump the cover to loosen the gasket, then remove the cover.

5. Remove the nut (**Figure 99**) and pull the impeller from the shaft.

6. If the seals (**Figure 100**) are leaking, remove the engine and separate the engine crankcase as described in this chapter.

7. Clean all old gasket material from the back of the coolant pump cover (**Figure 101**) and the mating surface of the crankcase.

8. Install the impeller and tighten the retaining nut to the torque listed in **Table 3**.

9. Install the pump cover using a new gasket. Tighten the retaining screws in a crossing pattern to the torque listed in **Table 3**.

10. Attach the coolant hoses. Fill the cooling system with a mixture of antifreeze and water as described in Chapter Three.

CRANKCASE

Disassembly

The crankcase contains the crankshaft, the balance shaft and the oil pump assembly. The crankshaft is made of several pieces pressed together and

includes the connecting rod. Service to these components is often better performed by properly trained technicians. Use extreme caution whenever you separate and rejoin the crankcase. The importance of absolute cleanliness during internal engine service cannot be over emphasized.

Crankcase Separation

1. Remove the engine as described in this chapter.
2. Remove the cylinder head and cylinder as described in this chapter.
3. Remove the camshaft drive (lower) sprocket from the engine crankshaft as outlined in this chapter.
4. Remove the coolant pump cover and impeller as described in this chapter.
5. Remove the ten screws attaching the crankcase halves together.
6. Remove the flywheel key from the crankshaft.

NOTE
The crankcase separation tool is much like a puller that is attached to one side of the crankcase with the puller screw placed at the center of the crankshaft. The tool pushes the crankshaft out of the right side main bearing without damaging the crankshaft. Pounding on the end of the crankshaft can knock the crankshaft out of alignment as well as damage the threaded end.

7. Attach a crankcase separation tool to the magneto side of the crankcase.
8. Bump the end of the coolant pump shaft while tightening the center screw of the crankcase separation tool. Be prepared to catch the crankcase halves when the bearings become free of the shafts. Refer to **Figure 102** for PTO side crankcase half and related components.
9. Remove the thrust washer from the pump shaft (A, **Figure 102**), then lift the drive gear from the shaft.
10. Remove the screws (**Figure 103**) attaching the oil pump to the crankcase, then remove the oil pump.

CAUTION
The balance shaft may be equipped with shim washers. Be careful not to loose or damage these washers.

11. Lift the balance shaft (B, **Figure 102**) from its bearing in the case.

CAUTION
*Be careful to support the case and press only on the center of the crankshaft (C, **Figure 102**). Do not drop the crankshaft when it releases from the bearing.*

12. Press the crankshaft from the left crankcase half using the crankcase separation tool.
13. Refer to the appropriate sections in this chapter for inspection and service to the crankshaft, oil pump and crankcase bearings.

Assembly

1. The crankshaft bearings are damaged while separating the case halves. New bearings must be installed during reassembly.
2. Always install new seals before assembling the crankcase.
3. Lubricate the bearings and seals located in the crankcase halves.
4. Select the correct thickness of shims for the crankshaft and balance shaft. Refer to *Crankshaft, Balance Shaft, Bearings and Seals* section in this chapter for determining the correct thickness of shims to install.

CAUTION
Always use the special crankshaft installation tool (part No. 2871283) when assembling the crankcase. The crankshaft may be damaged while assembling the crankcase halves, if the special crankshaft installation tool is not used. Thread the installation tool into the left (PTO) end of the crankshaft at least 25.4 mm (1 in.) to be sure the threads are not damaged during assembly.

5. Use crankshaft installation tool (part No. 2871283) to pull the crankshaft through the left (PTO) side main bearing.
6. Install the balance shaft with the marked tooth of the balance gear aligned with the marked valley as shown in **Figure 104**. Make sure the balance shaft is fully seated in the bearing.
7. Apply a light film of oil to the oil pump mounting surface and install the oil pump. Refer to **Table 3** for the recommended torque for the pump mounting screws (**Figure 103**).

8. Align the drive pin with the hole in the drive gear and install the oil pump drive gear (**Figure 103**).
9. Position the correct thickness of shims on the pump shaft, crankshaft and balance shaft. Refer to *Crankshaft, Balance Shaft, Bearings and Seals* section in this chapter for determining the correct thickness of shims to install.
10. Apply Loctite 515, Loctite 518 (or equivalent) to the mating surface of the crankcase halves.
11. Make sure the alignment dowels are in place.
12. Set the right (magneto) side of the crankcase over the crankshaft and coolant pump shaft. Be careful not to damage the shaft seals.
13. Use the crankshaft installation tool (part No. 2871283) to pull the crankshaft through the right (magneto) side main bearing. Tap the case around the pump to make sure that the case is installed straight. Make sure the case is fully seated before installing the retaining screws. Do not attempt to pull the case halves together with the retaining screws.
14. Install the ten screws retaining the case halves together. Tighten the screws in several steps using a crossing pattern. Gradually increase the torque to the value listed in **Table 3**.
15. Install the oil/coolant pump shaft mechanical seal from the outside as follows:
    a. Make sure the seal bore is clean.
    b. Position the new seal in the seal drive collar and install them over the shaft.
    c. Screw the guide onto the end of the pump shaft.
    d. Install the washer and nut. Tighten the nut to push the seal into place until fully seated.
    e. Remove the guide adapter.

16. The remainder of the assembly is the reverse of the separation procedure.

CRANKSHAFT, BALANCE SHAFT, BEARINGS AND SEALS

Inspection/Installation/Adjustment

CAUTION
The crankshaft bearings are damaged while separating the crankcase halves. Install new bearings when assembling. If the old bearings must reused, inspect the bearings very carefully and do not remove them from their bores.

1. Use suitable pullers to remove the bearings and seals from the crankcase halves. Note the original direction of the shaft seals. The oil/coolant pump shaft mechanical seal should be removed by driving it out toward the outside.

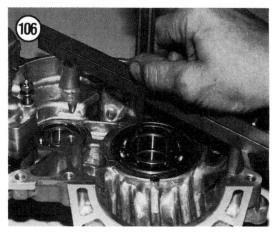

NOTE
Install the new mechanical seal from the outside after the crankcase is assembled.

2. Clean the crankcase halves, both inside and out with a suitable solvent and dry thoroughly. Be sure to remove all traces of old gasket material and sealer from mating surfaces.

3. Inspect the crankcase halves carefully for cracks, fractures or other damage. Inspect the bearing bores for damage and be sure that all oil passages are absolutely clean.

4. Install new bearings in the crankcase with the manufacturer's numbers visible. Press bearings into their bores using drivers that are the correct size to press only on the outside race. The outer diameter of the various bearings are:

    a. Crankshaft main bearings, 70 mm (2.755 in.).

    b. Balance shaft, 46 mm (1.810 in.).

    c. Oil/cooling pump shaft, 28 mm (1.100 in.).

5. Check the condition of the connecting rod bearing. It is difficult to clean this bearing and its condition is usually determined by turning the connecting rod and noting any roughness or noise. Additional tests are as follows:

    a. Measure connecting rod side play with a feeler gauge as shown in **Figure 105**. Compare the side play with the specification listed in **Table 4**.

    b. Measure connecting rod radial play with a dial indicator and compare with the recommended limit listed in **Table 4**.

    c. Mount the crankshaft in a truing stand or in V-blocks and measure the runout at the shaft ends. Compare the runout with the recommended limit listed in **Table 4**.

6. If the crankshaft and connecting rod assembly is damaged, take it to a Polaris dealer for further evaluation.

7. Determine the correct shim thickness necessary to establish the correct crankshaft, balance shaft and oil pump end play inside the crankcase. The first step is to accurately measure the distance between the inner races of the bearings.

8. Make certain the crankshaft and balance shaft bearings are fully seated in both crankcase halves. Also, make certain the oil pump shaft bearing is fully seated in the magneto side crankcase half.

9. Position a straightedge across the PTO side crankcase half as shown in **Figure 106**.

10. Using a dial-type vernier caliper or depth gauge, *carefully* measure the diatance from the top of the straightedge to the PTO side crankshaft bearing. See **Figure 106**.

11. Next, measure the thickness of the straightedge as shown in **Figure 107**. Subtract the thickness of the straightedge from the measurement taken in Step 10. The remainder is the distance from the mating surface of the PTO side crankcase half to the crankshaft bearing. Record this measurement.

12. Repeat Steps 9-11 to measure the magneto side crankcase half. Do not forget to subtract the thickness of the straightedge from the measurement.

13. Then, add the magneto side and the PTO side measurements together to obtain the total distance between the crankshaft bearings.

14. Measure the width of the crankshaft at the bearing seats as shown in **Figure 108**. Record the measurement.

15. Subtract the width of the crankshaft (Step 14) from the total distance determined in Step 13. This value, minus the preferred crankshaft end play specification (**Table 4**), is the shim thickness necessary to establish the correct crankshaft end play. Replace the original crankshaft shim(s) if not the correct thickness.

16. Again, place the straightedge across the PTO side crankcase half and measure the distance from the top of the straightedge to the balance shaft bearing. See **Figure 106**, typical. Subtract the thickness of the straightedge (**Figure 107**) from the measurement and record the remainder.

17. Repeat Step 16 on the magneto side crankcase half. Do not forget to subtract the thickness of the straightedge. Add this measurement to the distance obtained in Step 16 to determine the total distance between the balance shaft bearings.

18. Measure the width of the balance shaft between the bearing seats. **See Figure 109**. Subtract the balance shaft width from the total distance determined in Step 17. This value, minus the preferred balance shaft end play specification (**Table 4**), is the shim thickness necessary to establish the correct balance shaft end play. Replace the original balance shaft shim(s) if not the correct thickness.

19. Next, place the straightedge across the magneto side crankcase half. Measure the distance form the top of the straightedge to the oil pump shaft bearing. Subtract the thickness of the straightedge (**Figure**

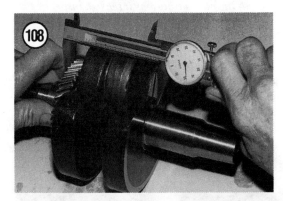

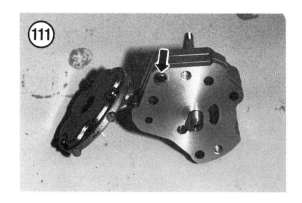

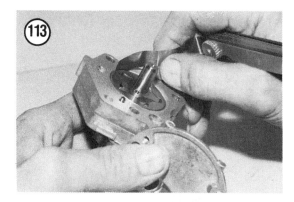

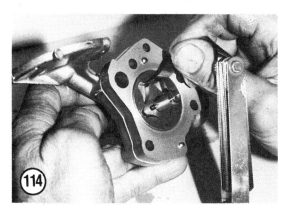

107) from the measurement and record the remainder.

20. Install the oil pump drive gear on the pump shaft. Using a dial-type caliper or micrometer, measure the width of the oil pump and drive gear. Record this measurement.

21. Subtract the width of the pump and gear assembly from the measurement obtained in Step 19. This value, minus the preferred oil pump end play specification (**Table 4**), is the shim thickness necessary to establish the correct oil pump end play. Replace the original pump shim(s) if not the correct thickness.

22. Install the oil/coolant pump oil seal from the outside of the crankcase before assembling the crankcase as follows:

   a. Coat the lip of the seal with grease.

   b. Use a 25 mm (0.985 in.) seal driver to install the seal with the spring loaded lip toward the inside. Drive the seal into its bore until the outside is flush with the bottom of the mechanical (cooling) seal bore.

   c. Install the mechanical seal from the outside after the crankcase is assembled. Refer to the procedure described in crankcase assembly in this chapter.

OIL PUMP

Disassembly/Inspection/Assembly

The oil pump can be removed after separating the crankcase halves as described in this chapter.

1. Remove the three screws attaching the pump intake screen and remove the screen from the pump. Refer to **Figure 110**.

2. Clean and inspect the screen. Check for damage to the screen and for other damage indicated by metal particles in the screen.

3. Remove the screw (**Figure 111**) and separate the cover from the pump body as shown in **Figure 112**.

4. Use a feeler gauge and measure the clearance between the outer rotor and the pump body as shown in **Figure 113**. Recommended clearance is listed in **Table 4**.

5. Use a feeler gauge and measure the clearance between the tip of the inner rotor and the outer rotor as shown in **Figure 114**. Recommended clearance is listed in **Table 4**.

6. Use a straightedge and feeler gauge as shown in **Figure 115** to measure the end play of the pump rotors. Recommended end play is listed in **Table 4**.

7. Remove the inner rotor, outer rotor and pump body from the pressure pump to expose the scavenge pump rotors and body.

8. Measure the clearances for the scavenge pump following the description in Steps 4-6. Recommended clearances are the same as those for the pressure pump and are listed in **Table 4**.

9. Clean and dry all parts thoroughly.

NOTE
Do not use any sealer when assembling the pump. Also, make sure the pump is absolutely clean when assembling.

10. Coat all parts of the pump with clean engine oil and assemble the pump without using sealer. Tighten the pump cover screws securely.

ONE WAY CHECK VALVE

The one way check valve is located under the flanged plug on the left side of the engine crankcase near the external oil pipes. Refer to **Figure 116**. The PVT (drive and driven pulleys) and the inner cover must be removed before the check valve can be removed. Usually, the one way check valve and spring (**Figure 117**) are only removed, cleaned and

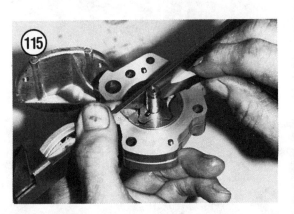

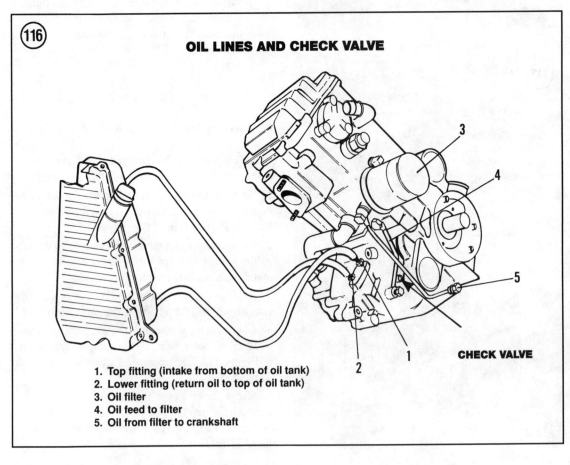

OIL LINES AND CHECK VALVE

CHECK VALVE

1. **Top fitting (intake from bottom of oil tank)**
2. **Lower fitting (return oil to top of oil tank)**
3. **Oil filter**
4. **Oil feed to filter**
5. **Oil from filter to crankshaft**

reassembled when the engine is removed and being overhauled. If engine oil drains from the reservoir into the engine crankcase when the engine is stopped, the check valve is probably leaking. Refer to **Table 3** for torque recommended when installing the one way check valve plug.

BREAK-IN PROCEDURE

If the rings were replaced, a new piston installed, the cylinder rebored or honed or major lower end work performed, the engine should be broken-in just as though it were new. The performance and service life of the engine depends greatly on a careful and sensible break-in.

For the first 5-10 hours of operation, use no more than 1/3 throttle, and vary the speed as much as possible within the 1/3 throttle limit. Avoid hard acceleration in addition to prolonged steady running at one speed, no matter how moderate.

After the initial 5-10 hours of operation, use progressively more throttle (with short bursts of speed) until the ATV has run for 10-15 hours.

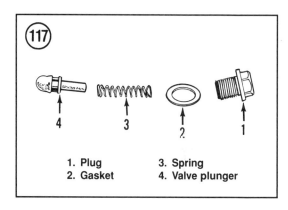

(117)

| 1. Plug | 3. Spring |
| 2. Gasket | 4. Valve plunger |

5

Table 1 4-STROKE ENGINE SPECIFICATIONS

Engine model	Bore mm (in.)	Stroke mm (in.)	Disp. cc (cid.)
1995			
Magnum 2 × 4 and 4 × 4			
EH42PLE-01	87.9	70	425
	(3.4606)	(2.578)	25.9

Table 2 ENGINE LUBRICATION

Engine oil*		
API type	SE or SF	
Viscosity	10W-40	
Oil capacity	1.89 L	2 qt.
Oil pressure at 5,500 rpm		
Normal	138 kPa	20 psi
Minimum limit	83 kPa	12 psi
* The manufacturer recommends Polaris 40W/40 engine oil.		

Table 3 TIGHTENING TORQUES MAGNUM 4-STROKE ENGINE

	N·m	ft.-lb.
Breather union	8.97-15.2	6.5-11
Cam drive sprocket nut	48.3-70.4	35-51
Cam driven sprocket screws	6.9-8.28	5-6
Cam chain tensioner slider	6.9-8.28	5-6
Cam chain tensioner plug	19.3-26.2	14-19
Carburetor flange	16.6-19.3	12-14
Coolant pump cover	6.9-8.97	5-6.5
Coolant pump impeller	6.9-8.97	5-6.5

(continued)

Table 3 TIGHTENING TORQUES MAGNUM 4-STROKE ENGINE (continued)

	N·m	ft.-lb.
Crankcase		
8mm	19.3-20.7	14-15
Crankcase drain bolt	19.3-23.5	14-17
Cylinder head bolts		
6mm	8.29	6
11mm	See text for procedure	
Cylinder head cover	8.28	6
Cylinder base bolts		
6mm	6.9-8.28	5-6
10mm	62.1-67.6	45-49
Flywheel	80.0-99.4	59-73
Oil delivery pipe bolts	24.8-34.5	18-25
Oil filter union	49.7-59.3	36-43
Oil hose union	8.97-15.2	6.5-11
Oil pressure blind plug	8.97-15.2	6.5-11
Oil pump mount bolts	6.9-8.97	5-6.5
One way valve plug	19.2-6.2	14-19
Recoil starter	6.9-8.97	5-6.5
Rocker arm support brackets	11.0-12.4	8-9
Rocker arm adjuster nut	8.28-9.66	6-7
Rocker shaft locating screw	8.28	6
Spark plug		
New	12.0-15.2	8.7-11
Old	23.5-27.6	17-20
Starter motor	6.9-8.97	5-6.5
Stator plate	6.9-8.97	5-6.5
Oil pump case screws	2.76	24 in.-lb.

Table 4 SERVICE SPECIFICATIONS

	mm	in.
Balance shaft end play	0.2-0.4	0.008-0.016
Cam chain tensioner spring		
Free length	58.9	2.320
Camshaft		
Exhaust cam lobe height	32.726-32.826	1.2884-1.2924
Wear limit	32.426	1.2766
Inlet cam lobe height	32.726-32.826	1.2884-1.2924
Wear limit	32.426	1.2766
Journal O.D.	38.005-38.025	1.4963-1.4970
Journal to bore clearance	0.055-0.090	0.0022-0.0035
Wear limit	0.10	0.0039
Connecting rod small end I.D.	23.007-23.020	0.9058-0.9063
Bearing radial clearance	0.007-0.026	0.0003-0.0010
Bearing wear limit	0.05	0.0020
Connecting rod big end		
Side clearance	0.1-0.65	0.0039-0.0256
Wear limit	0.80 mm	0.0315
Bearing radial clearance	0.011-0.038	0.0004-0.0015
Wear limit	0.05	0.0020
Crankshaft end play	0.2-0.4	0.008-0.016
Crankshaft runout limit	0.06	0.0024
Cylinder		
Bore diameter	87.900-87.920	3.4606-3.4614
Taper/out of round limit	0.050	0.002
Piston clearance	0.015-0.045	0.0006-0.0018
Wear limit	0.060	0.0024

(continued)

Table 4 SERVICE SPECIFICATIONS (continued)

	mm	in.
Cylinder head		
Standard height	98.3	3.870
Warpage limit	0.05	0.0020
Inlet valve		
Margin limit	0.8	0.031
Overall length	101-0	3.976
Seat width	0.7-1.4	0.028-0.055
Stem diameter	5.950-5.965	0.2343-0.2348
Stem to guide clearance	0.035-0.062	0.0014-0.0024
Exhaust valve		
Margin limit	0.8	0.031
Overall length	101.2	3.984
Seat width	1.0-1.8	0.039-0.071
Stem diameter	5.945-5.960	0.2341-0.2346
Stem to guide clearance	0.040-0.067	0.0016-0.0026
Oil pump		
Inner rotor tip clearance	0.127	0.005
Wear limit	0.2032	0.008
Outer rotor to pump body	0.0254-0.0762	0.001-0.003
Wear limit	0.1016	0.004
Rotor end clearance	0.0254-0.0762	0.001-0.003
Wear limit	0.1016	0.004
Shaft end play	0.2-0.4	0.008-0.016
Piston		
Standard diameter	87.875-87.885	3.4596-3.460
Pin bore diameter	23.0-23.006	0.9055-0.9057
Clearance in cylinder		
Desired	0.015-0.045	0.0006-0.0018
Wear limit	0.060	0.0024
Piston pin O.D.	22.994-23.0	0.9053-0.9055
Clearance in piston	0.004-0.008	0.0002-0.0003
Piston rings		
End gap		
Top, desired	0.20-0.36	0.0079-0.0138
Wear limit	1.0	0.039
Second, desired	0.20-0.36	0.0079-0.0138
Wear limit	1.0	0.039
Oil control, desired	0.20-0.70	0.0079-0.0236
Wear limit	1.5	0.059
Side clearance		
Top, desired	0.040-0.080	0.0016-0.0031
Wear limit	0.15	0.0059
Second, desired	0.030-0.070	0.0012-0.0028
Wear limit	0.15	0.0059
Rocker arms		
Bore clearance	0.020-0.054	0.0008-0.0021
Wear limit	0.10	0.0039
Shaft O.D.	21.987-22.0	0.8656-0.8661
Valve seat and face angle	45°	
Valve guide I.D.	6.0-6.012	0.2362-0.2367
Protrusion	17.5-18.0	0.689-0.709
Valve springs		
Distortion limit	1.9	0.075
Standard free length		
Orange paint	44.05	1.7342
Yellow paint	42.0	1.654
Minimum free length		
Orange paint	42.05	1.656
Yellow paint	40.0	1.575

5

FUEL AND EXHAUST SYSTEMS

The fuel system consists of the fuel tank, fuel pump, fuel shutoff valve, carburetor and air filter.

The exhaust system consists of an exhaust pipe and muffler assembly.

This chapter includes service procedures for all parts of the fuel system and exhaust system. Air filter service is covered in Chapter Three.

Carburetor specifications are covered in **Table 1**, located at the end of this chapter.

CARBURETOR OPERATION

An understanding of the function of each of the carburetor components and their relation to one another is a valuable aid for pinpointing a source of carburetor trouble.

The carburetor's purpose is to supply and atomize fuel in correct proportions with air drawn into the engine through the air intake. At the primary throttle opening (idle), a small amount of fuel is siphoned through the pilot jet by the incoming air. As the throttle is opened further, the air stream begins to siphon fuel through the main jet and needle jet. A tapered needle is positioned in the needle jet and the effective flow capacity of the needle jet is increased as the needle is lifted.

At full throttle, the carburetor venturi is fully open and the needle is lifted far enough to permit the main jet to flow at full capacity.

The starting enrichment circuit is a starting jet system in which the choke lever opens a fuel enrichment valve rather than closing an air restricting butterfly. In the open position, the jet discharges a stream of fuel into the carburetor venturi to enrich the mixture when the engine is cold.

2-stroke models are equipped with a Mikuni VM carburetor. 4-stroke models are equipped with a Mikuni CV carburetor.

CARBURETOR
(MODELS WITH 2-STROKE ENGINES)

Refer to **Figure 1** and the following paragraphs when disassembling the carburetor.

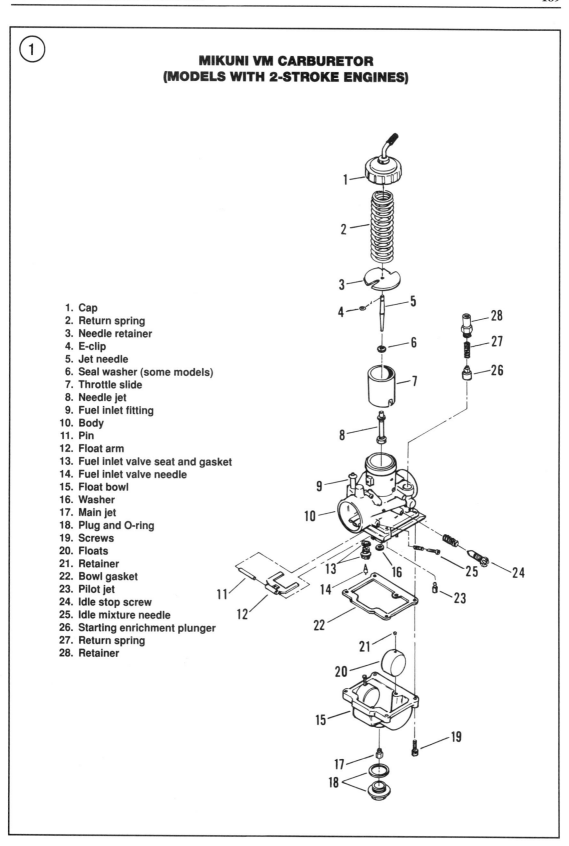

MIKUNI VM CARBURETOR
(MODELS WITH 2-STROKE ENGINES)

1. Cap
2. Return spring
3. Needle retainer
4. E-clip
5. Jet needle
6. Seal washer (some models)
7. Throttle slide
8. Needle jet
9. Fuel inlet fitting
10. Body
11. Pin
12. Float arm
13. Fuel inlet valve seat and gasket
14. Fuel inlet valve needle
15. Float bowl
16. Washer
17. Main jet
18. Plug and O-ring
19. Screws
20. Floats
21. Retainer
22. Bowl gasket
23. Pilot jet
24. Idle stop screw
25. Idle mixture needle
26. Starting enrichment plunger
27. Return spring
28. Retainer

Table 1 lists the carburetor originally installed and the original specifications. Some specifications may be different than listed to compensate for altitude, optional equipment or abnormal operating conditions.

Removal/Installation

1. Place the vehicle on level ground and set the parking brake.
2. Remove the seat and interfering panels.
3. Remove the fuel tank as described in this chapter.
4. Loosen the clamp at the rear of the carburetor and slide the air hose from the rear flange of the carburetor. It may be easier on some models to remove the air filter and inlet housing to provide more room.
5. Note the routing of the carburetor vent and overflow tubes prior to removing the carburetor. It is easier to attach the lines if they are marked before detaching them from the carburetor.
6. Unscrew the carburetor cap (**Figure 2**), then pull the throttle slide from the carburetor.

NOTE
As soon as it is removed, wrap the throttle slide in a shop towel to protect the slide and jet needle from damage.

7. Loosen the clamp (**Figure 3**), slide the carburetor back to free it from the intake adapter, then move it to the side.
8. Unscrew the starting plunger retainer (28, **Figure 1**) from the carburetor body and withdraw the starting enrichment plunger.
9. Refer to *Remove Throttle Slide* description in this chapter if the throttle slide is to be detached from the throttle cable.
10. Place a clean shop towel into the intake manifold and air box boot openings to prevent the entry of foreign material.
11. Install by reversing these removal steps, noting the following.
    a. If separated, attach the throttle cable to the throttle slide as described in this chapter. Make sure that the valve needle is correctly seated, needle clip is in the correct groove and the retainer plate is in place between the throttle return spring and the throttle slide. Check throttle operation and be sure that the end of the cable is seated in recess of throttle slide.
    b. Insert the throttle slide into the carburetor, aligning the jet needle with the needle jet. The groove on the left side of the throttle slide must be aligned with the guide pin in the carburetor bore.
    c. Install the cap (**Figure 2**) and tighten securely.
    d. After installing, operate the throttle lever and the starting enrichment (choke) at the handlebar a few times. Make sure the throttle slide and starting enrichment valve operate properly without hanging up or binding.
    e. Adjust the throttle cable free play as described in Chapter Three.
12. Insert the carburetor into the adapter and tighten the clamp (**Figure 3**).

Throttle Slide
Removal/Installation

Refer to **Figure 1**.
1. Unscrew the cap (**Figure 2**) from the Mikuni VM carburetor.

CAUTION
If the throttle slide cannot be easily removed from the carburetor bore, have a Polaris dealer inspect the condition of the carburetor. Do not cause additional damage by attempting to force the slide from the bore.

2. Withdraw the throttle slide, cap and cable.
3. Compress the spring by pressing the throttle slide against the cap. Push the end of the cable to the side and disengage the throttle cable from the throttle slide.

4. Withdraw the cable from the throttle slide and cap. Separate the cap, throttle slide and spring slowly.

5. Lift the retainer plate, jet needle and needle clip from the throttle slide. Some models may have a seal washer located between the needle clip and the throttle slide.

6. Attach the throttle slide to the cable by reversing the procedure. Make sure the throttle cable end is seated in the throttle slide relief.

NOTE
Engage the groove in the side of the throttle slide with the alignment pin in the left side of the carburetor bore. The slide should move freely without binding.

7. Insert the throttle slide into the carburetor, making sure to align the jet needle with the needle jet.

8. Tighten the cap (**Figure 2**) securely.

Disassembly

1. Remove the Mikuni VM carburetor as described in this chapter.

CAUTION
*If possible, remove the plug (18, **Figure 1**) and float bowl (15, **Figure 1**) while holding the carburetor upright. If the carburetor is turned upside down, sediment from the bottom of the float bowl may be dumped into the small passages located in the upper part of the carburetor.*

2. Remove plug (18, **Figure 1**) and O-ring from bottom of float bowl.

3. Remove screws (19, **Figure 1**) and separate the float bowl from the carburetor body. Be careful not to lose or damage the floats (20, **Figure 1**), or retainers (21, **Figure 1**), when removing the float bowl. Inspect the float bowl for sediment.

4. Remove pin (11, **Figure 1**), then remove the float arm (12, **Figure 1**), and the fuel inlet needle (14, **Figure 1**).

NOTE
*Before removing the idle mixture needle (25, **Figure 1**), check its current setting as follows. Observe the location of the slot in the idle mixture needle and turn it clockwise until lightly seated while noticing how far the needle has turned from its initial setting. Record the original setting as turns or parts of turns from the seated position. Compare the observed setting with the suggested setting in **Table 1**. Large differences may indicate improper setting or attempts to compensate for other problems.*

5. Remove the idle mixture needle and spring (25, **Figure 1**).

6. If not already removed, remove the carburetor throttle slide (7, **Figure 1**) as described in this chapter.

7. Remove the idle speed screw, O-ring and spring (24, **Figure 1**) from the carburetor body.

8. If not already removed, remove the retainer (28, **Figure 1**) and withdraw the starting enrichment plunger (26, **Figure 1**) and spring (27, **Figure 1**).

9. Remove the main jet (17, **Figure 1**) and washer (16, **Figure 1**).

10. Push the needle jet (8, **Figure 1**) up and out of the carburetor body.

11. Remove the fuel inlet seat (13, **Figure 1**).

CAUTION
*The pilot jet (23, **Figure 1**) can be easily damaged by attempting to remove it with a screwdriver that is the wrong size.*

12. Carefully remove the pilot jet (23, **Figure 1**).

13. Carefully remove the float retainers (21, **Figure 1**) and pull floats from the posts in the float bowl. The posts and the floats should be clean and smooth. The floats must move easily on the posts.

14. Clean and inspect all parts as described in this chapter.

Cleaning and Inspection

1. Initially clean all parts in a petroleum based solvent, then clean in hot soapy water. Rinse parts with cold water and blow dry with compressed air.

> *CAUTION*
> *Do not dip the carburetor body or any of the O-rings in a carburetor cleaner or other solution that can damage the rubber parts and seals.*

> *CAUTION*
> *If compressed air is not available, allow the parts to air dry or use a clean lint-free cloth. Do not use a paper towel to dry carburetor parts, as small paper particles may plug openings in the carburetor body or jets.*

> *CAUTION*
> *Do not use wire or drill bits to clean jets as minor gouges in the jet can alter flow rate and upset the fuel/air mixture. Plugged jets can sometimes be cleared by using compressed air, but be careful that the obstruction is removed, not just more deeply seated.*

2. Make sure the overflow and vent tubes are clear. Blow tubes, fittings and passages out with compressed air if necessary.

3. Inspect the float bowl gasket for damage or deterioration; replace if necessary.

4. Inspect the fuel inlet valve assembly (13 and 14, **Figure 1**) as follows:

   a. Be sure that all of the gasket is removed from the carburetor body and the valve seat. Always install a new gasket when assembling.

   b. Inspect the end of the fuel inlet valve needle (14, **Figure 1**) for wear or damage.

   c. Check the inside of the fuel inlet valve body (seat) (13, **Figure 1**) uneven wear or other damage.

   d. If the fuel inlet valve needle and/or body (seat) are damaged, replace the fuel valve assembly as a set. Damage to these parts will result in flooding and an excessively rich fuel mixture.

5. Inspect the idle mixture needle (25, **Figure 1**) and spring for damage. Replace the needle if the tip or threads are damaged.

6. Inspect the O-ring on the idle speed screw (24, **Figure 1**) for excessive wear, hardness, cracks or other damage. Replace if necessary.

7. Inspect the float for deterioration or damage. If the float is suspected of leakage, place it in a water filled container and push it down. If the float sinks or if bubbles appear (indicating a leak), the float must be replaced.

8. Move the throttle slide (7, **Figure 1**) up and down in the carburetor bore and check for free movement. If it does not move freely or if it sticks in any position, determine the cause and repair or install a new throttle slide and carburetor body.

9. Inspect the orifices in the pilot jet (23, **Figure 1**) and the needle jet (8, **Figure 1**). Check for damage caused by improper removal procedures and use care not to damage the openings while cleaning.

10. Make sure all passages and openings in the carburetor body are clear. Clean any that are plugged.

Assembly

1. Insert the needle jet (8, **Figure 1**) into the carburetor body. Align the notch in the jet with the pin in its bore.

2. Install washer (16, **Figure 1**) and main jet (17, **Figure 1**).

3. Install the fuel inlet valve seat (13, **Figure 1**) using a new gasket.

4. Install the idle mixture needle and spring (25, **Figure 1**). Turn the needle clockwise until lightly seated, then back it out the number of turns noted during disassembly. Refer to **Table 1** for standard setting.

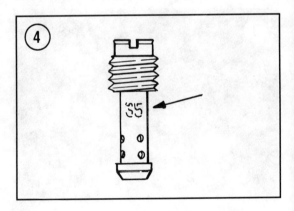

CAUTION
Do not overtighten the pilot jet when installing. The pilot jet can be easily damaged by careless installation procedures.

5. Install and tighten the pilot jet (23, **Figure 1**). The jet size is stamped on the side as shown in **Figure 4**. Refer to **Table 1** for standard size jet.

6. Insert the fuel inlet needle (14, **Figure 1**) into the seat assembly.

7. Position the float arm over the fuel inlet needle and between the attaching brackets, then install the pivot pin.

NOTE
Do not bend the float arms to change their position. Both arms should be at the same height and both are changed by bending the small tang in the center of the arms.

8. Turn the carburetor body upside down and observe the position of the float arm. The float arm should be parallel (**Figure 5**) with the gasket surface of the body. If necessary, bend the small tang that contacts the fuel inlet needle to adjust the float arm setting.

9. Install the floats (20, **Figure 1**) over the pins in the float bowl. The small pins on the sides of the floats should be facing toward the bottom of the float bowl.

10. Install the retainers (21, **Figure 1**) and make sure the floats move freely.

11. Install the float bowl using a new gasket (22, **Figure 1**). Tighten screws (19, **Figure 1**) securely.

12. Install the plug (18, **Figure 1**) on the bottom of the fuel bowl using a new O-ring.

13. Compare the number stamped on the side of the jet needle (5, **Figure 1**) with the standard size listed in **Table 1**. The number following the "-" indicates the standard position of the E-ring (4, **Figure 1**). Number "2" indicates that the E-ring should be installed in the second groove from the top of the jet needle.

14. Position the jet needle and E-clip in the throttle slide (7, **Figure 1**). Some carburetors may have a sealing washer (6, **Figure 1**) located between the E-ring and the throttle slide.

15. Thread the throttle cable down through the cable guide in the cap (1, **Figure 1**), spring (2, **Figure 1**) and retainer (3, **Figure 1**). Compress the spring and thread the throttle cable through the throttle slide (7,

Figure 1). Push the cable to the side and seat the end in the pocket.

16. Install the throttle (idle speed) stop screw, spring and O-ring (24, **Figure 1**). Adjust the initial position of the stop screw as follows.

    a. Insert the throttle slide into the carburetor bore and thread the cap (1, **Figure 1**) onto the carburetor body.

    b. Tighten the stop screw (24, **Figure 1**) just enough to begin lifting the throttle slide (7, **Figure 1**). The stop screw increases the idle speed by holding the slide open a small amount.

    c. The carburetor cap (1, **Figure 1**) and throttle slide (7, **Figure 1**) can be removed after setting the initial adjustment of the throttle stop screw. Carburetor installation may be easier with throttle slide removed until after installation to the engine.

17. Thread the starting enrichment (choke) cable through the retainer (28, **Figure 1**) and return spring (27, **Figure 1**). Attach the end of the cable to the starter plunger (26, **Figure 1**).

18. Install the carburetor as described in this chapter, then install the throttle slide and the starting enrichment plunger. Check for proper operation of the starting enrichment (choke) and throttle controls.

19. Adjust the carburetor as described in this chapter after assembly and installation are complete.

Mixture Adjustments

The fuel inlet valve is controlled by the float to maintain a constant fuel level in the carburetor float bowl. The height of the fuel affects the fuel/air mixture throughout the engine's operating range, so the position of the float arm (**Figure 5**) should be adjusted as described in this chapter.

Adjustment of the idle mixture needle (25, **Figure 1**) is described in Chapter Three. The initial setting listed in **Table 1** is recommended for operation at ambient temperatures of 5-26° C (40-80° F) at altitudes of 0-900 M (0-300 ft.). Adjustment will probably be required (to lean the mixture) for improved performance at higher altitudes and at warmer temperatures. Turning the mixture needle out (counterclockwise) will lean the mixture.

The size of the pilot jet (23, **Figure 1**) also affects the fuel/air mixture for low speed throttle settings, but the size will probably not require changing.

The position and size of the jet needle (5, **Figure 1**) affects the fuel/air mixture for intermediate (medium) throttle openings. The E-clip (4, **Figure 1**) is located in one of the grooves at the top of the jet needle. **Table 1** lists the standard size jet needle and the number following the "-" identifies the original position of the E-ring. The position number indicates the number of grooves from the top of the needle. Installing the E-clip in a groove closer to the top of the jet needle will lower the needle and lean the mixture during mid-throttle opening. Moving the E-clip to a groove further from the top of the jet needle will raise the needle and enrich the mid-range mixture.

The size of the main jet (17, **Figure 1**) affects the fuel/air mixture during wide-open throttle operation. Different size main jets are available and can be installed to change the wide-open throttle mixture. The size is stamped on the jet. The size listed in **Table 1** is recommended for operation at ambient temperatures of 5-26° C (40-80° F) at altitudes of 0-900 M (0-3000 ft.). A smaller size main jet may be required for optimum performance at higher altitudes and at warmer temperatures. A larger main jet may be used at colder temperatures.

CARBURETOR
(MODELS WITH 4-STROKE ENGINES)

Refer to **Figure 6** and the following paragraphs when disassembling the carburetor. Mikuni CV carburetors are used on Magnum (4-stroke) models.

Table 1 lists the carburetor originally installed and the original specifications. Some specifications may be different than listed to compensate for altitude,

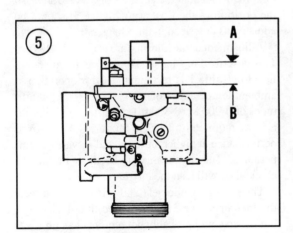

MIKUNI CV CARBURETOR
(MODELS WITH 4-STROKE ENGINES)

1. Body
2. Screw
3. Float bowl
4. Plug
5. O-ring
6. Float
7. Filter screen
8. O-ring
9. Fuel inlet valve seat
10. Screw
11. Fuel inlet valve needle
12. Pilot (fuel) jet
13. O-ring
14. Washer
15. Spring
16. Idle mixture needle
17. Idle speed stop screw
18. Washer
19. Spring
20. Screw
21. Cover
22. Spring
23. Spring seat
24. E-ring
25. Jet needle
26. Spacer
27. Diaphragm and vacuum slide assembly
28. Needle jet
29. Screw
30. Jet block assembly
31. Washer
32. Main jet
33. Pilot (air) jet
34. Starting enrichment valve
35. Spring
36. Retainer
37. Screw
38. Cover
39. O-ring
40. Cable guide
41. Throttle shaft
42. Screws
43. Ring
44. Return spring
45. Seal
46. Throttle valve
47. Seal
48. Packing
49. E-ring
50. Cap
51. Pin

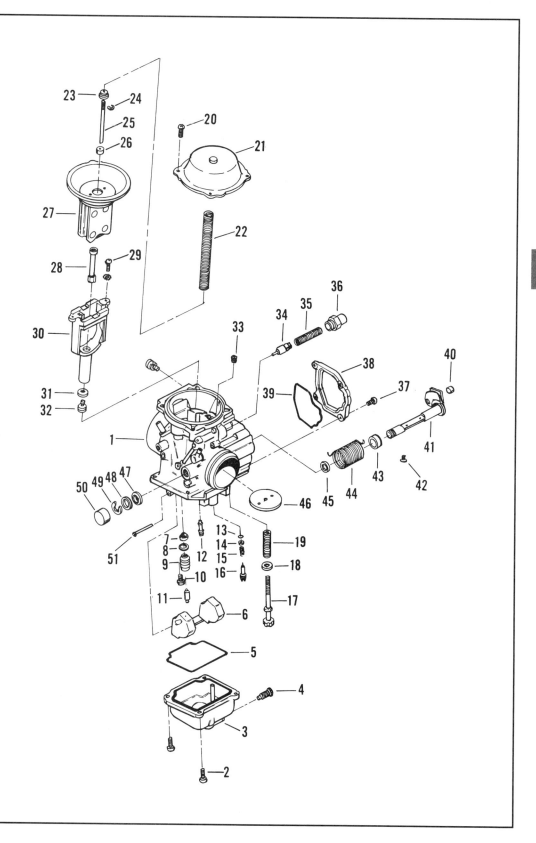

optional equipment or abnormal operating conditions.

Removal/Installation

1. Place the vehicle on level ground and set the parking brake.

2. Remove the seat and interfering panels.

3. Remove the fuel tank as described in this chapter.

4. Loosen the clamp at the rear of the carburetor and slide the air hose (A. **Figure 7**) from the rear flange of the carburetor. It may be easier to remove the air filter and inlet housing to provide more room.

5. Remove the carburetor attaching nuts (B, **Figure 7**).

6. Note the routing of the carburetor vent and overflow tubes prior to removing the carburetor. It is easier to attach the lines if they are marked before detaching them from the carburetor.

7. Loosen the clamp (C, **Figure 7**), slide the carburetor back to free it from the intake adapter, then move it to the side.

8. Move the carburetor to the side so the control cables (A, **Figure 8**) can be detached more easily. Remove the carburetor side cover screws and remove the side cover (B, **Figure 8**).

9. Detach the throttle cable from the throttle lever (**Figure 9**). Loosen the locknut on the throttle cable adjuster, unscrew cable adjuster, then withdraw the throttle cable.

10. Place a clean shop towel into the intake manifold and air box boot openings to prevent the entry of foreign material.

11. Install by reversing these removal steps, noting the following.

   a. Insert the throttle cable into the body and attach the cable end to the lever (**Figure 9**).

   b. Tighten the cable adjuster (A, **Figure 10**) into the carburetor and tighten the locknut.

   c. Insert the starting enrichment valve into the carburetor bore and tighten the retainer (B, **Figure 9**).

   d. Operate the throttle lever and the starting enrichment (choke) controls a few times. Make sure the throttle lever moves smoothly at the carburetor with no binding and that the cable end does not pop out.

   e. Adjust the throttle cable free play as described in Chapter Three.

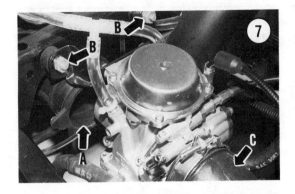

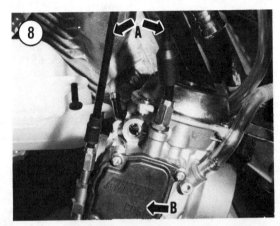

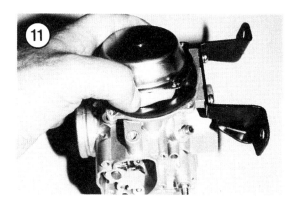

f. Adjust the starting enrichment cable as described in this chapter.

g. Install the cover (B, **Figure 8**) and tighten the screws securely.

12. Insert the carburetor into the front adapter and tighten the clamp (C, **Figure 7**).

13. Reverse removal procedure to complete installation.

Diaphragm/Vacuum Slide/Jet Needle Removal/Installation

1. Remove the top cover screws and the cover (**Figure 11**).

2. Remove the spring (**Figure 12**).

3. Remove the diaphragm and vacuum slide assembly (**Figure 13**).

4. Push the jet needle up to dislodge the spring seat (23, **Figure 6**). Remove the jet needle (25, **Figure 6**), E-ring (24, **Figure 6**) and spacer (26, **Figure 6**).

5. Refer to **Table 1** for standard size jet needle. E-ring (24, **Figure 6**) is originally installed in the third groove from the top of the jet needle as indicated by the "3" at the end of the jet needle size in **Table 1**.

6. Reinstall the diaphragm, vacuum slide and jet needle (**Figure 14**).

7. Install spring (**Figure 12**) in the center of the diaphragm.

8. Make sure that the diaphragm is correctly positioned, then install the cover (**Figure 11**). Tighten the retaining screws securely.

Idle Speed Adjustment

Adjustment of the idle speed stop screw (17, **Figure 6**) is covered in Chapter Three.

Fuel Inlet Valve

The fuel inlet needle (11, **Figure 6**) is moved by the float to allow fuel to enter the float bowl or to stop the flow of fuel into the float bowl. If the fuel inlet valve sticks shut and does not open, the engine will starve for fuel. If the valve does not close completely, the engine will flood with fuel.

The carburetor has to be removed and partially disassembled to remove and install the fuel inlet valve.

1. Remove the carburetor as described in this chapter.

2. Remove the screws (2, **Figure 6**) securing the float bowl and remove float bowl.

3. Use a small punch to push the pin (51, **Figure 6**) from the bracket for the float.

4. Remove the float (6, **Figure 6**) and the fuel inlet needle (11, **Figure 6**). Inspect the tip of the inlet needle (**Figure 15**).

5. Remove screw (10, **Figure 6**) and pull valve seat (**Figure 16**) from the carburetor body bore. Filter screen (B, **Figure 17**) should be over the end of the valve seat.

6. Reassemble using a new O-ring (A, **Figure 17**), seat (C, **Figure 17**) and needle (**Figure 15**). Hook the wire clip on the inlet needle to the tang of the float as shown in **Figure 18**.

7. Refer to *Float Adjustment* in this chapter for setting the fuel level.

8. Reassemble by reversing the disassembly procedure.

9. The float valve can be checked using a small pressure checker connected to the fuel inlet as shown in **Figure 19**. The valve should hold 34.5 kPa (5 psi) indefinitely.

Float Adjustment

The fuel inlet valve is controlled by the float to maintain a constant fuel level in the carburetor float bowl. Because the height of the fuel affects the fuel/air mixture throughout the engine's operating range, make sure the float position is correctly adjusted.

The carburetor assembly has to be removed and partially disassembled for this adjustment.

1. Remove the carburetor as described in this chapter.

2. Remove the screws (2, **Figure 6**) securing the float bowl and remove float bowl.

> *NOTE*
> *Be sure that the weight of the float is not pushing the fuel inlet valve needle down when checking the float setting.*

3. Hold the carburetor on its side so the tang in the middle of the float arm is just touching the fuel valve. Use a float level gauge, vernier caliper or small ruler as shown in **Figure 20** to measure the distance from the carburetor body gasket surface (gasket removed)

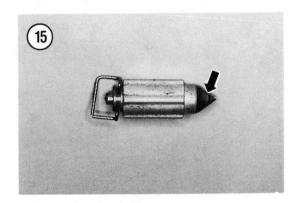

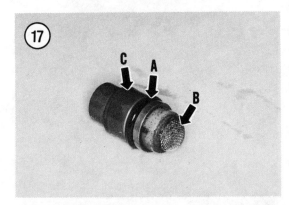

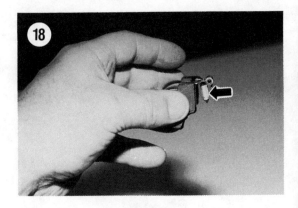

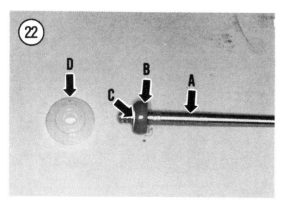

to the float. The correct distance is 14.5-14.7 mm (0.53-0.61 in.).

4. If the float setting is incorrect, adjust as follows:

   a. Carefully bend the tang in the center of the float arm (**Figure 21**) with a small screwdriver to adjust the float level.

   b. Recheck the float level as described in Step 3. Repeat until the float level adjustment is correct.

5. Reassemble and install the carburetor.

Jet Needle Adjustment

The position of the jet needle can be adjusted to affect the fuel/air mixture for medium throttle openings.

1. Remove the *Diaphragm/Vacuum Slide/Jet Needle* (**Figure 14**) as described in this chapter.

2. Push the jet needle up to dislodge the spring seat (23, **Figure 6**). Remove the jet needle (A, **Figure 22**), spacer (B), E-ring (C) and spring seat (D).

3. Refer to **Table 1** for standard size jet needle. The E-ring (C, **Figure 22**) is originally installed in the third groove from the top of the jet needle as indicated by the "3" at the end of the jet needle in **Table 1**.

NOTE
Record the clip position prior to removal.

4. Raising the needle (lowering the E-ring) will enrichen the mixture during mid-throttle opening, while lowering the needle (raising the E-ring) will lean the mixture.

5. Install the jet needle, vacuum slide and diaphragm as described in this chapter.

Main Jet

The size of the main jet (32, **Figure 6**) affects the fuel/air mixture during wide-open throttle operation. Different size main jets are available and can be installed to change the mixture for operation at high engine speeds.

The carburetor assembly has to be removed and partially disassembled to remove the main jet.

1. Remove the carburetor as described in this chapter.

2. Remove the screws (2, **Figure 6**), securing the float bowl and remove float bowl.

3. Remove the main jet and washer (**Figure 23**).

4. The size is stamped on the jet. The main jet size listed in **Table 1** is recommended for operation at ambient temperatures of 5-26° C (40-80° F) at altitudes of 0-900 m (0-3000 ft.). A smaller size main jet may be required for optimum performance at higher altitudes and at warmer temperatures. A larger main jet may be used at colder temperatures.

5. Install the main jet and reassemble the carburetor by reversing the disassembly procedure.

Idle Mixture Adjustment

Adjustment of the idle mixture needle (16, **Figure 6**) is described in Chapter Three. The initial setting is listed in **Table 1**.

The size of the pilot (fuel) jet (12, **Figure 6**) and the air jet (33, **Figure 6**) also affects the fuel/air mixture for low speed throttle settings. The pilot fuel jet (A, **Figure 24**) can be removed after removing the carburetor and float bowl as described in the preceding *Main Jet* paragraphs. The pilot air jet (**Figure 25**) can be removed after removing the *Diaphragm/Vacuum Slide/Jet Needle* as described in this chapter. The starter jet (B, **Figure 24**) cannot be removed.

THROTTLE CABLE REPLACEMENT

The throttle cable on models with 2-stroke engines branches into 2 cables. 1 branch of the cable controls the carburetor and the other controls the oil injection (lubrication) pump. If the cable is damaged at any location, the cables must be replaced as an assembly.

A single throttle cable connects the speed control at the handlebar with the carburetor on models with 4-stroke engines.

1. Place the vehicle on level ground and set the parking brake.

2. Remove the seat.

3. Remove the fuel tank cover and front fender as described in Chapter Fifteen.

4. Remove the fuel tank as described in this chapter.

5. Disconnect the throttle cable from the carburetor as described under *Carburetor Removal/Installation* in this chapter.

6. On 2-stroke models, disconnect the throttle cable from the oil injection pump. Refer to **Figure 26**.

7. Disconnect the throttle cable from the handlebar mounted throttle lever as follows:

a. Slide the rubber boot (A, **Figure 27** or A, **Figure 28**) off the cable adjuster.

b. Remove the screws from the cover.

c. Loosen the throttle cable adjuster to provide as much cable slack as possible.

d. Detach the cable from the throttle arm (B, **Figure 27** or B, **Figure 28**). If you can't disconnect the cable end, remove the throttle arm nut, washer and lever, then disconnect the cable.

e. Withdraw the cable from the throttle housing.

8. Disconnect the throttle cable from any clips holding the cable to the frame.

NOTE
A string can be attached to the cable before withdrawing it, so the original path of the cable is occupied with the string. The new cable can be attached to the string and pulled into the path of the original cable.

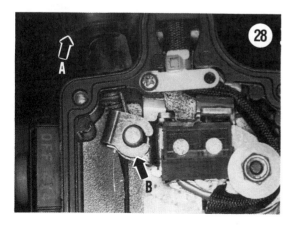

9. Make a note of the cables routing path through the frame, then remove it.

10. Lubricate the new cable(s) as described in Chapter Three.

11. Reverse Steps 1-8 to install the new cable assembly.

12. The junction block of the throttle and oil injection pump cables should be attached securely to the frame with a cable tie.

13. Reattach the throttle cable to the carburetor as described under *Carburetor Removal/Installation* in this chapter.

14. Apply grease to the handlebar end of the cable and attach it to the throttle lever and housing.

15. On 2-stroke models, attach the cable to the oil injection pump control lever (**Figure 26**).

16. Adjust the cable free play as described in Chapter Three.

17. On 2-stroke models, adjust the oil injection pump as described in Chapter Three.

18. Operate the throttle lever and make sure the carburetor throttle linkage is operating correctly with no binding. If operation is incorrect or there is binding, make sure the cable is attached correctly and there are no tight bends in the cable.

19. Test ride the vehicle and make sure the throttle is operating correctly.

CHOKE CABLE

The choke control provides a rich fuel/air mixture for starting the engine. This starting enrichment is accomplished by opening a valve in the carburetor that permits the flow of more fuel. This starting enrichment (choke) valve is shown at 26, **Figure 1** or 34, **Figure 6**. The valve is attached to the choke control knob by a cable, which must be free to open and close the valve. Starting may be difficult if the valve cannot open and the mixture is too rich to run correctly, if it does not close.

Removal/Installation

The starting enrichment valve is shown at 26, **Figure 1** for Mikuni VM carburetors used on models with a 2-stroke engine. The similar valve is shown at 34, **Figure 6** for the Mikuni CV carburetor used on Magnum models with a 4-stroke engine.

1. Locate the choke cable at the carburetor and remove the retainer (28, **Figure 1** or 36, **Figure 6**).

2. Withdraw the cable, retainer, spring and valve (26, **Figure 1** or 34, **Figure 6**) from the carburetor bore.

3. Inspect the operation as follows.

  a. Hold the choke valve end of the control cable and operate the choke knob.

  b. Observe the movement of the valve at the end of the cable.

  c. The cable should move easily inside its housing and the spring should move the valve smoothly. The pressure of the spring must be sufficient to move the cable and close the valve.

  d. Inspect the valve for scratches or other damaged surfaces that would affect smooth movement or cause leakage.

4. Compress the spring (27, **Figure 1** or 35, **Figure 6**) and detach the valve from the control cable.

5. Detach the upper end of the choke cable and remove any clips holding the cable to the frame.

6. Make a note of the cable's path through the frame, then remove it.

7. Lubricate the new cable as described in Chapter Three.

8. Reverse the removal procedure to install the new cable assembly.

9. On Magnum models with Mikuni CV carburetor, adjust the choke cable as follows.

  a. Remove the fuel tank as described in this chapter.

  b. Remove the *Diaphragm/Vacuum Slide/Jet Needle* as described in this chapter.

  c. The choke lever has three positions, choke off, 1/2 choke and full choke. Move the choke to OFF position and observe the small hole shown in **Figure 29**. The starting enrichment plunger should close the hole.

  d. Move the choke control to the 1/2 choke position and observe the small hole **Figure 29**. The hole should be half-way covered by the valve.

  e. Move the choke control to the FULL choke position and observe the small hole **Figure 29**. The hole should be fully open. The choke valve should not cover any part of the hole when the choke control is in the FULL choke position.

  f. If the choke control does not move the valve to each of the three positions shown in **Figure 29**, loosen the locknut and turn the cable adjuster (**Figure 30**) as necessary. Tighten the

locknut on the cable adjuster when adjustment is complete.

  g. Reinstall the diaphragm, vacuum slide and jet needle.

  h. Reinstall the fuel tank.

FUEL TANK

Removal/Installation

Refer to **Figure 31** or **Figure 32** for this procedure.

1. Place the vehicle on level ground and set the parking brake.

2. Remove the seat.

3. Disconnect the battery negative lead.

WARNING
Several different types of shut-off valves are used. If the shut-off valve is attached directly to the fuel tank, it can be turned off and remain attached to the tank. If fuel hoses run from the tank to a shut-off valve that is attached to the frame, the

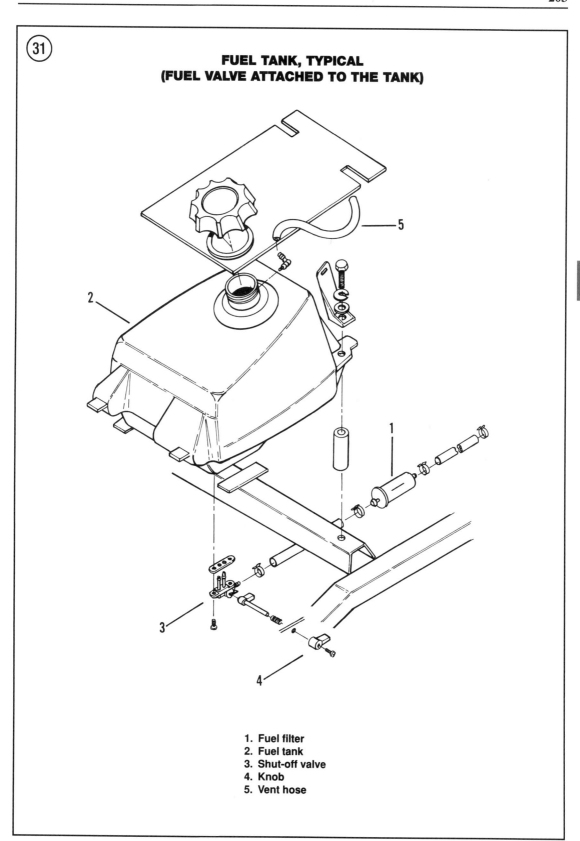

31

FUEL TANK, TYPICAL
(FUEL VALVE ATTACHED TO THE TANK)

6

1. Fuel filter
2. Fuel tank
3. Shut-off valve
4. Knob
5. Vent hose

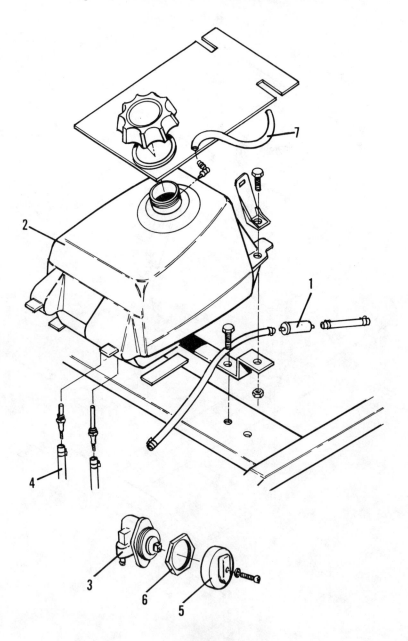

③②

FUEL TANK, TYPICAL
(FUEL VALVE INLINE WITH HOSES)

1. Fuel filter
2. Fuel tank
3. Shut-off valve
4. Hoses from tank to valve
5. Knob
6. Nut
7. Vent hose

tank should be drained and the hoses plugged. It is unsafe to disconnect both hoses and attach them together, because of the hazard of spilled fuel.

4. Drain all fuel from the tank.

5A. On models with the shut-off valve attached to the tank, refer to **Figure 31** and proceed as follows.

   a. Turn the fuel shutoff valve to the OFF position.

   b. Disconnect the fuel line from the valve and plug the open end to prevent contamination.

5B. On models with the shut-off separate from the fuel tank as shown in **Figure 32**, proceed as follows.

   a. Loosen the clamps on hoses (4, **Figure 32**) leading from the fuel tank to the shut-off valve.

   b. Disconnect both fuel lines and plug all of the openings to prevent contamination.

6. Remove the screws attaching the fuel tank cover (**Figure 33**), then remove the cover.

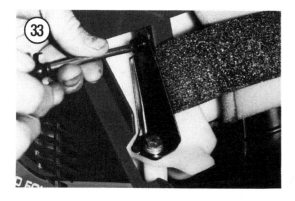

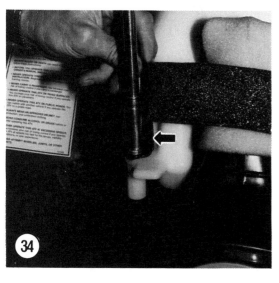

7. Remove the fuel tank mounting bolts (**Figure 34**), washers and collars, then lift the fuel tank from the frame.

8. Inspect the tank for any damage or leaking.

9. Store the tank in a place where there is little chance for fire and where the tank will not be damaged.

10. Install by reversing these removal steps, check for fuel leakage after installation is completed. Tighten fuel tank mounting bolts securely.

FUEL SHUTOFF VALVE

Refer to **Figure 31** and **Figure 32**. Several different types of shut-off valves have been used.

WARNING
All service to the fuel system is somewhat dangerous because of the flammable nature of gasoline. It is extremely unsafe to attempt removal of the shut-off valve in any way that increases the hazard of spilled fuel.

1. Drain all of the gas from the fuel tank. Store the fuel in a can approved for gasoline storage.

2A. If the shut-off valve is attached directly to the fuel tank as shown in **Figure 31**, proceed as follows.

   a. Remove the fuel tank as described in this chapter.

   b. Remove the screws securing the fuel shutoff valve to the fuel tank and remove the valve and gasket.

2B. If fuel lines run from the tank to a shut-off valve that is attached to the frame as shown in **Figure 32**, proceed as follows.

   a. Loosen the clamps on hoses (4, **Figure 32**) leading from the fuel tank to the shut-off valve.

   b. Disconnect both fuel lines from the tank and the third fuel line from the carburetor. Plug all of the openings to prevent contamination.

   c. Remove the screw from the knob (5, **Figure 32**), then pull the knob from the valve.

   d. Remove the nut (6, **Figure 32**) and withdraw the valve (3, **Figure 32**) from the frame mount.

3. The valve should not be disassembled. Install a new valve assembly if the old valve has failed in any way.

4. Install by reversing these steps.

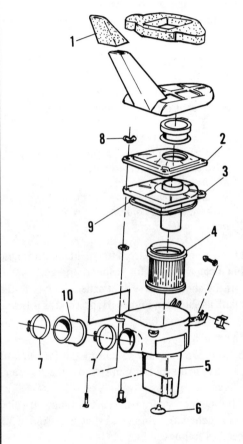

**AIR BOX ASSEMBLY
(TYPICAL, 2-STROKE MODELS)**

1. Pre-filter
2. Top cover
3. Bottom cover
4. Filter element
5. Air box
6. Vent valve
7. Clamp
8. Wing nut
9. Gasket
10. Hose

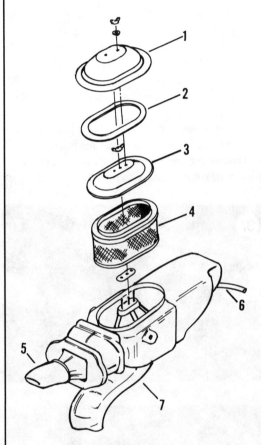

**AIR BOX ASSEMBLY
(TYPICAL, 4-STROKE MODELS)**

1. Access cover
2. Gasket
3. Filter cover
4. Air filter element
5. Pre-filter
6. Sediment drain tube
7. Air box

5. If the valve is attached to the bottom of the tank, install a new fuel shutoff valve gasket and tighten the screws securely.

6. Check for fuel leakage after installation is completed.

AIR BOX

The air box is mounted underneath the seat. The air box shown in **Figure 35** is typical of 2-stroke models. Magnum models with 4-stroke engines are equipped with the air box and filter shown in **Figure 36**.

Removal/Installation

Refer to **Figure 35** or **Figure 36** for this procedure.

1. Place the vehicle on level ground and set the parking brake.

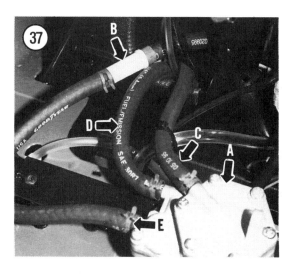

2. Remove the seat.

3. Unbolt and remove the top cover(s) and air filter (2, 3 and 4, **Figure 35** or 1, 2, 3 and 4, **Figure 36**).

4. If the rear fenders or other body panels interfere, remove the panels as described in Chapter Fifteen.

5. Loosen the hose clamp securing the air box (5, **Figure 35** or 7, **Figure 36**) to the carburetor.

6. Remove the screw attaching the air box to the frame and lift the air box from the frame.

7. Cover the carburetor opening to prevent dust from entering.

8. Inspect all rubber components of the air box assembly and replace any that are damaged or beginning to deteriorate.

9. Install by reversing these removal steps, making sure the carburetor-to-air box hose clamp is seated properly and tightened securely.

10. Service the pre-filter (1, **Figure 35** or 5, **Figure 36**) as described in Chapter Three.

FUEL PUMP

A fuel pump is installed on Magnum models to deliver fuel to the carburetor. The pump (A, **Figure 37**) is mounted on a brace between the front fenders as shown. The inline fuel filter (B, **Figure 37**) is located in the hose between the fuel tank and the pump.

1. Remove the headlight cover and cowling.

2. Loosen the clamp, then detach the impulse hose (C, **Figure 37**) from the pump.

3. Check the impulse hose for signs of fuel leakage. The presence of fuel in the impulse hose indicates a broken diaphragm.

4. Attach a hand vacuum pump such as a Mity-Vac (part No. 2870975) to the impulse port of the pump.

5. Apply a vacuum equal to 5 in. Hg to the port and observe any leakage. The pump diaphragm should hold the vacuum indefinitely.

6. Alternating pulses of pressure and vacuum at the impulse port of the pump should pump fuel.

7. If the pump is damaged, turn the fuel off at the tank shut-off valve.

8. Loosen the clamp, then disconnect the fuel inlet hose (D, **Figure 37**) from the pump.

9. Loosen the clamp, then detach the fuel outlet hose (E, **Figure 37**) from the pump.

10. Drill the rivets from the fuel pump bracket as shown in **Figure 38**.

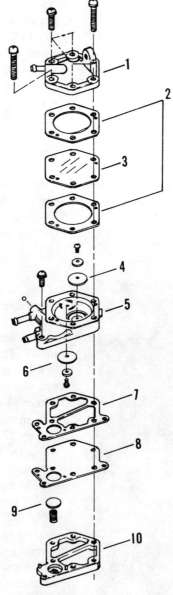

FUEL PUMP
(MAGNUM MODELS)

1. Cover
2. Gaskets
3. Diaphragm
4. Check valve
5. Pump body
6. Check valve
7. Gasket
8. Diaphragm
9. Pressure regulator
10. Cover

NOTE
Do not disassemble the pump unless new diaphragms, gaskets and valves are available.

11. If service parts are available, refer to **Figure 39** and disassemble the pump.

12. Reassemble and install the pump by reversing the procedure.

EXHAUST SYSTEM

Check the exhaust system for deep dents or fractures and repair or replace parts as required. Check the mounting flanges (**Figure 40**) on the muffler and the frame for fractures. Replace broken or missing springs (**Figure 41**). Replace or tighten any missing or loose bolts. Check the mounting flange attached to the cylinder (2-stroke models) or cylinder head (4-stroke models) for tightness. A loose exhaust pipe connection will cause excessive exhaust noise and reduce engine power.

The stock exhaust system consists of the exhaust pipe, muffler, gaskets and mounting fasteners.

Removal/Installation

1. Place the vehicle on level ground and set the parking brake.
2. Remove any interfering panels as described in Chapter Fifteen.
3. Remove attaching springs.
4. Loosen mounting bolts.
5. Loosen or remove any exhaust pipe to muffler clamps.
6. Remove the muffler mounting bolts and remove the muffler.
7. Remove the exhaust pipe.
8. Remove the nuts attaching the exhaust flange to the cylinder or cylinder head and remove the flange.
9. Install by reversing these removal steps, noting the following.
10. Inspect the gasket between the cylinder or cylinder head and the exhaust flange. Replace the gasket if damaged or leaking and always install a new gasket if the flange was removed.
11. After installation is complete, start the engine and make sure there are no exhaust leaks.

Table 1 is on the following pages.

Table 1 CARBURETOR SPECIFICATIONS

	Carb. model	Main jet	Needle jet	Jet needle	Pilot jet	Idle needle	Idle rpm
1985							
Scrambler & Trail Boss	VM30SS	155	O-6(169)	5DP7-3	30	1 1/2	800
1986							
Scrambler & Trail Boss	VM30SS	145	O-0(169)	5DP7-3	50	1	800
1987							
Trail Boss	VM30SS	145	O-0(169)	5DP7-3	50	1	800
Cyclone	VM34SS	200	O-4(166)	6DH5-3	40	1	800
Trail Boss 4 × 4	VM30SS	145	O-0(169)	5DP7-3	50	1	800
1988							
Trail Boss 2 × 4 and 4 × 4	VM30SS	145	O-4(169)	5DP7-3	35	1	800
Trail Boss 250 R/ES	VM38SS	230	O-2(247)	6DH4-3	45	1 1/2	800
1989							
All models	VM30SS	145	O-4(169)	5DP7-3	40	1	800
1990							
Trail Blazer, Trail Boss 250, 2 × 4, 4 × 4 and Big Boss 4 × 6	VM30SS	145	O-4(169)	5DP7-3	40	1	700
Trail Boss 2 × 4 350L and 4 × 4 350L	VM34SS	200	O-6(480)	6DH29-2	30	1 1/2	700
1991							
Trail Blazer, Trail Boss 250, 2 × 4, 4 × 4, Big Boss 4 × 6 and 6 × 6	VM30SS	145	O-4(169)	5DP7-3	40	1	700
Trail Boss 2 × 4 350L and 4 × 4 350L	VM34SS	200	O-6(480)	6DH29-3	30	3/4	700
1992							
Trail Blazer, Trail Boss 250, 2 × 4, 4 × 4, Big Boss 4 × 6 and 6 × 6	VM30SS	145	O-4(169)	5DP7-3	40	1	700
Trail Boss 2 × 4 350L and 4 × 4 350L	VM34SS	200	O-6(480)	6DH29-3	30	3/4	700
1993							
Trail Blazer, Trail Boss 250 2 × 4, 250 4 × 4 and 250 6 × 6	VM30SS	145	O-4(169)	5DP7-3	40	1	700
Sportsman 350 2 × 4, 4 × 4 and 6 × 6	VM34SS	200	O-6(480)	6DH29-3	30	3/4	700
1994							
Trail Blazer and Trail Boss	VM30SS	145	O-4(169)	5DP7-3	40	1	700

(continued)

Table 1 **CARBURETOR SPECIFICATIONS** (continued)

	Carb. model	Main jet	Needle jet	Jet needle	Pilot jet	Idle needle	Idle rpm
1994 (continued) Sport, Sports-man 4 × 4, 400 2 × 4, 4 × 4 and 6 × 6	VM34SS	200	O-6(480)	6DH29-3	30	1 1/2	700
300 2 × 4, 4 × 4 and 6 × 6	VM30SS	155	O-4(169)	5DP7-3	40	1 1/2	700
1995 Trail Blazer and Trail Boss	VM30SS	145	O-4(169)	5DP7-3	40	1	700
300 2 × 4, 4 × 4	VM30SS	155	O-4(169)	5DP7-3	40	1 1/2	700
Scrambler	VM34SS	240	O-6(480)	6DH29-2	30	1 1/2	700
400 2 × 4, 6 × 6, Sport, Sportsman 4 × 4 and Xplorer	VM34SS	200	O-6(480)	6DH29-3	30	1 1/2	700
Magnum 2 × 4 and 4 × 4	CVBST34	140	P-8	5F81-3	42.5	1 3/8	1,200

6

COOLING SYSTEMS

POLARIS VARIABLE TRANSMISSION (PVT) COOLING SYSTEM

Air is circulated around the Polaris Variable Transmission (PVT) assembly to cool the primary drive pulley (clutch), belt and driven pulley. Refer to **Figure 1**, **Figure 2** or **Figure 3**. Reasonably clean and dry air from under the fuel tank is drawn into the system to the port in the left side of the crankcase. The fins (**Figure 4**) on the back of the drive pulley act as a centrifugal fan to move the air. The air is finally exhausted from the air outlet duct attached to the clutch outer cover.

For the system to operate properly, all covers, ducting, seals and hoses must be in place and properly attached. The air circulating around the PVT pulleys and belt should be cool and dry. If water enters the PVT cooling system, shift the transmission to neutral, increase engine speed and allow the system to dry before proceeding.

Clutch Outer Cover/Ducting Removal/Installation

An obstruction in the ducting, missing parts or leaking connections can increase the operating temperature and shorten the life of the pulleys and the belt. Loose connections can also allow water to enter the system. Refer to **Figure 1** for PVT cooling covers and ducts typical of models with round frame tubes. Refer to **Figure 2** for most models with square frame tubes except Magnum. **Figure 3** is typical of PVT cooling system for Magnum models.

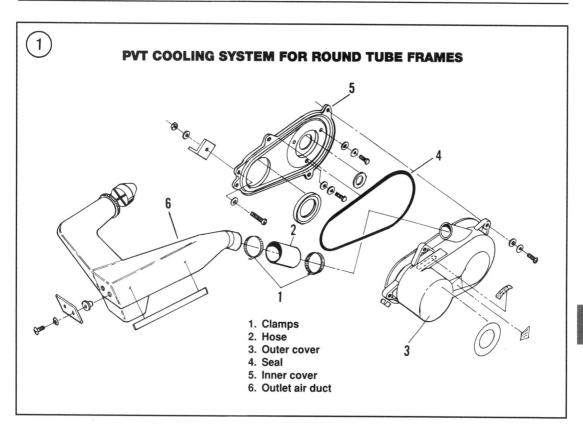

PVT COOLING SYSTEM FOR ROUND TUBE FRAMES

1. Clamps
2. Hose
3. Outer cover
4. Seal
5. Inner cover
6. Outlet air duct

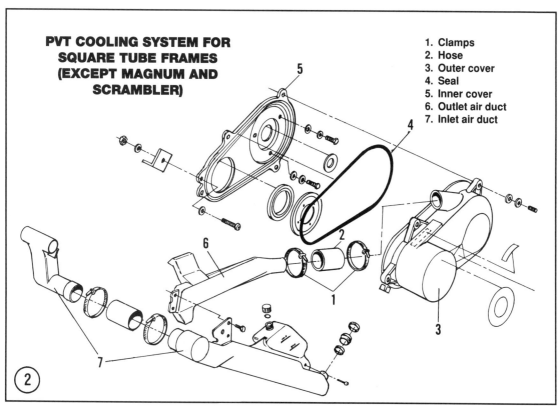

PVT COOLING SYSTEM FOR SQUARE TUBE FRAMES (EXCEPT MAGNUM AND SCRAMBLER)

1. Clamps
2. Hose
3. Outer cover
4. Seal
5. Inner cover
6. Outlet air duct
7. Inlet air duct

7

1. Remove any interfering body panels as described in Chapter Fifteen.

2. Loosen clamps (A, **Figure 5**, typical) and slide the connecting hose (B, **Figure 5**) from the clutch cover.

3. Remove the screws (C, **Figure 5**) attaching the clutch cover, then carefully remove the cover.

4. The procedure for removing the ducting depends on the model and type of service required. Refer to **Figure 1**, **Figure 2** or **Figure 3** for typical ducting.

5. The clutch inner cover (5, **Figure 1**, **Figure 2** or **Figure 3**) can be removed after removing the drive and driven pulleys as described in Chapter Eight.

6. Inspect the seal (4, **Figure 1**, **Figure 2** or **Figure 3**) and replace it if damaged.

7. Assemble by reversing the disassembly procedure. Tighten hose clamps and attaching screws securely, but do not damage parts by overtightening.

ENGINE COOLING
(AIR COOLED MODELS)

The engine on all 250 and 300 models is cooled by air circulating around the cylinder and cylinder head cooling fins. Some 250 models and all 300 models are originally equipped with an electric fan (**Figure 6**) that circulates air around the engine to assist cooling. The manufacturer recommends that a fan kit be installed on 250 models not originally equipped with a fan if the ATV is operated:

    a. At constant low ground speed.

    b. Pulling heavy loads.

    c. In commercial use.

    d. In agricultural use.

When installing the fan motor, the wiring and the vent line should exit down. Tie the wires to the frame

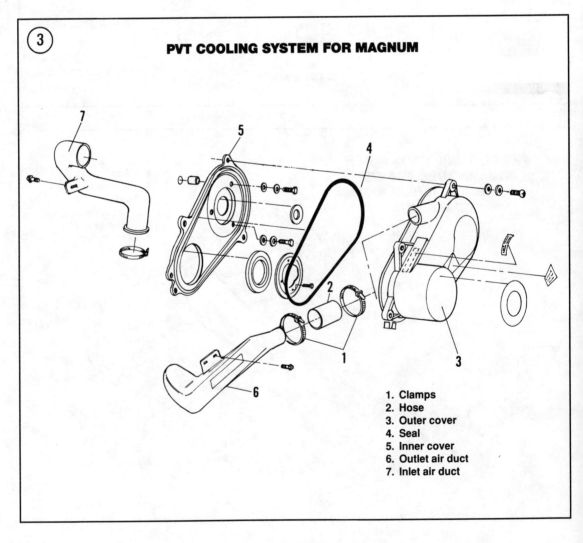

(3)

PVT COOLING SYSTEM FOR MAGNUM

1. Clamps
2. Hose
3. Outer cover
4. Seal
5. Inner cover
6. Outlet air duct
7. Inlet air duct

for the fan motor as shown at A, **Figure 6**. Make sure that loose wires, hoses or other objects cannot contact the fan blades. Install the fan blades with their raised ribs (B, **Figure 6**) facing back toward the engine.

Dirt, dried mud or other material can block the circulation of air for cooling. It is suggested that the engine be cleaned with water and inspected occasionally to assist cooling and to locate broken cooling fins or other problems that would affect cooling.

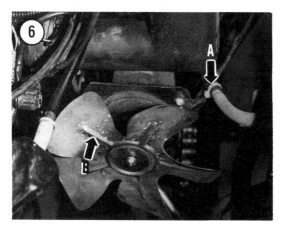

ENGINE COOLING
(LIQUID COOLED MODELS)

The engines on 350L, 400L and Magnum models are cooled by liquid coolant circulated within the cooling passages inside the cylinder, cylinder head and radiator by an impeller type pump. Refer to **Figure 7**, typical. The coolant pump is mounted on the right side of the engine crankcase. The liquid coolant is a mixture of ethylene glycol antifreeze and water. On Magnum (4-stroke) models, a thermostat is located in the cylinder head, under the outlet housing.

During normal engine operation, the coolant heats and expands. Pressure caused by this expansion is controlled by the radiator cap and excess pressure is released into the coolant recovery tank (A, **Figure 8**). As the engine cools, the pressure decreases and coolant is drawn from the coolant recovery tank back into the engine's cooling system. The amount of pressure maintained in the system, while it is warm, is determined by the radiator cap.

This chapter describes service to the liquid cooling system. Normal maintenance procedures are described in Chapter Three. Service to the engine gaskets, seals and coolant pump is described in Chapter Four (2-stroke engines) or Chapter Five (4-stroke engines).

Safety Precautions

Certain safety precautions must be kept in mind to protect yourself from injury and the engine from damage. For your own safety, the cooling system must be cool before removing any part of the system, including the radiator cap.

> *WARNING*
> *Do not remove the radiator cap when the engine is hot. The coolant is very hot and is under pressure. Severe scalding could result if the coolant comes in contact with your skin.*

To protect the engine cooling system, keep the system filled with a mixture of ethylene glycol anti-

7

freeze (that is formulated for use in aluminum engines) and distilled water.

CAUTION
Never fill the cooling system with water only, even in climates where low (freezing) temperatures do not occur. The aluminum will oxidize and severely damage the engine internally.

WARNING
Antifreeze has been classified as an environmental toxic waste by the EPA.

Dispose of it according to local regulations. ANTIFREEZE IS POISONOUS. Do not store coolant where it is accessible to children or pets. Open containers of drained antifreeze are especially dangerous.

Coolant (Antifreeze)

The coolant should be maintained at the proper level as described in Chapter Three. The radiator must be full and the coolant level should always be

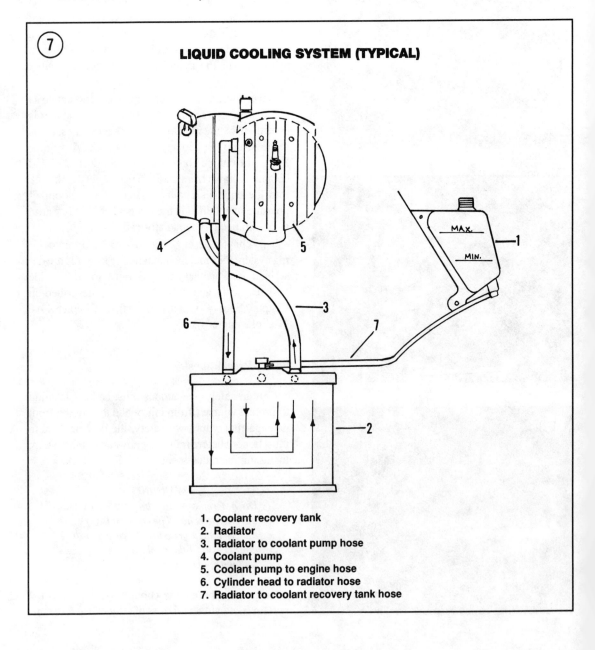

LIQUID COOLING SYSTEM (TYPICAL)

1. Coolant recovery tank
2. Radiator
3. Radiator to coolant pump hose
4. Coolant pump
5. Coolant pump to engine hose
6. Cylinder head to radiator hose
7. Radiator to coolant recovery tank hose

between the minimum and maximum marks on the coolant recovery tank (1, **Figure 7**). The system contains only a small amount of coolant and it is important that it remains filled with the proper solution.

The manufacturer recommends that the cooling system be drained and refilled with a new mixture of antifreeze and water at regular intervals as described in Chapter Three. It is important to use the type of antifreeze for recommended for use in aluminum engines, mixed in the suggested ratio both cold and warm operating environments.

Coolant Pump

The coolant pump (4, **Figure 7**) is located on the right side of the engine. The pump cover can be removed for inspection and service to the impeller. To install new seals for the coolant pump shaft, remove and disassemble the engine as described in Chapter Four (2-Stroke Models) or Chapter Five (4-Stroke Models).

The coolant pump shaft on 2-stroke engines is an extension of the balance shaft. Refer to Chapter Four to service the balance shaft and bearings.

The coolant pump shaft on 4-stroke engines is an extension of the oil pump shaft. Refer to Chapter Five to service the oil pump.

Hoses

Coolant is circulated between major components of the cooling system through hoses (3, 5 and 6, **Figure 7**), which can be punctured, cut, chafed or otherwise damaged allowing the coolant to escape.

The hoses may also be damaged while removing the hoses for other service and hoses deteriorate with age. A spray of hot coolant can injure the rider and the loss of the coolant can cause the engine to overheat quickly and damage the engine.

When any component of the cooling system is removed, inspect the connecting hoses and determine if replacement is necessary. If the hose has not been detached for some time, the hose will probably be hardened and a new hose should be installed.

The recommended time interval before routinely installing new hoses depends on many factors, including the heat and humidity of the environment. It is a good practice to test the flexibility of the hoses occasionally before starting the engine. Hardening of the rubber in the hose indicates an early stage of the aging process.

Engine Gaskets/Seals

A leaking gasket between the cylinder head and the cylinder usually leaks into the cylinder. If a sufficient amount of coolant enters the cylinder, it will be difficult to crank the engine with the starter. White smoke (steam) may be observed at the muffler when the engine is running. Coolant in the cylinder may prevent the engine from starting or make starting difficult. Refer to Chapter Four (2-stroke engines) or Chapter Five (4-stroke engines) to remove the cylinder head and install a new gasket.

A gasket is located between the coolant pump cover and pump body. Refer to Chapter Four (2-stroke engines) or Chapter Five (4-stroke engines) to install a new gasket.

Coolant may leak into the lubricating oil for the counterbalancer on 350L and 400L (2-stroke) engines or the crankcase on Magnum (4-stroke) engines. This mixture of coolant and oil can quickly cause serious damage. It is important to immediately disassemble and clean the engine, then install new seals to correct the leakage. Refer to Chapter Four (2-stroke engines) or Chapter Five (4-stroke engines) to disassemble the engine and install new seals.

Cooling System Inspection

The cooling system is equipped with a coolant recovery tank (**Figure 8**) and the coolant level can be checked without removing the radiator cap. Coolant is usually added to the coolant recovery tank. If the cooling system requires frequent refilling, there is probably a leak in the system.

If the engine overheats, allow the engine to cool completely, then remove the cap from the radiator and check the fluid level in the radiator. The radiator should always be completely full. If the level of fluid in the radiator is low, refer to Chapter Three for filling and bleeding air from the system.

To pressure check the cooling system, proceed as follows:

1. Remove the radiator cap access panel located in front of the headlight housing.
2. Detach the hose (7, **Figure 7**) leading from the radiator (near the cap) to the coolant recovery tank.
3. Attach a hand operated pump such as Mity Vac (part No. 2870975) to the connection on the radiator and pressurize the radiator to 69 kPa (10 psi).
4. Pressure in the cooling system should remain the same for at least five minutes. If a loss of pressure is evident, determine the cause. Some possible sources of leaks are:

   a. Leaking radiator cap.
   b. Leaking coolant hose connection.
   c. Leaking cylinder head gasket.
   d. Leaking coolant pump shaft seal.

5. Remove the radiator cap (**Figure 9**) and inspect the rubber cap seal for tears or cracks. Check the metal parts of the cap for dents, bends or distortions that could cause leakage. Rinse the cap under warm tap water to flush away loose dirt particles.
6. On Magnum models with the 4-stroke engine, check the thermostat as described in this chapter.

Thermostat

Magnum (4-stroke) engines are equipped with a thermostat located in the cylinder head under the coolant outlet housing.

1. Drain the cooling system as described in Chapter Three.
2. Loosen the 2 screws attaching the outlet housing (A, **Figure 10**) to the cylinder head and move the housing out of the way.
3. Withdraw the thermostat (A, **Figure 11**) from the cavity in the cylinder head.
4. Check the thermostat for opening temperature by heating in a pan of water while observing the tem-

perature. Refer to **Table 1** for the thermostat opening specifications.

5. Clean the surfaces of the cylinder head and the outlet housing.

6. Use a new seal and install the thermostat. The air bleed hole must be toward the top screw hole as shown at B, **Figure 10**.

7. Install the outlet housing and connect the hose if detached.

> *NOTE*
> *It is important to bleed all air from the cooling system when filling a system*

that was drained. Capacity of the cooling system is small and air pockets will result in overheating very quickly.

8. Fill and bleed the cooling system as described in Chapter Three.

Temperature Sensors

On liquid cooled models, a temperature sensor is located on the engine as shown at B, **Figure 11** (for Magnum models with 4-stroke engines) or B, **Figure 12** (for 350L and 400L liquid cooled 2-stroke engines). Refer to **Table 1** for the temperature at which the sensor should close to turn on the engine HOT indicator light.

On liquid cooled models, a temperature sensor is also located on the top of the radiator that controls the operation of the electric fan (**Figure 13**). Refer to **Table 1** for the temperatures at which the sensor should open and close to turn the fan on and off.

On air cooled engines equipped with an electric fan, a sensor is located above the carburetor to control the operation of the electric fan. Refer to **Table 1** for the temperatures at which the sensor should open and close to turn the fan on and off.

7

Table 1 COOLING SYSTEM SPECIFICATIONS

	250/300 Air cooled	350L/400L Liquid cooled	Magnum 4-stroke
Cooling fan			
ON at degrees C (F)	113 (235)	96 (205)	105 (221)
OFF at degrees C (F)	93-104(200-220)	65-71 (149-159)	77-82 (170-180)
Engine HOT light			
ON at degrees C (F)	–	96 (205)	105 (221)
Radiator cap relief			
Pressure kPa (psi)	–	90 kPa (13)	90 kPa (13)
System capacity L (qt)	–	1.89 (2)	2.13 (2.25)
Thermostat			
Begin opening C (F)	–	–	80 (176)
Fully open * C (F)	–	–	96 (205)
* The valve opening is 8 mm (0.315 in.) when the thermsotat is fully open.			

CLUTCH/DRIVE BELT SYSTEM

The drive train includes the clutch/drive belt system, a transmission assembly and a final sprocket/chain drive. The clutch/drive belt system is also called the Polaris variable transmission or PVT. The clutch/drive belt system consists of a drive pulley mounted on the left end of the engine crankshaft, a driven pulley mounted on the left end of the transmission input shaft, and a belt connecting the two pulleys.

This chapter describes the service procedures for the clutch/drive belt system components. Drive belt specifications are listed in **Table 1**. **Tables 1-5** are at the end of the chapter. Service to the chain, gear, or gear and chain transmission assembly is described in Chapter Nine.

DRIVE UNIT

Torque is transferred from the engine crankshaft to the transmission by the Polaris variable transmission (PVT). The drive unit automatically changes the drive ratio to permit the machine to move from idle to maximum speed. Major components are the drive pulley assembly, driven pulley assembly and drive belt (**Figure 1**).

The drive and driven pulleys are basically 2 variable diameter pulleys that automatically vary the amount of reduction. Changes in the reduction ratio are possible by moving the sides of the pulleys closer together or further apart. Changing the gap between the sides of the pulley causes the belt to move up or down in the pulley groove, changing the effective diameter of the pulley. These changes in pulley diameter adjust to correspond with the prevailing load and speed conditions. See **Figure 2**.

The shift sequence is determined by a combination of engine torque and engine rpm. When the load (resistance) increases, such as when going up hill, the pulleys change the reduction ratio; engine rpm will remain nearly the same but the vehicle's speed will drop. When the load decreases, the pulleys automatically shift toward a higher ratio; engine rpm remains the same but the vehicle's speed will increase.

DRIVE PULLEY ASSEMBLY

Major components of the drive pulley assembly are the sliding pulley half (sheave), fixed pulley half (sheave), weight levers, spider and primary spring. The V-belt connects the drive and driven pulleys (**Figure 1**).

Fixed and Sliding Pulley Halves

The sides of the pulley are made of mild steel and the belt surfaces are precision machined to a smooth taper. The pulley is carefully balanced to prevent vibration. The tapered surfaces of both pulleys match the V-belt gripping surface (**Figure 3**).

The drive pulley assembly is mounted on the left end of the engine crankshaft. When the engine is at idle or stopped, the fixed and sliding halves of the pulley are held apart by the primary spring. At slow idle speed or when the engine is stopped, the groove should be wide enough for the V-belt to drop down between the sides of the pulley. There is no engagement because the width of the belt is *less* than the space between the sides of the drive pulley.

When the engine speed is increased from idle, centrifugal force causes the weight levers mounted on the sliding half of the drive pulley to swing out.

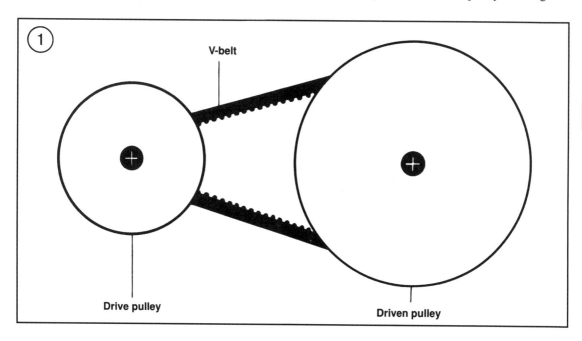

V-belt

Drive pulley

Driven pulley

8

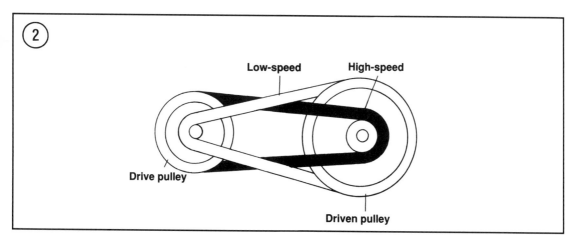

Low-speed   **High-speed**

Drive pulley

Driven pulley

When centrifugal force of the weights is sufficient to overcome the pressure of the primary spring, the sliding half of the pulley is moved closer to the fixed half. This movement narrows the groove between the pulley halves until the sides of the pulley grip the belt. The point at which the pulley grips the belt is called the engagement rpm. Engagement rpm will vary between models, but will occur at approximately 1,500 engine rpm. At low speed, the belt will be located as shown at the low-speed position in **Figure 2**.

As engine rpm is increased, centrifugal force causes the weights of the drive pulley to swing further out and force the sliding half of the pulley closer to the fixed half. As the groove of the drive pulley becomes narrower, the V-belt is forced upward in the groove toward the outer edge of the pulley. The V-belt is forced deeper into the groove of the driven pulley as indicated by the high-speed position of the belt in **Figure 2**.

Though not part of the drive pulley, it should be noted that the release (secondary) spring of the driven pulley forces the sides of the pulley together. Pressure against the sides of the driven pulley will force the sliding half away from the fixed side. Movement of the weight levers in the drive pulley will force the pulley halves together and the belt will move to the outer diameter of the drive pulley. At the same time the belt will force the sides of the driven pulley apart so that it can operate deeper in the groove.

Drive Pulley Spring

The clutch release spring of the drive pulley controls engagement speed. If a lighter spring is installed (or the weights are too heavy), the drive will upshift too fast and the engine will not be able to reach its operating range of 6,000 rpm. If a heavier spring is installed, the engine speed (rpm) will have to be higher to overcome spring pressure and allow engagement. If the spring is too stiff or the weights too heavy, the drive will not be able to move high enough in the pulley groove to attain high gear. Refer to **Table 2** for the original spring installed for your model. **Table 3** lists specifications for identifying the different springs. Actual performance depends upon a combination of characteristics, but generally, the springs are listed in **Table 3** from the strongest at the top to the least strongest at the bottom of the table.

Centrifugal Weight Levers

As previously noted, weighted levers in the drive pulley react to engine speed and swing out. The weights attached to the movable sheave press against rollers on the spider to move the sliding half of the drive pulley. Centrifugal force causes the weights to swing out as the speed of the engine increases. Movement of the weighted levers and the sliding half of the pulley is opposed by the pressure of the primary spring. Until engine speed reaches the engagement rpm, the weights have not yet moved the sliding half of the pulley enough to engage the belt. The force exerted by the weighted levers is controlled by engine rpm. The faster the crankshaft rotates, the farther the weights pivot out. Movement of the sliding half of the drive pulley is controlled by the balance of the spring pressure and the weight of the weighted levers. Refer to **Table 4** for the original weights installed in your model. Performance may be improved at higher altitudes by installing lighter weights as indicated in the table.

DRIVEN PULLEY

Major components of the driven pulley assembly are the sliding half, fixed half, release (secondary) spring and cam (helix). The pulley halves are made of mild steel. The belt surfaces are machined to a

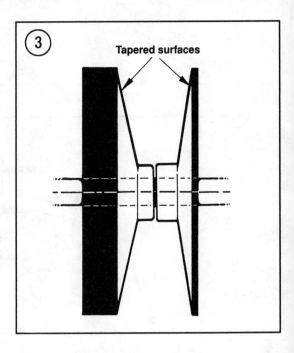

③ Tapered surfaces

smooth tapered surface. The tapered surfaces of the pulley halves match the V-belt gripping surface (**Figure 4**).

The driven pulley assembly is mounted on the left end of the transmission input shaft. When the engine is stopped or at idle, the driven pulley assembly is held in its low speed position by tension from the secondary (release) spring (**Figure 4**).

The driven pulley is a torque sensitive unit. If the ATV encounters an increased load condition, the cam helix forces the driven pulley to downshift by moving the driven pulley halves closer together. The speed of the vehicle will slow, but the engine will continue to run at a high rpm. By sensing load conditions and shifting accordingly, the engine can continue to operate in its peak power range.

Release Spring

The release spring located in the driven pulley assembly helps determine the shifting pattern. The spring is also used to keep the torque sensing cam (helix) in contact with the slider buttons. Spring tension can be changed by installing a different

spring or by repositioning the end of the spring in holes drilled in the cam. Observe the following:

a. Increasing release spring tension will prevent the belt from moving to a higher speed position until the engine speed is increased. If the drive pulley moves to a faster ratio too soon, engine rpm will drop and the engine will begin to bog down. For peak efficiency, the engine should operate within its optimum peak power range. Increasing spring tension may prevent upshifting too early. By not shifting up, the engine should continue to operate within its peak power range.

b. Decreasing secondary spring tension allows the belt to move to a higher speed position at a lower engine rpm. The engine will not operate as efficiently if it is running faster than its peak power range. Decreasing spring tension allows adjustment so that the drive system will shift into a higher ratio sooner to match the engine power.

The torque sensing cam angle will have more affect on the shifting sequence under heavy load than the release spring tension, but both are adjustable.

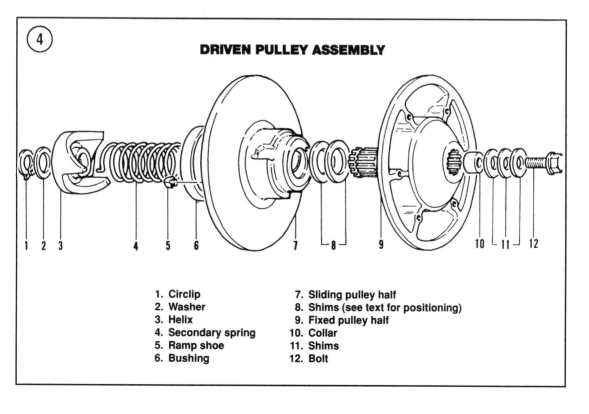

4

DRIVEN PULLEY ASSEMBLY

1 2 3   4   5   6   7 └ 8 ┘ 9   10 └ 11 ┘ 12

1. Circlip
2. Washer
3. Helix
4. Secondary spring
5. Ramp shoe
6. Bushing
7. Sliding pulley half
8. Shims (see text for positioning)
9. Fixed pulley half
10. Collar
11. Shims
12. Bolt

8

Refer to **Table 4** for the original position of the spring ends for your model.

Torque Sensing Cam Angle

The drive pulley spring tension and the cam angle of the torque sensing helix work together to control how easily the driven pulley will shift to a faster speed ratio. The helix cam pushes against the sliding pulley. If the cam angle is steep, the pulleys will shift to a faster speed ratio sooner and will not be as responsive to increases in load. Conversely, low cam angles will exert more side pressure and will slow shifts until the load is reduced and speeds are higher. Refer to **Table 4** for the standard helix (cam) angle.

DRIVE BELT

The drive belt transmits power from the drive pulley to the driven pulley. The belt provides a vital link in the operation and performance of the ATV. To insure top performance, the drive pulley, drive belt and driven pulley must be matched to each other and to the vehicle model. The correct size drive belt must be installed, because belt width and length are critical to proper operation. Belt wear affects clutch operation and shifting characteristics. Since normal wear changes the width of the belt, it is important to check the belt frequently and adjust the clutch as described in this chapter. See **Table 1** for the width of a new drive belt.

With general use, there is no specific mileage or time limit on belt life. Belt life is directly related to maintenance and the type of operation. The belt should be inspected at the intervals listed in Chapter Three. Early belt failure is abnormal and the cause should be determined to prevent subsequent damage. For proper belt cooling, it is important for all of the covers to be installed and joints (**Figure 5**) sealed as described in Chapter Seven.

Removal/Installation

1. Remove the outer cover as described in Chapter Seven.

2. Check the drive belt for manufacturers markings (**Figure 6**) so that during installation it will run in the correct direction. If the belt is not marked, draw

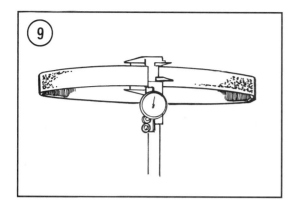

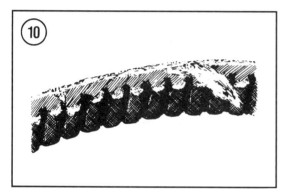

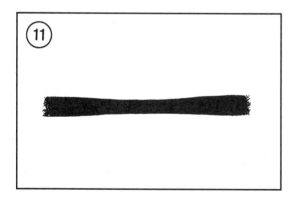

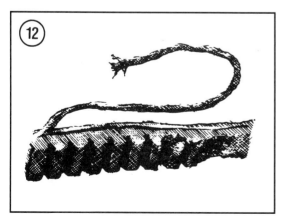

an arrow on the belt facing forward or install a new belt.

3. Push against the inner sheave of the driven pulley (**Figure 7**) and rotate it clockwise to separate the pulley halves. Then roll the belt out of the pulleys (**Figure 8**).

4. Inspect the drive belt as described in this chapter.

5. Perform the *Drive Belt Alignment* as described in this chapter.

6. Reverse Steps 1-3 and install the drive belt. If installing the original belt, make sure to install it so that the manufacturers marks on the belt (or those made before removal) faces in the same direction (forward). When installing a new belt, install it so that you can read the belt identification marks while standing on the left-hand side of the machine as shown in **Figure 6**.

Inspection

Inspect the drive belt weekly or every 150 miles (240 km) of operation.

1. Remove the drive belt as described in this chapter.

2. Measure the width of the drive belt at its widest point (**Figure 9**). Replace the belt if the width is less than the wear limit listed in **Table 1**.

3. Visually inspect the belt for the following conditions:

   a. *Frayed edge*—Check the sides of the belt for a frayed edge cord (**Figure 10**). This indicates drive belt misalignment. Drive belt misalignment can be caused by incorrect pulley alignment and loose engine mounting bolts.

   b. *Worn narrow in one section*—Examine the belt for a section that is worn narrower in one section (**Figure 11**). This condition is caused by excessive belt slippage probably due to engine idle speed adjusted too fast.

   c. *Belt disintegration*—Drive belt disintegration (**Figure 12**) is caused by severe belt wear or misalignment. Disintegration can also be caused by the use of an incorrect belt.

   d. *Sheared cogs*—Sheared cogs as shown in **Figure 13** are usually caused by violent drive pulley engagement. This is an indication of a defective or improperly installed drive pulley.

4. Replace a worn or damaged belt immediately. It is a good idea to always have a spare belt available for an emergency.

8

Drive Belt Deflection

Perform this procedure whenever a new drive belt is installed.

1. Check drive belt alignment as described in this chapter.

2. Position a straight edge across the top of the drive belt.

3. Press the drive belt down in the center and measure the deflection as shown in **Figure 14**. Belt deflection should be within specifications in **Table 1**.

4. If deflection is incorrect, disassemble the driven pulley as described in this chapter, then add or remove shims (**Figure 15**) as necessary. Observe the following.

   a. To tighten belt tension, remove some thickness from shims (**Figure 15**).

   b. To loosen belt tension, add thickness to shims (**Figure 15**).

NOTE
Always leave at least one shim (Figure 15) between the inner and outer sheaves of the driven pulley. If the deflection cannot be set correctly without removing the last shim, check the pulley center-to-center distance and the belt width.

   c. After adjusting belt deflection, rotate driven pulley to help seat the belt in the pulley grooves. Always recheck belt deflection after making any change.

Drive Belt Alignment

The center-to-center distance (A, **Figure 16**) from the drive pulley to the driven pulley, alignment of the pulleys (**Figure 17**) and the offset of the pulleys (**Figure 18**) must be correctly maintained for good performance and long belt life. Refer to **Table 1** for the recommended pulley center-to-center distance.

Correct center-to-center distance ensures correct belt tension and reduction ratio. If the center-to-center distance (A, **Figure 16**) is too short (or the belt is too long), the shift ratio will be too short. The proper size belt will not engage until it is too fast in the groove of the drive pulley. The engine speed will be too high when it engages, but the reduction ratio will not be high enough to easily start moving the vehicle.

If the centers of the pulleys (A, **Figure 16**) are too far apart (or the belt is too short), the drive belt will be pulled down too deep in the driven pulley groove too soon. The machine will not pull strongly because the pulleys are shifting too quickly towards the 1:1 ratio.

If the pulleys are not properly aligned (**Figure 17**) or if the pulley offset is incorrect (**Figure 18**), the belt will wear out prematurely.

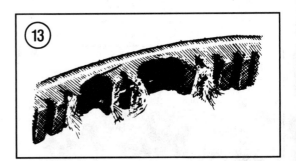

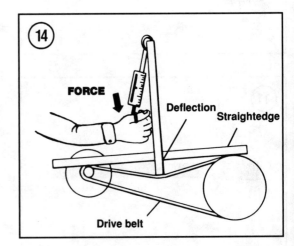

Deflection
Straightedge
FORCE
Drive belt

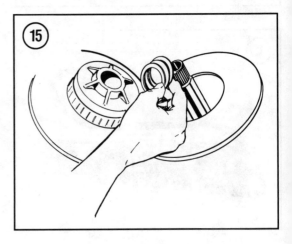

1. Remove the drive belt as described in this chapter.

2. Measure the distance (A, **Figure 16**) between the pulley centers. If the distance is different from the specification listed in **Table 1**, check the engine and transmission mounting bolts. If loose, tighten the bolts and recheck pulley center-to-center distance.

3A. If a Polaris offset alignment bar (part No. 2870654) is available, check the pulley offset and alignment as follows:

  a. Place the offset/alignment bar across the drive and driven pulleys as shown in **Figure 17**.

  b. Clutch alignment is correct when the bar fits easily over the drive pulley, contacts the rear edge of the driven pulley and has 3.2 mm (1/8 in.) clearance at the front edge of the driven pulley as shown at A, **Figure 17**.

  c. If alignment is incorrect, proceed to Step 4.

3B. If the Polaris alignment bar is *not* available, check the alignment as follows:

  a. Place a straightedge across the drive pulley making sure that it contacts the rim at both the front and rear of the pulley. See **Figure 18**.

  b. Measure the distance between the front and rear edges of the driven pulley and the straightedge.

  c. The clearance between the front of the pulley (A, **Figure 18**) and the straightedge should be 3.2 mm (1/8 in.) more than at the rear of the pulley (B, **Figure 18**).

  d. If alignment is incorrect, proceed to Step 4.

4. *Pulley Alignment*—If alignment is not correct, proceed as follows to change the alignment.

NOTE
*Small corrections in the adjustment may be made by adding or removing washers between the frame and the front, lower left engine mount. Add a washer to increase clearance at A, **Figure 17** or A,*

8

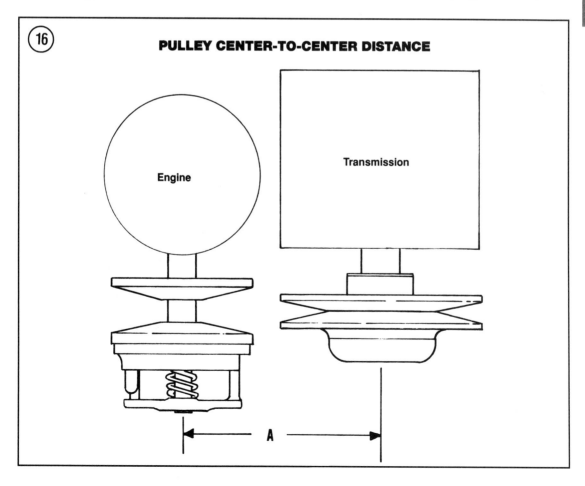

PULLEY CENTER-TO-CENTER DISTANCE

Engine

Transmission

A

Figure 18. *If there are washers between the engine mount and the frame, they can be removed to decrease the clearance at A,* **Figure 17** *or A,* **Figure 18**. *The normal adjustment procedure should be followed for large adjustments. Be sure that the bolts are tight before checking or changing the adjustment.*

a. Remove the drive and driven pulleys as described in this chapter.

b. Remove the inner clutch cover as described in this chapter.

c. Loosen the upper and lower mounts at the front of the engine.

d. Loosen the slotted rear mount (**Figure 19**).

e. Adjust the position of the engine as necessary to align the pulleys correctly, then tighten the engine mount bolts.

f. Temporarily install the pulleys, then refer to Step 3A or 3B to recheck alignment before installing the inner cover.

g. Check the pulley offset using the Polaris offset alignment bar (part No. 2870654) as described in Step 5.

5. *Pulley Offset*—To check pulley offset, place the Polaris offset/alignment bar (part No. 2870654) across the drive and driven pulleys as shown in **Figure 17**. Offset is correct if the rear of the tool just contacts the rear of the driven pulley inner half (B, **Figure 17**) and a 1.6-3.2 mm (1/16 to 1/8 in.) gap is present at the front of the pulley inner half (A, **Figure 17**). To adjust offset, remove the driven pulley assembly, and add or remove shims (**Figure 20**).

6. When the offset is correct and the pulleys are properly aligned, reinstall the inner cover as described in this chapter.

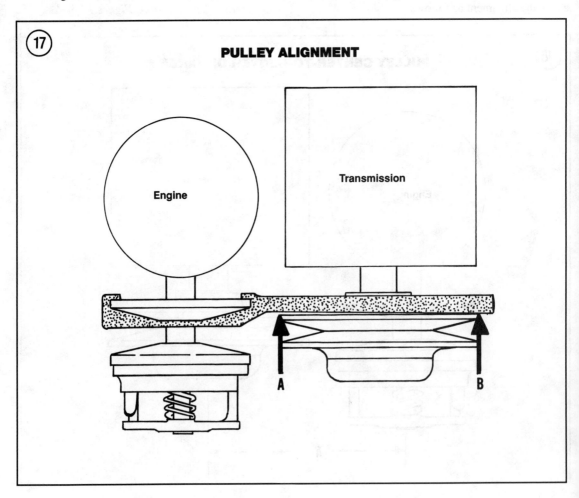

(17) **PULLEY ALIGNMENT**

Engine

Transmission

A

B

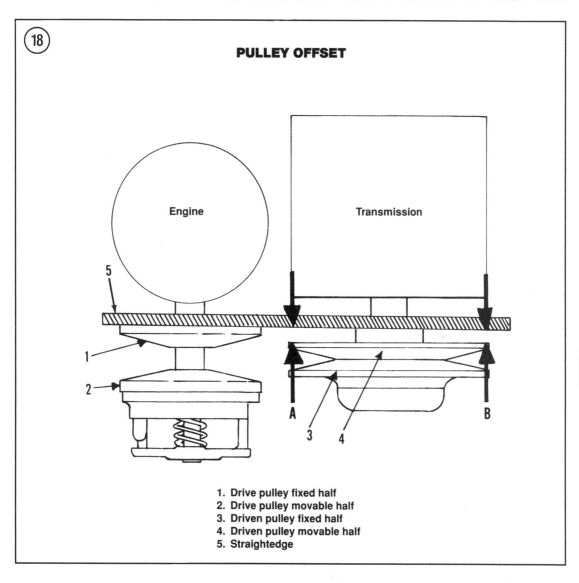

PULLEY OFFSET

Engine

Transmission

A

B

1. Drive pulley fixed half
2. Drive pulley movable half
3. Driven pulley fixed half
4. Driven pulley movable half
5. Straightedge

8

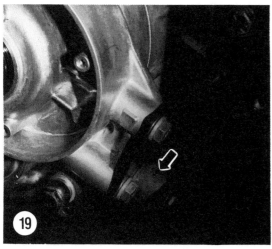

7. Install the drive and driven pulleys as described in this chapter.

8. Install the drive belt and check deflection as described in this chapter.

9. Install the outer cover. Be sure that the cover is properly sealed.

DRIVE PULLEY SERVICE

The drive pulley is mounted on the left end of the engine crankshaft. Refer to **Figure 21** when performing procedures in this section.

WARNING
The drive pulley is under spring pressure. Attempting to disassemble or reassemble the drive pulley without the use of the specified special tools may cause severe personal damage. If you do not have access to the necessary tools, have the service performed by a dealer or other ATV mechanic.

Removal

A special clutch holding tool and the drive pulley puller (part No. 2870506) should be used to remove the drive pulley.

1. Remove the drive belt as described in this chapter.

2. Loosen and remove the bolt and washer (**Figure 22**).

3. Use the special clutch holding tool (A, **Figure 23**) or equivalent to hold the drive pulley while using the puller (B, **Figure 23**) in Step 4.

4. Install the special puller (B, **Figure 23**) through the pulley. Tighten the puller screw to break the drive pulley loose from the crankshaft taper.

NOTE
It may be necessary to rap sharply on the head of the puller to shock the drive pulley loose from the crankshaft.

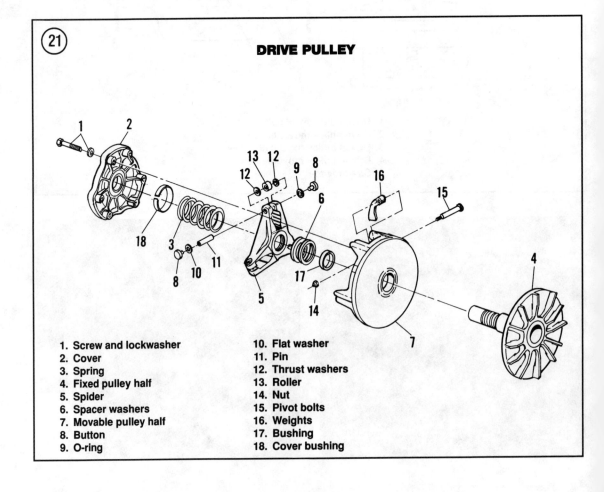

DRIVE PULLEY

1. Screw and lockwasher
2. Cover
3. Spring
4. Fixed pulley half
5. Spider
6. Spacer washers
7. Movable pulley half
8. Button
9. O-ring
10. Flat washer
11. Pin
12. Thrust washers
13. Roller
14. Nut
15. Pivot bolts
16. Weights
17. Bushing
18. Cover bushing

5. When the drive pulley is loose, remove the puller screw.

6. Remove the drive pulley assembly.

Disassembly

WARNING
Precise balance is critical to the operating safety of the drive pulley and it is important that nothing be done to disturb the balance of the unit. The manufacturer suggests that all disassembly and service be performed by an authorized Polaris dealer who is trained and equipped to disassemble, inspect and assemble the drive pulley. Inspect the drive pulley assembly before beginning to disassemble it to determine if any of the major components requires replacement. Install a new complete service drive clutch if the cover, fixed pulley half, spider or movable pulley half (2, 4, 5 or 7, Figure 21) is damaged. Never replace parts with similar used parts from another assembly.

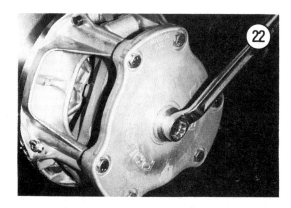

1. Before disassembling, use a felt tip permanent marker to mark the cover, spider, movable sheave and fixed sheave. The drive pulley (**Figure 21**) is balanced as an assembly and should be assembled in the same alignment as it was originally.

2. Loosen screws (1, **Figure 21**) evenly in a crossing pattern until all six are removed.

3. Lift cover (2, **Figure 21**) from the fixed pulley.

4. Remove the spring (3, **Figure 21**).

CAUTION
The remainder of disassembly should not be attempted unless the special holding fixture (part No. 2870547) and spider removal tool (part No. 2870341) are available. The spider is assembled very tightly and parts will probably be damaged if attempts are made to disassemble it without using the special tools. If these tools are not available, have a Polaris dealer disassemble, inspect and reassemble the drive pulley.

5. Attach the drive pulley fixed sheave (4, **Figure 21**) to the holding fixture.

6. Loosen the spider (5, **Figure 21**) using the special tool. Turn the spider counterclockwise to remove.

7. Remove all of the spacer washers (6, **Figure 21**) located between the spider and the movable sheave (7, **Figure 21**). Separate and identify these spacer washers so that the same washers (or same thickness) can be reinstalled when assembling.

NOTE
Several different types of buttons (8, Figure 21) have been used. If the buttons are replaced, make sure that the correct buttons are installed for your model. On some models, an O-ring is installed behind the driving side (9, Figure 21) and a flat rubber washer (10, Figure 21) is installed behind the trailing side buttons. Premature wear and excessive noise will occur if the O-ring and flat washer are improperly assembled.

8. Remove the buttons, O-rings and washers (8, 9 and 10, **Figure 21**).

9. If not already separated, separate the pulley fixed sheave (4, **Figure 21**) from the movable sheave (7, **Figure 21**).

NOTE
Use the special tool (part No. 2870910) or equivalent to remove the pins (11, Figure 21). Be careful not to damage the rollers, washers or the pins when removing or installing.

10. Remove one pin (11, **Figure 21**), then lift the two thrust washers and the roller (12 and 13, **Figure 21**) from the spider (5, **Figure 21**). Keep the pin, thrust washers and roller together as a set if they are to be reinstalled. Do not mix rollers and pins from the other two locations.

11. Repeat Step 9 for the other two pins to remove the remaining thrust washers and rollers.

12. Remove nuts and bolts (14 and 15, **Figure 21**) to remove the weights.

Inspection

1. Clean all parts thoroughly.

2. Remove all Loctite residue from the threads of all screws.

3. Check the pulley sheaves (4 and 7, **Figure 21**) for cracks or damage.

4. Check the drive belt surfaces of the pulley sheaves (4 and 7, **Figure 21**) for rubber or rust buildup. For proper operation, the surfaces must be *clean*. Remove debris with a fine grade steel wool. Clean with a piece of lint-free cloth.

5. Check the drive pulley spring (3, **Figure 21**) for cracks or distortion. The springs are color coded for correct application. Refer to **Table 2** for original spring application for your model. If the spring appears okay, measure its free length and compare with the free length specification listed in **Table 3**. Replace the spring with one of the same color code.

6. Check the weights (16, **Figure 21**) for:
   a. Outer surface of the weights for wear, dents or galling.
   b. Check the pivot bore for scoring or galling.
   c. Check the complete surface of the weights carefully for cracks, chips or broken ends. Damage to the weights is often an indication that the pin and roller (11 and 13, **Figure 21**) are also damaged.

WARNING
Refer to Figure 24 for the shape and gram weight of the drive pulley weights. It is important that all three weights are

exactly the same. Do not change the shape of the weights without a thorough understanding of PVT operation. Components of the drive and driven pulleys must be carefully matched for proper operation. Before changing the weights in the drive pulley, consult with your Polaris dealer.

7. Install new weights as a set if any are damaged. Weights are marked to indicate their original size and **Table 4** lists original application. It may be necessary to install lighter weights when operating at higher altitudes as indicated in **Table 4**.

NOTE
Special tools are required to install the bushings inspected in Steps 8 and 9. If you do not have access to the special tools, have the bushing replaced by a Polaris dealer.

8. Inspect the bushing (17, **Figure 21**) located in the movable sheave (7, **Figure 21**). The bushing is coated with Teflon and a new bushing should be installed if more brass is showing than Teflon. Do not remove the old bushing unless replacement is necessary. The bushing for 1985 and 1986 models is retained in position by a steel retainer that is installed after the bushing.

9. Inspect the bushing (18, **Figure 21**) located in the cover (2, **Figure 21**). The bushing is coated with Teflon and a new bushing should be installed if more brass is showing than Teflon. Do not remove the bushing unless replacement is necessary. The bushing for 1987 and later models is a steel backed split bushing.

10. Check for clearance between the buttons (8, **Figure 21**) installed on the spider and the towers of the movable sheave (7, **Figure 21**). The installation of new O-rings and flat rings (9 and 10, **Figure 21**) should remove all clearance.

11. Check the surfaces of the movable pulley towers contacted by the buttons (8, **Figure 21**). Install a new, complete driven pulley assembly if the spider or movable sheave is damaged.

12. Inspect the bushing contact areas of the fixed sheave (4, **Figure 21**) for wear, nicks or scratches.

13. If rollers (13, **Figure 21**) do not roll freely and smoothly on the pins (11, **Figure 21**), install new pins and rollers.

DRIVE PULLEY WEIGHTS
(PART NUMBERS AND WEIGHTS IN GRAMS)

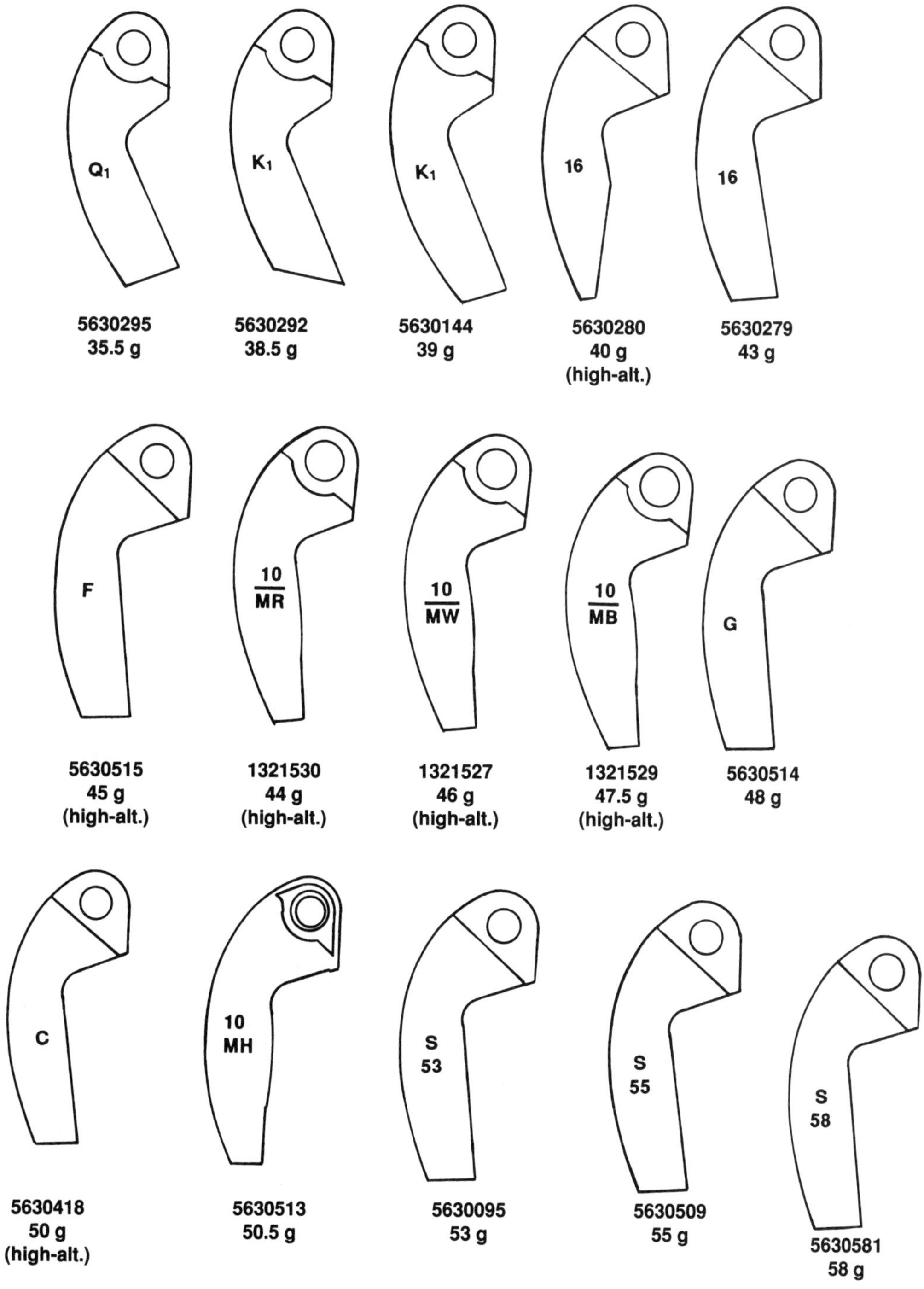

Q_1
5630295
35.5 g

K_1
5630292
38.5 g

K_1
5630144
39 g

16
5630280
40 g
(high-alt.)

16
5630279
43 g

F
5630515
45 g
(high-alt.)

$\frac{10}{MR}$
1321530
44 g
(high-alt.)

$\frac{10}{MW}$
1321527
46 g
(high-alt.)

$\frac{10}{MB}$
1321529
47.5 g
(high-alt.)

G
5630514
48 g

C
5630418
50 g
(high-alt.)

10
MH
5630513
50.5 g

S
53
5630095
53 g

S
55
5630509
55 g

S
58
5630581
58 g

8

14. If there is any doubt as to the condition of any part, replace it with a new one.

Reassembly

Refer to **Figure 21** for this procedure.

CAUTION
The drive pulley is assembled dry. Do not lubricate any component.

1. Assemble the rollers (13, **Figure 21**), thrust washers (12) and pins (11) in the spider (15). Make sure that the rollers turn freely on the pins after assembling.
2. Assemble the buttons (8, **Figure 21**), O-ring (9) and flat rubber rings (10). The O-rings *must* be located on the thrust side as shown at 9, **Figure 21**.
3. Assemble the movable sheave (7, **Figure 21**) over the fixed sheave (4, **Figure 21**).
4. Install the same spacer washers (6, **Figure 21**) as were originally installed. Install the washers over the shaft of the fixed sheave before installing the spider.
5. Align the previously affixed mark on the spider with the mark on the movable sheave, then thread the spider onto the fixed sheave.

CAUTION
Make sure that the spacer washers (6, Figure 21) remain in the recess of the spider while tightening. Misalignment will disturb the unit's balance.

6. Tighten the spider to the torque listed in **Table 5**.
7. Assemble the weights (16, **Figure 21**) and pivot screws (15) in the movable sheave. The weights should move easily on the pivot screws after assembling.
8. Install the clutch spring (3, **Figure 21**).
9. Align the previously affixed mark on the cover (2, **Figure 21**) with marks on spider and movable pulley, then install the cover. Tighten the screws (1, **Figure 21**) retaining the cover evenly, in a crossing pattern until they all reach the final torque listed in **Table 5**.

Installation

CAUTION
Do not apply antiseize lubricant or any other lubricant onto the crankshaft taper when installing the drive pulley assembly.

1. Clean the crankshaft taper with lacquer thinner or electrical contact cleaner.
2. Slide the drive pulley (**Figure 25**) onto the crankshaft (**Figure 26**).
3. Install the drive pulley retaining screw and lockwasher. Tighten the retaining screw to the torque listed in **Table 5**.
4. Install the drive belt as described in this chapter.
5. Check the outer cover seals and install as described in Chapter Three.

DRIVEN PULLEY SERVICE

The driven pulley is mounted onto the left-hand side of the transmission input shaft.

Removal

1. Remove the drive belt as described in this chapter.
2. Loosen and remove the driven pulley retaining screw (**Figure 27**).
3. Slide the driven pulley from the splined shaft.

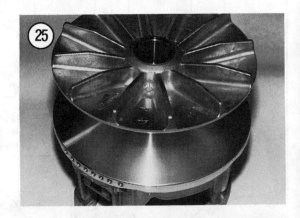

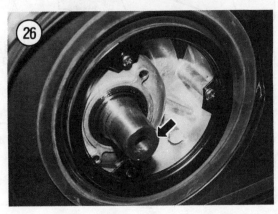

NOTE
*The shim(s) (**Figure 28**) installed behind the driven pulley are used to adjust the pulley offset. Do not remove the shims unless required for other service. Be sure to install the same shims before reinstalling the driven pulley.*

Installation

1. Make sure the shims (**Figure 28**) are installed on the transmission input shaft.
2. Clean the splines on the transmission input shaft and apply a light film of low temperature grease to the splines.
3. Slide the driven pulley onto the shaft, aligning the master splines of the shaft and pulley.
4. Install the screw retaining the driven pulley to the torque listed in **Table 5**.
5. Check the pulley offset as described in this chapter.

6. Install the drive belt as described in this chapter.
7. Check the drive belt deflection as described in this chapter.
8. Check the outer cover seals and install as described in Chapter Three.

Disassembly

1. Before disassembling driven pulley, locate the end of the spring in one of the two holes in helix (2, **Figure 29**). Mark the hole for identification of original setting.

WARNING
Wear eye protection and hold the helix cam securely when removing the snap ring in Step 2.

2. Set the driven pulley on a workbench with the outer sheave of the pulley down, push the helix (2, **Figure 29**) down and remove the snap ring (3, **Figure 29**). Slowly release the helix, allowing it to come up and turn.
3. Carefully remove the helix cam (2, **Figure 29**) from the spring, but leave the spring in the pulley.
4. Note the location of the end of the spring in the pulley movable half, then remove the spring. Mark the spring location in the movable half for identification of original setting. Suggested initial setting for new springs is listed in **Table 4**.

NOTE
*The spacer washers (9, **Figure 29**) located between the halves of the sheaves are used to adjust belt deflection. Do not lose or damage these spacer washers. At least one spacer should always be located between the sheaves.*

5. Slide the movable pulley half (7, **Figure 29**) from the fixed sheave (8, **Figure 29**).
6. The wear buttons (5, **Figure 29**) can be removed after removing the Torx screws (6, **Figure 29**).

Inspection

1. Clean all parts thoroughly.
2. Check the pulley halves (7 and 8, **Figure 29**) for cracks or damage.
3. Check the drive belt surfaces of the pulley halves (7 and 8, **Figure 29**) for rubber or rust buildup. For proper operation, the surfaces must be *clean*. Re-

8

move debris with a fine grade steel wool. Clean with a piece of lint-free cloth.

NOTE
Weakening of the driven pulley spring may be metal fatigue resulting from the constant twisting action. The driven pulley will open quicker than it should if the spring has weakened. This condition can be noticed when riding up steep grades or with a heavy load; the vehicle will be slower and have much less pulling power than normal. It is difficult to gauge spring wear, so you may choose to replace the spring when the unit is disassembled for service.

4. Check the driven pulley spring (4, **Figure 29**) for cracks or distortion. Check the alignment of the ends of the spring as shown in **Figure 30**. The ends of the spring are aligned when new. Replace the spring if necessary.

5. Check the wear buttons (5, **Figure 29**) for wear or damage. The wear buttons provide a sliding surface between the helix cam (2, **Figure 29**) and the movable pulley half (7, **Figure 29**). The buttons rub against aluminum and wear is usually minimal. The wear buttons can be reversed if the original wear surface is worn. When both sides are worn, install new wear buttons as a set.

6. Check the cam ramps on the helix (2, **Figure 29**) for scoring, gouging or other signs of damage. Smooth the ramp area with a #400 wet-or-dry sandpaper. If the ramp area is severely damaged, replace the helix.

7. Inspect the bushing (10, **Figure 29**) located in the movable sheave. The bushing is coated with Teflon and a new bushing should be installed if more brass

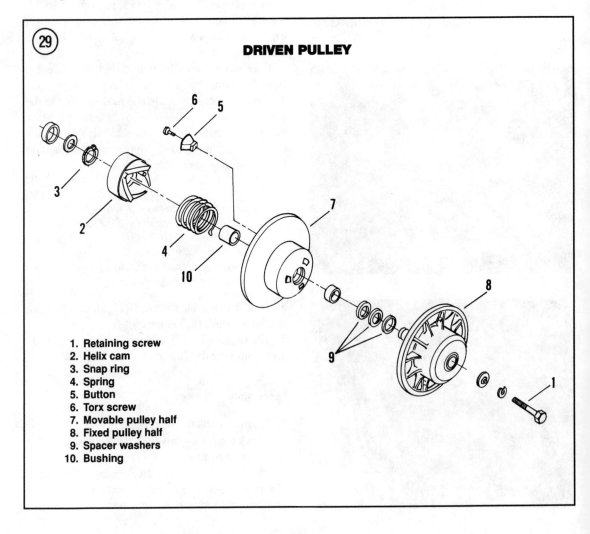

DRIVEN PULLEY

1. Retaining screw
2. Helix cam
3. Snap ring
4. Spring
5. Button
6. Torx screw
7. Movable pulley half
8. Fixed pulley half
9. Spacer washers
10. Bushing

is showing than Teflon. Do not remove the bushing unless replacement is necessary.

8. Inspect the bushing contact areas of the fixed pulley half (8, **Figure 29**) for wear, nicks or scratches.

9. If there is any doubt as to the condition of any part, replace it with a new one.

Assembly

1. Place the fixed pulley half (8, **Figure 29**) on the workbench so the shaft faces up.

2. Install the spacer washers (9, **Figure 29**) over the shaft. The spacer washers are used to adjust belt deflection and several may be installed, but there should always be at least one spacer between the sheaves.

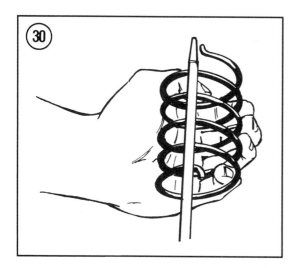

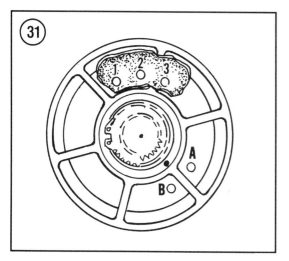

3. Install the movable pulley half (7, **Figure 29**) onto the fixed half so the belt surfaces face together.

NOTE
*The positioning of the ends of the spring will determine the shifting pattern. The greatest amount of spring tension will cause the engine rpm to be higher during upshift and will cause the unit to downshift sooner when the load is increased, such as going up a hill. Less spring tension will upshift faster and downshift slower. The actual position of the spring ends may be different from those listed in **Table 4** to suit the driver's preference. This is especially true for a spring that has been in service for some time. The spring tension should also be increased for operation at high altitudes.*

4. Install the spring (4, **Figure 29**) with one end in the hole (1, 2 or 3, **Figure 31**) marked during disassembly. Refer to **Table 4** to determine which of the three holes in the pulley was used on original assembly. The first part No. in the *Clutch Spring Position* column is the suggested hole in the movable pulley.

5. Install the helix (2, **Figure 29**) with the end of the spring in the hole marked during disassembly. Refer to **Table 4** to determine which of the two holes was used on original assembly. The second part No. is the hole in the helix suggested for the spring.

6. Install the helix and preload the spring approximately 1/3 turn as follows:

   a. Align up the master splines of the helix (2, **Figure 29**) and the shaft and push the helix partly onto the spline.

   b. Twist the movable pulley half (**Figure 32**) counterclockwise approximately 1/3 turn (120°). The location of the cam surfaces on the helix and the buttons (5, **Figure 29**) will determine actual position.

   c. Push the helix down onto splines against spring pressure, then install the snap ring (3, **Figure 29**).

   d. Make sure the snap ring is completely seated in the pulley shaft groove.

CLUTCH INNER COVER

The clutch inner cover is an important component of the PVT (belt drive) cooling system. The belt and other drive components can be quickly damaged by heat generated by normal operation if not properly cooled. Slippage caused by mud, water or oil entering the system can also quickly damage the drive system components. Refer to Chapter Seven for additional service to the system.

Removal/Installation

The clutch inner cover, outer cover and ducts are shown in **Figure 33**, **Figure 34** and **Figure 35** typical of all models.

1. Remove the outer cover (A, **Figure 33**, **Figure 34** or **Figure 35**) as described in Chapter Seven.

2. Remove the drive belt as described in this chapter.

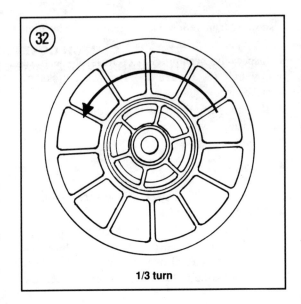

1/3 turn

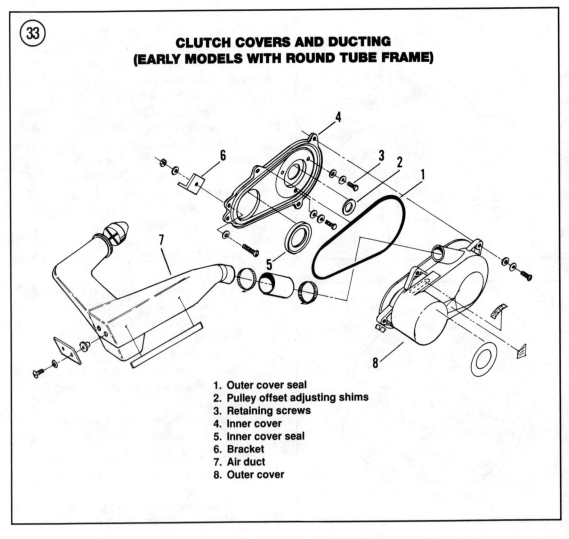

CLUTCH COVERS AND DUCTING
(EARLY MODELS WITH ROUND TUBE FRAME)

1. Outer cover seal
2. Pulley offset adjusting shims
3. Retaining screws
4. Inner cover
5. Inner cover seal
6. Bracket
7. Air duct
8. Outer cover

(34)

CLUTCH COVERS AND DUCTING
(MODELS WITH SQUARE TUBE FRAMES EXCEPT MAGNUM AND SCRAMBLER)

1. Outer cover seal
2. Pulley offset adjusting shims
3. Retaining screws
4. Inner cover
5. Inner cover seal
6. Retainer
7. Bracket
8. Air duct
9. Outer cover
10. Air duct

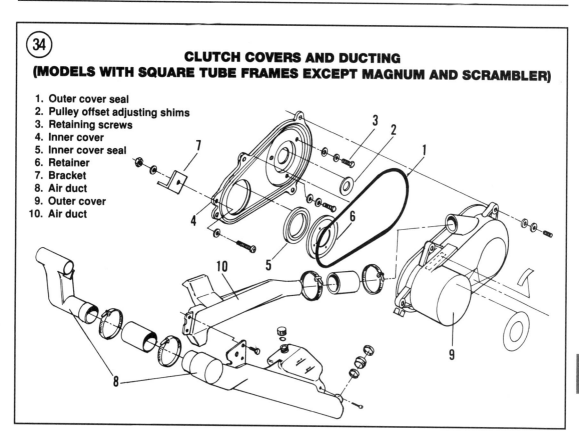

(35)

CLUTCH COVERS AND DUCTING
(MAGNUM MODELS)

1. Outer cover seal
2. Pulley offset
   adjusting shims
3. Retaining screws
4. Inner cover
5. Inner cover seal
6. Retainer
7. O-ring
8. Spacer
9. Outlet air duct
10. Inlet air duct
11. Outer cover

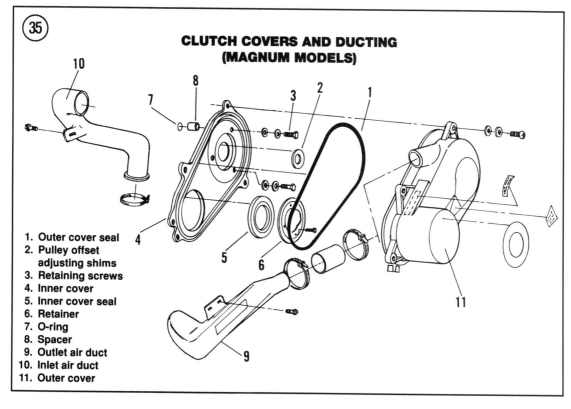

8

3. Remove the drive and driven pulleys as described in this chapter.

NOTE
Some models are not equipped with the retainer removed in Step 4. The screws attaching the inner cover vary and may be different from those shown in the illustrations.

4. Remove the screws attaching the front retainer (**Figure 36**) on models so equipped.

NOTE
*Screws (A, **Figure 37**) should be completely removed from the threads of the transmission housing, but do not lose the O-rings (A, **Figure 38**) and spacers (B). The O-rings (A, **Figure 38**) are used to hold the spacers (B) and bolts together to prevent their loss and to assist installation of the inner cover.*

5. Loosen the screws (A, **Figure 37**) attaching the inner cover to the transmission.

6. Check for any other screws (B, **Figure 37**) or bolts attaching the inner cover to brackets (6, **Figure 33** or 7, **Figure 34**). Remove any additional attaching screws.

7. Remove the inner cover after making sure all of the attaching screws are removed.

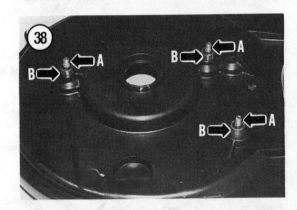

NOTE
Proper sealing of the clutch cover is important to prevent the entrance of water and to properly direct the flow of fresh air for cooling the belt drive system.

8. Inspect the inner cover and the seals (**Figure 39**) for damage. Make sure the front seal is attached to the cover with silicone sealer before installing the cover.

9. Inspect the inlet ducting for proper sealing. See **Figure 40**. Repair or replace any loose, damaged or missing parts of the PVT cooling system.

10. Position the inner cover and install the screws (A, **Figure 37**) loosely.

11. Make sure that the front of the inner cover is properly located and install the retainer (6, **Figure 34** or 6, **Figure 35**), if so equipped.

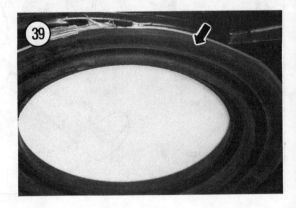

12. Install and tighten any screws attaching the inner cover before tightening the screws (A, **Figure 37**) attaching the cover to the transmission housing.

13. Tighten the screws (A, **Figure 37**) to the torque listed in **Table 5**.

14. Complete assembly by reversing the removal procedure.

8

Table 1 DRIVE BELT AND PULLEY SPECIFICATIONS

	cm	in.
Belt deflection	2.9-3.2	1 1/8-1 1/4
Belt width		
New	3.02	1.188
Wear limit	2.86	1.125
Pulley center-to-center distance	24.9-25.9	9.81-10.19

Table 2 OPERATING RPM AND DRIVE SPRING SPECIFICATIONS

Model No.	Operating RPM	Drive pulley spring color
1985		
Scrambler W857027 and		
Trail Boss W857527	5,800-6,200	Blue/green
1986		
Scrambler W867027, Trail Boss W867527		
and Trail Boss W867627	5,800-6,200	Blue/green
1987		
Trail Boss W877527, 4 × 4 W878027,		
4 × 4 W878127 and 4 × 4 W878327	5,800-6,200	Blue/green
Cyclone W877828	6,800-7,200	Brown
1988		
Trail Boss 2 × 4 W887527 and		
4 × 4 W888127	5,800-6,200	Blue/green
Trail Boss 250 R/ES X888528 and		
W888528	6,400-6,800	Yellow

(continued)

Table 2 OPERATING RPM AND DRIVE SPRING SPECIFICATIONS (continued)

Model No.	Operating RPM	Drive pulley spring color
1989		
All models	5,800-6,200	Blue/green
1990		
Trail Blazer W907221	5,800-6,200	Blue/green
Trail Boss 250 W908527, 2 × 4 W907527		
and 4 × 4 W908127	5,800-6,200	Blue/green
Trail Boss 2 × 4-350L W907539 and		
4 × 4-350L W908139	5,600-6,000	Blue/green
Big Boss 4 × 6 W908627	5,800-6,200	Blue/green
1991		
Trail Blazer W917221	5,800-6,200	Blue/green
Trail Boss 250 W918527, 2 × 4 W917527		
and 4 × 4 W918127	5,800-6,200	Blue/green
Trail Boss 2 × 4-350L W917539 and		
4 × 4-350L W918139	5,600-6,000	Blue/green
Big Boss 4 × 6 W918627 and		
6 × 6 W918727	5,800-6,200	Blue/green
1992		
Trail Blazer W927221	5,800-6,200	Blue/green
Trail Boss 250 W928527, 2 × 4 W92752		
and 4 × 4 W928127	5,800-6,200	Blue/green
Trail Boss 2 × 4-350L W927539 and		
4 × 4-350L W928139	5,600-6,000	Blue/green
Big Boss 4 × 6 W928627 and		
6 × 6 W928727	5,800-6,200	Blue/green
1993		
Trail Blazer W937221	5,800-6,200	Blue/green
Trail Boss 250 W938527, 2 × 4 W937527,		
4 × 4 W938127 and		
6 × 6 W938727	5,800-6,200	Blue/green
Sportsman W938039	5,600-6,000	Blue/green
350 2 × 4 W937539, 4 × 4 W938139 and		
6 × 6 W938739	5,600-6,000	Blue/green
1994		
Trail Blazer 2W W947221	5,800-6,200	Blue/green
Trail Boss 2W W948527	5,800-6,200	Blue/green
Sport W948540 and		
Sportsman 4 × 4 W948040	5,500-5,900	Blue/green
300 2 × 4 W947530, 4 × 4 W948130 and		
6 × 6 W948730	5,400-5,800	Blue/green
400 2 × 4 W947540, 4 × 4 W948140 and		
6 × 6 W948740	5,500-5,900	Blue/green
1995		
Trail Blazer W957221 and		
Trail Boss W958527	5,800-6,200	Blue/green
300 2 × 4 W957530 and		
300 4 × 4 W958130	5,400-5,800	Blue/green
400 2 × 4 W957540, Sport W958540 and		
Sportsman 4 × 4 W958040	5,500-5,900	Blue/green
Xplorer 4 × 4 W959140 and		
400 6 × 6 W958740	5,500-5,900	Blue/green
Scrambler W957840	5,800-6,200	White
Magnum 2 × 4 W957444 and		
Magnum 4 × 4 W958144	5,800-6,200	Blue/green

Table 3 DRIVE PULLEY SPRING SPECIFICATIONS

Color	Wire diameter mm	in.	Free length mm	in.	Part No.
Blue/gold	5.26	0.207	85.9-92.2	3.38-3.63	7041080
Gold	5.26	0.207	79.5-85.9	3.13-3.38	7041148
Silver	5.28	0.208	76.2-82.6	3.00-3.25	7041062
Red	4.88	0.192	92.7-99.1	3.65-3.90	7041083
Red/white	4.88	0.192	88.1-94.5	3.47-3.72	7041150
Brown	5.08	0.200	74.7-81.0	2.94-3.19	7041061
Orange	4.98	0.196	82.6-88.9	3.25-3.50	7041060
Pink	4.50	0.177	116.1-122.4	4.57-4.82	7041065
Yellow	4.88	0.192	71.1-77.5	2.80-3.05	7041102
Green	4.05	0.177	74.4-80.8	2.93-3.18	7041168
Purple	4.27	0.168	107.9-114.3	4.25-4.50	7041063
White	4.05	0.177	71.1-77.5	2.80-3.05	7041032
Plain	3.99	0.157	108.2-114.6	4.26-4.51	7041021
Blue/green	4.05	0.177	61.0-67.6	2.40-2.66	7041157
Black	3.56	0.140	104.8-111.1	4.13-4.38	7041022

Table 4 SHIFT WEIGHTS AND DRIVEN PULLEY SPECIFICATIONS

Model	Shift weights I.D. mark/weight Original position	Above 6,000 ft	Driven pulley Helix angle	Spring position*
1985				
Scrambler W857027 and Trail Boss W857527	5/45 g	16/40 g	40°	3-B
1986				
Scrambler W867027 and Trail Boss W867627	16/43 g	16/40 g	40°	3-B
1987				
Trail Boss W877527, 4 × 4 W878027, 4 × 4 W87812 and 4 × 4 W878327	16/43 g	16/40 g	40°	3-B
Cyclone W877828	16/43 g	–	44-36°	3-B
1988				
Trail Boss 2 × 4 W887527 and 4 × 4 W888127	16/43 g	16/40 g	40°	2-B
Trail Boss 250 R/ES X888528 and W888528	16/43 g	16/40 g	44-36°	2-B
1989				
All models	16/43 g	16/40 g	40°	2-B
1990				
Trail Blazer W907221	16/43 g	16/40 g	40°	2-B
Trail Boss 250 W908527, 2 × 4 W907527 and 4 × 4 W908127	16/43 g	16/40 g	40°	2-B
Trail Boss 2 × 4-350L W907539 and 4 × 4-350L W908139	S/53 g	–	40°	2-B
Big Boss 4 × 6 W908627	16/43 g	16/40 g	40°	2-B
1991				
Trail Blazer W917221	16/43 g	16/40 g	40°	2-B
Trail Boss 250 W918527, 2 × 4 W917527 and 4 × 4 W918127	16/43 g	16/40 g	40°	2-B
Trail Boss 2 × 4-350L W917539 and 4 × 4-350L W918139	S/53 g	–	40°	2-B

(continued)

8

Table 4 SHIFT WEIGHTS AND DRIVEN PULLEY SPECIFICATIONS (continued)

| Model | Shift weights I.D. mark/weight | | Driven pulley | |
	Original position	Above 6,000 ft	Helix angle	Spring position*
1991 (continued)				
Big Boss 4 × 6 W918627 and 6 × 6 W918727	16/43 g	16/40 g	40°	2-B
1992				
Trail Blazer W927221	16/43 g	16/40 g	40°	2-B
Trail Boss 250 W928527, 2 × 4 W927527 and 4 × 4 W928127	16/43 g	16/40 g	40°	2-B
Trail Boss 2 × 4-350L W927539 and 4 × 4-350L W928139	S/53 g	C/50 g	40°	2-B
Big Boss 4 × 6 W928627 and 6 × 6 W928727	16/43 g	16/40 g	40°	2-B
1993				
Trail Blazer W937221	16/43 g	16/40 g	40°	2-B
Trail Boss 250 W938527, 2 × 4 W937527, 4 × 4 W938127 and 6 × 6 W938727	16/43 g	16/40 g	40°	2-B
Sportsman W938039	S/53 g	C/50 g	40°	2-B
350 2 × 4 W937539, 4 × 4 W938139 and 6 × 6 W938739	S/53 g	C/50 g	40°	2-B
1994				
Trail Blazer 2W W947221	16/43 g	16/40 g	40°	2-B
Trail Boss 2W W948527	16/43 g	16/40 g	40°	2-B
Sport W948540 and Sportsman 4 × 4 W948040	S/55 g	S/53 g	44-36°	–
300 2 × 4 W947530, 4 × 4 W948130 and 6 × 6 W948730	G/48 g	F/45 g	44-36°	–
400 2 × 4 W947540, 4 × 4 W948140 and 6 × 6 W948740	S/55 g	S/53 g	44-36°	–
1995				
Trail Blazer W957221 and Trail Boss W958527	16/43 g	16/40 g	40°	2-B
300 2 × 4 W957530 and 300 4 × 4 W958130	G/48 g	F/45 g	44-36°	–
400 2 × 4 W957540, Sport W95854 and Sportsman 4 × 4 W958040	S/55 g	S/53 g	44-36°	–
Xplorer 4 × 4 W959140 and 400 6 × 6 W958740	S/55 g	S/53 g	44-36°	–
Scrambler W957840	S/55 g	S/53 g	40°	2-B
Magnum 2 × 4 W957444 and Magnum 4 × 4 W958144	10MH 50.5 g	10MW 46 g	40°	2-B

* The first number is the recommended position of the spring in the movable sheave and the second number is the location number of the hole in the cam helix.

Table 5 TORQUE SPECIFICATIONS

	N·m	ft.-lbs.
Drive pulley screw	54.2	40
Driven pulley screw	23.1	17
Inner cover screws	16.3	12
Drive pulley cover screws	10.2	7.5
Spider to fixed sheave	271	200

CHAPTER NINE

TRANSMISSION SYSTEM

Three different transmissions have been used. Refer to **Table 1** for the type of transmission installed in your model. If the service procedures are different for the various models, reference to the different types may be to "Type I, Type II,"or "Type III" as listed in **Table 1**.

TRANSMISSION OIL

Oil contained in the transmission housing lubricates the chain and sprockets or gears. Different oil is recommended for models with chain transmission (Type I) than for models with gear transmission (Type II) or gear/chain transmission (Type III). Refer to Chapter Three for recommended lubricant types and maintenance procedures.

TYPE I TRANSMISSION

The Type I transmission is a chain type that is used on all 1985-1986 models and some 1987-1990 models. Refer to **Table 1** for application.

Removal/Installation

1. Place the ATV on a level surface and block the wheels to keep it from rolling.
2. Remove the rear rack, cowling and fenders as described in Chapter Fifteen.
3. Remove the PVT outer cover as described in Chapter Seven.
4. Remove the drive belt, drive pulley, driven pulley and inner cover as described in Chapter Eight.
5. Loosen the rear chain adjuster as described in Chapter Three.

6. Remove the master link clip and master link from the rear drive chain, then remove the rear drive chain.

7. Loosen the swing arm bolts (A, **Figure 1**) on the left and right of the transmission enough to remove the transmission.

8. Remove the 2 attaching screws (B, **Figure 1**) from the left side of the transmission.

9. Remove the attaching screw from the bottom of the transmission.

10. Remove the disk brake cover, brake disc and caliper from the right side of the transmission as described in Chapter Fourteen.

11. Detach the air box from the carburetor and the frame tube, then remove the air box.

12. Lift the transmission from the frame.

13. Reverse the removal procedure to reinstall the transmission. Refer to **Table 2** for the recommended torque when tightening the swing arm transmission support bolt. Be sure to bend the locking tabs (**Figure 2**) around the screw heads after tightening.

14A. Adjust the optional torque stop available on 1985-1986 models as follows.

    a. Adjust the length of the stop (**Figure 3**) until it just contacts the transmission.

    b. Lengthen the stop 1 1/2 turns, then tighten the locknuts.

14B. Adjust the torque stop on 1987-on models as follows.

    a. Adjust the length of the stop until it just contacts the transmission.

    b. Lengthen the stop 1/2 turn, then tighten the lock nut.

Disassembly/Inspection/Reassembly

1. Remove the transmission as described in this chapter.

2. Drain oil from the transmission.

3. Remove the set screw, detent spring and ball (**Figure 4**).

4. Remove the reverse switch.

5. Remove the chain and sprocket guard (**Figure 5**).

6. Remove the output sprocket.

7. Remove the screws attaching the case halves and carefully separate the case halves (**Figure 6**).

8. Remove the shafts, sprockets and chain (**Figure 7**).

9. Clean the case, shafts, chain, sprockets and all other parts carefully.

10. Inspect the bearings, shift dogs, sprockets and chain carefully, and install new parts as necessary.

NOTE
Several changes have been made to this transmission, the most obvious is the change from a chain that is 15 links wide to a chain that is 11 links wide. Always

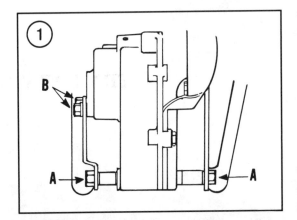

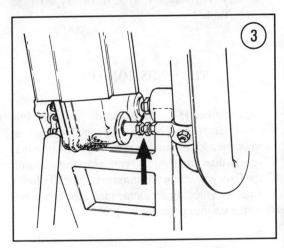

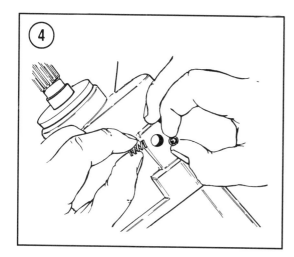

④

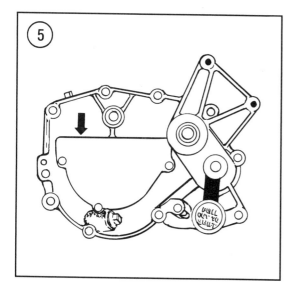

⑤

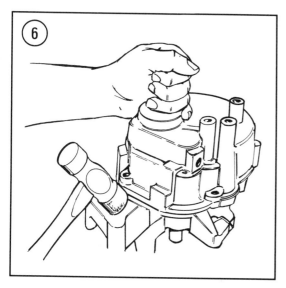

⑥

be sure to install parts that are correct for the transmission being serviced.

11. Reassemble the output shaft, gears, sprocket and bearings. Always install bearings onto shafts using drivers that contact the inner race.

12. Install the shifter shaft, input shaft, output shaft and chain in the right side of the case at the same time as shown in **Figure 7**.

13. Coat the mating surface of the right side case half with Loctite 515 Gasket Eliminator, or equivalent.

14. Install the left case half, making sure that the bearings are seated in their bores.

15. Install and tighten the screws attaching case halves together. Refer to **Table 2** for recommended tightening torque.

16. Install the detent ball, spring and set screw (**Figure 4**).

17. Install the reverse switch.

18. Install the shift handle.

19. Install the shaft seals as follows:

   a. Grease the shafts to prevent damage to the seals.

   b. Install the seals over the shafts by hand, being careful not to damage the lip of the seal.

   c. Seat the seal in case bore using the correct size driver that contacts the outer edge of the seal.

20. Fill the transmission with the correct type and quantity of lubricant as described in Chapter Three.

TYPE II TRANSMISSION

The Type II transmission is a gear type that is used on some 1987-1993 models. Refer to **Table 1** for application.

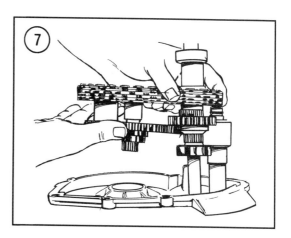

⑦

9

Removal/Installation

1. Place the ATV on a level surface and block the wheels to keep it from rolling.
2. Remove the seat.
3. Remove the rear rack, cowling and fenders as described in Chapter Fifteen.
4. Remove the air filter and silencer/air box.
5. Remove the shields from the exhaust, then remove the exhaust pipe and muffler as described in Chapter Six.
6. Remove the brake caliper and disc as described in Chapter Fourteen.
7. Remove the nut attaching the external shift arm (A, **Figure 8**) to the shift shaft, then pull the lever from the shift shaft. Move the lever and connecting rod out of the way.
8. Detach the wire (B, **Figure 8**) from the neutral light switch.
9. Detach the vent hose (C, **Figure 8**).
10A. On models with front wheel drive (4-wheel drive), proceed as follows.
   a. Unbolt and remove the front drive chain guard and the foot pad from the right side.
   b. Remove the screw and washers (**Figure 9**) attaching the front drive sprocket to the transmission output shaft.
   c. Slide the front drive sprocket from the output shaft.
   d. On early models equipped with a locking collar, loosen the set screw (**Figure 10**) in the collar, then rotate the collar out away from the inner race. Later models use a bushing carrier instead of the locking collar.

   e. Remove the bolts (**Figure 11**) attaching the outboard bearing flange to the frame plate.
   f. Clean the front drive output shaft thoroughly, then slide the bearing and flange from the shaft and the frame.

10B. On models with only rear-wheel drive, unbolt and remove the foot pad from the right side.

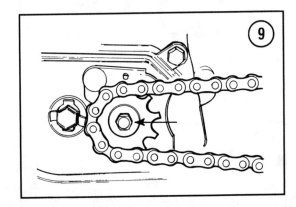

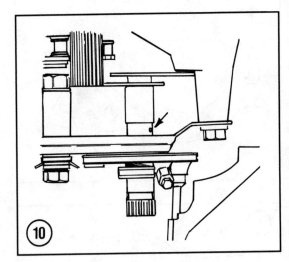

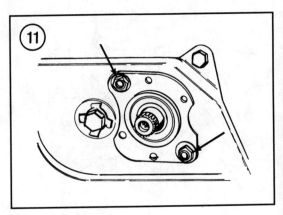

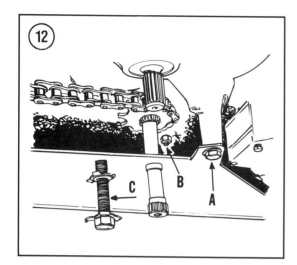

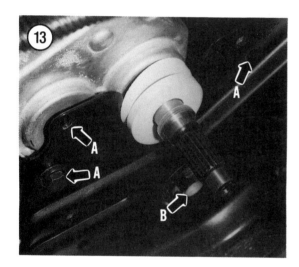

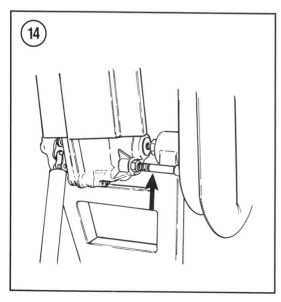

11. Remove the rear chain guard.

12. Loosen the rear drive chain and roll the chain off the transmission sprocket.

13. Remove the mounting screws (A and B, **Figure 12**).

14. Loosen the swing arm bolt (C, **Figure 12**) and pull the bolt part of the way out. Do not remove the swing arm bolt.

15. Remove the PVT outer cover as described in Chapter Seven.

> *CAUTION*
> *Be careful not to lose or damage the spacer washers located behind the driven pulley. These spacers are used to adjust the pulley offset and should be reinstalled.*

16. Remove the drive belt, drive pulley, driven pulley and inner cover as described in Chapter Eight.

17. Remove the 3 screws from their locations, A, **Figure 13**.

18. Loosen the swing arm bolt (B, **Figure 13**) enough to slide it outward part of the way. Do not remove the swing arm bolt.

19. Slide the transmission from the lower mounting brackets and sit it on the right side of the frame.

20. Loosen the locknut then remove the torque stop bolt (**Figure 14**).

21. Reverse the removal procedure to reinstall the transmission. Refer to **Table 2** for the recommended torque when tightening the swing arm pivot bolts and the transmission mounting bolts. Be sure to bend the locking tabs (**Figure 15**) around the bolt heads after tightening.

22. Adjust the torque stop as follows:

9

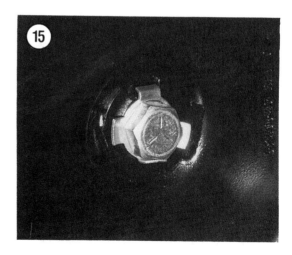

a. Adjust the length of the stop (**Figure 14**) until it just contacts the frame.

b. Lengthen the stop 1/2 turn, then tighten the lock nut.

23. Adjust the controls as described in this chapter.

Adjusting Controls

1A. On 1987-1988 models with Hi/Lo shift transmissions, adjust the shift linkage as follows:

a. If linkage is attached to the shift levers, detach the tie rod from the transmission shift lever.

b. Shift the shift lever on the transmission to NEUTRAL.

c. Move the hand shift lever to the NEUTRAL (N, **Figure 16**) position.

d. Adjust the length of the shift rod so that it can be connected without moving either lever, then attach the rod.

1B. On 1989-1993 models with Hi/Lo shift transmissions, adjust the shift linkage as follows:

a. Make sure that the hand shift lever is in NEUTRAL (N, **Figure 16**) and start the engine.

b. Slowly move the shift lever from the NEUTRAL position toward the "L" position until the gears just begin to clash, then return the lever to the "N" position. Note the location of the hand lever where the gears begin to clash.

c. Move the hand shift lever toward the "R" position until the gears just begin to clash, note the position of the hand lever, then return the lever to "N" position.

d. Adjust the length of the shift rod so the gears begin to clash equal distances from the "N" position (**Figure 16**).

> *CAUTION*
> *The transmission gears may be damaged by improper adjustment of the shift lock mechanism. Damage may also result from not lubricating the control cable properly.*

2. Models with a shift locking button on the hand lever (**Figure 17**) should be adjusted as follows:

a. Depress the shift lever button on the hand control lever.

b. Observe the position of the locking lever on the transmission. The lever on the transmission should be pulled forward in the shift position (**Figure 18**) and should be contacting the pin.

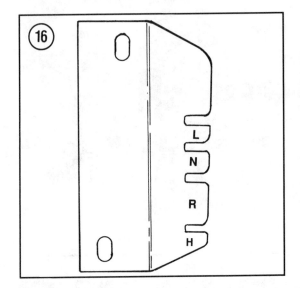

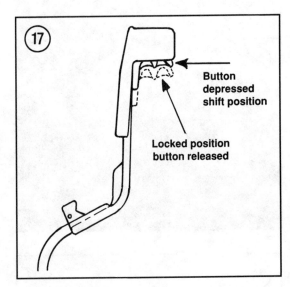

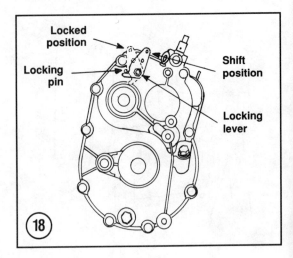

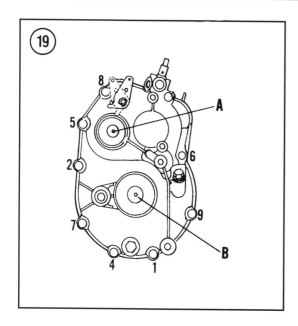

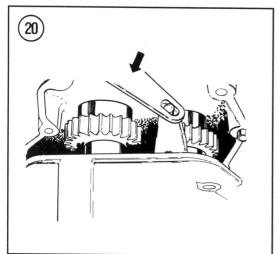

c. Release the button on the hand control lever and make sure that the lever returned to the locked position (**Figure 18**).

d. Adjust the cable as necessary to make sure that the locking lever releases fully when button is depressed and engages quickly and completely when the button is released. It is important to lubricate the cable frequently to keep it from catching in the housing.

Disassembly/Inspection/Reassembly

1. Remove the snap ring retaining the output sprocket, then slide the sprocket from the shaft.

2. Remove the nine bolts (**Figure 19**) that attach the case halves together.

3. Begin to separate the case halves by bumping the brake and output shafts (A and B, **Figure 19**) with a soft faced hammer while lifting the right half.

4. When the case halves have separated slightly, move the case half to disconnect the inner shift arm (**Figure 20**) from the shift fork pin, then complete removal of the right case half.

5. Lift the large output gear and shaft (**Figure 21**) from the case.

6. Remove the forward gear cluster (**Figure 22**).

7. Remove the shift fork and support shaft (**Figure 23**).

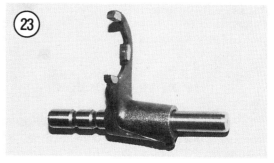

8. Remove the input shaft and sliding gear assembly (**Figure 24**).

9. If the shift lever and shaft must be removed from the case, it is necessary to first remove the pin (**Figure 25**). The pin fits in the groove in the shift shaft (**Figure 26**).

10. Clean the case halves and all parts thoroughly.

11. The output shaft should not have any side play in the case. Check the removed assembly for clearance between the gear and bearing on the short end of the shaft. Add shims between the left side bearing and the gear (**Figure 27**) if necessary to eliminate end play. Do not install too many shims or case will not close properly.

12. The forward cluster gear (**Figure 22**) should not have any side play in the case. Check the removed assembly with a feeler gauge for clearance between the collar and gear (**Figure 28**). Add shims between the bearing and gear at either end of the shaft to eliminate end play. Do not install too many shims or case will not close properly.

13. Inspect all parts for visible damage and install new parts as necessary.

14. Use properly fitting drivers to install seals and bearings. Install all seals flush with the case. Grease the shafts and the lips of seals before installing the shafts.

15. Assemble the shafts, gears, bearings and shift fork in the right case half as shown in **Figure 29**.

16. Make sure the 2 dowel pins are at locations indicated in **Figure 29**.

17. Clean the mating surfaces of both case halves and coat both surfaces with Loctite 515 gasket eliminator (or equivalent).

18. Install a new gasket and install the other case half. Bump the case halves together, then install the nine bolts (**Figure 19**). Refer to **Table 2** for recommended tightening torques.

19. Check transmission operation before installing, by turning the shafts by hand. The shafts should not have end play, but should not bind.

TYPE III TRANSMISSION

The Type III EZ Shift transmission is a gear/chain type and is used on some 1993 models and all 1994-on models. Refer to **Table 1** for application.

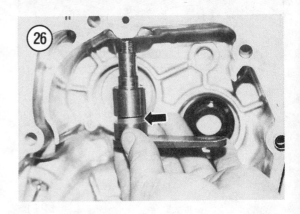

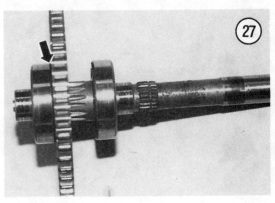

Removal/Installation

1. Place the ATV on a level surface and block the wheels to keep it from rolling.
2. Remove the seat.
3. Remove the rear rack, cowling and fenders as described in Chapter Fifteen.
4. Remove the air filter and silencer/air box.
5. Remove the shields from the exhaust, then remove the exhaust pipe and muffler as described in Chapter Six.
6. Remove the brake caliper as described in Chapter Fourteen.
7. Remove the nut attaching the external shift arms (A and B, **Figure 30**) to the shift shaft, then pull the levers from the shafts. Move the levers and connecting rods out of the way.
8. Disconnect the speedometer cable.
9. On models with front-wheel drive (4-wheel drive), proceed as follows:
    a. Unbolt and remove the front drive chain guard from the right side.
    b. Remove the screw and washers (**Figure 31**) attaching the front drive sprocket to the transmission output shaft.
    c. Slide the front drive sprocket from the output shaft.
10. Remove the brake disc as described in Chapter Fourteen.
11. Remove the bolts (A, **Figure 32**) attaching the outboard bearing flange to the frame plate.
12. Clean the front drive output shaft thoroughly, then slide the bearing and flange from the shaft and the frame.
13. Remove the rear chain guard.

14. Loosen the rear drive chain and roll the chain off the transmission sprocket.

15. Remove the mounting screw (B, **Figure 32**).

16. Remove the lower mounting screw using a socket and extension as shown in **Figure 33**.

17. Release the locking tab, loosen the swing arm bolt (C, **Figure 32**) and pull the bolt part of the way out. It is not necessary to remove the swing arm bolt.

18. Remove the PVT outer cover as described in Chapter Seven.

> *CAUTION*
> *Be careful not to lose or damage the spacer washers located behind the driven pulley. These spacers are used to adjust the pulley offset and should be reinstalled.*

19. Remove the drive belt, drive pulley, driven pulley and inner cover as described in Chapter Eight.

20. Remove the 3 screws from their locations, A, **Figure 34**.

21. Release the locking tab, loosen the swing arm bolt (B, **Figure 34**) enough to slide it outward part of the way. It is not necessary to remove the swing arm bolt.

22. Slide the transmission from the lower mounting brackets and sit it on the right side of the frame.

23. Loosen the locknut then remove the torque stop bolt (**Figure 35**).

24. Reverse the removal procedure to reinstall the transmission. Refer to **Table 2** for the recommended torque when tightening the swing arm pivot bolts and the transmission mounting bolts. Be sure to bend locking tabs around screw heads (C, **Figure 32** and B, **Figure 34**) after tightening.

25. Adjust the torque stop as follows:
    a. Adjust the length of the stop (**Figure 35**) until it just contacts the frame.
    b. Lengthen the stop 1/2 turn, then tighten the lock nut.

26. Adjust the controls as described in this chapter.

Adjusting Control Linkage

Adjust the shift linkage as the first step to correct transmission or shifting problems. Improper linkage adjustment may cause gears to clash, jump out of gear, gear noise when slowing down and prevent the use of a gear.

Also, adjust the linkage whenever the transmission has been removed or serviced. Always check the adjustment of both control rods, because changing one can affect the other.

1. Remove necessary body panels, exhaust heat shield and exhaust pipe from the right side to gain access to the shift controls.

2. Check and adjust the torque stop as follows:

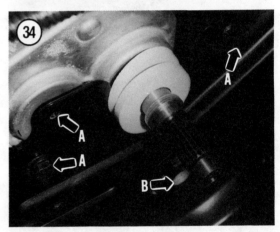

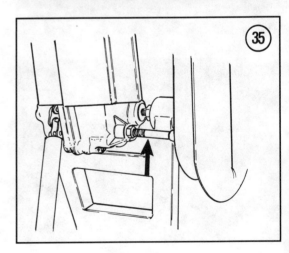

a. Adjust the length of the stop (**Figure 35**) until it just contacts the frame.

b. Lengthen the stop 1/2 turn, then tighten the lock nut.

3. Before adjusting the shift control rods, check for wear or improper installation as follows:

a. Check the ends of the shift control rods for looseness. Be sure that fasteners are tight and that rod ends are not worn.

b. Check to be sure that the control rods are attached correctly. The clevis or rod ends at the rear of the control rods should be on top of the transmission levers on all models. On 300 and Magnum 4 × 4 models, the inside rod end is attached under the shifter slide and the outside rod end is attached above the slide as shown in **Figure 36**. On Magnum 2 × 4 models, the front rod ends of both rods are attached to the top of the shifter slides. On 350 and 400 models, except 400 Sport, the outer rod end is attached under the slide and the inner rod end is attached above the slide. Sport 400 models

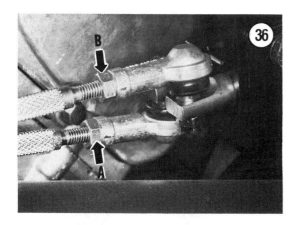

have only one control rod (forward/reverse) and the rod end is attached above the shifter slide.

c. Check to be sure that the shifter control is mounted solidly and that all of the attaching screws are tight.

d. Lubricate the rod ends with Polaris Cable Lube (part No. 2870510).

4. Loosen the locknuts at each rod end (**Figure 36** and **Figure 37**).

5. Detach both rod ends from the transmission levers (**Figure 37**).

6. Shift the hand lever to NEUTRAL and check the ends of the shift rails (**Figure 36**). When the control is in NEUTRAL, the rails will be even.

7. Shift both transmission levers to NEUTRAL (**Figure 37**). When the transmission is in NEUTRAL, the shift controls will be in a detent position and the levers will be perpendicular to the transmission parting line.

8. Change the length of the inside (Lo Range) control rod (A, **Figure 36** and A, **Figure 37**) if necessary to attach the rod to the rearmost shift lever. Attach the rod end to the lever and install the attaching nut. Leave the locknuts on the rod loose.

9. Adjust the length of the connecting control rod (A, **Figure 36** and A, **Figure 37**) as follows:

a. Turn the connecting rod clockwise until resistance increases slightly.

b. Mark the control rod with a line on the top to identify its position.

c. Count the turns of the rod while turning it counterclockwise until the same slight increase in resistance is felt. Count the turns of the rod by observing the mark while adjusting.

d. Turn the connecting rod clockwise again 1/2 the number of turns observed in sub-step 9c.

e. Tighten both rod end locknuts after setting the correct rod length. The two rod ends should be parallel after tightening the locknuts. Binding can occur if the rod ends are not straight. Check by rotating the control rod. Rod should rotate freely without binding.

10. Change the length of the outside (High/Reverse) control rod (B, **Figure 36** and B, **Figure 37**) if necessary to attach the rod to the rearmost shift lever. Attach the rod end to the lever and install the attaching nut. Leave the locknuts on the rod loose.

11. Adjust the length of the connecting control rod (B, **Figure 36** and B, **Figure 37**) as follows:

a. Turn the connecting rod clockwise until resistance increases slightly.

b. Mark the control rod with a line on the top to identify its position.

c. Count the turns of the rod while turning it counterclockwise until the same slight increase in resistance is felt. Count the turns of the rod by observing the mark while adjusting.

d. Turn the connecting rod clockwise again 1/2 the number of turns observed in sub-step 11c.

e. Tighten both rod end locknuts after setting the correct rod length. The two rod ends should be parallel after tightening the locknuts. Binding can occur if the rod ends are not straight. Check by rotating the control rod. Rod should rotate freely without binding.

12. If shifting difficulty is still encountered after adjusting, check the shifting effort required as follows.

a. Disconnect the shift control rods from the transmission shift levers (**Figure 37**).

b. Attach a torque wrench to the nut holding the levers (**Figure 37**) to the transmission shift shafts.

c. Make sure that both shift levers are in NEUTRAL. Both levers will be perpendicular to the parting line of the transmission case.

d. Roll the vehicle forward slowly, while shifting the transmission rear lever to forward gear using the torque wrench. Observe the torque required to shift the transmission.

e. Shift the transmission to NEUTRAL.

f. Roll the vehicle backward slowly, while shifting the transmission rear lever to REVERSE gear using the torque wrench. Observe the torque required to shift the transmission.

g. Check the torque required to shift the front (Lo Range) shift lever following a similar procedure.

h. If more than 13.6 N•m (10 ft.-lbs.) is required to shift the transmission, problems are indicated.

i. Reattach the control rods when testing is finished.

13. Check the distance the shifter slides move when changing gears. The shifter should move 7.6 mm (0.30 in.) each way from the center position. Total movement is 15.2 mm (0.60 in.) from the fully in to the fully extended position. Less than specified movement may indicate wear in the shifter assembly.

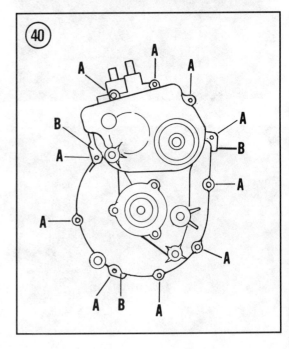

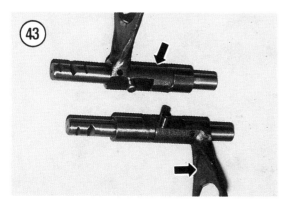

Disassembly/Inspection/Reassembly

1. Drain oil from the transmission and remove the dipstick.

2. Remove the output sprocket if not already removed.

3. Unbolt and remove the speedometer drive (**Figure 38**), then remove the seal (**Figure 39**).

4. Remove the ten screws (A, **Figure 40**) that attach the case halves together.

5. Separate the case halves by bumping the case at the three bosses (B, **Figure 40**) with a soft-faced hammer.

6. Remove the bearing (A, **Figure 41**) and thrust washer (B). It may be necessary to use a puller to remove the bearing from the shaft.

7. Use a dental pick or similar tool to remove the needle bearing (A, **Figure 42**), then remove gear (B, **Figure 42**) and thrust washer. This second thrust washer has a larger inside diameter than the first, removed in Step 6.

8. Turn the external shift shafts while removing the high/reverse (A, **Figure 43**) and low (B, **Figure 43**) shift rail and fork assemblies.

9. Remove the large output gear and output shaft assembly.

NOTE
*The input shaft must be moved slightly to clear the oil deflector (**Figure 44**) while removing it. DO NOT remove or bend the oil deflector.*

10. Remove the input shaft, high/reverse shaft and chain together (**Figure 45**).

11. Clean and inspect all parts thoroughly. Remove the shaft seals if replacement is necessary; however install the seals after the transmission is reassembled.

NOTE
*Use one screwdriver (A, **Figure 46**) to push the shift lock in, then use the second (B, **Figure 46**) to hold the shift lock until the shift rail is installed.*

12. Install the high/reverse shift fork and rail. Make sure the pin on the fork is located between the spring ends (A, **Figure 47**). Rotate the internal shift levers out while installing the shift forks and rails.

13. Insert the high/reverse shaft, chain and input shaft into the case as an assembly, while engaging the high/reverse shift fork with the inner shift dog.

NOTE
*A separate spacer is located on the rail **Figure 48** on early models. The spacer is integral with the high/reverse shift fork on later models.*

14. Hold the shift lock for the low range shift rail back using a procedure similar to that used for the high/reverse shift rail.

15. Install the low range shift fork and rail, engaging the fork with the shift dog. The pin on the shift fork must be located between the spring ends (B, **Figure 47**). **Figure 48** shows the relative location of the shift forks..

16. Install the output shaft and gear assembly.

17. Install the thrust washer with the *larger* inside diameter, then install the low gear with the engagement dogs toward the inside.

18. Install the needle bearing inside the low gear.

19. Install the thrust washer with the *smaller* inside diameter.

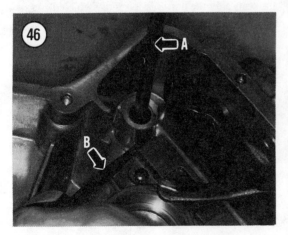

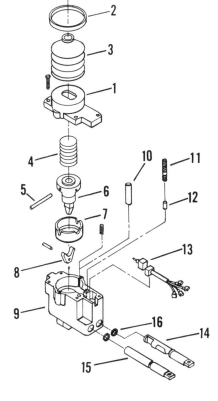

(51)

EZ SHIFTER

1. Cover
2. Clamp
3. Boot
4. Spring
5. Pin
6. Striker
7. Bearing cup
8. Interlock butterfly
9. Housing
10. Stop pin
11. Detent spring
12. Detent bullet
13. Switch
14. Right selector slide
    (3 notches)
15. Left selector slide
    (2 notches)

20. Install the bearing on the shaft. When properly assembled, the end of the shaft should be flush with the outside of the bearing race.

21. Clean the mating surfaces of both case halves and coat both surfaces with Loctite 515 gasket eliminator (or equivalent).

22. Make sure the dowel pins are properly installed, then install the left case half. Bump the case halves together, then install the ten screws (**Figure 40**). Refer to **Table 2** for recommended tightening torques.

23. Check transmission operation before installing, by turning the shafts by hand. The shafts should not have end play, but should not bind.

24. Use properly fitting drivers to install the seals flush with case. Grease the shafts and the lips of seals before installing.

EZ Shift Shifter Selector

The shifter is attached to the right side of the frame.

1. To remove the selector assembly, proceed as follows:
   a. Remove the fuel tank cover as described in Chapter Fifteen.
   b. Remove the cable ties that attach the wiring harness to the frame.
   c. Detach the wires from the terminal board (**Figure 49**).
   d. Pull the wiring harness through to the right side.
   e. Detach the control rods from the selector slides (**Figure 50**).

2. Disassemble the shifter assembly as follows:
   a. Remove the three screws attaching the shifter assembly, then lift the assembly from the mounting bracket.
   b. Remove the screws attaching the top cover (1, **Figure 51**), then lift the shift lever and cover from the housing.

NOTE
*The stop pin (10, **Figure 51**), spring (11) and detent bullets (12) may fall from the housing if it is turned upside down. Be careful not to lose parts while the cover is removed, especially when dumping oil out of the housing.*

9

c. Hold the interlock butterfly out and remove the shifter slides (14 and 15, **Figure 51**).

3. Flush the housing and check for moisture. Clean and inspect all parts thoroughly.

4. Assemble by reversing the disassembly procedure. Install the white bearing cup (7, **Figure 51**) after the detent bullets (12, **Figure 51**), spring (11) and stop pin (10) are installed.

NOTE
The wrong type or too much oil could cause shifting problems.

5. Fill the housing half way with 10W-40 oil (part No. 2871271), or equivalent.

NOTE
Be careful not to damage the selector switch while assembling.

6. Carefully install the switch (13, **Figure 51**). Position the switch toggle inside the hole in the striker (6, **Figure 51**).

7. Clean the housing and the cover (1 and 9, **Figure 51**), coat the mating surfaces with Loctite Primer and place a bead of Loctite 515 (or equivalent) completely around the edge of the housing.

8. Install the cover and tighten the retaining screws to the torque listed in **Table 2**.

9. Before installing the boot (3, **Figure 51**), apply RTV sealant to the selector shaft to seal the boot to

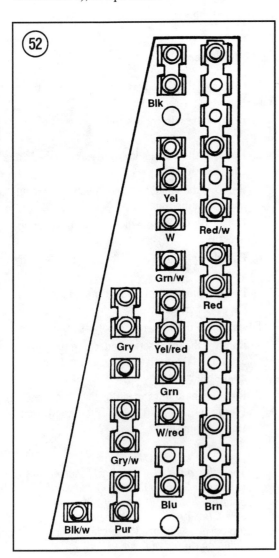

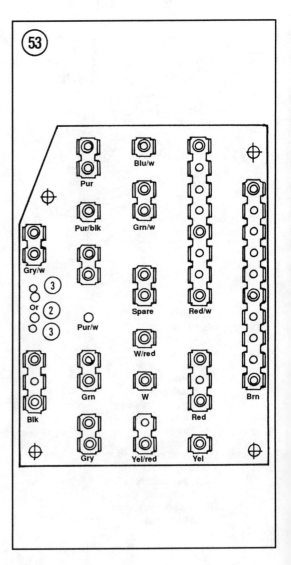

the shaft. Allow approximately 12 hours for the RTV to cure before moving the shift lever.

10. Install the shifter in the mounting bracket and install the three mounting screws.

11. Reattach the electrical wires to the terminal board. Refer to **Figure 52** for the terminal board on models with EZ Shift, except 1995 Scrambler and Xplorer models. Refer to **Figure 53** for terminal wire connections of 1995 Scrambler and Xplorer models. Attach wires to the frame with cable ties.

12. Attach and adjust the control linkage as described in this chapter.

Table 1 TRANSMISSION APPLICATION

Model No.	Transmission
1985 and 1986	Polaris, Type I, chain is 15 links wide
1987	
Trail Boss W877527	Polaris, Type I, chain is 11 links wide
Cyclone W877828	Polaris, Type I, chain is 11 links wide
Trail Boss 4 × 4 W878027, W878127	
and W878327	Gear (ME25P), Type II, Fuji
1988	
Trail Boss 2 × 4 W887527	Gear (ME25PR), Type II, Fuji
Trail Boss 4 × 4 W888127	Gear (ME25P3), Type II, Fuji
Trail Boss 250 R/ES X888528 and	
W888528	Polaris, Type I, chain is 11 links wide
1989	
Trail Boss W898527	Polaris, Type I, chain is 11 links wide
Trail Boss 2 × 4 W897527	Gear (ME25P6), Type II, Fuji
Trail Boss 4 × 4 W898127	Gear (ME25P3A or ME25P5), Type II, Fuji
Big Boss 4 × 6 X898627 and	
W898627	Gear (ME25P6), Type II, Fuji
1990	
Trail Blazer W907221	Polaris, Type I, chain is 11 links wide
Trail Boss 250 W908527	Gear (ME25P10), Type II, Fuji
Trail Boss 2 × 4 W907527	Gear (ME25P8), Type II, Fuji
T.B. 2 × 4-350L W907539	Gear (ME25P10), Type II, Fuji
Trail Boss 4 × 4 W908127	Gear (ME25P7), Type II, Fuji
T.B. 4 × 4-350L W908139	Gear (ME35P1), Type II, Fuji
Big Boss 4 × 6 W908627	Gear (ME25P8), Type II, Fuji
1991	
Trail Blazer W917221	Gear (ME25P10), Type II, Fuji
Trail Boss 250 W918527	Gear (ME25P10), Type II, Fuji
Trail Boss 2 × 4 W917527	Gear (ME25P8), Type II, Fuji
T.B. 2 × 4-350L W917539	Gear (ME25P2), Type II, Fuji
Trail Boss 4 × 4 W918127	Gear (ME25P7), Type II, Fuji
T.B. 4 × 4-350L W918139	Gear (ME35P1), Type II, Fuji
Big Boss 4 × 6 W918627	Gear (ME25P8), Type II, Fuji
Big Boss 6 × 6 W918727	Gear (ME35P1), Type II, Fuji
1992	
Trail Blazer W927221	Gear (ME25P10), Type II, Fuji
Trail Boss 250 W928527	Gear (ME25P10), Type II, Fuji
Trail Boss 2 × 4 W927527	Gear (ME25P8), Type II, Fuji
T.B. 2 × 4-350L W927539	Gear (ME25P2), Type II, Fuji
Trail Boss 4 × 4 W928127	Gear (ME25P7), Type II, Fuji
T.B. 4 × 4-350L W928139	Gear (ME35P1), Type II, Fuji

(continued)

9

Table 1 TRANSMISSION APPLICATION (continued)

Model No.	Transmission
1992 (continued)	
Big Boss 4 × 6 W928627	Gear (ME25P8), Type II, Fuji
Big Boss 6 × 6 W928727	Gear (ME35P1), Type II, Fuji
1993	
Trail Blazer W937221	Gear (ME25P10), Type II, Fuji
Trail Boss W938527	Gear (ME25P10), Type II, Fuji
Sportsman W938039	Type III Gear/chain (1341136)
250 2 × 4 W937527	Gear (ME25P8), Type II, Fuji
350 2 × 4 W937539	Gear (ME25P2), Type II, Fuji
250 4 × 4 W938127	Gear (ME25P7), Type II, Fuji
350 4 × 4 W938139	Gear (ME35P1), Type II, Fuji
250 6 × 6 W938727	Gear (ME35P1), Type II, Fuji
350 6 × 6 W938739	
Without EZ Shift	Gear (ME25P2), Type II, Fuji
With EZ Shift	Type III Gear/chain
1994	
Trail Blazer 2W W947221	Type III Gear/chain (1341124)
Trail Boss 2W W948527	Type III Gear/chain (1341124)
Sport W948540	Type III Gear/chain (1341124)
Sportsman 4 ×4 W948040	Type III Gear/chain (1341136)
300 2 × 4 W947530	Type III Gear/chain (1341125)
400 2 × 4 W947540	Type III Gear/chain (1341123)
300 4 × 4 W948130	Type III Gear/chain (1341136)
400 4 × 4 W948140	Type III Gear/chain (1341146)
300 6 × 6 W948730	Type III Gear/chain (1341136)
400 6 × 6 W948740	Type III Gear/chain (1341146)
1995	
Trail Blazer W957221	Type III Gear/chain (1341124)
Trail Boss W958527	Type III Gear/chain (1341124)
300 2 × 4 W957530	Type III Gear/chain (1341125)
400 2 × 4 W957540	Type III Gear/chain (1341123)
300 4 × 4 W958130	Type III Gear/chain (1341136)
Scrambler W957840	Type III Gear/chain (1341140)
Sport W958540	Type III Gear/chain (1341124)
Sportsman 4 × 4 W958040	Type III Gear/chain (1341146)
Xplorer 4 × 4 W959140	Type III Gear/chain (1341146)
Magnum 2 × 4 W957444	Type III Gear/chain (1341139)
Magnum 4 × 4 W958144	Type III Gear/chain (1341132)
400 6 × 6 W958740	Type III Gear/chain (1341146)

Table 2 TIGHTENING TORQUES

	N•m	ft.-lb.
Type I transmission		
Case halves	5.4	4
Swing arm pivot bolts	74.6	55
Type II transmission		
Case halves	23.0	17
Drain plug	19.0	14
Drive sprocket bolt	23.0	17
Output shaft bearing		
mounting nuts	16.3	12
Shift lever pivot	19.0	14
Speedometer angle drive	14.9	11
(continued)		

Table 2 TIGHTENING TORQUES (continued)

	N·m	ft.-lb.
Type II transmission (continued)		
Swing arm pivot bolts	74.6	55
Transmission mounting	33.9	25
Type III transmission		
Case halves	16.3	12
Shift lever nut	19.0	14
Drain plug	19.0	14
Speedometer angle drive	14.9	11
Transmission mounting	33.9	25
Drive sprocket	23.0	17
Output shaft bearing		
mounting nuts	16.3	12
Swing arm pivot bolts	74.6	55
Shift rod ends		
Lock nuts	3.95	2.9
EZ shift cover screws	16.3	12

9

CHAPTER TEN

FRONT DRIVE SYSTEM

The "Demand 4" front drive system is used on some 1987 and later models. This system permits the vehicle to be driven by the rear wheels as long as the front wheels rotate faster than the front drive axle. If the rotational speed of the front wheels slows to less than the speed of the drive axle, the front wheel hubs engage. The front hubs on 1987 and 1988 models are mechanical and the hubs for 1989-on models have electrical engagement control.

> *NOTE*
> *Tire size is important for proper operation on all models. If the tire size is changed, the engagement of the front drive may be erratic and could result in dangerous control problems. Refer to **Table 1** for original tire size for your model. Refer to Chapter Three for proper tire inflation.*

FRONT HUBS

Disassembly/Inspection/Reassembly

1. Place the ATV on a level surface so that all of the wheels can be raised off the ground at the same time.
2. Lift and block both the front and rear of the vehicle so that the front wheels can be removed and the rear wheels can be rotated.
3. Unbolt and remove the front wheels.
4. Clean the front hubs and brake assembly.
5. Unbolt and remove the front brake calipers as described in Chapter Fourteen.
6. Position a pan under the front hub and remove the hub cap. Refer to **Figure 1**.

> *NOTE*
> *The spindle nut on some 1987 models is locked with safety wire that must be removed before the nut can be removed. Some models may be equipped with a*

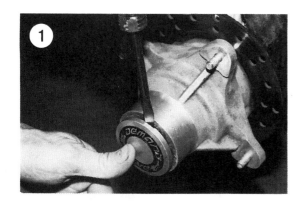

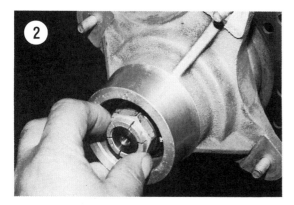

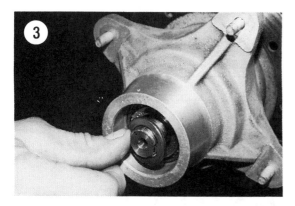

nut that is staked (bent in) to the keyway of the shaft. Do not attempt to remove the staked area and never reuse a nut that has been staked to the shaft keyway. A self locking FlexLoc nut should be installed on all models except the 1987 W878027 model. The manufacturer suggests that a new locking nut be installed when reassembling after service.

7. Remove the spindle nut (**Figure 2**). Some 1994 and all later models have a left-hand nut installed on the left axle. Turn the left-hand nut clockwise to remove it.

8. Remove the tang washer (**Figure 3**).

9. Remove the outer bearing (**Figure 4**).

10. Remove the wheel hub and brake rotor (**Figure 5**).

11. Remove the inner wheel bearing (**Figure 6**).

12. Remove the roller clutch assembly (A, **Figure 7**).

10

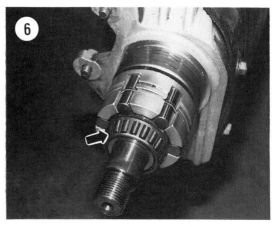

NOTE
*Do not mix the parts of one roller clutch with similar parts from another clutch. The cam (1, **Figure 8** or **Figure 9**) of some models is marked "Left" or "Right" and must be installed on the correct side.*

13. Remove the drive key (B, **Figure 7**) on models so equipped.

NOTE
*The clutch can usually be cleaned and inspected without removing the spring and rollers (2 and 4, **Figure 8** or **Figure 9**). If the rollers are removed, do not stretch the spring farther than necessary to remove one roller (4, **Figure 8** or **Figure 9**) at a time. If the spring is removed from the cage, it has been stretched far enough that a new spring should be installed.*

14. Thoroughly clean the roller clutch. Refer to **Figure 8** and **Figure 9** for exploded views of the types used.

15. On early (1987-1988) models with mechanical engagement, inspect the plunger (5, **Figure 8**), rubber support (6) and compression spring (7). Install new parts as necessary.

16. Inspect the cage and the rollers (3 and 4, **Figure 8** or **Figure 9**). Make sure the rollers move freely

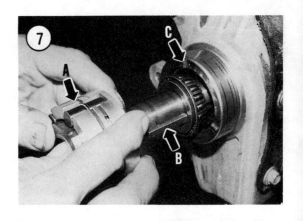

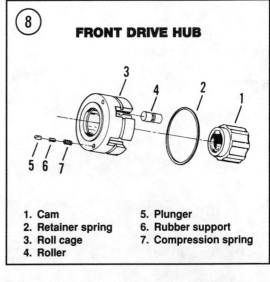

FRONT DRIVE HUB

1. Cam	5. Plunger
2. Retainer spring	6. Rubber support
3. Roll cage	7. Compression spring
4. Roller	

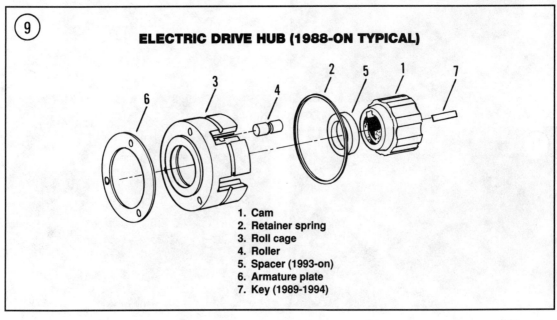

ELECTRIC DRIVE HUB (1988-ON TYPICAL)

1. Cam
2. Retainer spring
3. Roll cage
4. Roller
5. Spacer (1993-on)
6. Armature plate
7. Key (1989-1994)

within the sliding surfaces of the cage. Small burrs can sometimes be removed using fine emery cloth or small file, but be sure all of the parts are thoroughly clean before assembling.

NOTE
The retainer springs on models produced after 1989 are stronger than the spring used on earlier models. Be sure the correct spring is installed. Centrifugal force may engage the front drive at high speed if the spring is not strong enough. Refer to Table 2 for identification of springs by wire size.

17. Inspect the retainer spring (2, **Figure 8** or **Figure 9**) for irregular gaps, without removing it. Install a new spring if the gaps are not even and whenever the old spring has been removed. The old spring can be removed by cutting.

18. If removed, install the retainer spring using a special tool and the following procedure:

   a. Install the rollers in the cage.

   b. Position the special cone shaped tool (part No. 2870888) over the end of the cage.

   c. Hook the ends of the retainer spring together and carefully roll the spring over the tool. The spring should move evenly onto the cage and into the groove.

NOTE
The cam (1, Figure 8 or Figure 9) on some models is marked "Left" or "Right" and must be installed on the correct side. If the cam is not marked, the cam can be installed on either side.

19. Assemble the engagement cam (1, **Figure 8** or **Figure 9**) to the roller cage. The cam on 1987-1992 models has a shoulder that must be installed toward the inside. A spacer (5, **Figure 9**) is used on 1993 and later models.

20. To remove and install the hub inner seal, proceed as follows:

   a. Remove the four screws (**Figure 10**) attaching the brake rotor to the hub. The screws are installed with threadlocking compound and it is necessary to heat the hub near the threads before removing the screws.

   b. Continue to heat the hub around the seal area of the hub and pry the seal (**Figure 11**) from the hub.

10

NOTE
On 1987 Model W878027 vehicles, the seal should be recessed 0.2-0.3 mm (0.080-0.110 in.) below flush with the disk brake mounting surface. On all models except 1987 Model W878027, the seal should be flush with the brake disc mounting surface. On all models, make sure the seal is installed straight in the seal bore.

   c. Install the new seal (**Figure 11**) with the spring loaded lip toward the inside.

   d. Clean the brake disc, making sure that all oil, including oil from your hands, is removed from the disc.

   e. Coat the threads of the retaining screws (**Figure 10**) with medium strength threadlocking compound and install the brake disc. Refer to **Table 3** for tightening torque.

21. On 1987-1988 models, inspect the ramps (C, **Figure 7**). Install a new casting if the ramp is worn to less than 1/2 of its original height.

22. On models so equipped, install the key (B, **Figure 7**).

23A. On 1987-1988 models, install the plungers, rubber support and compression spring (**Figure 12**) in the bores of the roll cage.

23B. On 1989-on models, assemble the armature plate (6, **Figure 9**) with tabs in the holes of the roll cage as shown in **Figure 13**.

24A. Install and time the mechanically actuated front drive clutch as described in this chapter.

24B. Install and adjust the electrically engaging front drive clutch as described in this chapter.

Install and time the mechanically actuated front drive clutch

Improper installation and timing may cause loss of vehicle control. The drive clutches must be correctly installed for the front drive to function properly.

1. Rotate the front axles until the drive key is at the 12 o'clock (straight up) position as shown in **Figure 14**.

> *NOTE*
> *The cam on some models is marked "L" or "R" (**Figure 15**) indicating installation on the left or right side of the vehicle. If the cam is not marked, it can be installed on either side.*

2. Coat the drive assembly with Type F automatic transmission fluid and install the assembly (**Figure 16**) on the axle. The roll cage must be free to turn on the axle. The cam (1, **Figure 8**) must be installed with the correct side out.

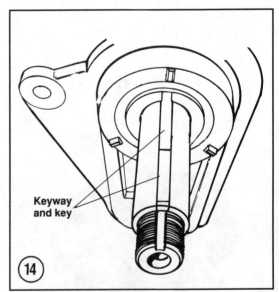

Keyway and key

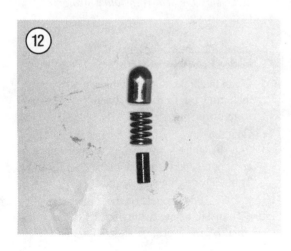

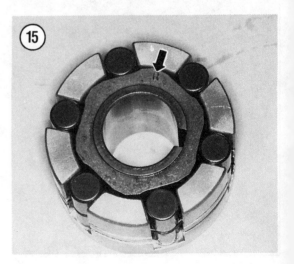

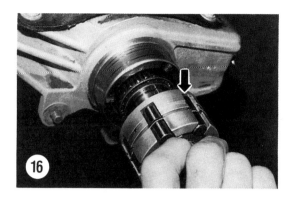

3A. On the right side of the vehicle, position the roll cage so the plunger (A, **Figure 17**) is just about to contact the ramp (B, **Figure 17**) if the cage rotates in the normal direction.

3B. On the left side of the vehicle, position the roll cage so the plunger (A, **Figure 18**) is just about to contact the ramp (B, **Figure 18**).

4. Install inner wheel bearing (**Figure 19**).

5. Coat the seal (**Figure 20**) with grease, then install wheel hub over the clutch. Be careful not to damage the seal.

6. Install the outer wheel bearing (**Figure 21**).

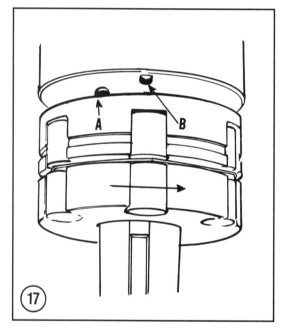

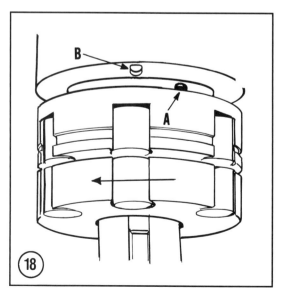

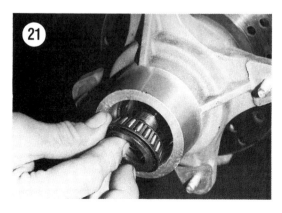

10

7. Install the tang washer (**Figure 22**) with tang engaging the keyway.

> *NOTE*
> *The axle nut on some 1987 models is locked with safety wire that must be installed after tightening the nut. Some models are equipped with a nut that is locked by staking (bending) the nut into the keyway of the shaft. Never reuse a nut that has been staked to the shaft keyway. Other models are equipped with a self-locking FlexLoc nut that must not be reused.*

8A. On 1987 W878027 models with the nut drilled for safety wire, install and tighten the nut as follows.

    a. Install the axle nut and tighten to 11.3 N•m (100 in.-lb.) torque.

    b. Rotate the wheel hub several revolutions. The front hub can be rotated by rotating the rear wheel.

    c. Tighten the axle nut to 8.47 N•m (75 in.-lb.) torque.

    d. Install safety wire to keep the nut from loosening.

8B. All 1987-1988 models except W878027, should be equipped with FlexLoc self-locking nuts (**Figure 23**). Some models were originally equipped with a nut that required staking, but this nut should be replaced by a new FlexLoc nut. Install and tighten this nut as follows:

> *NOTE*
> *The FlexLoc nut requires some force to turn on the thread before it is tightened. It is this force of 8.5-45.2 N•m (75-400 in.-lb.) torque that locks the nut to the threaded axle shaft. If this torque is less than 8.5 N•m (75 in.-lb.), install a new nut.*

    a. Measure and record the torque required to turn the nut before it tightens against the tang washer.

    b. Continue tightening the axle nut against the tang washer until the torque is 45.2 N•m (400 in.-lb.) torque more than the torque measured in sub-step a.

    c. Rotate the wheel hub several revolutions. The front hub can be rotated by rotating the rear wheel.

    d. Retighten the axle nut as described in sub-step b.

9. Install the hub cap.

10. Remove the fill plug (**Figure 24**).

11. Refer to Chapter Three to fill the hub with the proper quantity and type of lubricant.

12. Reinstall the plug (**Figure 24**).

13. Install front wheels. Refer to **Table 3** for tightening torque.

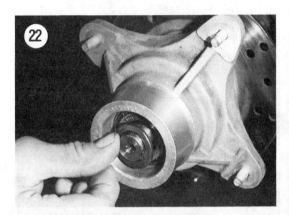

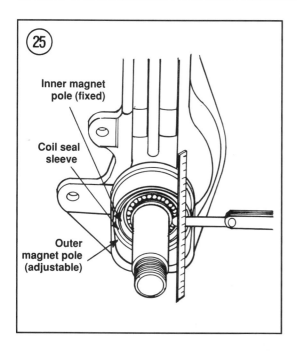

Inner magnet pole (fixed)

Coil seal sleeve

Outer magnet pole (adjustable)

Install and adjust the electrically–engaged front drive clutch

Improper installation and adjustment can result in a dangerous lack of vehicle control. The drive clutches must be correctly installed for the front drive to function properly.

1. Before installing the drive clutch, check for electrical problems as described in Chapter Eleven.

2. Use a depth gauge or a straightedge and feeler gauge to measure the distance from the outer pole (seal sleeve) to the inner pole as shown in **Figure 25**. Measure the pole gap in at least 3 locations and compare with the specification in **Table 2**.

3. If the pole gap measured in Step 2 is incorrect, move the outer magnet pole (seal sleeve) by tapping the seal sleeve.

4. Be sure the tabs of the armature plate are still engaging the holes in the roll cage as shown in **Figure 26**.

5. Install inner wheel bearing.

6. Coat the seal (**Figure 27**) with grease, then install the wheel hub over the clutch. Be careful not to damage the seal.

7. Install the outer wheel bearing.

8. Install the tang washer with the tang engaging the keyway.

> *NOTE*
> *Replace the self-locking FlexLoc nut during reassembly.*

9. All models are equipped with FlexLoc self-locking nuts (**Figure 23**). Install and tighten this nut as follows:

> *NOTE*
> *The FlexLoc nut requires some force to turn on the thread before it is tightened. It is this force of 8.5-45.2 N•m (75-400 in.-lb.) torque that locks the nut to the threaded axle shaft. If this torque is less than 8.5 N•m (75 in.-lb.), install a new nut.*

   a. Measure and record the torque required to turn the nut before it tightens against the tang washer.

   b. Continue tightening the axle nut against the tang washer until the torque is 45.2 N•m (400 in.-lb.) torque more than the torque measured in sub-step a.

10

c. Rotate the wheel hub several revolutions. The front hub can be rotated by rotating the rear wheel.

d. Retighten the axle nut as described in sub-step b.

10. Install the hub cap.

11. Remove the fill plug (**Figure 24**).

12. Refer to Chapter Three to fill the hub with the proper quantity and type of lubricant.

13. Reinstall the plug (**Figure 24**).

14. Install front wheels. Refer to **Table 3** for tightening torque.

FRONT DRIVE SHAFT BOOTS AND CV JOINTS

The front drive shafts connect the front drive eccentric shaft and the drive clutches located in the front wheel hubs. Service to the shafts is usually limited to installing new seal boots or installing the complete shaft and universal joints.

Replacement front drive shaft boots for 1987-1988 models are split and can be installed without disassembling the drive shaft. The boot kit (part No. 3260108) includes instructions for installation. It is important to keep any grease or oil from the splice area of the replacement boot. The splice is coated with an adhesive and will not hold together if contaminated.

On 1989-on models, the drive shaft boots can be replaced using the type originally installed. Remove the drive shaft as described, install a new boot, then reinstall the drive shaft.

Removal/Installation

1. Place the ATV on a level surface so that all of the wheels can be raised off the ground at the same time.

2. Lift and block both the front and rear of the vehicle so that the front wheels can be removed and the rear wheels can be rotated.

3. Unbolt and remove the front wheels from the hubs.

4. Clean the front hubs and brake assembly.

5. Unbolt and remove the front brake calipers as described in Chapter Fourteen.

6. Remove the front wheel drive hubs as described in this chapter.

7. Remove the outer bearing (**Figure 28**).

8. Remove the cotter pin and nut (A, **Figure 29**).

9. Detach the lower A frame (B, **Figure 29**) from the strut.

NOTE
It may be necessary to detach the steering rod from the strut and the top of the strut from the frame on some models. Be very careful not to damage the electrical wires to the front wheel drive engagement coils on 1989 and later models.

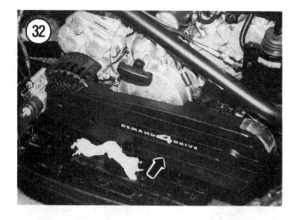

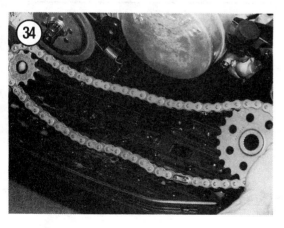

10. Carefully pull the strut out of the way while withdrawing the drive shaft from the strut.

11. The inner end of the drive shaft can be detached after removing the roll pin (**Figure 30** or **Figure 31**). The inner universal joint is splined to the front drive eccentric shaft.

12. Remove the clamps from the boot covering the CV joint. Be careful not to pull the splined end from the CV joint.

13. Slide the boot back onto the drive shaft, then pull the CV joint from the drive shaft.

14. Remove the boot from the drive shaft.

15. Clean the areas of the drive shaft and CV joint where the boot is attached.

16. Inspect the grease on the CV joint for contamination. If the boot has been damaged or if the CV joint is worn, the grease will indicate contamination. To clean and lubricate the CV joint, proceed as follows:

    a. Clean the CV joint using special cleaner (part No. 2870770) available from your Polaris dealer.

    b. After the CV joint is thoroughly clean, assemble the joint using special grease (part No. 3260110) available from your Polaris dealer. The grease will help to hold the parts of the CV joint in place while assembling.

17. Slide the small end of the boot over the drive shaft.

18. Slide the CV joint onto the splined end of the drive shaft.

19. Install the large end of the boot over the CV joint.

20. Install both clamps on the boot. Make sure that clamps are tight, but do not cut the rubber boot.

21. Reassemble by reversing the removal procedure. Refer to **Table 2** for tightening torques.

CENTER CHAIN AND SPROCKETS

1. Unbolt and remove the cover (**Figure 32**) from the chain.

2. Remove the retaining screws and washers (**Figure 33**).

3. Slide the sprockets from the shafts and remove the sprockets with the chain as shown in **Figure 34**.

4. Inspect the chain for wear or damage. A section of twenty pitches of the 520 chain should measure 32 cm (12.5 in.) when new. Install a new chain if any twenty pitches is more than 32.7 cm (12.875 in.).

10

Also check the chain for loose side plates, damaged O-rings, twists or other damage that would indicate replacement is necessary.

5. Check the sprockets for "hooked" or otherwise damaged teeth. Install new sprockets if the chain can be pulled 6 mm (0.25 in.) away from the sprocket. Always install new sprockets if installing a new chain.

6. Install the sprockets and chain by reversing the removal procedure. Install the *closed end* of the drive chain master link toward the direction of travel as shown at A, **Figure 35**.

7. Adjust center and front drive chains as described in Chapter Three.

FRONT CHAIN AND SPROCKETS

1. Loosen the front chain adjustment as described in Chapter Three, then remove the front chain.

2. To remove the front sprocket, it is necessary to remove the front drive axles as described in this chapter.

3. To remove the center sprocket, remove the center eccentric shaft.

4. Inspect the chain for wear or damage. Any section of twenty pitches of the 520 chain should measure 32 cm (12.5 in.) when new. Install a new chain if any twenty pitches is more than 32.7 cm (12.875 in.). Also check the chain for loose side plates, damaged O-rings, twists or other damage that would indicate that replacement is necessary.

5. Check the sprockets for "hooked" or otherwise damaged teeth. Install new sprockets if the chain can be pulled 6 mm (0.25 in.) away from the sprocket. Always install new sprockets if installing a new chain.

6. Adjust center and front drive chains as described in Chapter Three.

Eccentric Shafts

The center eccentric shaft and housing can be removed after removing the drive chains and the clamp bolts (B, **Figure 35**). To remove the front eccentric shaft, it is first necessary to remove the front drive axles as described in this chapter.

Table 1 TIRE SIZE AND PRESSURE		
	Front tires **kPa (psi)**	**Rear tires** **kPa (psi)**
1987		
Trail Boss 4 × 4 W878027		
Size	22 × 8.00 × 10	22 × 11.00 × 10
Pressure	27.6 (4)	20.7 (3)
Trail Boss 4 × 4 W878127		
Size	22 × 8.00 × 10	22 × 11.00 × 10
Pressure	27.6 (4)	20.7 (3)
Trail Boss 4 × 4 W878327		
Size	22 × 8.00 × 10	22 × 11.00 × 10
Pressure	27.6 (4)	20.7 (3)
(continued)		

Table 1 TIRE SIZE AND PRESSURE (continued)

	Front tires kPa (psi)	Rear tires kPa (psi)
1988		
Trail Boss 4 × 4 W888127		
Size	22 × 8.00 × 10	22 × 11.00 × 10
Pressure	27.6 (4)	20.7 (3)
1989		
Trail Boss 4 × 4 W898127		
Size	22 × 8.00 × 10	22 × 11.00 × 10
Pressure	27.6 (4)	20.7 (3)
1990		
Trail Boss 4 × 4 W908127		
Size	22 × 8.00 × 10	24 × 11.00 × 10
Pressure	27.6 (4)	20.7 (3)
Trail Boss 4 × 4 - 350L W908139		
Size	25 × 8.00 × 12	25 × 12.00 × 10
Pressure	27.6 (4)	20.7 (3)
1991		
Trail Boss 4 × 4 W918127		
Size	22 × 8.00 × 10	24 × 11.00 × 10
Pressure	27.6 (4)	20.7 (3)
Trail Boss 4 × 4 - 350L W918139		
Size	25 × 8.00 × 12	25 × 12.00 × 10
Pressure	27.6 (4)	20.7 (3)
Big Boss 6 × 6 W918727		
Size	22 × 8.00 × 10	22 × 11.00 × 10
Pressure	34.5 (5)	34.5 (5)
1992		
Trail Boss 4 × 4 W928127		
Size	22 × 8.00 × 10	24 × 11.00 × 10
Pressure	27.6 (4)	20.7 (3)
Trail Boss 4 × 4 - 350L W928139		
Size	25 × 8.00 × 12	25 × 12.00 × 10
Pressure	27.6 (4)	20.7 (3)
Big Boss 6 × 6 W928727		
Size	22 × 8.00 × 10	22 × 11.00 × 10
Pressure	34.5 (5)	34.5 (5)
1993		
Sportsman W938039		
Size	25 × 8.00 × 12	25 × 12.00 × 10
Pressure	27.6 (4)	20.7 (3)
250 4 × 4 W938127		
Size	22 × 8.00 × 10	24 × 11.00 × 10
Pressure	27.6 (4)	20.7 (3)
350 4 × 4 W938139		
Size	25 × 8.00 × 12	25 × 12.00 × 10
Pressure	27.6 (4)	20.7 (3)
250 6 × 6 W938727		
Size	22 × 8.00 × 10	22 × 11.00 × 10
Pressure	34.5 (5)	34.5 (5)
350 6 × 6 W938739		
Size	25 × 8.00 × 10	25 × 12.00 × 10
Pressure	34.5 (5)	34.5 (5)
1994		
Sportsman 4 × 4 W948040		
Size	25 × 8.00 × 12	25 × 12.00 × 10
Pressure	27.6 (4)	20.7 (3)

10

(continued)

Table 1 TIRE SIZE AND PRESSURE (continued)

	Front tires kPa (psi)	Rear tires kPa (psi)
1994 (continued)		
300 4 × 4 W948130		
Size	22 × 8.00 × 10	24 × 11.00 × 10
Pressure	20.7 (3)	20.7 (3)
400 4 × 4 W948140		
Size	25 × 8.00 × 12	25 × 12.00 × 10
Pressure	27.6 (4)	20.7 (3)
300 6 × 6 W948730		
Size	22 × 8.00 × 10	22 × 11.00 × 10
Pressure	34.5 (5)	34.5 (5)
400 6 × 6 W948740		
Size	25 × 8.00 × 12	25 × 12.00 × 10
Pressure	34.5 (5)	34.5 (5)
1995		
300 4 × 4 W958130		
Size	22 × 8.00 × 10	24 × 11.00 × 10
Pressure	27.6 (4)	20.7 (3)
Scrambler W957840		
Size	23 x 7.00 × 10	22 × 11.00 × 10
Pressure	27.6 (4)	20.7 (3)
Sportsman 4 × 4 W958040		
Size	25 × 8.00 × 12	25 × 12.00 × 10
Pressure	27.6 (4)	20.7 (3)
Xplorer 4 × 4 W959140		
Size	25 × 8.00 × 12	25 × 12.00 × 10
Pressure	27.6 (4)	20.7 (3)
Magnum 4 × 4 W958144		
Size	25 × 8.00 × 12	25 × 12.00 × 10
Pressure	27.6 (4)	20.7 (3)
400 6 × 6 W958740		
Size	25 × 8.00 × 12	25 × 12.00 × 10
Pressure	34.5 (5)	34.5 (5)

Table 2 FRONT WHEEL DRIVE HUB SPECIFICATIONS

	mm (in.)
Mechanically–engaged units	
1987-1988	
Retainer spring	
Part No.	3250021
Wire diameter mm (in.)	0.30 (0.012)
Free length, inside hooks	173 (6.85)
Electro–mechanical units	
1989-1994	
Retainer spring	
Part No.	3250022
Wire diameter	0.38 (0.015)
Free length, inside hooks	168 (6.63)
Pole gap (outer to inner)	0.05-0.1 (0.002-0.004)
1995-on	
Retainer spring	
Part No.	3250032
Wire diameter	0.45 (0.018)
Free length, inside hooks	177 (6.968)
Pole gap (outer to inner)	0-0.025 (0-0.001)

Table 3 TIGHTENING TORQUES

Ball-joint to A frame	
1987-1988 models	94.9 (70)
1989-on models	33.9 (25)
Brake disc screws	24.4 (18)
Chain adjuster eccentric pinch bolts*	
Center	65.1 (48)
Front	65.1 (48)
Front drive sprocket	40.7 (30)
Middle sprocket	
Drive	23.0 (17)
Driven	40.7 (30)
Wheel nuts	
Front	20.3 (15)
Rear	67.8 (50)

* Listed torque value does not include the torque required to move the self-locking nut. Measure the torque required to move the self-locking nut before the nut is tight, then add this to the value listed to determine the correct torque indicated by the torque wrench. The manufacturer recommends that new self-locking nuts be installed each time the nut is removed. The locking integrity of a used self-locking nut is not the same as when new.

Table 4 FRONT DRIVE CHAIN AND SPROCKETS

Model No.	Center sprockets	Center chain	Front sprockets	Front chain
1987				
Trail Boss 4 × 4 W878027	11/22	76 pitch	11/24	64 pitch
Trail Boss 4 × 4 W878127	11/22	76 pitch	11/24	64 pitch
Trail Boss 4 × 4 W878327				
1988				
Trail Boss 4 × 4 W888127	11/22	76 pitch	11/22	64 pitch
1989				
Trail Boss 4 × 4 W898127	11/22	70 pitch	11/22	64 pitch
1990				
Trail Boss 4 × 4 W908127	11/22	70 pitch	11/22	64 pitch
T.B. 4 × 4-350L W908139	11/22	70 pitch	12/22	64 pitch
1991				
Trail Boss 4 × 4 W918127	11/22	70 pitch	11/22	64 pitch
T.B. 4 × 4-350L W918139	11/22	70 pitch	12/22	64 pitch
Big Boss 6 × 6 W918727	11/24	72 pitch	11/22	64 pitch
1992				
Trail Boss 4 × 4 W928127	11/22	70 pitch	11/22	64 pitch
T.B. 4 × 4-350L W928139	11/22	70 pitch	12/22	64 pitch
Big Boss 6 × 6 W928727	11/24	72 pitch	11/22	64 pitch
1993				
Sportsman W938039	11/22	70 pitch	12/22	64 pitch
250 4 × 4 W938127	11/22	70 pitch	11/22	64 pitch
350 4 × 4 W938139	11/22	70 pitch	12/22	64 pitch
250 6 × 6 W938727	11/22	70 pitch	11/22	64 pitch
350 6 × 6 W938739	11/22	70 pitch	11/22	64 pitch
1994				
Sportsman 4 × 4 W948040	11/22	70 pitch	12/22	64 pitch
300 4 × 4 W948130	11/22	70 pitch	11/22	64 pitch
400 4 × 4 W948140	11/22	70 pitch	12/22	64 pitch
300 6 × 6 W948730	11/22	70 pitch	11/22	64 pitch
400 6 × 6 W948740	11/22	70 pitch	12/22	64 pitch

(continued)

10

Table 4 FRONT DRIVE CHAIN AND SPROCKETS (continued)

Model No.	Center sprockets	Center chain	Front sprockets	Front chain
1995				
300 4 × 4 W958130	11/22	70 pitch	12/22	64 pitch
Scrambler W957840	11/22	70 pitch	12/22	64 pitch
Sportsman 4 × 4 W958040	11/22	70 pitch	13/22	64 pitch
Xplorer 4 × 4 W959140	11/22	70 pitch	13/22	64 pitch
Magnum 4 × 4 W958144	11/22	70 pitch	11/22	68 pitch
400 6 × 6 W958740	11/22	70 pitch	12/22	64 pitch

ELECTRICAL SYSTEM

This chapter contains service and test procedures for all electrical and ignition components. ATV's are often exposed to moisture and water while operating under severe conditions, so it is important to keep all electrical connections firmly attached. Also, apply dielectric grease (available from automotive parts stores) to all electrical connectors before they are connected. Dielectric grease helps seal out moisture and helps prevent corrosion of the electrical connector terminals. Do not substitute another material such as grease or silicone sealant that can trap water and actually contribute to corrosion.

Information regarding the battery and spark plugs are covered in Chapter Three.

The electrical system includes the following systems:

  a. Charging system.
  b. Ignition system.
  c. Starting system.
  d. Lighting system.
  e. Other electrical systems and components.

Tables 1-4 are at the end of this chapter.

CHARGING SYSTEM

Models without electric start may use a charging system to operate lights, but are designed to operate without a battery or rectifier. As shown in **Figure 1**, a typical system consists of an alternator and the regulator unit.

> *CAUTION*
> *Models designed to have a battery will almost certainly damage any lights turned on while the engine is running, if the battery is not installed. Other components may also be damaged. The battery is needed to control the electrical system and helps dampens voltage surges.*

The charging system on models with electric starting typically consists of the battery, alternator, circuit

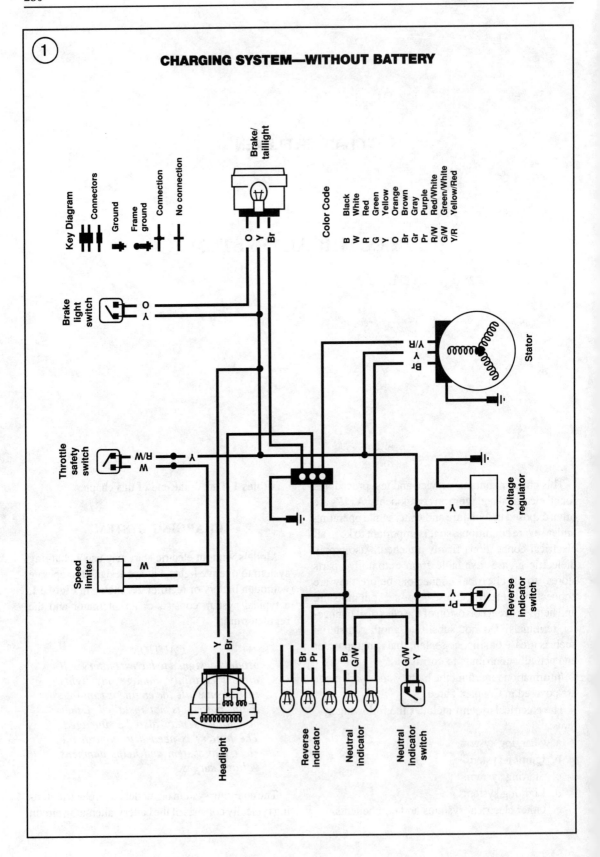

breaker and a voltage regulator/rectifier (**Figure 2**). Alternating current generated by the alternator must be rectified to direct current before it can be stored in the battery. The voltage regulator maintains the voltage at a level that will not harm the battery or other electrical components. The alternator, rectifier, regulator and battery combine to provide direct current at a constant voltage regardless of variations in engine speed and electrical loads such as lights and ignition.

Charging System Output Test

If charging system trouble is suspected, make sure the battery is fully charged and in good condition before going any further. Clean and test the battery as described under *Battery Testing* in Chapter Three. Make sure all electrical connectors in the charging system are tight, making good contact and free of corrosion. To test the system, proceed as follows.

1. If the electrical system seems to be dead, check battery cable connections and the main circuit breaker which is located adjacent to the battery. If the main circuit breaker is okay, proceed to the next step.

2. Test the battery specific gravity as described under *Battery Testing* in Chapter Three. Note the following:

    a. If the specific gravity reading is correct, continue to Step 3.

    b. If the specific gravity reading is not within the specified range, clean and recharge the battery as required. If it is physically damaged or if it will not hold a charge, install a new battery.

3. Connect a 0-20 DC voltmeter to the battery terminals. Connect an inductive tachometer to the spark plug following its manufacturer's instructions.

4. Start the engine and increase engine speed to 4,000 rpm. Read the voltage indicated on the voltmeter. It should be between 13-14.6 volts. Note the following:

    a. Charging voltage correct: The charging system is operating properly.

    b. Charging voltage incorrect: Test the stator charge coils as described under *Alternator Stator* in this chapter. Replace the stator coils if faulty. If the charging coils are okay, perform Step 5.

5. Check the charging system wiring harness and connectors for dirty or loose-fitting terminals; clean

and repair as required. If the wiring harness and connectors are okay, and you have not found the problem after performing the previous tests, the regulator/rectifier is probably faulty. Install a regulator/rectifier unit that is known to be in working order, then retest the charging system.

NOTE
Most ATV dealers and parts suppliers will not accept the return of any electrical part. If you are unable to determine the cause of the charging system malfunction, have a Polaris dealer retest the charging system to verify your test results. If you purchase a new regulator/rectifier, install it, and then find that the charging system still does not work properly, you will, in most cases, be unable to return the unit for a refund. Note also that service specifications for testing the regulator/rectifier unit are not available.

6. After the test is completed, disconnect the voltmeter and tachometer.

ALTERNATOR STATOR (CHARGING OR LIGHTING COIL)

Procedures for removing and installing the alternator rotor (engine flywheel) and stator assembly (**Figure 3** or **Figure 4**) are covered in Chapter Four (2-stroke models) and Chapter Five (4-stroke Magnum models).

Stator (Charging or Lighting) Coil Testing

It is not necessary to remove the stator coil to perform the following tests. To get accurate resistance measurements the stator assembly and coil must be approximately 20° C (68° F).

1. Remove necessary covers to locate the wires leading from the engine. Locate the connector containing the yellow and yellow/red wires.

NOTE
Models without a battery do not have the yellow/red wire. An additional yellow/brown wire is also used by the alternator on some later models.

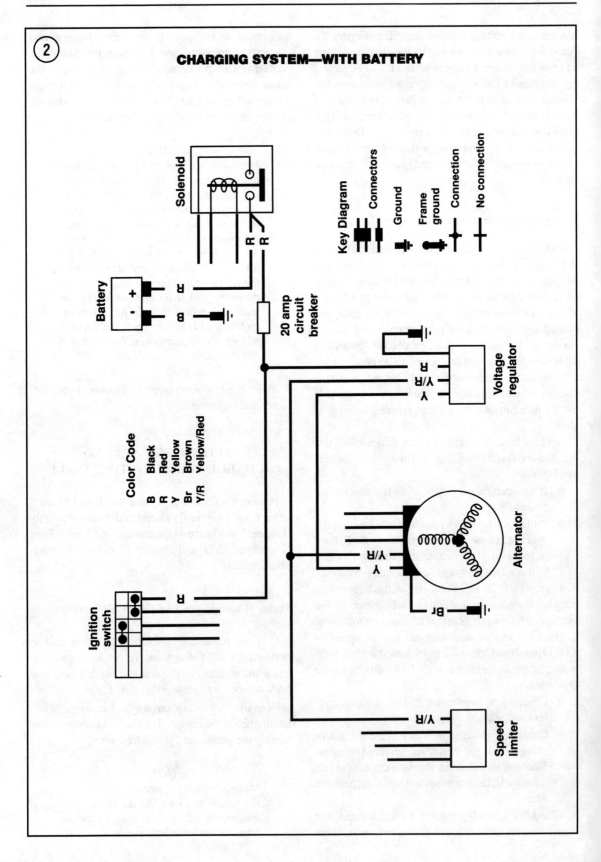

CHARGING SYSTEM—WITH BATTERY

2A. On models with a battery, separate the electrical connector containing the yellow and yellow/red wires from the alternator.

2B. On models without a battery, separate the electrical connectors containing the yellow wire and the brown wire from the alternator.

NOTE
Check resistance on the engine (alternator) side of the connectors.

3A. On models without a battery, check the resistance between the yellow and brown wires from the alternator.

3B. On models with a battery, check the resistance between the yellow wire and the yellow/red wires from the alternator.

4. The specified resistance is listed in **Table 2**. If there is continuity (indicated resistance) and it is within the specified resistance, the coil is good. If there is no continuity (infinite resistance) or the resistance is less than specified, the coil is defective and the stator assembly must be replaced (the individual coil cannot be replaced).

5. Apply dielectric grease (available from an automotive parts store) to the electrical connector prior to reconnecting it. This will help seal out moisture.

6. Make sure the electrical connectors are clean, free of corrosion and completely coupled.

VOLTAGE REGULATOR/RECTIFIER

Testing

Service specifications are not available for testing the voltage regulator/rectifier. To determine if the voltage regulator (**Figure 5**) is faulty, proceed as follows.

1. First check the condition of the battery.

2. Perform the *Charging System Output Test* as described in this chapter.

3. If the charging system output is determined to be low, check the resistance of the charging coils, described as *Stator (Charging or Lighting) Coil Testing* in this chapter. Before removing and installing the voltage regulator, it is advisable to check electrical connections. If all other possible sources of problems are eliminated, it is logical to suspect the voltage regulator.

Removal/Installation

1. Place the vehicle on level ground and set the parking brake.

2. Remove the covers necessary to locate the voltage regulator/rectifier. On most 1989 and later models, it is located under the headlight cover.

CAUTION
Do not attempt to detach any electrical connections with the engine running or

11

with the battery connected. Modern electrical components can be destroyed instantly by improper testing, servicing or handling. Dealers and parts suppliers will usually not accept the return of any electrical part.

3. Disconnect the ground (negative) cable from the battery.

4. Detach electrical connectors, remove attaching screws and remove the voltage regulator/rectifier unit.

5. Install by reversing these removal steps, noting the following.

6. Apply dielectric grease to the electrical connectors prior to reconnecting them. This helps seal out moisture.

7. Make sure all electrical connectors are clean, free of corrosion and completely attached.

CAPACITOR DISCHARGE IGNITION

All models are equipped with a capacitor discharge ignition (CDI) system, a solid-state system that uses no breaker points.

CDI Precautions

Certain precautions should be taken to reduce the chance of damaging the capacitor discharge ignition system. Instantaneous damage to the solid state components of the system may occur if the following precautions are not observed.

1. Never disconnect any electrical connection while the engine is running.

2. Apply dielectric grease to all electrical connectors (**Figure 6**) before connecting to help seal out moisture.

3. Make sure all electrical connections are clean, free of corrosion and completely attached.

4. The CDI unit is mounted within a rubber vibration isolator. Always be sure that the isolator is in place when installing the unit.

CDI Troubleshooting

Refer to Chapter Two.

CDI Unit Testing

Service specifications for testing the CDI unit are not available. Test all other ignition components and troubleshoot the CDI unit using a process of elimination.

CDI Unit Replacement

1. Place the vehicle on level ground and set the parking brake.

2. Disconnect the CDI unit electrical connectors.

3. Remove the CDI unit mounting bolts and remove the CDI unit from underneath the rear fender; see **Figure 7**.

4. Install by reversing these steps, plus the following.

5. Apply dielectric grease to the electrical connectors prior to reconnecting them. This helps seal out moisture.

6. Make sure all electrical connectors are free of corrosion and are completely coupled to each other.

IGNITION HIGH TENSION COIL

Testing

The ignition high tension coil (**Figure 8**) is a form of transformer which develops the high voltage required to jump the spark plug gap. The only maintenance required is that of keeping the electrical connections clean and tight and occasionally checking to see that the coil is mounted securely.

Comprehensive resistance tests of the coil's windings are described in Chapter Two. If the condition of the system is doubtful, the following quick check may help identify if the ignition is delivering a spark.
1. Disconnect the high voltage lead from the spark plug.
2. Remove the spark plug from the cylinder head.
3. Attach a test plug (**Figure 9**), a new spark plug or a used spark plug that is known to be good to the high voltage lead. Connect the spark plug base to a good ground like the engine cylinder head and position the plug so you can see the electrodes.

WARNING
If it is necessary to hold the high voltage lead, do so with an insulated pair of pliers. The high voltage generated by the CDI could produce serious or fatal shocks.

4. Turn the ignition ON and crank the engine with the electric or recoil starter while observing the spark plug electrodes.

NOTE
If the test plug electrodes are in too much light, it may be difficult to see the spark, but a snapping sound may be heard.

5. If a fat blue spark occurs between the electrodes of the test plug, the ignition is delivering a spark and the coil is in good condition. Failure to start or run may be a result of the spark occurring at the wrong time or may be caused by a problem in another system, such as the fuel system. Reinstall the spark plug in the cylinder head.

NOTE
Make sure that you are using a good spark plug for this test. If the test is conducted with a damaged, used spark plug, the test results may be incorrect.

6. If there is no spark at the test plug, check the emergency shut-off and safety switches. Additional tests of the ignition exciter, pulser and high tension coils are described in Chapter Two.

Removal/Installation

1. Place the vehicle on level ground and set the parking brake.
2. Locate the ignition high tension coil (A, **Figure 8**). It is attached to the frame above the engine. The coil is located under the headlight cover on late models.
3. Disconnect the black/yellow or black/white primary connector (B, **Figure 8**) from the high tension coil.
4. Disconnect the spark plug cap (secondary lead) from the spark plug.
5. Remove nuts (C, **Figure 8**) from the mounting screws, then remove the ignition coil from the frame.
6. Install by reversing the removal steps. Make sure all electrical connections are tight and free of corro-

sion. Apply dielectric grease to the electrical connectors before reconnecting, to help seal out moisture.

IGNITION STATOR COILS
(EXCITER AND PULSER)

The ignition exciter and pulser coils are located under the flywheel on all models, except 400L and 4-stroke models. See **Figure 10**, **Figure 11** and **Figure 12**. The pulser coil (2, **Figure 10**) is separate from the exciter coil (13, **Figure 10**) on 2-stroke models produced before 1988. On 1988 250 cc models and all 300 and 350L models, the exciter/pulser coil is a 1-piece assembly. On 400L models, and all 4-stroke models, the exciter coil is part of the stator assembly. See 2, **Figure 11** (400L models) or 2, **Figure 12** (4-stroke models). On these models, the pulser coil (**Figure 13**) is mounted outside the flywheel.

Procedures for removing the alternator rotor (flywheel) and stator assembly (**Figure 3** or **Figure 4**) are covered in Chapter Four (2-stroke models) or Chapter Five (4-stroke models). It is not necessary to remove the stator coils to test the exciter and pulser coils. Refer to Chapter Two for testing procedures.

ELECTRIC STARTING SYSTEM

The starting system consists of the starter motor, starter gears, solenoid and the handlebar mounted starter button (**Figure 14**).

An electrical diagram of the starting system is shown in **Figure 15**. When the starter button is pressed, it engages the starter solenoid switch that completes the circuit allowing electricity to flow from the battery to the starter motor.

CAUTION
Do not operate the starter for more than 5 seconds at a time. Let it rest approximately 10 seconds, then use it again.

Troubleshooting

Refer to Chapter Two.

Starter
Removal/Installation

1. Place the vehicle on level ground and set the parking brake.

2. Disconnect the negative (ground) lead (**Figure 16**, typical) from the battery.

3. On 2-stroke engines, remove the recoil starter as described in Chapter Four.

4. On 2-stroke engines, remove the two screws (**Figure 17**).

5. On 2-stroke engines, remove the belt drive and inner cover as described in Chapter Eight.

6. Pull back the rubber boot from the electrical connector and detach the starter cable (**Figure 18**, typical).

7. On Magnum models, remove screw (A, **Figure 19**) and detach the starter ground cable from the starter.

8A. On 2-stroke engines, remove the two screws (**Figure 20**).

8B. On Magnum models, remove screw (B, **Figure 19**) securing the starter to the crankcase.

9. Pull the starter toward the left side and remove it from the engine. The starter gear can be removed as shown in **Figure 21**.

10. Install by reversing these removal steps.

11A. On 2-stroke models, be sure to install the drive gears and the gasket (**Figure 22**).

11B. On Magnum models, install and lubricate the O-ring (**Figure 23**) before installing.

Disassembly

Refer to **Figure 24** for this procedure.

1. If not already marked (**Figure 25**), scribe an alignment mark across both end covers and the armature housing for reference during reassembly.

2. Remove the 2 screws (**Figure 26** or **Figure 27**), washers, lockwashers and O-rings.

NOTE
Record the thickness and number of shims (Figure 28) installed on the shaft as they are removed in the following steps. Be sure to install these shims in their same position when reassembling the starter. The number of shims used in each starter varies. The starter you are working on may use a different number of shims from that shown in the photographs.

3. Remove the rear cover (**Figure 29**, typical) and rear shim(s).

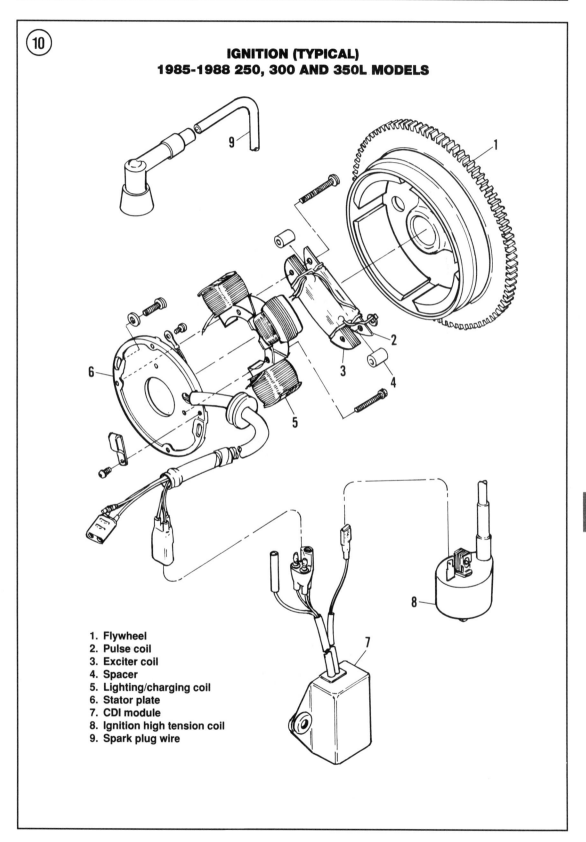

IGNITION (TYPICAL)
1985-1988 250, 300 AND 350L MODELS

10

11

1. Flywheel
2. Pulse coil
3. Exciter coil
4. Spacer
5. Lighting/charging coil
6. Stator plate
7. CDI module
8. Ignition high tension coil
9. Spark plug wire

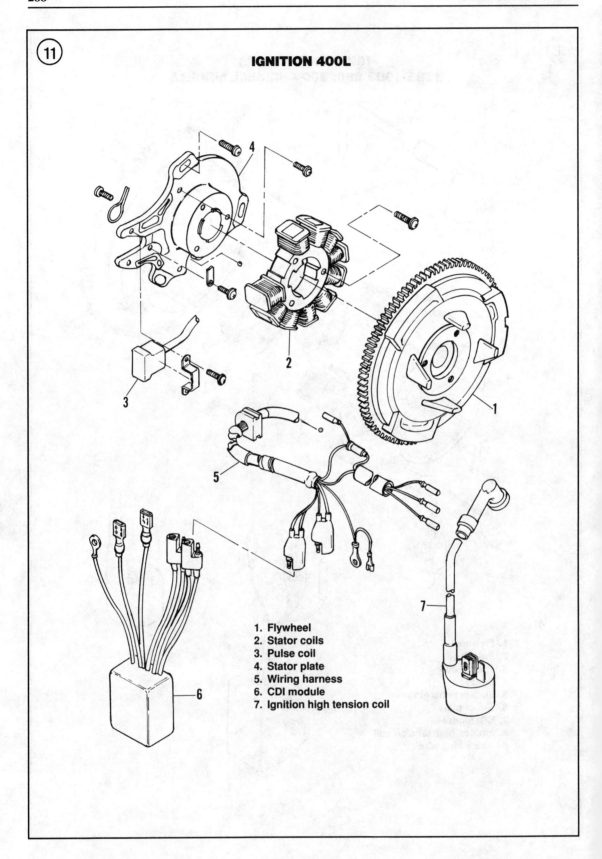

IGNITION 400L

1. Flywheel
2. Stator coils
3. Pulse coil
4. Stator plate
5. Wiring harness
6. CDI module
7. Ignition high tension coil

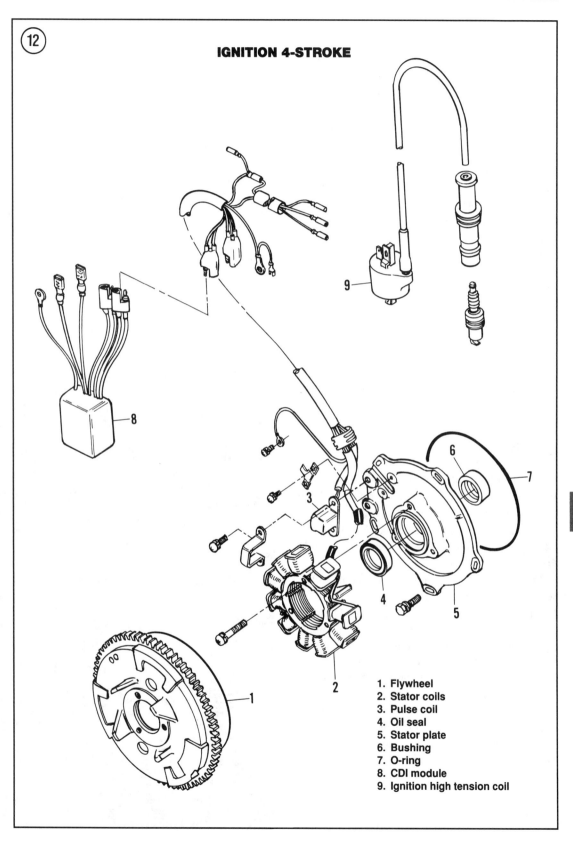

⑫

IGNITION 4-STROKE

1. Flywheel
2. Stator coils
3. Pulse coil
4. Oil seal
5. Stator plate
6. Bushing
7. O-ring
8. CDI module
9. Ignition high tension coil

11

4. Slide the front cover (**Figure 30**, typical) from the armature. Remove the shim(s).

> *NOTE*
> *Some starters have 2 brushes, while other starters have 4 brushes. Some starters may be slightly different from those shown.*

5. Remove the nut, washers, insulators (**Figure 31**, typical) and O-ring (**Figure 32**, typical), then remove the brush plate (**Figure 33**).

6. Slide armature from the housing.

7. Clean all grease, dirt and carbon from the armature, case and end covers.

> *CAUTION*
> *Be extremely careful when selecting a solvent to clean electrical components. Do not immerse any of the wire windings in solvent, because the insulation may be damaged. Wipe the windings with a cloth lightly moistened with solvent, then allow the solvent to dry thoroughly.*

Inspection

Starter motor specifications are listed in **Table 3**.

1. Pull the spring away from each brush and pull the brushes (**Figure 33**) from their guides.

2. Measure the length of each brush (**Figure 34**). If the length is equal to or less than the limit in **Table 3**, replace the brushes as a set.

3. Inspect the brush springs for damage or weakness. Replace springs if necessary.

4. Inspect the commutator (A, **Figure 35**). The mica should be below the surface of the copper commutator segments (**Figure 36**). If the commutator segments are worn to the same level as the mica insulation, have the commutator serviced by a dealer or electrical repair shop.

5. Inspect the commutator copper segments for discoloration. If the commutator segments are rough, discolored or worn, have the commutator serviced by a dealer or electrical repair shop.

6. Use an ohmmeter and perform the following:

    a. Check for continuity between the commutator bars (**Figure 37**); there should be continuity (indicated resistance) between pairs of bars.

    b. Check for continuity between the commutator bars and the shaft (**Figure 38**); there should be no continuity (infinite resistance).

    c. If the unit fails either of these tests, the starter assembly must be replaced. The armature cannot be replaced individually.

7. Use an ohmmeter to check for continuity between the starter cable terminal and the brushes. There should be continuity. Refer to **Table 3** for minimum measured resistance.

8. Inspect the bearing and seal (**Figure 39**) in the front cover for wear or damage.

9. Inspect the bushing (**Figure 40**) in the rear cover for wear or damage.

10. Inspect the starter housing for cracks or other damage.

11. Inspect inside the starter housing for loose, chipped or damaged magnets.

12. Inspect all the starter O-rings for deterioration, flat spots or other damage. Replace as required.

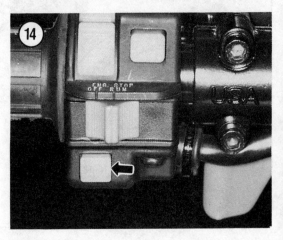

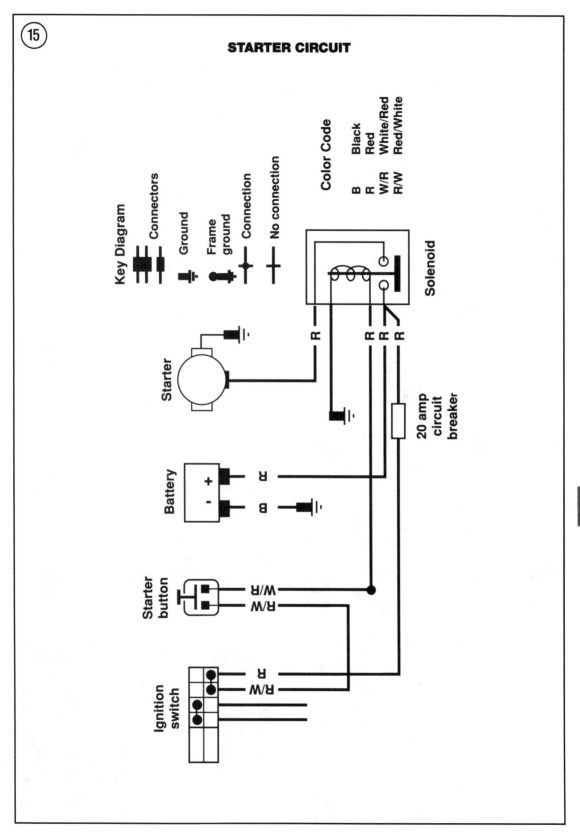

STARTER CIRCUIT

Key Diagram

Connectors
Ground
Frame ground
Connection
No connection

Color Code

B Black
R Red
W/R White/Red
R/W Red/White

Solenoid

Starter

R

R R R

20 amp circuit breaker

Battery

+
-

R

B

Starter button

W/R
R/W

Ignition switch

R
R/W

11

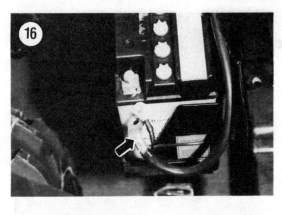

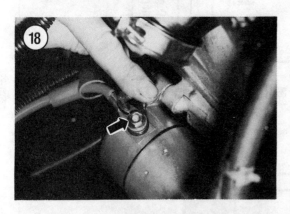

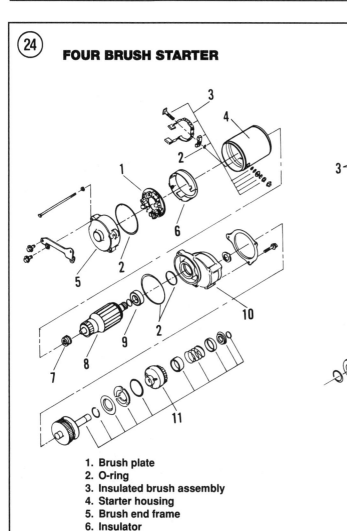

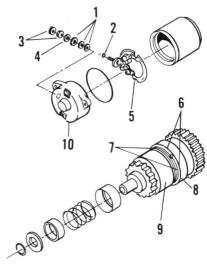

(24)

FOUR BRUSH STARTER

TWO BRUSH STARTER

1. Brush plate
2. O-ring
3. Insulated brush assembly
4. Starter housing
5. Brush end frame
6. Insulator
7. Thrust washers
8. Armature
9. Forward bearings
10. Drive end frame
11. Pinion gear assembly

1. Washer (insulating)
2. O-ring
3. Nut
4. Washer (metal)
5. Brush plate
6. Anti-kick out shoes
7. Alignment pins
8. Garter spring
9. Overrun clutch
10. Brush end frame

11

(25)

(26)

Assembly

1. If removed, install the brushes into their holders and secure the brushes with the springs.

2. Assemble the brushes, brush plate and end cover (**Figure 29**). Cover the threads of the terminal stud temporarily with plastic electrical tape when installing the O-ring (**Figure 32**) to keep from damaging the O-ring. Remove the tape after O-ring is installed.

3. Install the shims (B, **Figure 35**) over the armature shaft.

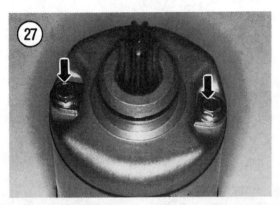

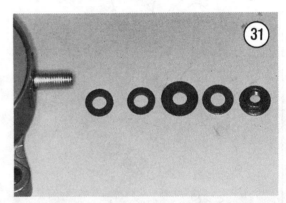

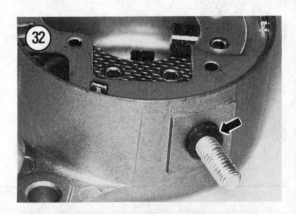

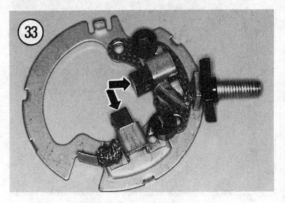

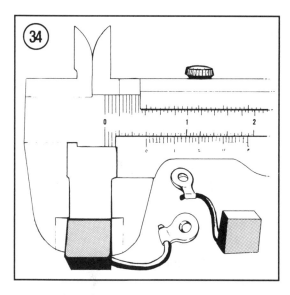

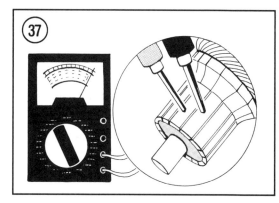

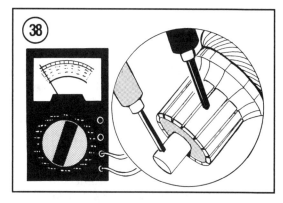

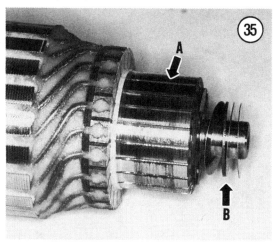

ARMATURE CONDITION

Good

Worn

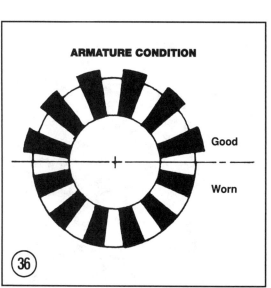

11

NOTE
Lubricate the end bushing with a silicone (nonpetroleum) grease before installing the end cover.

4. Compress the brushes against their springs, slide the brush plate over the commutator, then release the brushes (**Figure 41**).

NOTE
*Before installing the end frame, lubricate the large O-rings (**Figure 42**). Make sure that the O-rings are not twisted when installing the end covers.*

5. Assemble the end frame over the armature (**Figure 43**), aligning the mark on the cover with the matching mark on the housing (**Figure 44**). The tab (**Figure 45**) on the brush plate must also align with the notch in the brush end frame.

6. Install the previously used shim washers (**Figure 46**).

NOTE
Lubricate the end bearing with a silicone (nonpetroleum) grease before installing the end cover. Lubricate the large O-ring sealing the case before installing it. Make sure that the O-ring is not twisted when installing the end cover.

7. Install the drive end frame the armature, aligning the marks on the end frame and housing (**Figure 44**).

NOTE
*Make sure the O-rings are installed on the through bolts (**Figure 47**) before installing.*

8A. On 2-stroke engines, hold the end frames in place, align the marks (**Figure 44**, typical) and install the through bolts (**Figure 48**). If the bolts will not pass through the starter motor, the end frames and/or brush plate are installed incorrectly. Tighten the bolts securely.

8B. On Magnum models, hold the end frames in place, align marks (**Figure 44**) and install the through bolts (**Figure 49**). If the bolts will not pass through the starter motor, the end frames and/or brush plate are installed incorrectly. Tighten the bolts securely.

STARTER DRIVE GEARS

The electric starter operates through a set of reduction gears and an over running clutch. The starter pinion at the end of the armature shaft meshes with the larger gear. The larger starter drive gear engages the overrunning clutch, which drives the smaller of the two gears. The smaller drive gear engages the flywheel ring gear to start the engine.

On 2-stroke engines, the starter drive gears (**Figure 50**) are located between a bearing in the starter end frame and a bearing in the recoil starter housing. The starter drive gear and starter clutch assembly can be removed after removing the starter as described in this chapter.

On Magnum models, the starter drive gears (**Figure 51**) are located between a bearing in the crankcase and a bearing in the recoil starter housing. The starter drive gear and starter clutch assembly can be removed after removing the recoil starter as described in Chapter Five.

On some models, the garter spring is exposed and can be removed and a new spring installed. If the spring is damaged, the starter drive may not return

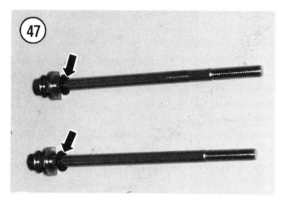

11

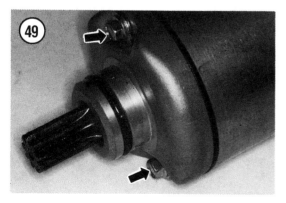

properly and drag on the flywheel. A replacement spring is available as a service part for these models.

When installing, be sure to lubricate and install the thrust washers (**Figure 52**).

STARTER SOLENOID

The starter solenoid (A, **Figure 53**) is mounted in front of the battery on the left-hand side.

Starter Solenoid Resistance Test

Test the starter solenoid with an ohmmeter as follows.
1. Turn the ignition switch OFF.
2. Separate the connector (B, **Figure 53**) of the small white/red wire attached to the starter solenoid.
3. Switch the ohmmeter to R × 1 and connect one lead to the small red wire attached to the solenoid and ground the other ohmmeter lead to the vehicle frame.
4. Measured resistance should be approximately 3.4 ohms.
5. Replace the starter solenoid if the resistance reading is too high.
6. Reconnect the solenoid electrical connector.

Removal/Installation

1. Remove the necessary covers to gain access to the solenoid (A, **Figure 53**).
2. Disconnect the battery negative (ground) lead.
3. Disconnect the battery cables and starter control wire from the starter solenoid electrical connectors.
4. Unbolt the solenoid from the frame.
5. Replace by reversing these removal steps, noting the following.
6. Attach both starter cables to the solenoid and tighten the nuts securely.
7. Make sure all of the electrical connectors are on tight and that the rubber boots are properly installed to keep out moisture.

LIGHTING SYSTEM

The lighting system consists of a headlight, taillight and instrument lights. **Table 4** lists replacement bulbs for these components.

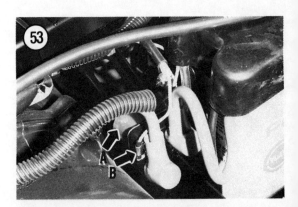

Always use the correct wattage bulb. The use of a larger wattage bulb will give a dim light and a smaller wattage bulb will burn out prematurely.

Headlight Bulb Replacement

Several different headlight configurations have been used. Refer to **Figure 54**, **Figure 55** or **Figure 56**.

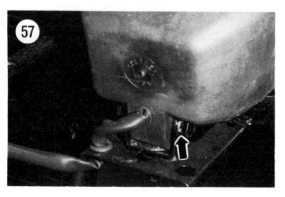

> *WARNING*
> *If the headlight has just burned out or turned off, it will be hot! Do not touch the bulb until it cools off.*

1. Remove the headlight guard or paneling, if so equipped.
2A. If so equipped, remove the screws from the trim or retaining ring.
2B. On some models, the headlight is held in place by a rubber retaining ring, that can be pulled back while pulling the headlight from its housing.
3. Remove the bulb.
4. Install by reversing these steps.

Headlight Adjustment

The headlight on some models is equipped with a vertical adjust screw located at the base of the headlight below the grille. To adjust the headlight vertically, turn the screw counterclockwise to move the light up and clockwise to move the light down.

The headlights on some models are adjusted by loosening the fasteners (**Figure 55**, **Figure 56** or **Figure 57**), repositioning the light, then tightening the fasteners. Vertical adjustment is accomplished with the bolt (**Figure 55** or **Figure 57**). Horizontal adjustment can be accomplished after loosening the nut (**Figure 56**).

Taillight Bulb and Lens Replacement

Refer to **Figure 58** for this procedure. Be sure that the connector (**Figure 59**) is securely attached and that electrical current is delivered to connector at the proper times.
1. Remove the 2 screws (**Figure 58**) and pull the lens from its housing.
2. After removing the lens, the bulb can be removed.

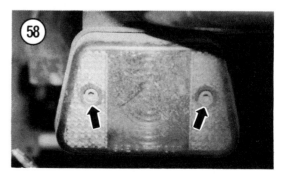

3. Replace the bulb with the type listed in **Table 4**.
4. Install by reversing these steps, noting the following.
5. Make sure the rubber gasket seal is seated all the way around the lens when assembling.

Instrument (Panel) Lights Lamp Replacement

Reverse and neutral indicator lights (**Figure 60** or **Figure 61**) are used on most models. Bulbs can be changed after removing the covers. On some models it is necessary to remove some panels to access the bulbs. Carefully remove the blown bulb, install the new bulb then install the bulb cover. Check that all wires are routed properly and connectors are securely fastened.

SWITCHES

Testing

Test switches for continuity using an ohmmeter (see Chapter One) or a self-powered test light at the switch connector plug by operating the switch in each of its operating positions and comparing results with its switch operating diagram. For example, **Figure 62** shows a continuity diagram for the starter switch. It shows which terminals should show continuity when the switch is in a given position.

When the starter switch is in the ON position, there should be continuity between the white/red and red/white terminals. This is indicated by the line on the continuity diagram. An ohmmeter connected between these 2 terminals should indicate little or no resistance, or a test light should light. When the starter switch is OFF, there should be no continuity between the same terminals.

When testing switches, note the following:

a. Check the battery as described under *Battery* in Chapter Three; if necessary, charge or replace the battery.
b. Disconnect the battery negative (ground) cable from the battery before checking the continuity of any switch.
c. Detach all connectors located between the switch and the electrical circuit.

CAUTION
Do not attempt to start the engine with the battery disconnected.

d. When separating 2 connectors, pull on the connector housings and not the wires.
e. After locating a defective circuit, check the connectors to make sure they are clean and properly connected. Check all wires going into a connector housing to make sure each wire is properly positioned and that the wire end is not loose.
f. To reconnect connectors properly, push them together until they click or snap into place.

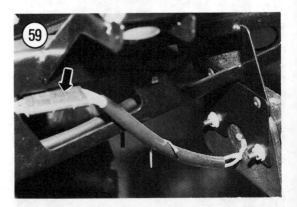

Figure 62 — STARTER SWITCH

Position \ Color	Red/white	White/red
FREE		
PUSHED	●——————●	

Figure 63 — KEY SWITCH

Position \ Color	Black	Brown	Red/white	Red
OFF	●————————●			
ON			●————————●	

Figure 64 — HEADLIGHT SWITCH

Position \ Color	Red/white	Green	Yellow
OFF			
LO	●————————●		
HI	●————————————————●		

Figure 65 — ENGINE SHUT-OFF SWITCH

Position \ Color	Black	Brown
OFF	●————————●	
RUN		

Figure 66 — ALL WHEEL DRIVE SWITCH

Position \ Color	Grey/white	Grey	Demand light	Brown
AWD OFF Button out				
AWD ON Button IN	●——————●			
	●——————————————●			●

If the switch or button does not perform properly, replace it. Refer to the following typical diagrams when testing the switches:

a. Starter switch: **Figure 62**.
b. Key switch: **Figure 63**.
c. Light switch: **Figure 64**.
d. Shut off switch: **Figure 65**.
e. All wheel drive switch: **Figure 66**.
f. Electronic throttle control switch: **Figure 67**.
g. Transmission switch: **Figure 68**.
h. Override switch: **Figure 69**.

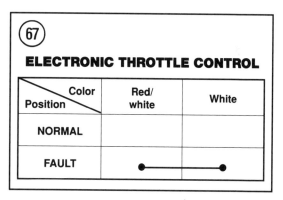

Figure 67 — ELECTRONIC THROTTLE CONTROL

Position \ Color	Red/white	White
NORMAL		
FAULT	●————————●	

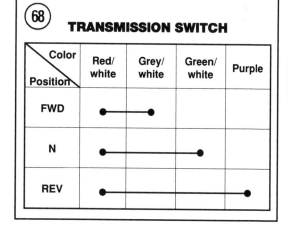

Figure 68 — TRANSMISSION SWITCH

Position \ Color	Red/white	Grey/white	Green/white	Purple
FWD	●————————●			
N		●————————●		
REV		●————————————————●		

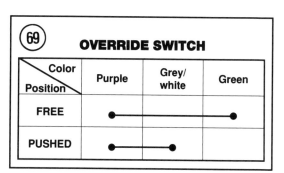

Figure 69 — OVERRIDE SWITCH

Position \ Color	Purple	Grey/white	Green
FREE	●————————————————●		
PUSHED	●————————●		

11

Right-hand Handlebar Switch Housing Replacement

The right-hand handlebar switch housing (**Figure 70**) is equipped with the following switches:

    a. All wheel drive switch (A, **Figure 70**).

    b. Electronic throttle control switch (B, **Figure 70**).

NOTE
The switches mounted in the right-hand handlebar switch housing may not be available separately. If one switch is damaged, it may be necessary to replace the housing as an assembly.

1. Remove any interfering panels as described in Chapter Fifteen.

2. Remove any clamps securing the switch wiring harness to the handlebar.

3. Disconnect the right-hand switch electrical connector.

4. Detach the throttle control cable as described in Chapter Six.

5. Remove the screws securing the switch to the handlebar and remove the switch and throttle control assembly (**Figure 71**).

6. Install by reversing these steps. Adjust the throttle cable as described in Chapter Three.

Key Switch Replacement

The key switch is mounted in the front panel.

1. Remove necessary covers (**Figure 72**).

2. Loosen the large plastic nut surrounding the key switch (**Figure 72** or **Figure 73**).

3. Disconnect the key switch electrical connector and remove the switch.

4. Install a new main switch by reversing these removal steps.

Left-hand Handlebar Switch Housing Replacement

The left-hand handlebar switch housing (**Figure 74**) is equipped with the following switches:

    a. Light switch.

    b. Override switch.

    c. Engine shut off switch.

    d. Starter switch.

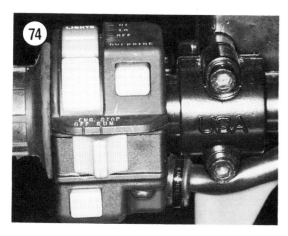

NOTE
The switches mounted in the left-hand handlebar switch housing may not be available separately. If one switch is damaged, it may be necessary to replace the housing as an assembly.

1. Remove any interfering panels as described in Chapter Fifteen.
2. Remove any clamps securing the switch wiring harness to the handlebar.
3. Disconnect the electrical connectors from the left-hand switch.
4. Remove the screws securing the switch to the handlebar and remove the switch (**Figure 74**).
5. Install by reversing these steps.

Transmission (Forward/Neutral/Reverse) Switches

The transmission switch of late models is mounted in the EZ shift control housing. Refer to Chapter Nine for service.

WIRING DIAGRAMS

Wiring diagrams for all models are located at the end of this book.

Tables 1-4 are on the following pages.

11

Table 1 CHARGING SYSTEM AND BATTERY SPECIFICATIONS

Model No.	Alternator output	Battery (amp hr.)
1985-1986		
Scrambler, Trail Boss	100 Watt	12V (14)
1987		
Cyclone	100 Watt	none
Trail Boss	100 Watt	12V (14)
1988		
Trail Boss	100 Watt	12V (14)
Trail Boss 250 R/ES	100 Watt	12V (14)
1989		
All models	* 150 Watt	12V (14)
1990-1992		
Trail Blazer	* 150 Watt	none
Trail Boss 250	* 150 Watt	12V (14)
Trail Boss 350L	* 150 Watt	12V (14)
Big Boss	* 150 Watt	12V (14)
1993		
Trail Blazer	* 150 Watt	none
Trail Boss	* 150 Watt	12V (14)
Sportsman	* 150 Watt	12V (14)
250 & 350	* 150 Watt	12V (14)
1994		
Trail Blazer	* 150 Watt	none
Trail Boss	* 150 Watt	12V (14)
Sport	* 150 Watt	12V (14)
Sportsman	* 200 Watt	12V (14)
300 models	* 150 Watt	12V (14)
400 models	* 200 Watt	12V (14)
1995		
Trail Blazer	* 150 Watt	none
Trail Boss	* 150 Watt	12V (14)
300 models	* 150 Watt	12V (14)
400 models	* 200 Watt	12V (14)
Scrambler and Sport	* 150 Watt	12V (14)
Sportsman and Xplorer	* 200 Watt	12V (14)
Magnum	* 200 Watt	12V (14)

* Output with engine operating at 4,000 rpm.

Table 2 CHARGING/LIGHTING COIL RESISTANCE SPECIFICATIONS

1985-1988 with 100 watt alternator	
Models without battery	
(yellow to yellow/red or brown)	0.45-0.60 ohms
Models with battery	
(yellow/red to yellow)	0.45-0.60 ohms
1989-on with 150 watt alternator	
250, 300, 350 & 400 engines	
(yellow/red to yellow)	0.25-0.35 ohms
400 & 425 engines with 200 watt alternator	
(yellow/red to yellow)	0.34 ohms
(yellow/brown to yellow)	0.17 ohms

Table 3 STARTER SPECIFICATIONS

Resistance tests	
Between two armature commutator segments	less than 0.3 ohm
Across the starter solenoid pull-in coil	3.4 ohms
Between starter Input terminal and brushes	less than 0.3 ohm
Between any commutator segment and armature ground	infinite
Brush wear limit	0.8 mm (5/16 in.)

Table 4 LIGHTS

Model No.	Headlight	Taillight	Instruments
1985-1987	45 Watts	5 Watts	–
	45/45 Stanley	GE 168	–
1988			
Trail Boss	45 Watts	5 Watts	–
	45/45 Stanley	GE 168	–
Trail Boss 250 R/ES	60 Watts	5 Watts	–
	60/60 Stanley	GE 168	–
1989-on	60 Watts	5 Watts	2 Watts
	60/60 Stanley	GE 168	Sylvania 12 POL

11

CHAPTER TWELVE

FRONT SUSPENSION AND STEERING

This chapter describes repair and maintenance of the front wheels, nondriving hubs, front suspension arms and steering components. Refer to Chapter Ten for service to the front drive hubs.

Refer to **Tables 1** for drive type and general front suspension specifications. **Tables 1-4** are located at the end of this chapter.

FRONT WHEEL
(4-WHEEL MODELS)

Removal/Installation

1. Place the vehicle on level ground and set the parking brake.
2. Mark the front tires with an "L" (left side) or "R" (right side) so that they can be installed onto the same side of the vehicle from which they were removed. If the tire is to be removed from the rim, also mark the tire with an arrow indicating the direction of rotation when traveling forward.
3. Loosen but do not remove the lug nuts (**Figure 1**) securing the wheel to the front hub.

4. Raise the front of the vehicle with a small hydraulic or scissor jack. Place the jack under the frame with a piece of wood between the jack and the frame.
5. Place block(s) under the frame to support the vehicle securely with the front wheels off the ground.
6. Remove the wheel nuts (loosened in Step 3) and remove the front wheel.
7. Clean the lug nuts in solvent and dry thoroughly.
8. Inspect the wheel for cracks, bending or other damage. If damage is severe, replace wheel as described under *Tires and Wheels* in this chapter.
9. Install the washers and nuts (**Figure 1**). Finger tighten the nuts until the wheel is positioned squarely against the front hub.

> *WARNING*
> *Always tighten the lug nuts to the correct torque specification or the nuts may work loose and the wheel could fall off.*

10. Use a torque wrench and tighten the lug nuts in a crisscross pattern to the torque specification listed in **Table 2**.

11. After the wheel is installed completely, rotate it; apply the front brake several times to make sure that the wheel rotates freely and that the brake is operating correctly.

12. Measure wheel runout with a dial indicator as described under *Front Hub* in this chapter.

13. Raise the front of the vehicle a little and remove the wooden block(s).

14. Let the jack down and remove the jack and wooden blocks.

FRONT WHEEL
(3-WHEEL SCRAMBLER MODEL)

Removal/Installation

Refer to **Figure 2** for this procedure.

1. Place the vehicle on level ground and block the rear wheels.

2. Loosen but do not remove the lug nuts securing the wheel to the front hub.

3. Loosen the front brake adjuster (**Figure 3**), then detach the lower end of the cable from the brake operating lever.

4. Use a small jack to lift the front of the vehicle off the ground.

5. Place block(s) under the frame to support the vehicle securely with the front wheel off the ground.

6. Remove the cotter pin from the axle nut, then remove the castellated axle nut and washer.

7. Withdraw the front axle from the fork tubes and the front hub.

8. Remove the spacer from the right side of the wheel hub.

9. Lower the wheel, hub and brake assembly away from the fork tubes.

10. Separate the brake hub from the brake drum.

11. Remove the lug nuts and separate the wheel from the hub.

12. Check the operation and condition of the front brake before assembling. Refer to Chapter Fourteen to service the brake.

13. Install the front wheel and hub by reversing the removal procedure. Make sure that the notch in the brake hub engages the lug on the left fork tube correctly.

14. Install the flat washer onto the axle.

15. Install the castellated axle nut, then tighten the nut to the torque specification in **Table 2**.

16. Check that one pair of openings in the castellated nut is aligned with the cotter pin hole in the axle. If not, align opening by tightening the axle nut. Do not loosen the axle nut to align the openings.

> *WARNING*
> *Always install a new cotter pin.*

17. Insert the new cotter pin through openings in the castellated nut and axle hole. Bend the cotter pin as shown in **Figure 4** to lock the nut.

18. Adjust the brake cable as described in Chapter Three.

FRONT HUB
(4-WHEEL MODELS WITHOUT
ALL-WHEEL DRIVE)

The nondriving front hub consists of 2 sealed bearings and a center hub spacer. On models with a drum type front brake, the drum is integral with the front hub. On models with a disc type front brake, the disc is bolted to the front hub.

Inspection
(Hub Installed)

Inspect the bearings for each wheel before removing bearings from the wheel hub.

> *CAUTION*
> *Do not remove the wheel bearings for inspection, because the bearings may be damaged during the removal process. Remove the wheel bearings only if they are to be replaced.*

12

1. Check that lug nuts (**Figure 1**) are tightened to the torque specified in **Table 2**.

2. Place the vehicle on level ground and set the parking brake. Block the rear wheels so the vehicle will not roll in either direction.

3. Lift the front of the vehicle with a small jack. Place the jack under the frame with a piece of wood between the jack and the frame.

4. Place wooden block(s) under the frame to support the vehicle securely with the front wheels off the ground.

5. Shake the wheel to check for play. If the wheel is loose, remove the hub cap and check the castellated nut (**Figure 5**). If the nut is tight, make sure that the looseness is located in the hub bearings.

6. Rotate the wheel and check for roughness. The hub should turn smoothly without roughness, exces-

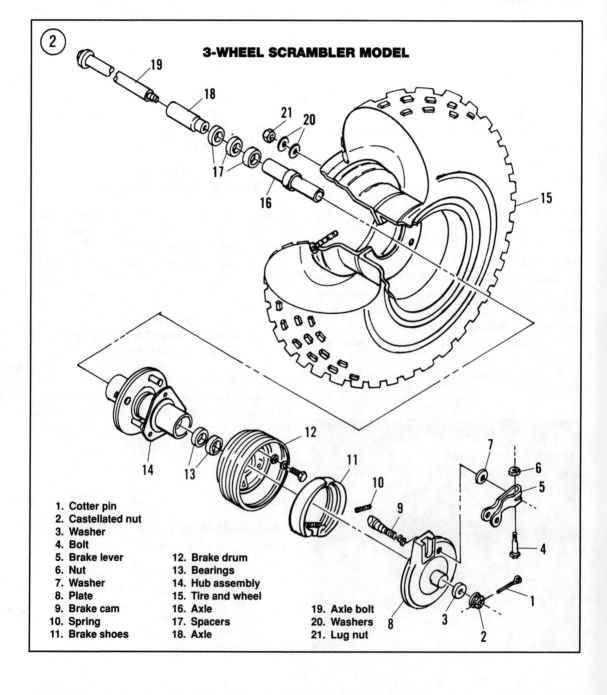

(2) 3-WHEEL SCRAMBLER MODEL

1. Cotter pin
2. Castellated nut
3. Washer
4. Bolt
5. Brake lever
6. Nut
7. Washer
8. Plate
9. Brake cam
10. Spring
11. Brake shoes
12. Brake drum
13. Bearings
14. Hub assembly
15. Tire and wheel
16. Axle
17. Spacers
18. Axle
19. Axle bolt
20. Washers
21. Lug nut

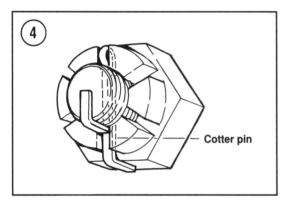

Cotter pin

sive play or other abnormal conditions. If hub does not turn smoothly, remove hub and check the bearings.

7. Mount a dial indicator against the wheel rim to measure radial and lateral runout. Turn the wheel slowly by hand and read movement indicated on dial indicator. If runout is excessive, check the condition of the wheel assembly. If the wheel is bent or otherwise damaged, it may require replacement.

8. If the wheel bearings are rough or otherwise damaged, remove the hub and install new bearings.

9. Remove the dial indicator and lower the vehicle to the ground.

Hub Removal

1. Remove the front wheel (A, **Figure 6**)as described in this chapter.

2A. On models with hydraulic disc brakes, remove the 2 brake caliper mounting bolts and lift the caliper away from the brake disc. Hang the caliper from the vehicle with a stiff wire hook.

NOTE
Insert a piece of vinyl tubing or plastic between the brake pads in the caliper, in place of the brake disc. That way if the brake lever is accidentally moved, the piston will not be forced from the cylinder. If the piston comes out of the cylinder, the caliper will have to be disassembled to reseat the piston and both front brakes will require bleeding. By blocking the brake pads, the piston cannot be forced out and bleeding the system should not be required.

2B. On models with mechanical drum brakes, it may be necessary to loosen the front brake adjuster.

3. Remove the hub cap (B, **Figure 6**).

4. Remove and discard the axle nut cotter pin.

5. Loosen and remove the axle nut (**Figure 5**).

6. Slide the front hub from the steering knuckle.

Inspection
(Hub Removed)

1. Remove the hub spacer from the outer seal.

2. Inspect the seals. Replace seals if cut, deteriorated or starting to harden.

12

3. Inspect the threaded studs on the front hub. Replace as necessary.

4. If necessary, remove the seals as described under *Disassembly* in this chapter.

5. Turn each bearing inner race with your fingers. The bearing should turn smoothly with no roughness, binding or excessive noise.

6. Inspect the play of the inner race of each hub bearing. Check for excessive lateral and radial play. Replace the bearings if play is excessive.

7. Always replace both bearings in the hub at the same time. When purchasing new bearings, write down the bearing manufacturer's code numbers from the old bearings (found on the outside of each bearing) and take them with you to ensure a perfect replacement.

Disassembly

The bearings are installed with a tight fit and force is required to remove them from the bores in the hub. Because of the close fit between the bearings and hub spacer, the center hub spacer may be damaged when removing the first bearing. Remove the bearings only if the bearings must be replaced. The inner and outer bearings and the inner and outer seals are different. Prior to removing the seals and bearings, write down the size code of each part so the replacement parts can be installed correctly.

1. Remove the outer seal by prying it from the hub.

CAUTION
When removing the bearings in the following steps, support the front hub carefully so that you do not damage the brake drum or disc.

2. To remove the front hub bearings without special tools:

  a. Using a long drift, tilt the center hub spacer away from one side of the outer bearing as shown in **Figure 7**.

NOTE
Try not to damage the hub spacer when positioning and driving against the long drift. You may have to grind a clearance groove in the drift to enable it to contact the bearing while clearing the spacer.

  b. Tap the bearing out of the hub with a hammer, working around the perimeter of the bearing's inner race.

  c. Remove the center hub spacer from the hub, noting the direction in which the spacer is installed in the hub, for reassembly reference.

  d. Use a large socket or bearing driver to drive the opposite bearing out of the hub.

3. Clean the hub and center hub spacer in solvent and dry thoroughly.

Assembly

Single row, deep groove ball bearings are used in the front hub. Prior to installing new bearings and seals, note the following:

  a. Install bearings so that the manufacturer's code marks and numbers face out.

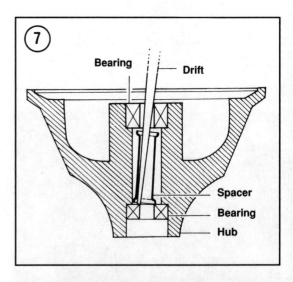

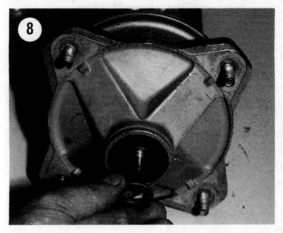

b. Install bearings by pressing them into hub with a socket or bearing driver that seats against the outer race only.

c. Install seals with their closed side facing out.

1. Pack the bearings with a good quality bearing grease. Work the grease in between the balls thoroughly. Turn the bearing by hand to make sure the grease is seated evenly inside the bearing.

2. Blow any dirt or foreign matter out of the hub and center hub spacer before installing the bearings.

3. Press the inner bearing into the hub until it bottoms in the bore.

4. Turn the hub over and install the center hub spacer so that its larger inner diameter seats against the inner bearing.

5. Press the outer bearing into the hub until it bottoms in the bore.

6. Fill the space inside the lip of each seal with a waterproof bearing grease.

7. Press in the inner seal until its outer surface is flush with the seal bore.

8. Press the outer seal until its outer surface is flush with the seal bore.

Installation

1. Clean the steering knuckle bearing surface, threads and axle nut with solvent. Blow dry with compressed air.

2. Install the hub spacer into the front hub outer seal.

3. Slide the front hub onto the steering knuckle.

4. Install the flat washer onto the steering knuckle as shown in **Figure 8**.

5. Install the castellated axle nut onto the steering knuckle, then tighten the nut (**Figure 5**) to the torque specification in **Table 2**.

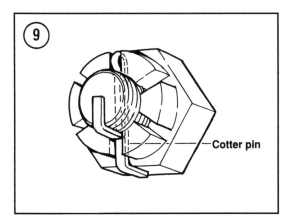

Cotter pin

6. Check that one pair of openings in the castellated nut is aligned with the cotter pin hole in the steering knuckle. If not, align opening by tightening the axle nut. Do not loosen the axle nut to align the openings.

WARNING
Always install a new cotter pin.

7. Insert the new cotter pin through the openings in the castellated nut and steering knuckle hole. Bend the cotter pin as shown in **Figure 9** to lock the nut.

8A. On models with disc brake remove the spacer previously installed between the brake pads and slide the brake caliper over the brake disc. Install the brake caliper mounting bolts and tighten to the torque specification in **Table 2**. Apply the front brake lever a few times to seat the pads against the disc.

8B. On models with drum brakes, adjust the brake cable as described in Chapter Three.

9. Install the front wheel as described in this chapter.

FRONT HUB
(3-WHEEL TRICYCLE MODELS)

The front hub consists of 2 sealed bearings and a center spacer. The front brake drum is bolted to the front hub.

Inspection
(Hub Installed)

Inspect the bearings for each wheel before removing bearings from the wheel hub.

CAUTION
Do not remove the wheel bearings for inspection, because the bearings may be damaged during the removal process. Remove the wheel bearings only if they are to be replaced.

1. Check that lug nuts are tightened to the torque specified in **Table 2**.

2. Place the vehicle on level ground and set the parking brake. Block the rear wheels so the vehicle will not roll in either direction.

3. Lift the front of the vehicle with a small jack. Place the jack under the frame with a piece of wood between the jack and the frame.

12

4. Place wooden block(s) under the frame to support the vehicle securely with the front wheel off the ground.

5. Shake the wheel to check for play. If the wheel is loose, check the castellated nut (2, **Figure 10**). If the nut is tight, make sure that the looseness is located in the hub bearings.

6. Rotate the wheel and check for roughness. The hub should turn smoothly without roughness, excessive play or other abnormal conditions. If the hub

does not turn smoothly, remove the hub and check the bearings.

7. Mount a dial indicator against the wheel rim to measure radial and lateral runout. Turn the wheel slowly by hand and read movement indicated on dial indicator. If runout is excessive, check the condition of the wheel assembly. If the wheel is bent or otherwise damaged, it may require replacement.

8. If the wheel bearings are rough or otherwise damaged, remove the hub and install new bearings.

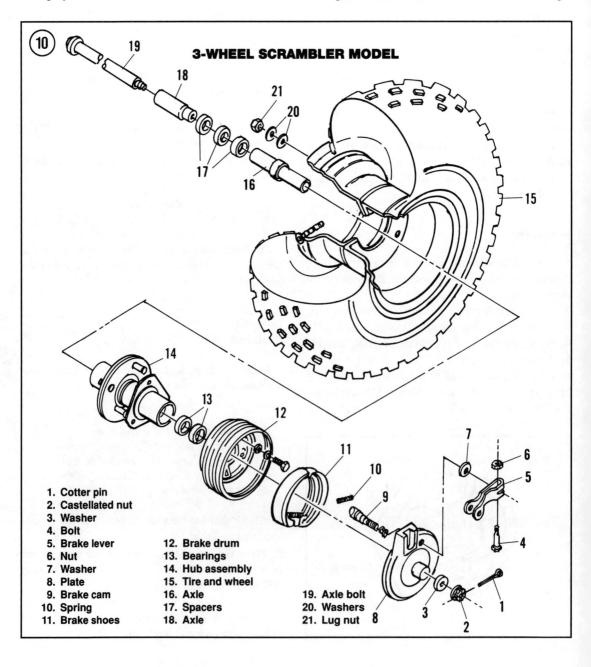

(10) **3-WHEEL SCRAMBLER MODEL**

1. Cotter pin
2. Castellated nut
3. Washer
4. Bolt
5. Brake lever
6. Nut
7. Washer
8. Plate
9. Brake cam
10. Spring
11. Brake shoes
12. Brake drum
13. Bearings
14. Hub assembly
15. Tire and wheel
16. Axle
17. Spacers
18. Axle
19. Axle bolt
20. Washers
21. Lug nut

9. Remove dial indicator and lower vehicle to ground.

Removal/Inspection/Installation

Refer to **Figure 10**.
1. Remove the front wheel as described in this chapter.
2. Unbolt the wheel and the brake drum from the hub.
3. Remove the hub spacers from the seals.
4. Inspect the seals. Replace seals if cut, deteriorated or starting to harden.
5. Inspect the threaded studs on the front hub. Replace as necessary.
6. If necessary, remove the seals as described under *Disassembly/Assembly* in this chapter.
7. Turn each bearing inner race with your fingers. The bearing should turn smoothly with no roughness, binding or excessive noise.
8. Inspect the play of the inner race of each hub bearing. Check for excessive lateral and radial play. Replace the bearings if play is excessive.
9. Always replace both bearings in the hub at the same time. When purchasing new bearings, write down the bearing manufacturer's code numbers from the old bearings (found on the outside of each bearing) and take them with you to ensure a perfect replacement.
10. Clean all parts including the axle and axle nut with solvent. Blow dry with compressed air.
11. Install the hub spacers into the front hub seals.
12. Attach the brake drum and front wheel to the hub and tightening the retaining bolts to the torque listed in **Table 2**.
13. Install the front wheel as described in this chapter.

Disassembly/Assembly

The front hub bearings are installed with a tight fit and force is required to remove them from the bores in the hub. Because of the close fit between the bearings and hub spacer, the center hub spacer might be damaged when removing the first bearing. Remove the bearings only if the bearings must be replaced. Before removing the seals and bearings, write down the size code of each part so the replacement parts can be installed correctly.
1. Remove the seals by prying them from the hub.

CAUTION
When removing the bearings in the following steps, support the front hub carefully so that you do not damage the brake drum or disc.

2. To remove the front hub bearings without special tools:
   a. Use a long drift to move the center hub spacer to one side of the bearing as shown in **Figure 7**.

NOTE
Try not to damage the hub spacer when positioning and driving against the long drift. You may have to grind a clearance groove in the drift to enable it to contact the bearing while clearing the spacer.

   b. Tap the bearing out of the hub with a hammer, working around the perimeter of the bearing's inner race.
   c. Remove the center hub spacer from the hub.
   d. Use a large socket or bearing driver to drive the opposite bearing out of the hub.
3. Clean the hub and center hub spacer in solvent and dry thoroughly.
4. Single row, deep groove ball bearings are used in the front hub. Prior to installing new bearings and seals, note the following:
   a. Install bearings so the manufacturer's code marks and numbers face out.
   b. Install bearings by pressing them into the hub with a socket or bearing driver that seats against the outer race only.
   c. Install the seals with their closed side facing out.
5. Pack the bearings with a good quality bearing grease. Work the grease in between the balls thoroughly. Turn the bearing by hand to make sure the grease is distributed evenly inside the bearing.
6. Blow any dirt or foreign material out of the hub and center hub spacer before installing the bearings.
7. Press one of the bearings into the hub until it bottoms in the bore.
8. Turn the hub over and install the center hub spacer so it is against the inner race of the installed bearing.
9. Press the other bearing into the hub until it bottoms in the bore.
10. Fill the space inside the lip of each seal with a waterproof bearing grease.

12

11. Press one seal in until its outer surface is flush with the seal bore.

12. Press the remaining seal in until its outer surface is flush with the seal bore.

FRONT FORK TUBES
(3-WHEEL SCRAMBLER MODEL)

These tricycle models are equipped with a telescopic front fork front suspension.

Removal/Installation

1. Place the vehicle on level ground and block the rear wheels.

2. Use a small jack to lift the front of the vehicle off the ground.

3. Place block(s) under the frame to support the vehicle securely with the front wheel off the ground.

4. Remove the front wheel and hub as described in this chapter.

5. Unbolt and remove the front fender.

6. Loosen the bolts that clamp the upper end of the fork tubes.

NOTE
Clean the outside of the front fork tubes before attempting to slide the tubes from the upper clamps.

7. Withdraw the fork tubes from the upper clamps.

8. Install dust boots on the outer fork tubes before installing the fork tubes. Do not clamp the boots in place.

9. Slide the fork tubes into the upper clamps until the top of the tubes are flush with the upper crown.

10. Tighten clamp bolts to the torque listed in **Table 2**. Make sure that the top of the inner tube remains flush with the top of the upper crown.

11. Route the breather tubes from the dust boots into the pivot tube of the clamp bracket, then attach the boots.

12. Reinstall the front fender.

13. Reinstall the front wheel.

Disassembly/Inspection/Assembly

To simplify fork service and to prevent the mixing parts, the fork legs should be disassembled and assembled individually.

1. Clamp the front axle boss at the bottom of the fork tube in a vise with soft jaws. Do *not* clamp the slider in a vise at any point except the fork axle boss.

NOTE
The Allen screw installed through the bottom of the slider has been secured using a locking and sealing compound and can be difficult to remove, because the damper rod will turn inside the slider. If you have access to an air-powered impact wrench, you can remove the Allen screw after removing the fork spring in the following steps. If you do not have access to an air-powered impact wrench, loosen the Allen screw before removing the fork spring. The fork spring will help keep the damper rod from turning and may allow the screw to be removed. If you are unable to remove the screw, take both fork tubes to a dealer and have the screws removed.

2. If you do not have access to an air-powered impact wrench, loosen but do not remove the Allen screw located at the bottom of the fork slider.

WARNING
The upper spring seat is under spring pressure. When removing, note that it may fly off. Keep your face away from the cap when removing it. Also make sure that the fork tube is fully extended. If the forks are damaged and stuck in a compressed position, the fork should be disassembled by a dealer or other qualified mechanic, because the upper seat may fly out of the fork tube with considerable force.

3. Pull the rubber cap from the top of the fork tube.

4. Press the upper spring seat down against spring pressure.

5. Remove the retaining ring from inside the fork tube.

6. Allow the spring to push the upper spring seat up and out of the fork tube.

7. Remove the fork spring and pour the oil from the fork into a clean container. Pump the fork several times to expel most of the oil. Check the oil for evidence of sludge or debris that would indicate worn or damaged parts. Properly dispose the oil after examining it.

8. Remove the retaining ring from the top of the lower slider.

CAUTION
Be careful not to damage the sealing surfaces of the fork tubes when removing the retaining ring or the seal.

9. Carefully pry the oil seal from the top of the lower slider.

10. Remove the Allen screw and washer from the bottom of the fork slider.

NOTE
The bushing installed in the slider is an interference fit. When separating the fork tube and slider, the bushing will be removed with the slider.

11. Grasp the slider in one hand and the fork tube in the other. Work the fork tube up and down to knock the upper bushing against the lower bushing.

12. Remove the tapered rebound sleeve from the end of the damper rod.

13. Inspect all parts for cracks, bends, dents, nicks, scratches or other obvious damage.

14. Compare the length of the springs to each other and to the specification listed in **Table 3**. Install new springs if distorted, broken or significantly shorter than new. Both springs should be nearly the same height.

15. Always install new fork seals. Install new fork seals by pressing against the outer edge of the seal. Install the seal retaining ring and make sure it is fully seated.

16. Install the damper rod in the inner fork tube. Hold the damper rod and install the tapered rebound sleeve on the end of the damper rod.

17. Coat the outer surface of the fork tube with oil before installing.

18. Hold the damper rod in place inside the fork tube and carefully install the lower slider over the fork tube.

19. Apply Loctite 680 to the Allen retaining screw and install the copper sealing washer over the screw. Continue holding the damper rod and install the Allen screw through the bottom of the slider. Tighten the screw to the torque listed in **Table 2**.

20. Place the fork in the upright position and pour the type and amount of fork oil recommended in **Table 3** into the fork tube. Work the fork up and down to bleed air from the lower surfaces.

21. Check the oil level before finishing assembly and installation. Compress the fork before installing the spring and measure the level of the oil from the top of the fork tube with the fork compressed fully. **Table 3** lists the correct oil level.

22. Extend the fork and install the spring with the closely wound coils at the top.

23. Make sure that the O-ring located on the spring seat is in good condition.

24. Hold the fork tube and compress the fork spring in the tube using the spring seat, then install the retaining ring. Make sure that the retaining ring is fully seated before releasing the spring.

25. Install the rubber cap in the top of the fork tube.

FRONT SUSPENSION
(4-WHEEL MODELS)

The front suspension on all 4-wheel models consists of two lower A-arms and strut type shock absorbers and springs. **Figure 11** shows a typical front suspension for 1985-1987 models without front drive. **Figure 12** shows a typical front suspension for later models without front drive. A ball-joint

(**Figure 12**) connects the lower A-arm to the steering knuckle on all models. The lower steering knuckle on 1987 models with all-wheel drive and all later models is an aluminum casting.

Steering is controlled by tie rods attached to the steering shaft and steering knuckle.

Front Suspension Tools

The threads of the tie rod ends and ball-joints are easily damaged. If you have difficulty removing the tapered studs of tie rods or ball-joints, have a dealer perform this operation. Using a forked tool (pickle fork) will almost certainly damage the boot.

In addition to common hand tools, a special tool set (part No. 2870871) will be required to remove and install the ball-joints from the steering knuckles. A special compressor tool (part No. 2870623) is available to compress the spring when removing or installing it.

A caster gauge (part No. 2870732) may be required to measure the front wheel caster on 1987 and 1988 models with all-wheel drive. The length of the A-arm rear tube is used to adjust the caster.

Suspension Unit
Removal/Installation

CAUTION
The steering knuckle or suspension unit can be removed by raising and blocking the front of the machine, but some prefer to pad the floor of the work area and tip the vehicle on its side. The method of gaining access is left to the discretion of the owner and mechanic, but care should be taken to prevent the ATV from falling.

1. Remove the front wheel as described in this chapter.

CAUTION
Do not hammer on the threaded stud of the tie rod ball-joint when trying to remove it. Doing so will damage the threads and requires installation of a new tie rod end or complete tie rod assembly.

2. Detach the tie rod end from the steering knuckle.

3A. On models with mechanical drum brakes, detach the brake cable from the brake arm.

3B. On models with hydraulic disc brakes, remove the 2 brake caliper mounting bolts and lift the caliper away from the brake disc. Hang the caliper from the vehicle with a stiff wire hook.

NOTE
Insert a piece of vinyl tubing or plastic between the brake pads in the caliper, in place of the brake disc. That way if the brake lever is accidentally moved, the piston will not be forced from the cylinder. If the piston comes out of the cylinder, the caliper will have to be disassembled to reseat the piston and both front brakes will require bleeding. By blocking the brake pads, the piston cannot be forced out and bleeding the system should not be required.

NOTE
If the CV joint in the steering knuckle is withdrawn, it must be reassembled as described in Chapter Ten. The drive axle can remain in the steering knuckle while servicing the strut if disassembly is not required.

4. On all models with all-wheel drive, remove the pin (**Figure 13**) from the inner universal joint and separate the inner universal joint from the center shaft. Hold the axle in place with wire to keep the CV joint from coming apart.
5. On 1989 and later 4-wheel drive models, detach the wires leading to the front wheel drive coil.
6. It is necessary to either separate the ball-joint from the steering knuckle or detach the inner end of

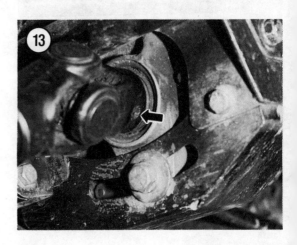

the A-arm from the vehicle frame. The procedure used should depend upon the service performed.

CAUTION
Be careful not to damage the ball-joint unless a new unit and the special tools to remove and install it are available.

 a. If the ball-joint is to be separated from the steering, remove the cotter pin and castellated nut (**Figure 12**) from the ball-joint. Separate the ball-joint from the A-arm.

 b. If the A-arm is to be separated from the vehicle frame, remove the bolts (**Figure 14**) from the inner ends of the A-arm. On models with all-wheel drive attach, the front drive axle to the A-arm to prevent the CV joint from coming apart. Refer to **Figure 15**.

7. Support the suspension unit, remove the nut (**Figure 16**) from the top of the suspension shaft, then withdraw the suspension unit (shock absorber, spring and steering knuckle).

8. Repeat for the other side as required.

9. Install by reversing the removal procedure. Refer to **Table 2** for tightening torques.

Spring
Removal/Installation

 The spring is installed on the hydraulically damped shock absorber. On all models, the shock damper unit is sealed and cannot be disassembled. Service is limited to removal and replacement of the damper unit, spring and mounting bushings.

WARNING
Do not remove the spring without a spring compressor. The spring on some models is under considerable pressure and may fly off and cause injury.

1. Attach a spring compressor to the shock absorber and compress the spring.

2. Remove the upper spring seat, then remove the spring (**Figure 17**).

3. Compare the spring free length with a new spring. Replace the spring if it is distorted, cracked, or otherwise damaged. If one spring is replaced, the other should be replaced also.

4. Reassemble by reversing the removal procedure.

12

Shock Absorber
Removal/Installation

Some conditions of the shock absorber can be evaluated before removing. If broken, bent or leaking fluid, replace the shock absorbers. The damper unit cannot be rebuilt and must be replaced as a unit. It is recommended to install shock absorbers for both sides at the same time.

1. To remove the shock absorber, first remove the spring as described in this chapter.

2A. On 1985-1987 rear wheel drive models, remove the attaching bolts (**Figure 18**), then separate the shock absorber from the steering knuckle.

2B. On 1988-on rear wheel drive models, remove the clamp bolts (**Figure 19** or **Figure 20**), then pull the shock absorber unit from the steering knuckle casting. It may be necessary to spread the clamp joint and to use penetrating oil before the unit can be withdrawn.

3. Clean the steering knuckle before installing the shock absorber.

4A. On 1985-1987 rear wheel drive models, do not tighten the lower bolts (**Figure 18**) until after completing the remainder of reassembly. These bolts should be tightened after setting the camber on the front wheels.

4B. On 1987 all-wheel drive models and all 1988-on models, install the shock absorber making certain that the unit is fully seated in the steering knuckle. Tighten the clamp bolts to the torque listed in **Table 2**.

5. Complete assembly by reversing the removal procedure. Refer to **Table 2** for recommended torque values.

6A. On 1985-1987 rear drive models, measure, set and adjust the front wheel camber as follows.

   a. Place the vehicle on a level surface with the vehicle weight on the wheels.

   b. Set a square against the wheel as shown in **Figure 21**, then measure the distance between the square and the wheel.

   c. The top of the wheel (A, **Figure 21**) should be tilted outward approximately 1 cm (0.4 in.) further than the bottom of the wheel (B).

   d. If the camber is incorrect, loosen bolts (**Figure 18**) and reposition the shock absorber and steering knuckle. Tighten bolts enough to maintain the setting, then recheck.

e. When the camber is set correctly, tighten the 2 bolts (**Figure 18**) to the torque listed in **Table 2**.

6B. On 1987 and 1988 all-wheel drive models, the length of the A-arm rear tube is adjustable to change the front wheel caster. The front shock absorber tube should be inclined to the rear about 2°. The special caster gauge (part No. 2870732) can be used to measure the caster.

6C. On 1988 rear wheel drive models and all 1989-on models, the caster and camber is not adjustable and should be correct unless parts are bent. If the frame or other components is bent, consult a Polaris dealer.

Steering Knuckle Removal/Installation

1A. On models with only rear wheel drive, remove the front hub as described in this chapter.

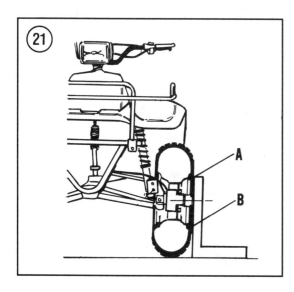

1B. On models with all-wheel drive, remove the front hub as described in Chapter Ten.

2. Use the procedure in this chapter to remove the suspension unit.

3. Remove the shock absorber from the steering knuckle as described in this chapter.

4. Install the steering knuckle by reversing the removal procedure.

Control Arm (A-Arm) Removal/Installation

CAUTION
The lower control arm (A-arm) can be removed by raising and blocking the front of the machine, but some prefer to pad the floor of the work area and tip the vehicle on its side. The method of gaining access is left to the discretion of the owner and mechanic, but care should be taken to prevent the ATV from falling.

1. Remove the front wheel as described in this chapter.

NOTE
If the CV joint in the steering knuckle is withdrawn, it must be reassembled as described in Chapter Ten. The drive axle can remain in the steering knuckle while servicing the strut if disassembly is not required.

2. On models with all-wheel drive, wire the axle to the steering knuckle to keep the CV joint from coming apart.

3. Remove the cotter pin and castellated nut (**Figure 22**) from the threaded stud of the ball-joint.

CAUTION
Be careful not to damage the ball-joint unless a new unit and the special tools to remove and install it are available. Do not hammer on the threaded stud of the ball-joint when trying to separate it from the A-arm. Doing so will damage the threads making it necessary to install a new ball-joint or steering knuckle assembly. Using a forked tool (pickle fork) will usually damage the boot.

4. Carefully withdraw the tapered ball-joint stud from the end of the A-arm.

5. Remove the bolts (**Figure 23** and **Figure 24**) from the inner ends of the A-arm, then remove the A-arm.

6. Several different spacers and bushings have been used in the A-arm. If replacement parts are required, be sure the parts are correct. If not properly maintained by greasing, the bushings may be stuck in the A-arm.

> *NOTE*
> *Do not intermix the pivot bolts, nuts, bushings and thrust covers when disassembling and cleaning the A-arms. Separate the parts so they can be installed in their original mounting positions.*

7. Clean parts in solvent and dry with compressed air.

8. Inspect the A-arm for cracks, fractures and dents. If damage is severe, replace the control arm. Never try to straighten a damaged or dented control arm, because it cannot be straightened properly.

9. Inspect each bushing, washer and spacer for severe wear or damage. Replace rusted or otherwise damaged parts.

10. Inspect attaching bolts for bending or other damage. Replace damaged bolts.

11. Inspect the attaching tabs on the frame for damage. If repair is required, consult a competent welder familiar with this type of repair.

12. Inspect ball-joints as described under *Ball-joint Inspection and Replacement* in this chapter before reassembling.

Ball-Joint Inspection/Replacement

A single ball-joint is located in the bottom of each steering knuckle and is attached to each lower control arm (A-arm). The ball-joints are a tight fit in the steering knuckle and should not be removed unless replacement is necessary.

1. Inspect the ball-joint rubber boot. The swivel joint is packed with grease. If the rubber boot or ball-joint is damaged, replace ball-joint as follows.

2A. On 1985-1987 models with rear wheel drive, the ball-joint is retained in the steering knuckle by the screw shown in **Figure 25**. Remove the screw and pull the ball-joint from the steering knuckle.

> *NOTE*
> *It may be easier to remove the ball-joints if the steering knuckle is first removed as described in this chapter. It may be necessary to heat the steering knuckle to soften the thread-locking compound applied to screw threads when removing the ball-joint from the steering knuckle.*

2B. On all except early (1985-1987) rear drive models, the ball-joint is held in place by a plate, which is

attached to the aluminum knuckle casting with 2 screws. The threads of the screws are coated with thread-locking compound and may be difficult to remove. Pull the ball-joint from the steering knuckle after removing the retaining plate.

3. Clean the pocket in the steering knuckle for the ball-joint and the retaining screw holes. If either is damaged, repair or replace the steering knuckle.

4. Install the new ball-joint and retaining screw(s). Refer to **Table 2** for correct tightening torque.

Handlebar Removal/Installation

CAUTION
Cover the fuel tank and front fender with a heavy cloth or tarp to protect them from any brake fluid that may be accidentally spilled. Use soapy water to wash any spilled brake fluid from painted or plated surface immediately to prevent damage to the finish. Rinse the area thoroughly with clean water making sure that brake fluid and soap are both removed.

1. Refer to Chapter Fourteen and remove the mechanical brake lever assembly or hydraulic brake master cylinder from the left side of the handle bar. Refer to **Figure 26**. Rest the brake on the front fender. Keep the hydraulic brake reservoir upright to keep fluid from spilling and to prevent air from entering the brake system. Do not detach the brake line from the master cylinder unless you are going to remove the master cylinder from the vehicle.

CAUTION
Do not allow the master cylinder to hang by its hose, because this could damage the hose.

2. Remove all ties or bands holding the wires and cables to the handlebar.

3. Remove the screws securing the left-hand switch assembly, then remove the switch housing from the handlebar. Refer to **Figure 26**. Lay the switch assembly on the front fender.

4. Remove the screws and clamp securing the throttle and switch assembly to the right side of the handlebar and remove the assembly. Lay the assembly on the front fender. Do not allow the cable to be kinked, crimped or damaged.

5. Remove the cover (**Figure 28**) from the handlebar center clamp (if used), then remove the screws attaching the handlebar clamp (**Figure 29**). Nuts are located under the top flange of the steering shaft.

6. Remove the handlebar.

7. To maintain a good grip on the handlebar and to prevent it from slipping, clean the knurled section of the handlebar with a wire brush. It should be kept rough so it will be held securely by the clamp. The center clamp should also be kept clean and free of any metal that may have been gouged loose by handlebar slippage.

12

8. Position the handlebar on the lower handlebar holder and hold it in place.

9. Install the upper handlebar clamp. On some models, a plate may be installed above the clamp as shown in **Figure 29**.

10. Install the handlebar retaining screws and nuts. Tighten the forward screws first and then tighten the rear bolts. Tighten all 4 screws to the torque specification listed in **Table 4**.

11. If you have installed a new handlebar, install new grips. Follow their manufacturer's directions for installing and sealing grips to the handlebar.

12. Position the left-hand switch housing (**Figure 26**) onto the handlebar and seat it next to the grip as shown. Tighten the switch screws securely.

13. Position the brake assembly on the handlebar and install the clamp.

14. Position the throttle and switch assemblies (**Figure 27**) onto the handlebar and secure with clamp screws.

15. Check the brake lever, throttle lever and switch positions on both sides of the handlebars while sitting on the seat. Tighten the clamp screws securely when controls are comfortably positioned.

16. If so equipped, install the handlebar cover (**Figure 28**).

17. After all assemblies have been installed, test each one to make sure it operates correctly with no binding. Correct any problem at this time.

18. Secure the housing wiring harness to the handlebar with wire and cable ties, making sure that wires and cables are properly routed with no sharp bends.

Tie Rod Removal/Installation

The tie rods connect the lever on the steering shaft to the steering arms on the steering knuckles. Each tie rod includes an inner and outer end attached to a threaded rod. The individual parts can be replaced separately. A puller may be required to separate the tie rod from the steering knuckle and steering shaft.

You can replace the outer tie rod ends (A, **Figure 30**) without detaching the tie rod inner end from the steering shaft. When replacing the inner tie rod end (**Figure 31**, **Figure 32** or **Figure 33**), first remove the complete tie rod from the vehicle so that the inner end and tie rod can be properly assembled.

1. Support the vehicle and remove the front wheel(s) as described in this chapter.

2. Before detaching either end of the tie rod, identify the placement of the ends. If improperly installed, the tie rod ends may hit other components causing damage and possible loss of control.

CAUTION
Do not hammer on the threaded stud of the tie rod when trying to remove it. Doing so will damage the threads and require installation of a new tie rod end. Using a forked tool (pickle fork) may damage the boot or the tie rod.

3. To disconnect the tie rod ball-joint from the steering knuckle:

  a. Remove the cotter pin from the tie rod ball-joint stud nut. Discard the cotter pin and always install a new pin when installing.

  b. Remove the castellated nut from the ball-joint stud.

NOTE
When installing the puller, make sure you do not damage the ball-joint rubber seal. If the angled arms on the puller are too thick, they can damage the seal.

  c. Attach a 2-jaw puller to the steering knuckle and center the puller's pressure bolt against the ball-joint stud.

  d. Tighten the puller to apply pressure against the ball-joint stud, checking that the puller is not cocked to one side.

NOTE
If the tie rod end does not move easily, it may be necessary to strike the top of the puller with a hammer to free the

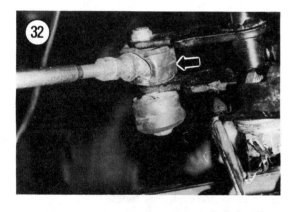

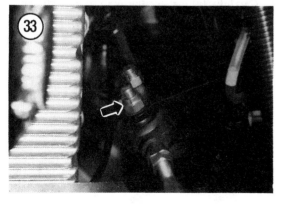

ball-joint from the steering knuckle. Keep the ball-joint stud under pressure by keeping the puller tight and support the steering arm to keep from damaging it.

4. If you are going to replace the outer tie rod end it is not necessary to detach the inner end.

5. To disconnect the inner tie rod end from the steering shaft:

  a. Remove the cotter pin from the tie rod stud nut. Discard the cotter pin. Some models are equipped with a self-locking nut.

  b. Remove the nut or bolt from the tie rod.

6. Detach the inner end of the tie rod from the lever on the steering shaft.

7. Inspect the tie rod shaft for damage. There should be no creases or bends along the shaft. Check with a straightedge placed against the tie rod shaft.

8. Inspect the rubber boot at the tie rod ends. If the rubber boot is damaged, dirt and moisture can enter the swivel joint and destroy it. If the boot is damaged in any way, disassemble the tie rod and replace the boot and the tie rod end.

9. Pivot the tie rod end back and forth by hand. If the tie rod end moves roughly or with excessive play, replace it.

10. Hold the tie rod end (A, **Figure 30**) with one wrench and loosen the locknut (B, **Figure 30**) with a second wrench.

NOTE
The tie rod ends marked with a groove (outer end), and the locknuts securing the outer tie rod ends have left-hand threads. The inner tie rod ends and locknuts have right-hand threads.

11. Unscrew and remove the damaged tie rod end(s).

12. Clean the threaded ends of the shaft and threads in the tie rod end with contact cleaner.

13. Thread a locknut and tie rod end onto each end of the tie rod shaft. Thread the ends on approximately the same distance as originally installed. Do not tighten the locknuts until the toe-out is adjusted as described in Chapter Three.

14. It is important to install the tie rods with the ends facing the correct direction so the tie rods and ends will not interfere with any other parts.

  a. On 1988-on models with rear wheel drive (except Magnum), the studs on the outer tie

12

rod ends should face up and the studs on the inner ends should face down as shown in **Figure 31**. Refer to **Table 2** for recommended tightening torques. Install new cotter pins in the castellated nuts at both ends.

b. On 1988-1992 all-wheel drive models, the stud on the outer ends should face down as shown in **Figure 30**. The inner end is attached with a bolt installed from the bottom with a self-locking nut on the top as shown in **Figure 32**. Refer to **Table 2** for recommended tightening torques. Install new cotter pins in the castellated nuts on the outer ends.

c. On rear wheel drive Magnum models, the studs at both ends of the tie rods should face down as shown in **Figure 30**. Refer to **Table 2** for recommended tightening torques. Install new cotter pins in the castellated nuts at both ends.

d. On 1993-on all-wheel drive models (except Xplorer and Scrambler), the stud on the outer ends should face down as shown in **Figure 30**. The inner end is attached with a bolt installed from the bottom with the self-locking nut on the top as shown in **Figure 32**. Refer to **Table 2** for recommended tightening torques. Install new cotter pins in the castellated nuts at the outside ends.

e. On 1995 all-wheel drive Xplorer and Scrambler models, the stud on the outer ends should face down as shown in **Figure 30**. The inner end is attached with bolts installed from the bottom with a self-locking nut on the top as shown in **Figure 33**. Refer to **Table 2** for recommended tightening torques. Install new cotter pins in the castellated nuts at the outside ends.

15. Install the front wheels as described in this chapter.

16. Check the front wheel toe-out and adjust as necessary before tightening the lock-nuts against the tie rod ends. Measure toe-out as described in Chapter Three.

STEERING SHAFT

Figure 34 and **Figure 35** are exploded views of the steering shaft and related components. The steering shaft pivots on split bearing blocks at the top and a bushing block at the lower end. Adjustable tie rods connect the steering shaft to the steering knuckles.

Removal/Installation

Refer to **Figure 34** (models prior to 1993) or **Figure 35** (1993-on models) for this procedure.

1. Remove the fuel tank as described in Chapter Six and the front fender assembly as described in Chapter Fifteen.

2. Remove both front wheels as described in this chapter.

CAUTION
Cover the frame with a heavy cloth or tarp to protect it from any brake fluid that may be accidentally spilled. Use soapy water to wash any spilled brake fluid immediately to prevent damage to the finish. Rinse the area thoroughly with clean water making sure that brake fluid and soap are both removed.

3. Remove the bolts that clamp the handlebar to the steering shaft. Remove the handlebar clamp.

4. Move the handlebar assembly back away from the steering shaft and place it on the frame. Keep the master cylinder upright to minimize the chance of spilling brake fluid and to keep air from entering the brake system. It is not necessary to detach the hydraulic brake line from the master cylinder.

5. Disconnect both tie rods from the steering shaft as described in this chapter.

6A. On early models, remove the cotter pin, nut and washer that secure the bottom of the steering shaft to the frame. See **Figure 34**, typical.

6B. On later models, remove the cotter pin, nut and washer that secure the bottom of the steering shaft. Refer to **Figure 36**.

7. Remove the bolts (21, **Figure 34** or 11, **Figure 35**) that hold the upper bearing blocks to the frame, then remove the clamp and block.

8. Carefully lift the steering shaft from the frame.

9. Install the steering shaft by reversing the removal procedure. Adjust the steering stops as described in this chapter.

Inspection

Refer to **Figure 34** (models prior to 1993) or **Figure 35** (1993-on models) for this procedure.

1. Wash all parts in solvent and dry thoroughly.

2. Inspect the steering shaft carefully. Check the bushing areas of the shaft for wear. Check the shaft

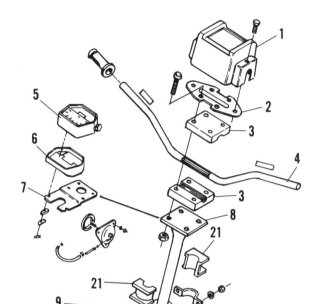

**STEERING AND SUSPENSION
(TYPICAL, MODELS PRIOR TO 1993)**

34

1. Cover
2. Plate
3. Clamp
4. Handlebars
5. Instrument
6. Pad
7. Plate
8. Steering shaft
9. Adjustable lock
   collar
10. Frame
11. Washer
12. Bearing housing
13. Washer
14. Tie rod
15. Steering knuckle
16. A-arm
17. Shaft
18. Bushing
19. Ball-joint
20. Boot
21. Upper bearing
    block
22. Clamp

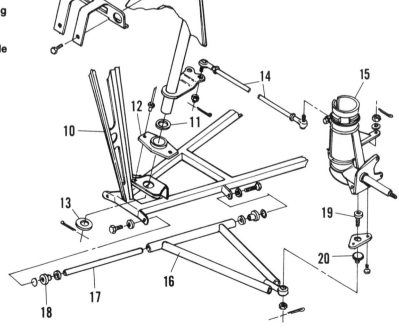

12

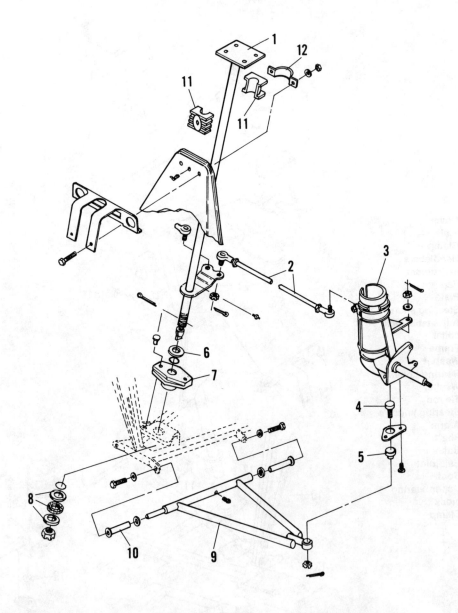

STEERING AND SUSPENSION
(1993-ON MODELS TYPICAL)

1. Steering shaft
2. Tie rod
3. Steering knuckle
4. Ball-joint
5. Boot
6. Washer
7. Lower bushing block
8. Thrust bearing
9. A-arm
10. Bushing
11. Upper bushing blocks
12. Clamp

for being bent, especially if the vehicle has been involved in a collision or spill. If the shaft is bent or twisted in any way it must be replaced. A bent shaft will cause rapid and excessive wear to the bushings and may stress other components in the frame and steering system. The shaft should be straight and can be checked between V-blocks.

3. Inspect the tie rod attachment holes in the lever on the lower section of the steering shaft. Check the hole(s) for elongation, cracks or wear. Check the steering shaft lever for being bent. Replace the steering shaft if necessary.

4. Inspect the upper bearing assembly for:

    a. Worn or damaged bearing block halves.

    b. Bent or damaged bolts or clamps.

    c. Worn or damaged upper collar (early models shown in **Figure 34**).

5. Inspect the lower steering shaft machined bushing surface and the threads on the end on later models. If severely scored or damaged, replace the steering shaft and the bushing assembly.

6. Inspect the steering shaft washers and bushing assembly. If the bushing is severely worn or damaged, replace the bushing block as described later in

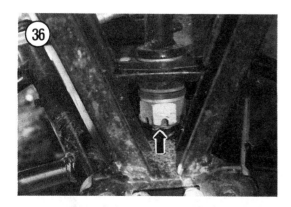

this chapter. If the O-rings (used on later models [**Figure 35**]) are worn, flattened, cut or swollen, replace both O-rings during reassembly.

Steering Shaft Bushing Replacement

All 4-wheel models are equipped with an upper bushing and lower bushing as shown in **Figure 34** or **Figure 35**. The upper bushing is a split block as shown and the lower bushing block is attached to the frame by rivets.

Use the procedure described in this chapter to remove the steering shaft for upper bearing removal. However the upper bushing can be removed before completely removing the steering shaft.

To remove the lower bushing block proceed as follows.

1. Remove the steering shaft from the frame as described in this chapter.

2. Drill out the rivets attaching the bushing block to the frame, then remove the bushing block.

3. Clean the frame bushing mounting area thoroughly.

4. Install the new bushing block using new hardened rivets.

5. Complete assembly by reversing the removal procedure. Coat the bushings with grease before assembling, then grease the bushings as described in Chapter Three again after assembly.

Adjust Steering Stops

The steering stop screws are located as shown in **Figure 37**. Adjust the stop screws so the front wheels will not turn shorter than 40° from straight ahead. Check to make sure that the wheels cannot contact any part of the vehicle while turning. Depending upon equipment installed on the ATV, it may be necessary to adjust the stops to limit the amount of turning to less than the recommended 40°. It is important that the wheels or tires never rub against any part to the vehicle.

TIRES AND WHEELS

The vehicle is equipped with tubeless, low-pressure tires designed specifically for off-road use only. Rapid tire wear will occur if the vehicle is ridden on paved surfaces. Due to their low-pressure require-

12

ments, they should be inflated only with a hand-operated air pump instead of using an air compressor, or the compressed air available at service stations.

> *CAUTION*
> *Do not overinflate the tires as they will be permanently distorted and damaged. If overinflated they will bulge out similar to an inner tube that is not within the constraints of a tire and will not return to their original contour.*

> *NOTE*
> *Additional inflation pressure in the stock tires will not improve the ride or handling characteristics of the vehicle. For improved handling, aftermarket tires may be installed.*

It's a good idea to carry a cold patch tire repair kit and hand held pump in the tow vehicle. Removing the tire from the rim is different than on a motorcycle or automobile wheel.

Tire Changing

The front and rear tire rims used on all models have a very deep built-in ridge (**Figure 38**) to keep the tire bead seated on the rim under severe riding conditions. This feature also tends to keep the tire on the rim during tire removal.

A special tool is required for tire changing on these models. A typical tool is shown in **Figure 39**.

1. Mark the tire with an arrow indicating the direction of rotation when moving forward. Also mark the tire to indicate its location on the vehicle.
2. Remove the valve stem cap and core and deflate the tire. Do not reinstall the core at this time.
3. Lubricate the tire bead and rim flanges with a liquid dish washing detergent or a rubber lubricant. Press the tire sidewall/bead down to allow the liquid to run into and around the bead area. Also apply lubricant to the area where the bead breaker arm will come in contact with the tire sidewall.
4. Position the wheel in the tire removal tool (**Figure 39**).
5. Slowly work the tire tool, making sure the tool is against the inside of the rim, and break the tire bead away from the rim.
6. Use your hands to press down on the tire on each side of the tool and break the rest of the bead free from the rim.

> *NOTE*
> *If the rest of the tire bead cannot be broken loose, raise the tool, rotate the tire/rim assembly and repeat Steps 4 and 5 until the entire bead is broken loose from the rim.*

7. Turn the wheel over and repeat Steps 4-6 to break the bead loose from the opposite side.
8. Remove the tire from the rim using tire irons and rim protectors (**Figure 40** and **Figure 41**).
9. Inspect the tire sealing surface of the rim. If the rim has been severely hit it will probably leak air. Repair or replace the rim as required.
10. Inspect the tire for cuts, tears, abrasions or any other defects.
11. Clean the rims and tire sealing surfaces.
12. Apply clean water to the rim flanges, tire beads and on the outer flange of the rim. Make sure the rim flange is clean. Wipe with a lint-free cloth.
13. Coat both of the tire beads with tire mounting lubricant or a liquid dish washing detergent.
14. Position the rim on the floor with the outside flange up.

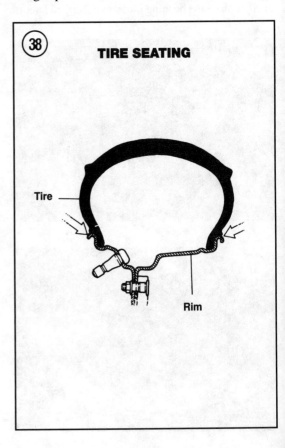

(38) **TIRE SEATING**

Tire

Rim

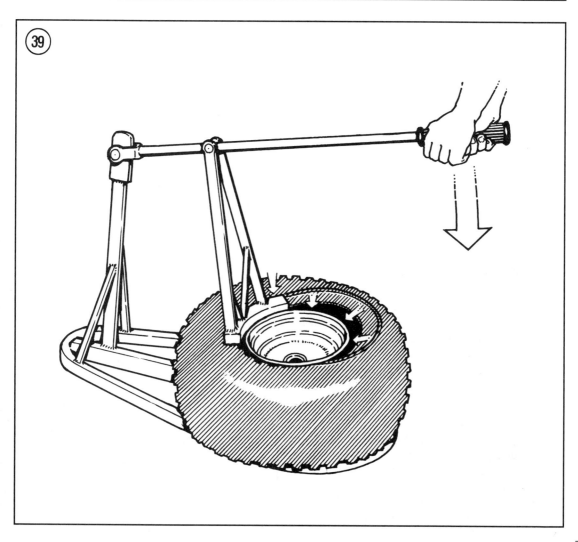

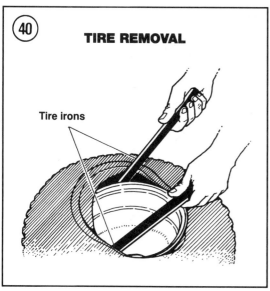

TIRE REMOVAL

Tire irons

TIRE BEAD INSTALLATION

12

15. Position the tire so the arrow on the tire points toward the direction of rotation while moving forward.

16. Start the inside bead of the tire onto the outside of the rim.

17. Press the inside bead of the tire onto the rim with your hands.

18. Press the outside bead onto the tire in a similar manner (**Figure 42**).

19. Apply tire mounting lubricant to both beads and inflate the tire to the pressure value listed in **Table 4**.

20. Deflate the tire and let it sit for about 1 hour.

21. Inflate the tire to the recommended air pressure. Refer to **Table 4**.

22. Check the rim line (**Figure 43**) molded into the tire around the edge of the rim. It must be equally spaced all the way around. If the rim line spacing is not equal, the tire bead is not properly seated. Deflate the tire and unseat the bead completely. Lubricate the bead and reinflate the tire.

23. Check for air leaks and install the valve cap.

Cold Patch Repair

This is the preferred method to patch a tire. The rubber plug type of repair is recommended only for an emergency repair, or until the tire can be patched correctly with the cold patch method.

Use the manufacturer's instructions for the tire repair kit you are going to use. If there are no instructions, use the following procedure.

1. Remove the tire as described in this chapter.

2. Prior to removing the object that punctured the tire, mark the location of the puncture with chalk or crayon on the outside of the tire.

3. On the inside of the tire, roughen the area around the hole slightly larger than the patch. Use the cap from the tire repair kit, a pocket knife or coarse sandpaper. Do not scrape too vigorously or you may cause additional damage.

4. Clean the area with a nonflammable solvent. Do not use an oil base solvent as it will leave a residue rendering the patch useless.

5. Apply a small amount of the special cement to the puncture and spread it with your finger.

6. Allow the cement to dry until tacky—usually 30 seconds or so is sufficient.

7. Remove the backing from the patch.

CAUTION
Do not touch the newly exposed rubber with your fingers or the patch will not stick firmly.

8. Center the patch over the hole. Hold the patch firmly in place for about 30 seconds to allow the cement to dry. If you have a roller use it to help press the patch into place.

9. Dust the area with talcum powder.

42 TIRE INSTALLATION

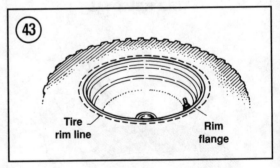

43

Tire
rim line

Rim
flange

Table 1 FRONT SUSPENSION AND FRONT WHEEL DRIVE

	Drive wheels	Type	Brake type
1985			
Scrambler W857027	Rear	Tricycle	Mech. drum
Trail Boss W857527	Rear	4-wheel	Mech. drum
1986			
Scrambler W867027	Rear	Tricycle	Mech. drum
Trail Boss W867527	Rear	4-wheel	Mech. drum
Trail Boss W867627	Rear	4-wheel	Mech. drum
1987			
Trail Boss W877527	Rear	4-wheel	Mech. drum
Cyclone W877828	Rear	4-wheel	Mech. drum
Trail Boss 4 × 4 W878027, W878127 & W878327	All	4-wheel	Hyd. disc
1988			
Trail Boss 2 × 4 W887527	Rear	4-wheel	Hyd. disc
Trail Boss 4 × 4 W888127	All	4-wheel	Hyd. disc
T. B. 250 R/ES X888528	Rear	4-wheel	Hyd. disc
T. B. 250 R/ES W888528	Rear	4-wheel	Hyd. disc
1989			
Trail Boss W898527	Rear	4-wheel	Hyd. disc
Trail Boss 2 × 4 W897527	Rear	4-wheel	Hyd. disc
Trail Boss 4 × 4 W898127	All	4-wheel	Hyd. disc
Big Boss 4 × 6 X898627	Rear	6-wheel	Hyd. disc
Big Boss 4 × 6 W898627	Rear	6-wheel	Hyd. disc
1990			
Trail Blazer W907221	Rear	4-wheel	Hyd. disc
Trail Boss 250 W908527, 2 × 4 W907527 & 2 × 4-350L W907539	Rear	4-wheel	Hyd. disc
Trail Boss 4 × 4 W908127	All	4-wheel	Hyd. disc
T.B. 4 × 4-350L W908139	All	4-wheel	Hyd. disc
Big Boss 4 × 6 W908627	Rear	6-wheel	Hyd. disc
1991			
Trail Blazer W917221	Rear	4-wheel	Hyd. disc
Trail Boss 250 W918527, 2 × 4 W917527 & 2 × 4-350L W917539	Rear	4-wheel	Hyd. disc
Trail Boss 4 × 4 W918127	All	4-wheel	Hyd. disc
T.B. 4 × 4-350L W918139	All	4-wheel	Hyd. disc
Big Boss 4 × 6 W918627	Rear	6-wheel	Hyd. disc
Big Boss 6 × 6 W918727	All	6-wheel	Hyd. disc
1992			
Trail Blazer W927221	Rear	4-wheel	Hyd. disc
Trail Boss 250 W928527, 2 × 4 W927527 & 2 × 4-350L W927539	Rear	4-wheel	Hyd. disc
Trail Boss 4 × 4 W928127	All	4-wheel	Hyd. disc
T.B. 4 × 4-350L W928139	All	4-wheel	Hyd. disc
Big Boss 4 × 6 W928627	Rear	6-wheel	Hyd. disc
Big Boss 6 × 6 W928727	All	6-wheel	Hyd. disc
1993			
Trail Blazer W937221	Rear	4-wheel	Hyd. disc
Trail Boss W938527	Rear	4-wheel	Hyd. disc
Sportsman W938039	All	4-wheel	Hyd. disc
250 2 × 4 W937527	Rear	4-wheel	Hyd. disc
350 2 × 4 W937539	Rear	4-wheel	Hyd. disc
250 4 × 4 W938127	All	4-wheel	Hyd. disc
350 4 × 4 W938139	All	4-wheel	Hyd. disc
250 6 × 6 W938727	All	6-wheel	Hyd. disc
350 6 × 6 W938739	All	6-wheel	Hyd. disc

(continued)

12

Table 1 FRONT SUSPENSION AND FRONT WHEEL DRIVE (continued)

	Drive wheels	Type	Brake type
1994			
Trail Blazer 2W W947221	Rear	4-wheel	Hyd. disc
Trail Boss 2W W948527	Rear	4-wheel	Hyd. disc
Sport W948540	Rear	4-wheel	Hyd. disc
Sportsman 4 × 4 W948040	All	4-wheel	Hyd. disc
300 2 × 4 W947530	Rear	4-wheel	Hyd. disc
400 2 × 4 W947540	Rear	4-wheel	Hyd. disc
300 4 × 4 W948130	All	4-wheel	Hyd. disc
400 4 × 4 W948140	All	4-wheel	Hyd. disc
300 6 × 6 W948730	All	6-wheel	Hyd. disc
400 6 × 6 W948740	All	6-wheel	Hyd. disc
1995			
Trail Blazer W957221	Rear	4-wheel	Hyd. disc
Trail Boss W958527, 300 2 × 4			
W957530 & 400 2 × 4 W957540	Rear	4-wheel	Hyd. disc
300 4 × 4 W958130	All	4-wheel	Hyd. disc
Scrambler W957840	Rear	4-wheel	Hyd. disc
Sport W958540	Rear	4-wheel	Hyd. disc
Sportsman 4 × 4 W958040	All	4-wheel	Hyd. disc
Xplorer 4 × 4 W959140	All	4-wheel	Hyd. disc
Magnum 2 × 4 W957444	Rear	4-wheel	Hyd. disc
Magnum 4 × 4 W958144	All	4-wheel	Hyd. disc
400 6 × 6 W958740	All	6-wheel	Hyd. disc

Table 2 TORQUE SPECIFICATIONS

	N·m	ft.-lb.
A-arm attaching bolt (inner end)	40.7	30
A-arm ball joint stud nut	33.9	25
Ball joint retainer plate screws	10.8	8
Fork tubes (3-wheel models)		
Lower retaining bolt*	23.0	17
Front axle nut (3-wheel models)	48.8	36
Front brake caliper bolts	24.4	18
Front hub nut (2 × 4)	54.2	40
Front wheel lug nuts	20.3	15
Handlebar clamp block	10.9-13.6	8-10
Wheel lug nuts	67.8	50
Steering crown (3-wheel models)		
Upper clamp bolts	19.0	14
Lower clamp bolts	29.8	22
Shock absorber (lower bolts)		
1985-1987, rear drive models	67.8	50
Shock absorber clamp bolts		
1988-on, all models	20.3	15
1987, all-wheel drive models	20.3	15
Tie rod attaching bolt	33.9-40.7	25-30
Tie rod castelated nut	31.2-32.5	23-24
Tie rod end jam nut	16.3-18.9	12-14
Top strut (shock absorber) nut	20.3	15
* Apply Loctite 680 to the threads before installing.		

Table 3 TRICYCLE FORK SPECIFICATIONS

Fork oil type	SAE 10
Capacity	117 mL (3.96 fl.oz.)
Level *	42 cm (16.5 in.)
Spring free length	50.1 cm (19.73 in.)
* Fork oil should be measured from top of inner tube with spring removed and tube fully compressed.	

Table 4 TIRE SIZE AND PRESSURE

	Front tires kPa (psi)	Rear tires kPa (psi)
1985		
Scrambler W857027		
Size	22 × 11.00 × 8	22 × 11.00 × 10
Pressure	20.7 (3)	20.7 (3)
Trail Boss W857527		
Size	22 × 8.00 × 10	22 × 11.00 × 10
Pressure	27.6 (4)	20.7 (3)
1986		
Scrambler W867027		
Size	22 × 11.00 × 8	22 × 11.00 × 10
Pressure	20.7 (3)	20.7 (3)
Trail Boss W867527		
Size	22 × 8.00 × 10	22 × 11.00 × 10
Pressure	27.6 (4)	20.7 (3)
Trail Boss W867627		
Size	22 × 8.00 × 10	22 × 11.00 × 10
Pressure	27.6 (4)	20.7 (3)
1987		
Trail Boss W877527		
Size	22 × 8.00 × 8	22 × 11.00 × 10
Pressure	27.6 (4)	20.7 (3)
Cyclone W877828		
Size	22 × 8.00 × 10	22 × 11.00 × 10
Pressure	27.6 (4)	20.7 (3)
Trail Boss 4 × 4 W878027		
Size	22 × 8.00 × 10	22 × 11.00 × 10
Pressure	27.6 (4)	20.7 (3)
Trail Boss 4 × 4 W878127		
Size	22 × 8.00 × 10	22 × 11.00 × 10
Pressure	27.6 (4)	20.7 (3)
Trail Boss 4 × 4 W878327		
Size	22 × 8.00 × 10	22 × 11.00 × 10
Pressure	27.6 (4)	20.7 (3)
1988		
Trail Boss 2 × 4 W887527		
Size	22 × 8.00 × 10	22 × 11.00 × 10
Pressure	27.6 (4)	20.7 (3)
Trail Boss 4 × 4 W888127		
Size	22 × 8.00 × 10	22 × 11.00 × 10
Pressure	27.6 (4)	20.7 (3)
Trail Boss 250 R/ES X888528		
Size	22 × 8.00 × 10	22 × 11.00 × 10
Pressure	27.6 (4)	20.7 (3)

(continued)

12

Table 4 TIRE SIZE AND PRESSURE (continued)

	Front tires kPa (psi)	Rear tires kPa (psi)
1988 (continued)		
Trail Boss 250 R/ES W888528		
Size	22 × 8.00 × 10	22 × 11.00 × 10
Pressure	27.6 (4)	20.7 (3)
1989		
Trail Boss W898527		
Size	22 × 8.00 × 10	22 × 11.00 × 10
Pressure	20.7 (3)	20.7 (3)
Trail Boss 2 × 4 W897527		
Size	22 × 8.00 × 10	22 × 11.00 × 10
Pressure	20.7 (3)	20.7 (3)
Trail Boss 4 × 4 W898127		
Size	22 × 8.00 × 10	22 × 11.00 × 10
Pressure	27.6 (4)	20.7 (3)
Big Boss 4 × 6 X898627		
Size	22 × 8.00 × 10	22 × 11.00 × 10
Pressure	27.6 (4)	34.5 (5)
Big Boss 4 × 6 W898627		
Size	22 × 8.00 × 10	22 × 11.00 × 10
Pressure	27.6 (4)	34.5 (5)
1990		
Trail Blazer W907221		
Size	22 × 8.00 × 10	22 × 11.00 × 10
Pressure	20.7 (3)	20.7 (3)
Trail Boss 250 W908527		
Size	22 × 8.00 × 10	22 × 11.00 × 10
Pressure	20.7 (3)	20.7 (3)
Trail Boss 2 × 4 W907527		
Size	22 × 8.00 × 10	24 × 11.00 × 10
Pressure	20.7 (3)	20.7 (3)
Trail Boss 2 × 4 - 350L W907539		
Size	22 × 8.00 × 10	24 × 11.00 × 10
Pressure	27.6 (4)	20.7 (3)
Trail Boss 4 × 4 W908127		
Size	22 × 8.00 × 10	24 × 11.00 × 10
Pressure	27.6 (4)	20.7 (3)
Trail Boss 4 × 4 - 350L W908139		
Size	25 × 8.00 × 12	25 × 12.00 × 10
Pressure	27.6 (4)	20.7 (3)
Big Boss 4 × 6 W908627		
Size	22 × 8.00 × 10	22 × 11.00 × 10
Pressure	34.5 (5)	34.5 (5)
1991		
Trail Blazer W917221		
Size	22 × 8.00 × 10	22 × 11.00 × 10
Pressure	20.7 (3)	20.7 (3)
Trail Boss 250 W918527		
Size	22 × 8.00 × 10	22 × 11.00 × 10
Pressure	20.7 (3)	20.7 (3)
Trail Boss 2 × 4 W917527		
Size	22 × 8.00 × 10	24 × 11.00 × 10
Pressure	20.7 (3)	20.7 (3)
Trail Boss 2 × 4 - 350L W917539		
Size	22 × 8.00 × 10	24 × 11.00 × 10
Pressure	27.6 (4)	20.7 (3)

(continued)

Table 4 TIRE SIZE AND PRESSURE (continued)

	Front tires kPa (psi)	Rear tires kPa (psi)
1991 (continued)		
Trail Boss 4 × 4 W918127		
Size	22 × 8.00 × 10	24 × 11.00 × 10
Pressure	27.6 (4)	20.7 (3)
Trail Boss 4 × 4 - 350L W918139		
Size	25 × 8.00 × 12	25 × 12.00 × 10
Pressure	27.6 (4)	20.7 (3)
Big Boss 4 × 6 W918627		
Size	22 × 8.00 × 10	22 × 11.00 × 10
Pressure	34.5 (5)	34.5 (5)
Big Boss 6 × 6 W918727		
Size	22 × 8.00 × 10	22 × 11.00 × 10
Pressure	34.5 (5)	34.5 (5)
1992		
Trail Blazer W927221		
Size	22 × 8.00 × 10	22 × 11.00 × 10
Pressure	20.7 (3)	20.7 (3)
Trail Boss 250 W928527		
Size	22 × 8.00 × 10	22 × 11.00 × 10
Pressure	20.7 (3)	20.7 (3)
Trail Boss 2 × 4 W927527		
Size	22 × 8.00 × 10	24 × 11.00 × 10
Pressure	20.7 (3)	20.7 (3)
Trail Boss 2 × 4 - 350L W927539		
Size	22 × 8.00 × 10	24 × 11.00 × 10
Pressure	27.6 (4)	20.7 (3)
Trail Boss 4 × 4 W928127		
Size	22 × 8.00 × 10	24 × 11.00 × 10
Pressure	27.6 (4)	20.7 (3)
Trail Boss 4 × 4 - 350L W928139		
Size	25 × 8.00 × 12	25 × 12.00 × 10
Pressure	27.6 (4)	20.7 (3)
Big Boss 4 × 6 W928627		
Size	22 × 8.00 × 10	22 × 11.00 × 10
Pressure	34.5 (5)	34.5 (5)
Big Boss 6 × 6 W928727		
Size	22 × 8.00 × 10	22 × 11.00 × 10
Pressure	34.5 (5)	34.5 (5)
1993		
Trail Blazer W937221		
Size	22 × 8.00 × 10	22 × 11.00 × 10
Pressure	20.7 (3)	20.7 (3)
Trail Boss W938527		
Size	22 × 8.00 × 10	22 × 11.00 × 10
Pressure	20.7 (3)	20.7 (3)
Sportsman W938039		
Size	25 × 8.00 × 12	25 × 12.00 × 10
Pressure	27.6 (4)	20.7 (3)
250 2 × 4 W937527		
Size	22 × 8.00 × 10	24 × 11.00 × 10
Pressure	20.7 (3)	20.7 (3)
350 2 × 4 W937539		
Size	22 × 8.00 × 10	24 × 11.00 × 10
Pressure	27.6 (4)	20.7 (3)

(continued)

12

Table 4 TIRE SIZE AND PRESSURE (continued)

	Front tires kPa (psi)	Rear tires kPa (psi)
1993 (continued)		
250 4 × 4 W938127		
Size	22 × 8.00 × 10	24 × 11.00 × 10
Pressure	27.6 (4)	20.7 (3)
350 4 × 4 W938139		
Size	25 × 8.00 × 12	25 × 12.00 × 10
Pressure	27.6 (4)	20.7 (3)
250 6 × 6 W938727		
Size	22 × 8.00 × 10	22 × 11.00 × 10
Pressure	34.5 (5)	34.5 (5)
350 6 × 6 W938739		
Size	25 × 8.00 × 10	25 × 12.00 × 10
Pressure	34.5 (5)	34.5 (5)
1994		
Trail Blazer 2W W947221		
Size	22 × 8.00 × 10	22 × 11.00 × 10
Pressure	20.7 (3)	20.7 (3)
Trail Boss 2W W948527		
Size	22 × 8.00 × 10	22 × 11.00 × 10
Pressure	20.7 (3)	20.7 (3)
Sport W948540		
Size	22 × 8.00 × 10	22 × 11.00 × 10
Pressure	27.6 (4)	20.7 (3)
Sportsman 4 × 4 W948040		
Size	25 × 8.00 × 12	25 × 12.00 × 10
Pressure	27.6 (4)	20.7 (3)
300 2 × 4 W947530		
Size	22 × 8.00 × 10	24 × 11.00 × 10
Pressure	20.7 (3)	20.7 (3)
400 2 × 4 W947540		
Size	22 × 8.00 × 10	24 × 11.00 × 10
Pressure	20.7 (3)	20.7 (3)
300 4 × 4 W948130		
Size	22 × 8.00 × 10	24 × 11.00 × 10
Pressure	20.7 (3)	20.7 (3)
400 4 × 4 W948140		
Size	25 × 8.00 × 12	25 × 12.00 × 10
Pressure	27.6 (4)	20.7 (3)
300 6 × 6 W948730		
Size	22 × 8.00 × 10	22 × 11.00 × 10
Pressure	34.5 (5)	34.5 (5)
400 6 × 6 W948740		
Size	25 × 8.00 × 12	25 × 12.00 × 10
Pressure	34.5 (5)	34.5 (5)
1995		
Trail Blazer W957221		
Size	22 × 8.00 × 10	22 × 11.00 × 10
Pressure	20.7 (3)	20.7 (3)
Trail Boss W958527		
Size	22 × 8.00 × 10	22 × 11.00 × 10
Pressure	20.7 (3)	20.7 (3)
300 2 × 4 W957530		
Size	22 × 8.00 × 10	24 × 11.00 × 10
Pressure	20.7 (3)	20.7 (3)

(continued)

Table 4 TIRE SIZE AND PRESSURE (continued)

	Front tires kPa (psi)	Rear tires kPa (psi)
1995 (continued)		
400 2 × 4 W957540		
Size	22 × 8.00 × 10	24 × 11.00 × 10
Pressure	27.6 (4)	20.7 (3)
300 4 × 4 W958130		
Size	22 × 8.00 × 10	24 × 11.00 × 10
Pressure	27.6 (4)	20.7 (3)
Scrambler W957840		
Size	23 × 7.00 × 10	22 × 11.00 × 10
Pressure	27.6 (4)	20.7 (3)
Sport W958540		
Size	23 × 7.00 × 10	22 × 11.00 × 10
Pressure	27.6 (4)	20.7 (3)
Sportsman 4 × 4 W958040		
Size	25 × 8.00 × 12	25 × 12.00 × 10
Pressure	27.6 (4)	20.7 (3)
Xplorer 4 × 4 W959140		
Size	25 × 8.00 × 12	25 × 12.00 × 10
Pressure	27.6 (4)	20.7 (3)
Magnum 2 × 4 W957444		
Size	23 × 7.00 × 10	24 × 11.00 × 10
Pressure	27.6 (4)	20.7 (3)
Magnum 4 × 4 W958144		
Size	25 × 8.00 × 12	25 × 12.00 × 10
Pressure	27.6 (4)	20.7 (3)
400 6 × 6 W958740		
Size	25 × 8.00 × 12	25 × 12.00 × 10
Pressure	34.5 (5)	34.5 (5)

12

REAR SUSPENSION

This chapter contains repair and replacement procedures for the rear wheel, rear hub and rear suspension components. Service to the rear suspension consists of periodically checking bolt tightness, replacing the swing arm bushings and servicing the rear spring/shock unit.

Drive chain size and the number of links are listed in **Table 1**. Tightening torques are listed in **Table 2**. **Table 3** lists the recommended tire sizes and inflation pressures. **Tables 1-3** are found at the end of this chapter.

REAR WHEELS

Removal/Installation

1. Park the vehicle on level ground and set the parking brake. Block the front wheels so the vehicle will not roll in either direction.

2. Lift the vehicle so both rear wheels are off the ground. Support the vehicle with jackstands or wooden blocks.

3A. To remove the tire/wheel assembly only, remove the four lug nuts that hold the rear wheel to the hub.

3B. To remove the tire/wheel and the rear wheel hub, remove the cotter pin, axle nut (**Figure 1**) and washer that hold the rear hub to the rear axle. Remove the tire/wheel and hub from the rear axle as an assembly.

4. Install by reversing these removal steps, noting the following.

5A. If only the tire/wheel reassembly was removed, perform the following:

    a. Place the tire/wheel assembly onto the rear hub studs.

    b. Install the wheel lug nuts that secure the rear wheel to the rear hub. First tighten the nuts finger tight, then torque to the specification listed in **Table 2**.

5B. If the tire/wheel and the axle hub were removed as an assembly, perform the following:

a. Slide the axle hub and wheel assembly onto the rear axle splines.

b. Install the washer and the axle nut (**Figure 1**) that secure the axle hub to the rear axle.

c. Tighten the rear axle nut to the torque specification listed in **Table 2**. Tighten the nut, if necessary, to align the cotter pin hole with the nut slot.

d. Insert a new cotter pin (**Figure 2**) through the slots in the nut and through the hole in the axle. Bend the ends of the cotter pin around the nut to lock it.

REAR TIRES

The procedure to remove and repair the rear tires is the same as for servicing the front tires. Refer to Chapter Twelve for tire service.

REAR AXLE

Figure 3 shows the rear axle and driven sprocket. Refer to the following for service to the rear axle on 3- or 4-wheel models. The same general procedures can be followed to service the center axle and the rearmost axle on 6-wheel models.

This section describes complete service to the axle, sprocket and center (bearing) housing. The driven sprocket can be removed with the rear axle installed on the vehicle. The axle and center (bearing) housing should be removed before disassembling the center housing or removing the axle from the bearings.

The swing arm can be removed from the vehicle before removing the rear axle and the center housing as described in the swing arm section of this chapter. If it is later determined that the rear spring, shock absorber and/or swing arm requires service, these parts can be removed after the rear axle.

Removal

1. Park the vehicle on a level surface and block the front wheels so the vehicle cannot roll in any direction.

NOTE
*Threads of the 2 large nuts (**Figure 4**) are coated with locking compound and are very fine threads. These nuts are very tight and may be difficult to remove, so be extremely careful. If necessary, apply heat to the nuts to soften the locking compound.*

2. If the center housing and sprocket hub are to be disassembled, it is often easier to loosen the 2 large nuts (**Figure 4**) before removing the axle.

3. Lift and support the rear of the vehicle. Secure the vehicle so it will not fall when removing the rear axle assembly. Allow sufficient room if the swing arm and/or the rear spring/shock absorber must also be removed.

NOTE
*It may be necessary to use a puller (**Figure 5**) to remove the wheel hubs from the ends of the axle.*

4. Remove both rear wheels as described in this chapter. The wheel hub (**Figure 6**) must be removed from the right side so the axle can be withdrawn from

13

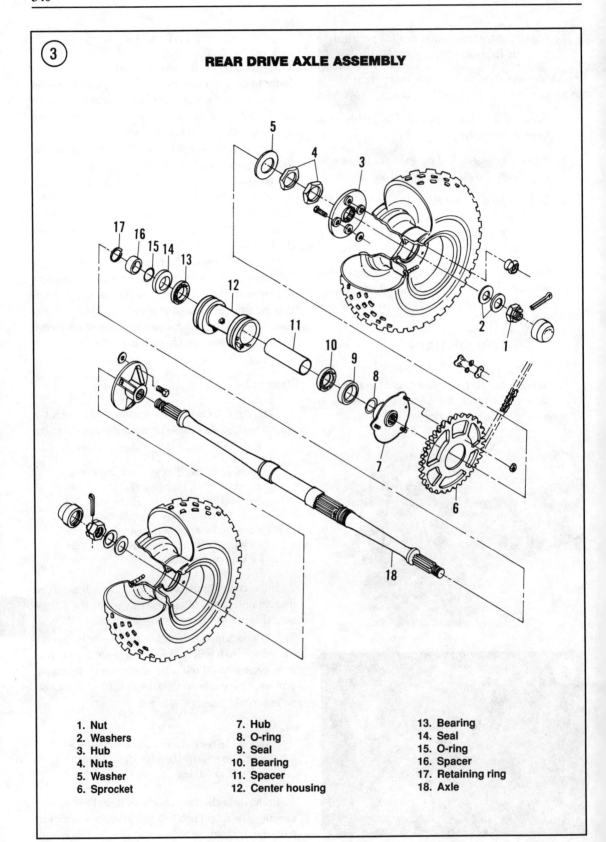

③ **REAR DRIVE AXLE ASSEMBLY**

1. Nut
2. Washers
3. Hub
4. Nuts
5. Washer
6. Sprocket
7. Hub
8. O-ring
9. Seal
10. Bearing
11. Spacer
12. Center housing
13. Bearing
14. Seal
15. O-ring
16. Spacer
17. Retaining ring
18. Axle

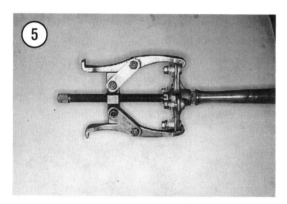

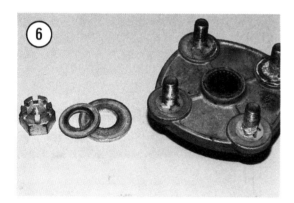

the swing arm. The hub must be removed from the right side to disassemble the axle and center housing.

5. Locate and remove the rear drive chain master link, then remove the drive chain.

6. Remove the two clamp screws (**Figure 7**).

7. Loosen the axle center housing by turning it in the swing arm clamp. If necessary, spread the rear clamps of the swing arm slightly to allow the center housing to be removed.

8. Withdraw the axle, sprocket and center housing from the vehicle.

Disassembly/Inspection/Reassembly

Refer to **Figure 1** for this procedure.

1. Remove the 2 large nuts (**Figure 8**) and washer.

NOTE
*Threads of the 2 large nuts (**Figure 8**) are coated with locking compound and are very fine threads. These nuts are very tight and may be difficult to remove, so be extremely careful. If necessary, apply heat to the nuts to soften the locking compound.*

2. Remove the sprocket and hub (A, **Figure 9**) from the shaft splines.

13

3. Remove the O-ring (B, **Figure 9**), then slide the rear axle from the center housing, bearings and seals.

> *NOTE*
> *Do not remove the axle seals or bearings for inspection, because they will be damaged during removal. Remove the seals and bearings only if replacement is necessary.*

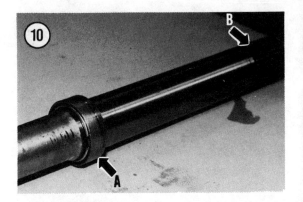

4. Turn the inner race of each bearing by hand. Make sure that the bearings turn smoothly. Some axial play is normal, but radial play should be negligible. The bearings should turn with no evidence of roughness or ratcheting.

5. Pry the seals from the housing with a wide-blade screwdriver. Pad the screwdriver to prevent it from damaging the axle housing bore.

6. Insert a drift into one side of the axle housing, push the spacer to one side and place the drift on the inner race of the opposite bearing.

7. Tap the bearing out of the hub with a hammer, working around the bearing's inner race to prevent the bearing from binding in the housing bore.

8. Remove the bearing and the center spacer.

9. Tap out the opposite bearing with a suitable driver inserted through the axle housing.

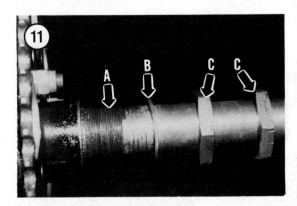

10. Clean the axle housing with solvent and dry with compressed air.

11. Clean the center spacer. Make sure that all corrosion and rust is removed.

12. Check the axle housing bores for cracks or other damage. Remove any burrs or nicks with a file or fine abrasive paper.

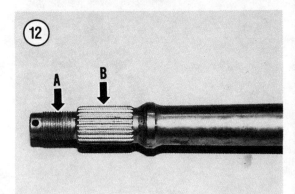

> *NOTE*
> *If one or both bearings are loose in the housing bore(s), do not attempt to repair the looseness by center punching or roughing up the area to tighten the bearing. This type of repair will not last long and the bearings will soon be loose again. If the bearing bores in the center housing are worn or damaged, install a new center housing.*

13. Inspect the seal ring (A, **Figure 10**) for damage. Replace the seal ring if the seal surface is rough.

14. Inspect the axle carefully as follows:
   a. Clean the axle completely and make sure the threads (**Figure 11**) are not damaged.

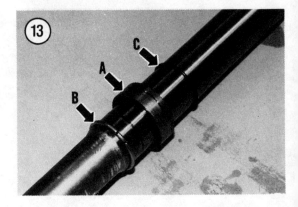

b. Inspect the threads (A, **Figure 12**) and splines (B) at the ends of the axle for damage.

c. Inspect the splines (B, **Figure 10**) near the center of the axle for damage.

d. Check the axle for straightness using a set of V-blocks and a dial indicator. Axle runout should not exceed 1.5 mm (0.06 in.). If runout is excessive, install a new axle.

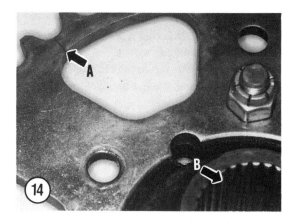

WARNING
Do not attempt to straighten a bent axle. Axle failure may occur during riding. A bent or a broken axle will cause loss of control that may result in personal injury.

15. Make sure the seal ring (A, **Figure 13**) is fully seated against the retaining ring (B, **Figure 13**), then install a new O-ring (C, **Figure 13**).

16. Blow any dirt or foreign matter from the housing and from the spacer before installing the bearings.

17. Press the first bearing into the center housing with its manufacturer's code numbers toward the outside. Make sure the bearing is bottomed in its bore.

18. Install the spacer and press the second bearing into the bore until it bottoms in the housing bore. The manufacturer's code numbers must be toward the outside.

19. Pack the lip of each seal with grease and press into the housing until the closed side of the seal is flush with or slightly below the edge of the housing bore.

20. Insert the axle assembly through the seals and bearings and into the center housing.

21. Inspect the sprocket and sprocket hub as follows:

a. Check the seal surface of the sprocket hub for roughness or other damage. Clean small imperfections using fine abrasive paper.

b. Check the sprocket for wear, cracks (A, **Figure 14**) or other damage. Make sure the sprocket is not bent.

c. Check the sprocket retaining bolts for tightness and condition. Install new bolts if damaged and tighten securely.

d. Check the hub for damaged splines (B, **Figure 14**).

22. Install O-ring (**Figure 15**) and slide the O-ring against the bearing.

23. Install the sprocket hub on the shaft splines and slide the hub into the seal.

24. Grease the unit through the fitting (**Figure 16**) until grease is expelled from the seals at both ends of the center housing. Make sure that the bearings and housing are filled with grease.

25. Make sure that the threads are cleaned, then apply Loctite 242 to the threads (A, **Figure 11**).

26. Install the washer (A, **Figure 17**) and the first nut (B, **Figure 17**).

13

27. Tighten the inner nut (B, **Figure 17**) to the specification in **Table 2**. Then install and tighten the outer nut (C, **Figure 17**) to the same specification (**Table 2**).

Installation

1. Insert the axle and center housing into the rear of the swing arm.

2. Install, but do not tighten the 2 clamp screws (**Figure 18**). The center housing must be free to rotate in the swing arm to adjust the drive chain.

3. Install the rear drive chain and install the master link so that the closed end of the retaining clip is toward the direction of chain movement as shown in **Figure 19**.

4. Adjust the chain free play as described in Chapter Three. Maintaining the correct chain adjustment is important.

5. Tighten the clamp screws (**Figure 18**) to the torque listed in **Table 2**.

> *WARNING*
> *Always install a new cotter pin.*

6. Install the rear wheel hubs and tighten the retaining nuts to the torque listed in **Table 2**. Install the locking cotter pins and bend the ends over the nut. If necessary, tighten the nut slightly beyond the recommended torque to install the cotter pin.

> *NOTE*
> *The nut should not be loosened to align slots in the nut with the hole in the axle.*

7. Install the rear wheels and tighten the lug nuts to the torque listed in **Table 2**.

DRIVE CHAIN

A 520 O-ring drive chain was originally installed on all models. O-ring drive chains are equipped with rubber O-rings between each side plate. The master link is equipped with 4 removable O-rings. O-ring chains are internally lubricated at the time of manufacture and assembly. The O-rings are designed to seal the chain's lubricant in while keeping dirt and moisture out.

Table 1 lists drive chain specifications.

Removal/Installation

1. Support the vehicle with both rear wheels off the ground.

2. Turn the rear axle and drive chain until the master link (**Figure 19**) is accessible.

3. Remove the master link spring clip with a pair of pliers.

4. Use a chain breaker to push the side plate from the master link. Remove the side plate and the 2 outside O-rings.

5. Push out the connecting link. Remove the 2 inside O-rings if required.

6. Lift the drive chain from the sprockets.

7. Install by reversing these removal steps, noting the following:

    a. Install an O-ring on each connecting link pin.

    b. Insert the connecting link through the chain to join it together.

    c. Install the 2 remaining O-rings onto the connecting link pins.

    d. Push the side plate onto the connecting link as far as it will go. Then press the side plate into position with a press-fit chain tool.

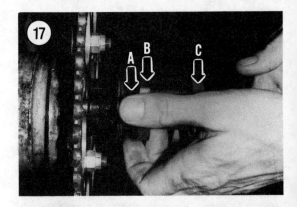

NOTE
Most commercial press-fit chain tools are designed to press the side plate onto the connecting link to its correct depth. If the side plate is pressed on too far, it will bind the chain where it joins the master link. If the side plate is not pressed on far enough, the spring clip cannot be installed correctly and may come off. What you are trying to do is press the side plate onto the connecting link until the slide plate is flush with both pin seating grooves in the connecting link.

CAUTION
Attempting to assemble a press-fit master link without the proper tools may cause damage to the master link and drive chain.

e. Install the spring clip on the master link so the closed end of the clip is facing the direction of chain travel (**Figure 19**).

8. Adjust the drive chain as described in Chapter Three.

Cutting A Drive Chain To Length

Table 1 lists the correct number of chain links required for stock gearing. **Table 1** also lists the number of teeth on standard sprockets. Be sure to count the number of teeth on the sprockets and count the chain links of the original chain before cutting the new chain. If your replacement drive chain is too long, cut it to length as follows.

1. Remove the new chain from its box and stretch it out on your workbench. Set the master link aside for now.

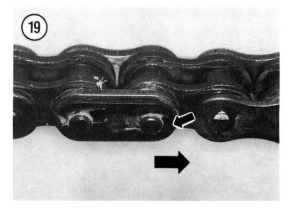

2. Determine the correct number of links for your chain by referring to **Table 1** or counting the number of links in the original chain.

3. Count the correct number of links on the new chain and mark the 2 chain pins to cut. Count the chain links one more time to make sure you are correct.

WARNING
A bench grinder or hand-operated high-speed grinding tool is required to grind the chain pins when cutting the chain. When using this equipment, safety glasses must be worn.

4. Use a bench grinder or other suitable grinding tool to remove the heads from the two marked pins. Grind the heads flush with the face of the side plate.

5. Use a chain breaker or a punch and hammer and lightly tap the pins from the side plate. Support the chain carefully while driving the pins from the side plate. If the pins are still tight, grind away more material, then try again.

6. Remove the side plate and push out the connecting link.

Drive Chain Cleaning/Lubrication

CAUTION
The O-rings in the drive chain can be easily damaged by improper cleaning and handling. Do not use a steam cleaner, a high-pressure washer or any solvent that may damage the rubber O-rings.

1. Remove the drive chain as described in this chapter.

2. Immerse the chain in a pan of kerosene and allow it so soak for about 30 minutes. Move the chain around and flex it while soaking so the dirt between the links, pins, rollers and O-rings will work its way out.

CAUTION
In the next step, do not use a wire brush to clean the chain or the O-rings will be damaged and the drive chain must be replaced.

3. Scrub the rollers lightly with a soft brush and rinse away loosened dirt. Do not scrub hard or use a stiff brush that might damage the O-rings. Rinse the chain a couple of times in kerosene to make sure all

dirt and grit are washed out. Hang the chain up over a pan and allow the chain to dry.

4. After cleaning the chain, examine it carefully for wear or damage. Check the O-rings for damage. Replace the chain if necessary.

5. Externally lubricate the chain with SAE 30-50 motor oil or a good grade of chain lubricant (non-tacky) specifically formulated for O-ring chains, following its manufacturer's instructions.

CAUTION
Do not use a tacky chain lubricant on O-ring chains. Dirt and other abrasive materials that stick to the lubricant will grind away at the O-rings and damage them. Remember, an O-ring chain is pre-lubricated during its assembly at the factory. External oiling is only required to prevent chain rust and to keep the O-rings pliable.

DRIVE AND DRIVEN SPROCKETS

The driven sprocket rides on a hub that is mounted on the rear axle. The driven sprocket can be removed without removing the rear axle from the vehicle. If the sprocket can not be easily and completely seen, it may be necessary to remove chain guards for proper inspection. See **Figure 20**.

The drive sprocket (**Figure 21**) is located on the output shaft of the transmission. Refer to the appropriate transmission section in Chapter Nine to remove the drive sprocket. On models with all wheel drive, it is necessary to remove the center chain and front drive sprocket as described in Chapter Ten before the rear drive sprocket. On models with the output shaft mechanical disc brake, the brake caliper and disc must be removed as described in Chapter Fourteen before the rear drive sprocket can be removed.

Inspection

Check the sprocket teeth for severe wear or undercutting. Clean the sprocket and inspect for cracks (**Figure 14**) or other damage. Check to see if the sprocket is bent. If the sprocket is damaged, replace both sprockets and the chain at the same time. Installing a new chain over severely worn or damaged sprockets will cause rapid chain wear.

Removal/Installation

Refer to the appropriate transmission section in Chapter Nine to remove the drive sprocket. On models with all wheel drive, it is necessary to remove the center chain and front drive sprocket as described in Chapter Ten before the rear drive sprocket. The sprocket is retained by a snap ring (**Figure 22**). On models with the output shaft disc brake, the brake caliper and disc (**Figure 23**) must be removed as

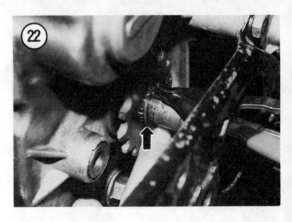

described in Chapter Fourteen before the rear drive sprocket can be removed.

1. Remove the right rear wheel and hub as described in this chapter.

2. Remove the drive chain as described in this chapter.

3. Remove nuts (**Figure 24**) from the bolts that hold the sprocket to the hub, then remove the sprocket.

4. Install by reversing these steps, noting the following.

5. Reinstall the chain guard and any spacers that were previously installed.

6. Tighten the sprocket nuts securely. Check to be sure the sprocket bolts are tight and hold the sprocket securely.

7. Refer to **Table 2** for the correct tightening torque when installing the rear hub.

TIRE CHANGING AND TIRE REPAIRS

The procedure for removing and repairing the rear tires are the same as for servicing the front tires. Refer to Chapter Twelve for tire service.

SHOCK ABSORBER

All models use a single rear shock absorber and spring unit. Some models are equipped with a gas (nitrogen) filled shock which has a remote gas/oil reservoir. The gas filled shock should be disassembled, rebuilt and filled by dealers trained and equipped for their service.

Removal/Installation

Refer to **Figure 25**.

1. Lift the rear of the vehicle off the ground, then block the rear, so that both rear wheels are off the ground, but the swing arm is not supporting any weight.

2. Remove the nut from the bolt (A, **Figure 26**) that attaches the lower end of the shock absorber to the swing arm.

3. Support the weight of the rear axle and swing arm, so the bolt (A, **Figure 26**) can be withdrawn, then lower the swing arm to the floor.

4. Remove the nut, washer and bolt that attaches the upper end of the shock absorber (**Figure 27**) to the frame and remove the shock absorber.

5. Install by reversing these steps. Note the following.

6. Clean the shock bolts, nuts, washers and collars in solvent. Dry thoroughly.

7. Position the upper end of the shock absorber in the frame, then install the upper shock mounting bolt. Install the washer and nut.

8. Position the lower end of the shock absorber, then install the washer and nut.

9. Tighten the upper and lower shock absorber mounting nuts to the torque specification listed in **Table 2**.

Shock Inspection

> *WARNING*
> *The shock absorber damper unit may contain nitrogen gas. Do not tamper with or attempt to open or disassemble the unit. Do not place it near an open flame or other extreme heat. Do not dispose of the damper assembly yourself. Take it to a dealer where it can be deactivated and disposed of properly. Read the WARNING label fixed to the reservoir.*

13

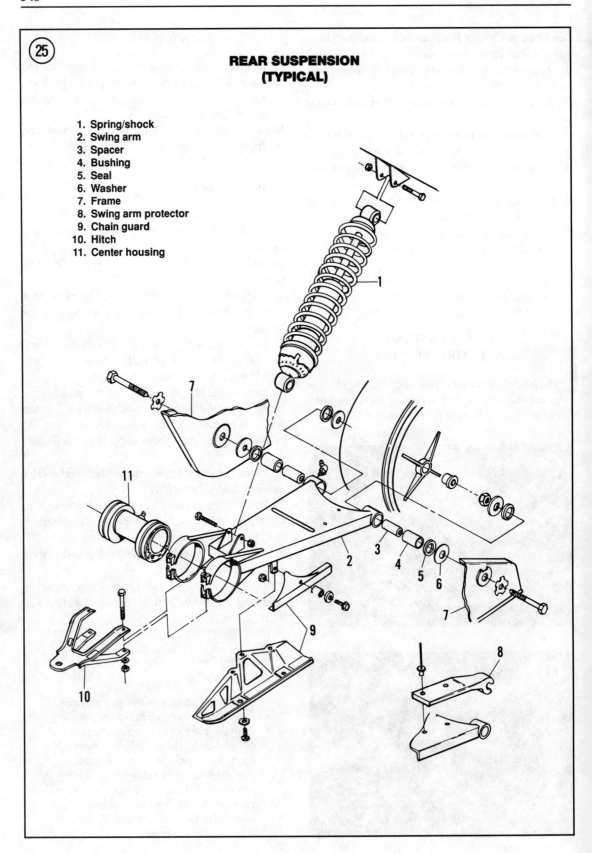

㉕

**REAR SUSPENSION
(TYPICAL)**

1. Spring/shock
2. Swing arm
3. Spacer
4. Bushing
5. Seal
6. Washer
7. Frame
8. Swing arm protector
9. Chain guard
10. Hitch
11. Center housing

1. Inspect the shock absorber for gas and oil leaks.

2. Check the damper rod for bending, rust or other damage.

3. Check the reservoir for dents or other damage.

4. Remove and inspect the spring as described in the following procedure.

Spring
Removal/Installation

In addition to the standard replacement shock spring, you can purchase shock springs from aftermarket suspension specialists, in a variety of spring rates. To replace a spring, perform the following.

1. Remove the shock absorber as described in this chapter.

2. If you are satisfied with the existing spring preload setting and want to maintain it, measure and record the spring preload position before removing the spring.

3. Use an appropriate spanner and adjust the spring tension to the lightest setting.

4. Secure the shock absorber upper mount in a vise with soft jaws.

5. Compress the spring using a suitable compressor tool (part No. 2870623).

6. Slide the rubber shock bumper down the shock shaft.

7. Remove the spring retainer, spring seat and spring from the shock.

NOTE
Some models may have a spacer installed below the spring as thick as 25.5 mm (1 in.). Suspension damage can be the result of setting the suspension too soft, when the operation is severe over rough terrain.

8. Measure spring free length and install a new spring if appreciably shorter than the free length of a new spring.

9. Install the spring by reversing these steps, noting the following.

10. Install the spring, spring guide and spring retainer. Make sure the spring guide and spring retainer seat flush against the spring.

11. Adjust the spring preload to the previous setting. Ride adjustment can be changed by turning the lower spring seat (B, **Figure 26**).

REAR SWING ARM

Figure 25 is a typical exploded view of the rear swing arm. Bearings are pressed into both sides of the swing arm. Size and design of the bushings, seals and inner spacers may be slightly different than shown.

Swing Arm and Bushings

Lubricate the swing arm bearings regularly as described in Chapter Three. If the swing arm appears to have an excessive amount of side-to-side play, the swing arm should be removed and the bearings inspected for wear or damage.

13

Inspection

1. Lift and support the rear of the vehicle so that the swing arm can be moved from side-to-side.
2. Make sure the chain has some free play and that the wheels are off the floor.
3. Have an assistant steady the vehicle, then grasp the rear of the swing arm and try to move it from side-to-side in a horizontal arc. There should be no noticeable side play.
4. If play is evident, check the pivot bolts for tightness as described in the following section. If the pivot bolts are tight, remove the swing arm and inspect the pivot bushings.

Removal

The rear axle does not need to be removed from the swing arm to inspect or install pivot bushings.
1. Lift and support the rear of the vehicle so the swing arm can be separated from the frame. Make sure that the support does not interfere with removal. Be sure the vehicle is securely supported and will not move when removing the swing arm.
2. Remove the drive chain as described in this chapter.
3. Remove the lower bolt (A, **Figure 26**) attaching the shock absorber to the swing arm.
4. Remove the drive belt and driven pulley as described in Chapter Eight.

NOTE
Some may prefer to remove the drive pulley and clutch inner cover as described in Chapter Eight instead of bending the inner cover.

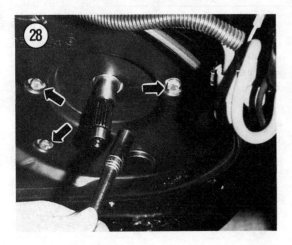

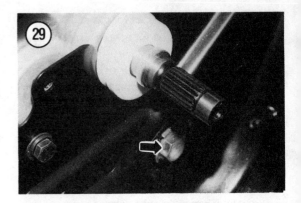

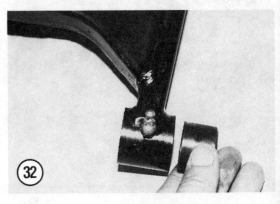

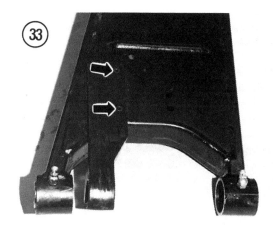

5. Unbolt the rear of the clutch inner cover (**Figure 28**) and pull the rear of the cover away from the frame far enough to remove the left swing arm pivot bolt (**Figure 29**).

6. Remove the brake assembly and covers as necessary to remove the swing arm pivot bolt (**Figure 30**) from the right side.

7. Pull the swing arm back, away from the frame.

8. Remove, clean and inspect bushings (**Figure 31** and **Figure 32**). Bushings may be slightly different than shown.

9. If worn or damaged, the swing arm chain protector can be removed after drilling out the attaching rivets (**Figure 33**).

10. Install by reversing the removal procedure and observing the following:

    a. Refer to **Table 2** for recommended tightening torques.

    b. Bend locking tabs (**Figure 34**) around the swing arm pivot bolts to prevent loosening.

    c. Grease the swing arm bushings when installing the bushings and after completing assembly of the swing arm.

    d. Refer to Chapter Eight for installation of the clutch inner cover. Make sure the inner cover is sealed properly.

    e. Refer to Chapter Eight for installation of the clutch driven pulley and drive belt.

13

Table 1 REAR DRIVE SPECIFICATIONS

Model No.	Sprocket teeth	Chain size	Chain pitch
1985			
Scrambler W857027	13/42	520	74
Trail Boss W857527	13/38	520	–
1986			
All models	13/42	520	74
1987			
Trail Boss W877527	13/42	520	74
Cyclone W877828	13/42	520	74
Trail Boss 4 × 4 W878027,			
W878127 & W878327	13/42	520	74
1988			
Trail Boss 2 × 4 W887527	13/38	520	72
Trail Boss 4 × 4 W888127	12/42	520	74
T. B. 250 R/ES X888528 &			
W888528	13/42	520	88
(continued)			

Table 1 REAR DRIVE SPECIFICATIONS (continued)

Model No.	Sprocket teeth	Chain size	Chain pitch
1989			
Trail Boss W898527	13/42	520	88
Trail Boss 2 × 4 W897527	13/38	520	86
Trail Boss 4 × 4 W898127	12/42	520	88
Big Boss 4 × 6 X898627 & W898627			
Center axle	12/42	520	88
Rear axle	30/30	520	108
1990			
Trail Blazer W907221	13/42	520	88
Trail Boss 250 W908527	13/34	520	84
Trail Boss 2 × 4 W907527	13/38	520	86
T.B. 2 × 4-350L W907539	13/34	520	84
Trail Boss 4 × 4 W908127	12/42	520	88
T.B. 4 × 4-350L W908139	13/34	520	88
Big Boss 4 × 6 W908627			
Center axle	12/42	520	88
Rear axle	30/30	520	108
1991			
Trail Blazer W917221	13/34	520	84
Trail Boss 250 W918527	13/34	520	84
Trail Boss 2 × 4 W917527	13/38	520	86
T.B. 2 × 4-350L W917539	13/34	520	84
Trail Boss 4 × 4 W918127	12/42	520	88
T.B. 4 × 4-350L W918139	13/34	520	88
Big Boss 4 × 6 W918627 & 6 × 6 W918727			
Center axle	12/42	520	88
Rear axle	30/30	520	108
1992			
Trail Blazer W927221	13/42	520	84
Trail Boss 250 W928527	13/34	520	84
Trail Boss 2 × 4 W927527	13/38	520	86
T.B. 2 × 4-350L W927539	13/34	520	84
Trail Boss 4 × 4 W928127	12/42	520	88
T.B. 4 × 4-350L W928139	13/34	520	84
Big Boss 4 × 6 W928627 & 6 × 6 W928727			
Center axle	12/42	520	88
Rear axle	30/30	520	108
1993			
Trail Blazer W937221	13/34	520	84
Trail Boss W938527	13/34	520	84
Sportsman W938039	12/34	520	84
250 2 × 4 W937527	13/38	520	86
350 2 × 4 W937539	13/34	520	84
250 4 × 4 W938127	12/42	520	88
350 4 × 4 W938139	12/34	520	84
250 6 × 6 W938727			
Center axle	12/42	520	88
Rear axle	30/30	520	108
350 6 × 6 W938739			
Center axle	13/42	520	88
Rear axle	30/30	520	108

(continued)

Table 1 REAR DRIVE SPECIFICATIONS (continued)

Model No.	Sprocket teeth	Chain size	Chain pitch
1994			
Trail Blazer 2W W947221	11/40	520	86
Trail Boss 2W W948527	11/40	520	86
Sport W948540	12/34	520	84
Sportsman 4 × 4 W948040	13/34	520	84
300 2 × 4 W947530	13/38	520	86
400 2 × 4 W947540	13/34	520	84
300 4 × 4 W948130	12/42	520	88
400 4 × 4 W948140	13/34	520	84
300 6 × 6 W948730			
Center axle	12/42	520	88
Rear axle	30/30	520	108
400 6 × 6 W948740			
Center axle	13/42	520	88
Rear axle	30/30	520	108
1995			
Trail Blazer W957221	12/42	520	88
Trail Boss W958527	12/42	520	88
300 2 × 4 W957530	13/38	520	86
400 2 × 4 W957540	13/34	520	84
300 4 × 4 W958130	13/40	520	88
Scrambler W957840	13/38	520	84
Sport W958540	12/34	520	84
Sportsman 4 × 4 W958040	13/34	520	84
Xplorer 4 × 4 W959140	13/34	520	84
Magnum 2 × 4 W957444	12/38	520	86
Magnum 4 × 4 W958144	12/38	520	86
400 6 × 6 W958740			
Center axle	13/42	520	88
Rear axle	30/30	520	116

Table 2 TORQUE SPECIFICATIONS

	N·m	ft.-lb.
Axle center housing clamp bolts	81.4	60
Rear shock bolt		
Lower	33.9	15
Upper	33.9	15
Rear sprocket hub retaining nuts	203.4	150
Rear wheel hub center nut	108	80
Rear wheel lug nuts	67.8	50
Swing arm pivot screws	74.6	55

13

Table 3 TIRE SIZE AND PRESSURE

	Front tires kPa (psi)	Rear tires kPa (psi)
1985		
Scrambler W857027		
Size	22 × 11.00 × 8	22 × 11.00 × 10
Pressure	20.7 (3)	20.7 (3)

(continued)

Table 3 TIRE SIZE AND PRESSURE (continued)

	Front tires kPa (psi)	Rear tires kPa (psi)
1985 (continued)		
Trail Boss W857527		
Size	22 × 8.00 × 10	22 × 11.00 × 10
Pressure	27.6 (4)	20.7 (3)
1986		
Scrambler W867027		
Size	22 × 11.00 × 8	22 × 11.00 × 10
Pressure	20.7 (3)	20.7 (3)
Trail Boss W867527		
Size	22 × 8.00 × 10	22 × 11.00 × 10
Pressure	27.6 (4)	20.7 (3)
Trail Boss W867627		
Size	22 × 8.00 × 10	22 × 11.00 × 10
Pressure	27.6 (4)	20.7 (3)
1987		
Trail Boss W877527		
Size	22 × 8.00 × 8	22 × 11.00 × 10
Pressure	27.6 (4)	20.7 (3)
Cyclone W877828		
Size	22 × 8.00 × 10	22 × 11.00 × 10
Pressure	27.6 (4)	20.7 (3)
Trail Boss 4 × 4 W878027		
Size	22 × 8.00 × 10	22 × 11.00 × 10
Pressure	27.6 (4)	20.7 (3)
Trail Boss 4 × 4 W878127		
Size	22 × 8.00 × 10	22 × 11.00 × 10
Pressure	27.6 (4)	20.7 (3)
Trail Boss 4 × 4 W878327		
Size	22 × 8.00 × 10	22 × 11.00 × 10
Pressure	27.6 (4)	20.7 (3)
1988		
Trail Boss 2 × 4 W887527		
Size	22 × 8.00 × 10	22 × 11.00 × 10
Pressure	27.6 (4)	20.7 (3)
Trail Boss 4 × 4 W888127		
Size	22 × 8.00 × 10	22 × 11.00 × 10
Pressure	27.6 (4)	20.7 (3)
Trail Boss 250 R/ES X888528		
Size	22 × 8.00 × 10	22 × 11.00 × 10
Pressure	27.6 (4)	20.7 (3)
Trail Boss 250 R/ES W888528		
Size	22 × 8.00 × 10	22 × 11.00 × 10
Pressure	27.6 (4)	20.7 (3)
1989		
Trail Boss W898527		
Size	22 × 8.00 × 10	22 × 11.00 × 10
Pressure	20.7 (3)	20.7 (3)
Trail Boss 2 × 4 W897527		
Size	22 × 8.00 × 10	22 × 11.00 × 10
Pressure	20.7 (3)	20.7 (3)
Trail Boss 4 × 4 W898127		
Size	22 × 8.00 × 10	22 × 11.00 × 10
Pressure	27.6 (4)	20.7 (3)

(continued)

Table 3 TIRE SIZE AND PRESSURE (continued)

	Front tires kPa (psi)	Rear tires kPa (psi)
1989 (continued)		
Big Boss 4 × 6 X898627		
Size	22 × 8.00 × 10	22 × 11.00 × 10
Pressure	27.6 (4)	34.5 (5)
Big Boss 4 × 6 W898627		
Size	22 × 8.00 × 10	22 × 11.00 × 10
Pressure	27.6 (4)	34.5 (5)
1990		
Trail Blazer W907221		
Size	22 × 8.00 × 10	22 × 11.00 × 10
Pressure	20.7 (3)	20.7 (3)
Trail Boss 250 W908527		
Size	22 × 8.00 × 10	22 × 11.00 × 10
Pressure	20.7 (3)	20.7 (3)
Trail Boss 2 × 4 W907527		
Size	22 × 8.00 × 10	24 × 11.00 × 10
Pressure	20.7 (3)	20.7 (3)
Trail Boss 2 × 4 - 350L W907539		
Size	22 × 8.00 × 10	24 × 11.00 × 10
Pressure	27.6 (4)	20.7 (3)
Trail Boss 4 × 4 W908127		
Size	22 × 8.00 × 10	24 × 11.00 × 10
Pressure	27.6 (4)	20.7 (3)
Trail Boss 4 × 4 - 350L W908139		
Size	25 × 8.00 × 12	25 × 12.00 × 10
Pressure	27.6 (4)	20.7 (3)
Big Boss 4 × 6 W908627		
Size	22 × 8.00 × 10	22 × 11.00 × 10
Pressure	34.5 (5)	34.5 (5)
1991		
Trail Blazer W917221		
Size	22 × 8.00 × 10	22 × 11.00 × 10
Pressure	20.7 (3)	20.7 (3)
Trail Boss 250 W918527		
Size	22 × 8.00 × 10	22 × 11.00 × 10
Pressure	20.7 (3)	20.7 (3)
Trail Boss 2 × 4 W917527		
Size	22 × 8.00 × 10	24 × 11.00 × 10
Pressure	20.7 (3)	20.7 (3)
Trail Boss 2 × 4 - 350L W917539		
Size	22 × 8.00 × 10	24 × 11.00 × 10
Pressure	27.6 (4)	20.7 (3)
Trail Boss 4 × 4 W918127		
Size	22 × 8.00 × 10	24 × 11.00 × 10
Pressure	27.6 (4)	20.7 (3)
Trail Boss 4 × 4 - 350L W918139		
Size	25 × 8.00 × 12	25 × 12.00 × 10
Pressure	27.6 (4)	20.7 (3)
Big Boss 4 × 6 W918627		
Size	22 × 8.00 × 10	22 × 11.00 × 10
Pressure	34.5 (5)	34.5 (5)
Big Boss 6 × 6 W918727		
Size	22 × 8.00 × 10	22 × 11.00 × 10
Pressure	34.5 (5)	34.5 (5)

(continued)

Table 3 TIRE SIZE AND PRESSURE (continued)

	Front tires kPa (psi)	Rear tires kPa (psi)
1992		
Trail Blazer W927221		
Size	22 × 8.00 × 10	22 × 11.00 × 10
Pressure	20.7 (3)	20.7 (3)
Trail Boss 250 W928527		
Size	22 × 8.00 × 10	22 × 11.00 × 10
Pressure	20.7 (3)	20.7 (3)
Trail Boss 2 × 4 W927527		
Size	22 × 8.00 × 10	24 × 11.00 × 10
Pressure	20.7 (3)	20.7 (3)
Trail Boss 2 × 4 - 350L W927539		
Size	22 × 8.00 × 10	24 × 11.00 × 10
Pressure	27.6 (4)	20.7 (3)
Trail Boss 4 × 4 W928127		
Size	22 × 8.00 × 10	24 × 11.00 × 10
Pressure	27.6 (4)	20.7 (3)
Trail Boss 4 × 4 - 350L W928139		
Size	25 × 8.00 × 12	25 × 12.00 × 10
Pressure	27.6 (4)	20.7 (3)
Big Boss 4 × 6 W928627		
Size	22 × 8.00 × 10	22 × 11.00 × 10
Pressure	34.5 (5)	34.5 (5)
Big Boss 6 × 6 W928727		
Size	22 × 8.00 × 10	22 × 11.00 × 10
Pressure	34.5 (5)	34.5 (5)
1993		
Trail Blazer W937221		
Size	22 × 8.00 × 10	22 × 11.00 × 10
Pressure	20.7 (3)	20.7 (3)
Trail Boss W938527		
Size	22 × 8.00 × 10	22 × 11.00 × 10
Pressure	20.7 (3)	20.7 (3)
Sportsman W938039		
Size	25 × 8.00 × 12	25 × 12.00 × 10
Pressure	27.6 (4)	20.7 (3)
250 2 × 4 W937527		
Size	22 × 8.00 × 10	24 × 11.00 × 10
Pressure	20.7 (3)	20.7 (3)
350 2 × 4 W937539		
Size	22 × 8.00 × 10	24 × 11.00 × 10
Pressure	27.6 (4)	20.7 (3)
250 4 × 4 W938127		
Size	22 × 8.00 × 10	24 × 11.00 × 10
Pressure	27.6 (4)	20.7 (3)
350 4 × 4 W938139		
Size	25 × 8.00 × 12	25 × 12.00 × 10
Pressure	27.6 (4)	20.7 (3)
250 6 × 6 W938727		
Size	22 × 8.00 × 10	22 × 11.00 × 10
Pressure	34.5 (5)	34.5 (5)
350 6 × 6 W938739		
Size	25 × 8.00 × 10	25 × 12.00 × 10
Pressure	34.5 (5)	34.5 (5)

(continued)

Table 3 TIRE SIZE AND PRESSURE (continued)

	Front tires kPa (psi)	Rear tires kPa (psi)
1994		
Trail Blazer 2W W947221		
Size	22 × 8.00 × 10	22 × 11.00 × 10
Pressure	20.7 (3)	20.7 (3)
Trail Boss 2W W948527		
Size	22 × 8.00 × 10	22 × 11.00 × 10
Pressure	20.7 (3)	20.7 (3)
Sport W948540		
Size	22 × 8.00 × 10	22 × 11.00 × 10
Pressure	27.6 (4)	20.7 (3)
Sportsman 4 × 4 W948040		
Size	25 × 8.00 × 12	25 × 12.00 × 10
Pressure	27.6 (4)	20.7 (3)
300 2 × 4 W947530		
Size	22 × 8.00 × 10	24 × 11.00 × 10
Pressure	20.7 (3)	20.7 (3)
400 2 × 4 W947540		
Size	22 × 8.00 × 10	24 × 11.00 × 10
Pressure	20.7 (3)	20.7 (3)
300 4 × 4 W948130		
Size	22 × 8.00 × 10	24 × 11.00 × 10
Pressure	20.7 (3)	20.7 (3)
400 4 × 4 W948140		
Size	25 × 8.00 × 12	25 × 12.00 × 10
Pressure	27.6 (4)	20.7 (3)
300 6 × 6 W948730		
Size	22 × 8.00 × 10	22 × 11.00 × 10
Pressure	34.5 (5)	34.5 (5)
400 6 × 6 W948740		
Size	25 × 8.00 × 12	25 × 12.00 × 10
Pressure	34.5 (5)	34.5 (5)
1995		
Trail Blazer W957221		
Size	22 × 8.00 × 10	22 × 11.00 × 10
Pressure	20.7 (3)	20.7 (3)
Trail Boss W958527		
Size	22 × 8.00 × 10	22 × 11.00 × 10
Pressure	20.7 (3)	20.7 (3)
300 2 × 4 W957530		
Size	22 × 8.00 × 10	24 × 11.00 × 10
Pressure	20.7 (3)	20.7 (3)
400 2 × 4 W957540		
Size	22 × 8.00 × 10	24 × 11.00 × 10
Pressure	27.6 (4)	20.7 (3)
300 4 × 4 W958130		
Size	22 × 8.00 × 10	24 × 11.00 × 10
Pressure	27.6 (4)	20.7 (3)
Scrambler W957840		
Size	23 × 7.00 × 10	22 × 11.00 × 10
Pressure	27.6 (4)	20.7 (3)
Sport W958540		
Size	23 × 7.00 × 10	22 × 11.00 × 10
Pressure	27.6 (4)	20.7 (3)

13

(continued)

Table 3 TIRE SIZE AND PRESSURE (continued)

	Front tires kPa (psi)	Rear tires kPa (psi)
1995 (continued)		
Sportsman 4 × 4 W958040		
Size	25 × 8.00 × 12	25 × 12.00 × 10
Pressure	27.6 (4)	20.7 (3)
Xplorer 4 × 4 W959140		
Size	25 × 8.00 × 12	25 × 12.00 × 10
Pressure	27.6 (4)	20.7 (3)
Magnum 2 × 4 W957444		
Size	23 × 7.00 × 10	24 × 11.00 × 10
Pressure	27.6 (4)	20.7 (3)
Magnum 4 × 4 W958144		
Size	25 × 8.00 × 12	25 × 12.00 × 10
Pressure	27.6 (4)	20.7 (3)
400 6 × 6 W958740		
Size	25 × 8.00 × 12	25 × 12.00 × 10
Pressure	34.5 (5)	34.5 (5)

CHAPTER FOURTEEN

BRAKES

This chapter describes service procedures for the front and rear brakes. Mechanical drum brakes are used on the front wheels on all 1985-1987 models with only rear wheel drive. A mechanical disc brake is used to stop the rear wheels on all 1985-1987 models with only rear wheel drive. Hydraulic disc brakes are used to stop the front and rear wheels of 1987 models with all wheel drive and all 1988-on models. The rear wheel brake disc is installed on a brake shaft or transmission output shaft. Refer to **Table 1** for brake application. **Tables 1-3** are located at the end of this chapter.

FRONT BRAKES
(DRUM TYPE)

The drum type front brakes are operated by the hand lever attached to the right side of the handlebar.

Refer to Chapter Three for the adjustment procedure.

Removal/Inspection/Installation

1. Refer to Chapter Twelve and remove the front brake drum and wheel hub (**Figure 1**). Procedures for both 4-Wheel and tricycle (Scrambler) models are described.

2. Pull the brake shoes and springs (**Figure 2**) from the anchor and cam.

3. Clean the backing plate (**Figure 3**) thoroughly.

4. Check the inner seal (A, **Figure 3**) for damage.

5. Check the cam (B, **Figure 3**) to make sure that it operates freely.

6. Measure the thickness of the lining on the brake shoes (**Figure 4**) and install new shoes if worn excessively.

14

7. Clean and inspect the brake drum (A, **Figure 5**) for wear, scoring or rust.

> *NOTE*
> *Do not remove parts from the hub and drum unless new parts are to be installed. Removal will almost certainly damage the seal and bearings.*

7. Clean and inspect the inner wheel bearing (B, **Figure 5**). If damaged, refer to Chapter Twelve for removing the wheel bearings. Bearings can be cleaned and repacked with fresh grease without removing them from the hub and brake drum.

8. Inspect the outer bearing and seal (**Figure 6**). If replacement is required, remove the seal, then remove the outer bearing.

9. Reinstall the brake shoes and return springs as shown in **Figure 7**.

10. Install the brake drum and wheel hub.

> *NOTE*
> *If necessary, tighten the castellated nut to align the slots in the nut with the hole in the axle. Do not loosen the nut after tightening to the correct torque.*

11. Tighten the castellated nut to the torque listed in **Table 2**, then install a new cotter pin. Bend the ends of the cotter pin as shown in **Figure 8**.

12. Refer to **Table 2** for recommended tightening torques.

HYDRAULIC BRAKES

The brakes on all 1988-on models and 1987 all wheel drive models are actuated by hydraulic fluid and controlled by a hand lever and master cylinder attached to the left side of the handlebar. As the brake pads wear, the brake calipers will automatically adjust the position of the pads and the fluid level in the reservoir will lower. Always be sure the reservoir is filled. Refer to Chapter Three.

When working on the hydraulic brake system, it is necessary that the work area and all tools be absolutely clean. Even very small particles of foreign matter and grit in the caliper or master cylinder can damage the components.

Observe the following when servicing the hydraulic disc brakes.

1. Use only DOT 3 brake fluid from a sealed container.

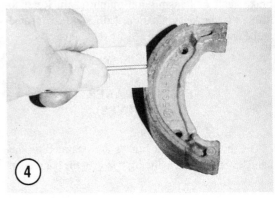

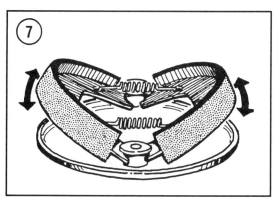

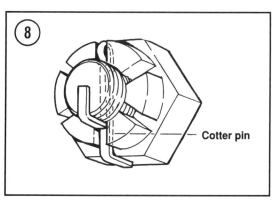

Cotter pin

2. Do not allow disc brake fluid to contact any plastic parts or painted surfaces as damage will result.

3. Always keep the master cylinder reservoir and extra containers of brake fluid closed to prevent dust or moisture from entering. Filling a brake system reservoir with contaminated fluid will be more costly than buying new fluid.

4. Use only disc brake fluid (DOT 3) to wash rubber parts. Never clean brake components with any petroleum base cleaners.

5. Whenever any component has been removed from the brake system the system is considered opened and must be bled to remove air bubbles. Refer to *Brake Bleeding* in this chapter for complete details.

6. A brake that feels spongy or soft, probably has air bubbles in the system and should be bled. Refer to *Brake Bleeding* in this chapter for complete details.

> *CAUTION*
> *Disc brake components rarely require disassembly, so do not disassemble unless absolutely necessary. Do not use solvents of any kind on the brake system's internal components. Solvents will cause the seals to swell and distort. When disassembling and cleaning brake components (except brake pads) use new DOT 3 brake fluid.*

> *CAUTION*
> *Never reuse brake fluid. Contaminated brake fluid can cause brake failure. Dispose of brake fluid according to local EPA regulations.*

FRONT BRAKE CALIPER (1987 MODELS WITH ALL-WHEEL DRIVE)

Refer to **Figure 9** when replacing the front brake pads or servicing the front brake caliper.

Front Brake Pad Replacement

There is no recommended time interval for changing the friction pads in the front brakes. Pad wear depends greatly on riding habits and conditions. Always replace both pads in both calipers at the same time.

14

1. Read the preceding information *Hydraulic Brakes* in this chapter.

2. Remove the front wheel as described in Chapter Twelve.

3. Remove the brake caliper mounting bolts, then move the caliper away from the brake disc.

4. Check the condition of the brake rotor (disc). If it requires removal, refer to Chapter Ten to remove the front drive hub.

5. Remove the 2 hanger pins (A, **Figure 10**) and brake pads (B, **Figure 10**).

6. Measure the thickness of each brake pad. Replace the brake pads if the thickness of any one pad is less than the service limit in **Table 3**. Replace brake pads as a set.

7. Inspect the brake pads for uneven wear, damage or grease contamination. Replace the pads as a set, if necessary.

8. Check the end of the piston for fluid leakage. If the seal is damaged and/or if there is fluid leakage, overhaul the brake caliper as described in this chapter.

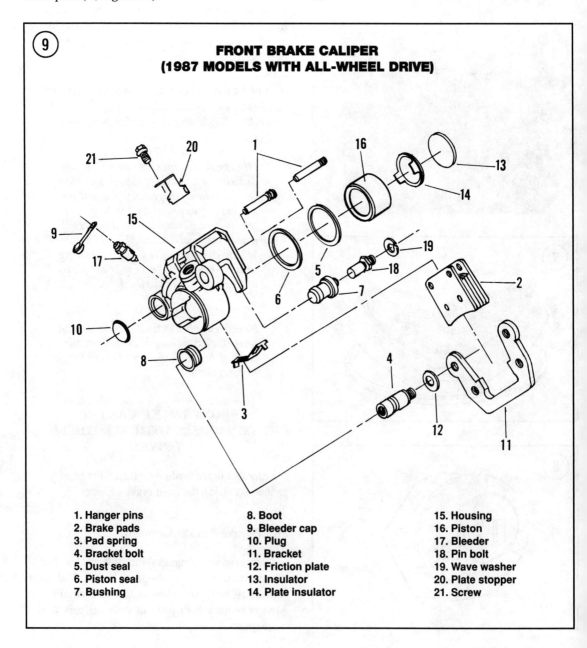

9

FRONT BRAKE CALIPER
(1987 MODELS WITH ALL-WHEEL DRIVE)

1. Hanger pins	8. Boot	15. Housing
2. Brake pads	9. Bleeder cap	16. Piston
3. Pad spring	10. Plug	17. Bleeder
4. Bracket bolt	11. Bracket	18. Pin bolt
5. Dust seal	12. Friction plate	19. Wave washer
6. Piston seal	13. Insulator	20. Plate stopper
7. Bushing	14. Plate insulator	21. Screw

9. To make room for the new pads, push the piston back into the caliper. This will force brake fluid to backup through the hose into the master cylinder reservoir. To prevent the reservoir from overflowing, it may be necessary to remove some of the brake fluid as follows:

   a. Clean the top of the master cylinder of all dirt.

   b. Remove the cover from the master cylinder.

   c. Temporarily install the inside brake pad into the caliper and slowly push the piston back into the caliper.

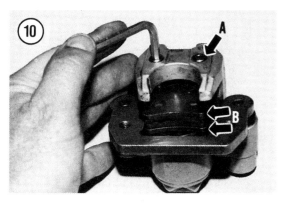

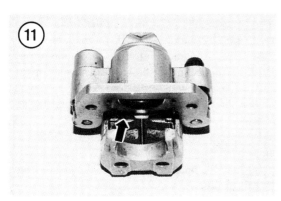

   d. Check the reservoir frequently to make sure brake fluid does not overflow. Siphon fluid from the reservoir, if necessary, before it overflows.

WARNING
Brake fluid is poisonous. Do not siphon with your mouth.

   e. The caliper piston should move freely in the caliper. If it does not, remove and overhaul the caliper as described in this chapter.

   f. Push the caliper piston in all the way to allow room for the new pads.

10. Check to be sure that the spring (**Figure 11**) is correctly in place and install new pads.

11. Install the hanger pins (**Figure 12**) and tighten to the torque listed in **Table 2**.

12. Install the caliper and tighten the retaining bolts to the torque listed in **Table 2**.

13. Repeat the procedure for the other front brake caliper.

WARNING
Use new brake fluid clearly marked DOT 3 from a sealed container.

14. Pull and release the brake lever a few times to seat the pads against each disc, then recheck the brake fluid level in the reservoir. If necessary, add fresh DOT 3 brake fluid.

15. Install the cover on the master cylinder reservoir and tighten the cover screws securely.

16. Install the front wheels as described in Chapter Twelve.

WARNING
Do not ride the vehicle until you are sure that all of the brakes are operating correctly with full hydraulic advantage. If necessary, bleed the brakes as described in this chapter.

14

Removal/Installation
(Caliper Will Not Be Disassembled)

If the brake caliper is to be completely removed but not disassembled, perform this procedure. If the caliper will be disassembled, refer to *Caliper Removal/Piston Removal* in this section.

If the caliper is being only partially removed, it is not be necessary to disconnect the brake line from the caliper. A wooden or plastic spacer block should be inserted in the caliper between the brake pads to keep the brake pads and piston in place.

NOTE
The spacer block prevents the piston from being forced out of the caliper if the brake lever is squeezed while the caliper is removed from the brake disc. If the brake lever is squeezed, the piston may be forced from its bore. If this happens, the caliper will have to be disassembled then reassembled to properly reseat the piston. Bleeding the system will also be required.

1. Remove the front wheel(s) as described in Chapter Twelve.
2. If the caliper is to be completely removed from the vehicle, loosen the brake hose fitting before removing the caliper.
3. Remove the brake caliper mounting bolts and pull the caliper assembly from the brake disc (rotor).
4. Remove the 2 hanger pins (A, **Figure 10**) and brake pads (B, **Figure 10**). New brake pads should be installed if the pads are contaminated with brake fluid.

NOTE
Prepare a container to catch the brake fluid released in Step 5.

5. Hold the brake hose fitting and turn the caliper to remove it from the brake hose.
6. Place the end of the brake hose in a container to prevent brake fluid from dripping onto the vehicle.
7. Place the caliper in a plastic bag and tie the bag closed. Remove the pads so the brake fluid cannot run down the side of the caliper and contaminate the pads.
8. Install the caliper by reversing these steps, noting the following.
9A. If the caliper was removed from the vehicle:
  a. Remove the caliper from the bag and install the brake pads. Make sure the brake pads are not contaminated with brake fluid.
  b. Attach the brake hose fitting to the caliper handtight.
  c. Slide the caliper into position on the brake disc.
  d. Install the caliper mounting bolt and tighten to the torque specification in **Table 2**.
  e. Tighten the brake hose fitting securely.

  f. Refill the master cylinder and bleed the brakes as described in this chapter.
9B. If the caliper was only partially removed from the vehicle:
  a. Remove the spacer block from between the brake pads.
  b. Slide the caliper into position over the brake disc.
  c. Install the caliper mounting bolts and tighten to the torque specification in **Table 2**.
10. Operate the brake lever a few times to seat the pads against the brake disc.

WARNING
Do not ride the vehicle until you are sure that the brakes are operating correctly with full hydraulic advantage. If necessary, bleed the brakes as described in this chapter.

Caliper Removal/Piston Removal (Caliper Will Be Disassembled)

If the caliper is to be completely disassembled, force from inside the caliper will be required to push the piston from the caliper. This force can be supplied by hydraulic pressure from the brake system itself, or from compressed air. If you are going to use brake system hydraulic pressure, you must do so before disconnecting the brake hose fitting from the caliper. The following procedure describes how to remove the piston while the brake hose is still attached.
1. Remove the brake pads as described in this chapter.
2. Operate the brake lever to force the piston from the caliper bore.

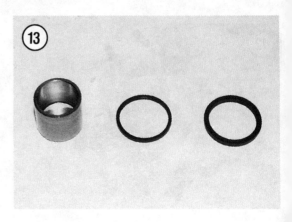

NOTE
If the piston will not come out, you may have to use compressed air. Refer to Disassembly in this chapter.

3. Support the caliper and loosen the attached brake hose fitting. After the hose fitting is loosened, hold the hose and turn the caliper to remove it from the brake hose. Place the end of the brake hose in a container to prevent brake fluid from dripping onto the vehicle.

4. Take the caliper to a workbench for further disassembly.

Disassembly

1. Remove the caliper as described in this chapter.

NOTE
If you have removed the piston, proceed to Step 3.

WARNING
Considerable force is required to force the caliper piston from its bore. Do not try to cushion the piston with your fingers, as injury could result.

2. Cushion the piston with a shop rag. Do not place your hand or fingers in the piston area.

3. Apply compressed air through the brake line port to force the piston out.

4. Remove the dust seal and piston seal from the caliper bore. Do not damage the bore.

5. Remove the bleed valve from the caliper.

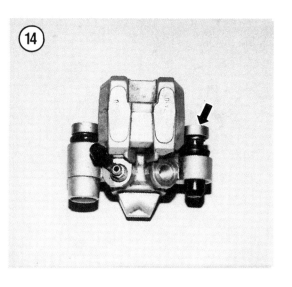

Inspection

1. Clean the caliper housing and dry thoroughly. Clean the dust and piston seal grooves with a soft-faced tool to avoid damaging the bore.

2. Discard the caliper seals. The seals should be replaced whenever the caliper is disassembled.

3. Clean the piston in clean DOT 3 brake fluid.

4. Inspect the piston and the caliper piston bore for deep scratches or other wear marks. Do not hone the piston bore. Replace the caliper if questionable.

5. Clean the bleed valve with compressed air. Check the valve threads for damage. Replace the dust cap if missing or damaged.

6. Measure the thickness of each brake pad and compare to the specification listed in **Table 3**. If the pad thickness is equal to or less than the wear limit, replace all 4 brake pads at the same time.

Assembly

Install a new caliper piston seal and dust seal (**Figure 13**) during reassembly.

NOTE
Use new, DOT 3 brake fluid when brake fluid is called for in the following steps.

1. Soak the piston seal (**Figure 13**) in brake fluid for approximately 5 minutes.

2. Coat the caliper bore lightly with brake fluid.

3. Install the new piston seal into the caliper bore groove.

4. Install the new dust seal into the caliper bore groove.

5. Wipe the piston O.D. lightly with brake fluid.

6. Insert the piston into the caliper bore.

7. Push the piston all the way into the bore.

8. Install and tighten the bleed screw.

9. Install the brake pads as described in this chapter.

14

Caliper Bracket
Removal/Inspection/Installation

1. Remove the brake caliper as described in this chapter.

2. Remove the caliper bracket mounting bolts (4, **Figure 9**) and remove the caliper bracket (**Figure 14**).

3. Inspect the bracket for cracks or other damage.

4. Install by reversing these steps. Apply a thin coat of PBC (Poly Butyl Cuprysil) grease (or equivalent) to sides of the caliper bracket mounting bolts (4, **Figure 9**). Be sure to install the dust cover and boot over the caliper mounting bolts.

> *CAUTION*
> *PBC grease is a special high-tempera-ture, water-resistant grease that can be used in braking systems. Do not use any other kind of lubricant as it may thin out and contaminate the brake pads.*

FRONT BRAKE CALIPER
(1988-ON)

Refer to **Figure 15** when replacing the front brake pads or servicing the front brake caliper. This caliper is also used for the brake on the rearmost axle of 6-wheel models.

Brake Pad Inspection

Measure brake pad wear with the brake caliper installed on the vehicle as follows.

1. Remove the front wheels as described in Chapter Twelve.

2. Measure the distance from the disc surface to the back of the pad's friction material. Replace the brake pads if the friction material thickness is equal to or less than the service limit specification in **Table 3**.

3. Install the front wheels as described in Chapter Twelve, or replace the brake pads as described in the following section.

Front Brake Pad Replacement

There is no recommended time interval for chang-ing the friction pads in the front brakes. Pad wear depends greatly on riding habits and conditions.

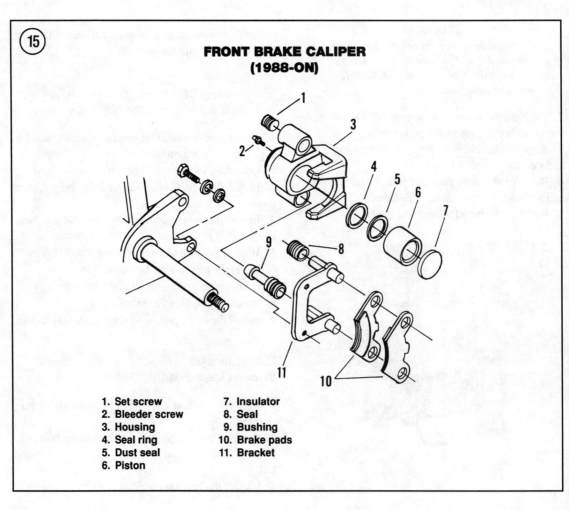

FRONT BRAKE CALIPER (1988-ON)

1. Set screw
2. Bleeder screw
3. Housing
4. Seal ring
5. Dust seal
6. Piston
7. Insulator
8. Seal
9. Bushing
10. Brake pads
11. Bracket

To maintain an even brake pressure, always replace pads in the calipers for both front wheels at the same time.

1. Read the information listed under *Hydraulic Brakes* in this chapter.

2. Remove the front wheel as described in Chapter Twelve.

3. Remove the brake caliper mounting bolts, then move the caliper away from the brake disc.

4. Remove the set screw (1, **Figure 15**).

5. Push the mounting bracket toward the piston and remove the brake pads.

6. Check the condition of the brake rotor (disc). If it requires removal, refer to Chapter Ten or Chapter Twelve to remove the front wheel hub.

7. Measure the thickness of each brake pad. Replace the brake pads if the thickness of any one pad is less than the service limit in **Table 3**. Replace brake pads as a set.

8. Inspect the brake pads for uneven wear, damage or grease contamination. Replace the pads as a set, if necessary.

9. Check the end of the piston for fluid leakage. If the seal is damaged and/or if there is fluid leakage, overhaul the brake caliper as described in this chapter.

10. To make room for the new pads, push the piston back into the caliper. This will force brake fluid to backup through the hose into the master cylinder reservoir. To prevent the reservoir from overflowing, it may be necessary to remove some of the brake fluid as follows:

   a. Clean the top of the master cylinder of all dirt.

   b. Remove the cover from the master cylinder.

   c. Temporarily install the inside brake pad into the caliper and slowly push the piston back into the caliper.

WARNING
Brake fluid is poisonous. Do not siphon with your mouth.

   d. Check the reservoir frequently to make sure brake fluid does not overflow. Siphon fluid from the reservoir, if necessary, before it overflows.

   e. The caliper piston should move freely in the caliper. If it does not, the caliper should be removed and overhauled as described in this chapter.

   f. Push the caliper piston in all the way to allow room for the new pads.

11. Install the caliper and tighten the retaining bolts to the torque listed in **Table 2**.

12. Repeat the procedure for the other front brake caliper.

WARNING
Use new brake fluid clearly marked DOT 3 from a sealed container.

13. Pull and release the brake lever a few times to seat the pads against each disc, then recheck the brake fluid level in the reservoir. If necessary, add fresh DOT 3 brake fluid.

14. Install the cover on the master cylinder reservoir and tighten the cover screws securely.

15. Install the front wheels as described in Chapter Twelve.

WARNING
Do not ride the vehicle until you are sure that the brakes are operating correctly with full hydraulic advantage. If necessary, bleed the brakes as described in this chapter.

**Removal/Installation
(Caliper Will Not Be Disassembled)**

If the brake caliper is to be completely removed but not disassembled, perform this procedure. If the caliper will be disassembled, refer to *Caliper Removal/Piston Removal* in this section.

If the caliper is being only partially removed, it is not necessary to disconnect the brake line from the caliper. A wooden or plastic spacer block should be inserted in the caliper between the brake pads to keep the brake pads and piston in place.

NOTE
The spacer block prevents the piston from being forced out of the caliper if the brake lever is squeezed while the caliper is removed from the brake disc. If the brake lever is squeezed, the piston may be forced from its bore. If this happens, the caliper must be disassembled then reassembled to properly reseat the piston. Bleeding the system will also be required.

1. Remove the front wheel(s) as described in Chapter Twelve.

14

2. If the caliper is to be completely removed from the vehicle, loosen the brake hose fitting before removing the caliper.

3. Remove the brake caliper mounting bolts and pull the caliper assembly from the brake disc (rotor).

4. Remove the two hanger pins (A, **Figure 10**) and brake pads (B, **Figure 10**). Replace the brake pads if the pads are contaminated with brake fluid.

> *NOTE*
> *Prepare a container for catching the brake fluid released in Step 5.*

5. Hold the brake hose fitting and turn the caliper to remove it from the brake hose.

6. Place the end of the brake hose in a container to prevent brake fluid from dripping onto the vehicle.

7. Place the caliper in a plastic bag and tie the bag closed. Remove the pads so the brake fluid cannot run down the side of the caliper and contaminate the pads.

8. Install the caliper by reversing these steps, noting the following.

9A. If the caliper was removed from the vehicle:
   a. Remove the caliper from the bag and install the brake pads. Make sure the brake pads are not contaminated with brake fluid.
   b. Attach the brake hose fitting to the caliper hand-tight.
   c. Slide the caliper into position on the brake disc.
   d. Install the caliper mounting bolt and tighten to the torque specification in **Table 2**.
   e. Tighten the brake hose fitting securely.
   f. Refill the master cylinder and bleed the brakes as described in this chapter.

9B. If the caliper was only partially removed from the vehicle:
   a. Remove the spacer block from between the brake pads.
   b. Slide the caliper into position over the brake disc.
   c. Install the caliper mounting bolts and tighten to the torque specification in **Table 2**.

10. Operate the brake lever a few times to seat the pads against the brake disc.

> *WARNING*
> *Do not ride the vehicle until you are sure that the brakes are operating correctly with full hydraulic advantage. If neces-*

sary, bleed the brakes as described in this chapter.

Caliper Removal/Piston Removal (Caliper Will Be Disassembled)

If the caliper is to be completely disassembled, force from inside the caliper will be required to push the piston from the caliper. This force can be supplied by hydraulic pressure from the brake system itself, or from compressed air. If you are going to use brake system hydraulic pressure, you must do so before disconnecting the brake hose from the caliper. The following procedure describes how to remove the piston while the brake hose is still attached.

1. Remove the brake pads as described in this chapter.

2. Operate the brake lever to force the piston from the caliper bore.

> *NOTE*
> *If the piston will not come out, use compressed air to remove it. Refer to Disassembly in this chapter.*

3. Support the caliper and loosen the attached brake hose fitting. After the hose fitting is loosened, hold the hose and turn the caliper to remove it from the brake hose. Place the end of the brake hose in a container to prevent brake fluid from dripping onto the vehicle.

4. Take the caliper to a workbench for further disassembly.

Disassembly

1. Remove the caliper as described in this chapter.

> *WARNING*
> *Considerable force is required to force the piston from the caliper bore. Do not try to cushion the piston with your fingers, as injury could result.*

2. Cushion the caliper piston with a shop rag, making sure to keep your fingers and hand away from the piston area. Apply compressed air through the brake line port to remove the piston.

3. Remove the dust seal and piston seal from the inside of the cylinder.

4. If necessary, remove the support bracket from the caliper.

5. Remove the bleed valve and its cover from the caliper.

Inspection

1. Clean the caliper housing. Remove stubborn dirt with a soft brush, but do not brush the cylinder bore as this may damage it. Clean the dust and piston seal grooves with a plastic tipped tool so that you do not damage them or the cylinder bore. Clean the caliper in hot soapy water and rinse in clear, cold water. Dry with compressed air.

2. Clean the piston with clean DOT 3 brake fluid.

3. Check the piston and cylinder bore for deep scratches or other obvious wear marks. Do not hone the cylinder. If the piston or cylinder is damaged, replace the caliper assembly.

4. Clean the bleed valve with compressed air. Check the valve threads for damage. Replace the dust cap if missing or damaged.

5. Clean and check the threads in the housing for damage.

6. Check the friction boot and dust cover. If swollen, cracked or worn, the entire brake caliper may have to be replaced.

7. Check the support bracket shafts for excessive wear, damage or uneven wear (steps). The shafts must be in good condition for the caliper to slide back and forth. Remove all grease residue from the bracket. If the support bracket is damaged, the entire brake caliper will have to be replaced.

8. Measure the thickness of each brake pad and compare to the specification listed in **Table 3**. If the pad thickness is less than the wear limit, install new pads.

9. Inspect the brake pads for uneven wear, damage or grease contamination. Replace the pads as a set, if necessary.

10. Replace the piston seal and dust seal as a set.

Assembly

> *NOTE*
> *Use only new, DOT 3 brake fluid when brake fluid is called for in the following steps.*

1. Soak the piston seal and dust seal in brake fluid for approximately 5 minutes.

2. Lightly coat the piston and cylinder bore with brake fluid.

3. Install a new piston seal into the second groove in the cylinder bore.

4. Install a new dust seal into the front groove in the cylinder bore.

> *NOTE*
> *Check that both seals fit squarely into their respective cylinder bore grooves. If a seal is not installed properly, the caliper assembly will leak and braking performance will be reduced.*

5. Install the piston—closed end first—into the cylinder bore.

6. If the support bracket was removed, perform the following:

   a. Apply a thin coat of PBC (Poly Butyl Cuprysil) grease or equivalent to the caliper bracket shafts.

> *CAUTION*
> *PBC grease is a special high temperature, water-resistant grease that can be used in braking systems. Do not use any other kind of lubricant as it may thin out and contaminate the brake pads.*

   b. Slide the support bracket shafts into the caliper. Slide the bracket back and forth, without removing it, to distribute the grease and to check the shafts for binding. The bracket must move smoothly; if any binding is noted, remove the bracket and inspect the shafts for damage. Wipe off any excess grease from the outside of the caliper or bracket.

7. If necessary, install the bleed screw and its dust cover. Tighten securely.

8. Install the brake caliper assembly and brake pads as described in this chapter.

MECHANICAL REAR BRAKE CALIPER (1985-1987 MODELS WITH REAR WHEEL DRIVE ONLY)

Disassembly/Inspection/Assembly

The rear brake caliper is attached to the transmission housing and surrounds the brake disc located on the brake shaft.

14

1. Remove the two bolts that attach the caliper housing to the transmission housing.

2. Remove the disc from the transmission brake shaft.

3. Remove the three caliper assembly screws.

4. Detach the brake cable from the operating lever.

5. Remove the adjusting ratchet from the caliper.

6. Use a screwdriver between the brake pads to push the pad from the housing.

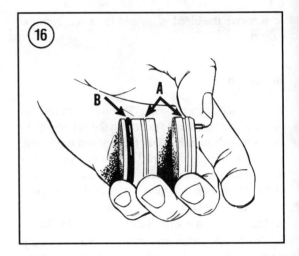

> *NOTE*
> *The brake pads may be corroded and stuck in the housing. Be careful not to damage the assembly when removing the brake pads.*

7. Inspect the brake pads for wear and corrosion. Install new pads if worn to the indicator groove (A, **Figure 16**) near the base of the brake pad.

8. Remove the O-ring (B, **Figure 16**) from the movable brake pad, then polish the movable pad and the bore in the caliper with light abrasive cloth.

9. Clean the caliper housing and the brake pad thoroughly, then install the O-ring (B, **Figure 16**).

10. Apply a thin coat of PBC (Poly Butyl Cuprysil) grease or equivalent to the housing bore, O-ring and sides of the brake pads.

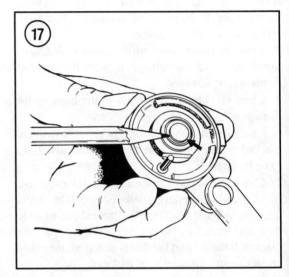

> *CAUTION*
> *PBC grease is a special high-temperature, water-resistant grease that can be used in braking systems. Do not use any other kind of lubricant as it may thin out and contaminate the brake pads.*

11. Reinstall the brake pads in the housing.

12. Rotate the ratchet clockwise until it is flush (**Figure 17**) with the housing.

13. Reattach the cable to the housing and ratchet arm.

14. Install the brake pads and the adjuster unit into the housing as an assembly. Refer to **Figure 18**.

15. Install cover and tighten the three assembly screws.

16. Reinstall the brake caliper and disc. Install and tighten the 2 attaching screws.

17. Adjust the brake cable by turning the adjuster located at the lever mounted on the right handlebar.

18. Apply the brake several times, then readjust the cable as necessary to obtain slight freeplay a the handlebar lever.

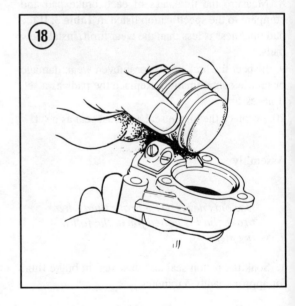

HYDRAULIC REAR CALIPER
(1987 MODELS WITH ALL-WHEEL DRIVE AND ALL 1988 MODELS)

The rear wheel brake on 1987 models with all wheel drive (AWD) and all 1988 models is equipped with a hydraulic caliper that operates against the brake disc on the transmission.

Brake Pad Inspection

Measure brake pad wear with the brake caliper installed on the vehicle. Replace the brake pads if the friction material thickness is equal to or less than the service limit specification in **Table 3**.

Brake Pad Replacement

There is no recommended time interval for changing the friction pads in the front brakes. Pad wear depends greatly on riding habits and conditions. Always replace both pads at the same time.

1. Remove the brake caliper mounting bolts, then move the caliper away from the brake disc.
2. Check the condition of the brake rotor (disc). Install a new disc if it is damaged.
3. Remove the screw (**Figure 19**) and retainer plate (**Figure 20**).
4. Push the pad hanger pins (**Figure 21**) from the housing and remove the brake pads.
5. Inspect the brake pads for uneven wear, damage or grease contamination. Measure the thickness of each brake pad. Replace the brake pads if the thickness of any one pad is less than the service limit in **Table 3**. Replace brake pads as a set.
6. Check the end of the piston (**Figure 22**) for fluid leakage. If the seal is damaged as indicated by fluid leakage, overhaul the brake caliper as described in this chapter.
7. To make room for the new pads, push the piston back into the caliper. This will force brake fluid to backup through the hose into the master cylinder reservoir. To prevent the reservoir from overflowing, it may be necessary to remove some of the brake fluid.
8. Push the caliper piston in all the way to allow room for the new pads. The caliper piston should move freely in the caliper. If it does not, overhaul the caliper as described in this chapter.

14

9. Position new brake pads in the caliper and install the hanger pins.

10. Install the retainer plate (**Figure 20**) and screw (**Figure 19**).

11. Separate the brake pads and install the caliper over the brake disc.

12. Tighten the retaining screws to the torque listed in **Table 2**.

13. Pull and release the brake lever a few times to seat the pads against the disc.

WARNING
Use new brake fluid clearly marked DOT 3 from a sealed container.

14. Recheck the brake fluid level in the reservoir. If necessary, add fresh DOT 3 brake fluid.

WARNING
Do not ride the vehicle until you are sure the brakes are operating correctly with full hydraulic advantage. If necessary, bleed the brakes as described in this chapter.

Removal/Installation
(Caliper Will Not Be Disassembled)

If the brake caliper is to be completely removed but not disassembled, perform this procedure. If the caliper will be disassembled, refer to *Caliper Removal/Piston Removal* in this section.

If the caliper is being only partially removed, it will not be necessary to disconnect the brake line from the caliper. Insert a wooden or plastic spacer block between the brake pads to keep the brake pads in place.

NOTE
The spacer block prevents the piston from being forced out of the caliper if the brake lever is squeezed while the caliper is removed from the brake disc. If the piston is forced from its bore, the caliper must be disassembled then reassembled to properly reseat the piston. Bleeding the system will also be required.

1. Remove any panels that interfere with the removal of the brake caliper.

2. If the caliper is to be completely removed from the vehicle, loosen the brake hose fitting before removing the caliper.

3. Remove the brake caliper mounting bolts and pull the caliper assembly from the brake disc (rotor).

NOTE
Prepare a container for catching the brake fluid released in Step 4.

4. Hold the brake hose fitting and turn the caliper to remove it from the brake hose.

5. Place the end of the brake hose in a container to prevent brake fluid from dripping onto the vehicle.

6. Plug the opening for the brake hose fitting to keep the fluid inside the caliper and to keep dirt out.

7. If the brake pads are to be reused, remove the brake pads or protect the brake pads from becoming covered with brake fluid. New brake pads must be installed if the pads are contaminated with brake fluid.

8. Install the caliper by reversing these steps, while noting the following.

9A. If the caliper was removed from the vehicle:

   a. Make sure the brake pads are not contaminated with brake fluid.

   b. Attach the brake hose fitting to the caliper hand-tight.

   c. Slide the caliper into position on the brake disc.

   d. Install the caliper mounting bolts and tighten to the torque specification in **Table 2**.

   e. Tighten the brake hose fitting securely.

   f. Refill the master cylinder and bleed the brakes as described in this chapter.

9B. If the caliper was only partially removed from the vehicle:

a. Remove the spacer block from between the brake pads.

b. Slide the caliper into position over the brake disc.

c. Install the caliper mounting bolts and tighten to the torque specification in **Table 2**.

10. Operate the brake lever a few times to seat the pads against the brake disc.

WARNING
Do not ride the vehicle until you are sure that the brakes are operating correctly with full hydraulic advantage. If necessary, bleed the brakes as described in this chapter.

Caliper Removal/Piston Removal (Caliper Will Be Disassembled)

If the caliper is to be completely disassembled, force from inside the caliper is required to push the piston from the caliper. This force can be supplied by hydraulic pressure from the brake system itself, or from compressed air. If you are going to use brake system hydraulic pressure, you must do so before disconnecting the brake hose from the caliper. The following procedure describes how to remove the piston while the brake hose is still attached.

1. Remove the brake pads as described in this chapter.

2. Operate the brake lever about 3 times to force the piston from the caliper bore.

NOTE
If the piston will not come out, remove it using compressed air. Refer to Disassembly in this chapter.

3. Support the caliper and loosen the attached brake hose fitting. After the hose fitting is loosened, hold the hose and turn the caliper to remove it from the brake hose. Place the end of the brake hose in a container to prevent brake fluid from dripping onto the vehicle.

4. Take the caliper to a workbench for further disassembly.

Disassembly

1. Remove the caliper as described in this chapter.

WARNING
Considerable force is required to force the piston from the caliper bore. Do not try to cushion the piston with your fingers, as injury could result.

2. Cushion the caliper piston with a shop rag, making sure to keep your fingers and hand away from the piston area. Apply compressed air through the brake line port to remove the piston.

CAUTION
Do not remove the seal rings unless new rings are available to be installed. Removing the rings from grooves in the caliper housing will damage even new rings. If the seals are removed, be extremely careful not to scratch or nick the bore. If the bore is scratched or nicked, it may be impossible to seal properly the brake.

NOTE
A suitably shaped seal pick can be used to remove the seal rings. A wire paper clip or similar stiff wire can also be bent to remove the seal rings.

3. Use an appropriate tool to remove the 2 seal rings from the caliper bore. Refer to **Figure 23**.

4. Remove the bleed valve and its cover from the caliper.

Inspection

1. Clean the caliper housing. Remove stubborn dirt with a soft brush, but do not brush the cylinder bore as this may damage it. Clean the dust and piston seal grooves with a plastic tipped tool so that you do not damage them or the cylinder bore. Clean the caliper in hot soapy water and rinse in clear, cold water. Dry with compressed air.

2. Clean the piston (**Figure 24**) with clean DOT 3 brake fluid.

3. Check the piston and cylinder bore for deep scratches or other obvious wear marks. Do not hone the cylinder. If the piston or cylinder is damaged, replace the caliper assembly.

4. Clean the bleed valve with compressed air. Check the valve threads for damage. Replace the dust cap if missing or damaged.

5. Clean and check the threads in caliper housing for damage.

14

6. Check the pad hanger pins (**Figure 21**) for excessive wear, damage or uneven wear (steps). The pins must be clean and in good condition for proper operation.

7. Measure the thickness of each brake pad and compare to the specification listed in **Table 3**. If the pad thickness is less than the wear limit, install new pads.

8. Inspect the brake pads for uneven wear, damage or grease contamination. Replace the pads as a set, if necessary.

9. Replace both of the piston seals as a set.

Assembly

NOTE
Use only new, DOT 3 brake fluid when brake fluid is called for in the following steps.

1. Soak the piston seals in brake fluid for approximately 5 minutes.

2. Coat the piston and cylinder bore with brake fluid.

3. Install the larger piston seal into the second (farthest) groove in the cylinder bore.

4. Install smaller seal into the front groove in the cylinder bore.

NOTE
Make certain both seals fit squarely into their respective cylinder bore grooves. If a seal is not installed properly, the seals will be ruined when the piston is installed, the caliper assembly will leak and braking performance will be reduced.

5. Install the piston in the cylinder bore with the tapered end (**Figure 24**) first.

6. Install the bleed screw and its dust cover.

7. Install the brake caliper assembly and brake pads as described in this chapter.

HYDRAULIC REAR BRAKE CALIPER (ALL 1989-ON MODELS)

Brake Pad Inspection

Measure brake pad wear with the brake caliper installed on the vehicle. Replace the brake pads if the friction material thickness is equal to or less than the service limit specification in **Table 3**.

Brake Pad Replacement

There is no recommended time interval for changing the friction pads in the front brakes. Pad wear depends greatly on riding habits and conditions. Always replace both pads at the same time.

1. Disconnect the foot brake linkage.

2. Remove the brake caliper mounting bolts, then move the caliper away from the brake disc.

3. Check the condition of the brake rotor (disc). Install a new disc if it is damaged.

4. Push the pad hanger pins (**Figure 25**) from the housing and remove the brake pads.

5. Inspect the brake pads (**Figure 26**) for uneven wear, damage or grease contamination. Measure the thickness of each brake pad. Replace the brake pads if the thickness of any one pad is less than the service limit in **Table 3**. Replace brake pads as a set.

6. Check the end of the piston for fluid leakage. If leaking, overhaul the brake caliper as described in this chapter.

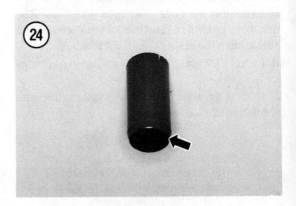

7. To make room for the new pads, push the piston back into the caliper. This will force brake fluid to backup through the hose into the master cylinder reservoir. To prevent the reservoir from overflowing, it may be necessary to remove some of the brake fluid.

8. Push the caliper piston in all the way to allow room for the new pads. The caliper piston should move freely in the caliper. If it does not, overhaul the caliper as described in this chapter.

9. Position new brake pads in the caliper and install the hanger pins.

10. Separate the brake pads and install over the brake disc.

11. Tighten the retaining screws to the torque listed in **Table 2**.

12. Reattach the foot brake linkage.

13. Operate the brake lever and pedal a few times to seat the pads against the disc.

> *WARNING*
> *Use new brake fluid clearly marked DOT 3 from a sealed container.*

14. Recheck the brake fluid level in the reservoir. If necessary, add fresh DOT 3 brake fluid.

> *WARNING*
> *Do not ride the vehicle until you are sure that the brakes are operating correctly with full hydraulic advantage. If necessary, bleed the brakes as described in this chapter.*

Removal/Installation (Caliper Will Not Be Disassembled)

If the brake caliper is to be completely removed but not disassembled, perform this procedure. If the caliper will be disassembled, refer to *Caliper Removal/Piston Removal* in this section.

If the caliper is being only partially removed, it is not necessary to disconnect the brake line from the caliper. Insert a wooden or plastic spacer block between the brake pads to keep the brake pads in place.

> *NOTE*
> *The spacer block prevents the piston from being forced out of the caliper if the brake lever is squeezed while the caliper is removed from the brake disc. If the piston is forced from its bore, the caliper must be disassembled then reassembled to properly reseat the piston. Bleeding the system will also be required.*

1. Remove any panels that interfere with the removal of the brake caliper.

2. If the caliper is to be completely removed from the vehicle, loosen the brake hose fitting to the caliper before removing the caliper.

3. Disconnect the foot brake linkage.

4. Remove the brake caliper mounting bolts and pull the caliper assembly from the brake disc (rotor).

> *NOTE*
> *Prepare a container for catching the brake fluid released in Step 5.*

5. Hold the brake hose fitting and turn the caliper to remove it from the brake hose.

6. Place the end of the brake hose in a container to prevent brake fluid from dripping onto the vehicle.

7. Plug the opening for the brake hose fitting to keep the fluid inside the caliper and to keep dirt out.

8. If the brake pads are to be reused, remove the brake pads or carefully protect the brake pads from becoming covered with brake fluid. Replace the brake pads if the pads are contaminated with brake fluid.

9. Install the caliper by reversing these steps, noting the following.

10A. If the caliper was removed from the vehicle:

    a. Make sure the brake pads are not contaminated with brake fluid.

    b. Attach the brake hose fitting to the caliper hand-tight.

    c. Slide the caliper into position on the brake disc.

14

(26)

   d. Install the caliper mounting bolts and tighten to the torque specification in **Table 2**.

   e. Tighten the brake hose fitting securely.

   f. Refill the master cylinder and bleed the brakes as described in this chapter.

10B. If the caliper was only partially removed from the vehicle:

   a. Remove the spacer block from between the brake pads.

   b. Slide the caliper into position over the brake disc.

   c. Install the caliper mounting bolts and tighten to the torque specification in **Table 2**.

11. Reattach the foot brake linkage.

12. Operate the brake lever and pedal a few times to seat the pads against the brake disc.

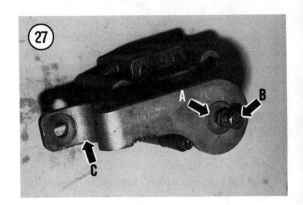

> *WARNING*
> *Do not ride the vehicle until you are sure that the brakes are operating correctly with full hydraulic advantage. If necessary, bleed the brakes as described in this chapter.*

Caliper Removal/Piston Removal (Caliper Will Be Disassembled)

If the caliper is to be completely disassembled, force from inside the caliper can be used to push the piston from the caliper. This force can be supplied by hydraulic pressure from the brake system itself, or by compressed air. If you are going to use brake system hydraulic pressure, you must do so before disconnecting the brake hose fitting from the caliper. The following procedure describes how to remove the piston while the brake hose is still attached.

1. Remove the brake pads as described in this chapter.

2. Operate the brake lever about 3 times to force the piston from the caliper bore.

> *NOTE*
> *If the piston will not come out, remove it using compressed air. Refer to **Disassembly** in this chapter.*

3. Support the caliper and loosen the attached brake hose fitting. After the hose fitting is loosened, hold the hose and turn the caliper to remove it from the brake hose. Place the end of the brake hose in a

container to prevent brake fluid from dripping onto the vehicle.

4. Take the caliper to a workbench for further disassembly.

Disassembly

1. Remove the caliper as described in this chapter.

> *WARNING*
> *Considerable force is required to force the piston from the caliper bore. Do not try to cushion the piston with your fingers, as injury could result.*

2. Cushion the caliper piston with a shop rag, making sure to keep your fingers and hand away from the piston area. Apply compressed air through the brake line port to remove the piston.

3. Loosen the locknut (A, **Figure 27**), remove the adjusting screw (B, **Figure 27**), then remove the lever (C, **Figure 27**).

4. Remove the two screws (**Figure 28**), then remove the stationary ramp and movable ramp (**Figure 29**).

5. Remove the brake apply pin and spring (**Figure 30**).

> *CAUTION*
> *Do not remove the seal rings unless new rings are available. Removing the rings from grooves in the caliper housing will damage even new rings. If the seals are removed, be extremely careful not to scratch or nick the bore. If the bore is scratched or nicked, it may be impossible to seal properly the brake.*

> *NOTE*
> *A suitably shaped seal pick can be used to remove the seal rings. A wire paper clip or similar stiff wire can also be bent to remove the seal rings.*

6. Use an appropriate tool to remove the 2 seal rings from each of the caliper bores. Refer to **Figure 31** and **Figure 32**.

7. Remove the bleed valve and its cover from the caliper.

Inspection

1. Clean the caliper housing. Remove stubborn dirt with a soft brush, but do not brush the cylinder bore as this may damage it. Clean the dust and piston seal grooves with a plastic tipped tool so that you do not damage them or the cylinder bore. Clean the caliper in hot soapy water and rinse in clear, cold water. Dry with compressed air.

2. Clean the piston (**Figure 33**) with clean DOT 3 brake fluid.

3. Check the piston and cylinder bore for deep scratches or other obvious wear marks. Do not hone the cylinder. If the piston or cylinder is damaged, replace the caliper assembly.

4. Clean the bleed valve with compressed air. Check the valve threads for damage. Replace the dust cap if missing or damaged.

5. Clean and check the threads in caliper housing for damage.

6. Check the pad hanger pins (**Figure 25**) for excessive wear, damage or uneven wear (steps). The pins must be clean and in good condition for proper operation.

14

7. Measure the thickness of each brake pad (**Figure 26**) and compare to the specification listed in **Table 3**. If the pad thickness is less than the wear limit, install new pads.

8. Inspect the brake pads for uneven wear, damage or grease contamination. Replace the pads as a set, if necessary.

9. Replace both of the piston seals as a set.

Assembly

NOTE
Use only new, DOT 3 brake fluid when brake fluid is called for in the following steps.

1. Soak the piston seals in brake fluid for approximately 5 minutes.

2. Coat the piston and cylinder bore with brake fluid.

3. Install the thicker piston seal into the second (farthest) groove in the cylinder bore. Refer to **Figure 31**.

4. Install thinner seal into the outside groove in the cylinder bore. Refer to **Figure 31**.

5. Install the thicker seal ring into the inside groove of the bore for the pedal piston. Refer to **Figure 32**.

6. Install the thinner seal ring in the outside groove of the bore for the pedal piston. Refer to **Figure 32**.

NOTE
*Make sure all 4 seals (**Figure 31** and **Figure 32**) fit squarely into their respective cylinder bore grooves. If a seal is not installed properly, the seals will be ruined when the piston is installed, the caliper assembly will leak and braking performance will be reduced.*

7. Coat the piston (**Figure 33**) with clean DOT 3 brake fluid and install the piston in the cylinder bore with the tapered and open end first.

8. Coat the brake apply pin (**Figure 30**) with clean DOT 3 brake fluid and install the pin and spring for the pedal.

9. Check the condition of the seal in the stationary ramp (**Figure 34**). If damaged, install a new seal.

10. Inspect the condition of the movable ramp (**Figure 35**) and if not damaged, install inside the stationary ramp.

NOTE
*In Step 11, the longer side of the movable ramp (**Figure 35**) will point toward the bleeder valve.*

11. Install the ramps with the flats of the movable ramp (**Figure 35**) perpendicular (90°) to the stationary ramp mounting holes (**Figure 34**).

12A. On models without an adjuster screw, install the brake lever (**Figure 36**), retaining washer and screw.

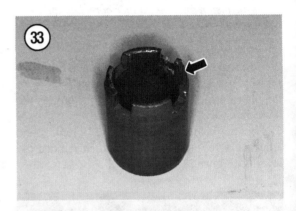

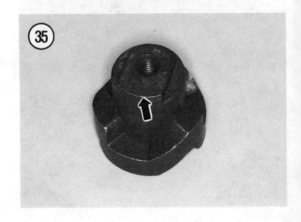

12B. On models with a brake adjuster screw (**Figure 37**), install the brake lever (**Figure 36**), retaining washer, lock nut and adjusting screw (**Figure 37**). Turn the adjuster screw in only far enough to just contact the pedal piston, then tighten the lock nut enough to hold the lever in place. Adjust the brake as described in Step 16 after the brake is installed.

13. Install the bleed screw and its dust cover.

14. Install the brake caliper assembly and brake pads as described in this chapter.

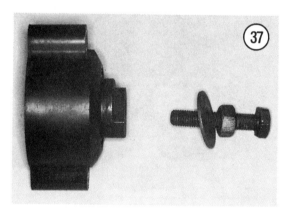

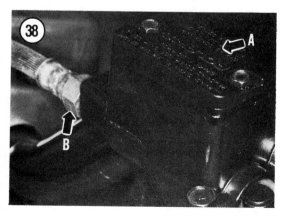

15. Operate the brake several times and check for leaks.

16. If foot pedal travel is excessive, proceed as follows:

   a. Place the transmission in neutral.

   b. Tighten the adjusting screw (**Figure 37**) until the brake pads rub on the disc.

   c. Loosen the adjusting screw (**Figure 37**) approximately 1/2 turn until the disc is free to rotate, then tighten the lock nut.

17. Check the brake fluid level in the handlebar mounted reservoir as described in Chapter Three.

MASTER CYLINDER

The handlebar on early (1987-1988) models passes through the master cylinder. The master cylinder and lever of these early models is clamped to the handlebar with a set screw that enters from the bottom of the master cylinder casting.

The master cylinder on later models is attached to the handlebar with 2 screws and a removable clamp.

Read the information listed under *Hydraulic Brakes* in this chapter before servicing the master cylinder.

Removal/Installation

1. Park the vehicle on level ground and block the wheels so the vehicle cannot roll.

2. Cover the area under the master cylinder to prevent brake fluid from damaging any component that it might contact.

> *CAUTION*
> *If brake fluid should contact any surface, wash the area immediately with soapy water and rinse completely. Brake fluid will damage plastic, painted and plated surfaces.*

3. Remove the master cylinder cover (A, **Figure 38**) and diaphragm.

4. Use a clean syringe to remove the brake fluid from the reservoir. Discard the brake fluid.

5. Detach the brake hose (B, **Figure 38**) from the master cylinder, then seal the brake hose to prevent brake fluid from draining out.

6A. On models without a clamp (1987-1988), it is necessary to remove the grip and interfering switches from the handlebars. Loosen the set screw

14

located under the master cylinder and slide the master cylinder from the handlebar.

6B. On models with the clamp shown in **Figure 39**, remove the two screws and the clamp that attach the master cylinder to the handlebar, then remove the master cylinder.

7. If necessary, service the master cylinder as described in this chapter.

8. Clean the handlebar, master cylinder and clamp mating surfaces.

9A. On early (1987-1988) models, slide the master cylinder onto the handlebar, then install the grip and switches.

9B. On later models with clamp (**Figure 39**), position the master cylinder against the handlebar, then install the two screws and clamp.

10. Move the master cylinder to a position where the brake lever suits your riding position, then tighten the set screw or the two mounting screws securely.

11. Attach the brake hose to the master cylinder and tighten the fitting securely.

12. Refill the master cylinder with DOT 3 brake fluid and bleed the brake as described in this chapter.

> *WARNING*
> *Do not ride the vehicle until the brakes are working properly. Make sure that the brake lever travel is not excessive and that the lever does not feel soft or spongy. If either condition exists, bleed the system again.*

Disassembly

1. Remove the master cylinder as described in this chapter.

2. Remove the brake lever pivot bolt (**Figure 40**) from the master cylinder and remove the brake lever.

3. If not already removed, remove the screws attaching the master cylinder cover, then remove the cover and diaphragm (**Figure 41**).

> *NOTE*
> *If there is brake fluid leaking from the piston bore, the piston cups are worn or damaged. Replace the piston assembly during reassembly.*

4A. On early (1987-1988) models, carefully remove the piston and spring (**Figure 42**) from the master cylinder bore.

4B. On 1989-on models, insert the push rod from special service tool (part No. 2870962) into the opening for the hose fitting as shown in **Figure 43**.

> *CAUTION*
> *Do not remove the seals from the piston (**Figure 42**). The seals are not available separately and will be destroyed by removing from the piston.*

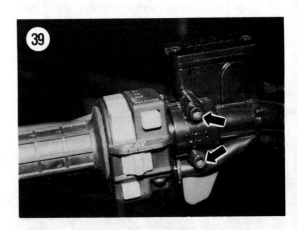

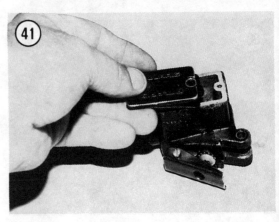

Inspection

Worn or damaged master cylinder components will prevent the master cylinder from building enough pressure to stop the vehicle. Proper brake operation will result in a feel that is firm, solid and sure. Air in the system, internal leakage or external leakage will cause the brake to feel soft, weak and indistinct.

1. Wash the piston and cylinder with clean DOT 3 brake fluid.

> *CAUTION*
> *Do not attempt to remove the seals (**Figure 42**) from the piston. Removal will damage the seals, which are not available separately from the piston.*

2. Install a new return spring (**Figure 42**) if broken, distorted or collapsed.

3. Inspect the piston assembly for the following defects:
   a. Worn, cracked, damaged or swollen seals (**Figure 42**).
   b. Scratched, scored or damaged piston.

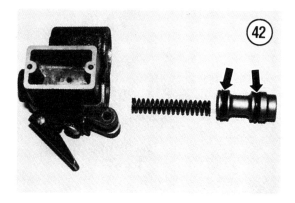

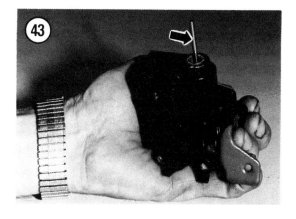

4. Install a new piston and seal assembly if either of the seals or the piston is damaged.

5. Inspect the master cylinder bore. If the bore is corroded, scored or damaged in any way, replace the master cylinder assembly. Do not hone the master cylinder bore to remove scratches or other damage.

6. Check for plugged supply and relief ports in the master cylinder. Clean with compressed air.

> *NOTE*
> *A plugged relief port will cause the pads to drag on the disc.*

7. Check the brake lever and pivot bolt for worn or damaged parts.

8. Check the reservoir cover and diaphragm for damage. Check the diaphragm for cracks or deterioration. Replace damaged parts as required.

9. Check all of the threaded holes in the master cylinder housing. Clean with compressed air. The small screws used to secure the reservoir cover are easily damaged. Check the screw heads and threads for damage and replace or repair if necessary.

Assembly

Use new DOT 3 brake fluid when brake fluid is called for in the following steps.

1. If you are installing a piston repair kit, note the following:
   a. Check the repair kit to make sure that it contains all of the necessary new parts.
   b. Wash the new parts in new brake fluid. It is important to remove all paper and dust from the new parts.

2. Coat the piston assembly and cylinder bore lightly with brake fluid.

> *CAUTION*
> *When installing the piston assembly in Step 3, make sure the primary and secondary seals (cups) do not tear or turn inside out; both seals are slightly larger than the bore.*

3A. On early (1987-1988) models, install the piston and spring as shown in **Figure 42**. Compress the piston into the bore and install the brake lever (**Figure 40**). Push and release the piston a few times to make sure it moves smoothly in the cylinder bore.

3B. On 1989-on models, assemble the piston and related parts as follows:

14

a. Lubricate the piston, seals (A, **Figure 44**) and the special installing tool (B) (part No. 2870962) shown in **Figure 44**.

b. Install the piston in the installing tool. The inner end of the piston and the return spring should be at the undercut end of the installing tool.

c. Install the inner washer at the inside of the master cylinder bore.

d. Slide the special installing tool, piston and spring into the master cylinder bore (**Figure 45**), and push the piston into the bore.

e. Hold the piston in place and remove the special tool.

f. Install the dust seal with its lips toward the outside, then press the seal into place with the end of the special tool that is not under cut. Refer to **Figure 46**.

g. Reinstall the brake lever.

h. Operate the hand lever several times to make sure the lever moves freely with no sign of binding.

BRAKE HOSE REPLACEMENT

Replace the brake hoses if they show signs of wear or damage.

1. Place a container under the brake line.

2A. If the fitting is a banjo bolt, remove the banjo bolt and sealing washers.

2B. To detach a compression fitting, hold the stationary fitting with a wrench and loosen the fitting on the brake hose with another wrench. It may be necessary to hold the brake hose with a wrench. If the hose fitting can not be turned without twisting the hose, it may be necessary to either loosen the other end of the hose first or to turn the component to detach it from the hose.

3. Place the end of the brake hose in a clean container. Operate the brake lever to drain fluid from the master cylinder and brake hose.

> *CAUTION*
> *Dispose of all used brake fluid. Never reuse brake fluid that has been drained from the system. Old fluid contains contaminants that can damage the brake system components.*

4. Install a new brake hose in the reverse order of removal.

5. Install new sealing washers and banjo bolts if necessary.

> *CAUTION*
> *Do not overtighten or crossthread banjo bolts or compression fittings. Overtightening will distort the fitting and may cause leakage.*

6. Tighten the banjo bolts and compression fittings securely.

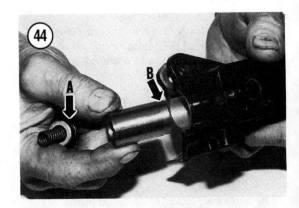

7. Refill the master cylinder with fresh brake fluid clearly marked DOT 3. Bleed the brake as described in this chapter.

WARNING
Do not ride the vehicle until you are sure
that the brakes are operating properly.

BRAKE DISC

Front brake discs are attached to the front hubs. The rear brake disc is located on a splined shaft that exits the right side of the transmission. On some models, the rear brake disc is located on the output shaft, while a separate brake shaft is used on some transmissions.

Inspection

It is not necessary to remove any brake disc to inspect it. Small marks on the disc are not important unless they are cracks. Radial scratches deep enough to snag a fingernail will reduce braking effectiveness and cause the brake pads to wear too quickly. If deep grooves are evident and the brake pads are wearing rapidly, replace the disc.

When servicing the brake discs, do not machine the discs to remove scratches or to compensate for wear or warpage. The discs are thin and grinding will reduce their thickness, causing them to warp quite rapidly. If a disc is warped, the brake pads may be dragging on the disc, causing the disc to overheat. Overheating can also be caused by unequal brake pad pressure on both sides of the disc. The main causes of unequal pad pressure are: the floating caliper is binding on the caliper bracket shafts, thus preventing the caliper from floating (side-to-side) on the disc; the brake caliper piston seal is worn or damaged; the small master cylinder relief port is plugged; and the primary cup on the master cylinder piston is worn or damaged.

1. Support the vehicle with all 4 wheels off the ground.

2. Remove the front wheels as described in Chapter Twelve.

3. Measure the thickness around the disc at several locations with a micrometer. Refer to **Figure 47**. Replace the disc if the thickness varies at different locations around the disc.

4. On the front wheel discs, make sure the disc bolts are tight prior to performing this check. Use a magnetic stand with the dial indicator stem against the brake disc. Turn the hub and measure the runout. If the runout exceeds 0.15 mm (0.006 in.), replace the disc.

5. Clean any rust or corrosion from the disc and wipe the disc clean with lacquer thinner. Never use oil based solvent that may leave an oil residue on the disc and do not touch the disc with fingers after cleaning.

Removal/Installation

1A. To remove the front brake disc:
   a. Remove the non-driven front hub(s) as described in Chapter Twelve.
   b. Remove the driven front hub(s) as described in Chapter Ten.
   c. Remove the screws securing the disc to the wheel and remove the disc.

1B. To remove the rear brake disc:
   a. On All Wheel Drive models, remove the front drive chain guard, chain and sprocket (A, **Figure 48**) as described in Chapter Ten.
   b. Remove the brake caliper assembly (B, **Figure 48**) as described in this chapter.
   c. On models with only rear wheel drive, remove the bolt or snap ring retaining the disc on the splined transmission shaft.

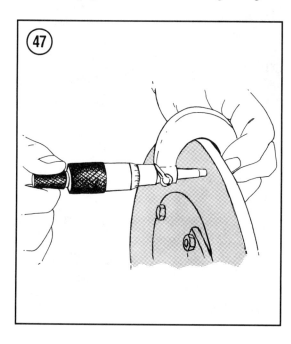

(47)

14

d. Pull the disc from the shaft splines.

2. Install by reversing the removal steps. Tighten the front wheel disc screws to the torque listed in **Table 2**.

BRAKE BLEEDING

This procedure removes air bubbles and pockets of air from the brake fluid. Bleed air from the fluid if the brakes feel spongy, a component has been replaced, a leak in the hydraulic system has been repaired or the brake fluid has been replaced.

NOTE
During this procedure, it is important to check the fluid level in the master cylinder frequently. If the reservoir runs dry, air will enter the system which will require starting over.

1. Locate the brake bleeder valve at each brake caliper. Flip the dust cap from the bleeder valve (**Figure 49**) and wipe off the valve.

2. Bleed the rear caliper first, then bleed each of the front calipers.

3. Connect a length of clear tubing to the bleeder valve on the caliper. Place the other end of the tube into a clean container. Fill the container with enough fresh brake fluid to keep the end submerged. The tube should be long enough so that a loop can be made higher than the bleeder valve to prevent air from being drawn into the caliper during bleeding.

CAUTION
Cover all parts which could become damaged by accidentally spilling brake fluid. Use soapy water to wash any spilled brake fluid immediately and rinse area completely with freshwater.

4. Clean the top of the reservoir cover, then remove the cover and diaphragm. Fill the reservoir to the level listed in **Table 3**. Install the diaphragm and cover to prevent the entry of dirt and moisture.

WARNING
Use brake fluid clearly marked DOT 3 only. Others may vaporize and cause brake failure. Always use the same brand and type. Do not intermix brake fluids, because some brands are not compatible.

NOTE
During this procedure, it is important to check the reservoir fluid level periodically to make sure it does not run dry. If the reservoir should run dry, air will enter the system and the bleeding procedure must be started over.

5. Bleed air from the bleeder valve as follows:
   a. Hold the brake lever in the applied position.
   b. Open the bleeder valve (**Figure 49**) by turning counterclockwise about 1/2 turn. Do not release the brake lever or pedal while the bleeder valve is open.
   c. As the bleeder valve just opens, you will feel the lever loosen a bit as it moves to the limit of its travel.
   d. Tighten the bleeder screw, then release the brake lever. Do not release the brake lever or pedal while the bleeder valve is open.

NOTE
As the brake fluid enters the system, the fluid level in the reservoir will drop. Maintain the correct level specified in

Table 3 to prevent air from being forced into the system.

6. Repeat Step 5 until no more air can be expelled from this bleeder. If you are replacing the fluid, continue until the fluid emerging from the hose is clean.

> *NOTE*
> *If bleeding is difficult, it may be necessary to allow the fluid to stabilize for a few hours. The air in the system will collect and form larger bubbles which must then be bled from the system. Repeat the bleeding procedure when the tiny bubbles in the system settle out.*

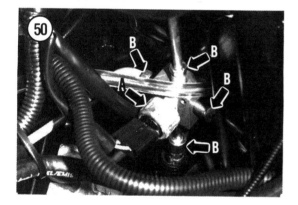

7. Hold the lever in the applied position and tighten the bleeder valve. Remove the bleeder tube and install the bleeder valve dust cap.

8. Check the fluid level in the reservoir and add fluid to the master cylinder reservoir if necessary.

9. Attach the bleeder hose to the next bleeder valve and bleed air from that valve following the procedure beginning with Step 3. Bleeding should begin with the rear caliper, proceed to one of the front calipers, then the other front caliper.

10. Test the feel of the brake lever. It should feel firm and should offer the same resistance each time it's operated.

11. If the brake lever doesn't yet feel solid, allow the fluid in the system to stabilize for a few hours. The air in the system will collect and form larger bubbles which are easier to bleed from the system. Repeat the bleeding procedure.

12. If air continues to enter the system, check for a leak. Check the brake switch (A, **Figure 50**) and all of the fittings for tightness, including those at T-connections (B, **Figure 50**).

> *WARNING*
> *Before riding the vehicle, make certain that the brakes are working correctly by operating the lever. Make the test ride (a slow one at first) to make sure the brakes are working correctly.*

Tables 1-3 are on the following page.

14

Table 1 BRAKE TYPE

1985-1986	Mech. Drum
1987	
Trail Boss W877527 & Cyclone W877828	Mech. Drum
Trail Boss 4 × 4 W878027, W878127 & W878327	Hyd. Disc
1988-On	Hyd. Disc

Table 2 TORQUE SPECIFICATIONS

	N·m	ft.-lb.
Front axle nut (3-wheel models)	48.8	36
Front brake caliper bolts	24.4	18
Front brake disc screws	24.4	18
Front brake hanger pins	16.3	12
Front hub nut (2 × 4)	54.2	40
Front wheel lug nuts	20.3	15
Master cylinder clamp screws	5.08-6.21	3.75-4.58
		45-55 in.-lb.

Table 3 BRAKE SPECIFICATIONS

	mm	in.
Minimum disc brake pad thickness	2.0	0.075
Fluid level in reservoir, measured from top		
1987-1988	3	1/8
1989-on	6-8	1/4-5/16

CHAPTER FIFTEEN

BODY

This chapter contains procedures to remove and install the body panels and seat. It is suggested that as soon as the part is removed from the vehicle, all mounting hardware (small brackets, bolts, nuts and washers) be reinstalled so they will not be lost.

SEAT

Refer to **Figure 1**.

Removal/Installation

1. Lift the seat latch at the rear of the seat and remove the seat.

2. To install the seat, engage the front seat bracket with the frame, then push the rear of the seat down to lock it in place.

3. Lift up on the seat and make sure it is properly secured at the front and rear.

FUEL TANK COVER

Refer to **Figure 1**.

Removal/Installation

The fuel tank on some models is covered and this trim material must be removed before removing the fuel tank. Refer to **Figures 2-4**.

1. Remove the seat as described in this chapter.

2. Remove the front and rear screws (**Figures 2-4**) that attach the fuel tank cover.

3. Lift the fuel tank cover from the vehicle.

4. Install the fuel tank cap.

5. Install by reversing these steps.

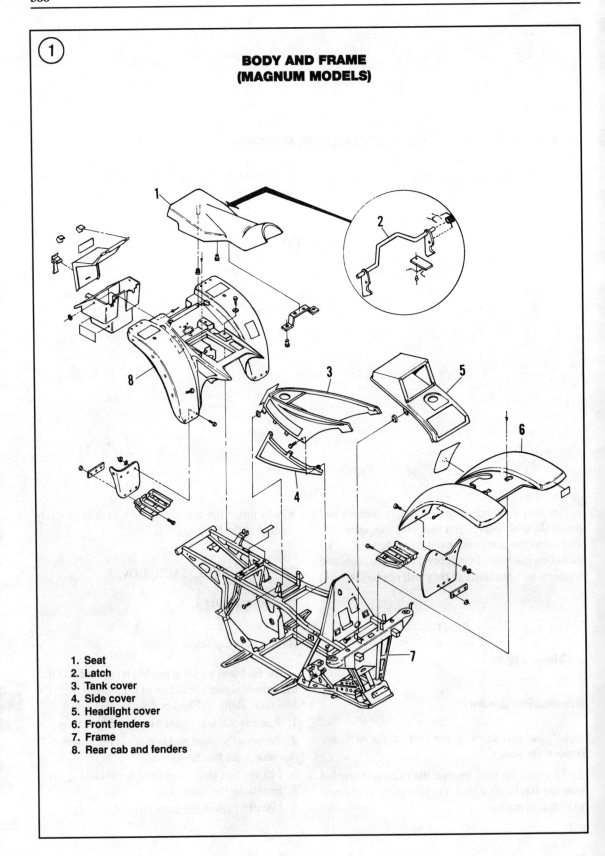

**BODY AND FRAME
(MAGNUM MODELS)**

1. Seat
2. Latch
3. Tank cover
4. Side cover
5. Headlight cover
6. Front fenders
7. Frame
8. Rear cab and fenders

FRONT PANEL

Refer to **Figure 1**.

Removal/Installation

1. Remove the fuel tank cover as described in this chapter.

2. Detach wires from the headlight.

3. Remove the screws attaching the headlight cover (**Figure 3** and **Figure 4**), then remove the cover.

4. Install by reversing these removal steps.

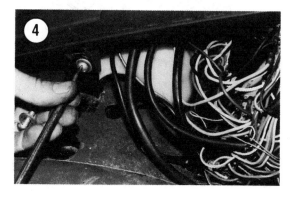

FRONT FENDER
(EXCEPT XPLORER AND SCRAMBLER)

Refer to **Figure 1**.

Removal/Installation

1. Remove the fuel tank cover and headlight cover as described in this chapter.

2. Remove the bolts and washers securing the front fender to the frame.

3. On models with a fuel pump mounted as shown in **Figure 5**, proceed as follows

    a. Unbolt the fuel pump bracket from the frame rails and move the fuel pump out of the way.

    b. Drill out the rivets (**Figure 6**) attaching the front fenders to the frame.

4. Carefully pull the front fender away from the frame, then toward the front.

5. Install by reversing these removal steps, noting the following.

6. Do not overtighten the bolts as the plastic fender may fracture.

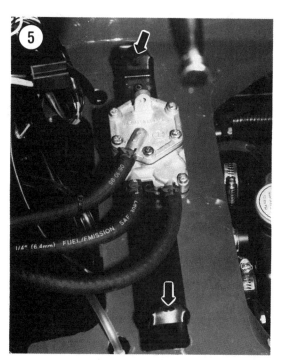

15

FRONT FENDER
(XPLORER)

Refer to **Figure 7**.

Removal/Installation

1. Remove the side panels.
2. Remove the front panel.
3. Remove the handlebar assembly (**Figure 8**).
4. Remove the the fuel cap.
5. Remove the screws, rivets, bolts and washers securing the front fender.
6. Carefully pull the front fender up, away from the frame, then lift the fender off.
7. Reinstall the fuel tank cap.
8. Install by reversing these removal steps. Do not overtighten the bolts as the plastic fender may fracture.

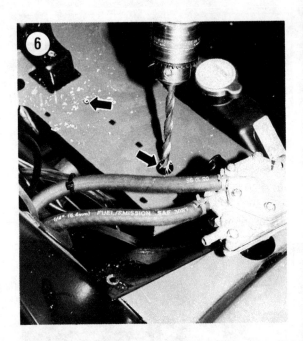

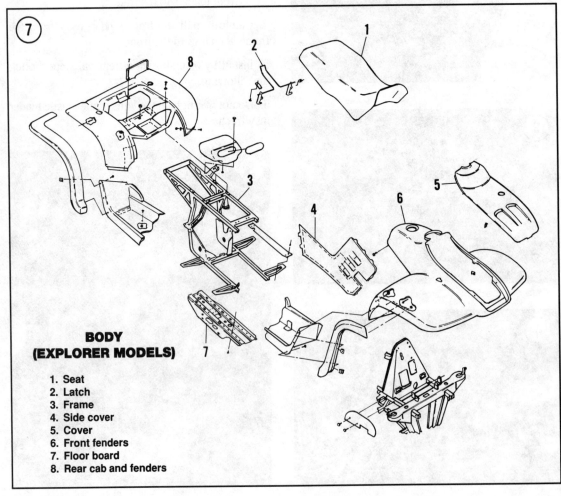

**BODY
(EXPLORER MODELS)**

1. Seat
2. Latch
3. Frame
4. Side cover
5. Cover
6. Front fenders
7. Floor board
8. Rear cab and fenders

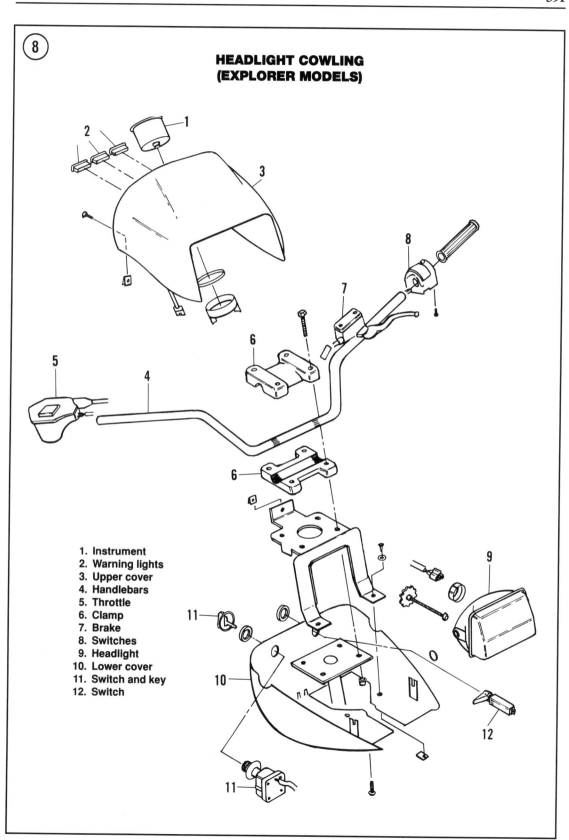

⑧

**HEADLIGHT COWLING
(EXPLORER MODELS)**

1. Instrument
2. Warning lights
3. Upper cover
4. Handlebars
5. Throttle
6. Clamp
7. Brake
8. Switches
9. Headlight
10. Lower cover
11. Switch and key
12. Switch

15

FRONT FENDER (SCRAMBLER)

Refer to **Figure 9**.

Removal/Installation

1. Remove the front panel.
2. Remove the handlebar assembly.
3. Remove the the fuel cap.
4. Remove the screws securing the front fender.
5. Carefully pull the front fender up, away from the frame, then lift the fender off.

6. Reinstall the fuel tank cap.
7. Install by reversing these removal steps. Do not overtighten the attaching screws as the plastic fender may fracture.

REAR FENDER

Refer to **Figure 1**, **Figure 7** or **Figure 9**

Removal/Installation

1. Remove the seat and any interfering side panels.

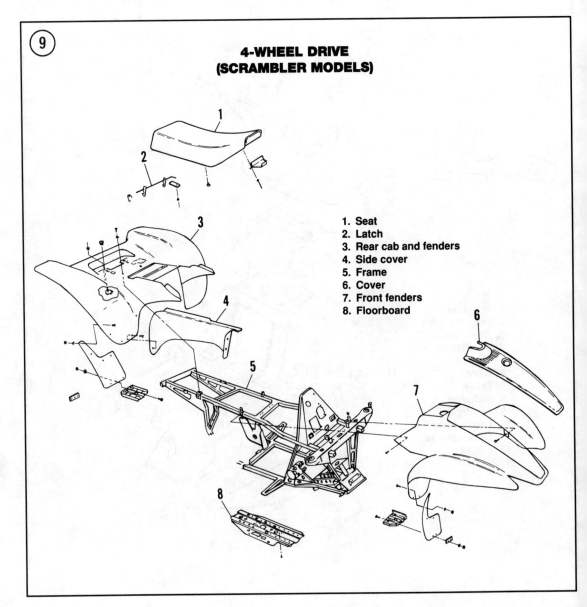

9

4-WHEEL DRIVE (SCRAMBLER MODELS)

1. Seat
2. Latch
3. Rear cab and fenders
4. Side cover
5. Frame
6. Cover
7. Front fenders
8. Floorboard

2. On some models the rear frame or other attachments may need to be removed befroe the rear fenders.

3. Remove the screws attaching the rear fender.

4. Lift the rear fender up slightly and remove the rear fender.

5. Install by reversing these steps, noting the following.

SIDE PANELS
(XPLORER MODELS)

Refer to **Figure 7**.

Removal/Installation

The side panels may be difficult to remove until they have been removed several times.

1. Remove the seat.

2. Hold the side panel near the rear and pull the panel forward and toward the outside to disengage the two rear tabs.

3. Push the panel down to disengage the front and top tabs.

4. When assembling, align the front and top tabs.

5. Push the panel forward and up until the tabs lock.

6. Bend the panel and insert the rear tabs.

7. Push the panel in until the tabs are all locked.

INDEX

16

16

1985-1988 MODELS
(EXCEPT CYCLONE)

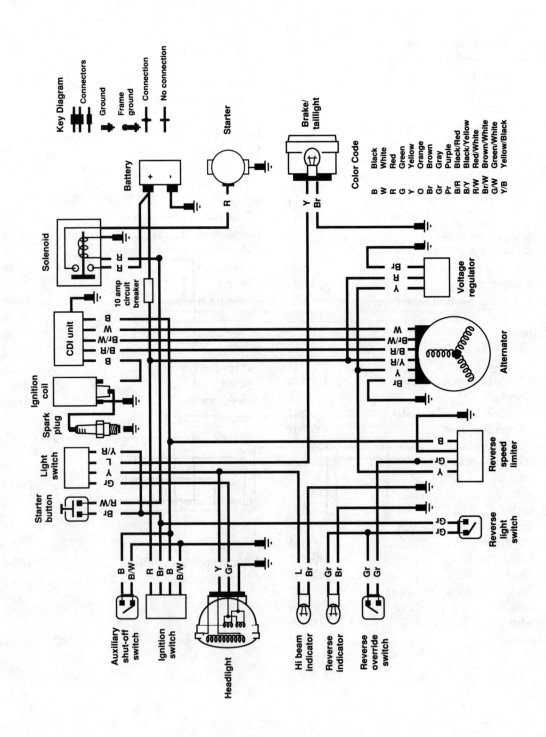

1987 CYCLONE

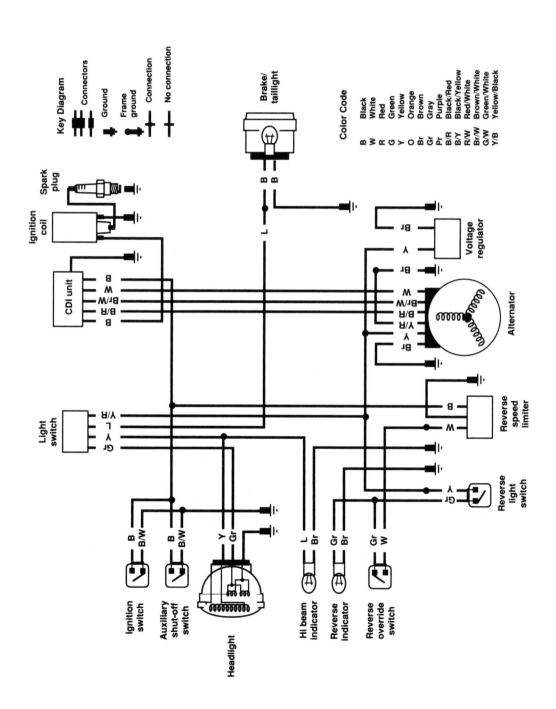

1989-1994 TRAIL BOSS MODELS

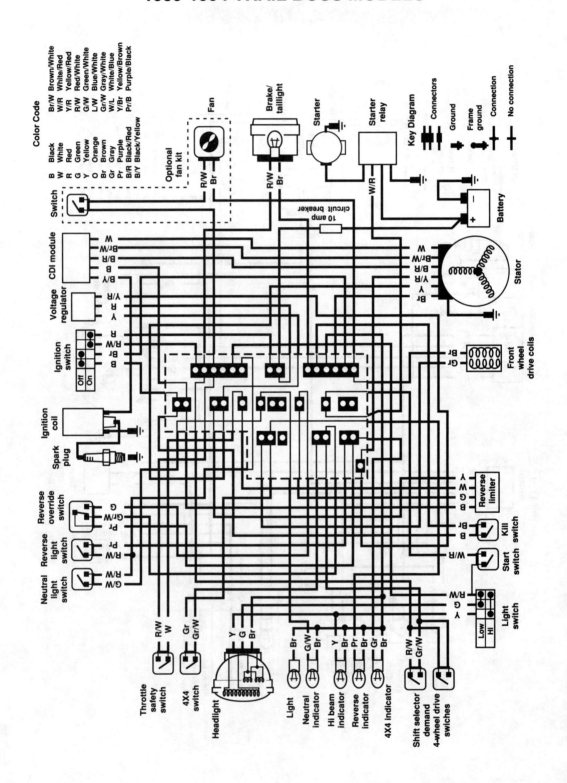

1993-ON 300, 400L 4×4, SPORTSMAN 6×6 AND 1995 EXPLORER

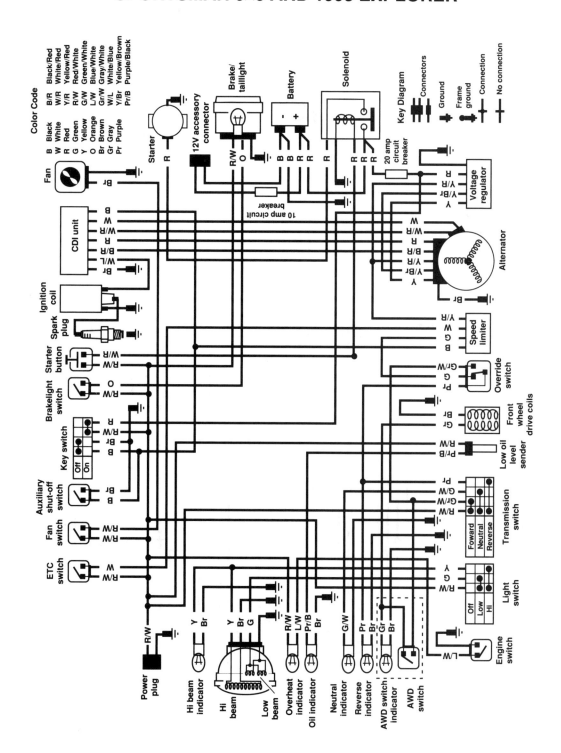

1990-1995 TRAIL BLAZER

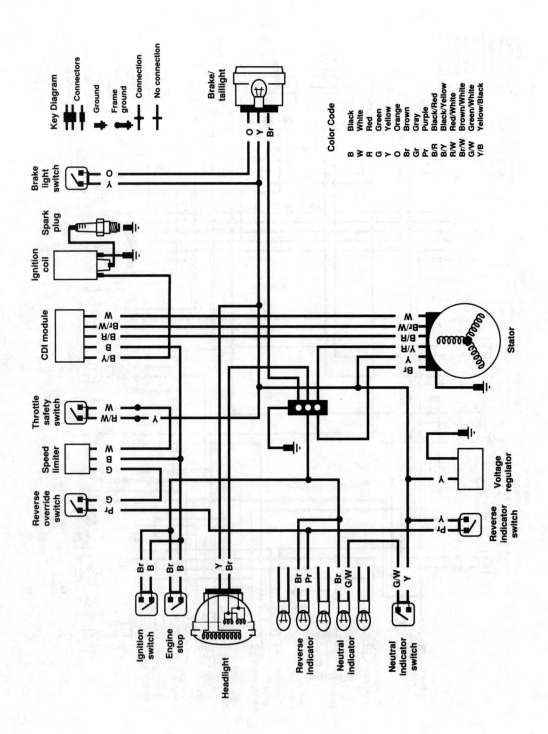

MAGNUM 2-WHEEL DRIVE

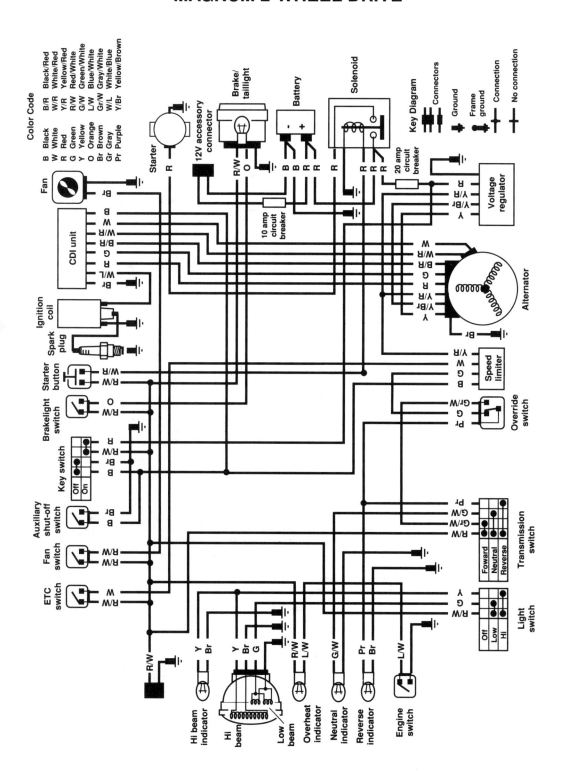

MAGNUM 4×4

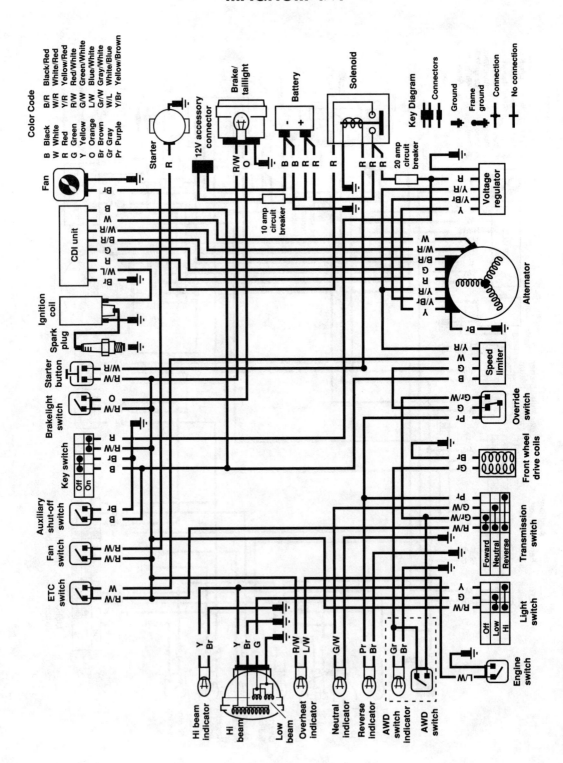

NOTES

NOTES

MAINTENANCE LOG

Date	Miles	Type of Service

BMW

M308	500 & 600 CC Twins, 55-69
M309	F650, 1994-2000
M500-3	BMW K-Series, 85-97
M502-3	BMW R50/5-R100 GSPD, 70-96
M503-2	R850, R1100, R1150 and R1200C, 93-04

HARLEY-DAVIDSON

M419	Sportsters, 59-85
M428	Sportster Evolution, 86-90
M429-4	Sportster Evolution, 91-03
M418	Panheads, 48-65
M420	Shovelheads,66-84
M421-3	FLS/FXS Evolution,84-99
M423	FLS/FXS Twin Cam 88B, 2000-2003
M422-3	FLH/FLT/FXR Evolution, 84-99
M430-2	FLH/FLT Twin Cam 88, 1999-2003
M424-2	FXD Evolution, 91-98
M425-2	FXD Twin Cam, 99-03

HONDA

ATVs

M316	Odyssey FL250, 77-84
M311	ATC, TRX & Fourtrax 70-125, 70-87
M433	Fourtrax 90 ATV, 93-00
M326	ATC185 & 200, 80-86
M347	ATC200X & Fourtrax 200SX, 86-88
M455	ATC250 & Fourtrax 200/250, 84-87
M342	ATC250R, 81-84
M348	TRX250R/Fourtrax 250R & ATC250R, 85-89
M456-3	TRX250X 87-92; TRX300EX 93-04
M446-2	TRX250 Recon 97-04
M346-3	TRX300/Fourtrax 300 & TRX300FW/Fourtrax 4x4, 88-00
M200	TRX350 Rancher, 00-03
M459-3	TRX400 Foreman 95-03
M454-2	TRX400EX 99-03
M205	TRX450 Foreman, 98-04
M210	TRX500 Rubicon, 98-04

Singles

M310-13	50-110cc OHC Singles, 65-99
M319	XR50R-XR70R, 97-03
M315	100-350cc OHC, 69-82
M317	Elsinore, 125-250cc, 73-80
M442	CR60-125R Pro-Link, 81-88
M431-2	CR80R, 89-95, CR125R, 89-91
M435	CR80, 96-02
M457-2	CR125R & CR250R, 92-97
M464	CR125R, 1998-2002
M443	CR250R-500R Pro-Link, 81-87
M432-3	CR250R, 88-91 & CR500R, 88-01
M437	CR250R, 97-01
M352	CRF250, CRF250X & CRF450R, 02-05
M312-13	XL/XR75-100,75-03
M318-4	XL/XR/TLR 125-200, 79-03
M328-4	XL/XR250, 78-00; XL/XR350R 83-85; XR200R, 84-85; XR250L, 91-96
M320-2	XR400R, 96-04
M339-7	XL/XR 500-650, 79-03

Twins

M321	125-200cc, 65-78
M322	250-350cc, 64-74
M323	250-360cc Twins, 74-77
M324-5	Twinstar, Rebel 250 & Nighthawk 250, 78-03
M334	400-450cc, 78-87
M333	450 & 500cc, 65-76
M335	CX & GL500/650 Twins, 78-83
M344	VT500, 83-88
M313	VT700 & 750, 83-87
M314	VT750 Shadow, 98-03
M440	VT1100C Shadow , 85-96
M460-3	VT1100C Series, 95-04

Fours

M332	CB350-550cc, SOHC, 71-78
M345	CB550 & 650, 83-85
M336	CB650,79-82
M341	CB750 SOHC, 69-78
M337	CB750 DOHC, 79-82
M436	CB750 Nighthawk, 91-93 & 95-99
M325	CB900, 1000 & 1100, 80-83
M439	Hurricane 600, 87-90
M441-2	CBR600F2 & F3, 91-98
M445	CBR600F4, 99-03
M434-2	CBR900RR Fireblade, 93-99
M329	500cc V-Fours, 84-86
M438	Honda VFR800, 98-00
M349	700-1000 Interceptor, 83-85
M458-2	VFR700F-750F, 86-97
M327	700-1100cc V-Fours, 82-88
M340	GL1000 & 1100, 75-83
M504	GL1200, 84-87
M508	ST1100/PAN European, 90-02

Sixes

M505	GL1500 Gold Wing, 88-92
M506-2	GL1500 Gold Wing, 93-00
M507	GL1800 Gold Wing, 01-04
M462-2	GL1500C Valkyrie, 97-03

KAWASAKI

ATVs

M465-2	KLF220 & KLF250 Bayou, 88-03
M466-4	KLF300 Bayou, 86-04
M467	KLF400 Bayou, 93-99
M470	KEF300 Lakota, 95-99
M385	KSF250 Mojave, 87-00

Singles

M350-9	Rotary Valve 80-350cc, 66-01
M444-2	KX60, 83-02; KX80 83-90
M448	KX80/85/100, 89-03
M351	KDX200, 83-88
M447-3	KX125 & KX250, 82-91 KX500, 83-04
M472-2	KX125, 92-00
M473-2	KX250, 92-00
M474	KLR650, 87-03

Twins

M355	KZ400, KZ/Z440, EN450 & EN500, 74-95
M360-3	EX500, GPZ500S, Ninja R, 87-02
M356-4	Vulcan 700 & 750, 85-04
M354-2	Vulcan 800 & Vulcan 800 Classic, 95-04
M357-2	Vulcan 1500, 87-99
M471-2	Vulcan Classic 1500, 96-04

Fours

M449	KZ500/550 & ZX550, 79-85
M450	KZ, Z & ZX750, 80-85
M358	KZ650, 77-83
M359-3	900-1000cc Fours, 73-81
M451-3	1000 &1100cc Fours, 81-02
M452-3	ZX500 & 600 Ninja, 85-97
M453-3	Ninja ZX900-1100 84-01
M468	ZX6 Ninja, 90-97
M469	ZX7 Ninja, 91-98
M453-3	900-1100 Ninja, 84-01
M409	Concours, 86-04

POLARIS

ATVs

M496	Polaris ATV, 85-95
M362	Polaris Magnum ATV, 96-98
M363	Scrambler 500, 4X4 97-00
M365-2	Sportsman/Xplorer, 96-03

SUZUKI

ATVs

M381	ALT/LT 125 & 185, 83-87
M475	LT230 & LT250, 85-90
M380-2	LT250R Quad Racer, 85-92
M343	LTF500F Quadrunner, 98-00
M483-2	Suzuki King Quad/ Quad Runner 250, 87-98

Singles

M371	RM50-400 Twin Shock, 75-81
M369	125-400cc 64-81
M379	RM125-500 Single Shock, 81-88
M476	DR250-350, 90-94
M384-2	LS650 Savage, 86-03
M386	RM80-250, 89-95
M400	RM125, 96-00
M401	RM250, 96-02

Twins

M372	GS400-450 Twins, 77-87
M481-4	VS700-800 Intruder, 85-04
M482-2	VS1400 Intruder, 87-01
M484-3	GS500E Twins, 89-02
M361	SV650, 1999-2002

Triple

M368	380-750cc, 72-77

Fours

M373	GS550, 77-86
M364	GS650, 81-83
M370	GS750 Fours, 77-82
M376	GS850-1100 Shaft Drive, 79-84
M378	GS1100 Chain Drive, 80-81
M383-3	Katana 600, 88-96 GSX-R750-1100, 86-87
M331	GSX-R600, 97-00
M478-2	GSX-R750, 88-92 GSX750F Katana, 89-96
M485	GSX-R750, 96-99
M377	GSX-R1000, 01-04
M338	GSF600 Bandit, 95-00
M353	GSF1200 Bandit, 96-03

YAMAHA

ATVs

M499	YFM80 Badger, 85-01
M394	YTM/YFM200 & 225, 83-86
M488-5	Blaster, 88-05
M489-2	Timberwolf, 89-00
M487-5	Warrior, 87-04
M486-5	Banshee, 87-04
M490-3	Moto-4 & Big Bear, 87-04
M493	YFM400FW Kodiak, 93-98
M280-2	Raptor 660R, 01-05

Singles

M492-2	PW50 & PW80, BW80 Big Wheel 80, 81-02
M410	80-175 Piston Port, 68-76
M415	250-400cc Piston Port, 68-76
M412	DT & MX 100-400, 77-83
M414	IT125-490, 76-86
M393	YZ50-80 Monoshock, 78-90
M413	YZ100-490 Monoshock, 76-84
M390	YZ125-250, 85-87 YZ490, 85-90
M391	YZ125-250, 88-93 WR250Z, 91-93
M497-2	YZ125, 94-01
M498	YZ250, 94-98 and WR250Z, 94-97
M406	YZ250F & WR250F, 01-03
M491-2	YZ400F, YZ426F, WR400F WR426F, 98-02
M417	XT125-250, 80-84
M480-3	XT/TT 350, 85-00
M405	XT500 & TT500, 76-81
M416	XT/TT 600, 83-89

Twins

M403	650cc, 70-82
M395-10	XV535-1100 Virago, 81-03
M495-3	V-Star 650, 98-04
M281	V-Star 1100, 99-04

Triple

M404	XS750 & 850, 77-81

Fours

M387	XJ550, XJ600 & FJ600, 81-92
M494	XJ600 Seca II, 92-98
M388	YX600 Radian & FZ600, 86-90
M396	FZR600, 89-93
M392	FZ700-750 & Fazer, 85-87
M411	XS1100 Fours, 78-81
M397	FJ1100 & 1200, 84-93
M375	V-Max, 85-03
M374	Royal Star, 96-03
M461	YZF-R6, 99-04
M398	YZF-R1, 98-03
M399	F21, 01-04

VINTAGE MOTORCYCLES

Clymer® Collection Series

M330	Vintage British Street Bikes, BSA, 500–650cc Unit Twins; Norton, 750 & 850cc Commandos; Triumph, 500-750cc Twins
M300	Vintage Dirt Bikes, V. 1 Bultaco, 125-370cc Singles; Montesa, 123-360cc Singles; Ossa, 125-250cc Singles
M301	Vintage Dirt Bikes, V. 2 CZ, 125-400cc Singles; Husqvarna, 125-450cc Singles; Maico, 250-501cc Singles; Hodaka, 90-125cc Singles
M305	Vintage Japanese Street Bikes Honda, 250 & 305cc Twins; Kawasaki, 250-750cc Triples; Kawasaki, 900 & 1000cc Fours